MUHAMMAD ALI

His Life and Times

Books by Thomas Hauser

GENERAL NON-FICTION

Missing
The Trial of Patrolman Thomas Shea
For Our Children (with Frank Macchiarola)
The Family Legal Companion
Final Warning: The Legacy of Chernobyl (with Dr. Robert Gale)
Arnold Palmer: A Personal Journey
Confronting America's Moral Crisis (with Frank Macchiarola)
Healing: A Journal of Tolerance and Understanding

MISCELLANEOUS

With This Ring (with Frank Macchiarola)
A God to Hope For

ABOUT BOXING

The Black Lights: Inside the World of Professional Boxing
Muhammad Ali: His Life and Times
Muhammad Ali: Memories
Muhammad Ali in Perspective
Muhammad Ali & Company
A Beautiful Sickness
A Year at the Fights
Brutal Artistry
The View from Ringside

FICTION

Ashworth & Palmer
Agatha's Friends
The Beethoven Conspiracy
Hanneman's War
The Fantasy
Dear Hannah
The Hawthorne Group
Martin Bear & Friends
Mark Twain Remembers
Finding the Princess

MUHAMMAD ALI

His Life and Times

THOMAS HAUSER

With the co-operation of Muhammad Ali

Foreword by Hugh McIlvanney

PORTICO

For Howard Bingham,
There's no-one like him.

First published in the United Kingdom in 1991 by
Portico
1 Gower Street
London
WC1E 6HD

An imprint of Pavilion Books Company Ltd

ISBN 978-1-907554-80-3

10 9 8 7 6 5 4

Grateful acknowledgment is made for permission to reprint from the
following material:
'The Greatest Love of All', by Michael Masser and Linda Creed;
copyright 1977 by Gold Horizon Music Corporation and Golden Torch Music
Corporation; international copyright secured; made in USA; all rights reserved;
used by permission.

'Forever Young' by Bob Dylan; copyright 1973, 1974 by Ram's Horn Music;
nternational copyright secured; all rights reserved; reprinted by permission.

A CIP catalogue record for this book is available from the British Library.

Printed and bound by CPI Group (UK) Ltd, Croydon, CR0 4YY

This book can be ordered direct from the publisher at www.pavilionbooks.com.

Contents

Praise for Thomas Hauser's *Muhammad Ali: His Life and Times:*

'Hauser's achievement in chronicling the life of Muhammad Ali is monumental . . .
triumphant and harrowing at one and the same time.'
The Guardian

'Hauser has come up with a superb book . . . hilarious, sad, moving, and hopeful.
Muhammad Ali: His Life and Times gradually reveals itself as a portrait of an
American generation rather than a slice of boxing history.'
The Times

'Hauser's previous boxing book, *The Black Lights*, deservedly became a classic.
So will this magnificent, fascinating book.'
Boxing News

'. . . the most significant boxing book ever written. Hauser has examined Ali as both
man and fighter, and placed his life in social, political, and religious perspective.
No one has ever done it better. Read this extraordinary work.'
Ring Magazine

'Hauser's approach has been so comprehensive, his research so thorough, that the
result is a tour de force.'
The Observer

'Ali was bigger than boxing, and so is this book.'
The Nation

'. . . a monumental achievement, a carefully orchestrated account through the words
of a vast and varied range of people whose lives were touched by Ali. It documents
every facet of his extraordinary life.'
The Daily Telegraph

'Hauser's skill gives this rich and absorbing portrait a flow and drive that create a
delightful summer read, and his training as a lawyer offers a precision that creates a
new foundation for all future Ali scholarship.'
The Los Angeles Times

'Thomas Hauser's fine new book, *Muhammad Ali: His Life and Times*, is a considerable
achievement and probably as thorough a look as we'll get at this remarkable man.'
Wall Street Journal

'Thomas Hauser has produced the definitive extraordinary story of an extraordinary man.'
Los Angeles Daily News

'. . . compassionate, intelligent, fair-minded, definitive, and certainly exhaustive.'
The New York Review of Books

'We now have the definitive biography of Muhammad Ali, who transcended sports as
no other athlete ever has.'
New York Daily News

Foreword

The simplest and best tribute I can pay to Thomas Hauser's book is to say that it is worthy of its subject. No single volume could ever tell all that deserves to be told about the greatest figure in the history of sport, but there is never likely to be a better attempt than is made in these pages to capture and preserve a vibrant sense of Muhammad Ali and the career that caused him to become the most widely recognised member of the human race.

When I first learned that this biography was to take the form of a vast accumulation of oral testimony, I suspected that the method would struggle to do justice to the complex strands and sweeping implications of Ali's story. Previous publications (*Missing* in particular) showed that Hauser was bringing formidable skills, as both writer and researcher, to the job. I was, however, unprepared for the tour de force of diligence, comprehensiveness and perception that is this book. It was not so much the choice of technique as the execution of it that made the results thoroughly remarkable. The judgment exercised in deciding which witnesses could best recreate incidents or elucidate themes was demonstrably matched by the conscientiousness and energy that ensured they were heard. Another vital element was obviously the quality of interviewing discernible in the liveliness and relevance of what emerged.

Linking the powerful individual statements – and unfailingly keeping them in context for the reader – are reportorial passages quietly impressive for their clarity, and an enthusiasm for pertinent detail. Whether dealing with boxing – and the terrible medical problems it ultimately inflicted on its nonpareil champion – with religious and political issues (which were inevitably intertwined by the Muslim affiliations) or with

Ali's marriages, his relations with his parents and other areas of his personal life, the narrative mechanism chosen by Hauser works extraordinarily well, not least because of his readiness to quote differing or even contradictory versions of events. The effect is not to damage coherence but to underline the value of flesh-and-blood perspectives.

Many of the voices that talk to us across the years are familiar to me and, naturally, Ali's is most familiar of all. I was enthralled and entertained by it in any number of unlikely locations, and some pretty strange circumstances, during the two decades I spent chronicling his activities around the world.

Because I had the luxury of a weekly deadline that came with working for a Sunday newspaper, the *Observer* in London, I was able to make myself available for every opportunity to get close to him in those periods when he was separated from the clamour of his public existence. That advantage yielded a wealth of occasions when I was in his company for hours as an audience of one, or perhaps with only my close friend and fellow reporter Ken Jones or the brilliant photographer Chris Smith sharing the privilege. Jones and I couldn't believe our luck back then and we still can't now, especially when we recall the surreal interview that began with Ali lying naked under the stars on the tiny patio of a modest suburban house in a street called Topaz in New Orleans (he had just done a road run as part of the preparation for the return fight with Leon Spinks, which marked his Third Coming as heavyweight champion) or the two-and-a-half hours when we had him to ourselves in the curtained coolness of a villa by the Zaire River on the day that had begun with the pre-dawn wonders of the Rumble in the Jungle.

For any journalist who wasn't willing to settle for Ali's performer persona, who had the time and patience to seek him out in his quieter, more reflective moods, the rewards were substantial. Even in his own day, we knew he was telling the truth when he said he was making himself more reachable than any great athlete had ever been before, or would ever be again. Looking back from the present, an age when many second-rate sportsmen have to be approached through agents or sponsors, when reporters are routinely fobbed off with press conferences and sound bites rather than real communication, we can appreciate him as a miracle of accessibility.

But the more we learned about him, the more we wanted to know, and the need for a serious and ambitious biography had to be met. Fifteen years ago it was, unorthodoxly but triumphantly. This new paperback edition once again emphasises that all of us who cherish the impact of Muhammad Ali on our lives have reason to be grateful to Tom Hauser.

Hugh McIlvanney

Preface

In October 1988, I met with Muhammad Ali and his wife, Lonnie, at their request to explore the possibility of writing this book. "People don't know the real Muhammad," Lonnie told me at our first session. "All they see is the man the media has exposed them to, but there are so many more sides to Muhammad. He has deep personal convictions, and lives up to those convictions every day. He's gentle and caring with a heart purer than any I've ever known. I want people to understand who Muhammad is, what he stands for, and what he's accomplished throughout his life."

Muhammad Ali: His Life and Times is an attempt to achieve that goal. There have been more words written about, more photographs taken of, and more attention lavished upon Ali than any athlete ever. Yet for all his years in the spotlight, the true Ali is largely unknown. Stories about him have been embellished and retold to the point where they assume biblical proportions. People worldwide recognize his face. Yet, even as the Ali chronicles grow, new generations are born, and to them Ali is more legend than reality, part of America's distant past. Indeed, for millions of young men and women today, the name Cassius Marcellus Clay is unknown—and that's a shame, because to understand Ali, one must understand where he came from.

This book is not an attempt to mythologize Ali. It's an effort to show him as he was and is: a superb human being with good qualities and flaws. In his twenties, he was arguably the greatest fighter of all time. But more importantly, he reflected and shaped the social and political currents of the age in which he reigned. Ali in the 1960s stood for the proposition that principles mattered, that equality among people was just and proper, that the war in Vietnam was wrong. Inevitably, the sixties passed. Ali evolved from a feared warrior to a benevolent monarch and ultimately to a benign venerated figure. He is today a deeply religious man, who evokes feelings of respect and love wherever he travels throughout the world.

In preparing this book, I've had a very special opportunity and also a special obligation. I've spent thousands of hours with Ali, the members of his family, his associates, and his friends. I believe Muhammad has been completely honest with me, and to the extent that people have related stories that might be critical of him for use in this book, it's not a case of telling tales out of school. Rather, Muhammad has personally asked each contributor to this project to be fully candid and open. Like most authors, I relied on a wide range of sources. Space does not allow me to list all the archival material and publications reviewed. However, I'm particularly indebted to the many individuals listed in the Appendix who granted interviews for this project.

Throughout the manuscript, a variety of opinions are expressed. I would like to remind readers of the distinction between opinion and fact, and note that I don't necessarily agree with every statement quoted. Rather, I've sought to incorporate as many divergent views as possible. Whenever a quotation appears in the manuscript, I've indicated its source in the Notes at the end of the book unless it comes from an interview conducted specifically for the book. I have often joined separate quotations from the same speaker and excerpted statements to facilitate reporting on a particular thought or event. This editing has been necessary to accommodate the hundreds of speakers whose voices are heard and who cover the full scope of Ali's life. I'm confident that in so doing I've done nothing to distort what was said or otherwise compromise the fairness of the book. In reporting on the early years of Ali's life, I've employed the name "Cassius Clay," not as a sign of disrespect but because it's the name Ali himself used and was known by then. To avoid confusion, I've tried to remain constant in the use of other names throughout the book. For example, Belinda Ali has changed her name to Khalilah Ali and Herbert Muhammad is now known as Jabir Muhammad. But most people I interviewed referred to them by their original names, and I have used those names for reasons of clarity. Again, no disrespect is intended.

Let me also add a word about Muhammad's health. That subject is dealt with extensively in the later pages of the book, but it was a threshold issue for me before becoming involved. Like millions of people, I'd seen Muhammad on television in recent years. Sometimes he looked well. Other times, his face was frozen; he moved slowly; the life seemed all but gone from his eyes. I didn't want to involve myself in this project unless Muhammad wanted it and was capable of making a significant contribution to the recounting of his life. And toward that end, before making a commitment, I spent five days with Muhammad and Lonnie Ali at their home in Michigan. It was the first of many times we spent together, and I was enormously relieved by what I found. Muhammad's speech is not what it once was, but his thought processes are still clear. His memory is good; his mind is sharp. And despite his physical difficulties, Muhammad is healthier, happier, more alert, and more content than most people realize. He enjoys his life; he believes he's doing God's work, and he's as satisfied with each day as anybody I know.

Thomas Hauser
New York, N.Y.

1

Origins

Each day at 5:00 A.M., a forty-nine-year-old man rises from bed on a small farm in Berrien Springs, Michigan. Quietly, as mandated by the Qur'an, he washes himself with clear running water. Then he puts on clean clothes, faces Makkah with his hands at his sides, and says to himself, "I intend to perform the morning prayer as ordered by Allah, the Lord of all the worlds." Outside, it is dark. The only sounds are the wind in winter and the blending of birds and insects when the weather is warm. The man changes position. "Allahu Akbar. Pure and glorified are You, O Allah. Blessed is Your Name and exalted is Your Majesty, and there is nothing worthy of worship except You. I seek refuge with Allah from Satan, the accursed."

The man is Muhammad Ali, the most recognizable person on earth. For half a century, he has walked among us, his face as familiar as that of a close friend. Somewhere in time, he captured a blend of mayhem and magic that carried him deep into the collective psyche of us all. The world didn't just see or hear Ali; it felt him. And if he hasn't always been part of the landscape, it somehow seems that way now.

One of life's lessons is that dreams and fantasies aren't bound by the same rules as reality, but time and again Ali made them coincide. In the ring, he was the most beautiful fighting machine ever assembled. One mark of a great champion is the ability to win his title at a young age and hold on to it until he's old. When Ali made his professional debut, Dwight D. Eisenhower was president of the United States, and several countries in which he later fought didn't exist at all. Ali fought through the terms of seven presidents, holding center stage for twenty years. In all of boxing history, only two men won the heavyweight championship at a younger age. And only one prevailed in a heavyweight title bout when he was older than Ali, who at thirty-six years eight months toppled Leon Spinks to recapture his crown. All told, Ali challenged for the heavyweight championship five times and successfully defended it on nineteen occasions. And in the process, he altered the consciousness of people the world over. Ali was black and proud of it at a time when many black Americans were running from their color. He was, to some, the greatest hero to come out of the Vietnam War. With the exception of Martin Luther King, no black man in America had more influence than Ali during the years when Ali was in his prime.

Cassius Marcellus Clay, Jr., as Ali was once known, was born in Louisville General Hospital at 6:35 P.M. on January 17, 1942. His father, Cassius Marcellus Clay, Sr., earned a living painting billboards and signs. According to court records, Ali's paternal grandparents could read and write, and all four of his paternal great-grandparents were listed as "free colored" on Kentucky's census rolls. While historical records offer no proof that members of the Clay family were held as slaves, in all likelihood at one time they were. Ali's mother, Odessa Grady Clay, worked as a household domestic when her children were young. One of her grandparents, Tom Moorehead, was the son of a white Moorehead and a slave named Dinah. Mrs. Clay's other grandfather was a white Irishman named Abe Grady, who emigrated to the United States from County Clare, Ireland, soon after the Civil War and married a "free colored woman" whose name is unknown.[1]

MUHAMMAD ALI: "My mother is a Baptist, and when I was growing up, she taught me all she knew about God. Every Sunday, she dressed me up, took me and my brother to church, and taught us the way she thought was right. She taught us to love people and treat everybody with kindness. She taught us it was wrong to be prejudiced or hate. I've changed my religion and some of my beliefs since then, but her God is still God; I just call him by a different name. And my mother, I'll tell you what I've told people for a long time. She's a sweet, fat, wonderful woman, who loves to cook, eat, make clothes, and be with family. She doesn't drink, smoke, meddle in other people's business, or bother anyone, and there's no one who's been better to me my whole life."

CASSIUS CLAY, SR.: "He was a good boy. Both them boys, him and his brother, were good boys growing up. They didn't give us any trouble. They were church boys, because my wife brought them to church every Sunday. She was a good Baptist. I was a Methodist. But my daddy used to say to me, 'Let them follow their mother because a woman is always better than a man.' So that's what I did, and their mother taught them right; taught them to believe in God and be spiritual and be good to everybody. He was a good child and he grew up to be a good man, and he couldn't have been nothing else to be honest with you because of the way his mother raised him. Sunday school every Sunday. I dressed them up as good as I could afford, kept them in pretty good clothes. And they didn't come out of no ghetto. I raised them on the best street I could: 3302 Grand Avenue in the west end of Louisville. I made sure they were around good people; not people who would bring them into trouble. And I taught them values—always confront the things you fear, try to be the best at whatever you do. That's what my daddy taught me, and those are things that have to be taught. You don't learn those things by accident."

ODESSA CLAY: "I had a pretty hard life when I was young. My mother and father separated when I was a child, so I never saw much of my father or knew much about where he came from. My mother had three children and couldn't raise us all, so very often I stayed with my aunt. I started working to buy clothes so I could go to school. And then, when I was sixteen, I met Mr. Clay. He was walking home from work while I was talking to a friend one afternoon, and my friend—she knew him—called across the street and told him to come over and say hello. He's four years older than I am, so that would have made him twenty at the time.

"We called Muhammad 'GG' when he was born because—you know how babies jabber at the side of their crib—he used to say 'gee, gee, gee, gee.' And then, when he became a Golden Gloves champion, he told us, 'You know what that meant? I was trying to say Golden Gloves.' So we called him GG, and sometimes I still do. When he was a child, he never sat still. He walked and talked and did everything before his time. When he was two years old, he'd wake up in the middle of the night and throw everything from his dresser onto the floor. Most boys run around flat-footed or walk; GG went around on his tip-toes all the time. He used to stuff cake in his mouth and his mouth would be full, but he'd still say, 'More cake, Mommy; more cake.' And by the time he was four, he had all the confidence in the world. Even when he played with older children, he always wanted to be the leader. He'd tell them, 'Okay, today I'm going to be the daddy.' Then his little brother, Rudolph, was born. And if I had to spank Rudolph, GG would run and grab me and say, 'Don't you hit my baby.' One time, he tied a string to our draperies in the bedroom, and ran the string out the window around the house to his own room. Then he waited until we were ready to go to bed, and pulled on the string to make the curtains move. Everything he did seemed different as a child. He even had measles and chicken pox at the same time. His mind was like the March wind, blowing every which way. And whenever I thought I could predict what he'd do, he turned around and proved me wrong.

"He had confidence in himself, and that gave me confidence in him. He started boxing when he was twelve, and we'd sit at night, and he'd tell me how someday he was going to be champion of the world. It made me nervous watching him in the ring, but I believed that he could take care of himself. Then he joined the Nation of Islam, and I felt, well, this is the land of the free; worship as you please. If that's what he wanted to do, it was all right. The important thing was that he had a belief in God. The controversy with the Army worried me a lot. I wanted him to join, because at the time, I thought that was the right thing to do, but he had to make up his own mind. And now I worry about his health. I think rest is the best thing for him. When he gets his rest, you can tell the difference. But that's in God's hands, and I can't tell you what God is going to do. I always felt like God made Muhammad special, but I don't know why God chose me to carry this child."

CASSIUS CLAY, SR.: "When the boys got older, I took them with me on jobs; taught them how to paint pretty good. Before he started fighting, Muhammad could lay out a sign. Draw letters, do the spacing, mix the paint, and fill it in right. That was my living before I had a heart attack. I can't do too much now. But I was an artist, not just a sign painter. I was born painting, and if it wasn't for the way things were at the time, a lot more people would have known what I could do. I don't have a favorite of the paintings I've done. To be honest with you, they're all good. One time, I had these paintings I did in the basement. They were like snow scenes. I don't know where they are now; I haven't got them anymore. And by having lights turn on them, Christmas lights on a motor, it looked like you had an orange sun, and the sun and clouds were moving across the snow. My paintings are in most of the churches down here. Almost every Baptist church in Louisville, Kentucky, has a mural I done for them."

RAHAMAN ALI (formerly Rudolph Arnette Clay): "Louisville was segregated, but it was a quiet city, very peaceful and clean. There wasn't much crime; no drugs; very little drinking or prostitution. Things were different from the way they are now. Growing up, the only problems Muhammad and I had with whites were if we were walking in a certain part of town. If we were in the wrong place, white boys would come up in a car and say, 'Hey, nigger, what are you doing here?' I never got into any fights. No one attacked me. It wasn't like in the Deep South, but people would call us nigger and tell us to get out if they thought we were someplace we didn't belong.

"Muhammad and I had a few fights between us. All brothers do. But it was nothing serious; more like tests of strength, wrestling. He always had to be the leader, and we let him because he was very intelligent and quick. Outside of boxing, he never played much sports. Now and then, we'd play touch football on the street, and he was fast. It was hard for the rest of us to make a tag on him because of his speed. But tackle football, he didn't like. He wouldn't play because he thought it was too rough. He was a great marbles player; he loved to shoot marbles. And that was it, except all the time, he used to ask me to throw rocks at him. I thought he was crazy, but he'd stand back and dodge every one of them. No matter how many I threw, I could never hit him."

In some ways, the Clays were a closely knit family, but as with most families, there were problems. Louisville police records reveal that Cassius Clay, Sr., was arrested four times for reckless driving, twice for disorderly conduct, once for disposing of mortgaged property, and twice for assault and battery. His penchant for women led to discord at home, and he sometimes turned violent under the influence of alcohol. On three occasions, Odessa Clay called the police for protection from her husband. Ali prefers not to talk about those times, but they weighed upon him, as did the "ugly etiquette" of the South. Segregation was a way of life in Kentucky, and reminders of second-class citizenship were everywhere.

MUHAMMAD ALI: "When I was growing up, too many colored people thought it was better to be white. And I don't know what it was, but I always felt like I was born to do something for my people. Eight years old, ten years old; I'd walk out of my house at two in the morning, and look up at the sky for an angel or a revelation or God telling me what to do. I never got an answer. I'd look at the stars and wait for a voice, but I never heard nothing. Then my bike got stolen and I started boxing, and it was like God telling me that boxing was my responsibility. God made us all, but some of us are made special. Einstein wasn't an ordinary human. Columbus wasn't an ordinary human. Elvis Presley, the Wright brothers. Some people have special resources inside, and when God blesses you to have more than others, you have a responsibility to use it right."

The saga of Cassius Clay's red-and-white Schwinn bike has been told often over time. In October 1954, he and a friend rode their bicycles to the Columbia Auditorium, which was hosting an annual black bazaar called The Louisville Home Show. For much of the afternoon, they canvassed the floor, eating free popcorn and candy. Then, when it was time to go home, Clay discovered his bike had been stolen. Meanwhile, a Louisville policeman named Joe Martin was at work in the basement, teaching youngsters how to box.

JOE MARTIN: "I was down at the gym one night, and there was something else going on in the building, a display of merchandise that the Negro merchants put on once a year for their customers. And one night this kid came downstairs, and he was crying. Somebody had stolen his new bicycle, and of course he was very upset about that and wanted to report it to the police. And as I was a police officer, well, someone told him there's a police officer downstairs in the gymnasium, go down and tell him about it. And he was having a fit, half crying because someone stole his bike. He was only twelve years old then, and he was gonna whup whoever stole it. And I brought up the subject, I said, 'Well, you better learn how to fight before you start challenging people that you're gonna whup.' "[2]

"To all intents and purposes," Wilfred Sheed later wrote, "Cassius Clay was born at the age of twelve, the day he entered the gym and started fighting."[3] As part of the Columbia Gym's amateur program, Martin produced a local television show called *Tomorrow's Champions*, which offered instant celebrity status to his young charges. Six weeks after joining the gym, eighty-nine-pound Cassius Marcellus Clay, Jr., made his ring debut, winning a three-minute, three-round split decision over another novice named Ronnie O'Keefe.

JOE MARTIN: "I guess I've taught a thousand boys to box, or at least tried to teach them. Cassius Clay, when he first began coming around, looked no better or worse than the majority. If boxers were paid bonuses on their potential like ballplayers are, I don't know if he would have received one. He was just ordinary, and I doubt whether any scout would have thought much of him in his first year. About a year later, though, you could see that the little smart aleck— I mean, he's always been sassy—had a lot of potential. He stood out because, I guess, he had more determination than most boys, and he had the speed to get him someplace. He was a kid willing to make the sacrifices necessary to achieve something worthwhile in sports. I realized it was almost impossible to discourage him. He was easily the hardest worker of any kid I ever taught."[4]

MUHAMMAD ALI: "When I started boxing, all I really wanted was someday to buy my mother and father a house and own a nice big car for myself. I figured if I could turn pro and get on Saturday night fights, I could make four thousand dollars just for one night. Then my dreams started to grow. In school, sometimes I'd pretend they were announcing my name over the loudspeaker system, saying 'Cassius Clay, heavyweight champion of the world.' Other times, I'd draw a picture of a jacket on a piece of paper, like a high school football jacket; only on back of the jacket I'd write 'National Golden Gloves Champion' or 'Cassius Clay, World Heavyweight Champ.'

"Joe Martin was the man who started me in boxing, but sometimes I trained with a black man named Fred Stoner. I trained six days a week, and never drank or smoked a cigarette. The only thing I ever did like drugs was twice I took the cap off a gas tank and smelled the gas, which made me dizzy. Boxing kept me out of trouble."

JOE MARTIN: "Only once did I ever see him knocked out, knocked cold, and that was in the gymnasium, working out with an amateur named Willy Moran. Moran was a good hitter. Later he turned pro. Anyway, he really flattened Cassius that day. Cassius had been talking to me about wanting a scooter, and when he regained consciousness, he said to me, 'Mr. Martin, which way was that scooter going that hit me?' The scooter was on his mind. That was the only time I ever saw him knocked cold, and it didn't faze him. He was back working out with Moran again the next day."[5]

One of Clay's contemporaries in Louisville was Jimmy Ellis, who later held the World Boxing Association heavyweight championship during Ali's exile from boxing.

JIMMY ELLIS: "When I met Ali, he was about fourteen. I saw him fight on television against a friend of mine and he beat my friend, and I said, 'I can beat this guy,' so I started going to the gym. That's what got me into boxing. We fought twice against each other in the amateurs. I was older, by two years, but he was bigger than me even then. The first time we fought, he won. It was close but he got the decision, and it was the first time I ever got beat in a fight. Then we fought again; it was close, and I won. I knew it was a good guy that beat me the first time and it didn't bother me, and I think he figured the second time it was a good guy that beat him. After that, we became friends. Boxing is that way. You know, you can run together, talk together, and wind up fighting each other the next night; but when the fight is over, you shake hands and be friends. And I can tell you, Ali spent all his time in the gym. That's where he lived. He wanted to box and he wanted to be great, and that's what his life was all about. I never saw him fight in the streets. I never saw him pushing or shoving outside the ring. But in the gym, he took his boxing very seriously. Even then, he did a lot of talking, telling guys they couldn't beat him, saying he was gonna knock everyone out. But he learned about what went on in the ring, because he was working at it constantly and had the desire to fight. I mean, he was a fighter. Even when he was young, he had a fighting heart. I saw him get knocked down and get up to knock other guys out. He could be in a hole, getting beat, and still come back to win."

Chuck Bodak, an amateur boxing official, recalls Cassius Clay in the ring at that time.

CHUCK BODAK: "I was on the Golden Gloves coaching staff for the *Chicago Tribune,* which conducted the National Golden Gloves Tournament in Chicago. When Cassius first came in, he looked like a young colt, very spindly legged and wiry. Framework was just about all he had, but even then there was an aura about him. People would stop and look and not know what they were looking at, but they were looking at him. He lost that first year to a kid named Kent Green, who was an older, seasoned amateur from Chicago. But Cassius had talent; he made an impression. And each year after that, the improvement was obvious. The more he matured, the sharper he got. I mean, you'd of had to be blind not to see how good this kid was. I told his mother once, 'Cassius must be from outer space, because I've never seen anyone like him in my life.' "

Bob Surkein, an Amateur Athletic Union referee and judge, supplements Bodak's recollections.

BOB SURKEIN: "I'd been refereeing boxing since 1943, and the first time I stepped in the ring with this kid, I didn't know who he was. I knew he was a young fighter from Louisville with a white police officer who was handling him. And I saw him with his hands down, standing there, looking like he was going to get bombed out, and all of a sudden realizing that God had given this kid reflexes like no one had ever seen. Because even in the amateurs, he had the same reflexes and skills he had later on. Normally, you saw an amateur fighter jump out of harm's way. Cassius would stand there, move his head two inches, turn his body another six inches, and just slide over. I said to myself, it can't be, but after watching him in the ring many times, I knew this kid had it.

"Personality-wise, I don't think he ever changed. I remember, one time we were staying at a hotel for a tournament out-of-town. Cassius had won his first bout on a knockout. The next morning, I went down to the hotel coffee shop for a newspaper. I bought one, took it up to my room, and couldn't find the sports section. So I went back downstairs and there were ten or fifteen papers there; no sports sections. And I got to thinking. I said, 'I know where the damn sports sections are.' So I went up to Cassius's room, and he was sitting on the floor with a pair of scissors, cutting his picture out of all the sports sections where it had been that day. But he was always a likable youngster. A couple of years later, when we were training at Fort Dix for the Olympics, we went to Atlantic City for a day, just to relax. We were walking along the boardwalk, and he was so innocent, so in awe of everything. He looked out at the ocean and said, 'Man, that's the biggest damn lake I've ever seen.' I still see him from time to time. And to this day, I carry a picture in my wallet of him and me together when he was seventeen."

FEDERAL BUREAU OF INVESTIGATION REPORT (dated May 31, 1966): "[Name deleted by the United States Government] of Central High School, 1130 West Chestnut Street, Louisville, Kentucky, furnished the following information from records of the school. [Person X] emphasized that he was furnishing information for the assistance of the U.S. Government and did not want the data made public.

"Cassius Clay entered Central High School in the 10th grade on September 4, 1957, having completed the 9th grade at DuValle Junior High School. Clay's record contained a notation that he had attended elementary school in Louisville, Kentucky, at the Virginia Avenue School, and there was a notation that he had a special interest in art.

"On March 31, 1958, Clay voluntarily withdrew from Central High School. No reason for the withdrawal is shown on the records, but the records reflect that during the 1957–1958 school year Clay made poor grades, receiving a 65 in English, 65 in American history, 70 in biology and a 70 in general art. Clay re-entered Central High School in September of 1958, and remained until he graduated June 11, 1960. He ranked 376 out of a graduating class of 391. His average grades for the 9th, 10th, 11th and 12th years was 72.7.

"On January 3, 1957, Clay was given the Standard California Intelligence Quotient Test and attained a rating of 83. On February 15, 1960, he took a College Qualifications Test and scored a percentile of 27. That is, 73 percent of those taking the test scored better than Clay.

"At the time Clay attended Central High School, it was necessary for a student to earn 16 units during his 9th through 12th grades in order to graduate. Clay earned 16 units, earning them in the following subjects:

Subject	Units Earned	Grades Attained
English	4	75 70 73 74
Mechanical drawing	2	70 71
Choral music	2	70 71
Social studies	1	75
General science	1	70
Biology	1	70
General art	1	70
American history	1	75
Algebra I	1	70
Foods	1	83
Metal work	1	93

16 Total

"[Person X] advised that, during the time that Clay was attending high school, a passing mark was 70. Clay's record also reflected that he was rated as follows with respect to the following:

Emotional control	Fair
Intellectual ability	Average
Leadership	Fair
Health	Above average
Initiative	Average
Social attitude	Average
Effort	Average
Honesty	Average
Scholastic zeal	Average"

Devoting his energies almost exclusively to boxing, Cassius Clay fought 108 amateur bouts, winning six Kentucky Golden Gloves championships, two National Golden Gloves tournaments, and two National AAU titles by the time he was eighteen. Still, to the public at large, he was unknown. Then came the 1960 Rome Olympics— although after prevailing in the Olympic trials, Clay almost didn't go to Rome.

JOE MARTIN: "He was afraid of flying. We had a rough flight going to California for the trials, and so when it came time to go to Rome, he said he wasn't gonna fly, and that he wouldn't go. I said, 'Well, you'll lose the opportunity of being a great fighter,' and he said, 'Well, I'm not gonna go.' He wanted to take a boat or something. Anyway, I finally took him out to Central Park here in Louisville and we had a long talk for a couple or three hours, and I calmed him down and convinced him if he wanted to be heavyweight champion of the world, that he had to go to Rome and win the Olympics."[6]

So Cassius Marcellus Clay, Jr., went to Rome. Before the games, *Sports Illustrated* declared him "the best American prospect for a gold medal [in boxing]," adding, "Clay likes to display supreme confidence by doing intricate dance steps between passages of boxing."[7] Other observers were less impressed, but concurred with the view that Clay was "one of the best-known, best-liked athletes in the Olympic Village."[8] "You would have thought he was running for

Mayor," one teammate opined. "He went around introducing himself and learning other people's names and swapping team lapel pins. If they'd had an election, he would have won in a walk."[9]

Clay won his first three fights in the 178-pound division, scoring two unanimous decisions and a second-round knockout. Then, in the finals, he faced Zbigniew Pietrzykowski of Poland—a three-time European champion and bronze medalist from the 1956 Olympic Games. British journalist John Cottrell described the bout:

> In the first round, it seemed that Clay would be badly mauled. He was confused by his opponent's southpaw style, took some heavy punishment, and once showed his inexperience by closing his eyes in the face of a barrage of blows. Clay managed to keep out of trouble in the second round, and in the last minute he abandoned his show-off style with the fancy footwork and dropped hands, and stood his ground to throw four hard rights to the head. Even so, he was still behind on points at this crucial stage. "I knew," he explained afterwards, "that I had to take the third round big to win."
>
> Clay did finish big. In that final round he suddenly found his top form, moving in and out with expert judgment, punching crisply and with perfect timing. This sharper, better coordinated Clay stormed back with a torrent of combination punching that left Pietrzykowski dazed. He no longer relied too much on his left jab, but made equal use of his right to penetrate the southpaw's guard. Ripping into the stamina-lacking Pole, he drew blood and came preciously close to scoring a knock-out. At the final bell, Pietrzykowski was slumped helplessly against the ropes. There was no doubting the verdict. All the judges made Clay the points winner.[10]

Clay's roommate at the Rome Olympics was Wilbert "Skeeter" McClure, who won back-to-back National Golden Gloves and AAU championships, and gold medals at the 1959 Pan American and 1960 Olympic games. Now a psychotherapist and president of a Massachusetts consulting firm, McClure puts young Cassius Clay in perspective.

WILBERT "SKEETER" MCCLURE: "I first heard of Cassius Clay back in 1959 at the National Golden Gloves Tournament in Chicago. All the fighters were staying at the same hotel. I was in the lobby, and there was this kid there, and I heard him whispering to some other guys, 'There goes Skeeter McClure.' That's because I had won the Nationals in '58 and was coming back for more. Anyway, he and I both won the Nationals, and were part of a team that represented Chicago in an inter-city tournament against New York. We trained together, and I remember Cassius kept bugging everybody on the team, saying, 'Man, there are all these pretty girls on the streets; all these pretty girls walking around; we got to meet some of these girls.' And the rest of us weren't interested in that. We were just there to fight. But he kept agitating and asking and saying, 'Come on, let's put on our jackets and go someplace to impress the girls.' So finally the coaches set it up. It was all Cassius's doing. They took us to Marshall High School, which was a huge school in Chicago. We had pretty girls as hostesses to show us around. Then we went into the cafeteria for lunch, which was filled with more pretty girls. There were pretty girls sitting everywhere. And the guy who'd been agitating just sat there, staring at the food on his tray the whole time. He didn't say a word. I mean, he was so shy. We teased him about it for days afterward, and all he did was look at us and shrug his shoulders. He was very, very shy around girls.

"After that, maybe a month later, the National AAUs were held in my hometown of Toledo. He was there. Both of us won, and I invited him home to meet my parents and brother and sister. And we were together again for the Pan American trials at the University of Wisconsin, where he lost to Amos Johnson. Johnson was a grown man, a Marine, and a southpaw. I think that was the last fight Ali lost until Joe Frazier beat him twelve years later. And what I remember most about that time was, my dad had driven over from Toledo and a bunch of us went out for dinner afterward. We were in this restaurant, and Cassius was philosophical. All he said was, 'I just couldn't figure him out.' And if you think about it, when you're seventeen years old and you meet a man who's twenty-five or twenty-six, in the service, who fights left-handed, that's a big disadvantage. But he didn't grumble or moan or complain. He just said like a champion, 'I couldn't figure him out.'

"Then we made the Olympic team together. And in those days, being an Olympian was purely amateur; not like it is now. An amateur was an amateur. In fact, I almost didn't go to the Olympics because I had one more semester to finish at the University of Toledo. I was paying my own way through college, and I didn't think I'd be able to afford to go to the games and go to school at the same time, until finally the university gave me a scholarship for the last semester so I could afford to go to Rome. That wouldn't happen today. Now the money is there to get the talented fighters to where they have to go. A gold medal is seen as a marketing tool. But back then, we weren't fighting to form the cornerstone of a professional career. We were fighting for pride.

"On the plane going to Rome, I remember, we were trying to decide who would win gold medals, and Cassius led the conversation. He was voluble even then. As I recall, he was afraid of flying, and he talked about that too. But once we got airborne he managed to distract his fears by talking a lot. He said, 'Now, I'm gonna win a gold, and Skeeter's gonna win a gold.' And there was a welterweight who got killed after we came back, Harry Campbell. He said, 'Campbell's gonna win a gold.' And there were two others he predicted, too. We talked about our personalities and boxing styles and how we were nice clean-cut wholesome kids, and we thought that would appeal to the judges.

"In Rome, he was outgoing but he was seriously into boxing. I don't know of anybody on any team who took it more seriously than he did. We'd walk around and he'd go up to people and shake hands with them, but he had his mind on training. He worked for that gold medal. He trained very, very hard. We all did. You don't slough off and play games when you're trying to become an Olympic champion. And certainly, when I watched him train, he was one of the hardest trainers I'd ever seen.

"The boxers all trained together. We ate together. We interacted well as a team. I remember, one night I was in bed—we had three rooms for the boxing team with those awful bunk beds—and I was in my bed writing a love letter to my girl back in the States. Cassius came over and asked what I was writing. I told him, and he asked if I'd write one for him, too. I said, 'Sure.' So he told me what to write, and I wrote it out for him and handed him the letter. I don't know if he copied it over before he sent it back to her or not, but when I wrote it out, he said, 'Wow, that's nice.' He was very pleased. And even though he was a year older than when we'd met in Chicago, he was still very shy around girls. In the ring he could dance, but at the Olympic Village, we went to one of the Olympic canteens, and he didn't dance at all. And I went to several parties with him later on, and he didn't dance there either. He just didn't dance. This was part of that shyness around women. I guess he never learned how to dance and was too shy to go out and do it on his own.

"So that's the way he was. And looking back—and I believe this;

I've told Ali this several times—I've told him that he was fated. It's like there was a star when he was born that fated him to do what he was going to do and to have impact on mankind around the globe, and there's nothing he could have done to prevent it and nothing he could have done to make it happen. It's just one of those things. You know, psychology is a science, but there's some slippage in there. There's still some philosophy, and we're still trying to understand and explain human behavior, and some things we just can't explain. And when you think about this young man's life—when I first saw him when he came to our home in Toledo, his pants were up at his ankles, his sports coat was too short, but it's like the clothing was irrelevant because he glowed. Even then, you knew he was special; a nice, bright, warm, wonderful person. That was thirty years ago, and I guess if someone had told me back then that Cassius Clay would become the most famous person in the world, I never would have believed them. It just didn't seem possible, but look at him now."

2

The Entertainer

Following the 1960 Olympics, Cassius Clay was perfectly positioned for a love-in with the American people. Young, handsome, entertaining, and gifted, he radiated the aura of an All-American boy. When a Soviet reporter asked how it felt to win a gold medal for his country when there were restaurants in the United States he couldn't eat in, Clay looked his questioner in the eye and answered, "Tell your readers we got qualified people working on that problem, and I'm not worried about the outcome. To me, the USA is the best country in the world, including yours."[1]

Dick Schaap, assistant sports editor for *Newsweek* in 1960, remembers what Cassius Clay was like at the time.

DICK SCHAAP: "I first met him in New York, when the Olympic team gathered before it left for Italy, and I absolutely fell in love with him. He was an irrepressible, charming, totally natural young man. As many of us do when we're young, I had a lot more time to spend with my subjects in those days, so I took him and three of the other Olympic fighters to Sugar Ray Robinson's restaurant in Harlem for dinner. I remember him being very excited by whatever color shade of pastel Robinson's Cadillac was that year. Then, after dinner, we went outside, and on the corner of Seventh Avenue and 125th Street, he saw what was possibly the first black nationalist speaker he'd ever seen—a man standing literally on a soapbox. And as I recall, the speaker's message was 'buy black,' which seems like an awfully mild message now. But at the time, I remember Cassius was stunned that a black man would stand up and say those things in public. And of course, in Louisville, Kentucky, something like that would never have happened.

"Then, a month later, he came back from Rome. I met him at Idlewild Airport, and looking back, I suppose it's ironic that within four years both Cassius Clay and the airport changed their names. That night, we went out alone, just the two of us. We went to Times Square, and he had a phony newspaper printed up which said, 'Clay signs to fight Patterson.' Floyd Patterson, of course, was heavyweight champion of the world at the time. Then we went to Jack Dempsey's restaurant, and he saw this big cheesecake under glass behind the counter and looked at it rather longingly and asked me, 'Do you have to eat the whole thing, or can I buy just one piece?' I assured him that he could buy just one piece, so he had a piece of the famous Jack Dempsey cheesecake. We went to Birdland, which was across the street from Jack Dempsey's, and he ordered a soft drink and asked them to put one drop, literally one drop of liquor in it. He was eighteen, so he was old enough to drink in New York, but he'd never had a drink before and this way he could say he'd had a drink, but it was really just one drop. And he was quite pleased that, everywhere we went, people recognized him. Of course, his fight against the Pole had been on television just a few nights before. And the fact that he was wearing his Olympic jacket with the letters U.S.A. emblazoned six inches high on the front didn't hurt. Also, he was wearing his gold medal around his neck. Finally, we got back to the hotel—it was around one-thirty in the morning—and he made me stay for another hour looking at pictures he'd taken with his camera in Rome. It was quite a night, one of the more memorable nights of my life. And I suppose that's only fitting, because Ali is probably the most memorable person I've known."

After a brief stay in New York, Clay returned to a welcoming throng at the Louisville Airport, and recited what would become his first published poem:

How Cassius Took Rome

To make America the greatest is my goal,
So I beat the Russian, and I beat the Pole,

And for the USA won the Medal of Gold.
Italians said, "You're greater than the Cassius of Old."
We like your name, we like your game,
So make Rome your home if you will.
I said I appreciate your kind hospitality,
But the USA is my country still,
'Cause they waiting to welcome me in Louisville.[2]

Then came the inevitable pursuit of his talents by managers and promoters from around the world.

CASSIUS CLAY, SR.: "There were a lot of people who wanted to take him over when he came back from the Olympics. And I saw he could take care of himself in the ring, but I wanted to see that he was well taken care of out of it too. He was underage, and didn't know exactly how to handle himself in business. And I was aware that, without the right backing, he wouldn't have much success, so it was very important to me that he get off in the right hands. And that's what happened. I got him a good contract with people that could promote him. I'm responsible for his starting out right. All sorts of people were talking big, but nobody really backed it up the way I thought they should except for the Louisville Sponsoring Group."

The Louisville Sponsoring Group was a collection of eleven white men between the ages of twenty-five and seventy, ten of whom were millionaires or heirs to old-line Kentucky fortunes. William Faversham, the eleventh, brought the group together. A former investment counselor and vice-president of Brown-Forman Distillers Corporation, Faversham estimated the cost of launching Clay as a professional at $25,000 to $30,000. Accordingly, each member of the syndicate was asked to pay $2,800, except for Faversham, who was given a $1,400 discount for his organizational efforts.

The investors were motivated by varying considerations. Some saw the syndicate as a chance to make money. Others were guided by the desire to safeguard a local hero, or simply have a bit of fun. Regardless, the contract signed by Cassius Clay and cosigned by his parents was fair and generous for its time. Clay received a $10,000 signing bonus and, for the first two years, a guaranteed draw of $333 a month against earnings. The sponsoring group had options to extend the contract for up to four additional twelve-month periods. Earnings would be split fifty-fifty for the first four years and sixty-forty in Clay's favor thereafter. All management, training, travel, and promotional expenses, including a trainer's salary, would come out of the syndicate's end. And 15 percent of Clay's income would be set aside in a pension fund, which he could not touch until he reached age thirty-five or retired from boxing.

On October 29, 1960, three days after signing the managerial contract, Clay made his professional debut in Louisville's Freedom Hall before six thousand partisan fans. The opponent was Tunney Hunsaker—a part-time fighter with a seventeen and eight record, whose regular job was serving as police chief of Fayetteville, West Virginia. Big, white, cumbersome, and slow, Hunsaker, as expected, lost a six-round decision.

TUNNEY HUNSAKER: "Before the fight, I heard he'd won the Olympics so I knew I was meeting a tough bird. But I don't think there ever was a fighter, not a good one anyway, who went in the ring thinking he was gonna get beat. I know I never did.

"The afternoon of the fight, I met Clay downtown in a sporting goods store. He came in—he knew I was there—and he fooled around a little, bounced a basketball or something, and I could see he was nervous. But the night of the fight, he was fast as lightning, and he could hit from any position without getting hit. I tried just about every trick I knew to throw him off balance, but he was just too good. After the fight, when I got home that night, Judge Abbott—he's a judge here now, but he was an attorney then—he asked me, 'What do you think about the boy?' And I told him, 'Mr. Abbott, he'll be heavyweight champion of the world someday.' And I've got to tell you, looking back over the years, I'm honored, highly honored, to have been the first person Muhammad Ali fought in his professional career. I'm still the police chief here in Fayetteville. The kids here know who Muhammad Ali is, so they know who I am too. And it was an honor for me to have been in the ring with him; a real honor. That's all I can say."

Clay trained with Fred Stoner for the Hunsaker fight, but the Louisville Sponsoring Group felt that more experienced guidance would be necessary as his career progressed. Thus, in November 1960, he was sent to California to train with a living legend who was still fighting at age forty-seven—Archie Moore.

ARCHIE MOORE: "I love Ali because he's the goose that laid the golden egg. You see, guys like myself, we had to beat a pathway, and then Ali broke the door down. In the beginning, I fought for ten dollars a fight. Sometimes I was given a promise, nothing more. Guys like me, we were always marching, fighting, marching, fighting; and most of the time, it wasn't much fun. It didn't get to be fun until I began to make money, and nobody would give me a fight for the championship until I got old.

"And then I met Ali. Of course, he was Cassius Clay then. He had sought the services of Ray Robinson as a trainer, but Robinson was still in the ring and had no time for this brash young man. He couldn't afford to squander time in his remaining years with an amateur who was turning pro, regardless of how much potential Cassius Clay had, and I think it hurt Ali that the great Sugar Ray refused to be with him. But then people said, 'Well, there's a man out on the Coast who's a pretty good fighter. Why don't you go see him?' So Ali came out to train with me. I had a camp at the time called the Salt Mine in Ramona, California, about thirty-five miles from San Diego, and I thought this would be a fine place for a youngster to train. He stayed with me for a few days at my home in San Diego. My children were very small. I had two girls who were four and five years old at the time, and he was crazy abut them and they were crazy about him. It was love at first sight, and I could see that he came from a nice family and had a nice upbringing as far as children were concerned. Then we went to camp. There was a gymnasium in the barn called Bucket of Blood, and I had a skeleton's head and the name Bucket of Blood printed on the barn door. And I had these rocks all over the place; great big boulders with the names of great fighters printed on them. Ali looked at all that and said, 'Wow, this is great, man. I'm gonna get me a camp like this some day.'

"I admired his stamina when he first came to the Salt Mine. I saw him run up a hill that was at a thirty-five-degree angle. He ran up that hill twice, came down, ran over to me, and asked, 'Want me to do it again?' He had all the natural talent in the world, but he wasn't always willing to learn. I wanted to teach him the tricks of longevity, so when he was fighting as an older man he wouldn't take the punishment he eventually took in the ring. I said to him, 'Son, I want to teach you how to punch.' He knocked a lot of guys out, but he did it his way, with a lot of energy and a lot of strain. I said to him, 'I want to teach you how to be a real power puncher so you get your man out of there in one or two rounds. We don't want you to go fifteen rounds. We don't want you to go ten rounds. We don't want you to waste your stamina. Knock these guys out quick, because your body just has a certain number of hard fights in it.' And I thought it would have been nice for him to listen to that, but he told me, 'I don't want to box like Archie Moore. I want to box like Sugar Ray Robinson. Sugar Ray's my man.' I said, 'Son, you don't want to do like that. You want to go out, slide underneath the punch, and whap, knock the guy out, and then go on to the next guy. You'll fight a lot more fights like that.' And he said, 'I don't want to fight to be an old man. That's all right for you, but I'm gonna only fight five or six years, make me two or three million dollars, and quit fighting.' That was the big vision in front of him, a couple of million dollars, and then he'd retire as a young man and marry and raise his family. And that looks beautiful, even today, to a young man."

Meanwhile, Moore had his own ring career to tend to, and his new charge was driving him to distraction. Dick Sadler, Moore's trainer at the time, recalls life with young Cassius Clay.

DICK SADLER: "I rode with Clay from the west coast down to Texas, where Archie had this fight [on November 28, 1960, against Buddy Thurman in Dallas]. We went by train, and it was a pretty wild ride. First the kid would be standing shouting out of the carriage. 'I am the greatest. I am the greatest!' He'd shout this at the passing cars and sheep and fields and stuff. Then after a while he started singing this number by Chubby Checker about the twist. He didn't know the words, just kept on and on singing, 'Come on baby, let's do the twist; come on baby, let's do the twist!' And it got to me. It was driving me crazy, to tell you the truth. I said, 'Jesus, son, you done twisted all across California and Arizona.' By the time we got to New Mexico, I told him, 'Look, sing the Charleston or the Boogaloo or any damned thing, but get off the twist.' Seven hundred miles of twisting, twisting, and 'I am the greatest!' It drove me crazy!"[3]

ARCHIE MOORE: "I knew he was going to be a great fighter, but I wanted him to respect me as a man and as an instructor and fall in line in the learning process. And that seemed to amuse and sometimes anger him. He felt I was ordering him, and who was I to order him to do certain things, so he challenged me to spar with him. I didn't accept the challenge. I said, 'No, I don't box with amateurs.' At the time, I was light-heavyweight champion of the world, and that's not the way to work with a young man. I was his instructor, not his sparring partner. And there were other things he didn't take to kindly that were expected of him. We washed our own dishes and did our own cooking at the Salt Mine. I didn't have the money and wherewithal like the big timers to hire people. So I said to him, 'You've got to wash dishes on Wednesday and scrub floors on Thursday, and you can help me cook on Friday.' I told him how we divided up the chores. We had other men at the camp, and each person pulled his load. And he said to me, 'Archie, I didn't come here to be a dishwasher.' I told him, 'You're not a dishwasher, but you have to carry your own load.' He said, 'I ain't gonna wash no dishes like a woman.' So I said to him, 'Okay, you ain't gonna eat.' And so he said all right, he'd wash dishes, and he looked at me with those pretty eyes and was scowling at me the whole time he was washing. And then the next day came and it was time to mop the floors, and he said okay, okay, he mopped the floors. But just as soon as I thought he was becoming disciplined, he said, 'I'm tired of this, I want to go home.' Christmas was coming up, and he said he wanted to go home for Christmas. Christmas was a good excuse for him to go. And I said, 'Okay, how do you want to go; do you want to fly?' He said, 'No, don't want to go on no plane.' I asked, 'Do you want to go on a bus?' He said, 'No, I want to go on a train.' So I put him on a train and sent him home to see his folks in Louisville for Christmas, and he never came back again. I had an idea he wasn't going to return. I was putting pressure on him to bring him under discipline, and this was the thing that Ali did not get. He was always trying to discipline his superiors, the people who were working with him. To tell you the truth, the boy needed a good spanking, but I wasn't sure who could give it to him. And the saddest time I had with him was when he left the Salt Mine. I had to keep my propriety up. I'm a great instructor and a great teacher, but I was sad when he left. I loved him like a son and I could see a lot of revenue leaving with him, but I had my dignity. So I had to say, 'Well, go ahead. If you want to go, I don't want to prevent you from doing anything you want to do. If you want to go home, that's your prerogative.' And then, after he left, there was nothing for me to do but watch his rise and eventually his fall. As his career progressed, we began to bring his name up against Joe Louis, and I believe in my mind and heart that Ali would have beaten Joe. If they'd fought five times, I believe Ali would have won four. The only man that I could see—and I've only seen him perform on old motion pictures—the only man that I could see Ali not being able to beat might be Jack Johnson, because Johnson was a dancing man himself. Jack Johnson was a defensive man. He was a hard hitter and a master boxer."

Once Clay returned to Louisville, the search for a new trainer began. Initially, the Sponsoring Group leaned toward Ernie Braca, but Braca was committed to Sugar Ray Robinson. Fred Stoner was considered, but found wanting in experience on the professional level. Finally, William Faversham telephoned Madison Square Garden and asked Harry Markson (president of MSG Boxing) for a recommendation. Markson suggested Angelo Dundee.

ANGELO DUNDEE: "The first time I met Cassius was 1957. I was in Louisville with Willie Pastrano to fight John Holman, who was a pretty good banger. We were in the hotel watching television, when the phone rang. And it was this kid saying, 'Mr. Dundee, my name is Cassius Marcellus Clay; I'm the Golden Gloves champion of Louisville, Kentucky.' And he gave me a long list of championships he was planning to win, including the Olympics and the heavyweight championship of the world, and then he said he wanted to come up to the room to meet us. I put my hand over the mouthpiece and said to Willie, 'There's a nut on the phone; he wants to meet you!' And Willie said, 'What the heck; there's nothing good on television.' So a few minutes later, the kid was in our room with his brother, Rudy. Both of them were handsome, well-mannered boys. Mostly we talked about boxing, and they stayed for three or four hours.

"Then, in 1959, Willie and I were back in Louisville for a fight against Alonzo Johnson. This time, Cassius came to the gym and asked if he could spar with Willie. I don't like pros sparring with amateurs; it's a good way to get someone hurt. But Willie was willing, and I figured why not let them go a round? Cassius was seventeen. Willie was a professional on his way to winning the light-heavyweight championship of the world. And I gotta tell you, Cassius won that round. So when Bill Faversham called [in December 1960], I was well acquainted with Cassius Clay. Faversham explained the situation to me, and came down to Miami with some of his partners to interview me. I liked them. They were satisfied with the training program I had in mind. And then it was time to talk money. They gave me a choice—$125 a week guaranteed, or 10 percent off the top. I took the guarantee, which wasn't the smartest move I've made in my life, although after the second Liston fight, we worked out a percentage deal. Anyway, once the money was set, I suggested waiting until after Christmas and then bringing Cassius to Miami to train. That was fine with them, but ten minutes later, they called back and told me, 'Listen, the kid wants to come to Miami now. He wants to fight. He says when he's fighting every day is Christmas.' "

On December 19, 1960, Clay began working with Dundee in Miami's Fifth Street Gym. Eight days later, he knocked out Herb Siler in the fourth round, and the bond between fighter and trainer was formed.

MUHAMMAD ALI: "Angelo Dundee was with me from my second professional fight. And no matter what happened after that, he was always my friend. He never interfered with my personal life. There was no bossing, no telling me what to do and not do, in or out of the ring. He was there when I needed him, and he always treated me with respect. There just wasn't any problem ever between us."

ANGELO DUNDEE: "The fun I had during those early years together was second to none, because it was just me and Muhammad. I had to hire guys out of town to work his corner. Gosh it was fun, absolute joy. And that was the whole key to Muhammad; when you have fun you can excel.

"Training him was a whole different ballgame from most fighters. You didn't have to push. It was like jet propulsion. Just touch him and he took off. The important thing was, always make him feel like he was the guy. He used to say, 'Angelo doesn't train me.' And I didn't; he was right. I directed him, and made him feel that he was the innovator. He'd come out of the ring after a sparring session, and I'd say, 'You threw a great left hook, the way you turned your shoulder with it, your body with it, your toe with it, fantastic.' The next time he sparred, he'd throw it that way. Same thing with his balance and not touching the ropes with his shoulders. These are things I learned from Charlie Goldman [Rocky Marciano's trainer]. Make the star feel that he's doing it on his own."

Angelo Dundee was, and is, one of the most respected trainers in boxing. "He's a pure boxing guy," says Ferdie Pacheco. "In a title fight, Angelo would work for nothing if he had to, because the fact that he impacts on the match is his identity." "In a sport not known for its decency," adds Dick Schaap, "Angelo Dundee is a decent man." Even boxing's most angry critic, Howard Cosell, concurs. "If I had a son who wanted to be a fighter and I couldn't stop him," says Cosell, "the only man I'd let train him is Angelo."

ANGELO DUNDEE: "In choosing opponents early in Ali's career, I tried not to give away too many things. Too much maturity; too much strength; too much speed, although no one was quicker than Cassius. His third fight was against Tony Esperti, and he knocked him out in the third round. Then he knocked out Jim Robinson in one. And around that time, he sparred with Ingemar Johansson. That was really something."

Johansson, the former heavyweight champion, was in Florida training for a rematch with Floyd Patterson. Harold Conrad, who coordinated promotion for that bout, recalls the Clay-Johansson sparring session.

HAROLD CONRAD: "The promoters decided to bring Ingemar to Miami to sell some tickets for the fight. Whitey Bimstein was his trainer. We got to Miami, and there weren't any sparring partners. So I asked Angelo, 'Do you have someone who can work with this guy?' Angelo said, 'Yeah,' and yelled, 'Hey, Cash.' And this big beautiful-looking young man—he must have been eighteen or nineteen—floated over, literally danced over. Angelo asks, 'You wanna work with Johansson?' And the kids says, 'Johansson?' Then he starts singing. 'I'll go dancin' with Johansson. I'll go dancin' with Johansson.' I said to Angelo, 'What the hell is this?' And Angelo says, 'You ain't seen nothing yet with this crazy bastard.' Anyway, they got in the ring, and Johansson had a great right hand but two left feet, and Cassius started dancing, popping him. Now remember, Johansson was getting ready to fight for the heavyweight championship of the world, but Cassius handled him like a sparring partner. And when I saw Clay's jab, I sat up and said, 'Jesus, that's it!' You know, guys around the fight business, you don't have to look at a fighter very long. Some of them you look at, and right like that, you know they have it. And the whole time, Clay doesn't shut up. He keeps talking to Johansson, saying, 'I'm the one who should be fighting Patterson, not you. Come on, here I am; come and get me, sucker. Come on, what's the matter, can't hit me?' Johansson was furious. I mean, he was pissed. He started chasing Clay around the ring, throwing right hands and missing by twenty feet, looking ludicrous. At the end of the second round, he was so exhausted that Whitey Bimstein just called it off."

Another witness to the sparring session was Gil Rogin—now corporate editor for Time, Inc., publications, but then a staff writer for *Sports Illustrated*.

GIL ROGIN: "When he sparred with Johansson, it was the greatest defensive boxing exhibition I'd ever seen. Here was a man, a boy really, who'd had four professional fights, and he made a monkey out of Johansson. I'd never seen anything like it before, and I've never seen anything like it since. As soon as I got back to New York, I told the editors at *Sports Illustrated*, 'This guy is going to be heavyweight champion someday. You have to write about him.' I didn't know he was going to beat Sonny Liston; Liston wasn't even champion yet. But I knew at some point it was a lock, a no-brainer, that Cassius Clay would be heavyweight champion of the world.

"*Sports Illustrated* was a relatively young magazine then. We were only six or seven years old, struggling through a period of emergence. And over the next few years, Ali was terribly important to the magazine. Obviously, both he and the magazine would have succeeded without the other, but clearly, it was a mutually beneficial relationship. And I'll tell you something funny. Even when he was young, Ali used to fall asleep sometimes when we were talking. Now when he falls asleep, people assume it's brain damage, but he always did it. With the energy he expended, he had to be tired a lot of the time. He'd be sitting there talking and I'd be taking notes, and soon his voice would start running down like one of those old record players, and then he'd be asleep. He did it a lot, and it didn't surprise me because he expended so much energy. His whole life was this energetic display that would exhaust absolutely anybody."

ANGELO DUNDEE: "After the Johansson sparring session, Cassius fought Donnie Fleeman—a Texas kid, very tough, but he couldn't cope with Muhammad's speed. Then we went home to Louisville for Lamar Clark, a real beauty. Clark was from Utah, and was knocking everybody out, but Muhammad ended it in the second round. After that, it was Duke Sabedong, and this was interesting. Sabedong was a tough fighter, a big tall Hawaiian, and he went the full ten rounds. But the main thing was, while we were in Las Vegas for the Sabedong fight, Cassius met Gorgeous George."

MUHAMMAD ALI: "A couple of days before I fought Sabedong, I did a radio program with Gorgeous George. First, they asked me about my fight. And I can't say I was humble, but I wasn't too loud. Then they asked Gorgeous George about a wrestling match he was having in the same arena, and he started shouting, 'I'll kill him; I'll tear his arm off. If this bum beats me, I'll crawl across the ring and cut off my hair, but it's not gonna happen because I'm the greatest wrestler in the world.' And all the time, I was saying to myself, 'Man, I want to see this fight. It don't matter if he wins or loses; I want to be there to see what happens.' And the whole place was sold out when Gorgeous George wrestled. There was thousands of people including me. And that's when I decided I'd never been shy about talking, but if I talked even more, there was no telling how much money people would pay to see me."

The truth is, Cassius Clay was mouthing off long before he met Gorgeous George. But after the Sabedong fight, he elevated bragging as an art form to a new level. "One of these days," he told Huston Horn of *Sports Illustrated*, "they're liable to make the house I grew up in a national shrine." Others were treated to similar sentiments, and on any given day, anyone within earshot might be informed, "I got the height, the reach, the weight, the physique, the speed, the courage, the stamina, and the natural ability that's going to make me great. Putting it another way, to beat me you got to be greater than great."[4] Before long, Angelo Dundee was moved to proclaim, "There's only one Cassius Clay—thank God."[5]

ANGELO DUNDEE: "The truth is, I never understood the resentment about his popping off. Maybe later, when he got into issues like the war and religion, I could understand it, even though I always believed he had the right to speak his mind. But before that? Hey, I remember people complaining because Joe Louis didn't talk. All a fighter would say in those days was, 'I'm looking forward to the fight, and I'll do my best.' That doesn't sell tickets. Muhammad changed the way things work. In promoting boxing, he made the fighter the main guy."

One reason Clay was so successful at self-promotion was that he had the personality to carry it off. What might have been insufferable in another fighter was considered charming in him until he challenged the establishment. Also helpful was the fact that he was extraordinarily handsome; better looking than most movie idols. And he benefited enormously from Dundee's advice regarding the media.

DICK SCHAAP: "All the writers liked Angelo, and he was very good back then at schooling Ali, telling him this is this writer and this is that writer, and this is how to make the relationship work. Cassius had a good memory. Once he saw a face, even if he couldn't remember the name, he could pick that person out of a crowd. And of course, he liked to talk, with the result being that he probably granted more interviews than anyone else in the history of the earth. I can't imagine a politician or show business figure who talked to as many people so many times for as long as he did. As he got on in his career, the act began to get stale. By the time we were in Manila, a lot of it was boring. He'd end a training session by going on the ropes and reciting old poetry and talking to the crowd. And while it was very entertaining the first ten times, by the twentieth time you'd say, 'Hey, let's go out to lunch.' But in the early days, when he was fresh, every minute with him was exciting. And even when he got old, it was still more fun being bored by Ali than being fascinated by just about anybody else."

ANGELO DUNDEE: "He was the most available superstar of our era, and I pride myself on that. I used to point the newspaper guys out to him and say, 'These are your people. Open up to them. Work with them. They can help.' You know, it's funny. Muhammad was never as talkative as people thought. In private, even twenty-five years ago, a lot of the time he was real thoughtful and quiet. But he knew how to promote himself. God, he could do that."

Neil Leifer, possibly the best sports photographer of his generation, covered Ali for *Time* and *Sports Illustrated* from the early 1960s through Ali's fight against Larry Holmes.

NEIL LEIFER: "How good was Ali at self-promotion? Let me tell you a story that shows his genius. After he turned pro, *Sports Illustrated* did a piece on him. They assigned a free-lance photographer named Flip Schulke, and Ali—he was Cassius Clay then—asked, 'Who do you work for?' Schulke told him he did a lot of work for *Life*. This was when *Life* was the biggest magazine in the country, and Ali wasn't that big then. He'd won the gold medal, but that was it. There was no reason for Ali to be in *Life* magazine, so when he said, 'Man, how about shooting me for *Life*,' Schulke told him, 'I'd love to, but I'd never get it past the editors.' Well, Ali accepted that, but a few minutes later, he was asking questions again. 'Tell me some of the photographs you've done.' And Schulke explained that he did a lot of underwater photography; that was his specialty. And Ali thought of something on the spur of the moment, which shows what an absolute genius he was. His eyes widened, and he told Schulke, 'I never told nobody this, but me and Angelo have a secret. Do you know why I'm the fastest heavyweight in the world? I'm the only heavyweight that trains underwater.' Schulke said, 'What do you mean?' And Ali explained, 'You know why fighters wear heavy shoes when they run? They wear those shoes because, when you take them off and put the other shoes on, you feel real light and you run real fast. Well, I get in the water up to my neck and I punch in the water, and then when I get out of the water, I'm lightning fast because there's no resistance.' Schulke was skeptical, but Ali swore it was the truth, and to prove his point, he told Schulke, 'Tomorrow morning, you can see me do it. I do it every morning with Angelo, and no one's ever seen it before. I'll let you photograph it for *Life* magazine as an exclusive.' So Schulke called up *Life* and suggested the piece, and I think they ran five pages of Ali up to his neck in a swimming pool. And the two things I remember most about that were, first, Ali couldn't swim, not a bit; and second, Ali had never thrown a punch underwater in his life. It was a total bullshit story he made up, but it got him in *Life*, and *Life* didn't do it as a joke. They were convinced he trained underwater. Now that's a genius you don't see in people very often. Genius and a bit of a con man, too."

Clearly, Cassius Clay could publicize and self-promote, but the question remained: How well could he fight? By holding his hands low and leaning away from instead of slipping punches, he seemed perpetually on the verge of disaster. That might make for entertaining fights, but a number of experts doubted his skills. They saw Clay as a runner, not a dancer. His jab, to their way of thinking, was a flick, not a punch. His natural ability and speed were such that he could outrun the mistakes he made against novices. But once he moved to more competitive opposition, a lack of fundamentals would bring him down. Indeed, A. J. Liebling, the dean of boxing writers, opined, "I watched Clay's performance in Rome, and considered it attractive but not probative. Clay had a skittering style, like a pebble over water. He was good to watch, but he seemed to make only glancing contact. It is true that the Pole finished the three-round bout helpless and out on his feet, but I thought he had just run out of puff chasing Clay, who had then cut him to pieces. A boxer who uses his legs as much as Clay used his in Rome risks deceleration in a longer bout."[6]

MUHAMMAD ALI: "People said I held my hands too low and did other things wrong, but when I was young, my defense was my legs. My style in the ring was to keep my distance, don't get too close, stay just out of range, get in just enough to punch, and get out."

ANGELO DUNDEE: "In the beginning, a lot of people criticized Ali for not being able to take a punch. That's why he danced around the ring, they thought. Those guys didn't know what they were talking about. Ask any fighter and he'll tell you, you don't get hit because it's fun. You get hit because sometimes you can't avoid it, and if you can avoid it, more power to you. Another thing they said was, 'All Cassius had was a jab.' Well, he had a lot more than that, but remember, a jab is a punch in the face. And the way Ali threw it, he could stun you or cut you up. He was a marksman with that jab. Before every fight, I'd tell him, keep that jab in the other guy's face. Stuff it in so hard it comes out the back of his head."

After his victory over Duke Sabedong, Ali became the first young fighter just out of an amateur career to have his bouts televised nationally. Teddy Brenner was the matchmaker for Madison Square Garden Boxing at the time.

TEDDY BRENNER: "I'd met Ali in the summer of 1960, just before he went to Rome. I was in my office at the Garden. He came in and asked, 'Are you Teddy Brenner?' I said, 'Yeah'; and he introduced himself. He said, 'My name is Cassius Clay; I'm going to the Olympics; I'm gonna win a gold medal; I'm gonna be the next heavyweight champion of the world; and I want to borrow ten dollars.' He was going up to Harlem and wanted to have a good time. So I lent him the money; I never figured I'd get it back. But after the Olympics, he came into my office and actually paid me.

"Those were the days when Madison Square Garden arranged fifty television fights a year for the *Gillette Cavalcade of Sports*. Naturally, we put a lot of fights on in the Garden, but when the Garden wasn't available, we used arenas around the country. What we'd do is, ask a promoter to put on a show, pay the main event fighters ourselves, keep TV rights, and let the promoter have the gate. So after the Olympics, I watched Clay very closely, because at some point, I knew, the Garden would want to use him.

"The first fight we did together was televised from Louisville; Clay against Alonzo Johnson [on July 22, 1961]. Johnson was a proven fighter; not a big puncher, but experienced and smart. Clay won a ten-round decision, and then we matched him against Alex Miteff. That one was in Louisville too, and a couple of hours before the fight, we realized that no one had brought boxing gloves. The stores were closed; it was too late to bring gloves in from someplace else. Finally, we found two pairs that were half horsehair and half foam rubber. Most gloves are all horsehair, but these were half-and-half. They'd been lying around in some gym for a long time, and were hard as a rock. We thought it would help Miteff. He was a good puncher, and Clay couldn't punch. In the fifth found it was an even fight, but Miteff figured to come on in the late rounds, because he was a slow starter and a good body puncher. Then in the sixth, Clay hit him on the chin and knocked him out with one punch. Miteff had never been knocked out before. And in the dressing room afterward, he kept asking what happened. He couldn't believe that Cassius Clay had knocked him out."

After Miteff, Clay fought again in Louisville—this time against Willie Besmanoff. Before his previous bout, the hometown hero had advised reporters, "My plan for fighting Alex Miteff is two fast left jabs, a rapid right, and a left hook. And if he's still standing and the referee isn't holding him up, then I'm gonna run." Now, preparing for Besmanoff, Clay declared, "I'm embarrassed to get into the ring with this unrated duck. I'm ready for top contenders like Patterson and Sonny Liston. Besmanoff must fall in seven."[7] And that was precisely what happened. Besmanoff was a hopelessly outmatched fighter, whom Clay could have knocked out from the early rounds on. But mindful of his prediction, and ignoring Dundee's pleas to "stop playing," Clay extended the bout until the seventh round. Now there was yet another story for the media to write. For the first time in memory, a fighter was announcing the round in which he would dispose of opponents, and then making good on his prediction. With media attention rapidly growing, Madison Square Garden decided to showcase Clay in New York.

TEDDY BRENNER: "We matched him against Sonny Banks, and it figured to be a tough fight. Banks was young, a converted southpaw, and he could punch. I wanted to see if Clay could fight. And

I wanted to see if he could draw fans someplace besides Louisville and Miami. John Condon was our director of publicity, so it was his job to help put people in the seats. Right away, John and Clay hit it off."

JOHN CONDON: "We were in the old Garden then, the one on Eighth Avenue between Forty-ninth and Fiftieth. And Cassius Clay was a publicist's dream. Fighters today feel they get paid to go up the steps, get in the ring, fight, and that's it. You have limousines pick them up at the hotel for *Live at Five*, and they don't understand why *Live at Five* can't come to the hotel. And you try to explain, 'Hey, it's called *Live at Five*; it's not on tape.' And you've gone out and busted your ass to get this interview, and they're bitching about the fact that they have to go across the street in a limousine to the studio. Or they come to New York for a press conference, and you get them booked on a radio show and two TV shows, and they don't want to do it. They say, 'Why can't these people come to the press conference; that's what I'm doing the press conference for.' But with Cassius, the moment I met him, he said, 'Hi, John. What do you want me to do?'

"He wore a bow tie all the time in those days. Everything was brand new to him, and he was full of life. A pleasure to watch, a pleasure to talk to, and a pleasure to be with. He used to say to me, 'Let's go watch the foxes, John.' The foxes were girls, and we'd stand out in front of Jack Dempsey's restaurant on Forty-ninth Street and Seventh Avenue and watch the girls go by. He wouldn't say anything to them. He wouldn't flirt or bother them. He just looked. He might say something to me about how she's pretty or whatever, but he never said anything nasty, derogatory, or harassing to any of the women.

"I was like a lot of other people, I didn't know what to make of him; he was so new and refreshing and so likable. I'm a New York City guy, so naturally I thought it was an act. I was convinced it was an act, and in a way it was. In a lot of ways, he was putting everybody on, because if you sat down and talked to him alone, he was a different person. He would become serious in a man-to-man conversation. But when he was on, so to speak, he just ate everybody up and had everybody falling in love with him.

"He used to walk up to people on the street and say, 'My name is Cassius Clay, and I'm going to be heavyweight champion of the world.' He'd go on the subways and say, 'I'm Cassius Clay; I'm going to be heavyweight champion of the world, and I'm fighting at Madison Square Garden on such and such a date.' The one thing he always worried about was not enough people would come to see him fight. And he charmed everybody. It was very hard to resent anything he did. A lot of people might have if it had been somebody else, but the way he did it, he just had a certain quality where everybody took an immediate liking to him. I know I certainly did. Maybe that's because I was a publicist and I realized what I could do with this product, so to speak. I saw a million things that I could do to promote him and get the world to know about him. And everything I did, everything I suggested, there wasn't a single thing I ever suggested that he didn't agree to do. We used to sit down at night in the Midtown Motor Inn, and think of things we were going to do. He would think of things, or I'd think of something and he'd embellish it. A lot of fighters, you suggest something, and they say, 'Nah, I don't want to do that.' And then the manager gets into the picture, and it's awful. But with Cassius, there was never any trouble. Promoting his fights, it didn't even take two to tango, because he did it all for you. Nobody could get you more publicity than he did. He charmed everybody. His round predictions alone were worth the price of admission. He did everything except grab the microphone during the prefight introductions. And I'm sure, if he'd thought of it, he'd have done that too."

After Madison Square Garden's prefight promotion was complete, there remained the formality of fighting Sonny Banks. Clay had predicted a fourth-round knockout. Gil Clancy was one of his cornermen for the bout.

GIL CLANCY: "Angelo and I had been partners back in 1951 before he moved to Florida, and when he came up to New York, he needed somebody to work the corner for the Banks fight. He asked if I would, and I said sure.

"Before the fight, in the dressing room, whenever there was more than one other person around, Clay seemed very confident, very cocky, telling everyone what he was gonna do, and so on. It was like self-hypnosis. He couldn't be beat. Then, just before we went to the ring, I was alone with him and his mood changed. For a few seconds, whatever his big mouth said he was gonna do, this wasn't the same cocky kid I thought. He looked at me, and asked, 'Hey, Gil, do you really think I can beat this guy?'

"And it was a good fight. Banks was a puncher. That's all; he didn't have much else, but he could punch. Halfway through the first round, he nailed Cassius on the chin with a left hook, and Cassius went down like a sack of wheat. Angelo turned pale. I thought I was going to have to revive Angelo instead of the fighter. People ask now, what went through my mind when he went down. And the truth is, I've seen lots of fighters go down. I wanted to see if he'd get up. And he did. I think he was more embarrassed than hurt. He got up throwing punches, ran rings around Banks, and knocked him out in the fourth round just like he said he would."

ANGELO DUNDEE: "Each fight proved a little something to me, and I started to realize the talent I had in my hands. Banks hit Muhammad right on the jaw, and on the way down, his eyes were closed. But when his butt hit the canvas, he woke up. That's when I saw his recuperative powers.

"Then [on February 28, 1962] he fought Don Warner. Warner was tough, another left-hooker, from Philadelphia, but Cassius kept him off balance. The guy would cock his hook, and Cassius would feint, stick, and move away from the punch. He knocked him out in the fourth round. And all the reporters wanted to talk about was his prediction, because he'd promised everyone it would be the fifth. So Cassius told them that Warner wouldn't shake hands before the fight, which made him mad, so he subtracted one round for poor sportsmanship."

On April 23, 1962, Clay ran his record to thirteen wins and no losses by knocking out George Logan in Los Angeles. The fight itself was hardly memorable, but the trip was important because Los Angeles was where Clay met Howard Bingham.

MUHAMMAD ALI: "Everybody says I love people, so it's only fair that I have the best friend in the world, and that's Howard Bingham. He never asks for anything; he's always there when someone needs him. There's no one like him. He's the best there is. And if you write that, I don't want Howard to think I'm getting soft, so write down that he's lucky I'm his friend too. And tell him I said I'm the only person in the world who likes him."

For twenty-nine years, Howard Bingham, in many ways, has been the closest person to the most famous man on earth. A free-lance photographer who has been under contract to *Life*, *Sports Illustrated*, and numerous other publications, he has taken over five hundred thousand photos of Ali, and stands in contrast to the hustlers and exploiters who later invaded Ali's life. If Ali was Don Quixote, then Bingham was his Sancho Panza.

HOWARD BINGHAM: "I was with a black newspaper in Los Angeles called *The Sentinel*. And my assignment that day was to cover Ali at a news conference to announce a fight at the Los Angeles Sports Arena against George Logan. I'd never heard of Cassius Clay, but I went to the news conference, introduced myself, took a couple of photos, and left. Then, that afternoon, I was driving downtown and saw these two guys on the corner of Fifth and Broadway, Cassius Clay and his brother Rudolph. I asked if they wanted a ride someplace because it looked like they were waiting for a bus, and they said no. They were just watching the girls go by. So I asked if they'd like to take a ride with me. They got in the car, and I had some errands to do. Then I took them by a bowling alley, to my mother's house, and a couple of other places and we hit it off good.

"That was in the spring. Ali came back to Los Angeles a couple of months later to fight Alejandro Lavorante, and then again at the end of the year for Archie Moore. Both times, I showed him around. He and Angelo offered me money to be a press secretary or guide, and I did all that stuff, but I never took the money. It wasn't something I wanted to get paid for. As far as I was concerned, we were friends.

"Then, on New Year's Day 1963, Ali called me up and asked if I wanted to come to Miami and hang out with him for a while. I said yeah. I'd never been on an airplane before. I arrived in Miami on a Sunday night. Ali met me at the airport, and the next morning we drove to Louisville to his parents' home. After that, we went to Pittsburgh, where he had a fight against Charlie Powell. I'd never been in cold weather before, so he bought me earmuffs, an overcoat, and long underwear. And we hung out together until March, when my draft board started messing with me. That took a while, getting Uncle Sam off my back. As far as the Army was concerned, I didn't want to go, and I'd heard that if you drank a lot of 7-Up, you'd have sugar in your blood. And also, I have a speech impediment [Bingham stutters], and I really let them hear it. It was a real handicap that day when I went in for my physical. But Ali would always call and see how I was doing and how my mother was doing. And finally, when I got things settled with the Army, we got back together again."

ANGELO DUNDEE: "After Logan, he fought Billy Daniels at St. Nicholas Arena in New York. Daniels was undefeated, a real cute sucker. It was a tough fight until Muhammad busted him up. Then we went back to Los Angeles, and he looked like a million dollars against Alejandro Lavorante. Against Lavorante, he looked the way he looked against Cleveland Williams. Now everybody in the business was talking about him, and we figured he was ready to fight Archie Moore."

Clay versus Moore was typical of boxing. A young up-and-coming fighter against an over-the-hill "name" opponent. Invariably, the older man has little chance of winning. He's being paid for the marquee value of his name. Yet certain elements of the match-up were intriguing. Clay had been in fifteen professional fights. Moore was a veteran of over two hundred. Clay, of course, had trained briefly with Moore. And most important, from a financial point of view, they were boxing's greatest outside-the-ring showmen, as the prefight promotional build-up confirmed:

Cassius Clay: "I do notice a lot of press releases and radio statements and TV announcers complaining about how I talk too much and I'm cocky and I need a good beating. And it's true. I do talk a lot but everything I say I mean to back up. I notice Archie Moore said the empty wagon makes the most noise. Well, I don't know too much about wagons, but that old man won't go but four rounds with me."

Archie Moore: "The only way I'll fall in four is by toppling over Clay's prostrate form. He belittles people too much. Even his contemporaries hope I beat the socks off him. As I've said, Clay can go with speed in all directions, including straight down if hit properly. I have a good solid right hand that will fit nicely on his chops."[9]

Cassius Clay: "I realize that Archie's a great fighter, but Archie is a great older fighter. Archie Moore is going around saying he's developing a lip buttoner for me. See, I've earned a reputation as the Louisville Lip. He says he's gonna invent a punch called the Lip Buttoner, but I'm the one who's gonna use it. Why doesn't somebody just get that old guy a pension; why doesn't somebody just retire him? He's too old, he's old enough to be my grand-daddy. I wish people would get together and work out a pension or something for him or I'm gonna have to do it once and for all."[10]

Archie Moore: "I view this young man with mixed emotions. Sometimes he sounds humorous, but sometimes he sounds like a man that can write beautifully but doesn't know how to punctuate."[11]

Cassius Clay: "Archie's been living off the fat of the land; I'm here to give him his pension plan. When you come to the fight, don't block the aisle and don't block the door. You will all go home after round four."[12]

"This fight," Arthur Daley wrote in *The New York Times*, "has assumed the magnitude, conversationally, of The Battle Of The Century."[13] By fight time, Clay was a three to one favorite, and 16,200 fans paid a California indoor record $182,600 to see the bout.

ARCHIE MOORE: "I had to fight him for financial reasons. It wasn't what either of us wanted, but I was in a bind financially. I was getting on in years, and had gone to Canada for a fight that didn't come off. And when I came back, I had to face a lot of debts. There was a promoter who wanted to showcase Cassius and thought that I was right for him, and so I took the money that they offered me to box.

"We had a tournament of words before the fight. He was full of poetry and brash statements, and I certainly never did lack for verbosity or elocution. But he outdid me in the area of poetry and the area of prose, too, because he was so naturally gifted in those areas. Then we fought and he knocked me out. My plan when I went into the fight was to move around and catch him with hooks to the body, because no one had hit him to the body much. Slow him down, and then maybe get him with a sneaky right hand. But his speed was too much for me, and I was made for him in that I used a wrap-around defense to cover up. I would leave the top of my head exposed, and that's what he wanted. You see, he had a style, he would hit a man a lot of times around the top of the head. And if you hit the top of a man's head, you shake up his thought pattern. You disturb his thoughts. A fighter has to think, but if someone is plunking you on top of the head, you cannot think correctly. And this is what he did. He made me dizzy and he knocked me out.

"People ask me now, if I'd fought Clay when I was young, would the outcome have been different? I don't think so. One never knows for sure, but I told you before, Ali would have beaten Joe Louis four times out of five. And I was a pretty good light-heavyweight, but I think Joe Louis would have beaten me."

Two months after defeating Archie Moore, Clay stepped into the ring in Pittsburgh against Charlie Powell and knocked him out as predicted in the third round. "When he first hit me," Powell said after the bout, "I thought to myself, I can take two of those to get in one of my own. But in a little while, I found out I was getting dizzier and dizzier every time he hit me, and he hurt. Clay throws punches so easily you don't realize how much they shock you until it's too late."[14]

Mort Sharnik, who covered Ali for twenty years, was in Pittsburgh for the Powell fight.

MORT SHARNIK: "I was with him on many occasions, but I remember him best when he was young. One time, the Sponsoring Group threw a luncheon for him in Louisville, and of course, Cassius was the centerpiece. There were some very beautiful young black girls there. Clearly, they were interested in him, and he didn't give out any vibrations toward them at all. I asked myself, 'What is this?' He was so dynamically handsome, and I didn't understand why he didn't seem interested. At his age, I might have said, 'I'm going to be cool; I'm going to be in control.' But I would have given off some sexual vibrations, and there weren't any coming from him. The girls were kind of puzzled by it too, because they were smitten with him and would have loved to flirt a little. I even wondered if he was gay, which in light of how he lived later on was as far from the mark as I could be.

"But getting to the Powell fight, as usual Cassius was talking all that jive, making predictions, and doing routines with his greeting-card poetry. He was very imaginative and he was talking about Powell as if he were a child fantasizing. You know, I'll do this to that old monster; he's Frankenstein; I'll turn him inside out. And that's fine until you meet Frankenstein. And now he was face-to-face with Charlie Powell at the weigh-in. And Charlie Powell was an ex–football player, very big, very strong, much more muscular than Clay. And Cassius looked at him at the weigh-in, and all of a sudden a touch of reality began to creep in. They started rapping at one another. Cassius seemed a little apprehensive, and Powell's brother, Art, who was a football player—he was there, and he's a talker too. Well, finally Cassius got really agitated. He'd taken his shirt off for the weigh-in, his undershirt, and then he put it back on backwards, which of course Powell pointed out. So Clay fumed and fussed and announced, 'I'm going,' and he opened the door and stomped into a broom closet.

"But it was at that fight that I recognized he was an extraordinary fighter. In the second round, Powell hit him a shot to the solar plexus, a right hand underneath and a left hand on top, and the shot to the solar plexus sunk in, it seemed, up to his elbow. Clay was hurt, but he controlled everything. Outside of that grunt, that oomph, when a man is hit—and physically you can't do anything about that, it's compression of air—outside of that, you saw nothing. He sagged for a split second, but there was no change in his facial muscles. And when Powell went to follow up, Clay incredibly just fired back. Before the round was over, he had Powell cut over the eye, and he stopped him one round later.

"I also remember that fight, because it was while we were in Pittsburgh that Cassius said some fascinating things to me about spiritualism. He was talking about his own spirituality, and he never touched on that with me again. It wasn't publicly known he was a Muslim then. I certainly didn't know it. But he was talking about his own religiosity and how spiritual he was, and he asked why couldn't he have visitations from God. Now, you're talking about something close to thirty years ago, so it's hard to remember everything. But he was saying that Moses spoke to God and the prophets spoke to God, and why couldn't he speak to God? And I had the feeling he sensed he was a special vessel, that he might be ordained for special things."

Clay had now captured the public imagination, and expectations were running high. Seven of his previous eight fights had ended in the predicted round. His poetry was being widely quoted, and *Life* magazine published an entire poem.[15] The time was ripe to return to New York, and Madison Square Garden signed him to fight Doug Jones. But no sooner had contracts been signed than a massive promotional problem loomed. New York City was in the midst of a 113-day newspaper strike, and it fell upon Clay to publicize the bout virtually on his own. For two weeks, he moved around the city, visiting bowling alleys, nightclubs, and television studios. When a Greenwich Village coffee house offered him a forum, he declared himself a beatnik and predicted doom for Doug Jones:

> This boy likes to mix
> So he must fall in six.

Later, the forecast was adjusted by two rounds:

I'm changing the pick I made before
Instead of six, Doug goes in four.

"I'm not even concentrating on Doug Jones," Clay proclaimed.
"He's nothing but a bum. If Jones upsets me, I'll quit fighting." As
for the strike, Clay solemnly assured his fans, "Yes, they have a
newspaper strike in New York, and I'm making an appointment with
President Kennedy to talk to him to see if he can't do something
about it, because there's a lot of people who want to read about my
fight and see my picture, and it's really embarrassing to go into the
city and there's no newspapers."[16]

Then came the bout, and the magnitude of Clay's drawing power
was revealed.

A. J. LIEBLING: "I shoved my way through shoals of pedestrians
coming from the Garden half an hour before the first preliminary
to the Jones fight. They were coming away from it because the house
was sold out—a report that they had refused to believe—and the
cops were chasing them out of the lobby, where they were blocking
the entrance. I had to show a ticket to get off the sidewalk. Inside
the lobby, the public-address system was happily blaring, 'This performance sold out. Only ticket holders in the lobby, please.' I hadn't
seen anything like it since the Louis-Marciano fight in 1951. But
Louis was an immortal, making a last stand against a coming immortal, while Clay and Jones had records like semifinalists. In the
jubilant lobby, the Garden special cops were laughing as they
chucked out the gate-crashers, and the life-size bronze statue of Joe
Gans, the old lightweight champion, seemed to have broken into a
sweat of excitement."[17]

But the fight itself verged on disaster. Clay fought one of the
worst fights of his career, and Jones fought one of his best. The
result was a boring bout, lacking in entertainment value. Once the
fourth round passed and Clay had failed to make good on his prediction, the crowd turned against him as though he had lost—which
he almost did. In the end, both judges scored the bout five rounds
to four in Clay's favor, with one round even. The referee, whose
mind must have been elsewhere, marked his scorecard eight-one-
one for the victor.

After the bout, Clay tried to remain upbeat. "The referee was
the most accurate," he said. "See, I'm as pretty as a girl. There isn't
a mark on me." As for his flawed prediction, he told reporters, "First,

I called it in six. Then I called it in four. Four and six, that's ten, right?"[18]

But the damage had been done. Soon, New York newspapers were publishing again, and Pete Hamill wrote, "Cassius Clay is a young man with a lot of charm who is in danger of becoming a dreadful bore."[19] Arthur Daley, who had once viewed Clay as "a refreshing highly personable young man,"[20] now saw him in a different light. "The time has come," Daley wrote, "for the precocious Cassius Marcellus to modify his public image. He's a handsome kid with so engaging a personality that he instantly attracts and wins everyone he meets. This amusing charmer uses the device of constant braggadocio to gain attention. However, his boasting now begins to irritate. What began as an amusing byplay has started to pall. The exceedingly likable Clay is lousing up his public relations by his boasting and it's high time he eased off."[21]

Clearly, some form of rehabilitation was necessary, and it came three months later in London, although again, Clay flirted with disaster. This time, the opponent was Henry Cooper, the reigning British heavyweight champion. Clay came into the ring wearing a red robe that bore the legend "Cassius the Greatest" and a crown embedded with imitation precious stones. Fifty-five thousand fans were on hand, mindful of the American's prediction that Cooper would fall in the fifth round.

For three rounds, two minutes and fifty-five seconds, everything went as planned. From the opening bell, Clay was in control. Soon Cooper was badly bloodied and hurt, fighting on courage alone. But each time the Englishman seemed ready to fall, Clay would drop his gloves, step back, and dance. At one point, William Faversham left his seat, moved as close to the ring as security allowed, and shouted to Dundee, "Angelo, make him stop the funny business."[22] But Dundee had no more control over his fighter than Faversham did. Clay was determined to carry his opponent and redeem himself as a prognosticator of rounds.

By round four, Cooper was apparently defenseless. Blood cascaded from a cut above his left eye. Clay, meanwhile, was dancing and mugging, periodically gazing toward the crowd. Then the Englishman let fly with "Henry's Hammer" — a devastating left hook; the one lethal weapon that remained in his arsenal. "The punch," one ringsider later wrote, "came from a long way back, with Cooper lunging forward as hard as he could. It caught Clay on the side of the jaw, and Cassius went over backwards through the ropes. He rolled back into the ring, then got dazedly to his feet. He was gazing off into the distance again, but this time starry-eyed. He wobbled forward, gloves low. He started to fall, but his handlers caught him, the round had ended. No one had heard the bell. Wembley Stadium was in an uproar."[23]

For the first time in his professional career, Cassius Clay was in desperate trouble. What followed is now boxing lore.

Angelo Dundee: "He split his glove on the seam near the thumb. Actually, it happened in the first round. I spotted the tear then and told him, 'Keep your hand closed.' I didn't want anyone to see it because everything was going our way, if you know what I mean. Then, at the end of the fourth round, he got nailed. And Cooper could do one thing; he could whack with that left hand. Cassius was hurt; no doubt about it. He got hit with that hook right on the button. So when he came back to the corner, I gave him smelling salts. One of the cornermen put ice on his back and down around his lower extremities to give him some feel. Then I helped the split a little, pulled it to the side, and made the referee aware that there was a torn glove. I don't know how much time that got us. Maybe a minute, but it was enough. If we hadn't gotten the extra time, I don't know what would have happened. I think Cassius would have made it through, but we don't have to answer that question because the horsehair really was coming out of the glove."

No extra gloves were available, so the bout resumed, split seam and all. Robert Daley of *The New York Times* described the next bloody round:

Clay, on dream street sixty seconds before, sprang into the center of the ring and laced into Cooper. The first jab snapped Cooper's head back, and opened the eye as a cleaver would have. There were so many punches that Cooper could not have known from whence they were all coming. Cassius was grim, absolutely ruthlessly concentrated. In 2 minutes 15 seconds, he nearly tore Cooper's head off his shoulders. Few men have absorbed such a beating in so short a time. Blood was everywhere. It now was gushing out of Cooper's wounds. Cooper was covering up as best he could. People were screaming, "Stop the fight!" At last, referee Tommy Little did stop it.[24]

Now the whole sports world was talking about Cassius Marcellus Clay. "I'm not the greatest," he proudly proclaimed. "I'm the double greatest. Not only do I knock 'em out, I pick the round. I'm the boldest, the prettiest, the most superior, most scientific, most skill-fullest fighter in the ring today. I'm the onliest fighter who goes from corner to corner and club to club debating with fans. I've received more publicity than any fighter in history. I talk to reporters till their fingers are sore."[25]

But to fulfill his goal of becoming heavyweight champion, Clay still had one more mountain to climb—Sonny Liston, the most feared fighter in the world.

3

"I Am the Greatest!"

"It may not seem like much that a fighter should size up the fight business as show business, but damned few before Cassius Clay ever did."[1]

So wrote Tom Wolfe in 1963, after Clay again broke new ground by recording an album for Columbia Records. The LP consisted of monologues and poems devoted largely to the recording artist's own greatness: "I'm so great, I impress even myself. . . . It's hard to be modest when you're as great as I am. . . . They all must lose in the round I choose. . . . I'm a perfect role model for children; I'm good-looking, clean-living, cultured, and modest."[2] Some of the material was written by Clay, the rest by employees of Columbia Records. Released in September to a barrage of publicity, the album enjoyed moderate commercial success and further enhanced Clay's marketability.

But who was Cassius Clay? What really went on inside his head? Only in isolated moments did he open up and truly speak his mind:

To Huston Horn: "Man, all the time somebody is telling me, 'Cassius, you know I'm the one who made you.' I know some guys in Louisville who used to give me a lift to the gym in their car when my motor scooter was broke down. Now they're trying to tell me they made me, and how not to forget them when I get rich. And my daddy, he tickles me. He says, 'Don't listen to the others, boy; I made you.' He says he made me because he fed me vegetable soup and steak when I was a baby, going without shoes to pay the food bill. Well, he's my father and I guess more teen-agers ought to realize what they owe their folks. But listen here. When you want to talk about who made me, you talk to me. Who made me is me."[3]

To Robert Lipsyte: "When I get that championship I'm gonna put on my old jeans and get an old hat and grow a beard and I'm gonna walk down an old country road where nobody knows me till I find a pretty little fox who don't know my name, who just loves me for what I am. And then I'll take her back to my $250,000 house overlooking my million dollar housing development, and I'll show her all my Cadillacs and the indoor pool in case it rains, and I'll tell her, 'This is yours, honey, 'cause you love me for what I am.' "[4]

To Huston Horn, again: "The hardest part of the training is the loneliness. I just sit here like a little animal in a box at night. I can't go out in the street and mix with the folks out there 'cause they wouldn't be out there if they was up to any good. I can't do nothing except sit. If it weren't for Angelo, I'd go home. Here I am, surrounded by showgirls, whiskey and nobody watching me. All this temptation and me trying to train to be a boxer. It's something to think about."[5]

To Dick Schaap: "I dream I'm running down Broadway. That's the main street in Louisville, and all of a sudden there's a truck coming at me. I run at the truck and I wave my arms, and then I take off and I'm flying. I go right up over the truck, and all the people are standing around and cheering and waving at me. And I wave back and I keep on flying. I dream that dream all the time."[6]

Flying over trucks. Throngs cheering. At one time or another, most people dream about being Superman. Saying anything they want, and knowing they can back it up. How many people have fantasized about taunting Mike Tyson or the functional equivalent? Telling him how ugly he is, how they're going to whip him in the ring, make him crawl, and then going out and doing just that. That's what Cassius Clay did to Sonny Liston.

HAROLD CONRAD: "Sonny Liston was a mean fucker. I mean, he had everybody scared stiff. People talk about Tyson before he got beat, but Liston, when he was champ, was more ferocious, more indestructible, and everyone thought, unbeatable. This was a guy who got arrested a hundred times, went to prison for armed robbery, got out, went back again for beating up a cop, and wound up being managed by organized crime. When Sonny gave you the evil eye— I don't care who you were—you shrunk to two feet tall. And one thing more: He could fight like hell. They forget it now, but when Liston was champ, some people thought he was the greatest heavyweight of all time."

The sole blot on Liston's record was a 1954 decision loss to Marty Marshall, avenged by knockout seven months later. Thereafter, Liston improved as a fighter, wreaking havoc in the heavyweight division, and capturing the heavyweight crown by knocking out Floyd Patterson in one round. Ten months later, on July 22, 1963, Liston and Patterson met again, and Patterson fell in two minutes ten seconds. "A prizefight is like a cowboy movie," Liston gloated. "There has to be a good guy and a bad guy. People pays their money to see me lose. Only in my cowboy movie, the bad guy always wins."[7]

And what did Cassius Clay have to say about Sonny Liston?

> Sonny Liston is nothing. The man can't talk. The man can't fight. The man needs talking lessons. The man needs boxing lessons. And since he's gonna fight me, he needs falling lessons. I'll hit Liston with so many punches from so many angles he'll think he's surrounded. I don't just want to be champion of the world, I'm gonna be champion of the whole universe. After I whup Sonny Liston, I'm gonna whup those little green men from Jupiter and Mars. And looking at them won't scare me none because they can't be no uglier than Sonny Liston.[8]

HAROLD CONRAD: "The campaign he launched to get a fight with Liston was genius. Right before the second Liston-Patterson fight, Clay followed Sonny out to Las Vegas. One night, Liston was in the casino—I think it was the Thunderbird Hotel—shooting craps. And Clay was standing against the wall, watching. Liston was a mean-tempered son-of-a-bitch, and he was losing, so naturally he's mad. Liston picks up the dice and throws craps and there's a big silence. Then a voice comes, 'Look at that big ugly bear; he can't even shoot craps.' Liston glared at him, picked up the dice, and rolled again. Another craps. 'Look at that big ugly bear. He can't do nothing right.' So Liston throws the dice down, walks over to Clay, and says, 'Listen, you nigger faggot. If you don't get out of here in ten seconds, I'm gonna pull that big tongue out of your mouth and stick it up your ass.' And Clay was scared. He walked; you better believe it. I asked him later, 'Were you scared?' And he said, 'Yeah, man; that big ugly bear scared me bad.' After that, people said Liston slapped him, but I was there, and I didn't see that. You know how those stories are; after a while, they get bigger and bigger. He didn't slap him, but he scared the shit out of him; you better believe it."

Still, several nights later, Clay was at ringside for the second Liston-Patterson fight. Brought into the ring during the customary prefight introductions, he shook Patterson's hand, looked toward Liston, threw his hands in the air in mock terror, and fled. Then, minutes after Patterson had been demolished, Clay was in the ring again. "The fight was a disgrace," he shouted into a microphone. "Liston is a tramp; I'm the champ. I want that big ugly bear. I want that big bum as soon as I can get him. I'm tired of talking. If I can't whip that bum, I'll leave the country."9

HOWARD BINGHAM: "I guess what Ali tried to do was drive Sonny Liston crazy. We had this bus. Ali bought it because he was afraid of flying. He used to say, one good thing about buses is, when they break down, they don't fall thirty thousand feet. Anyway, we were in Chicago one day, and Ali got the idea to go to Liston's house in Denver and drum up publicity to get the fight. We drove from Chicago just for that. It must have been a thousand miles each way. There was him and me and his brother Rudy and maybe a few others. We had a pretty good group. We took turns driving, and when one of us got tired, we changed in midroad. Whoever was driving would just lift up from the seat and the next guy would slide in. We got to Denver around two o'clock in the morning. Then Ali called some newspapers and radio stations, so by the time we got to Sonny's house, there was a bunch of people there. I was the one who got sent out of the bus to the house to knock on the door. Liston came to the door in his bathrobe, looked out the peephole, and said, 'What do you want, you black motherfucker.' You know that stare Sonny used to give opponents right before a fight when the referee was giving instructions. Well, that's the look I got from Sonny that night. So I got back to the bus pretty fast. One of the guys was in the bus, honking the horn, and Ali was on the lawn screaming and hollering about how he was gonna whup Liston bad. We all hollered for a while, and then Sonny came out on the lawn, so we took off. I had a good time that night."

MUHAMMAD ALI: "I was crazy then. But everyone wants to believe in himself. Everybody wants to be fearless. And when people saw I had those qualities, it attracted them to me. People ask me now, did I think out what I said and did ahead of time or did it just come to me? Some things I thought out, but most of the time, it just came to me. I guess it's like people say; you have to be a little crazy to be a fighter."

On November 5, 1963, Clay's promotional efforts came to fruition, and a contract to fight Sonny Liston was signed. "We did not want this fight so soon," Gordon Davidson, a lawyer for the Louisville Sponsoring Group, admitted in response to reporters' questions at a press conference. "But Cassius insisted and we had to give in. We argued that he needed more experience, that Liston was too strong right now. No use. He wasn't listening. We finally concluded Cassius doesn't try to learn anything from one fight to the next and really doesn't care about becoming one of the finest heavyweights who ever lived. All he wants is to be the richest. Wise or unwise, it's his decision and his career."[10]

MUHAMMAD ALI: "Everyone predicted that Sonny Liston would destroy me. And he was scary. But it's lack of faith that makes people afraid of meeting challenges, and I believed in myself. I was confident I could whup him. So what I did was, I studied his style, I trained hard, and I watched Liston outside the ring. I went to his training camp and tried to understand what went on inside his head, so later on I could mess with his mind. And all the time, I was talking, talking. That way, I figured Liston would get so mad that, when the fight came, he'd try to kill me and forget everything he knew about boxing."

The prefight buildup was vintage Clay:

Cassius Clay: "First five rounds, I'll be circling that big ugly bear, making him move. He's off balance whenever he reaches out with that jab, and every time he throws that jab I'll just counter over it. I'll be sticking and moving so fast the cameras won't be able to detect my speed. After he loses that zip in the sixth, I'll start pounding on him, Whop, Whop, Bop! Seventh round I'll continue shaking him up. Pop, Pop. Eighth round he'll be dazed, he'll be frustrated, he'll be tired and nervous. I'll meet him before he gets off of his stool and I'll be right on him faster than greased lightning. I'll be tagging him with left hooks, jabs to the body, crosses to the head. Whop! Whop! Bop! Bop! And Cassius becomes the champion of the world! I'll make him look so bad they'll call it a mismatch."[11]

Sonny Liston: "My only worry is how I'll get my fist outta his big mouth once I get him in the ring. It's gonna go so far down his throat, it'll take a week for me to pull it out again. That's my only worry, that loud-mouth."[12]

Cassius Clay: "I'm young, I'm handsome, I'm fast, I can't possibly be beat. I'm ready to go to war right now. If I see that bear on the street, I'll beat him before the fight. I'll beat him like I'm his daddy. He's too ugly to be the world champ. The world's champ should be pretty like me. If you want to lose your money, then bet on Sonny, because I'll never lose a fight. It's impossible. I never lost a fight in my life. I'm too fast; I'm the king. I was born a champ in the crib. I'm going to put that ugly bear on the floor, and after the fight I'm gonna build myself a pretty home and use him as a bearskin rug. Liston even smells like a bear. I'm gonna give him to the local zoo after I whup him. People think I'm joking. I'm not joking; I'm serious. This will be the easiest fight of my life. The bum is too slow; he can't keep up with me; I'm too fast. He's old, I'm young. He's ugly, I'm pretty. It's just impossible for him to beat me. He knows I'm great. He went to school; he's no fool. I predict that he will go in eight to prove that I'm great; and if he wants to go to heaven, I'll get him in seven. He'll be in a worser fix if I cut it to six. And if he keeps talking jive, I'll cut it to five. And if he makes me sore, he'll go like Archie Moore, in four. And if that don't do, I'll cut it to two. And if he run, he'll go in one. And if he don't want to fight, he should keep his ugly self home that night."[13]

Sonny Liston: "I might hurt that boy bad."[14]

Cassius Clay: "You tell this to your camera, your newspaper, your TV man, your radio man, you tell this to the world. If Sonny Liston whups me, I'll kiss his feet in the ring, crawl out of the ring on my knees, tell him he's the greatest, and catch the next jet out of the country. I'm the greatest. Everywhere I go, I draw sellout crowds. If it wasn't for me, the fight game would be dead. But for those of you out there who won't be able to see the eighth round of the fight, here's the eighth round exactly as it will happen:

> Clay comes out to meet Liston
> And Liston starts to retreat
> If Liston goes back any further
> He'll end up in a ringside seat
> Clay swings with a left
> Clay swings with a right
> Look at young Cassius
> Carry the fight
> Liston keeps backing
> But there's not enough room
> It's a matter of time
> There, Clay lowers the boom
> Now Clay swings with a right
> What a beautiful swing
> And the punch raises the bear
> Clear out of the ring
> Liston is still rising
> And the ref wears a frown
> For he can't start counting
> Till Sonny comes down
> Now Liston disappears from view
> The crowd is getting frantic
> But our radar stations have picked him up
> He's somewhere over the Atlantic
> Who would have thought
> When they came to the fight
> That they'd witness the launching
> Of a human satellite
> Yes, the crowd did not dream
> When they lay down their money
> That they would see
> A total eclipse of the Sonny
> I am the greatest!"[15]

HAROLD CONRAD: "Clay charmed; there was no doubt about it. While he was in Miami training for Liston, I took him to see Milton Berle at the Eden Roc Hotel. We're sitting in the audience, and Clay says to me, 'I can do what he does; I'm funnier than him.' Then Uncle Miltie called him up on stage to introduce him. And you have to remember, Milton Berle was big then. He might not have been Mr. Television anymore, but he was still big. He throws some lines at Cassius, using him as a straight man. And all of a sudden Cassius looks at him and says, 'Are you a big star?' Milton says, 'The biggest.' And Clay asks, 'How much are these people here tonight paying to see you?' And Milton tells him there's a twenty-dollar cover charge. Clay looks at him and says, 'Well, I'm bigger than you. People gotta pay a hundred dollars to see me when I work.'

"Then a week before the fight, I introduced him to the Beatles, who were in Miami Beach for the *Ed Sullivan Show*. Liston had already seen them. I took Sonny to the show so Ed Sullivan could introduce him on TV with a plug for the fight. And a couple of minutes after the Beatles started singing, Sonny sticks an elbow in my ribs and says, 'Are these motherfuckers what all the people are screaming about? My dog plays drums better than that kid with the big nose.' Anyway, after the show, I arranged for the Beatles to come to the gym to see Cassius, and he didn't know who they were. He had some idea they were rock stars from England, but that's all. And when he met them, they were all up in the ring together, talking about how much money they made. So Cassius pulled out a line he uses all the time. He looked at them and said, 'You guys ain't as dumb as you look.' And John Lennon looked him right in the eye and told him, 'No, but you are.' "

On the surface, it was fun and games. But behind the scenes, unbeknownst to many, a storm was brewing.

From the start of his career, Clay had been regarded as a "good colored boy." Indeed, that was how he'd justified his bragging. "Where do you think I'd be next week," he demanded of reporters, "if I didn't know how to shout and holler and make the public take notice? I'd be poor and I'd probably be down in my home town, washing windows or running an elevator and saying, 'yes suh' and 'no suh' and knowing my place. Instead of that, I'm one of the highest paid athletes in the world. Think about that. A southern colored boy has made one million dollars."[16]

Clay's image was one with which white America was comfortable. The syndicate that backed him was exclusively white. Dundee and

Ferdie Pacheco (the physician who worked with Dundee's fighters) were white. Howard Bingham was black, as was Drew "Bundini" Brown (who met Clay just before the Doug Jones fight and traveled with him). But Bingham and Brown were "the right kind of Negro." Now, for the first time in the Clay camp, a different kind of black man was coming into view.

The first public hint of a "problem" had occurred in September 1963, when the *Philadelphia Daily News* reported Clay's attendance at a "Black Muslim" rally in Philadelphia:

> Clay stood out in the crowd of some five thousand that heard Elijah Muhammad unleash a three-hour tirade against the white race and popularly accepted Negro leaders. Clay, who had come here from Louisville, Kentucky, for the rally, was among the throng that constantly applauded Muhammad as the Muslim leader called upon Negroes in this country and the entire world to form a solid front against the white race. Although he said he was not a Muslim, Clay said he thought Muhammad was "great."[17]

The Philadelphia report went largely unnoticed. Clay had not as yet signed to fight Sonny Liston, and the Nation of Islam (as the "Black Muslims" were properly titled) was still substantially unknown. Then, on January 21, 1964, Clay left training camp, and traveled from Miami Beach to New York. By this time, however, contracts for the championship bout had been signed; the fight was imminent; and Clay addressed the rally rather than simply attending. Also, Malcolm X traveled with him. The result was coverage on page one of the *New York Herald Tribune:*

> The brash young boxer, who celebrated his 22nd birthday last week, may not be a card-carrying Muslim. But, unquestionably, he sympathizes with Muslim aims and by his presence at their meetings lends them prestige. He is the first nationally famous Negro to take an active part in the Muslim movement. Yet he still has not formally announced support for the Muslims. He will not discuss the subject publicly. He will talk about his punches and his speed and his good looks, but he will not talk about the movement.[18]

The story was gathering steam. Two weeks later, the *Louisville Courier-Journal* published an interview in which Clay discussed his trip to New York: "Sure I talked to the Muslims," he acknowledged, "and I'm going back again. I like the Muslims. I'm not going to get killed trying to force myself on people who don't want me. I like my life. Integration is wrong. The white people don't want integration. I don't believe in forcing it, and the Muslims don't believe in it. So what's wrong about the Muslims?"[19]

Then, on February 7, 1964, eighteen days before the Liston fight, a *Miami Herald* article by Pat Putnam quoted Cassius Clay, Sr., as saying his son had joined the "Black Muslims."

PAT PUTNAM: "The *Herald* got a tip from an informant that the Muslims had threatened to kill Clay's father and mother and that, naturally, Cassius Senior was very upset. I thought he might want to talk about it, so I called Angelo and said, 'I want to do a story on the father; can you set it up?' Angelo didn't know what I was looking for. But he was always obliging with the press, and arranged for me to meet Mr. Clay in a restaurant aross the street from the Fifth Street Gym. We sat there and talked for about three hours, just me and the father. He told me Cassius had become a Muslim; that they'd brainwashed him to hate white people, and as soon as the fight was over he was going to change his name. He also claimed the Muslims were stealing his son's money and when he, the father, objected, they'd taken him out on a boat and threatened to drown him. I didn't interview anybody except Mr. Clay for the story. I wrote it strictly from his point of view, and it caused a stir. Then things got ugly. I began getting death threats; morons on the telephone calling up and saying, 'You're going to die.' That went on for a while, and then they started talking about my wife, how they were going to kill her too. And I got mad. I went over to Cassius's house one night around midnight when I got off work—he was living in a black neighborhood—and banged on the door, and told him what was happening. And I'll say this for him; whatever he went through, whatever he ever said or did, I don't believe he was ever antiwhite. And he said to me, 'Pat, don't worry about it; you'll never get another call.' I don't know what he did, but he must have put the word out to a lot of people, because that was the end of it. I never got a death threat again. And he never complained to me about that story or anything else I wrote, good or bad, the whole time I covered him."

HAROLD CONRAD: "When the Muslim story began to break, the people promoting the fight went bananas. The Muslims were unpopular in the United States, which is putting it mildly, but this was worse because the fight was in Florida, and Florida was a Jim Crow state. If you want to know what Florida was like, I'd been in Miami with Joe Louis and Max Schmeling two years earlier to promote the Patterson-Johansson fight. I was staying in a hotel and planned to have lunch with Louis in the dining room, and the owner of the hotel came over to me and said, 'Harold, could you do me a favor? Have lunch in your room this afternoon.' I said, 'What do you mean; why should I have lunch in the room?' And the owner said to me, 'This is a white man's hotel.' I looked at him, and I said, 'Wait a minute! Are you telling me that Joe Louis isn't good enough to eat in your dining room?' But that's the way it was. They'd let a Nazi in, and I don't mean Schmeling was a Nazi; I'm not saying that. But they'd let a Nazi in the dining room, and not Joe Louis. So when word got out that Clay was with Malcolm X and the Muslims, you can imagine what that did to the gate. The whole sales pitch for the fight had been Clay against Liston, white hat against black hat, and now it looked like there'd be two black hats fighting.

"Bill MacDonald was promoting the fight. He was a guy who'd made a big score in real estate or oil or something, and wanted everybody to love him. That's one of the reasons he was into promoting. He'd put up $625,000 to bring heavyweight championship boxing to Florida, and now his main drawing card was surrounded by blacks who were calling white people devils. So MacDonald called Cassius in and threatened to cancel the fight unless he publicly disavowed the Muslims, which Cassius wasn't about to do.

"That was that. It looked like the fight was off. But like I said, MacDonald wanted everybody to love him, and I said, 'Bill, you're gonna go down in history as the guy who denied a fighter a title shot because of his religion.' And MacDonald told me, 'Don't start hitting me with the Constitution. This is the South. I can't operate down here with these people.' So I asked him, 'If I get Malcolm X out of town, will you go ahead with the fight?' He said, 'Yeah, I guess so.' So I went to the house where Cassius was staying. And all the guys around him, they were black men wearing black suits and black ties, and when I got there, they were pretty nasty. Cassius had always been friendly to me, but this time he was cold, like I was a stranger. Malcolm X was there too, and I said to Malcolm, 'Look, the way things are now, the fight is off. Cassius will lose his chance to win the heavyweight championship, but you can save it for him.' Malcolm asked how, and I told him, 'You have to get out of town now. You're the focal point. You're the guy the press knows.' Malcolm thought about it. He was quiet for a long time. And then

he said, 'All right, I'll go; but I'm coming back for the fight.' That
was the deal. I stuck out my hand, but he wouldn't shake. He wasn't
into shaking hands with white people then. All he did was reach out
and touch my wrist with his finger. But thank God, the fight was
on again."

All that remained was the final build-up, but the consensus was
it wouldn't be much of a fight. Liston was an awesome fighter, with
polished skills and power in every punch. Clay was considered an
affable novice, who'd been knocked down twice by lesser opponents in a total of nineteen professional fights. The odds were
prohibitive—seven to one in Liston's favor. Las Vegas bookmakers
recorded five times as much wagering on which round Liston would
win in than on who would actually win the fight.

Clay's camp remained optimistic. "We have many assets," Dundee said a week before the bout. "Clay has a style Liston has never
seen before. He's much faster than Liston. He has the faculty of
getting under Liston's skin and won't be browbeaten by the champion. Deep down inside, Clay thinks he's unbeatable. And he can
hit Sonny with every punch he has. Sonny isn't hard to hit. We can
beat Liston with quantity and consistency. If you build a prototype
of what kind of fighter can whip Liston, you couldn't improve on
Clay."[20]

Still, the prevailing view among boxing's intelligentsia was that
Clay had little chance:

Robert Boyle: "Cassius must be kidding. If he isn't, he's
crazy to consider entering the ring against a virtually indestructible and demonstrably deadly fighting machine. Clay's
style is made to order for a massacre. He carries his hands
too low, he leans away from a punch, and he cannot fight a
lick inside. He will face in Liston an opponent with endurance, highly developed skills, deceptive speed, and strength
enough to stun an elephant with either hand."[21]

Jimmy Cannon: "Clay doesn't fight like the valid heavyweight he is. He seldom sets and he misses a lot. It should
be remembered he began fighting as an amateur weighing
118 pounds. His body grew but his style remained that of a
bantamweight. In a way, Clay is a freak. He is a bantamweight who weighs more than two hundred pounds. There
isn't a heavyweight now licensed who can handle Liston. No
big bantamweight is going to do the job."[22]

Arthur Daley: "An aura of artificiality surrounds Tuesday's heavyweight championship fight between Sonny Liston and Cassius Clay. It doesn't even rate being called a match made by popular demand. The only one who demanded it was Cassius, a precocious master of ballyhoo who lulls himself to sleep at night not by counting sheep but by counting money. He'll be seeing stars when Sonny hits him on Tuesday. On that evening, the loud mouth from Louisville is likely to have a lot of vainglorious boasts jammed down his throat by a ham-like fist belonging to Sonny Liston, the malefic destroyer who is the champion of the world. The irritatingly confident Cassius enters this bout with one trifling handicap. He can't fight as well as he can talk."[23]

Tex Maule: "Where Clay's jab stings, Liston's wounds. His arms are massively muscled, and the left jab is more than a jab. It hits with true shock power. Even when it is off target, which it seldom is, it explodes with enough force to knock the recipient off balance so that he must recover and set up again before he can attack. His left hook is as quick as a snake's strike and he does not have to coil to throw it. It follows the jab as rapidly as a drumbeat. It never occurs to Liston that he may lose a fight. He does not enter the ring hoping to outpoint his rival in 15 rounds and knock him out only if the opportunity offers. His aim is destruction. He may, in the course of a fight, hit his opponent low, in the kidneys, or on the back of the neck. The legality of his attack is of no concern to him. He cares less for points than he does for doing damage. This intended violence has given him command both physically and psychologically in past fights, and caused his opponents to fight in terror."[24]

Milton Gross: "Cassius the fighter, like Cassius the recording star, is a figment of somebody else's imagination. Only in this day of mediocrity could he be fighting for the world's heavyweight championship. Only in this time of soap bubble promotion could anybody take him seriously when he steps into the ring with Sonny Liston. The simple fact is, Clay doesn't know his business. He hasn't had time to learn it. He knows publicity and he is a charmer when it comes to popping off or popping setups. But he doesn't know the trouble he'll see when Sonny starts working

him over with malice aforethought to do a butchery job
on his pretty face."[25]

The day of the fight, February 25, 1964, was seasonally warm in
Miami Beach. With prebout preparations complete, Liston remained an overwhelming favorite. Former heavyweight champion
Rocky Marciano declared, "I don't consider Clay's decision to fight
Sonny Liston very smart."[26] Ninety-three percent of the sportswriters in attendance predicted the champion would retain his
crown. Then came a series of events that over the years have become
enshrouded in myth. And when February 25, 1964, was at an end,
the world of sports had irrevocably changed.

Robert Lipsyte, who covered the fight for *The New York Times*,
sets the scene.

ROBERT LIPSYTE: "I was doing feature stories in the sports department of the *Times*. And the editors didn't feel it was an important
enough fight to bother their main boxing writer, so they sent me
down. It was basically seen as a feature writer's story. Liston would
destroy Clay very quickly; the *Times* would do its usual antiboxing
editorial; and then they'd send the real boxing writer back to cover
whatever serious fights came along. In fact, when I went down to
Miami for the fight, my basic instruction was to find out the distance
from the arena to the nearest hospital, so I wouldn't waste deadline
time getting there after Clay was knocked out. And it was a great
feature writer's fight. So much was happening. There were wild
rumors, big ugly bears, Ali's charisma, and of course, the weigh-
in."

Before Clay's fight against Sonny Liston, championship bout
weigh-ins had been fairly standard and boring. But Muhammad Ali
reinvented the rituals of boxing, and after the show he put on in
Miami Beach, weigh-ins would never be the same.

At 10:30 A.M., wearing a blue denim jacket with the words "Bear
Huntin' " inscribed in red on the back, Clay entered the room where
the weigh-in would be held. Angelo Dundee, Bundini Brown, and
Sugar Ray Robinson were with him. Clay and Bundini were shouting
at the top of their lungs: "Float like a butterfly, sting like a bee;
rumble, young man, rumble." Then Clay took over on his own,
banging a walking stick on the floor and screaming, "I'm the champ!
I'm ready to rumble! Tell Sonny I'm here! He ain't no champ! Round
eight to prove I'm great! Bring that big ugly bear on."

Working their way through the crowd, Clay and his entourage retired to a dressing room, where he stripped down and put on a white terrycloth robe. Alarmed by what they'd seen so far, representatives of the Miami Beach Boxing Commission followed him in and warned of a fine if his behavior didn't change.

FERDIE PACHECO: "God, what a show Cassius put on that morning. In the dressing room, Angelo and Sugar Ray gave him a lecture. They said, 'Look, this is a weigh-in for the heavyweight championship of the world. Hundreds of members of the press are here. It's not for craziness.' And to be honest, I didn't think he'd have the nerve to pull it off. I mean, here's a twenty-two-year-old kid in front of boxing greats like Joe Louis and Ray Robinson, not to mention the entire news media. And even though he'd talked about psychological warfare before the fight, I just didn't think what happened would happen."

What happened was, at 11:09 A.M., Clay reentered the weigh-in room. Two minutes later, Liston appeared, and the challenger seemingly went wild. "I'm ready to rumble now," he screamed. "I can beat you anytime, chump! Somebody's gonna die at ringside tonight! You're scared, chump! You ain't no giant! I'm gonna eat you alive!" Bundini was shrieking, "Float like a butterfly, sting like a bee." Dundee, Robinson, and William Faversham were holding on to Clay, who seemed ready to attack Liston at any moment.

MORT SHARNIK: "I was there, and it looked to me like Cassius was having a seizure, all gathered up in his own hysteria, going on and on, totally out of control. It was hard to believe he could fight that night. Sugar Ray Robinson was trying to calm him down. There had to be six guys holding on to him, and it looked like he was struggling to throw all six around. Then, right in the middle of everything—and I don't know how many people saw this—he winked at Robinson. People were screaming and shoving and jockeying for better camera angles, and Cassius was probably having a ball."

Amidst the din, Morris Klein (chairman of the Miami Boxing Commission) moved to the microphone and announced, "Cassius Clay is fined $2,500." Meanwhile, Dr. Alexander Robbins (the commission's physician) managed to take Clay's blood pressure, and found his pulse rate to be 110 beats per minute, compared with a normal rate of 54. Pouring more fuel on the fire, Robbins announced that Clay was "emotionally unbalanced, scared to death, and liable to crack up before he enters the ring." Teddy Brenner, who had followed Clay since early in the fighter's career, opined, "My God; he's scared to death. This kid is out of his mind. He might not even show up for the fight."[27]

No one seemed to care very much that Liston weighed 218 pounds and Clay 210.

ROBERT LIPSYTE: "The weigh-in was like a police action, with an enormous amount of movement and noise exploding in a densely packed room. It was wild, but when it was over and we sorted out what had happened, it seemed to me that, while not everything had been carefully choreographed, Cassius was always in control. Even with all his ranting and raving, most things seemed to have been plotted out. And it was an absolutely extraordinary performance, because Liston took comfort in the fact that everybody was scared of him. I mean, who wouldn't be terrified of Sonny Liston? Well, the answer, of course, was a crazy person wouldn't be afraid, and now Liston thought Clay was crazy."

JERRY IZENBERG: "At the weigh-in, Clay sure as hell fooled me. I was covering the fight for the *Newark Star Ledger*, and I couldn't begin to get a handle on it at all. He behaved like an absolute lunatic. I remember Liston sitting there, watching him. Cassius had an African walking stick that he was banging on the floor, running back and forth, screaming, 'This is my destiny.' And Liston looked at him and said, 'Don't tell everybody,' and I didn't know what that was supposed to mean. The words were, 'Don't tell everybody.' And I think what he meant was, don't tell everybody what a fool you are, but even now I'm not sure.

"And there had been all sorts of crazy rumors flying around in the week leading up to the fight. We'd heard about fixes; we'd heard about Malcolm X. Then, the day before the fight, Clay went to Dundee and said, 'I gotta have two more tickets.' Angelo told him, 'You've already got enough tickets for all your aunts, your cousins, your uncles, your parents, your brother, your friends. I can't get you any more.' And Cassius said, 'These are very important. I gotta get two more tickets for the man in the speedboat.' Angelo asked, 'What man in what speedboat?' And Cassius said, 'The man in the speedboat who pulled me out of Biscayne Bay.' Angelo looked at him and, not really wanting to know the answer, said simply,

'When?' And Cassius told him, 'Yesterday.' Well, that was Cassius. He couldn't swim, but two days before the fight, he'd been out in a speedboat and the speedboat had capsized and some guy had pulled him out of the water. And when he discoverd who he'd saved, he said, 'I'd love to see the fight.' All Dundee said, was, 'I don't want to hear anymore. Don't tell me why you were in Biscayne Bay. I'll get you two tickets. See if you can behave yourself for the next twenty-four hours.'

"So what I'm saying is, things were absolutely crazy. I remember driving to the arena the night of the fight, and in the car, I heard a report on the radio that Clay had been seen at the airport buying a ticket to leave town. And I said to myself, 'I have no idea what's going on here.' I couldn't conceive of anything like this. Then I walked into the arena, and in the first or second bout of the evening, Muhammad's brother, Rahaman, made his pro debut. It was a bad crowd for the night, and early in the evening, it was positively empty, like a canyon. And I heard this voice, hollering. I turned around, and about halfway up the aisle, there was Cassius watching Rahaman, yelling instructions, really into the fight. And I said to myself, 'Lunatic, schmunatic, there's nothing wrong with this guy.' I still didn't think he was going to win. I've got to confess, at that point I didn't think Cassius could fight. But I said to myself, this might be an interesting night."

RAHAMAN ALI: "The greatest night of my life was February 25, 1964. That night was ecstasy, the epitome of joy. I made my debut against a fighter named Chip Johnson, who'd had about eight pro fights. I was nervous, and he shook me up in the first round. He had me in a daze. Then my head cleared in the rest period between rounds, and I won a unanimous decision. But what that night was about for me was my brother winning the heavyweight championship. I've always shared in my brother's joy. My whole life, his goals have been my goals. His happiness has been my happiness. His sorrow has been my sorrow. So when he became heavyweight champion of the world, I became champion too."

FERDIE PACHECO: "After Rahaman had his fight, things in the dressing room got pretty bizarre. The only people who were supposed to be there were Cassius, Angelo, Rahaman, Bundini, myself, and Luis Sarria (Clay's masseur). A few more came and went, but basically we were alone. Then Cassius assigned Rahaman to watch his water bottle. The bottle was taped shut. No one went near it. But every time Rahaman took his eyes off it, Cassius would take the tape off, empty it out, refill it, and tape it closed again. He did that three or four times, because he was worried that someone would try to drug him. And he was particularly suspicious of Angelo, because Angelo was Italian, and in his mind he'd begun to associate Angelo with the gangsters around Liston. Remember, the Muslims—and it was clear by then that Cassius was a Muslim—had never been in boxing before. All they had to go by were Hollywood movies where the mob fixed everything, and Liston was with the mob. It was crazy, but that's what Cassius thought. And in light of what happened in the fifth round that night, we were very lucky. I don't want to think about what might have happened if Angelo hadn't been on the ball."

Meanwhile, in Liston's dressing room, it was business as usual, as Liston's cornerman Milt Bailey recalls.

MILT BAILEY: "Sonny was a peculiar guy. He never really expressed his emotions. But before the fight, he was confident, just like all of us were. We thought Clay was crazy, because he was acting the way a crazy man acts. But we also knew he was afraid because of the way he was talking, and at the weigh-in, he seemed full of fear. So we didn't expect anything different that night. I know I didn't think Clay had a chance. Sonny was so powerful, and nobody had stood up to him. Then, in the first round—and it's been a long time; it's hard for me to remember round by round—but in the first round, Sonny couldn't catch up with Clay, and I thought we might have some trouble."

As the evening progressed and preliminary bouts passed, the crowd remained disappointingly small. High ticket prices, the prospect of a mismatch, and weeks of rumors had taken their toll.* Shortly before the fight, Les Keiter (who would broadcast the blow-by-blow description for ABC Radio) summed up the moment for a national audience: "Another boxing milestone is at hand. In just a

---

*There were 8,297 paid admissions in a hall that seated 15,744. Bill MacDonald, who paid a site fee of $625,000 plus $140,000 in expenses, lost $363,000. After closed-circuit television and other revenues were factored in, Clay and the Louisville Sponsoring Group received $630,000 split fifty-fifty between them. Liston received $1,360,500, although it's unclear how that money was divided. Liston's backers (Intercontinental Promotions, Inc.) collected $813,000 for their role in the promotion.

few minutes, Louisville's Cassius Marcellus Clay climbs the steps into the ring here in Convention Hall to face the target of his constant needling, to run head-on into the punches of the heavyweight champion, Sonny Liston. The man who has been screaming to the heavens that he's the greatest meets his destiny—the awesome Liston, a man cut from the mold of Joe Louis; a man who can take a man out with either hand; a ring executioner who has disposed of his opposition in the first round the last three times he has answered the bell. And now, as the electric moment draws near, the more than one hundred writers from all over the globe here for the title clash have gone down the line for the champ, giving the challenger no chance at all."[28]

Then the fighters entered the ring.

ANGELO DUNDEE: "You have to understand boxing to understand Muhammad. Most people look at fights, and even knowledgeable fans forget sometimes that what they're watching is real. The punches, the blood, the hurt, the pain. When all the training and promotion is done, it comes down to what a guy does in the ring.

"I was confident that Cassius would beat Liston. I felt he'd win, because he had the speed to offset Liston's jab, and Liston's jab was the key to everything. Liston had a jab that was like a battering ram. If he got you at the end of that jab, you were gone. But Cassius was able to surround the jab, side to side, either side, with quickness and agility. The question was, would he fight up to his potential or would Liston intimidate him the way he intimidated most people. Sonny made a science of intimidation. He used to put towels under his robe to make his shoulders look bigger. And when the ref gave instructions, he'd stare you down like you were a dead man. I told Cassius, 'Look, when you get in the ring with this guy, stand tall so he sees you're as big as he is.' But no matter what you say, no matter how you prepare for a fight, when all the preparation and mind games are done, there's that moment of truth right before the opening bell. And if you care about your fighter, either you love that moment or you hate it. I love it. That's why I'm in boxing."

MUHAMMAD ALI: "Just before the fight, when the referee was giving us instructions, Liston was giving me that stare. And I won't lie; I was scared. Sonny Liston was one of the greatest fighters of all time. He was one of the most scientific boxers who ever lived; he hit hard; and he was fixing to kill me. It frightened me, just knowing how hard he hit. But I was there; I didn't have no choice but to go out and fight.

"The first round, I was dancing, moving back and side-to-side. I hit him with a couple of combinations, and he got me once with a right hand to the stomach. At the end of the round, I went back to my corner, and I felt good because I knew I could survive. Round two, I made a mistake and he caught me against the ropes. I got away from most of the punches, but he hit me good with a left hook that shook me up. Round three, I changed my strategy. I'd planned to fight hard the first two rounds, and then coast while Liston got tired. That way, by round five or six, I'd be rested and he'd be out of energy, and I'd start coming on strong. But at the start of round three, I could see he was frustrated and getting tired already, so I decided to test him then."

MORT SHARNIK: "In the third round, Cassius went after Liston. And you have to understand, up until that moment, Sonny Liston had seemed indestructible. But Cassius had incredibly swift hands and a manner of punching where he twisted his fist at the moment of impact, which had the effect of a pretty sharp knife. He hit Liston with a one-two combination; a jab followed by a straight right. And it was like the armor plate on a battleship being pierced. Cassius pulled his jab back, and there was a mouse underneath Sonny's right eye. Then he pulled his right hand back, and there was a gash underneath the other eye. Liston's skin had seemed so thick, I didn't think it could possibly burst like that. And I said to myself, 'My God; Cassius Clay is winning this fight.' "

For most of round four, Clay coasted. Then came the most dramatic moments of the fight, the stuff of which legends are made.

ANGELO DUNDEE: "Near the end of the fourth round, Cassius started having trouble with his eyes. To this day, nobody knows exactly what the problem was. It might have been liniment from Liston's shoulder. My guess is, it was the coagulant that his corner used on the cuts. Probably, Cassius got the solution on his gloves, and when he brushed them against his forehead, it left a layer of something that trickled down with the perspiration into his eyes. Whatever it was, he came back to the corner after the fourth round and started shouting, 'I can't see! My eyes!' And something was wrong. His eyes were watery. He was saying, 'Cut the gloves off! We're going home!' And you can imagine what was going through his mind. He was winning the fight, winning easily, and all of a sudden he can't see. I told him, 'Forget the bullshit. This is the championship. Sit down.' I pushed him down, took a towel, and started cleaning out his eyes. Then I threw the towel away, grabbed a sponge, rinsed his eyes and threw the sponge away. There was something in his eyes, definitely, because I put my pinky in the corner of his eye, and then I put it in my own eye, and it stung, it burned. I only had a minute between rounds, and Barney Felix, the referee, was coming toward us to see what the problem was. Cassius was hollering, 'I can't see,' and I was scared they'd stop the fight. So I got his mouthpiece back in, stood him up, and said, 'This is the big one, daddy. Stay away from him. Run!' "

FERDIE PACHECO: "All those bullshit boxing stories people write; pretty soon, everyone starts believing them. Angelo cut the gloves in the first Cooper fight. Bullshit. Sit him down, and he'll tell you that the gloves were already split. He just helped them along a little. Angelo loosened the ropes for the Foreman fight in Zaire. Bullshit again. Angelo and Bobby Goodman tried to tighten the ropes right until the opening bell. Most of it's nonsense, and Angelo will be the first person to tell you the truth because he's a very modest guy. But one thing that truly belongs in the legend category was what went on between the fourth and fifth rounds of the Liston fight. Cassius couldn't see; he was ready to quit. And it had nothing to do with lack of courage, because this was a kid who'd been fighting since he was twelve years old. And in those years when he'd been learning how to box, he'd been poked and banged and busted and clobbered many times, and took on all comers his whole amateur career. He'd made his accommodation by then with the normal pains and blows of boxing, but this was something beyond what he'd experienced, and I was there. I could see it. His eyes were aflame. And Angelo was spectacular. He's not one of the best, he's the best cornerman I've ever seen. And what he did between rounds was the best example I can give you of a cornerman seizing a situation and making it right. Now, he had a willing subject, because as the world later learned, Muhammad Ali was as courageous as any man who ever put on a pair of boxing gloves. But that moment belonged to Angelo. And if Cassius had been with a corner of amateurs, there would never have been any Muhammad Ali. The fight would have been over. Liston would never have fought him again. And as a member of the Muslims, who were about as popular then as the PLO, Cassius would have sunk from view. And don't think the Muslims didn't know it. Look at what happened later on. Even though Angelo's influence diminished because of the Ali circus and its Byzantine squabbles, Ali's people never got rid of Angelo. Angelo was there till the very end."

ANGELO DUNDEE: "I didn't see too much of the fifth round; not the first minute, anyway. Everybody knew Liston was a tough guy with connections, and certain individuals had been fueling Cassius's imagination about white people being out to destroy him. As soon as I got down the steps in the corner, my brother Jimmy ran over all excited and said, 'Ang, show these guys you didn't do nothing. They're looking to do a number on you.' Because there were two Muslims standing there, looking at me in a definitely hostile way, figuring I'd done something wrong. So I said, 'Are you guys nuts? I want to win this thing as much as you do.' I threw water from the bucket in my eyes. I showed them everything I could. And then I went back to watching Cassius kick Sonny Liston's butt."

FERDIE PACHECO: "Just going out for the fifth round was an incredibly brave thing to do. Liston was considered as destructive as Mike Tyson before Tyson got beat. It was like blinding someone and sending them out to fight Tyson, and Cassius was absolutely brilliant then. The things he did, staying out of range, reaching out with his left hand, touching Liston when he got too close to break Sonny's concentration. It was an amazing, astonishing, breathtaking performance. Here's a fighter who's supposed to be Godzilla, who will reign for maybe a thousand years. Nobody can stand up to him in the ring. Cassius can't see, and still Liston couldn't do anything with him. What can I say? Beethoven wrote some of his greatest symphonies when he was deaf. Why couldn't Cassius Clay fight when he was blind?"

Midway through the fifth round, Clay's eyes cleared, and for the rest of the round, the two men fought on even terms. Round six belonged to the challenger. He hit Liston at will; Liston couldn't hit him. Just before the start of round seven, Howard Cosell (who was doing color commentary with Les Keiter's radio blow-by-blow) told his audience, "All I can say is, this is hard to figure out. Clay looked like he'd about had it—"

A roar from the crowd interrupted the thought, and then Cosell was screaming, "Wait a minute! Wait a minute! Sonny Liston is not coming out! Sonny Liston is not coming out! He's out! The winner and the new heavyweight champion of the world is Cassius Clay."[29]

Sonny Liston had quit on his stool, the first heavyweight champion to surrender his crown in that fashion since Jess Willard against Jack

Dempsey on July 4, 1919. But Willard had suffered a broken jaw, a broken nose, cracked ribs, and six broken teeth. Liston's excuse? His shoulder was hurt. As the defeated champion spat out his mouthpiece, Clay rose with both arms in the air. To say he danced would be an injustice. His feet skimmed back and forth with incredible speed, barely touching the canvas, as though he was levitating. And then, amidst the bedlam, he was shouting, "I am the greatest! I am the greatest! I'm the greatest! I'm the king of the world! I've upset the world! Give me justice! I told you! If he want to go to heaven, I'll get him in seven. I am the king! I am the king! I am the king!"

"What made him so easy for you," Cosell, who had climbed into the ring, demanded.

"I'm too fast. He was scared."

"Who gave you your plan, Angie Dundee?"

"No; myself."

"Was there any single point where you knew you had him?"

"I knew I had him in the first round. Almighty God was with me. I want everybody to bear witness. I am the greatest! I shook up the world! I'm the greatest thing that ever lived. I don't have a mark on my face, and I upset Sonny Liston, and I just turned twenty-two years old. I must be the greatest. I showed the world, I talk to God every day. I shook up the world. I'm the king of the world! I'm pretty! I'm a bad man! I shook up the world! I shook up the world! I shook up the world! You must listen to me. I am the greatest! I can't be beat! I am the greatest! It was no match. I want the world to know, I'm so great that Sonny Liston was not even a match. I don't have a mark on my face. In the fifth round, I couldn't see a thing. My face was burning, and I whupped him. He couldn't hurt me. I'm the prettiest thing that ever lived. I shook up the world. I want justice."[30]

MUHAMMAD ALI: "Twenty-six years, more than half my life, has gone by since then. Did Liston really hurt his shoulder? I can't say for sure, but I don't think so. My eyes burned bad in the fifth round. I could see a little, but not much. I wanted to stop. Angelo pushed me out. And I never knew for sure what caused the problem, but at the end of my career, before I fought Larry Holmes, a man from Philadelphia came to me. He had a bottle with a yellow liquid inside. He didn't ask for money. All he said was he wanted to help, and he told me, 'Put this on your gloves if you get in trouble. It won't hurt Holmes, but it will blind him temporarily.' I said no, that it would be against my religion. I'd never try to win a fight that way. But when we had that conversation, it reminded me of my fight against Sonny Liston. Twenty-six years. I can't believe all that time has gone by. When I listen to the tapes, what I said that night, I was great, but man, I was crazy."

CASSIUS CLAY (to reporters in his dressing room after the fight): "What are you gonna say now, huh? 'He can't go one round. He might go two. He holds his head back. He holds his hands too low.' Well, I'm still pretty. All you reporters made it hard on Liston. Never write about me like that. Never make me six to one; it just makes me angry. Never make me no underdog, and never talk about who's gonna stop me. Ain't nobody gonna stop me. Not a heavyweight in the world fast enough to stop me. Liston's one of the powerfulest in the world, and he looked like a baby. I held my hands down. I just played with him. I shook all of you up. Oh, I whupped him so bad; wasn't that good? Oh, I shook up the world. I whupped him so bad he has to go to the hospital, and I'm still pretty. What you gonna say about that, huh? I don't have a mark. The bear couldn't hurt me. I put him in the hospital. He's never been stopped. He's never been whupped. I'm so great. I'm so great. I shook up the world. Wasn't that so good? Oh, I shook up the world. Tell me, I am the greatest. I'm gonna show you how great reporters are. Who's the greatest? [There was no response.] No justice. I don't get no justice. No one's gonna give me justice. I'll give you one more chance. Who's the greatest? ['You are,' several reporters answered]."[31]

MORT SHARNIK: "After the fight, I went with Sonny to St. Francis Hospital, where they stitched him up. Jack Nilon [Liston's manager] and I were the only ones with him. Nobody else was there. Sonny looked like the loneliest person in the world. They X-rayed him, and put in sutures. And let me tell you, if anyone thought the fight was fixed, this guy was beaten up. His face was all swollen, chopped, and chewed up. In a way, he'd quit, but only after the fight was lost. He quit because he knew he was going to get knocked out; probably in the next round, which was what Cassius had predicted.

"Nilon and I were standing, talking over Sonny, while he was lying on one of those metal tables. All Sonny said was, 'That's not the guy I was supposed to fight. That guy could punch!' Then Nilon looked at me and asked, 'What in the world will we do with Sonny?' But for a moment, my mind was somewhere else. I was back with Cassius in my office in the Time-Life Building, looking out over the twinkling lights of Manhattan. We'd been there together a few months before, and I'd said to him, 'Now, Cassius, tell me the truth. Put aside all the hoopla, all the bravado. What do you think about Sonny Liston?' And he'd started, 'Oh, that big ugly bear.' I said, 'Forget that, and tell me the truth. What's going to happen?' And Cassius got very thoughtful, and then he said, 'Well, I'm like Columbus. I think the world is round, but I'm a little scared because now I'm reaching the point where I'll find out if it's really round and I can sail around it or is it flat and will I fall off. I think I can beat him. I think I'm going to do what I say. But I won't know for sure until I get there.''

ROBERT LIPSYTE: "Looking back, I suppose what interests me most about the whole experience in Miami Beach was the generational aspect of the coverage of the fight. A lot of things were happening then. John Kennedy's assassination, the start of our military build-up in Vietnam, black America rising to assert itself. But one very personal memory stands out in my mind.

"Joe Louis was down there. He was getting walking-around money from Sonny Liston's camp, and I think his wife might have been Liston's lawyer. And there was a very clear distinction between the younger reporters such as myself who saw Cassius Clay as the story and the older reporters who flocked around Liston and Joe Louis. I remember talking with one of the older writers, Barney Nagler— they were all around Louis—and I asked him, 'How can you hang around that old mumbling has-been, when here's this young beautiful hope of the future?' and Nagler said to me, 'You don't understand; he was so good when he was young.' And I didn't understand that until many years later when I was at the Mike Tyson–Larry Holmes fight, and I was one of the old reporters hanging around an aging mumbling ex-fighter once known as Cassius Clay, who'd been so wonderful and given us all so much to treasure when he was young.''

4

The Birth of Ali

Before February 25, 1964, it seemed as though almost everything Cassius Clay did fit within the context of establishment white values. He wasn't white, but he was "the next best thing." Tall, handsome, witty, charming; a good boy, whose ambitions in life were wealth and the heavyweight championship of the world. A prescient few might have divined that whenever Clay looked in the mirror and preened, "I'm so pretty," he was voicing a precursor of the theme "black is beautiful." Indeed, as early as March 1963, *Ebony* magazine declared, "Cassius Marcellus Clay—and this fact has evaded the sportswriting fraternity—is a blast furnace of racial pride. His is a pride that would never mask itself with skin lighteners and processed hair, a pride scorched with memories of a million little burns."[1] But *Ebony* was a black publication with limited readership, and its observation quickly sank from view. To white America, Clay remained a toy that presumably could be discarded as soon as his entertainment value waned.

Then things began to get complicated. The morning after his victory over Sonny Liston, the new champion appeared at a Miami Beach press conference to answer questions about the fight. Yes, he was pleased to be heavyweight champion. No, he wasn't surprised he won. He'd beaten Liston because he was a better boxer. For the first time in memory, his voice was subdued. "I'm through talking," he told his audience. "All I have to do is be a nice clean gentleman."[2]

Then came the question: "Are you a card-carrying member of the Black Muslims?"

"Card carrying; what does that mean?" Clay answered. "I believe in Allah and in peace. I don't try to move into white neighborhoods. I don't want to marry a white woman. I was baptized when I was twelve, but I didn't know what I was doing. I'm not a Christian anymore. I know where I'm going and I know the truth, and I don't have to be what you want me to be. I'm free to be what I want."[3]

Although the response stopped short of an unequivocal declaration, it left little room for doubt. Then, the following morning at a second press conference, Clay put any ambiguity to rest:

Black Muslims is a press word. It's not a legitimate name. The real name is Islam. That means peace. Islam is a religion and there are 750 million people all over the world who believe in it, and I'm one of them. I ain't no Christian. I can't be, when I see all the colored people fighting for forced integration get blowed up. They get hit by stones and chewed by dogs, and they blow up a Negro church and don't find the killers. I get telephone calls every day. They want me to carry signs. They want me to picket. They tell me it would be a wonderful thing if I married a white woman because this would be good for brotherhood. I don't want to be blown up. I don't want to be washed down sewers. I just want to be happy with my own kind.

I'm the heavyweight champion, but right now there are some neighborhoods I can't move into. I know how to dodge boobytraps and dogs. I dodge them by staying in my own neighborhood. I'm no troublemaker. I don't believe in forced integration. I know where I belong. I'm not going to force myself into anybody's house. I'm not joining no forced integration movement, because it don't work. A man has got to know where he belongs.

People brand us a hate group. They say we want to take over the country. They say we're Communists. That is not true. Followers of Allah are the sweetest people in the world. They don't carry knives. They don't tote weapons. They pray five times a day. The women wear dresses that come all the way to the floor and they don't commit adultery. All they want to do is live in peace. They don't want to

stir up any kind of trouble. All the meetings are held in secret, without any fuss or hatemongering.

I'm a good boy. I never have done anything wrong. I have
never been in jail. I have never been in court. I don't join
any integration marches. I don't pay any attention to all
those white women who wink at me. I don't carry signs. I
don't impose myself on people who don't want me. If I go in
somebody's house where I'm not welcome, I'm uncomfortable, so I stay away. I like white people. I like my own people. They can live together without infringing on each other.
You can't condemn a man for wanting peace. If you do, you
condemn peace itself. A rooster crows only when it sees the
light. Put him in the dark and he'll never crow. I have seen
the light and I'm crowing.[4]

ROBERT LIPSYTE: "I've been in sports and the media business
for most of my adult life, and that press conference was one of the
most remarkable things I've ever seen. The way Clay had played
the press from the beginning was extraordinary. He'd made us all
accomplices in his promotions with total self-awareness of what he
was doing and done it better than anyone before or since. He knew
the game. Still, before the Liston fight, even the old-line columnists—the ones like Jimmy Cannon and Dick Young who were hostile to him—didn't feel threatened by him because they knew he
was going to lose. If anything, Clay gave them a chance to fulminate
about how boxing was taking yet another bad turn. First you had
the criminal element, and now you had the encroachment of a show-
business clown. They took boxing kind of seriously, totally out of
proportion to its true worth. And they had an attitude of contempt
toward Clay. He gave us all such good copy, in a way it seemed to
be the journalistic equivalent of an easy lay.

"Then, after Liston, the press had no choice. We were hooked
into the story and had to follow it to the end. Clay was not dis-
missable. Most of the writers, particularly the older ones, felt more
comfortable with the mob figures around Liston than with the Muslims around Clay. The older reporters were saying, 'This is the worst
thing that ever happened to boxing.' And soon, that escalated to,
'This might be the worst thing that ever happened to the youth of
America, which needs a proper role model.' But regardless of what
they thought, they were stuck. And this garbage about the heavyweight champion being a role model; basically, what they were
talking about was the heavyweight champion, usually black, always

poor, being a safe role model for the underclass. The heavyweight championship was a way for the white establishment to say to black America, 'You should channel your rage and energy into going out and being someone who fights to entertain us within very specific carefully bounded areas. You can go out, eat glass, get drunk, get laid, do whatever you want as long as you stay within the parameters of what a member of the underclass is. Choke down your rage at how your people are getting screwed over, work very hard, make millions of dollars, have your pleasures in stereotypical ways, cars, women, wine, song, ultimately self-destruct, and keep our stereotypes in order.' And now, all of a sudden, these people were stuck with a heavyweight champion who said at the press conference the day after the fight, 'I don't have to be what you want me to be.' He understood. 'I don't have to be what you want me to be; I'm free to be me.' And among the things he didn't have to be were Christian, a good soldier of American democracy in the mold of Joe Louis, or the kind of athlete-prince white America wanted."

What Cassius Clay chose to be was inextricably linked to an organization known as the Nation of Islam and a man named Elijah Muhammad.

Elijah Muhammad was born in Georgia in 1898, and given the name Elijah Poole by his parents. In 1923, he moved to Detroit, where eight years later, he was visited by a man who identified himself as a silk merchant from the East named W. D. Fard. Fard was half-black and half-white, which he said enabled him to be accepted by black people in the United States and lead them, while at the same time, moving undiscovered among whites to understand the true nature of the enemy. He taught Elijah Poole and his wife for three-and-a-half years. Finally, Elijah asked, "Who are you? What is your true name?" And Fard revealed, "I am the one the world has been waiting for for the past two thousand years. I have come to guide you into the right path."

The heart of Fard's teachings began with Original Man, a black people who lived in the Holy City of Makkah. Approximately 6,600 years ago, there was born among them a child with an unusually large head, who came to be known as Mr. Yacub. Yacub began school when he was four, and by age eighteen had completed a full curriculum at all the universities in the land. Then he began preaching dissension in the streets, gathering adherents in defiance of God. Subsequently exiled to the island of Patmos with 59,999 followers, he decided as revenge to create a devil race of genetically engineered white people.

Yacub knew from his schooling that blacks had two genes, black and brown, but that the brown gene remained dormant because it was the weaker of the two. However, one out of every three children born to his followers had some visible trace of brown. Thus, Yacub decided to create a progressively lighter race through genetic matching—a race that, as it evolved, would become weaker because of its color and more susceptible to evil. Only adults bearing traces of brown were permitted to marry. Then, if a child of their union was born brown, the mother was instructed to care for it well. But if a black child was born, it was fed to wild beasts or a sharp needle was stuck in its brain, and the mother was falsely told that she had given birth to an angel baby that had gone to heaven.

Yacub never saw the devil race he engineered. He died at age 152, but left a legacy of laws and procedures to be followed. After two hundred years, all black people had been eliminated from the island of Patmos and only brown people remained. Two hundred years after that, brown people had been genetically eliminated and replaced by a yellow race. Finally, six hundred years after Yacub's experiment began, Patmos was inhabited by a race of pale-skinned, blond, blue-eyed devils.

Six hundred years after its creation, the white race emigrated to the mainland. Soon, through lies that set black people against one another, they transformed what had been an idyllic land into a strife-torn nation. Realizing this, the black people exiled the evildoers across the Arabian desert to the caves of Europe. Two thousand years after that, God sent Moses to civilize the devil race, which enabled them to rule for six thousand years. But ultimately, it was prophesied, the original black people would give birth to One whose wisdom, knowledge, and power were infinite. W. D. Fard was that One, and he taught that the white devil's civilization was about to be destroyed. There was in the sky a wheel-shaped Mother of Planes one-half mile wide, the largest man-made object in the sky. The finest minds in the world had built it. It was manned by black men, and circled the earth at night. Eight to ten days before Allah's chosen day of retribution, Arabic-language pamphlets would be dropped from the Mother of Planes, and righteous people would be told where to go to survive. Then fifteen hundred planes from the Mother of Planes would drop deadly explosives—"the type used in bringing up mountains on the earth"—and all but the righteous would be destroyed.

Elijah Poole believed Fard to be the manifestation of God in person. Fard gave him the name "Elijah Muhammad," and missioned him to educate and emancipate the black race in America. Then Elijah Muhammad's crusade began. He taught that God's true name was Allah, and that his true religion was Islam. However, his teachings differed greatly from those of the prophet Muhammad thirteen hundred years before. Orthodox Muslims rejected, and still reject, the view of white people as "devils." Mr. Yacub as described by Fard appears nowhere in the Qur'an. And while the concepts of Heaven and Hell are central to traditional Islamic thought, Elijah Muhammad rejected both. "No already physically dead person will be in the hereafter," he wrote. "That is slavery belief, taught to slaves to keep them under control."[5] Still, to a segment of black America in the 1930s and thereafter, Elijah Muhammad's message was a powerful one:

On the white enemy: "You and I, here in America, are licking the boots of the slave-master, begging him for the right of independent people. 'Sir, let me shine your shoes?' You have been doing that for approximately four hundred years. Today, if one rises up in your midst and says, 'We should not lick the slave-master's boots, we should lick our own boots,' you would say, 'He should be killed because he is teaching us to hate.' The American white people delight in mistreating us, their former slaves. There is no justice for us among such people, the devils in person. They hate us if we try being good."

On Christianity: "You are a people who think you know all about the Bible, and all about Christianity. You even are foolish enough to believe that nothing is right but Christianity! There is no hope for us in Christianity. It is a religion organized by the enemies of the Black Nation to enslave us to the white race's rule."

On self-love: "One of the great handicaps among the so-called Negroes is that there is no love for self, nor love for his or her own kind. This not having love for self is the root cause of hate, disunity, disagreement, quarreling, betraying, fighting, and killing one another. How can you be loved, if you have no love for self? Love yourself and your kind. It is a fool who does not love himself and his people. Your black skin is the best. Never try changing its color."

On separation of the races: "Our people are the fools of the nations. Integration means self-destruction. The black people throughout the earth are seeking independence for their own, not integration into white society. What do we look like, trying to integrate with our four-hundred-year-old enemies? We want our people in America whose parents or grandparents were descendants from slaves to be allowed to establish a separate state or territory of their own—either on this continent or elsewhere. We believe that our former slave-masters are obligated to provide such land and that the area must be fertile and minerally rich. Since we cannot get along with them in peace and equality after giving them four hundred years of our sweat and blood and receiving in return some of the worst treatment human beings have ever experienced, we believe our contributions to this land and the suffering forced upon us by white America justifies our demand for complete separation in a state or territory of our own."[6]

In 1934, W. D. Fard disappeared from view. Meanwhile, that same year, after establishing a University of Islam to educate his and other black children in Detroit, Elijah Muhammad was arrested on charges of contributing to the delinquency of minors. Released on the condition that he return his own children to public schools, he refused, and in September 1934, moved to Chicago. In 1942, he was arrested again, this time for refusing to register for the draft, and sentenced to five years in prison. Paroled in 1946, he reestablished his primacy within the Nation of Islam, but the movement itself languished until 1954, when a young black man named Malcolm X was designated leader of its Mosque No. 7 in Harlem.

Malcolm was a spellbinding charismatic speaker, capable of appealing both to the masses and to the growing number of black intellectuals, writers, and artists who were achieving prominence in the black community. Unlike Elijah, he was skilled at media manipulation. And over time—through rallies, sermons, radio appearances, and press conferences—the message Malcolm was preaching was heard:

My black brothers and sisters of all religious beliefs or of no religious beliefs; we all have in common the greatest binding tie we could have—we all are black people! I'm not going to take all day telling you some of the greatnesses of

The Honorable Elijah Muhammad. I'm just going to tell you now his greatest greatness! He is the first, the only black leader to identify, to you and me, who is our enemy! The Honorable Elijah Muhammad is the first black leader among us with the courage to tell us, out here in public, something which, when you begin to think of it back in your homes, you will realize we black people have been living with, we have been seeing, we have been suffering, all of our lives! Our enemy is the white man!

And why is Mr. Muhammad's teaching such a great thing? Because when you know who your enemy is, he can no longer keep you divided and fighting one brother against the other! Because when you recognize who your enemy is, he can no longer use trickery, promises, lies, hypocrisy, and his evil acts to keep you deaf, dumb, and blinded! When you recognize who your enemy is, he can no longer brainwash you, he can no longer pull wool over your eyes so that you never stop to see that you are living in pure hell on this earth, while he lives in pure heaven right on this same earth!

This enemy tells you that you are both supposed to be worshiping the same white Christian God. I know you don't realize the enormity, the horrors, of the so-called Christian white man's crime. Not even in the Bible is there such a crime! God in His wrath struck down with fire the perpetrators of lesser crimes! One hundred million of us black people! Your grandparents! Mine! Murdered by this white man. To get fifteen million of us here to make us his slaves, he murdered one hundred million! I wish it was possible for me to show you the sea bottom in those days; the black bodies, the blood, the bones broken by boots and clubs! The pregnant black women who were thrown overboard if they got too sick! Thrown overboard to the sharks that had learned that following these slave ships was the way to grow fat! Why, the white man's raping of the black race's women began right on those slave ships! The blue-eyed devil could not even wait until he got them here! Why, brothers and sisters, civilized mankind has never known such an orgy of greed and lust and murder.

Brothers and sisters here for the first time, please don't let that shock you. I know you didn't expect this. Because almost none of us black people have thought that maybe we

were making a mistake not wondering if there wasn't a special religion somewhere for us; a special religion for the black
man. Well, there is such a religion. It's called Islam. Let me
spell it for you, I-s-l-a-m! Islam![7]

MUHAMMAD ALI: "The first time I heard about Elijah Muhammad was at a Golden Gloves Tournament in Chicago [in 1959]. Then,
before I went to the Olympics, I looked at a copy of the Nation of
Islam newspaper, *Muhammad Speaks.* I didn't pay much attention
to it, but lots of things were working on my mind.

When I was growing up, a colored boy named Emmett Till was
murdered in Mississippi for whistling at a white woman. Emmett
Till was the same age as me, and even though they caught the men
who did it, nothing happened to them. Things like that went on all
the time. And in my own life, there were places I couldn't go, places
I couldn't eat. I won a gold medal representing the United States
at the Olympic Games, and when I came home to Louisville, I still
got treated like a nigger. There were restaurants I couldn't get served
in. Some people kept calling me 'boy.' Then in Miami [in 1961], I
was training for a fight, and met a follower of Elijah Muhammad
named Captain Sam. He invited me to a meeting, and after that,
my life changed."

ABDUL RAHAMAN (formerly known as Sam Saxon): "I was born
in Atlanta in 1931, and first heard the teaching in 1955. A brother
named James, who Elijah Muhammad sent to Atlanta, taught me.
I was what you'd call a sportsman; a man who shot pool, played
poker, and attended sporting events. That's the kind of life I was
living at the time. But the first time I heard the word of the Honorable Elijah Muhammad, I knew it was the truth. I was convinced
God had sent us a Messenger. After that, I went from Atlanta to
Los Angeles, and then my wife got a job teaching with Elijah Muhammad in Chicago. We stayed there for three years, until 1961,
when the Messenger said to me that he had many good people in
Chicago but needed help elsewhere, and since I was someone who
knew his teachings, he was sending me to Miami.

"The minister in charge of the temple in Miami was a man named
Ishmael Sabakhan, and the Messenger told him to make me his
captain. That wasn't like being a military captain. My job was to see
that the men in the temple were trained to be good providers for
their family, made physically fit, and taught how to live right. Once
you become a Muslim, you have to study, and I was also in charge

of helping everybody in the mosque with that. There weren't many members who attended regularly. Realistically, in Miami, we had about thirty. More than that believed, but only about thirty came regularly. This is 1961 I'm talking about. And when I wasn't in the temple, I ran concessions at Hialeah Race Track, Gulfstream, and Tropical Park. One track runs at a time in Miami, and when the first closes, the next opens up. You know the men's rooms, where you see those brothers in there with shaving lotion and Bromo Seltzer and the towels? I had those concessions and the shoeshine stands. There were three brothers working for me, one track after the next.

"I met Ali—I think it was in March of 1961—when I was selling *Muhammad Speaks* newspapers on the street. He saw me, said 'Hello brother,' and started talking. And I said, 'Hey, you're into the teaching.' He told me, 'Well, I ain't been in the temple, but I know what you're talking about.' And then he introduced himself. He said, 'I'm Cassius Clay. I'm gonna be the next heavyweight champion of the world.' I said, 'I know you, man. I followed you in the Olympics.' Then he asked, 'Do you want to come around and look at my scrapbook?' so I went to his hotel room. He was sharing it with another fighter. The scrapbook was full of articles about himself, and I looked at it real good. He was interested in himself, and he was interested in Islam, and we talked about both at the same time. He was familiar in passing with some of our teachings, although he'd never studied or been taught. And I saw the cockiness in him. I knew if I could put the truth to him, he'd be great, so I invited him to our next meeting at the mosque."

MUHAMMAD ALI: "The first time I felt truly spiritual in my life was when I walked into the Muslim temple in Miami. A man named Brother John was speaking, and the first words I heard him say were, 'Why are we called Negroes? It's the white man's way of taking away our identity. If you see a Chinaman coming, you know he comes from China. If you see a Cuban coming, you know he comes from Cuba. If you see a Canadian coming, you know he comes from Canada. What country is called Negro?' Then Brother John said, 'We don't even have our names.' And I said to myself, 'What's he talking about; I got my name.' But I kept listening, and he explained, 'If Mr. Chang is coming, you know he's a Chinaman. If Mr. Goldberg is coming, you know he's a Jew. Mr. O'Reilly is an Irishman. Rolling Thunder and Silver Moon are Indians. But if someone says here comes Mr. Jones or Mr. Washington, you don't know what's coming. We were named after our white slavemasters. If Mr. Jones had fifty slaves, they were Mr. Jones's niggers and they were named after him. Then, if Mr. Washington bought those slaves, they became Mr. Washington's niggers and changed to his name.' That was plain to me. I could reach out and touch what Brother John was saying. It wasn't like church teaching, where I had to have faith that what the preacher was preaching was right. And I said to myself, 'Cassius Marcellus Clay. He was a Kentucky white man, who owned my great-granddaddy and named my great-granddaddy after him. And then my granddaddy got named, and then my daddy, and now it's me.'

"So I liked what I heard, and wanted to learn more. I started reading *Muhammad Speaks* every week, went to meetings, and listened to a phonograph record they gave me called 'A White Man's Heaven Is a Black Man's Hell.' I had respect for Martin Luther King and all the other civil rights leaders, but I was taking a different road."

Soon after he began attending meetings, Clay was introduced to his next teacher—a man named Jeremiah Shabazz.

JEREMIAH SHABAZZ: "I was born in Philadelphia and raised in the Christian church. When I was fourteen, I heard the teachings of Islam from a barber who'd been imprisoned with some Muslim brothers down in Virginia. I'd never heard about Islam before. I'd heard about Muhammadanism, but the way this brother was talking, even though it was strange to me, it definitely had the ring of truth. By 1961, I was the Nation of Islam's minister over the Deep South, which was Georgia, South Carolina, Alabama, Mississippi, Louisiana, and Florida. That was my area, given to me by my leader, the Honorable Elijah Muhammad. And although I was headquartered in Atlanta, I moved back and forth like a circuit man from one town to the next.

"I wasn't there when Cassius Clay first came to the temple. And contrary to what has been portrayed in the movies and written in some books, Malcolm X was not his first teacher. The person to educate him first regarding Islam and the teachings of Elijah Muhammad was our minister in Miami, Ishmael Sabakhan. Cassius's reaction to what was being taught was so good that eventually they called me in Atlanta to say they had Cassius Clay down there, and I went down about a week later. We had a meeting, and he told me that he liked what he'd heard; he'd never heard anything like it before. It was new, it was strange, but it was also the truth, and he said he'd seriously consider becoming a Muslim. So we continued to talk with him, encouraging him to come to our meetings, which he did. He didn't come to every meeting, but he attended like once a week. And what we taught was different from what Martin Luther King was teaching. We dealt with the reality of the situation, not the way everybody wanted it to be.

"We taught him first that God is a black man. Everybody else has a God that looks like them. The Chinese have a Buddha who looks Chinese. Africans have God on a stick that looks like them. The Europeans have a Jesus. And as far as white people were concerned, we taught him that the white man is the devil. There's no devil in the ground. The devil we know on top of the ground is far worse than the one we don't know that they claim is in the ground. To us, God is real, the devil is real, heaven is a place here on earth. When you die, you're finished. You go in the ground; there's no hell in the ground. They've dug down in the ground and they haven't found no hell down there, and if anybody found it, it would have been us because we've had picks and shovels in our hands all our lives and we haven't found any hell down there. Hell is here on earth. And when somebody does to a people what whites have done to us for no reason whatsoever other than that our skin is black, then they must be evil for the sake of evil. And that makes them the devil. Their hatred of us has no grounds. There's no reason for it. We didn't do anything to them. It'd be different if there had been a war between Europe and Africa and Europeans had to wage war and take prisoners and then make them slaves to save lives. But what happened to us had no reason for it except greed, where they brought us over here to use our labor. And after using it, then they turned on us and killed us and treated us worse than animals. They used us up until we couldn't serve them no more, and then they killed us. This is what whites have done to blacks here in America. They have a propaganda campaign going against us to this very day whereby they hate us without cause. Nobody worked harder for the white man than black people did. We dug every trench, every canal, carried every brick all the way to the top of the Empire State Building. Black people made America what it is today. The country became great because it had hundreds of years of cheap labor and black slaves. And after giving America our blood, sweat, and tears, you'd think America would reward us, but no, they hate us now worse than they hated us before. What is the reason for this? Why are we so hated and despised when we've done nothing but work and slave for the white man all of our days? Today it's sophisticated slavery, but we're still slaves and the white man still hates us. He'll tolerate everybody but us. A Korean can come over here and he's all right. The damn Germans; they killed thousands of American soldiers, but they come over here and they're all right. The Japanese; they bombed Pearl Harbor, that was a horrible war, and they're all right too. And I still don't know why the white man hates us so. What have we done to him that makes him hate us, come in lynching, killing black people, kicking and stomping on black women, for what? All black people are doing is going to church singing songs, and praising the God white people taught us about, and they're still beating us and killing us and burning our homes. So there's no devil in the ground. The man that's inherently evil and has hated us ever since we've been here is the white man. Don't look for something that doesn't exist in the ground; look for something that you see every day.

"So that's how we began teaching Cassius, and he didn't have problems with our claim that the white man was evil. Sometimes he'd ask questions like, 'Wait a minute; what about a baby? A baby is born white; how is it the devil?' And I'd explain, if a lion gives birth, it can't give birth to anything except a lion. No pregnant lion is giving birth to a lamb. This was in 1961, and there was a lot of outright injustice going on. You could see it. You could pick up the newspaper every day, and see white police cracking black skulls and siccing dogs on us. And the thing that really got Cassius was when we began to explain that for someone to do this to other human beings, they can't be what he thought they were. They can't be God's people and mistreat other people the way white folks were doing.

"He was a young man, but he was a wise young man, so he was able to see that what we were teaching had truth. He had trouble worshiping a God other than Jesus, because he'd been raised in a Christian church. But we had a way back then which was, I guess you could say, a system of teaching that had been sophisticated to the point where we could go into history, biology, genetics and everything to prove our point of black goodness as opposed to white hatred. And the more Cassius saw, the more he questioned; and the more he questioned, the more he convinced himself that what we were telling him was right. He had been raised in Louisville, Kentucky. He saw what had happened all of his life. He'd seen the white man mistreating black people, saw his father and mother being disrespected and mistreated. So the real problem we had with him was not convincing him we were right. It was fear. Whenever we talked to black people, they had misgivings about what we were saying because black people generally feared whites, particularly in the South. That's what I saw at my post when I first went to Georgia. The biggest thing I saw down there was fear. And my leader, the Messenger, had told me to teach those people to overcome that fear because every black person knew one thing about the white man— if you said something he didn't like, he was going to get you, and fear of the white man's retribution was greater than any fear of God. So this was something Cassius wrestled with. He wanted to know how we could believe these things and say these things and keep walking around without the white man retaliating, because white people were killing black people every day. Cassius wasn't fearful of being shot or hung, but he had this great respect for the white man's power. From the president on down, the white man was it, and Cassius was asking, 'How are you going to overcome it? Even if what you're saying is right, how are you gonna beat the white man?' And we convinced him that the white man could be beaten, not by false alarms and violence, but by the power of Allah himself. We read him passages from the Qur'an, showing him, although sometimes the people of God appear to be outnumbered and defeated, always God has turned the tide of battle in their favor. That was the sort of thing that brought him around; that the forces of evil just cannot win because Allah is the God of everything, of the heavens and the earth. And if he has the power to create a sun a thousand times bigger than the earth, to cause the planets to go whirling around the sun, that kind of power has power over all things, and is not limited like the power of the white Jesus, who we were taught to believe in by our slavemasters. We had to convince him that the God we served was greater and more powerful than the white man; that Allah had power over all things. That was our message. The teachings of Elijah Muhammad were designed to convince black people that there was a higher power than the white man. Having been brainwashed, we really believed that there was no power greater than the white man, and that the white man was not just great here on earth, that he was also great up in heaven. That God was white, Jesus was white, all the angels were white. Everything having to do with the afterlife was white. So the black person didn't see himself a winner, living or dead. His relief would only come if the white man's heart would change or maybe God would turn him white and then he'd have a chance, but as long as he was a black man on earth or in heaven, he didn't stand a chance. The teachings of the Honorable Elijah Muhammad were such that they would convince the black person that God was indeed a powerful prayer-answering God, who, when you called on him, you didn't have to worry whether he was going to come to your rescue. You knew that, when you called on him, he would answer. And thousands of people became convinced that at last there was a God who would defend them against the white man. Jesus never did it. We called out Jesus' name while they were putting ropes around our necks. Thousands of our people got murdered down in Mississippi, Alabama, and Georgia. Those folks' prayers didn't do them any good. And we were able to convince black people that all of their prayers wouldn't stop white brutality and white inhumanity, but if they accepted Islam and prayed to Allah, then Allah would be there when they needed him."

HUSTON HORN: "Ali believed. Nobody entered the Nation of Islam for laughs, but he camouflaged his feelings well. I remember, in 1961, I went to Louisville and spent several days with him and his family, mostly at home, for Sports Illustrated. Then, the next time I saw him, he was on his way to Miami to train for a fight. We met at the airport in New Orleans; that was our rendezvous point. There was time between planes, so we went to a root beer stand. And what I remember is, they served mine in a frosted glass mug, but they filled a paper cup for him and said, 'This one's for the boy.' I was embarrassed and angry, but he wasn't. At least, it didn't seem that way. He said something—and I'm paraphrasing now—he said something to the effect that he was accustomed to that sort of treatment and had too much self-respect to define himself by the way other people defined him.

"Then we got to Miami, and he checked into the hotel that Angelo Dundee had arranged for him. It was in the black part of town; a scruffy motel actually, not a hotel, not a very nice place. And he said, 'You can stay here, too.' But, you know, I was from a big magazine in New York. I had reservations at a fancy hotel in Miami Beach. And I was embarrassed by that because it meant I was participating in the same sort of thing I'd seen at the root beer stand, but I didn't like the look of the place he was in, so I opted for the fancy hotel. I think about that sometimes now. I'm not proud of myself, but that's what I did. And despite those incidents and others like them, when he joined the Muslim movement, I still felt resentful and betrayed. I can back away from that now. I've grown up a lot since then. And objectively speaking, white Christianity was, and still is, something to look at real critically if you're black. But I'm cut from the Martin Luther King mold, not the mold of Elijah Muhammad. I thought Elijah Muhammad was a sinister man."

ABDUL RAHAMAN: "As things went along, I began to teach Cassius the tricks of the white man; how we were made slaves and manipulated and deceived in this country. I told him about the kingdoms of Africa, great empires that flourished while the white man was in caves. I taught him straight, like it really was, the same way I'd teach anybody else. The only difference between him and the other brothers was, because of his profession, he didn't have the same duties in the temple. But except for that, he was treated like everyone else.

"We used to eat together at the Famous Chef Café. And when I first sat down with Cassius, no one had taught him about not eating pork. But it wasn't hard to get him to change. He didn't drink or smoke or do drugs, and he didn't mind changing what he ate at all. At the meetings, he never talked much. He just sat there, listening, wanting to learn. He was a beautiful young man. All he wanted was what was right for our people. The Messenger taught, and it's definitely true, that we're no greater than the least one of us. If we don't pull the little man that society rejects up out of the mud, then we as a people are nothing. That's how you prove the coming of God; by making something out of nothing. And Cassius understood that. He could have been a thousand miles away, and it would still feel good just knowing a brother like that was in the world."

JEREMIAH SHABAZZ: "After Cassius had been with us about a month, he sent for his brother Rudolph, or Rahaman. And Rahaman was even more enthused than he was. Cassius had a cautious side. Once he got his heart in it, he was with us all the way, but he was skeptical in the beginning. Some of the things he was hearing for the first time, he wanted to roll over in his mind and look at from different angles. Rahaman, on the other hand, was gung ho from the start. He grabbed the whole thing and said, 'That's right; I want it!' Even though it was Cassius who first became interested, Rahaman actually joined the Nation before he did. And when Cassius finally did join, we chose to make certain accommodations. We had a champion in the making, a celebrity, and everybody was very happy about that; particularly those of us in the South, because most of the brothers in the North didn't know about him except for the few who followed boxing. But at that time, the Honorable Elijah Muhammad was the most hated man in the country among whites and also among the so-called Negro leadership. And we knew that if Cassius made a public declaration of faith, he'd never get to fight for the championship. So we decided he'd keep his feelings to himself. That was the safest thing to do. And the truth is, the Messenger didn't even show much interest in him at first. When I telephoned John Ali, our national secretary, to tell him, 'We got this fighter coming to our meetings,' I was roundly condemned for being involved with a boxer. The Messenger told me I'd been sent to the South to make converts, not to fool around with fighters."

MUHAMMAD ALI: "For three years, up until I fought Sonny Liston, I'd sneak into Nation of Islam meetings through the back door. I didn't want people to know I was there. I was afraid, if they knew, I wouldn't be allowed to fight for the title. Later on, I learned to stand up for my beliefs. And since then, my beliefs have changed. I don't believe in Mr. Yacub and the spaceship anymore. Hearts and souls have no color. I know that too. But Elijah Muhammad was a good man, even if he wasn't the Messenger of God we thought he was. If you look at what our people were like then, a lot of us didn't have self-respect. We didn't have banks or stores. We didn't have anything after being in America for hundreds of years. Elijah Muhammad was trying to lift us up and get our people out of the gutter. He made people dress properly, so they weren't on the street looking like prostitutes and pimps. He taught good eating habits, and was against alcohol and drugs. I think he was wrong when he talked about white devils, but part of what he did was make people feel it was good to be black. So I'm not apologizing for what I believed. I'm wiser now, but so are a lot of other people."

As 1961 progressed, Captain Sam Saxon became a regular at the Fifth Street Gym and traveled with Clay on various out-of-town trips. Then, at the start of 1962, Jeremiah Shabazz provided a Muslim cook to ensure that the fighter's meals were prepared in accordance with Nation of Islam dietary laws. Later that year, unbeknownst to the press, Clay drove from Miami to Detroit to hear Elijah Muhammad address a mass meting for the first time. The trip took on added importance when, in Detroit, Clay met Malcolm X.

BETTY SHABAZZ (widow of Malcolm X): "My earliest recollection of Muhammad Ali was from my husband, who said there was this young fighter who was at a great number of our meetings in different parts of the country. Then the next thing my husband said was that he was a convert, and all of us were very happy. Malcolm accepted Cassius, and loved him like a younger brother. He felt his job was to get this young man to believe in himself and stand squarely on both feet with his shoulders back. He did not want other people to exploit his talents, and felt he could do more and be more. But my husband felt that his conversion should in no way conflict with his role as a fighter, and that Cassius Clay shouldn't be made to publicly announce that he was in the movement. He felt that this young man's religion should be his own personal private concern for so long as he chose to keep it that way, and that he could gain great internal strength just from knowing that he had converted."

ATTALLAH SHABAZZ (daughter of Malcolm X): "I don't think the Nation of Islam was a religious organization at all. When Cassius Clay, which is what he was called then, joined the Nation, he underwent a social and political awakening. As spiritual as he was, and he's always had a relationship with God, he needed to belong to an organization that balanced out his Negritude, and the Nation was there for him. I'm glad that I personally was not indoctrinated in the Nation. In some respects, it was a positive force. It offered young black men and women who were victimized by circumstances an opportunity to move forward and like themselves. But it knocked other things down in order to build, and that's not a process that sat right with me.

"My father's relationship with Cassius Clay was not as a recruiter for the Nation so much as it was one individual meeting another and saying, 'Why don't you join me in this organization so you can have direction and a family of supporters.' It was more than counseling; it was a friendship. My father was an excellent big brother to many, and when he met Cassius, he saw greatness and wanted to offer a focus of motivation. My father loved Cassius like a brother, but once you were brought into the Nation, you became an entity of the Nation. Your allegiance was to the organization before it was to any individual except, perhaps in the eyes of some, to Elijah Muhammad."

MUHAMMAD ALI: "Malcolm was very intelligent, with a good sense of humor, a wise man. When he talked, he held me spellbound for hours. He introduced me to his wife and children. Then he sent a friend of his, Archie Robinson, to act as a sort of administrator or road manager. Archie looked over my contracts and helped run the training camp, but anything that had to do with boxing, like choosing sparring partners, was still decided by me and Angelo."

OSMAN KARRIEM (formerly known as Archie Robinson): "I was with Malcolm in a restaurant, talking, when a big red car pulled up and this kid jumped out. A bunch of people gathered around him, and I asked myself, 'What the hell is going on?' Then this wild kid, who was Cassius Clay, came into the restaurant, and Malcolm said, 'I want to introduce you. I think you should meet him.' So I went over, shook hands, and walked away. Malcolm and Cassius kept on talking, and I went home. Then, the next day, Malcolm told me, 'This young man needs some help; perhaps you should help him.' I said, 'I do not play with amateurs. I don't know anything about boxing except that I hate it. He's a clown.' But Malcolm wasn't really asking me; he was telling me. He said, 'It's not about boxing. One day this kid is going to be heavyweight champion of the world, and he's going to embrace the Nation of Islam. Do you understand what that could mean?' So I said 'yes' and talked with Cassius, and talking with him was like strange. Malcolm told him that I was a brother who would be there to advise him. And a day or two later, we had a meeting with Joe Glazer. I think that was why Malcolm wanted me involved. He wanted me to go with Cassius to that meeting.

"Joe Glazer was the president of Associated Booking, but he wasn't just a talent agent. For black entertainers and athletes, even though he was a Jew, he was the biggest talent agent around. When you started talking about blacks in show business—Duke Ellington, Sarah Vaughan, people like that—you were talking about Joe Glazer. If he was your agent, you worked, because there were nightclubs and record companies that he was in solid with. I knew him because, for a short while, I'd been road manager for the Platters, and he'd been their booking agent. And I'll say this; Joe Glazer was a man of his word. He always did what he said he would, and he'd earned a lot of respect in the black community.

"So I went to the meeting. Joe Louis's wife, Marva, had set it up. And the way I saw things, inherent in it all was a move on Joe Glazer's part to gain control of Cassius Clay. There were four of us in the room—Marva, Joe, Cassius, and myself. And I didn't waste time. I just looked at Joe and said, 'This kid is one you can't have.' "

Then came the build-up to the Sonny Liston fight, with Malcolm X becoming visible in the Clay camp.

Betty Shabazz: "Elijah Muhammad told my husband that he should not align himself too closely with Cassius Clay, because in the upcoming bout with Liston, he was more than likely to lose. Anyone looking at Liston, he said, could tell that Liston would prevail, and the whole fight would be an embarrassment to the Nation of Islam. Things by this time were not good between my husband and Elijah. Malcolm said he wished to go to Florida, not representing anyone, but to offer his personal support to Cassius Clay as a private person. And Elijah said to my husband, 'Yes, if you do go, it will be as a private person. You will not in any way be representing us, because it's impossible for Cassius Clay to win.' "

Abdul Rahaman: "At the time we were getting ready to fight Sonny Liston, Malcolm came down and asked would it be okay if he went over to the gym. I said, 'You know, everybody knows who you are, and it's better if you don't go,' because it wasn't acceptable in those days. But Malcolm didn't listen to me. He went over to the gym, trying to get the publicity for himself, and the promoters threatened to call the fight off. Cassius wasn't going to fight if they made him denounce the Nation. He was ready to walk. But I said to him, 'Brother, don't worry. They aren't gonna call this fight off, because they want the money they can get from it. Money is the white man's God.' "

Betty Shabazz: "Cassius was just about hysterical with apprehension of Sonny Liston. And my husband indoctrinated him continuously about the fact that, not only was he young, strong and skillful; he was a man who believed in God. They talked continuously about how David slew Goliath, and how God would not allow someone who believed in him to fail, regardless of how powerful the opponent was. As it turned out, of course, he beat Liston. And then all the people who said, 'Stay away from him, he can't do anything but bring disgrace to the Nation of Islam,' it was as if they hadn't said those things at all. All of a sudden, they were breaking their necks, trying to get close to the heavyweight champion. And my husband was just very happy for Cassius. He was pleased with the internal strength he'd shown."

Two days after Clay defeated Sonny Liston, Elijah Muhammad addressed five thousand followers at the Nation of Islam's annual convention in Chicago. "I'm so glad that Cassius Clay was brave enough to say that he was a Muslim," Elijah told the cheering throng.

"I'm happy that he confessed he's a believer. Clay whipped a much tougher man and came through the bout unscarred because he has accepted Muhammad as the Messenger of Allah."[8] Four days later, Clay himself journeyed to New York, where he checked into the Hotel Theresa in Harlem. Malcolm X had an office in the hotel, and the two men met in private for an hour before going to the Trans-Lux Theater, where a film of the Clay-Liston bout was shown. Then they toured the United Nations and were photographed with various African delegates. Alex Haley, who worked with Malcolm X on his autobiography and later authored *Roots*, was a witness to it all.

ALEX HALEY: "That was the first time I spent any length of time with Muhammad Ali, and it was a frustrating experience. I was at the Theresa to interview him for *Playboy* magazine, and was permitted to enter his room with many other people who wandered in and out. He was lying on the bed, lord of his kingdom, which is the way things are with most big fighters. And part of the problem was, I never got to be alone with him. The entourage was always filtering around, and someone always had something of urgent importance, a phone call or whatever, to keep his attention from a serious interview. He was very different from the person I'd seen in public; quiet, monosyllabic. It was all but impossible to get him to speak in personal terms. I couldn't figure out if he was putting me on or what, but sometimes I'd ask a question and there'd be no response. He appeared to be falling asleep. That happened several times, and it had nothing to do with the health problems he has now. I don't know if he was really tired, giving me the business, or what, but it wasn't an even interviewing pattern at all. I did well to get three questions with any substantive response in a session. Interviewing him was a matter of catching him for three questions, and then meeting him again to see if I could get in three more. The only time he broke that pattern was when he delightedly explained how he'd set up Liston. Everybody assumed Liston would kill him, and he'd played to that by leaking word to Liston's camp that he was scared to death. Liston believed this, and as a result, trained to fight only three rounds. And Muhammad, or Cassius Clay then, said to me with almost boyish joy, 'Do you remember at the end of the third round when I hollered something at him before I went to my corner?' And I said I did, although I didn't remember as specifically as I made it sound. And he told me, 'You know what I hollered at him? I hollered, "You big sucker; I got you now." ' "

While at the United Nations with Malcolm X, Clay was asked numerous times for his autograph. Several years earlier, he'd spoken with pride of the name Cassius Marcellus Clay. "Don't you think it's a beautiful name?" he'd said at the time. "Makes you think of the Coliseum and those Roman gladiators. Cassius Marcellus Clay. Say it to yourself. Feel the way it rolls out of your mouth. Say it out loud. Cassius Marcellus Clay. It's a beautiful name."[9] Now, however, he chose to sign "Cassius X Clay," incorporating the "X" as symbolic of his lost African identity. Then, on the night of March 6, in a radio broadcast from Chicago, Elijah Muhammad announced, "This Clay name has no divine meaning. I hope he will accept being called by a better name. Muhammad Ali is what I will give him for as long as he believes in Allah and follows me."[10]

MUHAMMAD ALI: "Changing my name was one of the most important things that happened to me in my life. It freed me from the identity given to my family by slavemasters. If Hitler changed the names of people he was killing, and instead of killing them made them slaves, after the war those people would have changed their slave names. That's all I was doing. People change their names all the time, and no one complains. Actors and actresses change their name. The pope changes his name. Joe Louis and Sugar Ray Robinson changed their names. If I changed my name from Cassius Clay to something like Smith or Jones because I wanted a name that white people thought was more American, nobody would have complained. I was honored that Elijah Muhammad gave me a truly beautiful name. 'Muhammad' means one worthy of praise. 'Ali' was the name of a great general [a cousin of the Prophet Muhammad, and the third Caliphate after the death of the Prophet]. I've been Muhammad Ali now for twenty-six years. That's four years longer than I was Cassius Clay."

The new name stuck in the public's collective craw. Almost unanimously, the media refused to use it. Then, on March 20, Ali went to Madison Square Garden to watch his stablemate, Luis Rodriguez, fight Holly Mims. Custom called for well-known fighters to be introduced from the ring, but Harry Markson (president of Madison Square Garden Boxing) maintained, "I cannot permit Clay's introduction under any name other than the one that's on his license at the State Athletic Commission office; Cassius Clay."[11] Ali threatened to leave the arena if his old name was used. Markson made good on his threat, and the champion left to a chorus of boos from the crowd—evidence that it wasn't only the media that was against him. Still, Ali continued to be heard:

> All I want is peace—peace for myself and peace for the world. I don't hate any man, black or white. I just want to live with my people. Is this a crime? Should I be condemned because I refuse to put my life in jeopardy over where I can drink a cup of coffee? I don't believe in forcing integration. I don't want to go where I'm not wanted. If a white man comes to my house, then he's welcome. But if he doesn't want me to come to his home, then I don't want to go. I'm not mad at the white people. If they like me, I like them. Milton Berle invited me to the hotel where he was performing and I went. But I wouldn't have gone there if I wasn't welcome. The NAACP and CORE have a right to do what they think, but I'm not going to get killed trying to force myself on people who don't want me. I like my life. Integration is wrong. The black man that's trying to integrate, he's getting beat up and bombed and shot. But the black man that says he don't want to integrate, he gets called a "hate teacher." Chubby Checker is catching hell with a white woman. And I'm catching hell for not wanting a white woman. People are always telling me what a good example I could set for my people if I just wasn't a Muslim. I've heard over and over, how come I couldn't be like Joe Louis and Sugar Ray. Well, they're gone now, and the black man's condition is just the same, ain't it? We're still catching hell.[12]

MUHAMMAD ALI: "I just spoke my mind; that's all. I said things black people thought, but were afraid to say. I didn't hate. Not then; not now. What I was doing was like a doctor giving someone a needle and hurting them a little to kill an infection. In the end it helps."

Maybe; but many people weren't buying. When Cassius Clay first announced his conversion to the Nation of Islam and later his name change, the prevailing attitude was to not take him seriously. Sports figures were supposed to be one-dimensional quasi-cartoon characters. Reporters were used to fighters telling them how much they weighed and what they ate for breakfast. Now, here was a young man whom a lot of people were starting to dislike. His carnival act seemed suddenly sinister to them, and the boxing establishment in particular responded with fury:

Jimmy Cannon: "The fight racket, since its rotten beginnings, has been the red-light district of sports. But this is the first time it has been turned into an instrument of mass hate. It has maimed the bodies of numerous men and ruined their minds but now, as one of Elijah Muhammad's missionaries, Clay is using it as a weapon of wickedness in an attack on the spirit. I pity Clay and abhor what he represents. In the years of hunger during the depression, the Communists used famous people the way the Black Muslims are exploiting Clay. This is a sect that deforms the beautiful purpose of religion."[13]

Abe Greene (commissioner of the World Boxing Association): "Clay should be given a chance to decide whether he wants to be a religious crusader or the heavyweight champion. As champion, he is neither a Muslim nor any other religionist because sports are completely nonsectarian. Clay should be given the choice of being the fighter who won the title or the fanatic leader of an extraneous force which has no place in the sports arena."[14]

Harry Markson: "Responsible promoters will hesitate to touch this kid. Clay's antics have been deplorable. You don't use the heavyweight championship of the world to spout religious diatribe. We've made so much progress in eliminating color barriers that it's a pity we're now facing such a problem, the heavyweight champion of the world preaching a hate religion."[15]

HARRY MARKSON: "When Cassius Clay won the Olympics and came back to the United States, he was a kid; a fun person to be around. Then, the night he won the title, he stood on a platform in the auditorium in Miami Beach and demanded, 'Who's the greatest?' And until the newspapermen answered, 'You are,' he refused to go on. People in the press, some people in the press, resented that. To demand adoration at a time when he really was an untested young fighter with one very questionable major victory to his credit was wrong. People were insulted by it. And then he converted to Islam. It's not that the media covering him changed; he changed. The Black Muslims stood for some pretty awful things. There was a positive side to what they were trying to accomplish, but I felt then and still feel that a lot of what they preached was wrong. And if you look at the reporters who covered Ali early in his career when he was Cassius Clay, a lot of them viewed him very differently from the reporters who dealt with him later on. Columnists like Dan Parker of the *Daily Mirror* were very angry at him. Joe Williams of the *World Telegram*, Dick Young and Jimmy Powers of the *Daily News*, Red Smith of the *Herald Tribune*, Gil Koram and Frank Graham of the *Journal American*, Jimmy Cannon. None of them were fond of Ali. The reporters who came later seemed almost to idolize him. There's an irony in the fact that, even though sports writing and writing in general has gotten more cynical in recent years, the later writers have near total adulation of Ali. They've totally accepted the Ali legend. As for myself, by and large, I don't regret what I've said and done in boxing. But I will confess, that night at Madison Square Garden when I refused to introduce him by his new name, I was wrong. If I had it to do over again, I'd introduce him as Muhammad Ali. But you have to put yourself back in that time. Twenty-five years ago, those were strange times. We've all learned a lot since then. But if I had it to do over, I'd introduce him as Eleanor Roosevelt if that's what he wanted."

Meanwhile, even as Ali was under attack, the Nation of Islam was being torn apart by a bitter rift between Elijah Muhammad and Malcolm X. The first public indication of a split had come in late 1963. Immediately after President Kennedy's assassination, Elijah had ordered his ministers to make no comment regarding the event. But in response to a question from the audience after a speaking engagement in New York, Malcolm termed the president's murder a case of "chickens coming home to roost," and added, "Being an old farm boy myself, chickens coming home to roost never did make me sad. They've always made me glad."[16] Elijah was livid and suspended Malcolm for ninety days to disassociate the Nation of Islam from his remarks. However, fundamental differences between the two men were far more serious than one isolated comment. Malcolm had become increasingly troubled by allegations of sexual misconduct and financial impropriety leveled against his leader, and had begun to question the path the Nation was taking. Soon it was clear that, one way or another, members of the Nation would have to take sides.

Ali aligned himself with Elijah. That he would do so became clear to those who knew him best within hours of his victory over Sonny Liston. Jim Brown of football's Cleveland Browns spent those hours with him.

JIM BROWN: "I was in Miami for the Runner-Up Bowl with the Browns, and although I'd met Ali before, this was the first time we'd talked seriously about important issues. Malcolm was planning to leave the Nation of Islam because of a falling-out with Elijah Muhammad, and wanted Ali to come with him. Then, the night of the fight, after Ali beat Liston, there was a huge party at the Fontainebleau Hotel with pretty girls and all the rest, but Ali didn't go. Instead, he took me to a little black motel with Malcolm and three or four other Muslim ministers. Malcolm said to me, 'Well, Brown, don't you think it's time for this young man to stop spouting off and get serious?' And I agreed, but that night made it clear to me that Malcolm's swan song was coming as far as Ali was concerned. Ali took me into a back room. It was just the two of us. We talked for about two hours. And he told me how Elijah Muhammad was such a little man physically but such a great man, and he was going to have to reject Malcolm and choose Elijah."

JEREMIAH SHABAZZ: "Malcolm's relationship with Ali wasn't what he thought it was. He thought he had enough pull with Ali to win him over. But having been one of Ali's early teachers, I knew how he thought, and I knew Malcolm could never sway him against Elijah Muhammad. Malcolm tried; there's no doubt about that. Malcolm actually tricked Ali into appearing in public with him. You see, Ali didn't know exactly what was happening in the day-to-day infighting and politics of the Islamic movement in America. Early on, he was going out and appearing everywhere. He didn't go to New York after the fight because he was aligned with Malcolm so much as he went to New York because that's where things were happening and Malcolm asked him. But Ali told me, 'That man can't convince me to go against the Messenger.' And that's when I realized Ali had arrived, that he had true understanding and respect for the teachings of Elijah Muhammad. He knew what Malcolm had forgotten; that Malcolm had been a pimp, a hustler, a junkie; that he'd been nothing until he heard Elijah Muhammad's teachings. Elijah cleaned Malcolm up, taught him how to eat, how to love himself and love other black people. Nobody knew Malcolm better than I did. Elijah Muhammad sent him to Philadelphia in 1954 after he got out of jail. Malcolm lived in a room with another brother and me for a year until he came to New York. So I got to know him well. I woke up in the morning next to him every day, and went to bed next to him every night. If anybody starts talking about Malcolm, they got to ask me; they can't tell me. And I'm telling you, when

Malcolm talked, people thought he was intelligent, and he was, but what he said came from Elijah Muhammad. Malcolm was taught by the wisest man on the planet Earth. It was what he got from Elijah Muhammad that he was saying. That's my view of it. And let me say one thing more. Malcolm didn't split from Elijah. He was kicked out. The whole history of Malcolm, like the history of Martin Luther King, has been rewritten and made palatable for the general public, but the truth is, Malcolm made a miscalculation. He thought he had strength enough among the Nation of Islam to make a bid for power and leadership. He thought he was strong. Because he was a great speaker, he thought that translated into real power and devotion from the followers of Elijah Muhammad, and it didn't. So when he failed, he knew he was doomed. In fact, he was questioned one time about saying the Muslims were going to kill him. Someone asked Malcolm, 'Why do you keep saying the Muslims are going to kill you?' And he answered, 'I know they're going to kill me because I taught them.' Malcolm had been the firebrand of Islam in America. He used to stand up and say, if someone stands against the Honorable Elijah Muhammad, death isn't good enough for him. He'd go into a harangue, rile people up and shout that anyone going against Elijah Muhammad deserved to have their bones burning in the pits of a triple hell. So when he went against the Messenger—who's the guy, the Frenchman, Guillotine, who invented the thing he died by— well, it was the same for Malcolm. He sowed the seeds of his own destruction."

In early spring 1964 with tensions between himself and Elijah rising, Malcolm embarked on a pilgrimage to Makkah, where his views underwent further transformation. Just as his eyes had been opened by Elijah to one new universe, now he was seeing another. "For twelve long years," he later wrote, "I lived in the narrow-minded confines of the straightjacket world created by a strong belief that Elijah Muhammad was a messenger direct from God and my faith in what I now see to be a pseudo-religious philosophy that he preaches."[17] This declaration was followed by another, branding Elijah a "religious faker."[18] But perhaps most important, in Makkah, Malcolm's attitude toward the white man changed, as reflected in an open letter he wrote for publication in newspapers and magazines throughout the United States:

My pilgrimage broadened my scope. It blessed me with a new insight. In two weeks in the Holy Land, I saw what I

never had seen in thirty-nine years here in America. I saw
all races, all colors—blue-eyed blonds to black-skinned Africans—in true brotherhood! In unity! Living as one! Worshiping as one! No segregationists; no liberals; they would not
have known how to interpret the meaning of those words. In
the past, yes, I have made sweeping indictments of all white
people. I never will be guilty of that again, as I know now
that some white people are truly sincere, that some truly are
capable of being brotherly toward a black man. The true
Islam has shown me that a blanket indictment of all white
people is as wrong as when whites make blanket indictments
agianst blacks.

Never have I witnessed such sincere hospitality and the
overwhelming spirit of true brotherhood as is practiced by
people of all colors and races here in this Ancient Holy
Land. For the past week, I have been utterly speechless and
spellbound by the graciousness I see displayed all around me
by people of all colors.

You may be shocked by these words coming from me. But
on this pilgrimage, what I have seen and experienced has
forced me to rearrange much of my thought-patterns previously held and to toss aside some of my previous conclu-
sions. This was not too difficult for me. Despite my firm
convictions, I have been always a man who tries to face facts,
and to accept the reality of life as new experience and new
knowledge unfolds it. During the past eleven days here in
the Muslim world, I have eaten from the same plate, drunk
from the same glass, and slept in the same bed (or on the
same rug)—while praying to the same God—with fellow
Muslims, whose eyes were the bluest of blue, whose hair
was the blondest of blond, and whose skin was the whitest of
white. And in the words and in the actions and in the deeds
of the "white" Muslims, I felt the same sincerity that I felt
among the black African Muslims of Nigeria, Sudan, and
Ghana. We were truly all the same (brothers) because their
belief in one God had removed the "white" from their
minds, the "white" from their behavior, and the "white"
from their attitude.[19]

Shortly after his return to the United States, Malcolm announced
establishment of the Organization of Afro-American Unity, which
he described as "a non-religious and non-sectarian group organized

to unite Afro-Americans for a constructive program toward attainment of human rights."[20] Meanwhile, on May 14, 1964, Ali left the United States for a month-long tour of Africa.

OSMAN KARRIEM: "I arranged the trip. To me, it was necessary to give the kid some breathing room. There was so much going on in his life, and this was a way to take him out of the line of fire. We'd been to the United Nations together, and a number of African ambassadors had stopped to acknowledge him. So I followed up on that, and kicked the idea around with Malcolm. I said, 'You know, this kid is under a lot of pressure. I don't know if he can go on like this, but I know I can't. The way it worked out, the trip also planted seeds for Ali's worldwide popularity, but I don't plan well enough to take credit for that. I'm not that smart. I had no way of knowing the impact that trip would have."

Ali's entourage in Africa included Rahaman, Howard Bingham, Osman Karriem, and Herbert Muhammad (one of Elijah Muhammad's eight children). It began in Ghana, where thousands of people cheered Ali's arrival and treated him like a national hero. In the capital, Accra, he kissed babies, boxed an exhibition, visited factories and schools, and met with Ghanaian President Kwame Nkrumah. "In America, everything is white," he told his audience. "I'm glad to be here with my true people."[21]

After two weeks in Ghana, Ali traveled to Nigeria, where he received a polite but less enthusiastic reception. Somewhat miffed, he cut short the visit and moved on to Egypt, where tumult and adulation reigned. Ali visited the pyramids, was extensively photographed riding a camel, and met with Egyptian President Gamal Abdel Nasser. Then he returned to the United States, leaving one memory in particular of his journey behind.

It happened in Ghana. Malcolm X was also in the country, readying to leave the day after Ali arrived. They crossed paths in the Hotel Ambassador on the morning of Malcolm's departure, and Ali snubbed him. "Did you get a look at Malcolm," the champion derisively told reporters. "Dressed in that funny white robe and wearing a beard and walking with that cane that looked like a prophet's stick? Man, he's gone. He's gone so far out, he's out completely. Nobody listens to Malcolm anymore."[22]

ALEX HALEY: "I recall principally the adoration between Malcolm and Muhammad Ali. I remember Malcolm's great pride when-

ever he would talk of, as he phrased it, 'My younger brother.'
Malcolm saw Ali as someone who had real capability to be a messenger in America and tell young black people what was going
on. It wasn't important to him that Ali take his side in his differences with Elijah Muhammad. He simply wanted Ali to be free and
strong.

"Malcolm was not one to talk much. He was very protective of
himself and his friends personally, so it was only very slowly and
subtly that I knew something was amiss. And then, finally, he told
me that, when he was in Africa, he had crossed paths with Muhammad Ali, and Ali had avoided him; they didn't speak. And I will tell
you, that hurt Malcolm more than any other person turning away
from him that I know of. Malcolm was very hurt by it all."

BETTY SHABAZZ: "I saw Ali right before my husband's assassination [in February 1965]. It was in Harlem, I think just inside the
door of the Theresa Hotel. This was while they were running my
husband all over the country, identifiable people. I said to Ali, 'You
see what you're doing to my husband, don't you?' And he said to
me with his hands in the air, 'I haven't done anything. I'm not doing
anything to him.'

"Since the assassination, Ali has not been a part of my life, and
I don't claim to know him well. I had the experience of being around
him for a short period, and that certainly should not constitute a
total life. I wish him well, as I wish the best for everyone. And in
a way, I'm glad Malcolm is not here at this point in time to see some
of the things that have happened to Ali. I don't want to go into what
they are. I care for Ali and his soul and his person, and I wouldn't
state what or why because it would be used for exploitative purposes,
and I am not that type of person. I would not want anyone to
interpret what I am saying by their own narrow definition. But I do
believe that there were people who saw Muhammad Ali only as a
bread ticket, and were not concerned for his person, soul, or future.
They cared about what Ali could do for them, rather than strength-
ening his character and beliefs as Malcolm sought to do. And that's
a shame, because Ali was important. He became a symbol for people
around the world, and particularly for young people, regardless of
ethnicity. We're constantly looking for signs and symbols for our
young people. We want not only to improve the environment they
live in, but also for them to understand that whatever it is we want
them to do, it can be done. If we have young people who dare to
be something, who dare to do something, who dare to make a con-

tribution, that is as much as we can ask for. And a lot of our young people would do better today if there was a Muhammad Ali in front of them, because a great number of young people once felt that they were the greatest because of him, and it's very evident now that a lot of our young people do not feel that they are the greatest."

ATTALLAH SHABAZZ: "Once my father wasn't allowed back into the Nation and people were taking sides, he was hurt that Ali didn't speak up on his behalf, but he also understood why. He cared about Ali. He never stopped loving him, and neither have I.

"I saw Ali for the first time after all the pain and changes in his life and my family's life in the late seventies. I think it was 1978. Some of Ali's artwork was being unveiled at the Waldorf-Astoria. I didn't know how he'd feel about seeing me because the Nation of Islam separated people. And yet, he'd been like a big brother to me. I missed not being able to have him. I went to the hotel, made my way into the room, and saw a crowd of people, security and others surrounding him. I didn't know if he would see me and recognize me, want me to leave because so many painful things had happened, or what. I just stood there. It had been thirteen years since I'd seen him before. My knees were weak. There was a knot in my stomach, thinking maybe he wouldn't like me anymore or that he'd stopped feeling a sense of family. Then, in that crowd, he did a double-take and recognized me. We're talking now, many inches difference from when I'd been young. He looked at me and said, 'Who are you?' I got 'Attallah' out of my mouth. And then in his playful way, he said, 'Attallah who?' and pulled me to his side. He kept me with him the entire day. And I felt that, despite the distance that had been perpetuated, even as my father missed him, Muhammad also missed being part of my father's life, that Muhammad missed his big brother, and that was very nice. We talked many times after that. He explored, and he asked me, 'What do you think happened? What went wrong?' And he sounded like a youngster; he sounded like the same twenty-two-year-old I'd known. He was, by that time, world-renowned, a man, a father; and yet there was still that vulnerable childlike quality about him."

MUHAMMAD ALI: "When Malcolm broke with Elijah, I stayed with Elijah. I believed that Malcolm was wrong and Elijah was God's Messenger. I was in Miami, training, when I heard Malcolm had been shot to death. Some brother came to my apartment and told me what happened. It was a pity and a disgrace he died like that, because what Malcolm saw was right, and after he left us, we went his way anyway. Color didn't make a man a devil. It's the heart, soul, and mind that counts."

OSMAN KARRIEM: "After a while, Ali and I got separated. There were forces at play to remove me from him. New people came in, people who weren't friendly with Malcolm, and I was perceived as Malcolm's man. But I'll remember that trip to Africa as long as I live, because that was where I saw Cassius Clay become Muhammad Ali. The first person had been a kid, scared, frightened to death of his own shadow. 'I'm the greatest.' But he was scared. Then I'd seen the emergence of someone who had real professional skills. He could fight. I'd developed a belief in his skills and grown to respect that this kid wasn't all nuts, but he still had a ways to go.

"It was in Africa that he became something he hadn't been before. We were driving down a road in Ghana. Usually, there was nobody on the roads. Outside of the capital, it was just towns forty miles apart with nothing in between. One day, we got in the car with no plan, and five minutes after we started driving, there was like a beating of drums. Then people started showing up on the road."

" 'Ali! Ali!'

"I'd never seen anything like it before. I was sitting there with this kid, and people were coming out of nowhere, lining the road, calling 'Ali! Ali!' I saw this kid sitting there. He didn't say anything. It's like he was hypnotized. Do you have any idea what it must have been like for him to see thousands of people materialize out of nowhere and know they were there just for him. That day, I saw the birth of a new human being. It was like Cassius Clay came to an end and Muhammad Ali emerged."

5

The Enemy

Ali may have been a hero in Africa. But in the United States, his mainstream appeal was plummeting as the faces around him continued to change. Still, when he returned in late June 1964, the newest face in his entourage went largely unnoticed.

Herbert Muhammad was the third of Elijah Muhammad's six sons. A short heavyset man, he operated a small photography studio in Chicago and was involved in publishing *Muhammad Speaks*, the Nation of Islam's weekly newspaper. Over time, his influence over Ali would grow to enormous proportions, and the bedrock of that influence was Elijah Muhammad.

HERBERT MUHAMMAD: "I'd seen Ali two or three times at our national gatherings, but I never met him up close until he came to my photography studio after he fought Sonny Liston. And right away, he trusted me because he loved and respected my father. That's the way things often were for me. Growing up as the son of the Honorable Elijah Muhammad put special pressures and special obligations on me, but the rewards were always greater. When Ali came to my studio, he was getting ready to make a trip to Africa. And because I'd been there, my father suggested that I guide him. Then, after the trip, we came back to Chicago, and that was when I introduced him to Sonji."

Sonji Roi was twenty-three years old, one year older than Ali. By all accounts, she was a strikingly sensuous woman, and remains so twenty-five years later. Her father had been killed in a card game when she was two. Six years later, her mother died. Brought up by godparents, Sonji gave birth to a son in her early teens, which forced her to withdraw from school. Thereafter, she supported herself with her looks: working in nightclubs, entering beauty contests, and modeling.

HERBERT MUHAMMAD: "A friend of mine had a tailor shop across the street from my photography studio, and Sonji used to get clothes made by him. One afternoon, he brought her over for me to take some photos, and I shot some very very good shots. Maybe a week later, I delivered them to her apartment. We talked for a while, and I told her I was going to Africa with Ali. So she handed me one of the pictures back, eleven by fourteen inches, and signed, 'From one champ to another.' I put it in my suitcase and forgot about it until we were in Egypt at the Nile Hilton. Ali was interested in one of the hotel waitresses. He'd taken one look at this girl, and was talking about marrying her. So I said to him, 'I got a girl in the States who's better looking than she is. I even have a photo of her.' I showed Ali the photo, and he said he liked the way Sonji looked. He wanted to meet her. And I told him, 'All right, as soon as we get back to the States, I'll introduce you.'"

SONJI CLAY (the name she prefers): "I remember things different from Herbert. I had a job as a cocktail waitress, and I'd done some modeling—photographers' modeling because I'm five-foot-three, which is too short for fashion work. I met Herbert because Herbert liked to take pictures of people. Then he gave me a job soliciting sales over the telephone for *Muhammad Speaks*. I was there about a week, when he told me he wanted me to meet Cassius Clay. I wasn't impressed. I didn't know anything about boxing. I didn't know who he was talking about, but I said okay. You're always meeting someone. Later, Herbert started bringing all sorts of women to Ali. Introducing women to Ali, is how I ought to say it. Ali liked pretty women. They both did. But I went and met him. We liked each other; and that was how it started."

JEREMIAH SHABAZZ: "Sonji was two cents slick, if you understand the term. She was a party girl, who lived life in the fast lane and came along at just the right time to catch Ali, a country boy coming out of Louisville. We warned Ali about her. She was very attractive, very popular in the nightclubs. Certain types of women would go in there at night, sit at the bar to be noticed, and people would seek them out. Sonji knew how to get the most out of being a beautiful woman in Chicago. She had her own apartment; she was streetwise; and Ali was smitten with her. I mean, he just fell head over heels in love with Sonji, and no one could tell him anything about her."

HOWARD BINGHAM: "Ali met Sonji on July 3, 1964. We had just come back from Africa, and Herbert introduced them so Ali could have some fun that night. At the time, Ali was very shy. I think Herbert paid Sonji for the first date, but I don't know for sure. And from that night on until the fourteenth of August when they were married, Ali never let Sonji out of his sight. Before that, there might have been one or two women, but Sonji taught him. He was crazy about her; after Sonji he was flying. And Sonji wasn't a bad person. I liked Sonji. She had her own convictions and her own way, but she wasn't a gold digger. She cared about Ali, and because she'd been out in the real world a long time, she could have been very good for him."

SONJI CLAY: "I met him, and he asked me to marry him that night. I didn't know if he was serious or not. I didn't know anything about him. But I was alone in the world. I didn't have a mother to go home and ask. I had to make the decision myself. After we spent some time together, I felt needed by him. He was strong, but he didn't know a lot of things. He needed a friend, and what better person than me? I said to myself, there's nothing else I'm doing with my life. I can do this. I can be a good wife to this man. Somebody had to be there for him, and I saw it as a chance for me to really help somebody. I wanted to be his wife and his best friend. I wasn't doing it for the money. It bothers me when people say that. And another thing that bothers me is when they say I taught him everything he knew about sex. That's not true either. It's like I'm some sort of sex object, and people still believe it. A couple of years ago, a friend of mine called from the University of Texas. She was taking a psychology course, and called to tell me that I was in one of her textbooks. I said, 'What! Send me the book.' She said it was an expensive book, but she sent me a Xerox of the pages. And for some reason, I was made reference to in this textbook on behavior patterns. The book said how Ali was torn, because he believed in his religion yet he loved me for my beauty and sensuality, and I carried myself in a manner that was unbecoming to the religion, but he was so mesmerized by my sexuality that he had to have me. And if you read this, you picture someone who's like running around in her underwear. So let me tell you, I didn't teach him nothing about sex. He knew what to do when I met him. It's just that I may have made him want to do it. All the things he knew he wanted to do, he just needed a reason to do them. If you're hungry and you sit down at a table and all your favorite dishes are on the table, what are you gonna do? I didn't teach him about sex. I gave him a reason to want to be sexy, let's put it like that, but I didn't teach him."

HERBERT MUHAMMAD: "The day after Ali met Sonji, he told me he was going to marry her. And I said, 'Man, you don't marry this girl. She works at a cocktail place wearing one of those little bunny things on her behind. You don't want to marry no girl like this. You don't even know this lady.' And he said no, he was gonna marry her. I said, 'Man, she's too experienced. You're just twenty-two years old. This girl knows what's happening out there.' But he wouldn't listen. Then, maybe three weeks later, he called me up and said he'd married her Islamically. He had one of the brothers perform the marriage, in a car with two witnesses, where he said before God that he accepted this woman to be his wife and all the responsibilities that went with it. And I said to him, 'Legally you still ain't married in the United States. If they find out you got this girl and you're running around to various places on the highway, you're gonna be in trouble.' But at that point I had to help him because he'd already told everybody he was married, and I suppose in the eyes of God he was. So we snuck him off to a justice of the peace, and the two of them were married according to the state."

Ali and Sonji Roi were formally married in Gary, Indiana, on August 14, 1964—forty-one days after they met. Then Ali returned to serious training in Miami in preparation for a rematch against Sonny Liston. The ring was still where he felt most comfortable, but considerable work lay ahead. For the first time in his life, he'd eaten himself out of shape, ballooning up to 231 pounds. And as happens with most champions, the number of handlers, hangers-on, and others around him continued to grow. Angelo Dundee, Bundini Brown, Howard Bingham, Luis Sarria, Ferdie Pacheco, Osman Karriem (then known as Archie Robinson), Abdul Rahaman (Captain Sam), and Ali's brother were still there. And three more regulars came on board.

One of the new arrivals—Booker Johnson—had been an assistant to Archie Moore in the 1940s, and joined the Nation of Islam in 1956. Most of his professional life had been spent as a road manager for musicians and an administrator for record companies. Johnson's first stay with the champion was only for a year, although he would resurface in the 1970s. However, two other arrivals—Walter Youngblood and Lana Shabazz—would have an effect on Ali throughout his career.

WALI MUHAMMAD (formerly known as Walter Youngblood—"Blood"): "I'm a street person. I was born in Louisiana, but grew up in Harlem, and I've been on the streets all my life. I took up boxing when I was young, but got cut bad and was advised by doctors that if I kept on fighting I'd probably lose my left eye, so I quit. After that, I went out to California just to see what it was like. I tried bartending, but I don't drink so I wasn't much of a bartender. After that, I did odd jobs, working mostly in a gym. In 1947, I met Sugar Ray Robinson. We got along, and he told me if I came back to New York I should look him up, so that's what I did. I started working for Ray in 1948 as sort of an assistant, and stayed with him until I joined Ali around the time he became champion. Ali brought me in as a security man. When I say security, it wasn't a violent job, but to make sure people didn't take advantage of him. And they also had me in charge of equipment at the gym. There was a room for me in the same house Ali lived in, and every place he went, I was with him. There weren't many times he talked with me about personal things. That wasn't his way. Most of the time when we talked in private, it was about religion. I'd been a Muslim since 1953, so he'd ask me questions. I wasn't the wisest man in the world, but I did my best to give him answers. And it was a true pleasure being with Ali. He never showed his greatness over other people. He always made me feel like family."

LANA SHABAZZ: "I first met Ali in 1962 when I worked at the Muslim restaurant on upper Fifth Avenue in Manhattan. Before that, I'd had two jobs. I worked in the Radio City Music Hall cafeteria—that was my main job—and also part-time at the temple restaurant. Then I lost the Radio City job because I was a Muslim. At that time, the FBI was running around, knocking on doors, saying things to employers. They'd come down to the stage door at Radio City, asking about me like I'd committed a crime, and I got fired, so the Muslim restaurant was the only job I had. One day, Cassius Clay came in, and I went out to wait on him. He was still Cassius

Clay, just beginning to learn about the religion, and he liked what we fed him. You see, we in the Nation of Islam were talking about healthy meals and balanced diets long before anyone else. It wasn't just what you shouldn't eat. It was also what you needed to be healthy. So whenever Ali was in New York, he came to our restaurant. I'd go out to wait on him, and he'd look at me and say, 'Sister, feed me.' I'd feed him lamb shanks, string beans, rice, carrots. I always believed in people eating right. I used to be famous for making bean pie, so I'd give him my bean pie and ice cream. It was good food because it was fresh, and he had a big appetite. As often as not, he'd eat two plates of food. He told me once, he said, 'Sister, I'm going to marry you, so you can cook for me.' But he was about twenty years old at the time and I was in my thirties with a fifteen-year-old daughter, so that didn't seem like such a good idea to me. My daughter—her name was Rebecca—was beautiful, and I think he wanted to marry her too.

"Then, after he beat Liston, I went to live in Miami. There was this huge house which Ali used only for training, and the rest of the time I lived there alone. I was still a young woman, so even when Ali was in town, I worked nights in the kitchen of the Barcelona Hotel. And let me tell you something. Folks don't know half of what Ali did for people. He'd have a sparring partner in camp, and the first thing he'd do is, if the guy wasn't dressed right, Ali would give him money and send him out to buy new clothes. Once, we had a sparring partner who got his eye injured, and any other fighter in the world, when that happens, they just let him go. Ali took him to the hospital, paid his bills, and made sure he was taken care of right. That's why I love him the way I do. That's why I gave my life to Ali. Sometimes I think I used to be his mother in another life; I just sense it. Ali would get up in the morning and say, 'Where's Lana?' Someone would tell him, 'She's sleeping,' and he'd say, 'Wake her up.' They'd wake me up at six o'clock in the morning. 'Lana, the champ wants you.' I'd go into the kitchen to be there when he came back from running. He'd say, 'Lana, make me a cup of tea.' And I'd make his tea with honey and it would be just right, just the way he wanted it. It's something to be with a person and to know them so well that you know just how much honey they want in their tea. But he'd want to see me even before he went out running. He'd want me up to make sure I was there. After a while, my children started complaining that I loved Ali more than I loved them. That wasn't so, but I stayed with Ali until he stopped fighting. I was there till the very end."

But not everything was harmonious in Ali's camp. Over the preceding two years, he'd grown torn between love for his parents and loyalty to the Nation of Islam. Ali's mother blamed the Louisville Sponsoring Group for her son's conversion. "The big mistake," she told a reporter, "was when they sent him to train in Miami all by himself. That's when the Muslims got him. That's how Sam Saxon talked all that Muslim stuff to him. This old Sam, the Muslim man, was in Cassius's room every night, brainwashing him. If somebody'd been with Cassius, they'd never have got to him."[1]

HOWARD BINGHAM: "What bothered Ali's dad wasn't so much the religious doctrine as the fact that he believed the Muslims were controlling Ali's life and taking his money. With his mom, it was more the nature of what they were teaching. But for both of them, it was like their son had joined some strange cult, and they didn't like it. They were worried for him.

"There were some pretty heated arguments in those days. Ali's father wasn't the kind to hold back. He always spoke what was on his mind. He'd say the Muslims were a racket and that Elijah Muhammad was just after Ali's money. And Ali would go crazy because he was really into the religion, and no one could say anything bad to him about Elijah Muhammad. There was some pushing here and there."

JEREMIAH SHABAZZ: "Old Cash was right, of course. He wasn't complaining about the teachings of Islam. What bothered him was the fact that certain people were out to steal his son's money. Not the Messenger. Elijah Muhammad had no desire to take Ali's money. In fact, he hardly got involved in Ali's career at all, because the Qur'an takes a very dim view of sports. The Messenger never even attended any of Ali's fights, but Herbert was another story. Ali asked the Messenger if there was someone in the Nation who could help look after his business dealings. And at that point, the Messenger said, 'I'll give you my son Herbert and my secretary John Ali to keep the white man from defrauding you.' That was their role. They were just supposed to shepherd Ali. But unfortunately, Herbert liked the boxing business and the money that was involved, and went further than his father wanted him to go. Mr. Clay saw what was happening. You couldn't put anything over on him. He saw what was going on around Ali, but Ali just wouldn't listen to him."

FBI REPORT (dated June 14, 1966): "[Name omitted] advised that he resides at [address] in Miami. He said that Cassius Clay when in Miami resides in the home next to his. [Person X] said he believes Clay's whole life is influenced and directed by Elijah Muhammad. He said there is no other person known to him who exerts as great an influence on Clay. He said that he believed Clay would blindly do whatever Elijah Muhammad would ask.

"[Person X] recalled that about a year ago, Clay's father arrived at Clay's house one evening obviously intoxicated. He had a knife in his hand, and started shouting about Clay's membership in the Muslims and the fact that his, the father's, name was being ruined by the Muslims. He said that he was going to kill all the Muslims around his son's house. [Person X] said that Clay got extremely upset at his father's statements and actions, and he attempted to attack his father, and had to be physically restrained from hurting him. When still being held, Clay was attempting to kick his father."

OSMAN KARRIEM: "I had trouble with Ali's father, almost to the point of being physical. There were things he said. There were things that he did, and I just rolled it off, because I don't get into stuff like that. It's not that I'm afraid to fight, but I'd rather not. I wasn't there to line my pockets, I was there to help Ali, because that's what Malcolm asked me to do. I can't say how the people who came later on felt about money. I can only tell you, that's not what I was there for. But Ali hit his father once about something because I wouldn't fight. It had to do with the Louisville Sponsoring Group. Mr. Clay felt that I was breaking their contract, and his boy wasn't going to have any money, and that the Nation and I were stealing it all from him. He got in my face and was saying things he didn't know nothing about.

"The other person I was at odds with back then was Howard Bingham. Howard and I were at each other's throats, and I accused him in my own mind of not being trustworthy, because he wasn't in the Nation and I didn't understand where he was coming from. But looking back—and I mean this; this is the truth—I think Howard has probably been the best friend Ali ever had. I didn't set out believing that. I was inclined to think he was a leech. But I've seen more integrity, more real love and loyalty in Howard than anybody who had a relationship with Ali."

Meanwhile, to the public at large, Ali remained a threatening force. Jimmy Cannon branded his ties to the Nation of Islam "the dirtiest in American sports since the Nazis were shilling for Max Schmeling as representative of their vile theories of blood."[2] Ali, in turn, drew his own analogy between his beliefs and the horrors of Nazi Germany, saying, "Elijah isn't teaching hate when he tells us about the evil things the white man has done any more than you're teaching hate when you tell about what Hitler did to the Jews. That's not hate; that's history."[3]

Jack Olsen, who covered Ali for *Sports Illustrated* and later authored *Black Is Best: The Riddle of Cassius Clay*, puts the time in perspective.

JACK OLSEN: "If there was an ugly period with Ali, that was it. *SI* sent me down to Miami, right into the middle of his training camp, which was all black except for Angelo. Ali was staying in a bungalow in the black part of town, and I got the cold shoulder from everybody. If I wasn't overtly treated rudely, I was spoken down to, or more often not spoken to at all. It was a fascinating experience in reverse racial prejudice. And I won't say it did me any good because I didn't feel I needed any lessons in racial fairness, but it's quite an experience to be the one white man in a whole group of blacks like that, all of them dedicated to one man. Ali's brother, Rahaman, was the worst. He wouldn't even say hello to me when I said hello. Ali himself wasn't personally abusive, but he didn't try to help my situation either. I remember we were sitting in his living room one evening watching television—five or six of his retainers, two or three sisters in their white outfits, and Ali. And it was like I wasn't there. Everybody's jacking around, talking. I said a few innocuous things, and was so thoroughly ignored that I shut my mouth and sat there and watched. It was the way a black person would have been treated in a group of six or eight southern whites, and Ali was part of that. He could have said, 'Look, Jack's here for *Sports Illustrated* doing his best, lighten up.' But he didn't. The one guy who was friendly to me was Howard Bingham. I said to him at one point, 'These guys are something else.' And Howard told me, 'No, in this group, you're something else.'

"I finally got one long terrific interview with Ali. There were several on the run, catch-as-catch-can conversations, but then I got a lulu. He was lying in bed. I was hanging around the house, and someone said, 'He wants to talk to you.' So into the bedroom I went, and he gave me a kind of Joycean stream of consciousness. That was real good, and revealing too. He put his act on for a while, and then he backed off and started talking about his momma and his poppa. He came from a very bright family. Later, I got to meet most of them. His aunt Coretta Clay was a wonderful woman. She said,

'Sure, you come in here; I'll tell you all about my nephew.' She pulled out a bottle of booze, opened it, sipped from it as we talked, and that was a terrific interview. But the truly marvelous stuff that happened to me with Ali was meeting his mother and father. There you saw the two component parts of Ali walking the earth in separate forms. The bombastic fast-talking father, the complete egoist, and that lovely, sweet, warm, wonderful mom. And one of the interesting things about Ali when I met him was, he had not integrated the maternal and paternal sides of his personality. You would see Cassius Senior come out in those pugnacious bellicose statements, and five minutes later you'd see his mother come out in some lovely sweet gesture or lyrical line. It was like a noninsane schizophrenia. And I guess what's happened over the years is he's integrated those personalities and now is on a more level plane."

JERRY IZENBERG: "There was a whole new atmosphere around Ali after he won the title and was getting ready for the rematch with Liston. It was a chilly atmosphere, and this was when he began to take on that dual personality which is long since gone but which lasted for a number of years. He'd be talking with you about something, and one of the Muslims would come into the room and the conversation would change completely. My feeling was, he wanted to please them. I think he was afraid of losing them, if that makes any sense to you. When he found the Muslims, he'd found an extraordinarily strong reason to be black. He was no longer somebody who could be cast aside because of his color. And I think he was afraid that if he didn't become SuperMuslim at that stage of his life, somehow that would mean he was failing them.

As for why he chose the Muslims, I guess no one knows for sure. Something happened in his upbringing that made him ripe for them. I'm not condemning Islam, but the Nation of Islam as it was constructed under Elijah Muhammad in that particular period was really more of a lodge and caste system than it was a religion. And for reasons that I don't know, I think Ali was an easy mark for them. Remember, there were other avenues to Islam in the early 1960s. It wasn't just the Nation of Islam, which even then was a radical splinter group. And to be honest, in the beginning, I think I knew more about the Nation of Islam than he did. I happened to know a fair amount from some things I'd written and was curious to find out just how much he knew and didn't know, so one afternoon I talked with him about it. Basically, what he knew was separation. I don't think he understood much more at all. But he wanted desperately to be taken seriously, to be respected, and told that he was special. I'm not a therapist, and even if I were, I wouldn't have all the answers. But I have the feeling that his father didn't pay much positive attention to him when he was a child. That's just my feeling; I could be wrong. And Elijah Muhammad paid an enormous amount of attention to him. I think it was a father-son thing, Elijah and Ali. And knowing what I know about Ali, I think he was looking for some group to belong to as well as a father figure. The Nation became Ali's family, even to the extent that he was able to bring his brother into it. And Elijah Muhammad became his father. That's my read. And it all fits in the same package, because somewhere in his life— very early, I think—Ali put up a shield. He feels for people; he hugs and he kisses. But he doesn't get close to many people on an adult level or allow them to get truly close to him. He loves people in groups, and they might hold his interest individually for a short period of time. But most of his interaction with people is centered on himself—not in an ugly way, but in a childlike way. I think the Nation keyed on that. And of course, there's irony in the fact that, although Ali might have professed allegiance to a religious movement that branded white people as devils, he had more white colleagues— people like Angelo Dundee and Ferdie Pacheco—than most black people did at that time in America, and continued to have them throughout his career."

Meanwhile, preparations for the second Liston bout, scheduled for November 16, 1964, went on. Once again, Liston was favored. Most observers thought Ali's victory in their first fight was a fluke. Some thought the bout had been fixed—a view based on unsubstantiated rumors of a late-money gambling coup by organized crime. Others attributed the upset to the shoulder injury Liston claimed to have suffered when he threw and missed with a left hook in the first round. A third theory was that the champion had simply taken the challenger too lightly in Miami Beach, and would be properly prepared when they met in Boston.

As Ali-Liston II drew closer, Ali for his part announced a newly refined "piston-drive punch" and decided to resume predicting rounds. "I figured nine at one time," he told reporters, "but I'm sharper than I thought. Maybe I'll cut him up and take him out in three. He's easy to cut, and if he tries to catch me, he'll fall flat on his face. Only fools believe I beat him by accident last time."[4] Even Angelo Dundee got in the act. Watching Liston go through a training exercise that involved handlers throwing a medicine ball against his stomach, Dundee asked, "Why don't they throw it in his face? That's where my guy is gonna hit him."[5] All but lost in the shuffle was the fact that Ali was an even more imposing physical specimen than he'd been before. After considerable work, his weight was down again to 210 pounds. His waist was still thirty-four inches, but two inches had been added to his biceps and thighs. And more important, he was growing as a fighter. Bill Cayton, who with Jim Jacobs co-managed Mike Tyson and built the largest fight film collection in the world, watched Ali grow.

BILL CAYTON: "I felt that his real style as a fighter didn't crystallize until the first Liston fight. He had such respect for Liston as a puncher that more than any other time before, he had to focus and concentrate on what he did right. That's when the focus of the world was on him, and in that theater suddenly everything he was came together. Ali grew up as a fighter in that fight, between round one when he was a very concerned young man and round six when he was a professional. That's what happened in those rounds. At the start, he was fueled by hysteria and fear. He was afraid he'd get hit and badly hurt. Then he realized he was better than Liston. And when Liston hit him, he handled that too. During that fight, Ali became a man. To withstand and beat the most ferocious fighter in the world; that, in my judgment, was the making of Muhammad Ali. He was a different person afterward than before, and Liston was, too. In fact, I believe that sometime between their two fights, Sonny Liston went on drugs. I've always believed that. The people handling him at that time, some of them at least, were heavily involved in the drug traffic, which back then meant heroin. And of course, in those days they didn't have drug tests for fighters, so if someone was on heroin you wouldn't know. But Liston deteriorated so much between the first and second fights. He wasn't anything in the second one. Even before he got hit, he looked awful. The right hand that knocked him out wouldn't have affected the old Liston."

On the night of Friday, November 13, three days before the scheduled rematch, Ali was in his suite at the Sherry Biltmore Hotel in Boston, watching an old Edward G. Robinson gangster film on television. Suddenly, he felt nauseated and began to vomit. Pain was spreading through his abdomen. "Something is awful wrong," he told his brother. "I'm real sick. Get me to a hospital."

The champion was suffering from an incarcerated inguinal hernia. A loop of his intestines had broken through the muscles lining his

abdomen and descended, causing swelling the size of a lemon in
the lower right bowel wall. Rushed to Boston City Hospital, he was
put under anesthesia and underwent an immediate seventy-minute
operation. "It was such a marvelously developed stomach, I hated
to slice it up," said one of the attending physicians.[6] The doctors
termed Ali's condition congenital. That is, the defect and potential
for harm had been present since birth. But when apprised of the
situation, Sonny Liston had a different view. "If he'd stop all that
hollering, he wouldn't have a hernia," Liston offered.[7]

In reality, the hernia was as much a setback for Liston as for Ali.
It meant their rematch would be postponed for six months. And
during that time, Ali as a young man would continue to mature
physically, while Liston's assets could only diminish. Meanwhile,
controversy continued to engulf the champion. The bout was rescheduled for May 25, 1965, but the same Massachusetts authorities
who had previously sanctioned it now refused to do so, ostensibly
because of fears that the promoter was tied to organized crime. Then,
on February 21, 1965, Malcolm X was assassinated. That night, a
fire of unknown origin occurred in Ali's apartment, and two days
later the Nation of Islam's headquarters in New York were bombed.
Presumably, the latter two incidents were acts of revenge for
Malcolm's death, which was believed by many of Malcolm's followers to have been ordered by Elijah Muhammad. Finally, amidst
threats, counterthreats, and rumors of violence, Ali-Liston II was
moved to St. Dominic's Arena—a small youth center in Lewiston,
Maine.

JERRY IZENBERG: "The atmosphere surrounding the fight was
ugly. Malcolm was dead, and there were rumors Ali was going
to be killed, maybe even in the ring, in retaliation. A lot of it
was hysteria fueled by the press, but even so, the fear was there.
Nation of Islam bodyguards were everywhere. And I've got to tell
you; I didn't like the way Ali handled himself then. I remember
being in a dressing room with him, and I don't mean the night of
the fight, but like a week before. He was on the rubbing table.
Luis Sarria was giving him a massage, and somebody asked something about Malcolm. It was a reporter who asked, 'You've heard
the stories about Malcolm's people making an attempt on your
life,' something like that. And Ali looked up and said, 'What
people? Malcolm ain't got no people.' And I remember, I got
mad, because in my mind Malcolm stood for certain things. And I
thought, 'You son of a bitch. One minute, Malcolm is great, and

then all of a sudden he's nobody because somebody tells you he's nobody.' I was really pissed about it."

MILT BAILEY: "All that talk about retaliating for Malcolm; none of that bothered Sonny. What hurt him most was when Ali had the hernia. At that time, Sonny was in the best shape I'd ever seen. And then, to have to wait six months and go through the training all over again; that definitely hurt physically and psychologically. Also, Ali had Sonny somewhat confused. We weren't sure what he'd do next. For instance, in their first fight, that round when Ali had trouble seeing, we couldn't tell if he was putting Sonny on or not, because he'd played so many jokes and everything. But I guess what it came down to both times was, Ali had a style that Sonny couldn't cope with. That's all. The moving and the running, and he hit pretty hard too. After they fought the second time, in the dressing room Sonny asked me for smelling salts. Don't let no one tell you that Ali couldn't punch."

ROBERT LIPSYTE: "The night before the second Ali-Liston fight, Dick Gregory and I went to see Liston. Dick had a program to give away turkeys on Thanksgiving in Mississippi, and we went to Liston's camp to get money. When we got there, Sonny was sitting in front of the television set, watching a movie called *Zulu*. There was a scene where three or four white guys with repeating rifles were mowing down the cream of the Zulu nation, wiping them out. Liston just sat there, staring at the television, and I had the sense his mind wasn't anywhere. Gregory said to me, 'His mind is blown. He's gonna lose fast.' "

Despite having lost in his previous fight with Ali, Liston entered the ring for their rematch a nine-to-five favorite. The announced attendance was 4,280, but more honest estimates were half that total. It was a short fight. Some fans missed it entirely:

Mickey Mantle: "Do you remember when Ali beat Sonny Liston; that second fight up in Maine? We were in Detroit. Half the Yankee team went to a theater where you have to pay to see the fight. Joe Pepitone was with us. We sent him out to get some popcorn. He came back with ten or twelve sacks, and everyone was leaving. Joe just threw the popcorn up in the air and asked, 'What the hell happened?' "

Lou Holtz: "I was an assistant football coach at the University of Connecticut in Storrs, and wouldn't have been able to

afford to watch it. But the TV station in Hartford responsible
for piping the fight into closed-circuit theaters invited certain
guests to the studio. I drove twenty-six miles, and walked in
just as they were getting ready to fight. All these hors
d'oeuvres were set out on a table. I went over to get some,
and when I came back the fight was over. I got in my car
and drove back to Storrs, missed the whole thing."

What Holtz and many others missed was a near-perfect punch
that some swore never landed. Ali landed only three blows of
consequence in the fight. The first came just after the opening
bell, when he rushed across the ring and surprised Liston with a
straight right. Then, a minute later, another right stunned the
challenger. Liston continued to move forward, trying desperately
to cut off the ring. He jabbed. Ali pulled back to make him miss,
planted his left foot for leverage, pivoted off his right foot for
power, and counterpunched with a straight right that landed flush
on Liston's jaw. The force of the blow lifted Liston's left foot, which
was balancing most of his weight, and sent the challenger tumbling
to the floor.

Then came a moment frozen in time. Instead of going to a neutral
corner, Ali stood over his fallen opponent, with his fist cocked,
screaming, "Get up and fight, sucker." At that point, Jersey Joe
Walcott, who was refereeing the fight, lost control. He should have
ordered Ali to a neutral corner, and refused to count until Ali went.
Instead, Walcott tried pushing the champion away from Liston—
an effort that failed until Ali began dancing around the ring with his
arms high. Seventeen seconds after landing on the canvas, Liston
struggled to his feet. The referee, who had never given him a count,
wiped his gloves as though the fight was still on. Ali charged back,
throwing punches. And then, above the din, Walcott heard Nat
Fleischer (the publisher of *Ring* magazine) shouting, "It's over! He's
out!" Turning his back on the fighters, Walcott walked toward
Fleischer, listened for a moment, returned to ring center, and
stopped the fight.

MUHAMMAD ALI: "The punch jarred him. It was a good punch,
but I didn't think I hit him so hard that he couldn't have gotten up.
Once he went down, I got excited; I forgot about the rules. I was
having fun, and wanted to give people their money's worth. Also,
people forget it now, but Liston said he lost the first fight because
he had a bad shoulder. Other people said maybe the first fight was

fixed. So the second time, I wanted to whup him bad. I didn't want him making excuses or quitting. I wanted him to get up, so I could show everyone how great I was."

Jose Torres, who two months earlier had captured the world light-heavyweight championship, was in Liston's dressing room after the fight.

JOSE TORRES: "The room was empty. Liston was embarrassed and very depressed. My first question was, 'Did you see the punch?' And he told me, 'Yes, but I saw it too late.' That was it. In boxing, the punch that knocks you out is not the hard punch. It's the punch you don't see coming. And Ali was a master at that. He punched so fast, he didn't give you a chance to prepare for the blow. If Ali had gone to a neutral corner, I don't know if Sonny could have gotten up by ten or not. He never got a proper count, but he was hurt, and I'm not sure he wanted to face Ali. Sonny was afraid of crazy people, and he thought Ali was crazy. Before the fight, he'd told me about his experiences in jail. I'd heard about what happens to prisoners with rape and sodomy, so I'd asked Liston if he'd had problems like that. And he told me no one had done anything like that to him because everyone in prison was afraid of him, but he had been afraid of the crazy prisoners."

SONNY LISTON (two years after the fight): "I can tell you what happened there. Ali knocked me down with a sharp punch. I was down but not hurt, but I looked up and saw Ali standing over me. Now there is no way to get up from the canvas that you are not exposed to a great shot. Ali is waiting to hit me, the ref can't control him. I have to put one knee and one glove on the canvas to get up. You know Ali is a nut. You can tell what a normal man is going to do, but you can't tell what a nut is going to do, and Ali is a nut."[8]

JERRY IZENBERG: "After Ali won the fight, that night, there was a moment I'll never forget. He and his entourage were staying at a hotel in Auburn, Maine. They were in the courtyard—Captain Sam, Archie Robinson; Blood might have been there too—and Ali was performing, laughing, hollering, carrying on. Then his wife, Sonji, came out onto the second-floor balcony, leaned over the railing, and called down. She was telling him, 'Come upstairs.' It was obvious there was great feeling between them. And the guys were saying, 'No, man; don't go. Stay down here.' Two or three of them were sitting on the stairs between the courtyard and the second floor. I'm watching this, saying to myself, 'There's a tug of war going on.' And it went on for about five minutes. Every time Ali started toward the stairs, they wouldn't move. They weren't barring his way saying, 'You can't go,' but they were using their territorial imperative to say, 'No, stick around.' I liked Sonji. No matter how her relationship with Ali might have started, I think she cared about him. And, of course, most of the Muslims didn't like her because she wore makeup, she wouldn't wear the veil and headdress, and she asked questions that maybe they didn't want asked. Anyway, back to the courtyard. Finally, Ali looked up at her, said, 'Go to bed,' and stayed downstairs. That scene always stayed with me. At that moment, I didn't like those guys on the stairs very much. I wanted to say to them, 'Why don't you leave this guy alone and leave her alone and see if they can get together and work out their lives?' And I felt sorry for Sonji, because I didn't think she was going to be around too long."

On June 23, 1965, twenty-nine days after defeating Sonny Liston in Maine, Ali filed a complaint in Dade County, Florida, Circuit Court seeking to annul his marriage. Among other things, the complaint claimed that, before the marriage, Sonji had been fully instructed in the tenets and beliefs of the Nation of Islam; that she had fraudulently promised to follow those tenets and beliefs for the purpose of inducing Ali to marry her; and that she had failed to live up to her promise. Numerous alleged transgressions were cited in the legal papers that followed. On January 10, 1966, a final decree of divorce was issued. Ali was ordered to pay his wife fifteen thousand dollars a year for ten years and an additional $22,500 to her lawyers. Just before the divorce became final, he sent Sonji a note that read, "You traded heaven for hell, baby."

MUHAMMAD ALI: "When Sonji and I split, I just about went crazy, sitting in my room, smelling her perfume, looking at the walls. But it was something that had to happen. She wouldn't do what she was supposed to do. She wore lipstick; she went into bars; she dressed in clothes that were revealing and didn't look right. She made vows, and then she broke them, and that brought on all sorts of quarreling. One time, I slapped her. It was wrong. It's the only time I did something like that, and after I slapped her I felt sorrier than she did. It hurt me more than it hurt her. I was young, twenty-two years old, and she was doing things against my religion, but that's no excuse. A man should never hit a woman.

"The whole time I was married to Sonji, I never went with another woman. I might have thought certain things sometimes, but I loved Sonji and never bothered with no one else. Then, about a month after we split, I was still feeling bad, and a friend took me to a party. I don't want to say which friend, but there was a room full of beautiful women. I was shy around women, but I met one; the prettiest woman in the room. Later, I learned that my friend had paid her to go to the party and meet me and entertain me. But before I learned, he was saying to me, 'You see, all you have to do is look at someone and you'll fall in love again. That's the way you are, Muhammad.' After that, I tried to make like everything was alright, but for a long time, I still missed Sonji."

SONJI CLAY: "He was a good husband. Looking back, I'll say that. He's precious; he's sweet; he's gentle. His only interest was making other people happy. He really had no care about anything else. He used to sing to me. Ben E. King, 'Stand By Me'; that was his favorite. And Sam Cooke. But 'Stand By Me' all the time. The best times we had together were when everybody else was gone and he could be himself, and it wasn't necessary for him to be the Muslim. And there were other good times. The world was at his feet, and I wasn't threatened by his popularity, because I'd been popular all my life. Not as much as him, but enough to know what it was like. I didn't have to be in the limelight. I didn't have to jump up in front of the cameras. I just wanted for us to be happy, and we would have been if people had left us alone.

"They say religion is what kept it from working between us, that I refused to accept his religion, but that isn't true. The problem was that certain people, not Muhammad but certain other people, couldn't control me the way they wanted to. It had to do with control. I told him, 'I'll wear the long clothes, I'll follow the diet, I won't wear makeup. It doesn't make sense, but I'll do all that if it's what you want me to do.' And even then, there were problems. I'd ask questions, and he'd say, 'You're always causing trouble, aren't you?' He'd be laughing when he said it, but part of him meant it. He'd look at me and say, 'Woman, you're too wise. Don't be asking them questions.' And the questions I was asking, I had a right to ask. We'd be sitting in Florida at night, looking up at the sky, and he'd point out the mother ship and say, 'It's gonna come save us when it destroys the rest of the world.' And we couldn't buy a house, because those men from the ship were gonna be here in three years, and when that happened, we'd be gone. And Elijah Muhammad, he lived in a nice big house in Chicago. So I'd ask, 'What does that mean? Elijah's not going?' Those are the kinds of questions I'd ask, because a lot of what Elijah was teaching him didn't make sense. Ali was telling me, we can't have a home; we can't do this; we can't do all the other things we could afford to enjoy because the mother ship was gonna come and take us away. Well, Elijah Muhammad obviously wasn't going because he had all those things. So there I'd be, in trouble because I was asking questions and saying things I wasn't supposed to say.

"So, like I said, it was a question of control. Those people had the man, he was heavyweight champion of the world, and they wanted to keep him. When Elijah was alive, he made the rules and Herbert carried them out. And I think Herbert made some of the rules himself. Herbert is very smart, very cunning. He has his ways; he gets what he wants. The last word on anything Muhammad Ali did depended on Herbert. And I saw no need for me to be married to one man and have another man control me. I told Ali, 'If you're telling me I have to abide by this man, then I should be married to him and not to you.' I mean, it was just so obvious to me, even then, that certain people were taking him for a ride. Ali doesn't wear jewelry. I don't know if he even has a watch. Somebody somewhere was benefiting from his wealth, but it wasn't him. And it wasn't just money. They wanted to control his entire life. When you went into the Nation, the first thing they taught you was, your brothers and sisters are in the temple and no one else matters. You can't have any other friends; you turn your back on everyone. Everything they want you to do, they got a place for you to do it. They got a temple where you pray; they got a restaurant where you eat; they got place where you buy your clothes. And to be honest, I don't know how much of their teachings Ali really believed. When nobody was around, he'd want one thing from me; and then in public, it was another. I couldn't understand his two faces. I mean, stand up for what you believe and feel and want, but don't do one thing for the Nation and another when you're alone with me like God can't see.

"Then we split up. Someone else made the decision—I'm sure of that—and it hurt me. I wanted to fight it; I loved the man. But I looked around and didn't see a friendly face in the crowd. I wasn't going to take on all the Muslims. If I had, I'd probably have wound up dead. After we separated, Ali wasn't supposed to be in my company. He was forbidden even to talk with me. I'd know he was someplace, I'd have a telephone number on the man. But if I called, the next day the number would be changed. That's how dangerous the Muslims thought I was. I mean, really! What kind of threat was I? And then the religion changed anyway. All those things Ali was taught to be against, suddenly they turned around and said it was okay. It's enough to drive a person crazy. One day, they're saying the white man is the devil, and then they say they didn't mean it. How do you turn around in midstream and say, no, it really isn't that way?

"It still hurts me. I'm affected by it even today, because I'm still walking in Ali's shadow. Ever since we were married, my life has been wide open, no privacy. I remarried, and I was still Muhammad Ali's wife. Then I got divorced again, and people kept talking about Ali. That's all they see; they don't know me. I'm more than just a pretty face who was once married to Muhammad Ali. I know how to cook. I'm strong. I'm a good person for people to know. I'm a good friend. I don't care if I get a wrinkle. I don't care if I get a gray hair. There's so much more to me than looking a certain way. I just want the chance to be me.

"And you know what I can't understand? Ali asks people even today, 'Where's my wife? Have you seen Sonji?' I don't mean to take anything away from the other woman. He's got a real good wife now, is what I hear. But when he comes to Chicago, if he sees someone he knew when we were together, he'll pull them over and ask, 'How's Sonji?' So he cares about me still, I guess. And it breaks my heart to see him today. This is a man who was so full of life, representing so much strength, not necessarily with his fists. There was so much he could have done besides fighting continuously. And to see him now, broken down to where he can't talk hardly, it makes my heart bleed. I think he fought so long because the ring was the only place he could control himself and be himself. Nobody could tell him what to do in there. But I'll always be hoping for him, wishing him nothing but the best. There was so much we had and so little time. And I know one thing. If somebody told me today that they loved me, I'd know whether it was true or not. I know what it's like to be loved, because he really loved me."

Meanwhile, following his first-round victory over Sonny Liston, public controversy continued to swirl around Ali. Once again, a heavyweight championship bout had ended in confusion and ambiguity. Some observers believed in Ali's talent. Former heavyweight champion James Braddock declared, "Clay is a pretty fair fighter. I have a feeling he's a lot better than any of us give him credit for."⁹ And writing in *Sports Illustrated*, Tex Maule opined, "Clay may be now—and certainly can be in time—the best heavy-weight ever."¹⁰ But Ali's detractors continued to attack his conduct in and out of the ring. "The trouble with Cassius Clay," wrote Jim Murray of the *Los Angeles Times*, "is that, if ever a guy misplayed a role in history, it was he. They gave Cassius the part of the marshal in *High Noon*, and he wanted to be the guy in the black hat."¹¹ Almost without exception, the media insisted upon continuing its practice of referring to the champion as "Cassius Clay." And various feuds began to simmer.

Perhaps the most noteworthy rift was between Ali and former heavyweight champion Joe Louis. Louis believed in certain prin-ciples, and was not averse to talking about them. "I'm against Black Muslims," he announced when Ali converted to the Nation of Islam. "I've always believed that every man is my brother. Clay will earn the public's hatred because of his connections with the Black Mus-lims. The things they preach are just the opposite of what we believe. The heavyweight champion should be the champion of all people. He has responsibilities to all people."¹²

Nor was Louis's criticism limited to Ali's religious views. "Clay has a million dollars worth of confidence and a dime's worth of courage," the former champion declared. "He can't punch; he can't hurt you; and I don't think he takes a good punch. He's lucky there are no good fighters around. I'd rate him with Johnny Paycheck, Abe Simon, and Buddy Baer. A lot of guys would have beaten him if he was around when I was. I would have whipped him. He doesn't know a thing about fighting on the ropes, which is where he would be with me. I would go in to outpunch him rather than try to outbox him. He'd be hit into those ropes as near a corner as I could get him. I'd press him, bang him around, claw him, clobber him with all I got, cut down his speed, belt him round the ribs. I'd punish the body, where the pain comes real bad. Clay would have welts on his body. He would ache. His mouth would shut tight against the pain, and there would be tears burning his eyes."¹³

Ali, of course, responded in kind. "What's this about Joe Louis beating me?" he demanded. "Slow-moving shuffling Joe Louis beat me? He may hit hard, but that don't mean nothing if you can't find nothing to hit. I'm no flat-footed fighter. Joe Louis, you're really funny. Joe Louis had a thing called the bum of the month club. The men that Joe Louis fought, if I fought them today in Madison Square Garden, they'd boo them out of the ring. Fat bellies, out of shape, awkward, had no stance, no stamina, no footwork. Joe Louis has never said nothing good about me. Every time I fought, Joe Louis picked the wrong man. I not only beat the man, I picked the round he'd go down in. Joe Louis never did that. Would Joe Louis have beat me? How would Joe Louis have knocked me out? What's he gonna do when I'm jumping and sticking and moving? And don't say I can only do it for a minute, because I can keep it up for fifteen rounds, three minutes a round. Now, how is Joe Louis gonna get to me? I just can't see slow Joe Louis, who is shorter than I am, fought at a lighter weight than I did, and wasn't half as fast, knock me out. Would I just quit dancing that night and stand there and let him hit me?"[14]

JOE LOUIS BARROW, JR.: "There were times when there was bad feeling between Muhammad and my father. He didn't like Muhammad's bragging, to be honest with you. That just wasn't his style. When my father was fighting, people would ask him, 'Are you better than Dempsey?' And what he'd say was, 'All you can do is be the best while you're around.' That was his answer, but he was very proud of his reign as champion and confident of his abilities in the ring. He wasn't going to let Muhammad take that away from him just by a lot of public shouting. Then Muhammad called my father an Uncle Tom. That came later, during the Vietnam era, when Muhammad chose to be a conscientious objector. During World War Two, my father had volunteered for the Army, conducted ninety-six exhibitions, and entertained two million troops, not to mention donating purses from two championship fights to the United States Army Relief Fund. That endeared my father to America, and during the war in Vietnam, people said to Muhammad, 'Why don't you go in the Army and serve your country in Special Services like Joe Louis?' I remember talking with my father about that, and about Muhammad's stance on the war. They were different wars at different times, but my father told me, 'Look, you might not believe in what this country does all the time, but it's still the greatest country in the world and you have to support it.' My father was a patriot. If his country's decision was to go into Vietnam, he supported it like many Americans did. So to the extent that Muhammad chose to be a conscientious objector, my father felt that Muhammad didn't support the country in a way he would have. Even with his religious beliefs, he felt Muhammad could have gone into the Army in a noncombat role."

As 1965 progressed, Ali's commitment to the Nation of Islam didn't waver. He studied its publications, attended meetings, sought converts to the religion, and spoke with Elijah Muhammad in person and by telephone regularly. Nor did his public pronouncements change. "Clay means dirt," he told one audience. "It's the name slave owners gave my people. My white blood came from slave-masters, from raping. The white blood harms us; it hurts us. When we was darker, we were stronger. We were purer. When I was growing up, what did I see? Jesus is white. Superman is white. The president is white. The angels is white. Santa Claus is white. That's brainwashing, the biggest lie ever told children. Every year, you buy toys, and your children wind up thinking they come from some white man with rosy cheeks. They think everything good has to come from someone white."[15]

For some, the impact of these statements was galvanic.

JEREMIAH SHABAZZ: "When Elijah Muhammad spoke, his words were confined to whatever city he had spoken in. But Ali was a sports hero, and people wanted to hear what he had to say, so his visibility and prominence were of great benefit to the Nation. His voice carried throughout the world, and that was a true blessing for us. There's no doubt, our following increased enormously, maybe a hundred percent, after he joined the Nation. When he went to a temple, there were overflowing crowds. And this stuff about hating; Ali didn't hate white people. He got along with white people. He dealt with white people every day. So did I; I still do. That doesn't mean I have to love them or marry one, but I talk with white people all the time. Look, I got along with Angelo; I respected Angelo. He did his job, and unlike some people, never tried to take advantage of Ali. I can deal with the reality of the situation. In the business Ali was in, sports in America, white people were, and still are, in charge."

The respect Jeremiah Shabazz had for Angelo Dundee was wide-spread throughout the Nation of Islam. Of all the people around Ali, Dundee, as much as anyone, was clear as to his own role. He was a trainer. Getting Ali ready to fight was his job. He didn't involve himself in Ali's religious, political, or social activities. Whatever opinions he had were kept to himself. The only demand Dundee made was, when the bell rang, he was the boss. During a fight, when he gave orders, the other cornermen were expected to obey. The formula worked; it lasted for twenty years.

By contrast, Drew Brown (better known as Bundini) had a stormy on-again off-again relationship with Ali. Born in 1929, he'd grown up "colored poor" in Florida and joined the Navy as a messboy at age thirteen. Discharged two years later for threatening an officer with a meat cleaver, Bundini entered the merchant marine, and spent twelve years traveling the world. He met Ali in March 1963, just before the Doug Jones fight in New York, and soon became court jester to the king. But those in the Ali camp saw Bundini as more than a mere source of amusement.

WALI MUHAMMAD ("Blood"): "Bundini was a great man for Ali. There was a bond between them; something really good. Nobody else could deal with Ali like Bundini. Ali would say, 'I don't feel like training today,' and Bundini would keep after him until finally the champ would say, 'All right, let's go.' He was like a cheerleader. He gave Ali spirit and got him to work right. Even with his drinking and fussing and all the other things he did wrong, we loved Bundini. We were a family, and we lost a very important member [in 1988] when Bundini died."

FERDIE PACHECO: "Bundini was a poet of the streets; a source of energy that Ali fed off constantly; someone who put words together in a way that connoted exactly what he meant and Ali could understand. 'Float like a butterfly; sting like a bee.' That was Bundini. He used to say that Ali and the entourage were like a cake, made with flour, eggs, sugar, and that he, Bundini, was the nutmeg which gave it that little extra taste. If you caught Bundini in one of his drinking swings, which happened from time to time, there might be a problem. But sober, he was the sweetest, nicest guy in the world.

"I don't know how many times Bundini was married; maybe just once, although he tried on several other occasions. In 1964, he came to my office in Miami for a blood test with a white woman. She was from a wealthy family that had thrown her out. She was a crazy lady, living in some sleazy hotel, and Bundini had decided he was going to marry her. No amount of talking could convince him otherwise, including reference to Florida's miscegenation laws. So they got their blood tests, went down to the courthouse, asked where the license bureau was, and a policeman directed them to the third floor. They waited on line, got to the desk, requested a license, and the clerk asked, 'Fishing or hunting?' Of course, what had happened was, the policeman who directed them couldn't imagine that a black guy and a white woman would be coming to the Dade County Courthouse to get married. The clerk asked, 'Fishing or hunting?' And Bundini screamed out, 'A fucking license.' They threw him out of the courthouse. And I told him afterward, I said, 'I tried to warn you that was going to happen.' But he was very upset. He was crying, and let's face it, the mores of the South were wrong.

"I also remember, ten years later when Ali fought George Foreman in Zaire, Bundini brought a white showgirl to Africa. This was a fight that was supposed to be an all-black show. A black promoter, two black champions, a black country, the height of black consciousness. And right in the middle of the whole thing, Bundini brings in a white woman, stashes her in his room, makes her wear a headband, and tells everyone she's an Indian. Angelo used to say, if you try to understand Bundini he'll drive you crazy, so don't even bother to try. But he was good for Ali. We miss him now that he's gone. And I do know that Bundini and his first wife, a white Jewish woman, had a wonderful son, a distinguished young man, who's a pilot now."

Drew Brown, Jr., was one of the first black jet attack pilots in the United States Navy. He now flies for Federal Express.

DREW BROWN, JR.: "There was something Ali got from my father that nobody else gave him: the truth. The people around Ali loved him, but anything he did was all right. It was like the people around the president. Whatever the man in the White House does, his staff says it's good because they want to keep their jobs. Ali had people around him, if his shoes weren't tied, those people would say, 'Man, isn't that cool how you don't tie your shoes.' My father would say, 'You big idiot, tie your shoes or you're gonna trip and break your head.' No one but my father would talk to him like that. And he was able to capture the truth in sayings that hit home and were easy to understand.

"In the ring, Ali could hear my father over everybody. It was the one voice he heard above the crowd. And it wasn't, 'Throw the left, throw the right.' It was, 'End the show.' You know, the last ten seconds of every round is when the judges pick up their pencils. That's when you have to put a whupping on the other guy. That's what wins the rounds. And, 'Dance, champ, dance.' Nobody said 'dance' before. It was, 'Move, run!' But my father was like a spirit, and he gave Ali spirit. Dance!

"My father used to call God 'Shorty.' Do you know why? Because it's always the little short man who gets pushed around and overlooked, and maybe that same person is the one who's taking notes on you. Maybe God is a little short man. And I'll give you another example of my father. My mother is Jewish; that's how I was raised. And at my bar mitzvah, my little cousin—she was born retarded, mongoloid—she was there. The photographer was taking all the pictures. You know, me and my grandfather cutting the challah; my mother and father; my grandmother. And my father brought my cousin into all the major pictures. Everybody was saying, 'Don't mess up the pictures.' And my father said, 'I'm not messing them up, and she will be there.' That day was the most important day of that little girl's life. Retarded people have feelings. They can feel themselves being pushed aside, always, and this was the first time in her life that she was in the spotlight for a whole day. I learned more from my father that day than he ever taught me. That's how Daddy was."

Bundini spoke often of his bond with Ali. "I get sick before a fight," he told one reporter. "It makes me feel like a pregnant woman. I give the champ all my strength. He throw a punch, I throw a punch. He get hit, it hurts me. I can't explain it, but sometimes I know what he's gonna do before he even knows."[16] Then, in mid-1965, tensions between the two men rose. Bundini's continuing relationships with white women angered many within the Nation of Islam. His drinking further violated their code. One story, bandied about humorously in white circles, recounted his drinking in a New York restaurant. Surrounded by those who believed in abstinence, Bundini took the waiter aside, ordered a martini in a water glass, called the waiter back, and whispered, "No olive." Members of the Nation didn't appreciate the humor. And when they learned Bundini had hocked Ali's championship belt to a Harlem barber for five hundred dollars, he was banished from the entourage—a separation that lasted for almost five years.

Meanwhile, Ali readied for his next ring challenge, this one against former heavyweight champion Floyd Patterson. Patterson was the darling of America's boxing establishment: soft-spoken, humble, the embodiment of what a sportsman and "good Negro" was supposed to be. After two first-round defeats by Sonny Liston, he'd come back to win five consecutive bouts, including decisions over Eddie Machen and George Chuvalo.

At first, Ali treated Patterson lightly. Dubbing his opponent "the rabbit" ("because he's scared like a rabbit"), the champion showed up at Patterson's training camp with two heads of lettuce and a half-dozen carrots. But soon, the prefight buildup turned ugly, as the challenger announced his intention to "reclaim the title for America":

> The Black Muslim influence must be removed from box-ing. I have been told Clay has every right to follow any reli-gion he chooses, and I agree. But by the same token, I have the right to call the Black Muslims a menace to the United States and a menace to the Negro race. I have the right to say the Black Muslims stink. I am a Roman Catholic. I do not believe God put us here to hate one another. I believe the Muslim preaching of segregation, hatred, rebellion and violence is wrong. Cassius Clay is disgracing himself and the Negro race. No decent person can look up to a champion whose credo is "hate whites." I have nothing but contempt for the Black Muslims and that for which they stand. The image of a Black Muslim as the world heavyweight champion disgraces the sport and the nation. Cassius Clay must be beaten and the Black Muslims' scourge removed from box-ing.[17]

Then it was Ali's turn to respond, attacking Patterson for moving into an all-white neighborhood and being an "Uncle Tom." "When he was champion," Ali declared, "the only time he'd be caught in Harlem was when he was in the back of a car waving in some parade. The big shot didn't have no time for his own kind, he was so busy integrating. And now he wants to fight me because I stick up for black people."[18]

There was a poetic assault by Ali:

> I'm gonna put him flat on his back,
> So that he will start acting black.
> Because when he was champ he didn't do as he should.
> He tried to force himself into an all-white neighborhood.[19]

And more:

> Patterson says he's gonna bring the title back to America.
> If you don't believe the title already is in America, just see

who I pay taxes to. I'm American. But he's a deaf dumb so-called Negro who needs a spanking. I plan to punish him for the things he's said; cause him pain. The man picked the wrong time to start talking to the wrong man. When Floyd talks about me, he puts himself on a universal spot. We don't consider the Muslims have the title any more than the Baptists thought they had it when Joe Louis was champ. Does he think I'm going to be ignorant enough to attack his religion? I got so many Catholic friends of all races. And who's me to be an authority on the Catholic religion? Why should I act like a fool? He says he's going to bring the title back to America. I act like I belong to America more than he do. Why should I let one old Negro make a fool of me?

This is going to be a beautiful fight. The people are going to see more of me. I'm going to show off, look pretty. I'm so elusive they ain't seen nothing yet. The ring's going to look like it got a gate on each corner. This little old dumb pork-chop-eater don't have a chance. From eating pork he's got trillions of maggots and worms settling in his joints. He may even eat slime of the sea. Before the first round is over, people will say, "Forget it." I got superior height, weight, balance, reach, speed, strength and youth. I'm going to point before I do it. Point at the spot where he's going to fall. That would be history, wouldn't it? When he's lying there, I'm going to stick a carrot in his mouth, a carrot with some green on it. "Nibble on it, Rabbit," I'll tell him. Don't you think that'll make him leave the country?[20]

The fight took place in Las Vegas on November 22, 1965—the second anniversary of John F. Kennedy's assassination. From the opening bell, it was no contest. Ali toyed with his opponent throughout the fight, not bothering to throw a punch in the first round. Midway through the bout, with Patterson on unsteady legs, a left jab knocked him down. Thereafter, it appeared Ali could end the contest at will, but each time the challenger seemed ready to collapse, the champion stepped back, enabling the torture to go on. Finally, in round twelve, with Angelo Dundee calling, "Ali, knock him out, for chrissake," referee Harry Krause stopped the fight. Later, Krause would explain, "I said, 'Man-to-man, Floyd, are you okay? Do you really want to go on?' He said, 'Yes, please.' It was hurting me to watch. Patterson was hopelessly outclassed. He lobbed his punches like a feeble old woman."[21]

FLOYD PATTERSON: "I never fought anyone who moved as well as he did. Of all the heavyweight champions, he stands out as far as that's concerned. He moved with such grace, three minutes of every round for fifteen rounds, and that's extraordinary. You see, moving takes a lot out of you, especially the way he did it. He never stopped. It's very hard to hit a moving target, and he was moving all the time. His legs were his strength. He was very much afraid of getting hit, which is not a bad way to feel, and his legs kept him out of trouble until he got old.

"When we fought—and I fought him again in 1972—there was a certain amount of bad feeling between us. You see, I'm a straightforward guy. I didn't like the Black Muslims. I don't like the Ku Klux Klan. I don't like any organization that thinks color counts for everything. I see all people as brothers and sisters, and I stood up for what I believed the same way he did. So that bad feeling did exist. He complained when I called him 'Cassius Clay,' but I didn't like it when he called me 'the rabbit' either. Then, maybe ten years ago when I was a commissioner for the New York State Athletic Commission, I visited his training camp and got to know him better. We sat and talked. And I kind of forgot all the derogatory things that happened in the past. When we talked in private, I was surprised at how much I liked him. He was a nice guy. Believe it or not, he even seemed a little shy."

In the aftermath of his victory over Floyd Patterson, the press descended on Ali as it never had before. *Life* magazine, which had been kind to him in the past, headlined its story on the fight, "Sickening Spectacle in a Ring."[22] Robert Lipsyte, another supporter, compared the champion's conduct against Patterson to "a little boy pulling off the wings of a butterfly piecemeal."[23] One day later, though, Lipsyte felt compelled to write again, conceding Ali's "incomparable artistry" in the ring: "Clay has never lost a fight," Lipsyte acknowledged, "and there are those who are beginning to think he never will."[24]

Perhaps Gil Rogin put man and moment in perspective best. "What strange times we live in," Rogin wrote. "What a strange uncommon man is Clay. Who can fathom him? We can only watch in wonder as he performs and ponder whether, despite his often truly affecting ways, he doesn't scorn us and the world he is champion of."[25]

6

"Ain't Got No Quarrel"

"Some kinds of fame, like Liberace's, are non-negotiable at the power bank. Others, like the Beatles', can cause convulsions."[1] So wrote Wilfred Sheed in an essay on Muhammad Ali.

In February 1966, twelve weeks after his victory over Floyd Patterson, Ali began to cause convulsions. The chain of events that would shake America and place Ali in the annals of United States constitutional law had begun on April 18, 1960, when eighteen-year-old Cassius Clay registered for the military draft with Selective Service Local Board 47 in Louisville. On March 9, 1962, he was classified 1-A (available for the draft). Then on January 24, 1964, one month before the first Liston fight, Clay was ordered to the Armed Forces Induction Center in Coral Gables, Florida, for the military qualifying examination. The physical portion of the exam was no problem, but the fifty-minute mental aptitude test was another matter. Clay had been a poor reader in high school, and had trouble with the exam, particularly the portion dealing with mathematics:

A man works from six in the morning to three in the afternoon with one hour for lunch. How many hours did he work?
   a) 7   b) 8   c) 9   d) 10

A vendor was selling apples for $10 a basket. How much
would you pay for a dozen baskets if one-third of the apples
have been removed from each of the baskets?

   a) $10   b) $30   c) $40   d) $80[2]

"When I looked at a lot of them questions," Ali said later, "I just
didn't know the answers. I didn't even know how to start about
finding the answers."[3] The result was an Army IQ score of 78, which
put him in the sixteenth percentile, well below the passing grade
of thirty. Two months later, he was retested to determine if the first
score was the result of true failure or malingering. Three Army
psychologists supervised the reexamination, and once again, Ali
failed. On March 26, 1964, he was reclassified 1-Y ("not qualified
under current standards for service in the armed forces").

Predictably, an uproar followed. How intelligent did a person
have to be to drive a truck and peel potatoes? The furor was such
that Secretary of the Army Stephen Ailes felt compelled to write
Carl Vinson (chairman of the House of Representatives Armed Services Committee) to explain the Army's point of view:

> Should Clay be drafted simply because of his national
> prominence? Should we act on the basis of the popular con-
> ception of his qualifications for induction, or on the basis of
> results of two written tests and time-evaluated opinions of
> three psychologists? To accept inductees on the basis of as-
> sumed rather than demonstrated ability would risk degrading
> the combat capability of the Army by inflicting potentially
> untrainable personnel on it. In my judgment, we must de-
> pend on the established standards which our mental tests
> measure in a very accurate degree. The requirements of to-
> day's Army do not allow for acceptance of those personnel
> not offering a reasonable value to the defense effort. The in-
> duction standards must be such that the new members of the
> Army are capable of learning new skills and applying them.
> In summary, it was my decision that Cassius Clay should be
> rejected for induction due to his inability to meet prescribed
> minimum standards.[4]

Ali, for his part, was embarrassed by the matter. "I said I was
the greatest, not the smartest," he told reporters.[5] But he was stung
by being publicly labeled "stupid," and embarrassed by the publicity
accorded his high school academic record. Thereafter, for two years,

the issue lay dormant. Then, in early 1966 with the war in Vietnam growing, the mental-aptitude percentile required by the military was lowered from thirty to fifteen, leaving Ali eligible for the draft. On February 14, 1966, his attorney appeared before Local Board 47 in Louisville to present a letter requesting deferment from military service on numerous substantive and procedural grounds. Three days later, the request was denied, and Ali was reclassified 1-A. Robert Lipsyte of *The New York Times* was with him when he heard the news.

ROBERT LIPSYTE: "I was in Miami on the lawn outside Ali's house, watching him watch the girls walk by. They'd slow down when they saw him, and from time to time, he'd sing, 'Hey little girl in the high school sweater.' Then, out of nowhere, a red television truck from one of the local stations pulled up and told him that his draft status had been changed. And to be honest, what I saw that afternoon wasn't particularly religious or political. That was a patina which came later. I saw a twenty-four-year-old scared of being drafted. It was, 'How can they do this to me? I don't want my career ruined.' He thought he'd put the draft behind, and now his life was about to be turned upside down. Someone had just told him he was going to Vietnam.

"Then the telephone started ringing; Associated Press, United Press International. And Ali's litany throughout the day was, 'This can't happen. How can they reclassify me when they haven't seen if I'm better or worser or smarter or dumber? For two years, they told everybody I was a nut, and made me and my parents ashamed.' And of course, the Muslims in the house were giving it to him. 'Yeah, man, they're gonna get your ass. They're gonna send you to Vietnam. Some white cracker sergeant is gonna put a shank in you.' As the afternoon went by, Ali got more and more agitated and the questions from reporters kept coming. 'How do you feel about the war in Vietnam?' 'I don't know nothing about Vietnam.' 'Do you know where Vietnam is?' 'Well, it's out there somewhere; I don't know.' 'Are you a hawk? Are you a dove? Is the war a just war?' And the Muslims were chortling, 'Oh, they're gonna get your ass. Some cracker sergeant is gonna kill you. They're gonna frag you with a grenade.' 'What do you think about the Gulf of Tonkin Resolution? What do you think about Lyndon Johnson? Could you kill a Vietcong? What if the Vietcong try to kill you?' He was going crazy, and it went on like that for I don't know how many hours.

"Finally after the tenth call—'What do you think about the Vietcong?'—Ali exploded. 'Man, I ain't got no quarrel with them Viet-cong.' And bang. There it was. That was the headline. That was what the media wanted."

JOHN CONDON: "Whatever the Muslims might have preached, Ali was never antiwhite. I'm a pretty tough Irishman; I'm sensitive to that type of thing; and I don't think he had a white-hate bone in his body. But then he made that statement—'I ain't got no quarrel with them Vietcong'—and it gave people who were already against him another reason to dislike him. First, they thought he was a loudmouthed nigger. And I don't like that word; I abhor it, but that's what they called him. Then he joined the Black Muslims. And now, on top of everything, he was refusing to serve his country, which to his enemies made him an unpatriotic draft-dodger."

The day after Ali made his "Vietcong" remark, it was front-page news across the country. America had not yet turned against the war, and the sporting press raged against him:

Red Smith: "Squealing over the possibility that the military may call him up, Cassius makes himself as sorry a spectacle as those unwashed punks who picket and demonstrate against the war."[6]

Milton Gross: "As a fighter, Cassius is good. As a man, he cannot compare to some of the kids slogging through the rice paddies where the names are stranger than Muhammad Ali."[7]

Murray Robinson: "For his stomach-turning performance, boxing should throw Clay out on his inflated head. The adult brat, who has boasted ad nauseam of his fighting skill but who squealed like a cornered rat when tapped for the Army should be shorn of his title. And to the devil with the old cliche that a ring title can be won or lost only in the ring."[8]

Jimmy Cannon: "Clay is part of the Beatle movement. He fits in with the famous singers no one can hear and the punks riding motorcycles with iron crosses pinned to their leather jackets and Batman and the boys with their long dirty hair and the girls with the unwashed look and the col-lege kids dancing naked at secret proms held in apartments and the revolt of students who get a check from dad every first of the month and the painters who copy the labels off

soup cans and the surf bums who refuse to work and the
whole pampered style-making cult of the bored young."[9]

Ali's next fight was scheduled for March 29, 1966, in Chicago,
and had loomed as a financial blockbuster. The opponent was to be
Ernie Terrell, who held the World Boxing Association's version of
the heavyweight championship (a title virtually no one honored) and
was a popular Chicago resident. Moreover, Chicago served as headquarters for the Nation of Islam. All signs were promising until Ali's
"Vietcong" remark. Then, virtually overnight, the climate changed.

On Sunday, February 20, 1966, the *Chicago Tribune* called on
the Illinois State Athletic Commission to rescind its sanction of the
bout. Chicago's other dailies followed suit, and Illinois Governor
Otto Kerner suggested the commission reexamine the fight. Soon,
newspapers across the country were demanding that the bout be
banned. Seeking to halt the tide of criticism, the fight's promoters
arranged for Ali to appear before the state commission, ostensibly
to apologize for his remark. But the hastily arranged session on
February 24 fell short of placating opponents of the bout.

"I'm not here to make a showdown plea or apologize the way the
press said I would," Ali told the commission. "I came here because
certain people would be hurt financially over what I said, and you
people were put on the spot before your governor and other authorities. If I've got any other apologizing to do, I'll do it to government officials and the draft board." Pressed further about
whether he was apologizing for the nature of his comments, Ali
answered, "I'm apologizing for making them to sportswriters and
newspapers." But he would go no further, finally stating, "I don't
have to apologize; I'm not in court."[10]

Later that day, without waiting for the commission to act, Illinois
Attorney General William Clark ruled that the Ali-Terrell bout violated state law. While Clark was vague regarding the basis for his
decision, it appeared to hinge on three provisions of the Illinois
Sports Act, none of which had been previously enforced. First, the
corporation promoting the fight had only two members instead of
the required fifty. Second, in applying for licenses, Ali and Terrell
had failed to file statements of fact showing that they were "of good
and stable moral character." And last, in applying for the license,
Ali had failed to sign his correct name.

With the fight less than five weeks away, the promoters now had
to find a new site. Louisville was considered, but the Kentucky State
Senate passed a resolution condemning Ali. "His attitude," the res-

olution read, "brings discredit to all loyal Kentuckians and to the names of the thousands who gave their lives for this country during his lifetime."[11] Thereafter, Miami, Pittsburgh, and a half-dozen other cities were considered, but in each instance political pressures vetoed the fight. Finally, Maple Leaf Gardens in Toronto was chosen, but by now Terrell wanted no part of the bout. Many of the theaters originally interested in the closed-circuit telecast had withdrawn from the promotion. And since the challenger was to be paid on a percentage basis, he saw little financial incentive to go forward. That left Ali without an opponent, and led to the substitution of Canadian heavyweight champion George Chuvalo. Thereafter, calls for a boycott of the fight escalated:

From the media; Arthur Daley of The New York Times: "Clay could have been the most popular of all champions. But he attached himself to a hate organization, and antagonized everyone with his boasting and his disdain for the decency of even a low-grade patriotism. This fight should not be patronized either in person or on theater TV. Not a nickel should be contributed to the coffers of Clay, the Black Muslims, or the promoters who jammed this down so many unwilling throats. A boycott is urged as the one effective way of showing resentment at a production that thumbs its nose at the public."[12]

From former champion Billy Conn: "I'll never go to another one of his fights. He is a disgrace to the boxing profession. And I think that any American who pays to see him fight after what he has said recently should be ashamed. They should stay away from those closed-circuit television shows."[13]

From members of Congress; Representative Frank Clark of Pennsylvania: "The heavyweight champion of the world turns my stomach. I am not a superpatriot. But I feel that each man, if he really is a man, owes to his country a willingness to protect it and serve it in time of need. From this standpoint, the heavyweight champion has been a complete and total disgrace. I urge the citizens of the nation as a whole to boycott any of his performances. To leave these theater seats empty would be the finest tribute possible to that boy whose hearse may pass by the open doors of the theater on Main Street, U.S.A."[14]

Still, plans for the fight went ahead, and Ali seemed relatively unaffected. In Toronto to train for the bout, he dubbed Chuvalo "the washerwoman" and announced, "I need some test harder than this to test me. A den full of poisoned rattlesnakes couldn't shake me. Allah would make the rattlesnakes' jaws lock. They'd have to tie me up in the hot sun in the den with the rattlesnakes, let them crawl all around me, take some boiling water and throw me in it, and that wouldn't scare me. Allah would cool it. This stuff ain't nothing."[15]

Meanwhile, Chuvalo had his own formula for success. "I'm a rough fighter," the Canadian said. "When I'm in close, I feel that I'm the boss, and I try to make sure my opponent knows it. I'll treat Clay as roughly as I can whenever I can. I plan to put pressure on Clay from the first bell and never let up. The hardest part of the fight for me will be the first ten rounds. After that, he'll be worn down. I think Clay will quit if he's hurt, and I intend to hurt him."[16]

Don Elbaum, who promoted club fights for decades, was in Canada for the buildup to the Ali-Chuvalo bout.

DON ELBAUM: "At the time, I was running shows in Toronto. Angelo called and asked if I'd get them a place to train, so I set them up in Sully's Gym. The deal was, I could charge admission and keep half the money, and the other half went to Ali. The gym held three hundred people. I charged five dollars a head, which was a lot for those days, and it was unreal. The place was jammed every day. You couldn't get in; I was pushing people in. Some would leave, and then we'd replace them, so we were pulling in two thousand dollars a day. At the end of each session, I gave Ali his money. So keep in mind, he was putting a thousand dollars a day in his pocket. Then we'd go back to our motel, and he'd give it all away. Kids would come and gather around him. There were thirty, maybe forty of them at first, although as word got around, the number grew. And what Ali did was set the kids up by size and ability in races. Every kid who was in a race got something. The winners got more, but the losers won too. And the way he worked it, fast kids were racing against other fast kids, and slow fat kids were racing against slow fat ones. The youngest were five or six years old, and the oldest he let participate were around twelve. I said to him after the second day, I said, 'Cassius'—by then he wanted to be called Ali, but I still slipped from time to time—I said, 'This is a hell of a story. I want to call the Toronto newspapers so they can come down and get a picture of it.' And he said, 'Please don't. I'm having too much fun. If the papers come and write about it, my people are going to get upset and I won't be able to do it anymore.' So I respected his wishes; I never told the press. And I gotta tell you, he had a ball."

The fight itself was one-sided from the start. Chuvalo was a warrior, virtually impossible to knock out. Rocky Marciano once said, "If all fights were a hundred rounds, George Chuvalo would be unbeaten in any era." But he lacked the tools to cope with Ali, who at times simply stood with his arms high and allowed Chuvalo to pound his body. Out of fifteen rounds, the challenger won only one.

GEORGE CHUVALO: "He was just so damn fast. When he got old, it was different. But when he was young, when he moved his legs and hands at the same time, when he synchronized them, he was great. When he was young, he threw his punches when he was in motion. That is, he'd be out of punching range, and as he moved into range, he'd already begun to throw the punch. So if you waited until he got into range to punch back, he beat you every time.

"Going into the fight, my tactics were, I was a short guy, I was a body puncher, I tried to nullify his speed by getting in close and not letting him use the whole ring, get him into the ropes, immobilize him. But he was so fast and so hard to trap. I wasn't totally dominated; I did some damage. They said he was peeing blood after the fight, but unfortunately that didn't do me much good. And it's funny. You fight your heart out with a guy. You do your best; he does his best. And when the fight ended, I liked him. We were both standing, and we'd forged a certain mutual respect.

"You know, I fought ninety-seven guys, and often you just see them at the weigh-in, there's a cursory glance, a handshake, you fight, win, lose or draw, and then you go separate ways. But it didn't happen that way with Muhammad. We saw each other a number of times afterward, and he was a real friendly sweet guy. Even now, every time I read about him, every time I see him, he's giving of himself to other people. It even happened with me. There was a testimonial dinner in my honor not long ago, and Muhammad came. He didn't have to. His expenses were taken care of, but he didn't get any money besides. And it was hard for him to communicate. He communicates more physically than verbally now because of his problem, but I could tell the good feelings were there. He's a man of integrity, a man with a good heart."

In the aftermath of the Chuvalo fight, Ali was more controversial than ever. Contrasts with Joe Louis appeared regularly in the press, and an increasing number of commentators began likening him to Jack Johnson. Ali enjoyed the latter comparison. "Jack Johnson was the most influential person in my career," he would say later. "He did things in the ring defensively that I saw on film and tried to copy. He came along at a time when black people felt they had nothing to be proud of, and he made them proud."

Then, six weeks after the Chuvalo fight, Ali, like Jack Johnson a half century before him, was placed under surveillance by the United States government. In part, this was the result of a May 13, 1966, letter from the United States Attorney's office in Louisville to the Federal Bureau of Investigation requesting data on which to base certain preliminary recommendations regarding Ali's draft status. But the scope of the investigation seemed to indicate that much more was involved. Dozens of acquaintances, past and present, were interviewed. Police records were combed and seven traffic violations over a five-year period in four states uncovered. The same investigation revealed that, on September 19, 1964, Ali had purchased a .22 caliber Colt derringer at a pawn shop in Miami, but that Sam Saxon had learned of the purchase and purportedly thrown the weapon in the Atlantic Ocean. An appearance by Ali on the *Tonight Show* with Johnny Carson was monitored and summarized in memorandum form for J. Edgar Hoover. Then the investigators turned their attention to Main Bout, Inc., a promotional firm set up to market ancillary rights to Ali's fights.

Main Bout was the creation of five men:

Bob Arum; then thirty-three years old. A former assistant United States attorney in the Southern District of New York, who had joined the law firm of Phillips, Nizer, Benjamin, Krim and Ballon in 1964.

Mike Malitz; the son of Lester Malitz, who had been a pioneer in closed-circuit telecasts.

John Ali; chief architect of the Nation of Islam. Elijah Muhammad was its spiritual leader, but as national secretary, John Ali performed the day-to-day operational work that held the Nation together.

Herbert Muhammad; son of Elijah Muhammad.

Jim Brown; who had retired from professional football after the 1965 season and became a leading proponent of black economic development.

BOB ARUM: "It was bizarre, really. Here were these guys, Herbert Muhammad and John Ali, from an organization that was considered very militant, very racist. There I was, a white Jewish lawyer. But we made the marriage.

"To understand how it began, you have to go back to when I joined Phillips, Nizer. Lester Malitz had a closed-circuit company, and asked me to represent them, which I did. Then Lester died, and his son Mike took over the business. We were doing a fight, George Chuvalo against Ernie Terrell, and things were going poorly, so I came up with what I thought was an ingenious idea. There had never been a black commentator, and wouldn't it be great if we had a black fight analyst because it would give the press something to say when they wrote about the fight. The first guy I went to was Willie Mays, but he didn't want to do it. Then someone suggested Jim Brown, who said yes, and we hit it off. At one point, Jim said to me, 'You know, you're really the promoter in this operation; why don't you promote fights?' And I didn't want to become involved in boxing, because from what I could see there was nothing in it except Muhammad Ali who I believed was tied up. But Jim said, no, Ali wasn't tied up and he'd talk to Ali's people to set up a meeting. Well, you know, people say a lot of things and don't deliver. But a couple of months later, we had a meeting attended by Jim, myself, Mike Malitz, Herbert Muhammad, and Muhammad Ali. A lot of what I said to them sounds pedestrian now, but at the time it was innovative. I told them that Ali could control the finances for his own fights, that he could get 60 percent of the gross instead of 40, and that we could get more black entrepreneurs involved in controlling closed-circuit outlets for his fights. Ali liked the idea. There were a number of trips back and forth between New York and Chicago, and finally we put together Main Bout, Inc. Herbert was president. The Muslims, meaning Herbert and John Ali, controlled 50 percent of the stock. Jim Brown had 20 percent, Mike Malitz 20 percent, and I had 10. Basically, I thought of myself as Malitz's lawyer. This was his business; he was my client. And while I had relatively little interest in boxing at that point, it was a fascinating experience for a young attorney to be involved with."

MIKE MALITZ: "The first fight we did as Main Bout, Inc., was a disaster. Ali-Terrell was what it was supposed to be. But then Ali made his Vietcong remark, the fight was canceled, Chuvalo was substituted, and we lost money. I can remember sitting at my desk with Jim Brown, Bob Arum, John Ali, and Herbert, having meetings, trying to figure out what to do next. I was married with three young children. This was how I was supposed to pay my bills, buy food, pay the rent at home, pay rent on the office. All I wanted was to earn a living, and it was tough. Between Herbert and John Ali, John was the bad guy, always second guessing whether or not Bob and I were stealing money. Herbert, on the other hand, was friendly and polite. Bob and I thought maybe they were playing us off— good cop, bad cop—but overall their dealings with us were sincere. Herbert was very inquisitive. He wanted to learn the business and not make mistakes, and there's no doubt that Bob taught him a lot. He relied very heavily on Bob Arum in that period. And I might add that Bob leased a 450-SLC Mercedes for Herbert, which was a big factor in keeping him happy."

BOB ARUM: "Later on, when the money became really big, Herbert took on an imperious presence. It was like visiting the emperor for an audience. But he was very accommodating in the early days. And you have to remember, the financial end of the boxing business was very different from what it is now. There weren't many fights on network television. As far as closed-circuit was concerned, there was less equipment and fewer screens. Pay-per-view didn't exist. No one had a handle on what was possible and what revenues might be brought in. Ali revolutionized the business of boxing. There's no doubt about it; he was the greatest promoter who ever lived. Fighting or not fighting, champion or not champion, he dominated the business for twenty years. But keep in mind, it was Ali, but it was also the fact that things were beginning to happen electronically. The equipment was getting more sophisticated. We'd never had satellites before, and now, for the first time, we could show a fight live from New York on television in the United Kingdom or vice versa. And those new markets were crucial, because after Chuvalo, Ali looked like dead merchandise in the United States. The only way we figured to make money was to have him fight overseas."

Thus it was that the heavyweight championship at long last was given to the world. On April 5, 1915, Jack Johnson had lost his title to Jess Willard in Havana. Thereafter, except for Primo Carnera against Paulino Uzcudun and Floyd Patterson versus Tom Mc-Neeley, the title had been contested exclusively on American soil for over five decades. Ali changed that. Beginning on March 29, 1966, in less than a year he defended his title seven times, four of them in foreign lands. George Chuvalo had been the first of those opponents. Now three European bouts were scheduled within the span of three-and-a-half months. Mickey Duff, England's preeminent fight manager and promoter, recalls them all.

MICKEY DUFF: "First, in May of 1966, Ali fought a rematch with Henry Cooper. That fight, without a doubt, was the biggest fight ever staged in England. A British heavyweight was fighting on home soil for the championship of the world, and because of the knockdown in their first fight, people thought Cooper had a chance. Ali cut him horribly over the left eye, one of the worst cuts I've ever seen, and the fight was stopped in the sixth round. Then, in August, Ali came back to England, and knocked out Brian London in three rounds. After that, he fought Karl Mildenberger in Frankfurt. Mildenberger was the first German to challenge for the championship since Max Schmeling. Jarvis Astaire and I were copromoters of the bout, and what I remember most about it is what happened afterward.

"Teddy Waltham had refereed the fight and done an excellent job. He stopped it in the twelfth round, and the stoppage was perfect; it came at just the right time. The next morning, we were all gathered to go back to London, and I saw Teddy, white as a sheet. We had paid him in cash right after the fight. We gave him a thousand pounds, which in those days was about twenty-four hundred dollars. He'd had the money in his pocket, and somebody picked his pocket. He'd lost it all. We got on the plane. Jarvis was sitting immediately behind me, so I turned my back to the front of the plane, leaned on my chair, and was telling Jarvis what had happened to Waltham, when suddenly I felt a tap on my shoulder. It was Ali, and Ali asked, 'Is that the guy who refereed my fight?' I said, 'Yeah.' Ali just shook his head and said, 'That's a shame; he worked so hard.' Anyway, when we got off the plane I saw Waltham, and he was looking quite happy. I said to him, 'You look like you found the money.' And he told me, 'Not exactly, but somebody must have told Ali because he just gave me a thousand pounds.' That was Ali. He'd asked somebody how much a thousand pounds was in American money, went into his own pocket, and gave it to Waltham."

Ali-Mildenberger was the first color telecast of a sports event ever transmitted by satellite. It also marked the last time Ali would fight on network television for seven years. In part, the hiatus was due to the superior profitability of closed-circuit telecasts. But it also came as a consequence of pressure from political leaders and advertisers not to showcase Ali on home TV. Meanwhile, controversy over his draft status continued to mount in a very public way.

On March 17, 1966, one month after being reclassified 1-A, Ali himself had appeared before Local Board 47 to request exemption from the draft. As in the past, he cited both the financial hardship he and his parents would suffer were he to be drafted and other procedural matters. However, this time, the focus of his plea was on a request for conscientious objector status. The request was denied. Six weeks later, the denial was sustained on appeal, and on August 23, 1966, Ali appeared at a special hearing to pursue the matter. The hearing officer was Lawrence Grauman, sixty-nine years old, a retired Kentucky State Circuit Court judge. Grauman's job was to hear evidence, consider the merits of Ali's application, and issue a recommendation to the Kentucky Appeal Board. In order to be eligible for conscientious objector status, Ali would have to convince Grauman of three things—(1) that his objection to military service was sincere; (2) that it was based on religious training and belief; and (3) that he was opposed to participation in all wars of any kind. At the start of the hearing, Ali handed Grauman a twenty-one-page letter, outlining the evolution and nature of his religious beliefs. Then he testified under oath as follows:

> Sir, I said earlier and I'd like to again make that plain, it would be no trouble for me to go into the Armed Services, boxing exhibitions in Vietnam or traveling the country at the expense of the Government or living the easy life and not having to get out in the mud and fight and shoot. If it wasn't against my conscience to do it, I would easily do it. I wouldn't raise all this court stuff and I wouldn't go through all of this and lose the millions that I gave up and my image with the American public that I would say is completely dead and ruined because of us in here now. I wouldn't jeopardize my life walking the streets of the South and all of America with no bodyguard if I wasn't sincere in every bit of what the Holy Qur'an and the teachings of the Honorable Elijah Muhammad tell us and it is that we are not to participate in wars on the side of nonbelievers, and this is a Chris-

tian country and this is not a Muslim country. We are not, according to the Holy Qur'an, to even as much as aid in passing a cup of water to the wounded. I mean, this is the Holy Qur'an, and as I said earlier, this is not me talking to get the draft board or to dodge nothing. This is there before I was born and it will be there when I'm dead and we believe in not only part of it, but all of it.[17]

At the close of the hearing, Grauman did what virtually no one expected him to do. He ruled that Ali was "of good character, morals, and integrity, and sincere in his objection on religious grounds to participation in war in any form."[18] Accordingly, he recommended that Ali's conscientious objector claim be sustained. Notwithstanding this recommendation, the Department of Justice wrote a letter to the Appeal Board opposing the claim. Drawing on the FBI's investigation of Ali, it argued that Ali's objection to war rested on political and racial rather than religious grounds, that he was opposed only to certain types of war, and that his beliefs were a matter of convenience rather than sincerely held. On August 25, 1966, L. Mendel Rivers (who had succeeded Carl Vinson as chairman of the House Armed Services Committee) addressed a Veterans of Foreign Wars convention in New York, and promised to seek "a thorough overhaul" of religious deferments if Ali's conscientious objector claim was upheld. "Listen to this," Rivers told his audience. "If that great theologian of Black Muslim power, Cassius Clay, is deferred, you watch what happens in Washington. We're going to do something if that board takes your boy and leaves Clay home to double-talk. What has happened to the leadership of our nation when a man, any man regardless of color, can with impunity advise his listeners to tell the President when he is called to serve in the armed forces, 'Hell no, I'm not going.' "[19]

Thereafter, despite Judge Grauman's recommendation, Ali's request for conscientious objector status was again denied. But now the battle lines had been drawn. Once again, Ali was fighting for a cause. "How can I kill somebody when I pray five times a day for peace?" he demanded. "Elijah Muhammad teaches us to fight only when we're attacked, and my life is in his hands."[20]

Then, in autumn of 1966, with the draft controversy raging, Ali took a step that further alienated the white power structure. His contract with the Louisville Sponsoring Group expired, and he retained Herbert Muhammad as his new manager. "We're not trying to be permanent people in the fistical world," Elijah Muhammad said shortly after the new arrangement was announced. "We know it's a crooked business, but we want Muhammad to get justice out of it."[21]

Upon becoming Ali's manager, Herbert Muhammad resigned as president of Main Bout, Inc., and was succeeded by John Ali. Bob Arum's law firm was retained as counsel to Ali in return for 5 percent of the aggregate proceeds paid to the champion in connection with his fights. Out of that amount, the firm was to pay all ordinary legal disbursements as well as the cost of an attorney retained separately to handle Ali's draft status. The firm also maintained its status as counsel to Main Bout, Inc., at a fee of four thousand dollars a month. A separate agreement between Herbert Muhammad and Angelo Dundee set Dundee's salary at a minimum of $10,000 per fight. Herbert was to be well-compensated as Ali's manager. His September 20, 1966, contract with Ali covered virtually all of Ali's income-producing activity, including but not limited to boxing, and was binding for a period of five years. Proceeds were to be split sixty-forty in Ali's favor, with all ordinary and necessary business expenses paid out of the manager's share. Then, less than a year later, given Ali's penchant for generous spending, the contract was amended to give him two-thirds of the proceeds, but with expenses paid off the top.

Ali's new management team intensified the controversy around him. More than ever, he now seemed to be breaking from the establishment. There'd always been a sense of the irrational about him; "The first symptom of a national nervous breakdown," Mark Kram called him.[22] But now he'd further broken the mold, and no one was quite sure what to make of him.

ROBERT LIPSYTE: "Most of the newspapermen in those days were older, set in their ways, and still refused to believe he was any good. They thought there was something freakish about him. They kept comparing him to people in the past. Joe Louis would have done this to him. Jack Dempsey would have done that. I guess when you're older, nothing new is any good; the best things were all long ago. But more important, most of the reporters failed completely to understand Ali's importance beyond the ring. A few did, but not many; and that continued to hold true for most publications.

"*The New York Times* position throughout the sixties, with which I had some terrible fights, was that his name was Cassius Clay, and he hadn't gone through a court of law to change it. If he did, they would call him whatever he wanted, but until then they would call him Cassius Clay. What generally happened was, I would use 'Muhammad Ali' in my articles and then some editor would change the copy to 'a/k/a Cassius Clay.' Once, I remember, I won the battle and they referred to him as Muhammad Ali throughout the piece, but the caption on a picture that ran with the story called him Cassius Clay. So Ali didn't get the support he deserved from the media. Attention, yes. Support, no. And a lot of the attention was focused on the wrong things. But there were several interesting media relationships that developed during that period, and the relationship between Ali and Howard Cosell was one of them."

HOWARD COSELL: "Muhammad Ali is a figure transcendental to sport. He's important to the history of this country because his entire life is an index to the bigotry lodged deep within the wellspring of this nation and its people. The only other person to come out of sports who might be as important as Ali was Jackie Roosevelt Robinson. And Ali had the advantage of coming in the 1960s. Look at what was happening then: the birth of the drug culture, the birth of the pill, riots in the streets, an ugly unwanted war, assassinations. Then you go into the 1970s. The most ignominious moment in the history of this country, the shootdown at Kent State. The betrayal of the presidency, Watergate. That time period was incredible, and Ali understood it; he was at the heart of it; he helped shape it all. And the powers he fought! The forces that lined up against him! Even I wasn't immune to fear. I supported him, but I often wondered how long ABC would back me. I'd come to the business at a very late age, and could have been snuffed out like that [Cosell snaps his fingers].

"I remember, once I was in London. This was in May of 1966, for the second Henry Cooper fight. I started an interview with Ali with the words, 'I am with Cassius Clay, also known as Muhammad Ali.' Ali had a huge sensitivity about him. He looked at me and said, 'Are you gonna do that to me too?' And I told him, 'No; I won't ever do that again as long as I live, I promise. Your name is Muhammad Ali.' And I went through it all; the pressure groups, the death threats. And I wondered, what is this country? How did it get this way? What happened to our heritage and our ideals? But I never stopped caring about Ali. I loved him; I worried about him. Even now, I dream about him. And one thing more about Ali. There were many things about him that impressed me, but one in particular was, he never listened to the sportswriters. Red Smith, Jimmy Cannon, Dick Young; they were horrible to him. If he'd listened to them, he'd have slugged it out with Sonny Liston in Miami Beach and danced against George Foreman in Zaire. He'd have gone into the Army, and been shipped off to Vietnam. Listening to his critics would have been the end of him, but he did what he wanted to do, and you never knew what reached him. He was much better at ignoring criticism than I was."

JOHN CONDON: "As far as Ali and Howard Cosell were concerned, it was a mutually beneficial relationship. Cosell knew that Ali was someone who looked great on television and would get him ratings. Ali knew that Cosell was a vehicle for reaching an audience that might otherwise have been shut off to him. But Ali made Cosell; it wasn't the other way around. If Ali had gone looking for a straight man, he couldn't have found a better one than Howard Cosell. In fact, I remember a fight we had here in the Garden; Ali against Zora Folley. Cosell was doing an interview; Ali was giving him a hard time; and finally Cosell accused him of being truculent. Ali just looked at him—and it was a wonderful moment—Ali looked Cosell right in the eye, and said, 'I don't know what truculent means, but if it's good, that's me.' Howard was just a supporting actor. Ali was the star, and he worked Cosell beautifully."

MUHAMMAD ALI: "I like Howard Cosell. He was a professional. He knew how to bring out the best in people. He respected the law, and had a sense of right and wrong and history. But he wouldn't have been nearly as big as he was without me, and I hope he knows it. I was big. All kinds of people came to see me. Women came because I was saying, 'I'm so pretty,' and they wanted to look at me. Some white people, they got tired of my bragging. They thought I was arrogant and talked too much, so they came to see someone give the nigger a whuppin'. Longhaired hippies came to my fights because I wouldn't go to Vietnam. And black people, the ones with sense, they were saying, 'Right on, brother; show them honkies.' Everyone in the whole country was talking about me."

With interest in Ali running high, in November of 1966 the champion readied for his next opponent—Cleveland "Big Cat" Williams. Williams had once been perhaps the hardest puncher in the heavyweight division. But in 1964, a traffic violation had led to his being shot with a .357 magnum in a confrontation with a Texas state highway patrolman. The bullet tore through his colon and right kidney before lodging deep in Williams's hip. After four operations, the fighter had returned to the ring, but was only a shell of his former self.

"Me and Cleve have it all figured out," said Hugh Benbow, Williams's manager. "We ain't gonna fight Clay's kind of fight. For the first time in his life, Clay is gonna have a big strong two-handed fighter in there with him. He's gonna be knocked out the first time Cleve gets to him, and the world will be well rid of the biggest mouth in boxing. Cleve don't fool around. He crushes their bones with either hand. He's knocked fifty guys deader than cow meat, and he broke one poor feller's back, put him on crutches for the rest of his life. I also want you to know that Cleve's a fine clean-living boy, goes to church on Sundays, don't drink, and is married to a preacher's daughter. He's gonna be a great champion, but Clay won't be around to know about it."[23]

Ali, for his part, approached the bout with equanimity, announcing that he would unveil a new dance step called "the Ali shuffle" against Williams—a step he promised would sweep the nation as the hottest dance innovation since the Twist.

JERRY IZENBERG: "I liked Cleveland Williams. He was an interesting guy, not a very sharp guy, much taken advantage of. But at one point in his career, he would have spelled real problems for Ali, because at his height as a puncher, Cleveland Williams hit harder than Liston. Before he got shot, the man was awesome. But afterward, he wasn't much of a fighter.

"The day before the fight, I was in a hotel room alone with Ali. He was lying on the bed, listening to a radio disc jockey who was talking about him, and every few minutes he'd call the disc jockey up and talk to him. It was a marvelous scenario. And then Ali said to me, 'I saw the greatest movie I've ever seen last night. It's the greatest movie ever made. It's called *Fantastic Voyage.*' Remember that old movie with Stephen Boyd and Raquel Welch? That was the one. And Ali went into great detail, telling me how they took these people and put a ray gun on them and made a teeny-tiny submarine, and injected them into a seriously ill person's body to save him. Ali took the submarine through the entire body for me, playing all the parts. Not only the part of Raquel Welch in a falsetto voice, but also the heart—'tha-bump, tha-bump.' The kidneys—'whoosh.' The lungs, the liver. He went through the whole body, and then he looked at me and said, 'You know what got those people in the submarine in trouble? It was the *white* corpuscles.'

"And then Ali said to me, 'You know this guy good, don't you?'

I said, 'What guy?' Because you know how Ali used to think. He was onto the next subject before you were finished with the first one. His mind would click, and sometimes he didn't express the subject matter he was talking about until he was well into it. So I asked, 'What guy?' And he answered, 'Williams. He could fight; he was a terrific puncher; but there's nothing much left now, is there?' I said, 'No.' And he said, 'It bothers me. It bothers me to fight him when he's like that.' And I told him, I said to Ali, 'If you want to do this guy a favor, knock him out as soon as you can. I mean it. Knock him out.' And I don't know if you remember that fight. Ali was not a great knockout puncher. But that night, as a puncher, he was the best he ever was. And strangely enough, I think that's because he didn't want to hurt Williams. Because if that fight had gone eight or nine rounds, Cleveland Williams would have been in terrible trouble."

A crowd of 35,460 attended the fight; the largest number of people up until that time to witness a boxing match indoors. Ali entered the Houston Astrodome a heavy five-to-one favorite.

MIKE MALITZ: "Right before the fight, there was a problem because Williams wouldn't go to the ring. Arum had to go back to his dressing room, screaming, 'You damn blankety-blank. Out into the ring now, or you don't get paid.' Williams was having second thoughts at that point. He was in way over his head, and obviously realized at the moment of truth that this was going to hurt. You know, he still had that bullet in him, and who knew what he thought would happen. The fight itself was pretty short. Ali was awesome. He absolutely destroyed him."

HOWARD COSELL: "The greatest Ali ever was as a fighter was in Houston against Cleveland Williams. That night, he was the most devastating fighter who ever lived. He dominated from the opening bell, knocked Williams down four times, and pummeled him until Williams was spitting blood. It was incredible that he could hand out a beating like that, and not once get touched himself. Ali had always been faster than his opponents, but now he was maturing and was bigger too. He was bold and young and strong and skilled, just coming into his prime as a fighter. That handsome child; all those years. It doesn't seem possible, but when I think about it, it's true—Ali is as old now as I was then."

The Williams fight removed any lingering doubts about Ali's abilities in the ring. He was so breathtakingly dominant that even his detractors were forced to admit his skill. His bouts had become performances rather than contests. He was so good, it seemed he might never lose.

LARRY MERCHANT: "Ali rode the crest of a new wave of athletes—competitors who were both big and fast. In basketball, slow lumbering centers and forwards were going the way of prehistoric mammals. In football, Jim Brown had just finished setting new standards for performance. Ali had a combination of size and speed that had never been seen in a fighter before, along with incredible will and courage. He also brought a new style to boxing. Babe Ruth upset and excited people by swinging for the fences and not being afraid to strike out. Jack Dempsey changed fisticuffs from a kind of constipated science where fighters fought in a tense defensive style to a wild sensual assault. Ali revolutionized boxing the way black basketball players have changed basketball today. He changed what happened in the ring, and elevated it to a level that was previously unknown."

Twelve weeks after the Williams fight, Ali returned to the Astrodome to fight Ernie Terrell. This was the bout that had been canceled in Chicago a year before. And while Ali was heavily favored, Terrell was considered the most dangerous opponent the champion had faced since Sonny Liston. The challenger was at the peak of his career and undefeated over the previous five years. During that time, he'd won fifteen fights, including victories over Cleveland Williams, Zora Folley, Bob Foster, Eddie Machen, George Chuvalo, and Doug Jones. His reach was three inches longer than Ali's, and he fought with a clutching grabbing style, which led Ali to label him "the octopus," but which some observers thought might give the champion trouble.

Ali began the prefight publicity in poetic fashion. "At the sound of the bell, Terrell will catch hell," he told reporters at a New York press conference.[24] But before long, the promotion turned ugly. Terrell, like Floyd Patterson, insisted on calling the champion "Clay." Moreover, he held the World Boxing Association version of the heavyweight crown, which had been taken from Ali after his conversion to the Nation of Islam. That, plus the fact that Ali and Terrell had once been sparring partners, led the champion to brand his opponent an "Uncle Tom" who had sold out for the white man's dollar.

"I had a question for him when we met to sign," Ali announced two days before the fight. "It was only three words—'What's my name?' And Terrell said, 'Cassius Clay,' using my slave name. That made it a personal thing, so I'm gonna whup him until he addresses me by my proper name. I'm gonna give him a whupping and a spanking, and a humiliation. I'll keep on hitting him, and I'll keep talking. Here's what I'll say. 'Don't you fall, Ernie.' Wham! 'What's my name.' Wham! I'll just keep doing that until he calls me Muhammad Ali. I want to torture him. A clean knockout is too good for him."[25]

ERNIE TERRELL: "The way the bad feeling started was, up until the fight, I thought it was just part of the promotion. I thought Ali and I had a relationship as friends. When you're a fighter coming up, you deal with lots of people, and for me Ali was one of them. I was a Golden Gloves champion right ahead of him. I turned pro a little before he did. In 1962, we sparred together in Miami. In fact, for about a week we shared a room. There were two hotels in Miami where blacks stayed. One was the Sir John, and the other was the Carver. The Sir John had a swimming pool, and that was where we were. I remember relaxing at the pool, and Ali coming around to start conversations with me about Islam. I don't think he'd converted yet, but he was into it; that's for sure.

"At the time, I was getting ready to fight Herb Siler, and he was on the same card against Don Warner. Both of us won, and afterward I was getting ready to take a plane home to Chicago. He had this big red Cadillac then, and offered to drive me as far as Louisville. Later on, I thought about that trip a lot, because on the way to Louisville we stopped at an all-black college in Chattanooga. He was popular because he was an Olympic champion, but nothing like what came later. And he tried to talk to some of the students. There was a group of ten or twelve of them, and he was talking about black people being stripped of their identity in the United States; except back then, most people used the word 'Negro.' And the students weren't relating to what he said. Times were different. He was saying, 'If you see a Chinaman, you know he comes from China. If you see a Canadian, you know he comes from Canada. If you see a Frenchman, you know he comes from France.' Then he asked, 'Now, tell me, what country is called "Negro"?' And one of the students looked at him and said, 'I don't know, but I never heard of a country called "white folks" either.' That made him angry. He told me, 'Come on, Ernie; let's get out of here.' And we drove on to Louisville, where I stayed overnight at his parents' house until I could catch a bus to Chicago in the morning.

"So that's how it was between us. And the way the name thing started; I didn't consciously decide to call him 'Clay.' What happened was, when we signed to fight, the promoter told us, 'You'll both have to be in Houston two weeks ahead of time and complete your training there to help the promotion.' And he asked me, 'Is that all right with you, Ernie?' And I said, 'It's all right with me if it's all right with Clay.' I wasn't trying to insult him. He'd been Cassius Clay to me all the time before when I knew him. Then he told me, 'My name's Muhammad Ali.' And I said fine, but by then he was going, 'Why can't you call me Muhammad Ali? You're just an Uncle Tom.' Well, like I said, I didn't mean no harm. But when I saw that calling him 'Clay' bugged him, I kept it going. To me it was just part of building up the promotion."

The bout itself was ugly and brutal. In the early rounds, Terrell suffered a fractured bone under his left eye and swelling of the left retina. Later, he charged that the injuries were caused by deliberate thumbing and aggravated further when Ali rubbed his eye along the upper strand of the ring ropes. Films of the fight are inconclusive regarding the cause of damage to Terrell's eye. However, no one disputed that it was a savage vicious fight. From the eighth round on, Terrell was virtually helpless. And from that point on, Ali taunted him mercilessly. Time and again, he shouted, "What's my name," and followed with a burst of blows to Terrell's eyes. "Uncle Tom! What's my name! Uncle Tom! What's my name!" "By the fourteenth round," wrote Tex Maule, "Terrell could no longer control his tormented body. Instead of reacting normally to a feint, he flinched instinctively with his whole being, and when he ventured to lead with his left, his recovery into a protective crouch was exaggerated and somehow pitiful. It was a wondeful demonstration of boxing skill and a barbarous display of cruelty."[26]

JERRY IZENBERG: " 'What's my name!' It wasn't a question. It was a demand. Ali was determined to make Terrell say it, and the fight was absolutely horrible. If Ali was an evil person, that's the kind of person he would have been all the time. It was a side of him—and let's be honest, it's a side that lives in each one of us with different motivations, different triggers—but somebody really pushed the wrong button that night because it was a side of him so out of character that to this day I find it hard to believe it was him. It wasn't really him, which I guess I shouldn't say—I guess it shows my affection for him—because he did it. Hey, I can't tell you he didn't do it. I saw it. I was there, and it was evil. He was trying to hurt Terrell. And it's funny to say a fighter is trying to hurt another fighter, but if you understand boxing, you know that means something very different from what the uninitiated think it means. Ali went out there to make it painful and embarrassing and humiliating for Ernie Terrell. It was a vicious ugly horrible fight."

ABDUL RAHAMAN: "I worked Ali's corner for that fight. There was me and Angelo and I don't remember who else. And I don't regret what Ali did to Terrell. Ernie knew us, because I had tried to convert him in Miami when he and Ali sparred together. He knew what we stood for, and still he gave comfort to our enemies by calling Ali 'Clay.' Before the fight, I had it in my mind that we were going to make him call Ali by his proper name. I told Ali that. And then during the fight, I reminded him, 'Make him call your name.' You know the beating Terrell took for not answering, but I don't see no need for an apology. The referee had authority to stop the fight. The doctor had authority to stop the fight. Terrell's corner could have stopped it if it was so cruel."

ERNIE TERRELL: "Before the fight, I was confident I could win. Then I got thumbed and everything changed. I thought the thumbing was intentional. I'm not trying to sound like sour grapes. The fight's over, and I have a lot of respect for Muhammad Ali. In the years since then, our association has been good. He even did a boxing exhibition to help me raise money for a fellow in Chicago who was in trouble. But Ali had a plan for everybody he fought. And when the stakes are high, I guess people do certain things. What he did was, he grabbed me around the neck and poked his thumb in my eye around three times. Then he got the top rope and rubbed my head across it. That's the reason I say it was done deliberately. And what happened was, his thumb went up and pushed my eye down to the bone. The bone broke, and the muscles that turn the eye got caught on the bone, and the eye wouldn't turn. It was jammed straight ahead. So the other eye would follow him around, but the hurt eye stayed straight and I had double vision. It wasn't like it was painful. I never thought of asking the referee to stop the fight. It was something I thought would go away, but it never did. The big thing was, I couldn't fight my regular fight because I was seeing two guys and didn't know which one to jab at. So I fought a kind of peek-a-boo style, walking straight toward him till I could see which one he was, and you just couldn't beat him that way. Afterward, I had to go to the hospital to get the muscle released from where it was hooked on the bone. People ask me now, how I feel about that fight. They're interested in Ali's talking to me. But to be honest, I didn't hear him saying, 'What's my name.' I had other things I was worrying about. He might have said it, but I wasn't concentrating on stuff like that. I wasn't listening to him that night. I was busy trying to survive."

Ali vehemently denies Terrell's charge that he employed dirty tactics. "It just never happened," he says. "People saw me fight for twenty years, and I was never a dirty fighter. To stick a thumb in another man's eye, to rub his eye against the ropes; that sort of thing is wrong, and I'd never do it on purpose. I'm not denying I tried to make him say my proper name. I was bad that night where that was concerned. But the thumbing and rubbing never happened, and I'm surprised Ernie would say that."

Still, the problem remained. After the Williams fight, Ali had enjoyed grudging respect from the media. The press might not have liked him much, but it had to admit he was an awfully good fighter. In the aftermath of Ernie Terrell, however, Ali's ring skills were largely forgotten. Gene Ward of the *New York Daily News* called the bout "a disgusting exhibition of calculating cruelty, an open defiance of decency, sportsmanship, and all the tenets of right versus wrong."[27] Arthur Daley branded Ali "a mean and malicious man whose facade continues to crumble as he gets deeper into the Black Muslim movement."[28] Milton Gross opined, "There should be dignity in the world's heavyweight title, but Cassius Clay demeans it. He has turned people's stomachs. One almost yearns for the return of Frankie Carbo and his mobster ilk."[29] And Jimmy Cannon raged, "It was a bad fight, nasty with the evil of religious fanaticism. This wasn't an athletic contest. It was a kind of lynching. This, the Black Muslims claim, is one of their ministers. What kind of clergyman is he? He is against all that ministers pray for in their churches. He agrees with the people who are the enemy of ministers. The Black Muslims demand that Negroes keep their place. They go along with the Klan on segregation. It seemed right that Cassius Clay had a good time beating up another Negro. This was fun, like chasing them with dogs and knocking them down with streams of water. The heavyweight champion is a vicious propagandist for a spiteful mob that works the religious underworld."[30]

In terms of public opinion and influencing the United States government, the Terrell fiasco couldn't have come at a worse time for Ali. Even as he was claiming "conscientious objector" status, the champion had brutalized an opponent beyond all apparent pretense of decency. Two weeks after the fight, Congressman Robert Michel of Illinois rose in the House of Representatives to condemn Ali. "I cannot understand," Michel declared, "how patriotic Americans can promote or pay for pugilistic exhibitions by an individual who has become the symbol of draft evasion. While thousands of our finest young men are fighting and dying in the jungles of Vietnam, this healthy specimen is profiteering from a series of shabby bouts. Apparently Cassius will fight anyone but the Vietcong."[31]

Still, as the days passed, Ali continued to stake his conscientious objector claim. In response to a reporter who asked, "What will you do if your appeals fall through; will you then resist going into the Army?" the champion answered, "The world knows that I am a Muslim. The world knows that I am a sincere follower to death of Elijah Muhammad. We say five times a day, 'My prayers, my sacrifices, my life, and my death are all for Allah.' I repeat, 'My prayers, my sacrifices, my life, and my death are all for Allah.' So this is what I sincerely believe. I've held my faith over the years. I gave up one of the prettiest Negro women in the country. The white businessmen in Louisville, Kentucky, will tell you that I've turned down eight million dollars in movie contracts, recordings, promotions, and advertisements because of my faith. And this was all before the draft started, so I don't see why I should break the rules of my faith now."[32]

Yet the noose was tightening. On March 6, 1967, the National Selective Service Presidential Appeal Board voted unanimously to maintain Ali's 1-A classification. Eight days later, he received a notice ordering him to report on April 11 for induction in Louisville. At the request of Ali's attorneys, the date was changed to April 28 and the site transferred to Houston, Texas. Meanwhile, on March 22, 1967, Ali fought Zora Folley in the first heavyweight championship bout at Madison Square Garden in sixteen years, and knocked Folley out in the seventh round. Afterward, Folley, a respected journeyman fighter, paid tribute to his conqueror, whom he called the greatest fighter of all time:

This guy has a style all his own. It's far ahead of any fighter's today. How could Dempsey, Tunney or any of them keep up? Louis wouldn't have a chance; he was too slow. Marciano couldn't get to him and would never get away from Ali's jab. There's just no way to train yourself for what he does. The moves, the speed, the punches, and the way he changes style every time you think you got him figured. The right hands Ali hit me with just had no business landing, but they did. They came from nowhere. Many times he was in the wrong position but he hit me anyway. I've never seen anyone who could do that. The knockdown punch was so fast that I never saw it. He has lots of snap, and when the punches land they dizzy your head; they fuzz up your mind. He's smart. The trickiest fighter I've seen. He's had twenty-nine fights and acts like he's had a hundred. He could write the book on boxing, and anyone that fights him should be made to read it.[33]

Then came the waiting for April 28, and as the days passed, if anything, Ali became more vocal in his stand. "Why should they ask me," he demanded, "to put on a uniform and go ten thousand miles from home and drop bombs and bullets on brown people in Vietnam while so-called Negro people in Louisville are treated like dogs? If I thought going to war would bring freedom and equality to twenty-two million of my people, they wouldn't have to draft me; I'd join tomorrow. But I either have to obey the laws of the land or the laws of Allah. I have nothing to lose by standing up and following my beliefs. So I'll go to jail. We've been in jail for four hundred years."[34]

Last-minute legal maneuvering was to no avail. Three days before his scheduled induction, Ali spoke again, prophesying what lay in store: "I've left the sports pages. I've gone onto the front pages. I'm being tested by Allah. If I pass this test, I'll come out stronger than ever. I've got no jails, no power, no government, but six hundred million Muslims are giving me strength. Why can't I worship as I want to in America? All I want is justice. Will I have to get that from history?"[35]

JERRY IZENBERG: "Right up until induction day, there were people who thought Ali would go in the Army. And, of course, most people thought he should. I can't tell you what I went through for defending him. All the cancellations of my newspaper column, the smashed car windows, the bomb threats; the thousands of letters from Army war veterans talking about Jews like me and concentration camps. I think I must have been in a different army from those guys when I was in Korea. But the people who judged him basically didn't know him. And that included most members of the press, who at that time—and I hate to say it this way—had intellectual limitations and read their own prejudices into what they saw in him. It worked both ways, of course. There were people who thought Ali was a saint, and obviously he wasn't. And then to others, he was the devil incarnate, which he wasn't either. But one thing I think everybody agrees on now is that the man was immense. Without meaning to, and surely without design, he's become a barometer for thirty years of change in American history. Look at the way the country has changed. Today you'd be hard pressed to find anybody— the guy would have to be a dyed-in-the-wool Nazi—who doesn't feel that Ali's stand on Vietnam was understandable and basically justified.

"But getting back to what I thought would happen; Ali didn't want to go to jail. And even though the Muslims were strongest in the prisons, I don't know how well he would have handled prison. But he was willing to go, that was for sure. I knew he'd see it through to the end, and I knew it, among other reasons, because of a conversation we'd had before the Chuvalo fight in Toronto. It was about ten days before the fight. His draft problems were starting to get serious, and Canada was becoming a refuge for a growing number of young men who were resisting the draft. I was alone with Ali in a dressing room at Sully's Gym, and I said to him, 'What I really want to know is, are you going to go home or stay here after the fight?' And I remember very clearly, he answered, 'Of course I'm going home. The United States is my birth country. People can't chase me out of my birth country. I believe what I believe, and you know what that is. If I have to go to jail, I'll do it, but I'm not leaving my country to live in Canada.' Then I asked him, 'How do you think it will come out?' and he said to me, 'Who knows; look what they done to sweet baby Jesus.' "

On April 28, 1967, at 8:00 A.M.—a half-hour ahead of schedule— Muhammad Ali arrived at the United States Armed Forces Examining and Entrance Station at 701 San Jacinto Street, Houston, Texas. The station processed an average of 440 inductees per month. Of the twenty-six young men called for induction that morning, twenty-five would be soldiers at Fort Polk, Louisiana, by day's end.

During the morning, the potential inductees filled out various forms and underwent physical examinations. At noon, they were given box lunches consisting of a beef sandwich, a ham sandwich, an apple, an orange, and a piece of cake. Ali threw away the ham sandwich and ate the rest. Then, at 1:05 P.M., he and the others were brought to the "ceremony room" to be inducted into the United States armed forces.

Outside the building, twenty demonstrators walked in a circle, carrying placards reading, "Draft beer—not Ali," "We love Ali," and "Ali, stay home." Inside, the potential inductees stood in a straight line as they were addressed by the induction officer:

> You are about to be inducted into the Armed Forces of the United States, in the Army, the Navy, the Air Force, or the Marine Corps, as indicated by the service announced following your name when called. You will take one step forward as your name and service are called, and such step will constitute your induction into the Armed Forces indicated.[36]

Then, one at a time, the names were called. At the sound of "Cassius Marcellus Clay" Ali remained motionless. When it became clear that he would not step forward, Lieutenant Clarence Hartman of the United States Navy touched his arm and asked Ali to accompany him to a room down the hall, which Ali did. There, Hartman advised him that refusal to accept a lawful induction order constituted a felony under the Universal Military Training and Service Act, punishable by up to five years' imprisonment and a five-thousand-dollar fine. Ali responded that he was aware of the consequences. Hartman then advised him that they would return to the ceremony room to repeat the induction order. But again, when Ali's name was called, he refused to step forward. At that point, Hartman asked for a written statement regarding the reason for the refusal, and Ali complied, writing, "I refuse to be inducted into the armed forces of the United States because I claim to be exempt as a minister of the religion of Islam."[37]

In anticipation of the moment, the station's commanding officer had prepared two statements for presentation to the media. The first read, "Ladies and gentlemen; Cassius Clay has just been inducted into the United States Army. Private Clay will leave Houston shortly. He will be transported by commercial bus to the reception center at Fort Polk, Louisiana, for further processing and assignment to a basic training unit. Private Clay has (has not) consented to speak to you."[38]

That statement was never read. Instead, the media was advised, "Ladies and gentlemen; Cassius Clay has just refused to be inducted into the United States Armed Forces. Notification of his refusal is being made to the United States Attorney, the State Director of the Selective Service System, and the local Selective Service Board for whatever action is deemed appropriate. Further questions regarding the status of Mr. Clay should be directed to Selective Service."[39]

Then Ali entered the media room and handed out copies of a four-page statement, thanking numerous individuals and organizations for their support. In part, Ali's statement read, "I am proud of the title 'World Heavyweight Champion,' which I won in the ring in Miami on February 25, 1964. The holder of it should at all times have the courage of his convictions and carry out those convictions, not only in the ring but throughout all phases of his life. It is in light of my own personal convictions that I take my stand in rejecting the call to be inducted into the armed services. I do so with full realization of its implications and possible consequences. I have searched my conscience, and find I cannot be true to my belief in my religion by accepting such a call. My decision is a private and individual one. In taking it I am dependent solely upon Allah as the final judge of these actions brought about by my own conscience. I strongly object to the fact that so many newspapers have given the American public and the world the impression that I have only two alternatives in taking this stand—either I go to jail or go to the Army. There is another alternative, and that alternative is justice. If justice prevails, if my constitutional rights are upheld, I will be forced to go neither to the Army nor jail. In the end, I am confident that justice will come my way, for the truth must eventually prevail."[40]

7

Exile

MUHAMMAD ALI: "I never thought of myself as great when I refused to go into the Army. All I did was stand up for what I believed. There were people who thought the war in Vietnam was right. And those people, if they went to war, acted just as brave as I did. There were people who tried to put me in jail. Some of them were hypocrites, but others did what they thought was proper and I can't condemn them for following their conscience either. People say I made a sacrifice, risking jail and my whole career. But God told Abraham to kill his son and Abraham was willing to do it, so why shouldn't I follow what I believed? Standing up for my religion made me happy; it wasn't a sacrifice. When people got drafted and sent to Vietnam and didn't understand what the killing was about and came home with one leg and couldn't get jobs, that was a sacrifice. But I believed in what I was doing, so no matter what the government did to me, it wasn't a loss.

"Some people thought I was a hero. Some people said that what I did was wrong. But everything I did was according to my conscience. I wasn't trying to be a leader. I just wanted to be free. And I made a stand all people, not just black people, should have thought about making, because it wasn't just black people being drafted. The government had a system where the rich man's son went to college, and the poor man's son went to war. Then, after the rich man's son got out of college, he did other things to keep him out of the Army until he was too old to be drafted. So what I did was for me, but it was the kind of decision everyone has to make. Freedom means being able to follow your religion, but it also means carrying the responsibility to choose between right and wrong. So when the time came for me to make up my mind about going in the Army, I knew people were dying in Vietnam for nothing and I should live by what I thought was right. I wanted America to be America. And now the whole world knows that, so far as my own beliefs are concerned, I did what was right for me."

Nineteen sixty-seven was the year that Muhammad Ali confronted the nation with his principles, and those in power struck back with a vengeance. One hour after Ali refused induction—before he'd been charged with any crime, let alone convicted—the New York State Athletic Commission suspended his boxing license and withdrew recognition of him as champion. Soon, all other jurisdictions in the United States followed suit, and the title Ali had worked for throughout his life was gone.

MARVIN KOHN: "I was press secretary for the New York State Athletic Commission at the time. And I remember very vividly sitting in the commission office with what was tantamount to an open line to the draft induction center in Houston. The chairman of the commission was Eddie Dooley. He'd been a football hero in college, and was a gung-ho rah-rah type, a former congressman from Westchester who'd lost his job in the Republican primary a few years before. Then he'd threatened to run in the general election, which would have split the Republican party. So to avoid that, Nelson Rockefeller, who was governor, named him chairman of the athletic commission.

"Dooley had heard that Muhammad would probably refuse induction. And the mood of the commission, which was the mood in many parts of the country, was if somebody was world heavyweight champion, why couldn't he go in the Army like Joe Louis? There might have been some consideration of the possibility that the courts might eventually uphold Ali's position, but that was secondary to Dooley's thinking. So what the commission did was prepare four options. If Muhammad went into the service, if he stepped forward and crossed the line, then it would issue a statement complimenting him. Or if he took limited conscientious objector service, they'd do something else. To my knowledge, the governor didn't exert any pressure in the matter. It was the three commissioners acting on their own.

"The day Ali refused induction, I was in the commission office with four press releases in front of me. There was a delicatessen downstairs and I'd stocked up on sandwiches, Cokes, and coffee, because I knew I might be in for a long siege, whatever happened. Then word came that he had refused to serve. I went into the chairman's office, and Dooley told me, 'All right, use the release that we're stripping him of his title and refusing to license him to fight further in New York.' That decision had been previously made, contingent on the action Ali took. Then I got on the phone and started calling the media, telling them what we'd done. And every other commission I know of followed our lead, although if we hadn't done it I'm sure most of them would have anyway."

HOWARD COSELL: "It was an outrage; an absolute disgrace. You know the truth about boxing commissions. They're nothing but a bunch of politically appointed hacks. Almost without exception, they're men of such meager talent that the only time you hear anything at all about them is when they're party to a mismatch that results in a fighter being maimed or killed. And what they did to Ali! Why? How could they? There'd been no grand jury impanelment, no arraignment. Due process of law hadn't even begun, yet they took away his livelihood because he failed the test of political and social conformity, and it took him seven years to get his title back. It's disgusting. To this day, I get furious when I think about it. Muhammad Ali was stripped of his title and forbidden to fight by all fifty states, and that piece of scum Don King hasn't been barred by one. What does that tell you about government, boxing, and the past twenty-five years in America? I still wonder how it could have happened in this country."

On May 8, 1967, ten days after refusing induction, Ali was indicted by a federal grand jury in Houston. That same day, he was photographed, fingerprinted, and released on five thousand dollars bail on the condition that he not leave the continental United States. Six years earlier, filling out a Selective Service questionnaire, Ali had misspelled his middle name. Thus, the title of the criminal case against him read "*United States of America* v. *Cassius Marsellus Clay.*" In one of history's ironies, the man who ultimately approved Ali's prosecution was Ramsey Clark—probably the most liberal attorney general the United States has known.

RAMSEY CLARK: "I opposed the war in Vietnam as early as I became aware of it, which was sometime in the mid-1960s. I probably didn't become aware of it as early as I should have because there was a period of about ten years during which I successfully kept television out of the house. In a sense, it was like living in another country, because the country everybody else was living in had television. Still I can remember the Gulf of Tonkin Resolution, and thinking that Wayne Morse and Earnest Gruening [the two senators who voted against the resolution] were heroes, and I remember William Fulbright's limited opposition to the war and thinking it was good but not enough.

"Then, in September 1966, I was named acting attorney general, and the appointment became final in February 1967. I can't say that I had a studied judgment on whether or not the war was legal, but I had grave doubts about it. I mean, if we're going to be a constitutional government, before we get a half million men in a foreign country shooting and killing, we ought to know whether it's constitutional and permissible to do it. Maybe as attorney general, I should have been out there saying, 'This war is against the law.' But I didn't, and part of the reason was I had come into the government in 1961 in the midst of the civil rights struggle. By 1967, it might have looked like things were going well, but the truth is we were very badly embattled. There was quite a bit of conflict between those who wanted to keep expanding in the area of civil rights and those who did not, and we were barely able to hold on. Also, I was opposing the death penalty. We had stopped federal executions in 1963, and 1968 would be the first year in the history of the United States that we didn't have a single execution despite the fact that that was the year Martin Luther King and Bob Kennedy were assassinated. Those struggles were very real and very important to me. There were a lot of people who wanted me to abandon them by resigning over the war in Vietnam, which was clearly the overriding moral issue in our society at the time. But in terms of all the things I believed in and all the causes in which I was involved, that would have let a lot of people down.

"Muhammad's conflict with the draft board was a great concern of mine, although I'd have to say, not as great as the concern I had for the poor young black kids from the ghettos or the rural poor from the South who never had a chance to question whether or not to go to Vietnam and who got brutalized and killed. My own personal view was that a person should have a right to conscientious objector status without professing a specific religious faith, and that one should be able to base it upon what you might call philosophical rather than religious grounds. But that of course was not the law then, nor is it now. I don't recall and doubt very much that I discussed the case with President Johnson. I had a strict policy not to discuss criminal cases with the president. I felt it would have been dangerous in appearance and potentially dangerous in fact to insert politics into a criminal matter, and the White House is a political office. Obviously, Muhammad's indictment involved some hard choices. But the good thing about it was, there was power on both sides to shape and test the issues. I wasn't particularly happy about it, but life is full of turbulence and conflict, and I never try to avoid either. In fact, I guess I seek them out because that's where the chance to make a difference is."

The head of the United States Attorney's Office for the Southern District of Texas at the time of Ali's indictment was Mort Susman, who recalls the early stages of the prosecution.

MORT SUSMAN: "We're talking about Muhammad Ali. Well, let's see. His draft board was originally in Kentucky, and he had it transferred to Houston because he bought a house here. He was heavyweight champion, and I believe the Vietnam War was going on pretty hot and heavy. Ali came down, refused induction into the Army, and was indicted. I was the U.S. attorney, and we had quite a few draft cases in our office. Ali's case was handled like everyone else's. We were sensitive to the fact that his rights should be fully respected, which we tried to do in all cases, and also to the perception of the general public that his rights were being protected. There'd been a lot of talk that the government was prejudiced against him because he was black or because he was a Muslim or because he had ideas that weren't consistent with the general run of ideas at that time. And we wanted everyone to know that, insofar as our office was concerned, that kind of talk just wasn't true. We were doing our job the way we saw it, and we felt the courts would deal with his case in a routine way.

"In retrospect, there's nothing I'd do differently with the case. After the indictment, we had a series of meetings with Ali and his lawyers at the Federal Building in Houston. If I remember right, his lawyers were trying to convince us that we didn't have a winning case. I think they felt they'd lose at trial, but had a good chance to win on appeal. Those discussions had to do with arguments on the law and technicalities of the Selective Service Act. And of course, we were trying to convince them that they didn't have a case, and that it would be in Ali's best interest to go into the armed forces. I assured them that I had a strong indication from the Army that Ali would be in Special Services; that he could continue fighting exhibitions; that he might go to Vietnam, but it would be to entertain the troops, not out in some rice paddy. We were talking about meaningful military service that would have bolstered the morale of our troops and been something Ali could have been proud of as a soldier. Beyond that, there wasn't much middle ground. It was either go in the Army or stand trial. And my belief is, Ali almost took us up on going into the service in a noncombat role. I think he found it personally unpleasant to be dragged through what was going on. As I recall, we had at least one discussion about whether he'd be publicly humiliated if he changed his position and went into the Army. And my own view, although I have nothing to prove it with, is he was very close to changing his mind but some of his advisors wanted to make a martyr out of him. Beyond that, all I can tell you is, he was a very charismatic, fascinating individual. I've never been to a prizefight; I don't watch them on television. I'm not a fight fan, and never will be. I don't see the point to it at all. But Ali was exceptionally friendly and charming. And I remember, when we talked, he was very proud of the fact that he was still handsome; that he didn't have a fighter's ears or scars."

JEREMIAH SHABAZZ: "Nobody put pressure on Ali not to go into the Army. The Messenger might have counseled him regarding what to say and what not to say, but the final decision was all his own. Now you know and I know that once Ali starts going in a direction, sometimes it's like a bulldozer with no driver. He just keeps going and going. But here, Ali had a belief and he stuck to it. He stood up for his religion, not in private among a few people, but to the world. And it was the right decision. Muhammad wasn't a serious student of history and politics. He never studied day-to-day current events like the thousands of white kids who opposed the war. But even though he was unsophisticated in his thinking, he knew it was a senseless, unjust war. And of course, in addition to that, Muslims following the Honorable Elijah Muhammad decided long ago that we weren't going to fight the white man's wars. If he starts them, he can fight them. Why should a slave who isn't going to benefit at all from the outcome take a gun, go fight, and come home to be mistreated, kicked around, abused, and persecuted again? So Muhammad saw it from that perspective as well, and his refusal to go into the Army affected many more lives than just his own. If Ali had consented to be inducted, thousands of young men would have followed him into the Army. But because he refused, thousands more were inspired to oppose military service and stay home."

HERBERT MUHAMMAD: "I know my father didn't want Ali to go in the Army. That war was wrong. But my father wasn't gonna tell Ali what to do. Because you have to realize, Ali was a young man then, and he might have gotten up and told the media, 'Elijah Muhammad told me not to go, so I'm not going.' And that was against the law. You couldn't counsel a young man to refuse the Army. So I told Ali to do what he wanted to do, but I reminded him that my father never went, and that was enough for him."

In the aftermath of Ali's refusal to accept induction, the sporting press again raged:

Milton Gross: "Clay seems to have gone past the borders of faith. He has reached the boundaries of fanaticism."[1]

Gene Ward: "I do not want my three boys to grow into their teens holding the belief that Cassius Clay is any kind of hero. I'll do anything I can to prevent it."[2]

Red Smith: "There are draft-dodgers in every war, and Clay isn't the only slacker in this one."[3]

Then, in early June in Cleveland, a remarkable gathering occurred. At the request of Herbert Muhammad, ten of the most prominent black athletes in the country met with Ali to discuss the possibility of his entering the Army. Three of those in attendance— Jim Brown, Kareem Abdul-Jabbar, and Bill Russell—recall the moment.

JIM BROWN: "Ali had the opportunity to make a deal; to go into the service and not see combat. And Herbert asked me to talk to him about it. I'll tell you the truth. Herbert would not have minded Ali going into the Army, because they were starting to make good money together, and I didn't think Herbert was necessarily wrong. If holding that meeting was a bad act, I wouldn't have done it, but when a man makes a decision of that magnitude he needs friends to help him sort things out. We wanted Ali to understand all the implications of his acts, and make sure he was given a choice. So I called some people into Cleveland. John Wooten, Walter Beach, and Sid Williams, from the Browns; Willie Davis, Curtis McClinton, Bill Russell, Kareem Abdul-Jabbar, Bobby Mitchell, Jim Shorter. We met at my office. They were beautiful guys, and some of them thought Ali should go into the service, but he was adamant. He said simply, 'I'm not going because it's against my religion,' and that was that. No one tried to convince him otherwise. We just wanted to discuss it with him, and I thought he showed tremendous courage."

KAREEM ABDUL-JABBAR: "I remember being very flattered and proud to be invited to the meeting, because these were professional athletes and I was just in college. And I was a hundred percent behind Muhammad's protesting what I thought was an unjust war. Jim Brown took the lead in the discussion, but he kept it as an open forum. He told us that our stature as heroes in the black community could help gather support for Ali. But Ali didn't need our help, because as far as the black community was concerned, he already had everybody's heart. He gave so many people courage to test the system. A lot of us didn't think he could do it, but he did and succeeded every time.

"Several years after that, I converted to Islam. My own decision wasn't influenced by Ali. I knew a lot of people who were in the Nation, and it just didn't appeal to me. I thought that what Malcolm was talking about was a much purer ideal. I never met Malcolm; his autobiography was what turned me around. Still, there's no doubt in my mind that public acceptance of what I did was greater because Muhammad lay the groundwork before me. He was, and is, one of my heroes. To do what he did outside the ring, on top of being a brilliant one-of-a-kind athlete; that's a very hard hat to wear, and he wore it like he was born with it on."

BILL RUSSELL: "I got a call from Jim Brown, who said that Ali was out there by himself and that we should support him in whatever he chose to do. So that was it, really. I didn't go to Cleveland to persuade Muhammad to join or not join the Army. We were just there to help, and I was struck by how confident he was, how totally assured he was that what he was doing was right. I never thought of myself as a great man. I never aspired to be anything like that. I was just a guy trying to get through life. But in Cleveland, and many other times with Ali, I saw a man accepting special responsibilities, someone who conducted himself in a way that the people he came in contact with were better for the experience. Philosophically, Ali was a free man. Besides being probably the greatest boxer ever, he was free. And he was free at a time when historically it was very difficult to be free no matter who you were or what you were. Ali was one of the first truly free people in America."

Shortly after the Cleveland meeting, Russell spoke publicly about Ali's draft status for the first time. "I envy Muhammad Ali," Russell said. "He faces a possible five years in jail and he has been stripped of his heavyweight championship, but I still envy him. He has something I have never been able to attain and something very few people I know possess. He has an absolute and sincere faith. I'm not worried about Muhammad Ali. He is better equipped than anyone I know to withstand the trials in store for him. What I'm worried about is the rest of us."[4]

On June 19, 1967, Ali's trial for refusing induction into the United States armed forces began. The judge was Joe Ingraham, a conservative jurist later elevated to the Fifth Circuit Court of Appeals. Most of the government's case was presented by Carl Walker—a black assistant United States attorney, who later became a state court judge in Houston. The first day at trial was devoted to choosing a jury of six men and six women with two male alternate jurors, all of whom were white. Then, at 9:00 A.M. the following day, the presentation of evidence began. The first three government witnesses were officers assigned to the induction station in Houston, who testified regarding the events of April 28. Then a legal officer from Selective Service headquarters identified Ali's Selective Service file, which was admitted into evidence. In response, the defense called two clerks from Local Board Number 47 in Louisville, who testified regarding the racial makeup of the board. At 5:50 P.M., the case went to the jury. Twenty minutes later, the jurors returned with a verdict of guilty. At that point, Ali told the judge, "I'd appreciate it if the court would give me my sentence now instead of waiting and stalling."[5]

Mort Susman, who was on hand for the proceedings, then stated that the government would have no objection if Ali received less than the maximum sentence allowed by law. "The only record he has is a minor traffic offense," Susman told the court. "He became a Muslim in 1964 after defeating Sonny Liston for the title. This tragedy and the loss of his title can be traced to that." Ali sat silent throughout Susman's remarks until the U.S. attorney stated that he had studied the Muslim order and found it "as much political as it is religious." "If I can say so, sir," Ali interrupted, "my religion is not political in any way."[6] Then Judge Ingraham imposed the maximum sentence allowable—five years' imprisonment and a fine of ten thousand dollars. Later Ingraham would say, "In my courtroom, he was a nice polite well-behaved young man. He said 'yes sir' and 'no sir,' and I gave him the sentence I did because that's what he deserved."

CARL WALKER: "I was the one who actually tried the government's case. Some people thought I was handpicked because I was black, but that wasn't true. I handled all the Selective Service cases in the office at that time. And I was very fond of Ali; I was a fight fan. I guess I got attracted to boxing during the Joe Louis era when I was in school, and I followed it all the way through. I rooted for Ali in all his fights, but as a lawyer, you have to put your personal feelings aside. Ali had to fight guys he liked, and sometimes I had to prosecute guys I liked. That was my job, and he understood that. I never felt any animosity from him at all.

"I would say it became a political case. I think politics got into it more than anything else. Back in those days, I was responsible for prosecuting all of what we called the 'draft evaders,' and this was the only case I know of where the hearing examiner recommended that conscientious objector status be given and it was turned down. As you know, Muhammad had joined the Muslims, who were a very unpopular religious group. In fact, to some people they weren't a religious group at all. They were looked upon like the Black Panthers or something along those lines, and there was a feeling that if Ali were allowed to escape the draft it would encourage other young men to join the Muslims. But under our Constitution, every religion has to be recognized, and I always felt it was a case the government would lose in the end. I knew we'd win at trial. At that time, any jury in the United States would have convicted him. But I also knew that Ali would take it all the way to the United States Supreme Court, and when the Supreme Court reversed his conviction, I wasn't surprised. I thought he should have been granted conscientious objector status all along, but that wasn't a decision anyone in our office could make.

"The trial itself was cut-and-dried. Based on the law, the jury had to find him guilty. The only real issue was whether his 1-A classification had been proper, and that issue had been decided by the Selective Service system and reviewed by the judge. So the only question at trial was whether he'd permitted himself to be inducted, and of course he hadn't. All the jury had to decide was whether or not he'd stepped forward to become a soldier. The only concern we had involved, not the trial, but rumors that there might be some sort of confrontation. We'd gotten word that twenty-five or thirty thousand Muslims might come to town to show moral support for Ali. Nothing violent, because the Muslims were of a nonviolent nature. But in those days, racial tensions in Houston were pretty high. Stokely Carmichael and Rap Brown came around from time to time, and we had a pretty tough police chief then. There'd been one incident out at Texas Southern University, where a couple of buildings got burned down and several people were killed. So we had a meeting with Ali in that regard. Mort Susman took us all, including Ali and his lawyers, to lunch in the Plantation Room at the Houston Club, which was a big deal. And after that meeting, at our request, Ali made a trip to Chicago and asked the Muslims to call the demonstration off. He was wonderful about that. Even with his own problems, he was concerned about someone else getting hurt."

Following Ali's conviction and sentencing, Judge Ingraham ordered that his passport be confiscated. Since Ali was already precluded from fighting in the United States by fiat of local boxing commissions, the court's action terminated his ring career. It also left boxing without a heavyweight champion, and Bob Arum stepped into the void. After shutting down Main Bout, Inc., Arum formed a new corporation, Sports Action, Inc., with Mike Malitz, Jim Brown, and Fred Hofheinz (whose father controlled the Houston Astrodome). Then Sports Action promoted an eight-man elimination tournament in conjunction with the World Boxing Association and ABC Television to determine a new heavyweight champion.

"Let them have the elimination bouts," Ali said when the tournament was announced. "Let the man that wins go to the backwoods of Georgia and Alabama or to Sweden or Africa. Let him stick his head in an elementary school. Let him walk down a back alley at night. Let him stop under a street lamp where some small boys are playing and see what they say. Everybody knows I'm the champion. My ghost will haunt all the arenas. I'll be there, wearing a sheet and whispering, 'Ali-e-e-e! Ali-e-e-e!' "[7]

BOB ARUM: "I wish I could say that I stood squarely with Ali on Vietnam, but I didn't. I thought what he was doing was horrible. You have to understand where I was coming from. I thought the war was good, and if not good, it was America. I considered myself a patriot, and like a lot of people, I was appalled by the position Ali took. I tried to help him. I even spoke to [Democratic fund-raiser]

Arthur Krim about making a deal with Lyndon Johnson that would allow Ali to go into the Army and not wear a uniform. He would have been able to continue fighting professionally. It was a real face-saving deal, but Ali turned it down, and I thought he was crazy. In the end though, it turned out he was right. It's amazing, really. Here he was, not an educated guy and certainly not at all knowledgeable about politics. And to my everlasting surprise, he was right about so many things where he didn't appear to have the background to know what he was talking about."

Meanwhile, Ali's life went on. Having been barred from the ring, he continued to attend Nation of Islam meetings, travel to mosques across the country, and study the teachings of Elijah Muhammad. Then, on August 17, 1967, he married seventeen-year-old Belinda Boyd.

JEREMIAH SHABAZZ: "After Ali and Sonji broke up, Ali was devastated, and he decided he just wanted a woman who was a good Muslim and would be a good wife. Belinda's mother worked as a sort of companion for the Honorable Elijah Muhammad's wife. At that time, there were a lot of Muslim sisters working in Muslim businesses, and Belinda was working at one of our bakeries. And the way I heard the story, Ali went over to the bakery one day. I don't know if he walked in by accident or not; I've heard it both ways. But he saw Belinda, liked what he saw, and started talking to her. Under the Islamic code, they weren't supposed to be talking. But as Elijah Muhammad used to say, you can't keep young people apart. So they found a way to talk, and Belinda was a wonderful young woman; fun-loving, tomboyish, very sincere. She'd been raised in the religion, and observed Muslim customs. She was tall, almost six feet, and that also appealed to Ali. He was like his daddy in that he fancied tall buxom women. And Belinda loved Ali. Muhammad has been married four times, and the wife he has now is the best thing that ever happened to him. But of the first three, Belinda was the best. She was a good wife; she was a good mother. When she and Ali were together, it was like a couple of kids. I remember, right after they got married, Ali gave Belinda a hundred dollars and told my wife to take her to the shopping center in Philadelphia so she could buy something nice for herself. And I'll never forget, Belinda couldn't figure out how to spend the whole hundred dollars. She bought a tie for Muhammad, a couple of blouses for herself. It came to about seventy dollars, and there was thirty dollars change left over. She never did get used to having money. In fact, about the only vice Belinda had was driving fast. She'd get in her car at my house in Philadelphia and swear she'd be home in half an hour, which no one could do. But sure enough, in half an hour, the phone would ring and it was Belinda saying, 'I'm home.' She must have burned up the highway."

BELINDA ALI: "To tell you the truth, we didn't actually meet in the bakery. The press saw me for the first time in the bakery, and we thought the story might help business, but that's not how we really met. I saw Ali for the first time in 1961, when he came to my school—the University of Islam, which was headquarters for the Muslim school structure in Chicago. Sister Christine was our principal. She introduced him to the students at an assembly, and he said he was going to be heavyweight champion of the world before he was twenty-one. I was eleven, I guess. And I got to meet him because I worked on the school newspaper and was first in my class academically. He called me 'the little Indian girl,' because I wore my hair real long in a braid. Then, I met him again at one of Elijah Muhammad's conventions in Chicago. I'd grown real tall by then, and he looked at me and said, 'Is that the little Indian girl I met before? Man, she's grown big.' By then, he was traveling all around the world. I'd read about him and was interested as a fan. I liked the way he said he was going to do something and went out and did it, and I was impressed by his dedication to his art. But being a very religious person, I wasn't impressed by his inner self because he was still a Christian. He hadn't fully converted yet. I'm very devoted to Islam. And for me, it was like, 'Your name is Clay; that means dirt. Why don't you get rid of your slave name?' Around that time, he also gave me his autograph, and I told him, 'Man, you scribble; you can't even write. You ought to go back to school and study how to read and write until you do it better.' That surprised him. He said, 'What's this girl talking to me like that for? This girl speaks her mind.' But I think my talking to him like that impressed him, because later on, after he converted, he called me before one of his fights. I think it was against George Chuvalo in Canada. And he told me, 'You know, sister, a lot of people want me to lose because I'm a Muslim. What do you think?' And I couldn't believe it. I mean, here I was, sixteen years old, and he was twenty-four and champion. But I said, 'Brother, God can't put you in top condition; that's up to you. Do your training, be dedicated, don't take any shortcuts. And if you do everything you can and say your prayers, Allah will help you the rest of the way. With his blessing, you can't lose.' He said, 'Okay, I like those words; I'll whup this guy for you.' And after he won, he called on the phone to tell me he'd done it.

"Then, when I was seventeen, Ali wanted to marry me. I think it was a challenge, because he'd become quite a guy with the women, and people said to him, 'It doesn't matter what you do, you'll never get to Belinda.' He'd tell them, 'Man, you're crazy! All women want me.' But they'd still say, 'No, Belinda is different. She's strict, she's strong, she's moral.' And I think it drove him crazy. If he'd asked me to marry him, I probably would have said no, but it didn't happen that way. He just kept coming around to the house a lot. My parents liked him. And finally, he didn't ask me, he told me. He just said, 'You're gonna be my wife.' I said, 'Right,' and that was it."

AMINAH ALI (formerly Aminah Boyd; the mother of Belinda Ali): "Muhammad was always a nice person. He loved children; he was truly generous. But what touched me most was when they wanted him to go into the service and he refused. I have great respect for anyone, regardless of what they believe, if they stand on conscience and don't let themselves be dissuaded. And that particular war wasn't right. America is a beautiful country, but it was in the wrong place in Vietnam. We were conscientious objectors in our family, but even if sometimes you have to fight, we had no business being in Vietnam. Killing somebody that didn't hurt you, going over there to fight people like that; it was just wrong. So when Muhammad wanted to marry my daughter, I wasn't sure Belinda was ready; she was only seventeen. But when they made their decision, I didn't want to interfere. It was a nice quiet ceremony in Chicago; simple and private. Herbert Muhammad was the best man. And I truly believe Belinda was a good wife to Muhammad."

BELINDA ALI: "He was my first love. He taught me everything I knew, and in the beginning he was beautiful. On the outside, he was always sure of himself, but inside, I could tell there was a little insecurity. Not about his boxing; he was very secure at that. But in other ways, I think he was unsure of himself, and spent a lot of his life searching for who he was.

"Muslim wives stay in the background. The woman can be powerful at home, but in public, that's not the wife's way. So I did the talking in the house, but when we got out in public, I didn't say anything. Sometimes, people would ask Ali, 'Does your wife speak English?' And he'd tell them, 'Yes, but she don't say nothing. There can't be but one big mouth in the family.' I liked it that way. And

God blessed us with four beautiful children. Maryum came first, about ten months after we were married. Then the twins—Rasheeda and Jamillah—were born, and finally, Muhammad Junior. Muhammad absolutely loved the children, but he didn't have the patience to spend full-time with them. He was good for about twenty minutes. 'Oh, this baby is so sweet; she's so cute!' And then it was, 'Please; take 'em.' He was definitely the buying kind of father. 'I want to buy them horses! I want to buy them every toy in the world!' And there was no way he'd ever discipline them. I'd get mad at something they did, and tell them to stay in their room all day; and a few minutes later, he'd go in and say, 'All right, you can come out.' They'd ask for a cookie or candy before dinner, and I'd tell them they had to eat their regular meal first. All they had to do then was look sad, and he'd say, 'Let 'em have it.' But overall, he was a good father, and we were very happy at first. The government had taken away his title, and we thought boxing was gone forever. We didn't have much money, but we said, 'It don't matter; we're gonna make it.' I didn't need money for my clothes. I sewed my own; I was trained that way. We did without, and we worked together. It was good, me and Ali. I was the first one to call him that. Everyone else would always say, 'Muhammad, Muhammad, Muhammad.' And whenever I wanted to get his attention, I'd just shout, 'Ali!' Soon everyone was doing it."

Several months after he was sent into exile, Ali found he could make money appearing on the college lecture tour. Initially, Jeremiah Shabazz arranged for appearances at Temple University and Cheney University for one thousand and five hundred dollars respectively. Then Ali signed with Richard Fulton, Inc., a national speakers bureau that mailed fifty thousand promotional flyers to customers around the country. Soon, Ali was appearing regularly on college campuses, lecturing on his view of life.

MUHAMMAD ALI: "Putting the lectures together was hard work. I had six of them, and first I wrote out all my ideas on paper. Then I wrote them again on note cards, studied them every day, and practiced giving speeches in front of a mirror with Belinda listening. Sometimes I tape recorded it so I could hear myself and learn how to improve what I said. I did that for about three months until I was ready, and the first speeches turned out good. Talking is a whole lot easier than fighting. I must have gone to two hundred colleges, and I enjoyed the speaking. It made me happy."

Ali's lectures were part sermon and part rap, bearing titles like "Friendship" and "The Intoxication of Life." Typically, he would start quietly, telling his audience, "As most of you know, I'm no longer in boxing, so I accept college invitations to come out and meet you." But soon, he'd be shouting, "Can my title be taken away without my being whupped?"

"No!" the audience would thunder.

"One more time?"

"No!"

"Now I'd like to hear this from you, and I want the world to hear. Who's the heavyweight champion of the world?"

"You are."

"One more time. We don't want no excuses. They might say the film was bad or the camera was broke. Who's the champ of the world?"

"You are!"[8]

JULIAN BOND: "I saw him on stage a couple of times when he was going around to college campuses, and he was just great. I make my living giving speeches; I labor over them. And this guy seemed to just stand up and talk. It was fantastic. He'd have a crowd, usually overwhelmingly white; some of them fight fans, many of them not. And Ali would have them in the palm of his hand. Many of the students had ideas about what he ought to say or be, but whatever that might have been, he was just himself. And I have to tell you, I was crazy about him. The more conservative black leadership was troubled by his opposition to the war. The civil rights movement at that time was split. There was one group of people who said, 'Let's not have any opinion about the war because this will alienate us from the powers that be, from President Johnson and successor presidents.' And there was another group that said, 'Listen, this war is wrong. It's killing black people disproportionately; it's draining resources that could be applied to the war on poverty; it's wrong in every respect. It doesn't matter who's president or what kind of access we have to the Oval Office.' So people in the first group were horrified by Ali. They thought he was a dunce manipulated by the Nation of Islam. And those in the second group felt entirely differently about him. I was in the second group, and I thought he was great. Certainly, there were others among the black leadership who took a stand against the war in Vietnam, most notably Martin Luther King with his Vietnam Summer. But most of the people who took an antiwar position tended to be organizational figures, and because

Ali stood on his own, his impact was special. He wasn't pursuing a political agenda; he wasn't bolstered by organizational support. He was simply a guy, not sophisticated, not well-learned, not an expert in foreign policy, but someone who knew right from wrong and was willing to risk his career for it. I look back on that time, and I feel very strongly that Ali is part of every American's heritage. Every American should view him with pride and love."

Time and again on college campuses, Ali sounded themes important to him:

On the war in Vietnam: "I'm expected to go overseas to help free people in South Vietnam, and at the same time my people here are being brutalized and mistreated, and this is really the same thing that's happening over in Vietnam. So I'm going to fight it legally, and if I lose, I'm just going to jail. Whatever the punishment, whatever the persecution is for standing up for my beliefs, even if it means facing machine-gun fire that day, I'll face it before denouncing Elijah Muhammad and the religion of Islam."[9]

On being stripped of his title and denied the right to fight: "The power structure seems to want to starve me out. The punishment, five years in jail, ten-thousand-dollar fine, ain't enough. They want to stop me from working, not only in this country but out of it. Not even a license to fight an exhibition for charity, and that's in this twentieth century. You read about these things in the dictatorship countries, where a man don't go along with this or that and he is completely not allowed to work or to earn a decent living."[10]

On the financial hardship he was enduring: "What do I need money for? I don't spend no money. Don't drink, don't smoke, don't go nowhere, don't go running with women. I take my wife out and we eat ice cream. My wife is such a good cook I never go to a restaurant. I give her twenty dollars for a whole week and it's enough for her. We can eat on three dollars a day. Look out there at that little robin pecking and eating. The Lord feeds the birds and the animals. If the Lord has this power, will the Lord let His servant starve, let a man who is doing His work go hungry? I'm not worried. The Lord will provide."[11]

On integration and segregation: "Why ask me if I believe in segregation. I recognize the fact that you believe in it. What do you mean, you don't believe in it? Oh, man, you're just crazy. Every city I go to, I can find a black neighborhood and a white neighborhood. How many Negroes live out here in this big old neighborhood? I'd like to see peace on earth, and if integrating would bring it, I'd say let's integrate. But let's just not stand still where one man holds another in bondage and deprives him of freedom, justice, and equality, neither giving him freedom or letting him go to his own."[12]

On lack of black pride: "We've been brainwashed. Everything good is supposed to be white. We look at Jesus, and we see a white with blond hair and blue eyes. We look at all the angels; we see white with blond hair and blue eyes. Now, I'm sure there's a heaven in the sky and colored folks die and go to heaven. Where are the colored angels? They must be in the kitchen preparing milk and honey. We look at Miss America, we see white. We look at Miss World, we see white. We look at Miss Universe, we see white. Even Tarzan, the king of the jungle in black Africa, he's white. White Owl Cigars. White Swan soap, White Cloud tissue paper, White Rain hair rinse, White Tornado floor wax. All the good cowboys ride the white horses and wear white hats. Angel food cake is the white cake, but the devils food cake is chocolate. When are we going to wake up as a people and end the lie that white is better than black?"[13]

On intermarriage: "You say maybe in another five thousand years or so, all races are going to be the same color. You say we'll be the color of that dog over there, but I don't want to be that color, and I don't want my children to be that color. No intelligent black man or black woman in his or her right black mind wants white boys and white girls coming to their homes to marry their black sons and daughters to produce little pale half-white green-eyed blond-headed Negroes. And no intelligent white man or white woman in his or her right white mind wants black boys and black girls comin' around their homes to marry their white sons and daughters and in return introducing their grandchildren as little mixed-up kinky-headed half-black niggers. You want your child to look like you."[14]

On the need for a separate black homeland: "We were brought here four hundred years ago for a job. Why don't we get out and build our own nation and quit begging for jobs? We want a country. Why can't I have my own land? Why can't I build me a house? Why can't we be free? We've been down so long we can't even imagine having our own country. You know, we're forty million people. We're the wisest black people on the planet; we learn everything the white man knows. Black people from Africa come here, learn half of what we know, and they go home and run their own country. We'll never be free until we own our own land. We're forty million people, and we don't have two acres that's truly ours."[15]

On hate: "I don't hate nobody and I ain't lynched nobody. We Muslims don't hate the white man. It's like we don't hate a tiger; but we know that a tiger's nature is not compatible with people's nature since tigers love to eat people. So we don't want to live with tigers. It's the same with the white man. The white race attacks black people. They don't ask what's our religion, what's our belief? They just start whupping heads. They don't ask you, are you Catholic, are you a Baptist, are you a Black Muslim, are you a Martin Luther King follower, are you with Whitney Young? They just go whop, whop, whop! So we don't want to live with the white man; that's all."[16]

On money versus principle: "I could make millions if I led my people the wrong way, to something I know is wrong. So now I have to make a decision. Step into a billion dollars and denounce my people or step into poverty and teach them the truth. Damn the money. Damn the heavyweight championship. I will die before I sell out my people for the white man's money. The wealth of America and the friendship of all the people who support the war would be nothing if I'm not content internally and if I'm not in accord with the will of Almighty Allah."[17]

BELINDA ALI: "On the road, talking at colleges; we were together, just him and me, eating in snack shops, thinking about the future. It was wonderful, but every time Ali spoke, there'd be hecklers. He'd be in the middle of a speech, and someone would shout

out, 'Nigger draft-dodger' or something like that. And it upset him. Finally, he told me, 'I ain't gonna do that no more.' And I said to him, 'Brother, all you gotta do is fight fire with fire. Next time, you go up there and someone heckles you like that, put him down.' And sure enough, we were speaking at Syracuse University, and somebody in the audience called him a draft-dodging nigger. And Ali said, 'Ladies and gentlemen, you know, a long time ago when I was a little boy, I used to always throw rocks at this donkey. And my grandma would say, "Cassius, quit throwing rocks at that donkey." I'd ask, "Why, grandma?" And she'd say, "Cause some day that donkey is gonna die and come back and haunt you."' Then Ali stopped and looked out at the audience and told them, 'Ladies and gentlemen, I know now that my grandma was right, because I believe that ass is in here tonight.' It brought down the house. And from that night on, any time there was a heckler, he'd tell that story."

ROBERT LIPSYTE: "The speeches were important, not just for Ali but for everyone who heard them. He was leading people into areas of thought and information that might not otherwise have been accessible to them. And a lot of young people wouldn't have thought this stuff through if it hadn't been a celebrity lightning rod telling it to them. Everywhere he spoke, there was excitement. He'd read his poetry and talk about the Nation of Islam. And a lot of what he said, the kids disagreed with. I remember, we were at a college in San Francisco, and he started complaining about the smell of marijuana in the air. On another campus, where the audience was dotted with black-white couples, he talked against interracial dating. And of course, that's always been Ali's way. He speaks his mind and marches to his own drummer. Liberals who adored him for opposing the war were appalled by his sexist attitude toward women and antigay sentiments. Blacks who applauded his battles against racism cringed every time he mocked Joe Frazier as a gorilla. But for me, the bottom line during his college speaking tour was, Ali was providing a window on a lot of social, political, and religious things that were going on in America; a window into the black world that wouldn't have been available to most of his listeners any other way."

Meanwhile, even though Ali's draft trial was over, the government continued its surveillance pursuant to a July 25, 1967, FBI memorandum, which declared:

Cassius Clay, alias Muhammad Ali, is an admitted active member of the Nation of Islam (NOI), which is a highly secretive organization whose membership is made up entirely of selected Negroes who advocate and believe in the ultimate destruction of the white race and complete control of the civilized world by the Negro cult. The Muslims, as members of this organization are referred to, hold highly secretive meetings which exclude all persons not Negro, which exclude members of the news media, and which generally exclude all non-Muslims. The Muslims promote segregation, and they advocate that their members not serve in the military service of our country. Within their organization, however, they train their members in military tactics, conduct classes in physical conditioning and karate, and utilize the paramilitary training normally used by secret militant type groups. Clay, who purports to be a minister in this organization, has utilized his position as a nationally known figure in the sports world to promote through appearances at various gatherings an ideology completely foreign to the basic American ideals of equality and justice for all, love of God and country.[18]

Each of Ali's public appearances was monitored. A typical surveillance report prepared by the United States Army Intelligence and Security Command read:

At 1555 hours 21 May 1968, Cassius Clay arrived at Lambert Field, St. Louis, Missouri. He proceeded to the Carousel Motel, North Kings Highway, St. Louis, Missouri, to change clothing. At 1900 hours 21 May 1968, he arrived at the Riviera Civic Center (a night club in an all-Negro area), 4460 Delmar Avenue, St. Louis to attend a Black Muslim convention sponsored by the Moslem mosque #28 of St. Louis, Missouri. About 600 persons were in attendance. Clay spoke for about 45 minutes, mostly about himself and about his cause, which is to avoid being placed in a white man's army. He stayed at the Riviera from 1900 hours to 2200 hours. He departed for the Carousel Motel at 2200 hours. Shortly thereafter, he left for Lambert Air Field, and departed for Chicago at 2350 hours, 21 May 1968.[19]

Then, in December of 1968, Ali actually went to jail, sentenced to ten days incarceration in Dade County, Florida, for driving without a valid license. "He got sentenced for being Cassius Clay," Ali's lawyer, Henry Arrington of Miami, told reporters shortly after sentence was passed. "Everyone is caught up in the hate Clay hysteria."[20]

MUHAMMAD ALI: "Jail is a bad place. I was there for about a week until they let us out for Christmas, and it was terrible. You're all locked up; you can't get out. The food is bad, and there's nothing good to do. You look out the window at cars and people, and everyone else seems so free. Little things you take for granted like sleeping good or walking down the street, you can't do them no more. A man's got to be real serious about what he believes to say he'll do that for five years, but I was ready if I had to go."

If a week in jail gave Ali second thoughts about refusing induction, it didn't show in public. Soon after his release, he declared, "If I go to jail, so be it. I'm not scared about going to jail. Somebody's got to do something to knock the fear out of some of these Negroes. Somebody's got to stand up. If I went to jail for robbing a bank or beating somebody up, I'd be going for nothing. But I don't mind going for what I believe in."[21]

Meanwhile, the case of *United States of America* v. *Cassius Marsellus Clay* was wending its way through the courts on a less-than-promising course. On May 6, 1968, the Fifth Circuit Court of Appeals affirmed Ali's conviction. The court acknowledged that blacks were underrepresented on draft boards throughout the country. For example, in Ali's home state of Kentucky, only one of 641 local board members was black; and in twenty-three states, there were no blacks on draft boards at all. Still, the court ruled that even the "systematic exclusion of Negroes from draft boards" would not render their acts null and void.[22] It then held that Ali was not entitled to a ministerial deferment because he was a professional boxer, not a minister, and that the Kentucky Appeal Board's decision that Ali did not meet the standards for conscientious objector status was binding. Thereafter, the government's case was temporarily derailed when it was revealed that, in the course of conducting surveillance of Elijah Muhammad and Martin Luther King, FBI agents had secretly monitored five telephone conversations involving Ali. However, after considering the matter, the court of appeals ruled that the wiretaps had "resulted

ABOVE–Cassius Clay, age twelve.
(Big Fights Inc.)

ABOVE RIGHT–At the Olympic Trials, San
Francisco, 1960. *(Big Fights Inc.)*

RIGHT–On the medal stand at the Rome
Olympics, 1960. From left: Giulio Sar-
audi, Tony Madigan, Clay, Zbigniew Pietrzykowski. *(Big Fights Inc.)*

With Malcolm X in New York, 1963.
(Howard Bingham)

Posing with one million dollars, December 1963.
(Howard Bingham)

Clowning with the Beatles, a week before the first Liston fight, February 1964. *(Wide World Photo)*

Fighting Sonny Liston in Miami Beach, February 1964. *(The Bettmann Archives)*

Spreading the word, New York, 1964. *(Howard Bingham)*

LEFT–With his first wife, Sonji, 1964.
(Howard Bingham)

ABOVE–Herbert and Elijah Muhammad, 1966.
(Howard Bingham)

BELOW–Preaching at a Muslim meeting, New York,
1967. *(Howard Bingham)*

With Lew Alcindor (later Kareem Abdul-Jabbar) at the Cleveland meeting, 1967. *(Howard Bingham)*

With attorneys Quinton Hodges and Hayden Covington, and federal prosecutor Mort Susman, 1967. *(Howard Bingham)*

Sparring with James Earl
Jones, with Burgess Mere-
dith refereeing, on the set of
The Great White Hope,
1970. *(Howard Bingham)*

With his second wife, Be-
linda (pregnant with Mar-
yum), 1967.
(Howard Bingham)

Ali-Frazier I in Madison Square Garden, 1971. *(Howard Bingham)*

in no prejudice and had no bearing on defendant's conviction."*[23]

Ali greeted each court setback with stoicism. "I'm being tested by Allah," he'd said on the day of his conviction. "I'm giving up my title, my wealth, maybe my future. Many great men have been tested for their religious belief. If I pass this test, I'll come out stronger than ever."[25]

But despite his claims to the contrary, Ali was troubled. Boxing had been his way of life and also his sole source of income. The college lecture circuit provided some revenue, but not enough to pay the burgeoning attorneys' fees, which had become his responsibility rather than Phillips, Nizer's once he had stopped fighting. Then another blow came his way: Elijah Muhammad suspended Ali from the Nation of Islam.

JEREMIAH SHABAZZ: "The Honorable Elijah Muhammad did not advocate professional boxing. He regarded it as an unnecessary display of brutality, which usually pitted one black man against another black man for the entertainment of a white audience. And of course, sports, not just violent sports but all sports, are frowned upon in Islam. Sport as a way of keeping your body fit is all right, but sport as a money-making venture is unacceptable. Now despite that, when Ali first joined the Nation, the Messenger let him continue his career. He understood that Ali had been raised as a Christian and that, by the time he joined the faith, he'd been led by circumstances to rely upon boxing for his livelihood. However, once Ali was driven from boxing, the Messenger told him, 'You don't have to go back to the ring. The world knows that America has wronged you. Your cause is worldwide, and you can use your fame to help our proselytizing.' That was fine with Ali. On several occasions, I heard him commit himself to not going back to boxing. And on those same occasions, I heard Elijah Muhammad tell him, 'Brother, don't worry

---

*As a consequence of the wiretaps, Ali was overheard talking with Elijah Muhammad, Martin Luther King, Herbert Muhammad, and John Ali. None of the conversations appeared legally significant, although this could not be proven with certainty since the tapes had already been destroyed. The court based its decision on logs provided by the FBI. For example, Ali's conversation with Martin Luther King had been summarized for FBI files as follows: "MLK spoke to Cassius, they exchanged greetings, MLK wished him well on his recent marriage, C invited MLK to be his guest at his next championship fight, MLK said he would like to attend. C said that he is keeping up with MLK, that MLK is his brother, and he's with him 100% but can't take any chances, and that MLK should take care of himself, that MLK is known worldwide and should watch out for them whities, said that people in Nigeria, Egypt and Ghana asked about MLK."[24]

about how you're going to eat or where you'll live. We'll take care of you.'

"Then, in early 1969, Ali was questioned on a television program about whether or not he'd go back to boxing. And Ali said something to the effect of, 'Yeah, I'd go back if the money was right.' And that comment angered the Messenger, because to him it was like Ali was saying he'd give up his religion for the white man's money. The Messenger sent for Ali, and I went with him to Chicago. I was there when the Messenger told Ali he was taking his name back and suspending him from the faith; that he didn't want to be involved with anyone who was so weak as to go crawling on hands and knees to the white man for a little money."

On April 4, 1969, the Nation of Islam newspaper, *Muhammad Speaks,* carried the following statement over the signature of Elijah Muhammad:

> We tell the world we're not with Muhammad Ali. Muhammad Ali is out of the circle of the brotherhood of the followers of Islam under the leadership and teaching of Elijah Muhammad for one year. He cannot speak to, visit with, or be seen with any Muslim or take part in any Muslim religious activity. Mr. Muhammad Ali plainly acted the fool. Any man or woman who comes to Allah and then puts his hopes and trust in the enemy of Allah for survival is underestimating the power of Allah to help them. Mr. Muhammad Ali has sporting blood. Mr. Muhammad Ali desires to do that which the Holy Qur'an teaches him against. Mr. Muhammad Ali wants a place in this sport world. He loves it. Mr. Muhammad Ali shall not be recognized with us under the holy name Muhammad Ali. We will call him Cassius Clay. We take away the name of Allah from him until he proves himself worthy of that name. This statement is to tell the world that we, the Muslims, are not with Mr. Muhammad Ali, in his desire to work in the sports world for the sake of a "leetle" money. Allah has power over the heavens and the earth. He is sufficient for us.[26]

LANA SHABAZZ: "I was working for the Messenger during that time when we weren't supposed to talk to Ali. I could have lived in the Messenger's house because I was taking care of the Messenger's wife, who was quite sick, and they wanted me there at all hours.

But I never liked to sleep on the job, so I had a room of my own that I went back to every night. Ali was such an outcast then that we weren't even supposed to talk about him. But even in the Messenger's home, his name came up every day. And I knew the Messenger still loved Ali even though he was punishing him.

"I loved the Messenger, but my heart was with Ali. In fact, I used to cook for Ali at my house while he was under suspension. And like I told you; we weren't even supposed to be talking about him or to him or anything. The mosque wasn't far from where I lived. Ali would come for dinner. I'd look out my door, see him coming, and there'd be a hundred people trailing behind. I'd say, 'Ali, why did you bring all these people to my house? You know I'm not even supposed to be talking to you, and here I am cooking for you. You're gonna get me thrown out of the mosque.' But fortunately, the Messenger let it pass. Then, finally, he started to accept Ali again, and Ali came to the Messenger's house for dinner. I was serving, and I told Ali, 'Whenever you're ready, I'm coming back to work for you.' He said, 'Lana, get out of here. You aren't gonna leave the Messenger for me.' But I told him, 'When you come back, I'm coming back,' and that's just what I did."

JEREMIAH SHABAZZ: "What happened eventually was, Herbert went to his father and pleaded Ali's cause. And the Messenger never really sanctioned Ali going back into the ring, but in the end he didn't publicly repudiate him for it, either. He just allowed Ali to go ahead and do what he wanted, because he didn't want to exercise authority that would interfere with Muhammad's livelihood. The Messenger was very understanding that way, and it helped that Muhammad was truly apologetic."

Meanwhile, Ali needed money, and as his exile from boxing dragged on, he embarked upon a series of ventures designed, if nothing else, to pay his bills.

BILL CAYTON: "Jim Jacobs and I have been involved with Ali since the Rome Olympics, when we first recognized him as an extraordinarily talented and engaging personality. Even then, we'd made an all-out effort to acquire film rights to his amateur fights, and that continued throughout his career. But we wanted to do more than that, because we felt that what Ali had done was right. I personally was very much against the war; I thought it was a horrible war. My son went into the Army. He volunteered, left school, and served as an officer in Da Nang because he thought the war was right. It was a reverse of the roles one expected from a father and son at that time. But Jim and I felt the war was wrong, and we told Ali, 'We'd like to do a documentary about you.' The first question he asked was, 'How much will I get paid?' And we said, 'We'll hire you for one week of shooting, and at the end of each day, we'll give you a thousand dollars cash.' He loved it. At the end of the first day, I gave him fifty twenty-dollar bills, and I don't think I'd ever seen him that happy. The film ultimately was titled *A/K/A Cassius Clay*. Ali, Cus D'Amato, and a narrator were on camera; and of course, we interspersed a lot of documentary footage. It was released as a theatrical feature just as Ali's exile from boxing was ending, and did quite well, which was a tribute to Ali's appeal. There's simply never been another athlete with his worldwide appeal and earning potential."

At the same time *A/K/A Cassius Clay* was on the drawing board, Ali entered into a second film venture—this one a "computer" fight against former heavyweight champion Rocky Marciano. Bert Sugar, the publisher of *Boxing Illustrated*, recalls that endeavor.

BERT SUGAR: "It began with an old concept. While Ali was in exile, an advertising executive named Murray Woroner put data on sixteen heavyweight champions into a computer and created a fictitious tournament which was broadcast on radio. And it was ludicrous, which became painfully apparent when Jack Johnson was outpointed by Max Baer in one of the tournament's early fights. Then Ali lost to Jim Jeffries, which was just as silly because Jeffries wouldn't have gotten out of the dressing room against Ali. And when that happened, Chauncey Eskridge, one of Ali's attorneys, filed suit, claiming that not only had the government taken away Ali's title, now Woroner was taking away his good name. But that gave Woroner an idea. Rocky Marciano had won the computer tournament. Both Marciano and Ali were alive. So why not match the two of them in a televised fight to buy Ali off and give him a chance to clear his reputation?

"Marciano had been retired for thirteen years. But he went on a diet, lost fifty pounds, put on the worst-looking toupee I've ever seen, and filmed with Ali for three days. They fought seventy-five one-minute-rounds, with Marciano trying his hardest and Ali playing the whole time. I don't know how many different endings were filmed. You had Ali by a knockout; Marciano by a knockout; decisions, a draw, the fight being stopped on cuts. Then, supposedly Woroner fed everything into a computer, comparing the fighters on a hundred different characteristics, and edited the film for closed-circuit viewing. Ali got ten thousand dollars and a percentage. Marciano got about the same. And no one knew who won until it was shown in the United States, and Marciano knocked Ali out in the thirteenth round. That played well in the United States, but it made people in Europe mad. So a week later, the BBC showed a different version in England with Ali stopping Marciano on cuts. It was silly, really; and also sad, because Marciano died in a plane crash three weeks after the show was filmed and went to his grave not knowing who won."

Soon after the computer bout was filmed, Ali tried his hand at another form of theater; this time on Broadway, where he played the title role in a musical called *Buck White*. At Ali's request, all profanity was removed from the script, and several lines were changed to conform to his religious views. "I feel like a tiger in a cage," he said of performing on stage each night. "People come to see the tiger, but the tiger does better when he's out free to roam around."[27] Still, the drama critics were pleasantly surprised by his performance:

Clive Barnes: "How is Mr. Clay? He emerges as a modest naturally appealing man. He sings with a pleasant slightly impersonal voice, acts without embarrassment, and moves with innate dignity. He does himself proud."[28]

Richard Watts: "Cassius Clay/Muhammad Ali is a handsome charming man, and he turns out to be a most likable actor. His lack of histrionic experience interferes somewhat, but he made up for it by his humor and appealing sincerity."[29]

Walter Kerr: "Mr. Clay does his chores well enough, whispering the evening's prettiest song, 'Black Balloons,' evocatively, and pushing the incantatory rhythms of 'Get Down' hard toward the floorboards, every muscle involved."[30]

Richard Cooke: "It is a strangely dignified and impressive appearance. Muhammad Ali sings distinctly and musically, and is much better at it than many other non-singing leading men who have taken top musical roles."[31]

JAMES EARL JONES: "I met Muhammad Ali for the first time shortly before he was on Broadway. It was backstage after a performance of *The Great White Hope,* in which I played the Jack Johnson character. Ali was still not allowed to fight, and meeting him was exciting, particularly given his response to the play he'd just seen. He said of Johnson, 'That's me. You take out the white woman, and that play is about me.' Then he told me, 'I want to go on stage and say those lines.' He was referring to the scene where the Jack Johnson character is in exile in Europe. He's been reduced to performances of *Uncle Tom's Cabin* to earn a living, and the powers that be keep pursuing him, hoping to get him to agree to a little fight with a prearranged loss. Finally, they talk him into coming back to fight, with the idea of turning the crown over to Jess Willard in Cuba. And the character says, 'Come get me; here I is.'

"We waited until the audience had left. Then Ali went out onto the stage and spoke to an empty theater. 'Here I is! Here I is!' He felt those lines expressed his life, and he spoke them with feeling. And what I wondered at the time was, could he translate that into the craft of acting, which is using somebody else's lines, which is the most difficult thing for any natural performer to do? I never saw him when he played in *Buck White,* because I was working somewhere else myself. I did see him on television much later in *Freedom Road.* And I played Malcolm X in two very short scenes in *The Greatest,* where Ali played himself but was essentially reading someone else's lines. And what I found was, given his own words he was a great performer, but given somebody else's words there was a self-consciousness that he was unable to overcome. So he wasn't a great craftsman in the art of acting, but that by no means takes away from his accomplishments. I'm not and never have been a fan of boxing. I had an unfortunate experience at a fight I went to long ago in Spain. A Nigerian fighter was killed in front of my eyes. But Ali represents America to me; power at its best, power well used, because real power is individual power. And each time we reconsider Ali now, we realize there's more to him and more value than we realized before."

All totaled, Ali spent three-and-a-half years in exile, years during which he was deprived of his title and denied the right to earn a living in the ring. But slowly, a significant change was occurring: America was turning against the war. Ali might not have been an intellectual, but he'd correctly perceived history's bend. The nation was growing weary of ritual body counts from Saigon. It was no longer willing to wait for the promised "light at the end of the tunnel." And just as important, it had become clear to all that, if nothing else, Ali was sincere. At a time when America was being torn apart, when the government was lying to its people, he was speaking the truth as he saw it, if not as it really was.

TED KENNEDY: "My brother Bob followed Muhammad's resistance to the Vietnam War. It was a commitment they shared. And I think Muhammad's actions contributed enormously to the debate about whether the United States should be in Vietnam and galvanized some of his admirers to join protests against the war for the first time. I respect the fact that he never backed down from his beliefs, that he took the consequences of refusing induction, and endured the loss of his title until after his conviction was reversed. He had a worldwide audience, and naturally, anyone with that wide an audience will have an impact when they take a stand. And it's to Muhammad's credit that he still uses his influence to fight for his principles. I have a picture of us together in the reception room of my Senate office alongside a pair of boxing gloves which he inscribed to me. He said he hoped the gloves would help me in the fight to knock out injustice. And certainly, he fought that fight too."

But Ali's reach wasn't confined to black audiences or the New York–Washington axis. He was touching nerves and winning respect throughout middle America as well.

JOE PATERNO (head football coach, Penn State University): "Ali was important. I think every black person who's able to overcome the problems that surround them as he did and serve as a role model is important. Kids today are in desperate need of role models who not only succeed in the sports world, but once they've done that, have the ability of a Jackie Robinson or a Muhammad Ali to change the social attitudes of black and white Americans, and make blacks understand that they don't necessarily have to do what whites want them to do to be respected. And Ali achieved that. I always admired him as an athlete, but I think the stand he took on the draft was what spoke most about him. That he had the courage to jeopardize his career and accept all the implications of his position showed a man of great principle.

"The world was different then. And it's hard for some people now to remember the—'despair' might be too strong a word, but the fear in young people over what was going on. I had a friend, a bright young man I admired greatly, who'd covered our team for the student newspaper here at Penn State. Then he'd become editor of the paper, and gone into the service after college. One day he came back to visit and had a long talk with me about deserting. He wanted to know how I'd react. And I said, 'Well, as far as our personal relationship is concerned, it would have no effect on me.' And he did desert. He went up to Canada, and wrote me every once in a while. And when he did that, and when Ali took his stand, it made me wonder, 'What the devil is going on?' I started thinking about what was happening in Vietnam. Now, if I'd been drafted, I probably would have gone because of my traditions, but that doesn't mean I'd have been right to go. And the truth is, I started to become very sympathetic to people like Ali and that young man. I began to understand that they had very good reasons for what they were doing. I began to see Vietnam as a white man's war in the sense that it was being fought by blacks, but in support of a white colonial mentality. I began to think that the war was very wrong."

JAMES MICHENER: "When Ali refused induction into the Army, as far as I was concerned he got into pretty rough seas. I'm a Quaker and would have been excused from World War II had I chosen to take the exemption, but I didn't do that. I volunteered against my own interests to go to the Pacific, because I saw Hitler and Tojo as terrible tyrants and knew they had to be grappled with. In my Quaker group at that time, men my age divided fifty-fifty. Half of them behaved like me and went to war. The other half, just as good, just as educated, just as patriotic, did not. And as you probably know, they served the nation in very useful ways; as guinea pigs in medical experiments, as ambulance drivers, and so on. So emotionally and intellectually, at first I took a harsh view of Ali's behavior. However, as time went by, I began to appreciate that this was a man with the courage of his convictions. And as I got to know him and better understand the splendid role he played in black American life, I excused him. I figured he had problems that I didn't have and he was solving them in ways that I would not have been brave enough to do, and I wound up being an unqualified admirer of his.

"I met him, actually, on several occasions. Once, I remember vividly, was in the lobby of a hotel in New York. He was waiting downstairs, and I wanted to tell him how fascinated I was by his track record as a citizen. We had a long discussion of about an hour-and-a-half. Time is somewhat confused in my memory; I do so many things and shift frequently from one to another. But I think the conversation came late in his career, after his great persona had been established. I doubt very much he knew who I was. To him,

I was just another person. But I have to say, I have enormous admiration for men and women who handle themselves well. I don't know any other phrase than that. And I particularly admire people who make a contribution, who take their knocks and come back. And Ali handled himself damn well under circumstances that were infinitely more difficult than any I ever faced. He performed heroically in and out of the ring. I guess he reminds me of the great mother mastodon I described in *Alaska*. A primitive force, almost irresistible, intelligent, and fighting going forth. He's that kind of person. His greatest contributions came in the 1960s. I don't know what role he'd play if he were young today, because so many of his battles have been fought and won. But a man has to be considered within his time frame; and within his milieu, Ali was brilliant."

JIM BROWN: "If you want to see man at his best, take a look at Ali in his prime. When Ali came back from exile, he became the darling of America, which was good for America because it brought black and white together. But the Ali that America ended up loving was not the Ali I loved most. I didn't feel the same about him anymore, because the warrior I loved was gone. In a way, he became part of the establishment. And I suppose, in a sense, there's nothing wrong with that, because if you can come to a point where you make all people feel good, maybe that's greater than being a fighter for black people, but I didn't like it.

"Ali, before he came back, was a true warrior. It was unbelievable, the courage he had. He wasn't just a championship athlete. He was a champion who fought for his people. He was above sports; he was part of history. The man used his athletic ability as a platform to project himself right up there with world leaders, taking chances that absolutely no one else took, going after things that very few people have the courage to go after. Ali was involved in the Vietnam War. Ali was involved in the struggle for racial equality. The Boston Celtics weren't involved in the 1960s. The Montreal Canadiens, the Green Bay Packers, the New York Yankees; they weren't involved in that. From the standpoint of his ability to perform and his ability to be involved with the world, Ali was the most important sports figure in history. To do what he did, to achieve the pinnacle of his profession, to fight for freedom for black people, to perform while being ostracized and still be a champion; Jackie Robinson died from that, and Ali was able to prevail.

"Take a look at black superstars today—Michael Jackson, Richard Pryor, Eddie Murphy—and look at them hiding behind the bushes with all the power they have. Watch them twist their mouths and make money and pretend, yet do virtually nothing but pay tokenism to black freedom. If Ali was Michael Jackson or Richard Pryor or Eddie Murphy, he'd risk everything for black people. These guys today are babies. Ali was a man. And Ali never wanted to rise above other people. The most common person in the world—black, white, whatever color—was always good enough for him. Sometimes, when we were together, he'd say, 'Come on, Jim. Let's walk through the ghetto and talk to people.' And we'd go into the ghetto; into barber shops, into stores, on the streets, and just talk to people. He was never above the people. His greatest attribute was, no matter how famous he was, he loved every person he saw."

The world was lucky. After three years in exile, Ali would return. And when he did, he would reach for heights no one had ever dreamed of before.

8

Joe

During his exile, Muhammad Ali grew larger than sports. He became a political and social force. Only two other fighters—Jack Johnson and Joe Louis—achieved similar stature. And while Ali was better known worldwide than Johnson or Louis, comparisons among them will endure forever. Three sports historians offer their perspective.

ARTHUR ASHE (author of *A Hard Road to Glory: A History of the African-American Athlete*): "I still think that, within the United States, Jack Johnson had a larger impact than Ali because he was first. Nothing that Frederick Douglass did, nothing that Booker T. Washington did, nothing that any African-American had done up until that time had the same impact as Jack Johnson's fight against Jim Jeffries on July 4, 1910. It was the most awaited event in the history of African-Americans to that date. Lincoln's Emancipation Proclamation was not done with widespread prior knowledge. Half of black America didn't know it was going to be issued, and even after it was, many African-Americans didn't know about it for weeks. But virtually every black American knew that Johnson versus Jeffries was going to take place. They knew it; they knew what was at stake; and they also knew they could get the results almost immediately because of the advent of the telegraph. And when Johnson won, there were racial reprisals all across the United States. I think the official tally was nineteen blacks killed and many more injured. But it completely destroyed one of the crucial pillars of white supremacy—the idea that the white man was superior in body and mind to all the darker peoples of the earth. That was just not true as far as anybody was concerned anymore, because now a black man held the title symbolic of the world's most physically powerful human being. It had an emotional immediacy that went beyond what Ali, Joe Louis, or even Jackie Robinson did, because it was the first time anything like that had ever happened. And black Americans were so far down in the pecking order, it provided a tremendous spiritual and emotional uplift.

"Then Joe Louis came on the scene. Joe was the first black American of any discipline or endeavor to enjoy the overwhelming good feeling, sometimes bordering on idolatry, of all Americans regardless of color. And he was schooled for this, particularly as a result of Jack Johnson's legacy. Joe Louis was told in no uncertain terms, 'You're not supposed to gloat after your victories. Never take a photograph alone with a white woman.' He was taught how to use a knife and fork correctly. He was given elocution and very simple English lessons. He was told to be kind and generous to people. And Joe Louis came along at just the right time for black and white Americans. The courts were still against us; the civil rights movement was just getting into gear. Because of the Depression, all America needed a shot in the arm spiritually, and then we needed someone to disprove Hitler's doctrine of Aryan supremacy. So what Joe Louis did in the ring was particularly important, but no more important than Ali.

"Muhammad was a great athlete. And if you're that good, if you're that superior at whatever you do, it's going to be important; people will listen to what you have to say. But Ali went beyond that. He combined his athletic talent with social action during the 1960s, when both he and the black social revolution reached their peak. And the result was that he became an icon for literally millions of black Americans.

"I never went along with the pronouncements of Elijah Muhammad that the white man was the devil and that blacks should be striving for separate development—a sort of American apartheid. That never made sense to me. It was a racist ideology, and I didn't like it. But I understood the motivation, and I can tell you that Ali was very definitely, sometimes unspokenly, admired by a lot of the leaders of the civil rights movement, who were sometimes even a little bit jealous of the following he had and the efficacy of what he did. There were a lot of people in the movement who wished that they held that sort of sway over African-Americans, but did not. I know, I personally can remember feeling all tingly when he refused to step forward at that induction center in Houston in 1967. I was sure the establishment would get Ali. I understood what he was sacrificing. In fact, I was convinced he was going to jail. I knew what they'd done to Jack Johnson in 1913, when they took the Mann Act, which had been erected to stop organized crime from transporting prostitutes across state lines, and gave it a personal application for his consorting with white women. Johnson was railroaded, and that's what I thought would happen to Ali. It wasn't just that he'd lose his title. I thought the man was going to jail. And I really believe that, if Ali hadn't done what he did, Harry Edwards wouldn't have gotten a fraction of the support he got in 1968 to boycott the Mexico City Olympics. Tommie Smith and John Carlos wouldn't have raised their fists. Ali had to be on their minds. He was largely responsible for it becoming an expected part of a black athlete's responsibility to get involved. He had more at stake than any of us. He put it all on the line for what he believed in. And if Ali did that, who were the rest of us lesser athletic mortals not to do it? I know, he certainly influenced me later in 1967 when the Davis Cup draw came up, and lo and behold, the United States was supposed to meet South Africa in the third round. I was thinking to myself, 'Oh, my God, just three months ago, Muhammad Ali refused to cross the line. And here I am, the only black player in tennis, the main member of the Davis Cup Team.' There's no question that Ali's sacrifice was in the forefront of my mind. Fortunately, the president of the United States Tennis Association then was Robert Kelleher, a wonderful man. We talked about it, and he suggested that the most effective way to deal with the situation would be for us to give up the home-court advantage. We had what was known as choice of ground. And Kelleher told me, 'Let's do something that's never been done in the history of Davis Cup competition. Let's offer to play South Africa in South Africa, and go down there and beat the crap out of them. Let South Africa see a black person win in their own backyard. It never came to that; South Africa lost to West Germany in the second round. But Ali was very much in my thoughts. And I can tell you, the 1960s would have been very different for black Americans without him."

RANDY ROBERTS (author of *Papa Jack: Jack Johnson and the Era of White Hopes*): "In truth, Ali and Jack Johnson were radically different figures. Their primary similarity was in how whites perceived them. Both were seen as threats to the racial status quo, which in Johnson's time was strict segregation, and in Ali's time a liberal consensus of integration. But otherwise, they were very different.

"Johnson was treated as a black menace, but he didn't have a highly developed racial consciousness. Most of his friends were white, and he made a number of derogatory comments about blacks, particularly black women, throughout his life. His lifestyle was hedonistic. If you took Jack Johnson out of the early 1900sand put him in the 1960s, I don't think you'd have much of a problem. You'd have a black man who might be disliked for cavorting with white women, but that wouldn't be unprecedented. Certainly, his integrationist position would have fit with the consensus of the times.

"By contrast, Ali's message was racial pride, the glorification of being black, a refusal to accept that black was anything less than best; a demand for dignity and full entitlements for all black people. He came alone at a time when the civil rights movement was maturing, and whites were willing to be pushed a bit. The possibility existed that you could offend white people and still prevail. Ali seized upon that moment and pushed to the limit. But if you put Ali in the early 1900s with his doctrines of separatism and black economic development; sure, whites would have disliked him, blacks would have liked him. But he wouldn't have caused as much of a stir as Jack Johnson."

JEFFREY SAMMONS (author of *Beyond The Ring: The Role of Boxing in American Society*): "You can't talk about Ali and Jack Johnson without talking about Joe Louis as a bridge, so let me start with Louis. I grew up listening to my parents and grandparents talk about Joe Louis. He was a hero in our home. The simple fact that he was fighting, let alone beating, white opponents was a victory. Joe Louis was a very important man, but he basically supported the system. Whites wanted to be reassured that he wasn't a threat, and Joe did that very well. Publicly, at least, he was an unassuming, God-fearing, mother-loving, Bible-reading guy. His vices were supposed to be overeating—too much chicken and ice cream—and voracious gum chewing. Of course we know today that Joe Louis was also quite a ladies' man and prone to drinking. And later in life, the drug problems surfaced. But the press gave us a model citizen who was white in every way except his color. In fact, Louis went against a lot of black people when he entered a segregated Army and was used by the government to boost black troop morale. There were critics who questioned his donating purses to the Army and Navy relief funds, especially the Navy, which was notoriously discriminatory; yet he felt it was the proper thing to do. What I'm saying is, history put a social importance on Louis, largely because of the era in which he lived and because he fought Max Schmeling in a fight that had become a test of Hitler's philosophy of Aryan supremacy. But Ali created his own history. He refused to drift with the tide, and created his own importance by joining the Nation of Islam, changing his name, opposing the war, and standing up proudly and at times defiantly for being black. He attacked injustice on black terms, and was always willing to face the consequences.

"As for Jack Johnson, clearly his effect on black Americans was enormous. Johnson, more than anyone else, shattered the myth of white physical superiority. For many blacks, he stood for the proposition that their place was greater than the white man had told them it was. I see Johnson as a forerunner of the new Negro who emerged during the period around World War I, when blacks became more assertive, less subservient, and more willing to defend themselves. But Johnson never saw himself as a racial symbol. He felt he was as good as anybody else and that he shouldn't be denied anything that anybody else had, but he didn't think in racial terms. He never became part of a movement or aligned himself in a crusade with others the way Ali chose to do."

In 1970, Muhammad Ali began a crusade to accomplish what Jack Johnson and Joe Louis were never able to do—recapture the heavyweight championship of the world. To many, it seemed a Quixotic quest. Stripped of his title, forbidden to fight, it was questionable whether he'd ever be allowed in the ring again, let alone permitted to fight for the title. Indeed, after the 1969 Ali-Marciano computer bout, Marciano had advised Belinda Ali, "Tell Muhammad to stop torturing himself. Get him out of boxing, and forget the whole thing." The advice had been well-intentioned and, to some, sound. But Belinda had answered, "He won it in the ring, and he'll lose it in the ring. That's the only way he'll give up his crown."

Meanwhile, during Ali's absence, professional boxing had gone on. Jimmy Ellis emerged from the World Boxing Association tournament with its version of the heavyweight crown. Almost simultaneously, Joe Frazier knocked out Buster Mathis to capture the

"New York World Heavyweight Championship." Frazier successfully defended his title four times, then knocked out Ellis in the
fifth round of a unification bout on February 16, 1970. Three weeks
later, *Ring* Magazine, which had steadfastly continued to recognize
Ali as champion, withdrew that recognition and acknowledged Frazier. Ali took the development in stride. "I can't blame Joe Frazier
for accepting the title under the conditions he did," he told on
interviewer. "Joe's got four or five children to feed. He's worked in
a meat-packing house all his life and deserves a break. He would
have fought me if he had the chance. Joe Frazier wasn't just given
the title. He had to fight for it, and he had to fight the best around
except for me, so I can't take nothing from him. He had to keep on
living, regardless of what happened to me."[1]

HAROLD CONRAD: "I spent three years of my life trying to get
Ali back into boxing. Twenty-two states I went to, trying to get him
a license to fight. We almost had it in California. The chairman of
the State Athletic Commission polled the members and said they
had the votes to give Ali a license. Then the governor, a fellow
named Ronald Reagan, said, 'That draft dodger will never fight in
my state, period.' And he didn't; they denied him the license. In
Nevada the governor was with us, but the mob killed the fight
through its political connections. In Montana, I was told by appropriate authorities that they'd sanction a fight if we put a hundred
thousand dollars in the right pockets. Once, I had a deal for Ali to
fight in a bull ring in Tijuana. I went to the Justice Department and
said, 'Look, you can send twenty marshals with him. They'll go across
the border, and be back in six hours.' And the Justice Department
said no. They wouldn't give him back his passport. It sucked. That's
all I can say. It really sucked. The man was heavyweight champion
of the world, and they wouldn't let him in a ring to fight. Politics
did it. Politics was what kept him out of boxing, and in the end, it
was politics that got him back. And it happened in the strangest
place—Atlanta, Georgia.

"There was no state athletic commission in Georgia, so as far as
boxing was concerned, the mayor of Atlanta, a Jewish fellow named
Sam Massell, could do just about anything he wanted. And there
was a black state senator named Leroy Johnson, who was important
in this too. What happened was, Bob Arum started trying to put
together Ali against Jerry Quarry. Then Bob Kassel, who worked
with Arum, called Harry Pett, a bigshot Atlanta businessman, who
went to Johnson. Johnson cut himself a piece of the promotion, and

after that visited Massell to call in his chits. Massell wasn't happy about the whole thing, but Johnson controlled a pile of black votes, so the mayor went along with it. That's what it took. People think now that the Supreme Court decision is what allowed Ali to fight, but that didn't come until later. All it took was politics and money and three years of trying until we worked things out in Georgia."

Even with Massell's cooperation, there was no guarantee that Ali would be allowed to fight. Georgia Governor Lester Maddox opposed any Ali bout, as did several members of Congress who called upon the Justice Department to find a way to thwart any comeback attempt. Thus, to test the waters, in early September Ali sparred with three opponents in an eight-round exhibition at Morehouse College in Atlanta. The event went off without a hitch. Then, seven weeks later, on October 26, 1970, he fought again; this time against Jerry Quarry.

Before his death, fight historian Jim Jacobs began the task of putting Ali's comeback in perspective.

JIM JACOBS: "In some ways, the exile from boxing was the best thing that could have happened to Ali. In terms of his skills, it was a tragedy. But in terms of his earning power, it was a plus. If you go back to the Folley fight, which was Ali's last before he refused induction, he was no longer commanding large amounts of money. A substantial portion of the American public disliked him, and worse, they were getting tired of hearing what he was about. But the exile turned all that around. It showed people that Ali was sincere. It made him an underdog. He became a symbol to people who had never been interested in boxing before. And traveling around the country, speaking on college campuses, Ali was able to bring his message to tens of thousands of young men and women. In a way, it was like a presidential candidate sowing the seeds for future caucuses and primaries. And of course, people began to feel that, whether or not they liked Ali, he shouldn't have been forced out of boxing for his beliefs. It was so obvious, really. He couldn't be beaten in the ring, so larger forces were brought in to do the job. People understood that if Ali had been the tenth-ranked heavyweight instead of champion, he never would have been denied a license to fight. So the bottom line was, when he came back, even though he'd been out of boxing for three-and-a-half years and even though he was only fighting a ten-round nontitle fight, Ali was paid more money for that fight than he'd ever been paid before."

As the fight approached, battle lines were drawn with no middle ground. Among other things, Quarry would be the first white American Ali had faced in the ring since George Logan, eight-and-a-half years before. But in contrast to the massive prefight buildup, the fighters themselves were largely subdued. "It's been so long," Ali told Mark Kram of *Sports Illustrated*. "I never thought I'd be back in my old life again."[2] Like everyone else, perhaps more so, Ali was aware of the stakes involved:

> I'm not just fighting one man. I'm fighting a lot of men, showing them here is one man they couldn't conquer. Lose this one, and it won't be just a loss to me. So many millions of faces throughout the world will be sad; they'll feel like they've been defeated. If I lose, for the rest of my life I won't be free. I'll have to listen to all this about how I was a bum, how I joined the wrong movement and they mislead me. I'm fighting for my freedom.[3]

Bert Sugar: "The first thing that comes to mind whenever I think of Ali is standing in the lobby of the Regency-Hyatt Hotel in Atlanta the night he fought Jerry Quarry. It was right before the crowd left for the arena. Ali was going up to his room in one of those glass elevators, ascending. And everybody in the throng below, his legion of followers who'd been waiting forever for his resurrection, looked up, cheering as he ascended. It was spine-tingling; it transcended anything I'd ever seen. I've had occasion to be with Ali, to broadcast with Ali, to write about him, laugh with him, cry with him. And that's still the moment I remember most, even after all these years.

"The fight itself was in an old arena with pillars that looked like something out of *Gone with the Wind*. It held maybe five thousand people, and the black community was there in force. It was probably the greatest collection of black power and black money ever assembled up until that time. Bill Cosby, Sidney Poitier, Jesse Jackson, Julian Bond, Ralph Abernathy, Andrew Young, Coretta Scott King, Whitney Young. People were arriving in hand-painted limousines, dressed in colors and styles I'd never seen. They'd come for the return of Muhammad Ali, and there was no doubt in their mind that he'd win. They weren't boxing fans; they were idolators."

Julian Bond: "My wife—she's now my ex-wife—went to a cocktail party with me two days before the fight. She was wearing a light blue dress. We chatted with Ali and told him we had seats in the third row. And he asked her, 'Are you wearing that dress to the fight?' She said, 'I don't know.' And he told her, 'Well, don't wear that dress, because I'm gonna spill blood all over you.'

"Then we went to the fight, and it was like nothing I'd ever seen. The black elite of America was there. It was a coronation; the King regaining his throne. I remember meeting Mary Wilson of the Supremes and saying, 'My God, Mary Wilson and I are at the same event.' The whole audience was composed of stars; legitimate stars, underworld stars. You had all these people from the fast lane who were there, and the style of dress was fantastic. Men in ankle-length fur coats; women wearing smiles and pearls and not much else. Then the fight started. I was sitting behind this youngish blond woman, and all through it I kept hitting her on the back in my excitement. And she was so excited, she never turned around and told me to stop. All I can remember saying was, 'Stick him, Ali! Stick him! Stick him!' It was more than a fight, and it was an important moment for Atlanta, because that night, Atlanta came into its own as the black political capital of America."

JERRY QUARRY: "I wasn't fighting for any race, creed, or color that night. I was fighting for money. The first home I had was a tent in Utah with my mom and dad and five of us children. Then we moved to California to work the fields. My heritage was *The Grapes of Wrath*. Before I got into boxing, I was making ninety-nine dollars a week changing tires on Greyhound buses. And to fight Ali, I got the biggest purse of my career, three hundred thousand dollars. After paying off everything—taxes, sparring partners, my trainer and manager—I netted ninety-five thousand. And if I'd won, which I thought I would, I'd have made millions.

"None of the noise surrounding the fight bothered me. The more attention and publicity, the better. The crowd was 90 percent black and all for Ali, but that didn't motivate me or intimidate me either. When I got in the ring, it was just another fight, even though the opponent was Ali. I wasn't fighting against a symbol. I was fighting a fighter, who had two arms and two legs just like me."

Quarry was first to enter the ring that night. Then came Ali, buffeted by near-hysterical screams from the crowd. As always, Angelo Dundee was his chief second, but Abdul Rahaman had been replaced in the corner by Wali Muhammad, and Bundini Brown had been allowed to return. Unlike the idolators, Ali's corner expected a hard bout. Quarry was a world-class fighter, strong and durable, with the ability to take a punch. He was also the first fighter Ali had faced as a professional who was younger than Ali. Looking out over the overwhelmingly black crowd, Bundini pointed to a handful of whites and labeled them "white buttons on a black silk shirt." Then he whispered to Ali, and would later shout throughout the fight, "Jack Johnson's ghost is watching you."

Tony Perez was the referee for the fight.

TONY PEREZ: "The first round was all Ali. He came out throwing punches, and landed almost everything he threw. Then, in round two, he started to slow down. Quarry hit him with a big hook to the body, and I said to myself, 'Oh, my God, maybe we have an upset.' By round three, Ali wasn't on his toes. Quarry was getting confident, and then—it came out of nowhere—Ali opened a huge cut over Quarry's eye. I'd never seen a cut like that before. You could see the bone. After the round, there was no doctor in Quarry's corner. There'd been a big controversy that day about whether the doctors would be black or white. Finally, they'd got four doctors, two of each color, but none of them were in the corner where they were supposed to be. That meant, I had to make a decision alone. Quarry wanted to keep going. He was screaming, 'No, no, Tony. Don't stop the fight!' But I had to stop it. His own trainer wanted me to. The eye was so bad, I just couldn't let it go on."

After the fight, Quarry accepted his defeat with grace. "It wasn't a butt," he said of the blow that caused the gash. "And I don't want anybody saying it was. It was a right hand."[4] Meanwhile, Ali's supporters were jubilant, but there was cause for concern. In defeating Quarry, Ali had been physically strong, perhaps stronger than in the past. But he'd also been slower, and that was an ominous portent.

FERDIE PACHECO: "When Ali was young, he was the best physical specimen I've ever seen. If God sat down to create the perfect body for a fighter, anatomically and physiologically, he'd have created Ali. Every test I did on him was a fine line of perfect. His blood pressure and pulse were like a snake. His speed and reflexes were unbelievable. His face was rounded, with no sharp edges to cut; and on top of that, his skin was tough. Blacks don't cut as easily as whites, and that's not a racist statement. Black fighters are just as smart and work just as hard as white fighters, but they also cut less, possibly because of the melanin in their skin, and Ali cut less than most blacks. In a tough situation, he could summon up enormous spurts of energy and recover quickly without the exhaustion that most fighters feel afterward. That enabled him to have those all-out rounds, where both guys fought the whole three minutes, and in the next round the opponent was out of gas while Ali still had it. His peripheral vision was incredible. And when you hit him, except for one time when he got whacked on the jaw in a freak occurrence after dental surgery, no matter how hard you hit him, nothing broke. In fact, up until the layoff, it was like a fraudulent representation to say I was Ali's doctor. I was his doctor in case something happened, but it never did. Being Ali's doctor meant I showed up at the gym once in a while and came to the fights.

"After the layoff though, it was a different story. For starters, there was a problem with his hands. A lot of boxers have bursitis in their hands. It's an inflammation of the knuckle joints, sometimes with calcium deposits. And with Ali, his hands were okay in the gym. Sparring, he used big gloves and didn't really bear down on his punches. But the actual fights were something else, particularly after the layoff when his hands got soft. After the layoff, when Ali fought he was in pain. So what we did, starting in 1970, was numb his hands. It was my idea; I was the doctor. The shots were administered in the dressing room right before each fight. One of Ali's peculiarities is that he's scared of needles, so first I'd numb him with ethyl chloride. Then I'd put one cc of cortisone and Xylacene in each hand; two shots to each hand, in the webs between the three middle fingers. The shots didn't violate any rules that I know of, although we didn't brag about them. And to be honest, if I hadn't shot Ali's hands, the outcome of his fights probably would have been the same. During a fight, when someone like Joe Frazier is trying to knock your head off, the adrenaline is pumping and you don't worry about your hands hurting. But the shots gave Ali comfort and the security of knowing he could punch without pain.

"His legs were a more serious problem. The legs are the first thing to go in a fighter. And when Ali went into exile, he lost his legs. Before that, he'd been so fast, you couldn't catch him, so he'd never taken punches. He'd been knocked down by Henry Cooper and Sonny Banks, but the truth is, he rarely got hit and he'd never taken a beating. In the gym, he'd work with Luis Rodriguez, who was the fastest welterweight in the world; and Luis, who was like lightning, couldn't hit him. Then, after the layoff, Ali came back and his legs weren't like they'd been before. And when he lost his legs, he lost his first line of defense. That was when he discovered something which was both very good and very bad. Very bad in that it led to the physical damage he suffered later in his career; very good in that it eventually got him back the championship. He discovered he could take a punch. Before the layoff, he wouldn't let anyone touch him in the gym. Workouts consisted of Ali running and saying, 'This guy can't hit me.' But afterward, when he couldn't run that way anymore, he found he could dog it. He could run for a round and rest for a round, and let himself get punched against the ropes while he thought he was toughening his body. I can't tell you how many times I told him and anyone else who'd listen, 'Hey, when you let guys pound on your kidneys, it's not doing the kidneys any good.' The kidneys aren't the best fighter in the world. They're just kidneys, and after a while, they'll fall apart. And of course, taking shots to the head didn't do much good either. But Ali was stubborn; he did what he wanted to do. And when he started to get lazy in the gym, which came before his greatest glories, that was the beginning of the end."

Six weeks after defeating Jerry Quarry, Ali fought again; this time in New York against Oscar Bonavena. That he was allowed to fight at all in New York resulted not from a change of heart by state authorities but from a court order. Acting on Ali's behalf, the NAACP Legal Defense Fund had filed suit in federal court, claiming that the denial of a ring license violated Ali's Fourteenth Amendment rights as a discriminatory departure from the state's practice of granting licenses to accused and convicted felons. To bolster their case, Ali's lawyers presented the court with a list of ninety people who had been licensed to box in New York despite having been convicted of crimes including murder, rape, armed robbery, child molestation, and military desertion. After weighing the evidence, District Judge Walter Mansfield branded the commission's action "astonishing" and "on its face, an intentional, arbitrary and unreasonable discrimination against [the] plaintiff, not the even-handed administration of law which the Fourteenth Amendment requires."[5] Three days later, Edwin Dooley announced that the State Athletic Commission would bow reluctantly to the judge's order.

HARRY MARKSON: "The fight against Bonavena was in Madison Square Garden on December 7, which was the anniversary of Pearl Harbor. That caused some protests from veterans' organizations, but everything went smoothly despite that problem. I guess what I remember most about it wasn't the fight but what happened after the weigh-in. Ali was walking across the floor of the arena. There was a basketball team practicing, and one of the players threw a ball to him. He was standing at midcourt, but he took a shot anyway, just flung the ball toward the basket. And I'll be damned if it didn't go in; swish. Everyone just stared in awe, but that was the kind of luck I figured followed Ali."

Then came the fight, and Ali looked mediocre. Gil Clancy, who trained Bonavena, recalls the encounter.

GIL CLANCY: "Nobody could handle Bonavena; he wouldn't pay attention to any trainer. He came to my gym and asked if I'd work with him for the fight, and I told him, 'Let me think about it; come back tomorrow.' So the next day, he came back, and I said to him, 'I'll train you for the fight, but this is how the deal is gonna work. I want half my money before we go to training camp, and the other half at the weigh-in, or I won't go in the ring with you.' That way, I figured he had to behave himself. Bonavena agreed, and I'll tell you, I never had one bit of trouble with him at training camp or anyplace else. He did his job every day. He worked hard; no nonsense. By fight time, he was ready and I figured he had a real shot. He was awkward; you never knew where his punches were coming from. All I did with him was, I said, 'Oscar, Ali is used to fighting with everybody chasing him. Then he gets into a rhythm and uses angles. What I want you to do is, back yourself into a corner so Ali has to punch at you. And when he punches, he has to be attached to his arm. So if he hits you or misses the punch, either way, he's at the other end of that arm. Every time you back yourself into a corner, as soon as he starts to punch, I want you to lash out and punch as hard as you can, because you're gonna hit something.' And that's what Bonavena did. He didn't chase Ali. He had Ali come to him, and then he tried to nail him. In the ninth round, he had Ali hurt. And by the fifteenth round, believe me, they were like two Golden Gloves kids. Whoever hit who, the other guy was gonna go. That's when Ali threw a left hook. His head was looking up toward the balcony somewhere, and he threw a left hook, hit Bonavena on the chin, and knocked him down. Bonavena got up, but he was out on his feet. Ali knocked him down three times that round, but after the first knockdown it was academic."

The Bonavena fight was another example of Ali's "magic." He'd looked awful; it was a boring fight. But the knockout had been so dramatic that afterward people forgot the first fourteen rounds. All they remembered was how he'd won. But as with Quarry, the danger signs were there.

FERDIE PACHECO: "Ali absorbed more punishment against Bonavena than he had in any previous fight; much more than people realized. Now, try to put things in perspective. He hadn't fought in three-and-a-half years. In October, he fought Quarry, which was a relatively easy fight. Then, in December with no rest in between, he fought Bonavena and took something of a beating even though he was clearly the better fighter. Now he'd fought himself back into shape, and what he should have done was let his body recuperate. Train for four or five months, and then go after Joe Frazier. Given time to get himself right, he would have beaten Frazier in their first fight. But the money was there; the opportunity was there. And Ali didn't know if he'd be fighting or in jail in four or five months, so he went after it."

Ali-Frazier.

Championship fights between great fighters are few and far between. Championship fights between great fighters with compelling action are an even rarer phenomenon. Over the course of four-and-a-half years, Muhammad Ali and Joe Frazier fought three fights that have become the pyramids of boxing. It was as great a rivalry as any sport has ever seen.

Frazier, one of thirteen children, grew up on a farm in Beaufort, South Carolina. He dropped out of school after ninth grade, and was as nonpolitical as a man could be. As a youngster, Frazier had fought for pride. Years later, at the end of his career, he would say, "Being a fighter made a good living for me, but that wasn't all. I loved fighting. I loved the competitiveness. I loved to stand on my own. People don't understand what an honor it is to be a fighter. It gave me the opportunity to prove myself, to stand up and say, "I'm the best; I matter; I am.""[6]

Four years after Cassius Clay won a gold medal in Rome, Frazier represented the United States at the Tokyo Olympic Games. Despite competing with a broken thumb, he prevailed in the heavyweight division and returned home to launch his professional career. Undefeated over six years, he'd scored twenty-three knockouts in twenty-six fights. Commenting on Ali and Frazier, Jimmy Cannon wrote, "Their race and trade are all they appear to have in common."[7]

After Ali was forced into exile, Frazier, on paper, became heavyweight champion of the world. Dave Wolf, who had been sports editor for *Life* magazine and later managed Ray Mancini and Donny Lalonde, was in Frazier's camp for several years.

DAVE WOLF: "Joe wanted Ali back in the ring, because Joe wanted universal acceptance as the best in the world, and he knew that wouldn't happen until he'd beaten Ali. But apart from his own self-interest, Joe was good to Ali during his years in exile. On several occasions, he engaged in prearranged publicity confrontations, which allowed Ali to remain in the limelight and earn money on the lecture tour. Joe even went to several Muslim services at Ali's suggestion, and had he been a less committed Baptist, who knows what might have happened? I do know that Joe got curious enough about the Muslims to do some homework on his own. I remember talking with him one night. He told me he'd learned that in many instances the guys on the street who sold *Muhammad Speaks*, the Islamic newspaper, were charged for the papers they didn't sell. And Joe found that upsetting, because his perception of these guys was that they didn't have much money and were out there working for the church, and if they didn't do well enough, they were fined. In his religion, he couldn't think of a parallel, and he just didn't think that was right. But Joe was genuinely religious, and initially he had a lot of respect for Ali's religious beliefs. When Ali got nasty before their first fight, when he started calling Joe an Uncle Tom, Joe's feelings changed. But up until then, Joe had no problem with Ali's decision not to serve in the Army. I remember his telling me, 'If Baptists weren't allowed to fight, I wouldn't fight either.' "

The first Ali-Frazier fight was the biggest event in the history of boxing. Due to changes in the industry, there have been subsequent fights that generated more revenue, but no fight ever transcended boxing as Ali-Frazier I did throughout the world. The bout was held in Madison Square Garden, but the driving force behind it came from California.

Jerry Perenchio was president of a Beverly Hills talent agency. Jack Kent Cooke was the multimillionaire owner of the Los Angeles Lakers and Los Angeles Kings. Until December 30, 1970, when the fight was signed, neither man had met Ali or Frazier. Yet they agreed to pay each fighter the previously unheard-of sum of $2,500,000.

TEDDY BRENNER: "Madison Square Garden wanted the fight, so Harry Markson and I went to Philadelphia to meet with Yank Durham, Frazier's manager. Yank told us that, whatever Joe was offered, he had an understanding with Herbert Muhammad that Ali would get the same. Then we talked to Herbert, and he said the same thing, so we made an offer of $1,250,000 against 35 percent of the gross to each fighter. That was a tremendous amount of money, unheard of at that time. Yank said it sounded good, but he wanted us to talk to his lawyer first. And the lawyer told us our offer was fine, but someone had just came into his office and offered two-and-a-half million dollars flat for each fighter. Even then, we were still in the running because we were offering a percentage of the gross. But Yank kept saying, 'Two-and-a-half million dollars! Ain't nobody ever got that.' And there was a funny scene; Yank, Joe, Harry Markson, and I sat down in Joe's gym with yellow pads and pens. I said, 'With our offer, you're going to get one million two hundred and fifty thousand dollars against 35 percent. Write that down.' And Joe started to write it down; Yank started to write it down; but they couldn't put the commas in the right spots. They kept writing the numbers, but the commas kept going in the wrong places. And finally Yank said, 'A million two hundred and fifty thousand dollars is a lot of money, but it's not as much as two million five hundred thousand, and that's what we're gonna take.'

"Fortunately, we weren't shut out of the promotion completely. We'd been instrumental in bringing Frazier along. He'd fought George Chuvalo and Oscar Bonavena in the Garden; won the title against Buster Mathis in the Garden; and defended it with us against Manuel Ramos, Jerry Quarry, and Jimmy Ellis. And Joe was loyal. Cooke wanted the fight at the Los Angeles Forum, which was his building, but Joe insisted that it be with us. Ali didn't care where it was; he just wanted to fight Frazier and get paid. But Joe said it had to be in the Garden. Perenchio and Cooke didn't like it, but they had no choice. So the way it worked was, Cooke put up $4,500,000, and the Garden put up five hundred thousand, which covered what the fighters were paid. For our share of the money, we got the live gate. Cooke and Perenchio got everything else, the most important part of which was the closed-circuit take. The Garden was scaled for $1,250,000, which was twice the old indoor record. We charged a one-hundred-fifty-dollar top, which was more than anyone had charged for ringside tickets before. And we sold out. A full month before the fight, there wasn't a single ticket left. Harry Markson was kicking himself for not charging two-fifty. But the people who really came up short were Ali and Frazier. To this day, I don't know what the fight grossed. But I've heard through the grapevine that, if they'd taken our offer of $1,250,000 each against 35 percent of the gross, each fighter would have made nine million dollars."

Once the fighters were signed the promotional buildup began, although it was a fight that largely promoted itself. For the first time in history, two undefeated heavyweights, each with a legitimate claim to the title, were meeting for the championship of the world. It was a classic matchup between boxer and slugger. Ali, at six-foot-three, had the speed of a welterweight and moved like Baryshnikov. Frazier, four inches shorter, was always moving forward in the ring, a brawler with the inexorable style of a threshing machine. It was Ali the draft-dodger versus patriotic Joe; Ali the loudmouth versus softspoken Joe; Ali the Muslim against honest Bible-reading Baptist Joe. "The thrust of this fight on the public consciousness is incalculable," wrote Mark Kram. "It has been a ceaseless whir that seems to have grown in decibel with each new soliloquy by Ali, with each dead calm promise by Frazier. It has cut deep into the thicket of our national attitudes, and is a conversational imperative everywhere from the gabble of big-city salons and factory lunch breaks to the ghetto."[8] But most of all, the fight was becoming black versus white, despite the fact that Joe Frazier was, if anything, more typical of black America than Ali.

DAVE WOLF: "From my perspective, which was that of someone close to Joe, I have some very negative recollections of Ali. Ali was a very bright, calculating guy. Very little that happened to him or around him in those days happened by accident. And what he did was turn Joe into a black white hope. He isolated Joe from the black community. He constantly equated Joe with the white power structure, and said things like, 'Any black person who's for Joe Frazier is a traitor.' He did it on purpose; he did it far beyond what was necessary to sell tickets. It was cruel; that's all.

"I remember watching TV one night with Joe. Ali was on some talk show, and he was saying, 'The only people rooting for Joe Frazier are white people in suits, Alabama sheriffs, and members of the Ku Klux Klan. I'm fighting for the little man in the ghetto.' And Joe was sitting there smashing his fist into the palm of his hand, saying, 'What does he know about the ghetto?' Joe perceived Ali as having come from a middle-class background, and whatever Ali's background was, it was middle-class compared to Joe's. Ali wasn't a street guy in any sense. Joe, as a result of his background and upbringing, was almost the stereotypic black person Ali claimed to be fighting for. Yet Ali demeaned Joe at every turn. He had almost a master plan of painting Joe into a corner. And after a while, it went so far beyond what was necessary, that it started to remind me of how Ali had been with Ernie Terrell. I wasn't particularly bothered by the beating he put on Terrell. In my mind, that went with the territory, but there was something more than that. It was a desire to strip away Terrell's manhood; to humiliate a guy who it had been clearly established rounds before was not competitive, so that it stopped being an athletic contest and began to be a form of public torture. And at the time, I thought I understood Ali's motivation, especially since I was not uncomfortable with Ali's politics. He'd been subjected to a lot and was letting it out on Ernie. But then I saw the same thing happen again with Joe. Just as Ernie hadn't been able to fight back physically, he wasn't competitive anymore; well, verbally and politically, Joe wasn't competitive with Ali. I'm sure Ali has forgotten most of what he did. There were moments when Joe was so hurt and which he remembers so vividly even now. And Ali probably doesn't remember them at all, but they were there. Look at the perception many people have today that Joe is stupid because he's not facile with the language and because his particular brand of South Carolina English isn't easily understood by people who don't come from that part of South Carolina. Joe is not dumb. But Ali stuck that saddle on him, and Joe will have to wear it forever. Joe is not, and never was, an Uncle Tom, whatever that means, but Ali branded him with that label too. And at the same time Ali was going around saying Joe was a tool of the white man, the significant people around Joe were a lot blacker than the significant people around Ali. Joe didn't miss for a moment the fact that Ali was dealing with an awful lot of whites.

"So those were some of Joe's frustrations, and they were compounded by the inability of many people to see what Ali was doing. Writers who should have known better bought the whole package of Joe as a dumb tool of the white establishment. A lot of it was calculated to give Ali a psychological edge in the fight, but Ali took it beyond that. There was a bullying sadistic quality to what he did, like pulling the wings off a dying insect. I think later on he mellowed. His own success and the changing social and political climate of the country combined to make him a different person. But the damage he did to Joe was never undone. And to my mind, it's very understandable that Joe, of all the people from that era, is the one who still harbors real ill will toward Ali."

In the war of words before the fight, clearly, it was Ali who prevailed:

• Frazier's no real champion. Nobody wants to talk to him. Oh, maybe Nixon will call him if he wins. I don't think he'll call me. But ninety-eight percent of my people are for me. They identify with my struggle. Same one they're fighting every day in the streets. If I win, they win. I lose, they lose. Anybody black who thinks Frazier can whup me is an Uncle Tom. Everybody who's black wants me to keep winning.[9]

• Joe Frazier is too ugly to be champ. Joe Frazier is too dumb to be champ. The heavyweight champion should be smart and pretty like me. Ask Joe Frazier, "How do you feel, champ?" He'll say, "Duh, duh, duh."[10]

• When he gets to ringside, Frazier will feel like a traitor. When he sees those women and those men aren't for him, he'll feel a little weakening. He'll have a funny feeling, an angry feeling. Fear is going to come over him, and he'll lose a little pride. The pressure will be so great that he'll feel it. It's going to be real frightful when he goes to his corner. He don't have nothing. But me, I have a cause.[11]

• Joe Frazier says he wants to be a singer; says he's got himself a band. Joe Frazier can't sing. Oh man, Joe; I can beat you singing too. Yes, I can. I can hold a note better than you and everything. I heard you on television singing, and everybody's talking about how you can't sing. I'm just gonna tell you the truth; everybody's talkin' about how you can't sing a lick; everybody.[12]

JOHN CONDON: "Ali-Frazier was the seventeenth world heavyweight championship fight to be held in Madison Square Garden, and unquestionably, it was the greatest event I've worked on in my life. I don't think I'll ever be involved with anything that gives me so much of a thrill and so much satisfaction. From the moment the fight was made until the very end, it was an electrifying experience. Patti Dreifuss and I were the Garden's publicists for the fight. I worked sixteen hours a day for two months and lost fifteen pounds. We didn't need gimmicks to sell it. There were more requests for press passes than for any event ever held in Madison Square Garden. We granted 760 press credentials, and turned down requests for five hundred more. We even had a correspondent from Israel, who told us he'd been having breakfast in Israel and his eighty-year-old mother asked him, 'Who's going to win, Ali or Frazier?' And he'd said to himself, 'My God, if my eighty-year-old mother is asking, we really have to cover this fight.' "

As the fight approached, public interest neared its peak. Contracts were signed to broadcast the bout live to a record thirty-five foreign countries. Several black organizations complained that the high cost of closed-circuit tickets meant much of Ali's constituency wouldn't be able to see the fight. That, in turn, brought a rebuff from Yank Durham, who also rejected suggestions that the fight should have been run by black promoters, with a portion of the proceeds being returned to the black community. "What do I care how much money go here and how much go there," Durham responded. "I got two-and-a-half million dollars each for the fighters, and nobody has ever given me nothing. No white group has ever given me nothing. No black group has ever given me nothing, I worked for everything I got. I worked on the railroad; I worked as a stevedore; I worked with fighters. I had a number of fighters who were fighting, and this is the only fighter I ever had that be successful, so I ain't giving up nothing. I think it's right for the fighter I'm working with, and that's all I'm interested in."[13]

In the last days before the fight, tensions continued to increase while the war of words ran apace:

Muhammad Ali: "Joe Frazier will be nothing but a target for me. I'll be dancing, moving, and hitting, and Frazier won't be able to find me. Joe Frazier will be reaching and straining with those hooks, and they'll get longer and longer, and he'll get more frustrated. Things are going to happen so fast, Joe Frazier won't be able to keep up with them. Pop, pop, pop! Plus I'm talking to him: Come on, Joe; come on, Joe; You're no champ. Come on, you lost three rounds already. Like my poem says:

> "Joe's gonna come out smokin'
> But I ain't gonna be jokin'
> I'll be pickin and pokin'
> Pouring water on his smokin'
> This might shock and amaze ya
> But I'm gonna destroy Joe
>   Frazier."[14]

Joe Frazier: "He can keep that pretty head; I don't want it.
What I'm going to do is try to pull them kidneys out. I'm
going to be at where he lives in the body. Then I'll be in
business. Watch him. He'll be snatching his pretty head
back, and I'll let him keep it until about the third or fourth
round, and then there'll be a difference. He won't be able to
take it to the body no more. Now he'll start snatching his
sore body away, and the head will be leaning in. That's
when I'll take his head, but then it won't be pretty, or
maybe he just won't care."[15]

Muhammad Ali: "Fifteen referees. I want fifteen referees to
be at this fight because there ain't no one man who can keep
up with the pace I'm gonna set except me. There's not a
man alive who can whup me. I'm too fast. I'm too smart. I'm
too pretty. I should be a postage stamp. That's the only way
I'll ever get licked.[16]

Joe Frazier: "I've been there before. You know what I
mean? I've been to the bad wars. As a fighter, I'm together.
I've proved I can take a punch, but what about Clay? Is he
together, or will he come apart when I put something on
him, when I start smoking where he lives. It ain't gonna be
easy. He's good and I'm good, and that's what fights should
be about."[17]

Muhammad Ali: "On that night, they'll be waiting everywhere; England, France, Italy. Egypt and Israel will declare
a forty-five minute truce. Saudi Arabia, Iraq, Iran; even Red
China and Formosa. Not since time began has there been a
night like this. People will be singing and dancing in the
aisles, and when it's all over, Muhammad Ali will take his
rightful place as champion of the world. And after I whup
this man, I don't want my title taken no more until someone
whups me in the ring."[18]

BRYANT GUMBEL: "Muhammad Ali; March 8, 1971. It was a
tumultuous night. I was living in a third-floor walkup on Forty-sixth
street between Eighth and Ninth avenues in New York. The only
way I could find out about the fight was to listen to the radio, and
after every round they gave a quick capsule. I nearly died that night.
I just died, because this was a night when it all came together, and
if Ali lost, it was as though everything I believed in was wrong.

"It's very difficult to imagine being young and black in the sixties and not gravitating toward Ali. He was a guy who was supremely talented, enormously confident, and seemed to think less of what the establishment thought of him than about the image he saw when he looked in the mirror. And to people who were young and black and interested in tweaking the establishment, and in some cases shoving it up the tail of the establishment, you had to identify with somebody like that. The fact that he won all the time made it even better. You know, for all our passions of those years, we didn't have a lot of victories. More often than not, we were on the losing side, so the fact that Ali won was gravy. He was a heroic figure, plain and simple. In every sense of the word, he was heroic. Would he have been something special if he wasn't black and had the same beliefs? Perhaps. But the fact that he was black made him all the more special. The fact that he was athletic made him all the more special. The fact that he was good-looking made him increasingly special. It's obvious that one of the great attractions of Ali was that he was extremely good-looking. And you'd have to be an idiot to believe that many of the racial problems in this country are not rooted deep down psychologically in the white man's fear that black men are sexually superior to them. The fact that this black hero was good-looking to boot spoke, among other things, directly to the core of racial problems in this country.

"So what you had that night were two undefeated heavyweight champions. One was the very symbol of black pride, parading black feelings about black heritage, speaking out against racial injustice. And the other guy was more like your parents were. He just kind of went along. He did his job. He wasn't a proponent of the old order, but he didn't fight it, either. One guy was dead set against the war. The other didn't seem to have much of a feeling about it, but was supported by those who backed the war. And it's hard to explain to people today how dominant Vietnam was in a young guy's life then. It tailored everything from the girl you went out with who you might not see again to your grades in school, because what the hell did you need a degree for if you weren't going to get a chance to use it? It was bizarre, and Ali fit so nicely into that. After a while, how you stood on Ali became a political and generational litmus test. He was somebody we could hold on to; somebody who was ours. And fairly or unfairly, because he was opposing Ali, Joe Frazier became the symbol of our oppressors.

"It's hard to believe twenty years have passed since then. And when Ali lost, I was devastated. It was awful. I felt as though everything I stood for had been beaten down and trampled. We'd all seen those pictures of the people with flags and hard hats beating up kids with long hair who were protesting, and this was our chance to get even in the ring. Our side was right, and their side thought it was right, and whoever won the fight, damn it, that's how it was. There was no middle ground. And it was a terrible, terrible night. I'll never forget it as long as I live. The feeling was like when Richard Nixon won that crushing reelection mandate a year later. That was devastating, but Ali losing was much more personal because we had the feeling on the political side that our opinion was in the minority anyway. We knew we'd lose going in. It was almost like being part of the chosen ones; we were the only ones who had the whole world figured out, but the majority didn't see it our way. We knew the numbers weren't in our favor. That's why Ali-Frazier was so important, because that was the test. That was the level playing field; one against one, man against man. Now we'll show you bastards."

On March 8, 1971, the eyes of the world were focused on a small square of illuminated canvas, which had become one of the great stages of modern times. Never before had so many people watched and waited for a single event. Tension, anticipation, and excitement were everywhere. The atmosphere was more like that of a closely contested presidential contest than a bout for the heavyweight championship of the world.

After the morning weigh-in, Garden officials decided it would be too complicated to send Ali back and forth between the arena and his hotel, so he spent the rest of the day on site. At one point, a Romanian diplomat handed him a native doll. Ali accepted the gift and listened patiently to a lengthly presentation speech until he realized he was being photographed. Then he gave the doll to Bundini with the words, "Take this; it don't look good for the heavyweight champion of the world to be playing with dolls."[19] At 2:30 P.M., he ate his last prefight meal. After that, he took a nap. Meanwhile, downstairs, another scene was unfolding.

JOHN CONDON: "I was in the main arena, in the press area, working on something. And Angelo came in, walked over to the ring, which had already been set up, and started loosening the ropes. I said, 'Angelo, what the hell are you doing? We'll have to tighten them all up again.' And he said, 'No, John, leave 'em alone.' I said, 'For Chrissake, I can't do that.' So in fairness to Frazier, I went to Yank Durham and said, 'Yank, you better check the ropes; okay?' Yank asked, 'Why, what's the matter with the ropes?' I said, 'Just check the ropes. I'm not telling you there's anything wrong with them. Just check the ropes yourself.' And when Yank checked the ropes, he went out of his mind. He started yelling, 'They're too loose! No one tightened the goddamn ropes.' And I said, 'Well, get someone to tighten them.' So Yank never knew that Angelo did it, and Angelo never knew—I guess until he reads this—that I told Yank.

"But all day long, the Garden was a madhouse. During the afternoon, I heard one of our security guys saying Frank Sinatra was going to be in the first row of the press section. And I stopped him. I said, 'Joe'—that was the guy's name—I said, 'There's no way in the world Sinatra's going to be in the working press tonight. Get it out of your mind now and please don't embarrass him or me, because if he's there, he's going to get thrown out.' That night, the Garden was like a combination of New Year's Eve and the Easter Parade. I don't think there's ever been a night like it. It was one of those evenings where everybody who was anybody was there. I look in the press section, and I see Sinatra. I'd just finished kicking out Dustin Hoffman and Diana Ross. So I went over to throw Sinatra out, and just as I got to him, one of the ABC cameramen said, 'He's got one of our tickets.' That meant I couldn't do anything about it. As long as he had a press ticket, he was entitled to be there. And it ended up that Sinatra photographed the fight for *Life* magazine, and took what turned out to be *Life*'s cover photo.

BUTCH LEWIS: "After Joe won the Olympics, a group of businessmen organized Cloverlay, Inc., to back his career. My father was one of them, and pretty soon I was traveling with Joe as his road buddy. That's how I got my start in boxing. And the night he fought Ali, their first fight, I couldn't stand it. I mean, the tension was just too much. It was more than my being personal with Joe, and more than my being involved with things leading up to the fight. There was something more to it than the fight. I remember, I went over to Ali's dressing room with Eddie Futch to watch him have his hands taped. I wanted to put my two cents in. I'm just bad; you know what I mean? Ali was sitting on the rubdown table. He saw me, and he must have figured the closest thing to getting the needle into Joe was getting it into me. So he looked at me and said, 'You take this back to Joe.' Then he gets off the table and starts moving his hands; jabbing, shuffling. 'You take this back to Joe Frazier.' Pop, pop, pop! Throwing punches. Pop, pop, pop! 'You tell Joe this is what I got for him.' And I said to myself, 'Holy shit, this fight is about to happen.' I mean, normally I'd say, 'Yeah, man; screw you. We're gonna mess you up bad.' But my heart was in my ears. I could hear it. I'm sweating, and Ali is jabbing and dancing, saying, 'Take this back to Joe; I'm gonna knock him out.' And I'm not responding. I'm doing nothing, because I'm messed up. I'm just standing there, with my mouth open. Then I go back to Joe's dressing room. Joe is done wrapping his hands, and he's working, standing up, throwing hooks. You know how he does it. He grunts when he throws the hooks. It's not pop, pop. It's uhgh! Uhgh! And the closed-circuit guys are there with their cameras. Joe's trying to move around to warm up. And one of the cameramen, I don't know what the son-of-a-bitch is trying to do, but he's talking at Joe and he's got the camera in Joe's face. And Joe's punching. He's going, 'Uhgh!—Yank—uhgh!—tell these motherfuckers—uhgh!—to get the fuck out of here—uhgh!' And again, I say to myself, 'Oh, shit. This fight is gonna happen. This fight is now.' Yank and Eddie are calm through the whole thing; they're professionals. They're saying, 'Come on, move the people out of here. Take it easy, champ.' But I was a wreck. I'm telling you, if I'd been an older person, I'd have had a heart attack. That's how hyped up I was. Then I go to my seat, and I'm still a wreck. I had a bottle of Crown Royal I'd put under my seat to get a hit to steady me down. And as the fighters enter the ring, Ali's coming down the aisle, and this guy behind me jumps up, kicks the bottle, and breaks it. Then, right after that, a fellow two rows behind me collapses, and they get a stretcher to take him out. And I say to myself, 'Oh, shit. The fight hasn't even started, and already they're carrying people away. I can't stand it. It's too dramatic. I don't know about Joe and Ali, but I'm not gonna make it through the night.' "

The night belonged to Joe Frazier. Ali was a master at psychologically breaking down his opponents. It was part of his fight plan, a weapon as potent as any punch he threw. But Frazier was too pure a fighter to be swayed by words. Like Ali, he had faith in himself. Like Ali, he knew he would win.

In the early rounds, the fight was even, but Ali took more punches than ever before. Too often, when his legs failed, he lay on the ropes, absorbing punishment, conceding points that would be crucial later on. In round eleven, the tide irrevocably turned. Frazier landed a crushing left hook, and Ali, hurt, wobbled backward across the ring. Four more rounds followed, each as brutal as the one before. "In round fifteen," recalls Ferdie Pacheco, "Ali was tired; he was hurt, just trying to get through the last round. And Frazier hit him flush on the jaw with the hardest left hook he'd ever thrown. Ali went down, and it looked like he was out cold. I didn't think he could possibly get up. And not only did he get up; he was up almost as fast as he went down. It was incredible. Not only could he take a punch. That night, he was the most courageous fighter I'd ever seen. He was going to get up if he was dead. If Frazier had killed him, he'd have gotten up."

Eddie Futch was the primary architect of Joe Frazier's strategy. Of Futch's importance, Yank Durham later said, "I might have cut the diamond, but Eddie polished it." Arthur Mercante, who has refereed close to a hundred world championship fights, was the third man in the ring. Futch, Mercante, Ali, and Frazier tell the story of March 8, 1971.

ARTHUR MERCANTE: "No one knew who would referee the fight. That morning, one of the local newspapers had photos of seven different referees, each of whom was a possibility, and one of them was me. We were all dying to get the job. And at four o'clock that afternoon, I received a call from Frank Morris of the New York State Athletic Commission asking me to go to the Garden. He didn't say I had the fight; just would I please go to the Garden for an assignment. That's when I knew I had it.

"The intensity level that night, in and out of the ring, was extraordinary. The smallest bit of action, and there was a lot of it, brought roars from the crowd. Refereeing a Muhammad Ali fight, you couldn't help but be aware of who he was. But I always try to remain neutral and not be in awe of any athlete. You have to say to yourself that these are just two young men in the ring; each one wants to win as badly as the other, and you treat them alike. And the truth is, refereeing an Ali fight was much easier than refereeing a lot of other fighters. He was basically a clean fighter. In clinches, if you said, 'Break,' he broke cleanly. He wouldn't attempt to hit on the break. He did a few things on the inside that were illegal, mainly pushing an opponent's head down as part of tying the opponent up. But if you could move with Ali, you had the best seat in the house.

"Ali and Joe did a lot of damage to each other that night. Both of their faces were misshapen afterward. Ali's face was no longer round. Frazier's was all bruised, swollen, and cut up. In a way, it was horrible watching their features change. But it was history in the making, an incredible fight. As the rounds went by, Ali talked to Joe a lot. He cursed a bit, and said things like, 'Come on, man. Is that the best you got?' Most of the time, I couldn't hear what he was saying because of the crowd and the positioning of the fighters. Joe rarely talked back. Mostly, it was Ali talking. A couple of times, I said, 'Ali, stop talking,' and he'd stop for a while before starting again. There were some parts of the fight I couldn't understand. At times, Ali just lay against the ropes, throwing pitty-pat punches while Frazier put it to him. Maybe he was resting; it might have been a psychological ploy. But those tricks weren't going to work against Joe that night, and Ali gave away rounds he neeed later.

"There were several moments that stand out in my mind. One of them, which I'm glad people don't remember, came in the tenth round. Frazier was a bull of a fighter. When I broke them apart, all I had to do was say, 'Break,' and Ali would float back, but I had to use physical pressure with Joe. Otherwise, he'd just keep coming in. Midway through the tenth round, I broke them, and Joe kept coming, right through me. The little finger of my right hand was extended. And of course, when you're refereeing, you keep your fingernails cut short and smooth so there's no problem. But my finger hit him in the bottom of the eye socket, stuck him hard. He looked at me and said, 'Goddamn, fuck, man; keep your hands off me.' And he turned to go back to his corner to clear his eye, saying, 'Damn, I got two men beating up on me.' And I said to myself, 'If he goes back to his corner, he's going to sit down and we'll have the controversy of the century.' So I put my arm around him, pushed him back into action, and they went at it until the bell rang. Then I went back to the corner with Joe to apologize to him, and Yank Durham bawled me out, not in particularly polite language. Both of them got on me pretty good. But Joe came back in the next round and hurt Ali.

"Except for incidents like the one I just mentioned, the only time I visit a corner is when I feel a fighter has been hurt. I'll go and listen in on what's being said and observe so I know what to do; whether I should call the doctor, whether I should stop the fight. And after the eleventh round, I went to Ali's corner to make sure he was all right. But it was the last round that I remember best. That round showed me that Muhammad Ali was the most valiant fighter I've ever seen. Frazier hit him as hard as a man can be hit. Ali was exhausted. He went down, and anyone else would have stayed on the canvas, but he was up in three seconds. I didn't even have time to pick up a count. I motioned Frazier to a neutral corner. Joe went right there, and when I turned around to face Ali, he was on his feet. I didn't ask if he was all right. The last thing you do is ask a fighter who's been beaten up or is dazed, a fighter who might be hurt, if he wants to continue; because if he's any kind of fighter at all, he'll say yes. And of course, Ali wasn't just any kind of fighter; he was possibly the greatest and most courageous fighter who ever lived. No, it's the referee's job to make a determination, and I never thought of stopping it. The fight was too close. And Ali, while it had been a devastating punch, was back up and very much in control of himself. In fact, he fought better in that round after the knockdown than before it.

"Those were the days when referees scored fights in addition to refereeing, and I scored it eight-six-one for Frazier. The two judges had it nine-six and eleven-four for Joe. Eight-six-one is a close fight. Muhammad could have had a draw on my card by changing one round, and he could have won the fight by changing two. As I said before, if he hadn't leaned against the ropes taking punches for a couple of rounds, he could have won that fight.

"Afterward, I didn't go to any of the postfight parties. I went right home. Refereeing the fight meant a lot to me. Even then, I knew I had taken part in a very important historical event. But at the time, I was doing public relations work for a beer company. That was my regular job, and the following morning, I was at my desk at eight o'clock as usual."

EDDIE FUTCH: "Yank was the boss, and Joe did the fighting; but I like to think I was helpful in defeating Ali. I was in Joe's camp for all three of the Ali-Frazier fights, and I was with Ken Norton the first two times he fought Muhammad. And each time, I saw flaws in Ali's style that could be exploited. With Joe, it was the way Ali pulled his head back from punches; not in the center of the ring, but when he was on the ropes. He would pull his head back from punches in a way that left his body exposed. So when Joe fought him, the first fight, the body attack was the key. Most fighters, when they boxed Ali, when he went to the ropes they'd go immediately to the head. Ali would pull back so the punches passed in front of him, and once he made you miss, he'd come off the ropes and hurt you. He had great maneuverability, the ability to stay out of danger and outpunch his opponents off the ropes. So Joe was instructed, when Ali was on the ropes, to work the body with both hands. Let Ali pull his head back, because if he leaned back against the ropes, he'd expose his body to hard shots. And then, eventually, instead of pulling back to avoid shots to the head, we knew Ali would bring his head forward in the process of protecting his body. And it worked. Ali's legs weren't what they once were, and Joe hurt him against the ropes. In fact, Joe should have knocked him out in the eleventh round, but Ali conned him out of it. We teased Joe about that later, because he didn't realize at the time that he was being conned. Ali was in trouble. He got hit with a left hook, and was hurt very badly, and he exaggerated the fact that he was hurt like he was clowning. He gave Joe exaggerated moves, and Joe walked casually to Ali all the way across the ring. We call that 'The Long March.' It gave Ali extra time and kept Joe from scoring a knockout. By exaggerating, Ali made Joe think that he was fooling. He conned him good."

MUHAMMAD ALI: "I always felt pressure before a big fight, because what was happening was real. Boxing isn't like a movie where you know how things will turn out in advance. You can get cut; you can get knocked out; anything can go wrong. Against Frazier, I knew he'd be tough. He was harder for me than Liston or Foreman, because he had what I was vulnerable to—a good in-close left hook. Foreman wasn't an infighter or a hooker. He was an uppercutter with a right hand and a jab, always looking you in the eye. Liston was scarier than Frazier, but I fought Liston when I was young. Joe stayed on me, always on my chest; and from out of nowhere he'd throw the hook. If I was young, I'd have danced for fifteen rounds, and Joe wouldn't have ever caught me. But the first time we fought, I was three-and-half years out of shape. He punched hard; he pressured me good. And laying on the ropes to save energy, I lost some rounds I could have won. But it would be wrong to say I gave the fight to Joe. I didn't give it away. Joe earned it."

JOE FRAZIER: "I never liked Ali. Sometimes, if we was alone talking about the wife and kids, he was okay. But as soon as someone else came in, he'd start up and I couldn't talk to him. Before we fought, the words hurt me more than the punches. Now he says he did it to help the gate, but the gate didn't have nothing to do with it. We had our guarantees—two-and-a-half million dollars each—and there wasn't nobody but the promoters getting a percentage. Calling me an Uncle Tom; calling me the white man's champion. All that was phoniness to turn people against me. He was helping himself, not black people. Ali wasn't no leader of black people. He didn't lead me, except when I was running. Doing roadwork, I'd set him up in my mind on the road in front of me and go four miles saying, 'I'm gonna catch you, Cassius Clay.' All his talking did was make me work harder. I didn't like that conversation at all. He had a lot of mouth, and his lips got in the way of his hands. I was mad as a junkyard dog at Ali. I used to watch him on television, talking about me before the fight, and I'd say, 'God, give him to me; I want him so bad.' But I shut his mouth. Yes, I did. A lot of people went to the fight that night to see Clay's head knocked off, and I did my best to oblige them. When he went down, we were both dead tired. Fifteen rounds; that's how long we'd been fighting. And the only thing going through my mind when he got up was what was going through my mind all night. Throw punches; just throw punches. Let Clay do the talking. All I had to do was punch."

DAVE WOLF: "After the fight, Joe's face was a mess. It was all lumped up; his eyes, his cheekbones, around the forehead. He was in a lot of pain, and I remember his saying, 'Can't somebody do something about this; it hurts.' He wasn't whining; he was very controlled, but it definitely wasn't matter of fact. He was hurting; he wanted help. One of the doctors gave him a painkiller, and he spent a long time soaking his face in ice water. Someone poured ice into the sink just off the dressing room. Joe put his head in and kept it there so long I thought he was going to drown. Then he remembered that, before the fight, Ali had said he'd crawl across the ring if Joe beat him. He'd made a big deal about it and everyone had forgotten, but suddenly Joe remembered. And he screamed at Yank, 'Go get Clay. Tell him to come in here and crawl across this room.' Yank's answer was, 'No.' But Yank did go over to Ali's dressing room and tell Ali he'd fought a hell of a fight."

FERDIE PACHECO: "The scene in Ali's dressing room after the fight was transient. We dressed him like a drunk; he just lay there limp. Then we put him in a limo and took him to Flower Fifth Avenue Hospital for X-rays because his jaw was swollen, all puffed up. I wanted to keep him overnight for observation but he said no. He didn't want anybody saying Joe Frazier had put him in the hospital. The X-rays were negative; I saw them wet. I never saw them dry because someone stole them before they reached that point."

In the aftermath of the bout, Ali's foes were joyful. The enemy had been crushed; the legend was dead. "If they fought a dozen times," wrote Red Smith, "Joe Frazier would whip Muhammad Ali a dozen times; and it would get easier as they went along."[20] Ali had lost; that was the key. That Frazier had won seemed almost irrelevant. As a man and as a fighter, Joe Frazier engendered relatively little response except insofar as he related to Ali. Those who hated Ali loved Joe. It was that simple, or complex.

Ali, for his part, was philosophical in defeat. Meeting with reporters the day after the fight, he said he thought he'd won by landing more punches than Frazier but he refused to be bitter about the loss. "Just lost a fight, that's all," he said. "There are more important things to worry about in life. Probably be a better man for it. News don't last long. Plane crash, ninety people die, it's not news a day after. My losing's not so important as ninety people dying. Presidents get assassinated, civil rights leaders get assassinated. The world goes on. You'll all be writing about something else soon. I had my day. You lose, you don't shoot yourself."[21]

"Last night," one of the reporters interrupted, "Joe said he didn't think you wanted to fight him again."

Ali's response was short and sweet: "Oh, how wrong he is."

9

The Underdog

MUHAMMAD ALI: "The whole time I wasn't allowed to fight, no matter what the authorities said, it felt like I was the heavyweight champion of the world. Then I lost to Joe Frazier. And what hurt most wasn't the money that losing cost me. It wasn't the punches I took. It was knowing that my title was gone. When I beat Sonny Liston, I was too young to appreciate what I'd won. But when I lost to Frazier, I would have done anything except go against the will of Allah to get my title back again."

Ali's loss was a stunning blow, not only to him, but to everyone who believed in him. Joe Frazier was a decent man. In some ways, he characterized the struggle of America's underclass far more than Ali. But in part by accident and partly by design, Frazier had become a symbol behind whom people who hated Ali could unite. Soon after he defeated Ali, Frazier was invited to address the legislature in his birth state of South Carolina. It was the first time in four decades that a black man had been accorded that honor. And regardless of how the invitation was phrased, Frazier wasn't being invited as heavyweight champion. Were that the case, the invitation would have been extended in 1970 after he'd unified the title by knocking out Jimmy Ellis. He was invited and accepted as the man who defeated Muhammad Ali.

Meanwhile, Ali began to chart his comeback. For the first time in his career, he was forced to rest after a fight to regain strength before training again. But that didn't stop plans from progressing for a bout, not against a legitimate heavyweight contender, but against a man who had never even been to a prizefight except as a spectator—Wilt Chamberlain.

BOB ARUM: "One of the things you have to understand is, in the beginning, I knew nothing about boxing. And even after I learned the business, for a long time I still knew nothing about the sport. I knew Ali was tremendously talented, but I didn't understand the skill involved. I remember being in London in 1966, and approaching Ali with the idea of his fighting Jim Brown. I had the absurd notion that, because Jim was big and strong and tough, it would be a competitive fight. We were in a park. Jim was there, and Ali said to him, 'Hit me as hard as you can. Don't hold back; don't worry about hurting me.' Jim tried. And he couldn't touch Ali; he kept hitting air. And Ali kept slapping him in the face, not hard, but hard enough and often enough to make the point that, as great an athlete as Jim was, he'd have no chance in the ring against Ali.

"But be that as it may, in 1971 before the first Frazier fight, I heard that Wilt Chamberlain wanted to fight Ali. So I went to Herbert, and we agreed that, whatever the merits of the fight, the gate would be tremendous. Then I went to see Wilt, and he told me his greatest dream was to fight for the heavyweight championship of the world. And we signed a contract. Wilt actually signed to fight Ali. But then Ali lost to Frazier, and Herbert came to me and said, 'There's no championship to fight for. What do we do now?' Well, we thought about it. And you have to understand, people pay millions of dollars to publicists and advertising agencies to promote themselves the way that Ali was instinctively able to. Even after he lost to Frazier—and later, when he lost to Norton and Spinks—he still overshadowed them all. So I told Herbert, 'Let's do the fight anyway.' "

WILT CHAMBERLAIN: "I knew Muhammad fairly well during his time of glory. Not as well as I would have liked but reasonably well, and the things that I would say about him aren't all flattering. I liked the man; I still do. But when he was held up as a spokesman for black people, I thought that was ludicrous because Muhammad could hardly speak for himself. I applauded some of the stands he took; for example, his refusal to go into the war. A great many people wouldn't have had the courage to do that. And I saw nothing wrong with his changing his name and establishing his own identity. But to hold up one person to represent any group of people, that person has to be pretty far-reaching, and Muhammad wasn't an appropriate spokesman for me. He was a guy writing lightweight poetry who happened to be a tremendous athlete, who was not educated in areas where somebody who speaks for a group of people should be. And to be honest, I don't think Muhammad really saw himself as a spokesman for black America. That might have been the role that some of those around him and the white media saw for him. But if somebody like Muhammad was speaking for black America, then black America was in bad shape.

"But getting to the fight, from the time I entered sports, guys tried to get me to become a fighter. Ask any boxing manager, if they had to pick an athlete from another sport to develop who they would choose, they'll say a basketball player. That's because of some very basic things basketball players have—size, speed, quickness, and hand-eye coordination. And I always thought that if I had to fight somebody, it would be Muhammad Ali for two reasons. Number one, he was the greatest of his era. And two, he was a kind person; so if it turned out that I was in over my head, he wouldn't take cruel advantage of it, where some other fighters might try to hurt me if I was vulnerable. And it almost happened; I came very close to fighting Muhammad. I was offered more money than I'd ever gotten. It would have been a scheduled ten-round fight, and I honestly believed I had a chance. I thought a man as great at his job as Ali was might take me lightly. I could see that happening. And also because of his nature, he'd want to have fun with this particular fight, which might give me an opening.

"I took it seriously enough that I spent some time training with Cus D'Amato. I remember, right at the start, I told him, 'Cus, I have a fear of being knocked on my ass.' And Cus said to me, 'If you didn't have that fear, I wouldn't train you, because without that fear people go into situations and fall victim to all the bad things that can happen to them. Fear is a very healthy emotion for a fighter.' That made me feel better about my apprehensions. And I believed I was capable of going out there and representing myself in a way that would not be embarrassing, because for me the most devastating thing I can think of is to be embarrassed at anything I'm doing. I could never go through what Kareem went through his last year with the Lakers. That's embarrassing, for three million, for five million, for however many dollars. But against Ali, I thought I could acquit myself reasonably well. I didn't have to learn how to become a complete boxer. I was going to learn for eight or ten months how to apply my strengths and skills against one person. One of the first things Cus said to me was, 'You're going to learn how to fight one man; that's all. We're going to have all the tapes of Ali. We're going to know all the things you have to do and what you possess to do it with against this one person. And there's no way that Ali can train to fight you. He won't know anything about you as a fighter, because there's only one of you and no tapes.' That was my edge. Ali would be coming in blind; he'd have no idea what he was facing, whereas I'd know what to expect. And of course, I had God-given strength, size, and athletic ability. If I'd been the odds-maker, I'd have made Muhammad a ten-to-one favorite. But I truly believed there was a chance for me to throw one punch and take Ali out."

At seven feet two inches, 275 pounds, Chamberlain would have been the most imposing figure in ring history, but the bout never happened. As to why not, there are differing views. Chamberlain says the deal fell apart because "the people controlling the fight weren't willing to relinquish a fair share of the ancillary rights." And certainly, it's true that most failed negotiations in boxing do break down over money. However, Bob Arum maintains that the stumbling block wasn't economic at all. "Chamberlain agreed to the fight," says Arum. "Everything had been negotiated; all we needed were the signatures. I was sitting in the Astrodome with Ali and Fred Hofheinz, waiting for Wilt and his lawyer so we could do a press conference announcing the fight. And I said to Ali, 'Ali, shut your mouth. Let's get him signed to the contract before you start riding him.' Ali told me, 'Don't worry.' Then Chamberlain comes in, and Ali shouts. 'Timber!' Chamberlain turns white, goes into the next room with his lawyer, comes out, and says he's not fighting. I think Ali intimidated him; that's all it was. At the moment of truth, Wilt realized that fighting Ali was a totally ridiculous concept."

Should the fight have happened? Chamberlain and his two greatest rivals—Bill Russell and Kareem Abdul-Jabbar—offer their views:

Bill Russell: "I can't speak for Wilt. I just know that I personally would never challenge a champion in his field of expertise. I would never get in a boxing ring with Ali or on the football field with Jim Brown or on a track with Carl Lewis. I would never impose my thoughts or motivations on someone else, but for me personally, that's just not the way I am."

Kareem Abdul-Jabbar: "Ali versus Wilt was something I didn't want to see happen. Wilt would never have put a glove on him. Fast people couldn't put a glove on Ali, and Wilt was never known for his speed. Either Wilt would have made a fool of himself, or he would have gotten hurt, and I didn't want Ali to be the one who turned Wilt's brain to mush. I just didn't want to see all that ego in competition."

Wilt Chamberlain: "It didn't happen, and it may be good for me that it didn't happen or it may be bad. I don't know. I'll just take it as a wash."

Muhammad Ali: "Timber!"

Meanwhile, on April 19, 1971, three days before the collapse of negotiations for the Ali-Chamberlain fight, two men had stood before the United States Supreme Court in Washington, D.C. One was Erwin Griswold, solicitor-general of the United States. The other was Chauncey Eskridge, one of several attorneys who had represented Ali in his draft litigation over the years. Four years had passed since Ali's refusal to step forward in Houston, and during that time the mood of the country had changed. Still, there were many who fervently believed that Muhammad Ali belonged in jail. Indeed, just three weeks earlier, Congressman George Andrews of Alabama had addressed the House of Representatives and demanded, "Where on earth is the Justice Department in this country? Why on earth is not that man Cassius Clay in the penitentiary where he should be?"[1]

ERWIN GRISWOLD: "The atmosphere in the court that day wasn't different from any other. I've argued 127 times before the United States Supreme Court, and this was just another case as far as I was concerned. I didn't have any personal feelings one way or the other about Mr. Ali. There's no reason why I should have. I'd never watched him fight. It's not my practice to watch fights on television or otherwise. I argued the case myself because the question of Selective Service was full of pressures and emotions, and I just thought I ought to take the case on. I thought it was a very close case. You win some, you lose some; and this one we lost."

On June 28, 1971, fifty months to the day after Ali had refused induction, the United States Supreme Court unanimously reversed his conviction. Thereafter, all criminal charges pending against him were dismissed. However, the Court's action was hardly the ringing declaration of religious freedom that some observers thought it to be. With Thurgood Marshall recusing himself, the justices had initially divided five to three in favor of affirming Ali's conviction. Then Justice Harlan, who was dying of cancer and would resign from the Court later that year, shifted his vote to even the balance at four and four. Had the tally stayed that way, the ruling of the lower court would have been upheld and Ali would have gone to jail. At that juncture, Justice Potter Stewart suggested a compromise.

In order to qualify for conscientious objector status, Ali had been required to show that (1) he was opposed to war in any form; (2) his opposition was based upon religious training and belief; and (3) his opposition was sincere. In opposing Ali's request for conscientious objector status, the Justice Department had initially advised the draft appeal board that, in its view, Ali failed to meet any of the three criteria. But in arguing before the Supreme Court, the government had conceded the second and third requirements and based its case solely on the claim that, because Ali would fight in a Muslim holy war, he wasn't opposed to "all war in any form." Seizing on the discrepancy, Stewart pointed out that the draft appeal board had never indicated the specific basis on which Ali's request for conscientious objector status had been denied. Thus, he argued, it was theoretically possible that the denial was based on a finding that Ali's position was not sincerely held or not based upon religious training and belief—positions that the government itself now conceded were wrong.

Stewart's argument appealed to the conservatives on the Court, because it meant that Ali's conviction could be reversed without ruling that members of the Nation of Islam were entitled to conscientious objector status. Only Chief Justice Warren Burger refused to go along with the proposal; and in the end, he too succumbed to Stewart's logic.

Ali was subdued when the court's decision was announced. "Blank," was how he described his emotions. "It's like a man's been in chains all his life, and suddenly the chains are taken off. He don't realize he's free until he gets the circulation back in his arms and legs and starts to move his fingers. I don't really think I'm going to know how that feels until I start to travel, go to foreign countries, see those strange people in the street. Then I'm gonna know I'm free."[2]

And there was one thing more Ali had to do. The Supreme Court couldn't give him back his title; he had to regain that himself in the ring. The quest began in the Houston Astrodome on July 26, 1971. Promoters dubbed it "the inevitable fight"—Ali against his boyhood friend and former sparring partner, Jimmy Ellis. But for the first time in ten years, Angelo Dundee wasn't in Ali's corner. Dundee was Ellis's trainer and manager, and had decided, with Ali's consent, to work with Ellis in training and during the bout. That way, he could collect his one-third share of Ellis's purse as opposed to the far smaller percentage that Ali paid him for fights.

JIMMY ELLIS: "Fighting Ali was strange after the good times between us. When he left home to work with Angelo, I stayed in Louisville. Then I realized I couldn't get anywhere boxing in Louisville, and Ali was the one who brought me to Miami. So that was good of him right there. He introduced me to Angelo, helped me meet different people, and encouraged me to build my career. We started sparring together before he fought Henry Cooper the first time, and stayed together pretty much until the layoff. And sparring, we were good for each other. He knew I always gave my best and he knew he always had to defend himself, because if he didn't, I'd tag him. I made him work, he made me work, and we got better together. Then they took his title away. That's when I won the tournament for the WBA championship, and he wasn't angry or anything like that. He was happy for me that I won it.

"As for when we fought each other, I thought I could beat him. We'd sparred a thousand rounds together, and I knew him good. There was nothing he could do to me that I hadn't seen before. I figured I had the style and speed to do what had to be done, and his legs weren't the same anymore. It was a fair fight, and he won. The shot I looked for all night long was the one that got me. He came over my jab with a right hand. I was looking for it; I'd gotten away from it all night. But in the end, that was what I got hit with, and he knocked me out in the twelfth round.

"Afterward, there wasn't any bitterness between us. I shook his hand and said, 'Hey, you got me.' And I still love and respect the man. Whatever he did, it came from the heart. He always treated me the way I wanted to be treated. I'm a Baptist, and no matter what was going on in his life, he never let religion come between us. From time to time, he talked to me about Islam, but I knew what I wanted to be and he never pushed me to join his religion. Once, some of the guys in training camp pressured me about it, but Ali told them, 'Jimmy is my friend and that's it; whatever he wants to do is his business.' And the way I feel about Ali, he could call me any time of the day or night, I don't care where he'd be, and I'd be there for him. People worry now about his health. But there's a God; and it don't matter if his name is Jehovah or Allah, you can call him anything you want—and God will look after Ali."

One month after Ali defeated Jimmy Ellis, he extended his managerial contract with Herbert Muhammad for an additional four years. Then he began training for his next bout, against Buster Mathis.

Mathis was a hard sell. After a promising amateur and early professional career, he'd given in to obesity and, in the words of Barney Nagler, "resembled nothing as much as a dancing elephant." "I'm gonna do to Buster what the Indians did to Custer," was Ali's tag line for the promotion.[3] Still, it was clear that the fight, which was being broadcast on closed-circuit television, could use some help.

Bobby Goodman, who handled publicity for the contest and later became director of Madison Square Garden Boxing, recalls Ali's efforts in that regard.

BOBBY GOODMAN: "My dad and I had our own publicity agency. We did most of the big closed-circuit fights, and Muhammad was always conscious of how a promotion was doing. He did everything possible to help, but for the Buster Mathis fight, we had a problem. The guys liked each other, it didn't shape up as the most competitive fight in the world, and ticket sales were lagging because we couldn't get Buster riled up. They were both such sweet guys. And every time they were together for an interview or press conference, Buster would start laughing; he couldn't control himself. So I went to Muhammad and said, 'We've got to come up with something. This is a closed-circuit fight; we have to generate some news.' Muhammad started thinking. Then all of a sudden, his eyes got real wide and he said, 'I've got it! I've got it! It'll make front-page headlines around the world.' I said, 'What is it?' I couldn't wait to hear what he had to say. And he said, 'You can have me kidnapped. Take me to a cabin in the woods. Just set up a ring and heavy bag and speed bag. Send somebody in to cook for me; get a couple of sparring partners. Everybody will think I'm kidnapped, and then a couple of days before the fight I'll show up again.' And I said to him, 'Muhammad, first of all, that would be fraud. There might be some problems with the police. And second, if people thought you were kidnapped, there wouldn't be any fight to sell tickets for.' And he seemed sort of disappointed with that, but he saw the logic of what I was saying and went on to think of something else. But that was Muhammad. Nothing was too bizarre, and nothing was beyond his imagination."

The fight itself was woefully one-sided. Ali won a lopsided decision, fighting almost gently, as reported by Tex Maule:

> At the start of the twelfth round, when Buster stood up, he staggered a couple of steps to his left before he caught himself and moved toward Ali. Ali reached out a long left and tapped Mathis rapidly on the forehead, like a man knocking on a door. Even these feathery punches made Buster's legs wobble, and when Muhammad hit him with a gentle right hand, he went down. He struggled to his feet, and Ali flicked him lightly with the left hand as he staggered around the ring and again hit him with a caressing right, and Buster was down again. To his credit, the big man hauled himself up once more and tried to return to the attack, while Ali patted him even more gently with the left and did not throw the right.[4]

Afterward, Mathis went to Ali's dressing room, crying. He thanked Ali for the opportunity to make money, and said it had been an honor to fight him. However, the sporting press was less moved. The same men who had savaged Ali for "torturing" Ernie Terrell now criticized his compassion in a business that required cruelty. But Ali held firm. "I don't care about all them people yelling, 'Kill him,' " he told reporters. "I see the man in front of me, his eyes all glassy and his head rolling around. How do I know just how hard to hit him to knock him out and not hurt him? I don't care about looking good to the fans, I got to look good to God. I got to sleep good at night. How am I going to sleep if I killed a man in front of his wife and son just to satisfy you writers?"[5]

Six weeks after beating Mathis, Ali was in Switzerland, where he knocked out a mediocre West German fighter named Jurgen Blin. Then, after a journey to Saudi Arabia, the Ali roadshow resumed. In April 1972, he traveled to Tokyo for a fifteen-round victory over Mac Foster. In May and June, he fought encores against George Chuvalo and Jerry Quarry, decisioning Chuvalo and knocking Quarry out in the seventh round. Next came a bout against Al "Blue" Lewis, notable primarily because it was held in Ireland.

HAROLD CONRAD: "It was always my dream to do a big heavyweight fight in Ireland. I'm not Irish, it's nothing like that, but Ireland is where fights started. You ever been there? They fight; they argue all the time. If you don't argue with them, they get mad at you in Ireland. And this guy, his name was Butty Sugrue, owned a pub in Dublin. He wanted to promote a fight, so I told him, 'Okay, for two hundred thousand dollars, you can have Ali.' And when Ali stepped off the plane onto Irish soil at the airport, the people went wild. He told them his great-grandfather was named Grady and had come from Ireland, and they loved it. Then, the next day, he called me up and asked, 'Where are all the niggers in this town?' That's Ali talking, not me. I told him, 'Ali, there aren't any,' and he said, 'Oh.'

"The night before the fight, I was in a pub talking with some guy who said he was going to the fight. I asked, 'Did you get tickets already?' And he said, 'Tickets? It's an insult for an Irishman to pay to see a fight.' I should have made a note of that, because the next day seven thousand people crashed the main gate, tore it down. Seven thousand got in for free. But it was a good fight. Ali had a little cold, and Lewis was there to win. He bloodied Ali's nose, but Ali chopped him down toward the end and stopped him in the eleventh round."

Back in the United States after the fight, Ali considered a brief diversion from his ring career. Well over a year had passed since his loss to Joe Frazier, and Frazier was showing no willingness to fight him again. However, other opportunities loomed. In August 1972, Bob Arum opened negotiations with Warner Brothers for Ali to play the lead in a remake of *Here Comes Mr. Jordan* entitled *Heaven Can Wait*. Over the next three months, details were hammered out, and by November a contract was ready to be signed. Ali would be paid $250,000 if the project went ahead, and receive "first star billing" in all advertising and the film itself. His name would appear above the title of the picture in a size "at least as large as that used to display the title." In the event the film earned a profit under Hollywood's convoluted accounting standards, he would also receive "ten percent of the gross after $10,000,000." In return, Ali would make himself available for twelve weeks of principal photography, and Warner Brothers could extend that time for up to three additional weeks at $25,000 per week. In deference to Ali's religious beliefs, he was to furnish Warner Brothers with "a clearly spelled out written list of guidelines to which the screenplay and photoplay must conform in the area of black-and-white race relations and treatment of sex."[6] The first draft of the screenplay had already been written by Francis Ford Coppola.

Ali was enthusiastic about the project, which involved a fighter being brought back to life after an untimely death and ultimately winning the heavyweight championship. However, there was one last hurdle to be cleared before the deal was finalized. It had to be approved by Elijah Muhammad, and that approval would not be forthcoming. A memorandum from Arum to his partner, Theodore Friedman, told the tale:

> Over the weekend Ali and Herbert talked with Elijah about the proposed picture to be made by Warner Brothers. Herbert had implied to me that he had discussed the matter with his father and that no problems were anticipated. At any rate, Elijah has now ruled that Ali cannot make the picture because the plot is contrary to Muslim beliefs. Apparently, the aspect of the picture where the fighter dies and then returns in the body of another man is objectionable on the grounds that Muslims don't believe in life after death. As a practical matter, this ends the project, since there is no way anyone can get into a theological discussion with Elijah.[7]

Ali was disappointed by the collapse of the film project. Meanwhile, however, another of his desires was about to be fulfilled. Twelve years earlier, training with Archie Moore, he'd vowed to someday have a training camp of his own. In autumn 1972, that dream came to fruition with the opening of a training facility in Deer Lake, Pennsylvania. The focal point of the camp was a fifty-by-sixty-foot gym built at a cost of $42,000. Other structures included a dining hall, a barn, a two-story bungalow, and cabins for sparring partners, guests, and friends. Huge boulders lay scattered about the land, with the names of former champions painted on. Ali would train at Deer Lake for the remainder of his career. And it was there that many members of his entourage found a home.

RALPH THORNTON: "I'd met Muhammad when he was in Miami training for Joe Frazier. Blood [Wali Muhammad] was a friend of mine, and invited me to visit. I had some money, so I went to Miami, and I was all excited about it, meeting the champ. Ali didn't know who I was. He asked, 'Do I know you, brother?' I said, 'Not really, champ. I just came down with Blood.' But he told me I could stay at the hotel with them.' I said, 'That's good, but all I want is the same room rate that you people get. I'll pay for myself.' So I stayed a while, and before I left, I paid like I said I would. The next time I saw him, it was a year later, and I was doing bad. I mean, I'm talking about bad. I had no money. Before, I'd worked in record stores and did some performing, singing and dancing. Things like that weren't recommended for Muslims so I kept it low key. But when I saw Ali the second time, I was out of work and flat broke. And he's very observant. Right away, he noticed my situation from the way I was dressed. He asked, 'What are you doing now?' I said, 'Not too much.' And he told me, 'I remember you. You're the only guy who paid his own hotel bill. Why don't you come work for me?'

"I went to Deer Lake, not knowing what I was going to do. I really had no function. Ali just said, 'I'm glad to see you. Find something to do.' So I started cleaning the gym; it was very dusty up there. And I'd park cars during training sessions, but mostly I kept the gym and basic areas clean. Later on, people started calling some of us in camp 'hangers-on.' And they didn't say it in a nice way. It was like, all we were doing was sitting around, laughing at Ali's jokes, taking his money. And it hurt me to hear them talk like that. You know, everybody is hanging on to something, and sometimes it's another person, because all you got in life are your relationships. And to be a servant, to be in this man's presence, was enough for me, and he wanted me there. I was employed. I didn't just join him for fights and ride around with him and sit in hotel restaurants and sign his name to checks. I had a job. I was keeping the training camp clean. I was living on his property. That was my home. I was receiving mail there. The bank had my address there. Sometimes people would say, 'Hey, man, you ain't doing nothing but hanging on.' But I knew that every morning I was sweeping the gym, cleaning up the facilities. That was work to me. And in return, Ali did more than pay me. He did more for me than anybody in my family ever did. He took me places I never would have been able to go on my own. We went first class and lived first class. As far as my life was concerned, Ali opened up the world."

BOOKER JOHNSON: "I'd been with Ali for a year after he won the title from Liston. Then Herbert took over and brought his own people in, and I was out of the picture for quite a while. But in 1972, when the camp at Deer Lake opened, Ali asked me back again. At first, I was like a man Friday. I did whatever was available for me to do. Then one day, Sister Lana asked Ali if I could help her in the kitchen because she didn't have an assistant at the time. He told her I could help for one day, and I wound up in the kitchen with Sister Lana for ten years. And it was beautiful in camp; we were a family. There was Ali, Khalilah [Belinda Ali's Muslim name], the children, Blood, Lana, Bundini, Ralph, the sparring partners, and so many more coming in and out. Gene Kilroy was sort of the administrator for the camp. He coordinated what was going on, made reservations for group travel, stuff like that. A lot of the time, Gene was the only white person in camp. Angelo would come in a few weeks before a fight, but Gene was always there. At first, he had to struggle some, because he was white and that didn't sit well with some members of the Nation. But he was good; he did his job. And after a while, everyone accepted him as part of the group."

GENE KILROY: "I met Ali in Rome at the Olympics. I was there as an officer with the United States Army fighters, but I didn't get close to him until later on. At the time he came back from exile, I was in marketing for Metro-Goldwyn-Mayer. I left that job, went to work with Ali, and never regretted it.

"People didn't have titles around Ali. He'd never say, 'This is my advisor; this is my business manager.' People did what they wanted to do and whatever Ali wanted them to do. Bundini had a saying— 'There's no big I's and little you's.' And that's the way it was. I had so many good times with Ali, I couldn't possibly pick out the best. He just never stopped giving of himself. I can't tell you how many times Muhammad went to hospitals without fanfare, without TV cameras. Day after day, he'd go into hospitals because he knew how happy it made people. I remember one time, we went to a Shriner's Hospital in Philadelphia. There was a little boy there who didn't have any legs; he just had stumps for legs. His legs were cut off at his knees and they had artificial legs for him, but he wouldn't wear them because he was used to walking on his knees, and he thought he could get around that way, and it was too hard for him to learn how to use the prosthetic legs. Ali held the kid in his arms and said to him, 'Listen, you can't quit now. You gotta keep going; you gotta fight hard. We're sending spaceships to the moon; you can do this. So I want you to learn how to use these things, and once you've learned how, I'm coming back and I'm gonna teach you the Ali Shuffle.'

"Another time, Ali went to a nursing home, and there was an old man with no teeth in bed. He was wrapped in a diaper. Muhammad went into the man's room with me. One of the nurses went over to the man and asked, 'Do you know who this is?' The man looked up and said, 'Oh, my God; it's Joe Louis. All my life I've wanted to meet you, Joe.' And I laughed. Muhammad bumped me in a chastising way. Then he looked back at the man and said, 'That's right, I'm Joe Louis.' And he hugged the man and said, 'God bless you.' Afterward, he told me, 'All his life, that man has wanted to meet Joe Louis. Who knows how much longer he's gonna live. But now he can die happy, knowing that he's met his hero.' "

RALPH THORNTON: "At first the neighbors were very unhappy when we moved into Deer Lake. There were a lot of rumors. A lot of people said, 'Don't go up there and have anything to do with the Muslims; they'll kill you.' I remember one incident when Khalilah and I went into town to shop. We were going to get some washing machines and refrigerators and other things for the camp. We went to this shopping center, and Khalilah was walking around asking, 'How much is this refrigerator?' The guy would tell her it's four hundred dollars. And she'd say, 'Okay, bring me two of these in white and two in the cream color.' And the salesman was looking at these two black people. I had on my work shoes, a sweatshirt, and jeans. Khalilah was dressed like a lady dresses. Then we left that department and went over to where the beds were sold, asking, 'Now, how many beds do we need? There's the rooms where the sparring partners are gonna stay; and this person, and that person. Well, that's sixteen beds.' Anyway, it got back to the store manager that two black people were making all these crazy orders, and the manager actually called the police. Then Khalilah explained who she was, and there were a lot of apologies. 'I'm so sorry, Mrs. Ali. I didn't know who you were.' And after a while, the neighbors came to like us. There was a road that ran to the camp from Route 61. It was terribly dusty and had never been paved, and Ali was successful in getting the county to pave that road all the way up the hill. That won the neighbors over. They said, 'Well, he got the road paved and we appreciate that.' Then people started coming around to meet the champ, and found out how friendly he was. After a while, they realized we were good neighbors. They knew we weren't going to threaten them in any way, and they became good neighbors too."

BOOKER JOHNSON: "Ali was different from any champion ever. His camp was open to the world. Floyd Patterson, when he was champ, had an armed guard with a rifle where he trained. Joe Louis, Rocky Marciano, Larry Holmes; they all shut people out. But anyone could walk into Deer Lake at any time. I remember, one day Khalilah put up a rope. People were standing on the other side waving at Ali, and he told them, 'Come on down, over here.' Well, someone pointed to the rope. Ali asked, 'Who put that there?' Khalilah said, 'I did.' And Ali told her, 'Take that down, and never put it up again.' That's just the way he was. Absolutely everyone was welcome."

RALPH THORNTON: "There was a boy, maybe twelve years old. He was in one of the local hospitals, dying of leukemia, and he asked his father if it would be possible to visit Deer Lake to see Ali. The father told me later that he'd been reluctant to do it because he didn't like Ali, but this was his son and the boy was dying. I happened to be in the front of the camp when the man drove up. He left his boy in the car, came over to me and said, 'Pardon me, Mister. I don't know whether this is possible, but I know the champ trains here. Do you think there's any way he could see my son? He's dying of leukemia. The doctors say he doesn't have long to live.' I said, 'Sure, he'll see him.' Now, this boy, from the treatments, he'd lost his hair and he was like a rail, very thin. He looked like he was dying. I took him and his father into the gym. Ali had just finished training. He was in the dressing room, so I knocked on the door, went in, and explained the situation. And the champ told me, 'Bring the boy in.' Well, he spent all afternoon, talking with that boy, playing with him, joking with him. The boy went back to the hospital after that. But the father came to see me later, almost in tears. He told me, 'Mister, I never liked Ali. I've hated him ever since I knew about him. I was always hoping someone would beat him, and beat him badly. But I'll never forget what he did for my son. He's a good man, and I'm sorry for the way I felt about him.'

"So that was Ali. He loved everyone. And for me, the time that showed it best was once they brought some children up to the camp, children who can't control themselves. They slobbered at the mouth; cerebral palsy, I think it was. Ali stopped training, got out of the ring, grabbed each one of those kids. And you know, if they tried to kiss me I'd probably have pulled away, but he kissed each one of them dead on the mouth, slobber all over him. The kids were laughing, waiting to be kissed by this man, and you could see how much they loved him."

On September 20, 1972, Ali fought a rematch with Floyd Patterson in Madison Square Garden, and knocked Patterson out in the seventh round. Then came a set of negotiations that culminated in Ali signing to fight in Johannesburg, South Africa. The bout, scheduled for November 18, 1972, against Al Jones, was to be promoted by Reliable N. E. Promotions (a South African partnership) in association with Top Rank (Bob Arum's new promotional company). Ali was to receive $250,000. Paragraph 8 of the promotional contract, signed by all parties, declared:

> Promoter acknowledges that Ali's party and Jones's party will be multiracial. Promoter agrees that hotel or residential accommodations to be provided by the Promoter for Ali and his party and for Jones and his party will not require any segregation whatsoever on the basis of race. Promoter also agrees that the audience at the bout will be multiracial. Seating at the bout will either be on an integrated basis, without regard to race, or on a segregated basis which will provide separate but equal seating for whites and non-whites.[8]

Ultimately, the Jones fight was canceled because Reliable N. E. Promotions failed to produce the necessary financial letters of credit. However, the fact remains that, at the time, Ali was willing to fight in South Africa. Herbert Muhammad, who negotiated the contract, justifies that willingness as follows: "The position of the Nation of Islam was that Ali was a fighter, and that as champion of the world, he should be able to fight anywhere on earth. We didn't get into that thing about South Africa. My father didn't look no different at South Africa than he did at the United States; he believed both of them were run by devils. And to say don't fight in South Africa because they're doing wrong; well, some of the same crimes are done in the United States against black people. So my father didn't have the attitude that you could fight in the United States but not in South Africa."

With the Jones fight canceled, Ali fought instead in Stateline, Nevada, on November 21, 1972, against light-heavyweight champion Bob Foster. Outweighed by forty-one pounds, Foster was knocked down seven times before being counted out in the eighth round. But in the fifth round, he did something no one had been previously able to do: He cut Ali—a wound beneath the left eyebrow that required five stitches to close.

BOB FOSTER: "The fight was in a nightclub. You go up in the ring, and there are people sitting there, eating dinner, having drinks all around you. But once the fight started, it was him and me and the referee. It didn't feel that different. My strategy going in was to hit him with jabs, because I had a stiff jab that would bust anybody up. That's all I wanted to do—jab, jab, jab, until I could drop the bomb—but Ali never stood in one place. The first round, I couldn't catch him. I couldn't see his hands at all. They say he slowed down after the layoff, but the guy was still just too fast. At the end of the round, I went back to my corner. My trainer, Billy Edwards, asked, 'Bobby, what do you see?' And I said, 'I can't catch this guy.' So Billy told me to counterpunch, and that's what I did. When Ali jabbed, I jabbed, and after a while I began to connect.

"Busting him up is what I remember most about the fight. It wasn't one punch. It was a lot of jabs that got the skin raw and finally cut him. I like to think that back then I had the hardest jab in boxing. I stopped a lot of guys with it by ripping them open in three or four rounds. Hey, I was the best light-heavyweight in the world; I figured I could beat Ali. But what happened was, his weight wore me down. He outweighed me by forty-something pounds, and after a while, the tugging and pulling and holding got me. People say now that I had Ali hurt early. I stung him bad, but he was able to con me. I could have won, but I didn't and it's history. I saw him a few years ago. I'm working now in the sheriff's office in Albuquerque, but I was in Las Vegas for the rematch between Larry Holmes and Michael Spinks. I walked over to Ali and said, 'How are you, champ?' but he didn't recognize me."

Two months after the Foster fight, Ali's plans took another turn. For almost two years, he'd been pointing toward a rematch with Joe Frazier. But on January 22, 1973, in Kingston, Jamaica, Frazier was dethroned. His conqueror was George Foreman, twenty-five years old, a pulverizing puncher who knocked Frazier down six times in two rounds. Now there were two dragons to slay. Ali wanted redemption against Frazier, but George Foreman held the crown.

On Valentine's Day 1973, Ali and Joe Bugner fought in Las Vegas, with Ali winning over twelve slow rounds. The most notable aspect of the fight was a flowing bejeweled robe bearing the legend "People's Champion," which Ali wore into the ring. Fashion experts, such as they are in boxing, observed that the attire was somewhat gaudy, but Ali had no choice—the robe was a gift from Elvis Presley, whom Ali had admired intensely since the age of fourteen.

The victory over Bugner was Ali's tenth in a row, and a title fight within the next year seemed likely. Then, on March 31, 1972, he entered the ring against Ken Norton in San Diego. Norton's most recent bout had been in front of seven hundred spectators for a purse of three hundred dollars. He was so lightly regarded as an opponent that Ali's promoters decided to forgo closed-circuit televison and show the fight live on network TV—the first time one of his fights had been televised in that manner in more than six years. Brimming with confidence, Ali trained less than three weeks, and much of that time he was hampered by a sprained ankle. "I was playing golf one day," he explained to reporters. "Revolutionizing the game. I was walking up to the ball, hitting it while I was walking, and knocking it three hundred, three-hundred-fifty yards. Then I figured I was gonna run up and hit the ball. First time, I hit the grass. Second time, I lost my balance and swung all the way around, fell down and twisted my ankle. Couldn't run no more before the fight, couldn't train right, nothing."[9]

The price he paid for overconfidence was disaster.

EDDIE FUTCH: "The people who picked Ali's opponents during his career did a masterful job. Sometimes, they had to bite the bullet and go after a Sonny Liston, Joe Frazier, or George Foreman. But apart from that, they generally choose fighters who were too old or too slow and never at their peak. Occasionally, they made a mistake. Doug Jones was a mistake. And of course, when Ali got old, any fight was dangerous. But the biggest mistake they ever made was putting him in the first time with Ken Norton. Norton had been sparring with Joe Frazier for several months. He'd gotten very sharp. Style-wise, he was hard for Ali, and he was just coming into his own as a fighter. I talked before about what we looked for in Ali that Frazier was able to exploit. With Norton, it was the way Ali held his hands. Not that they were too low the way people said, but the placement of his right hand when he threw the jab. When a man throws a jab, his right hand should be by his chin to parry the jab that's coming back, but Ali didn't keep it there. He'd move it to the right. Now Norton had four inches more height than Frazier. And he had a good jab; not as good as Ali's, but pretty good. So I told him to step toward Ali with his jab. Norton's right hand being in the proper position, Ali's jab would be blocked by Norton's right. And Norton's jab would hit Ali in the middle of the face, because Ali's right hand would be out of position. You do that a couple of times, being heavyweights in a twenty-foot-square ring, and Ali would be back against the ropes. Then Norton was instructed to shift from the head and go to the body."

WALI MUHAMMAD: "In the second round, Ali fell against the ropes, pulling away from a jab. Norton threw a straight right, nailed him, and broke his jaw. During fights, my job in the corner was, Angelo would take the mouthpiece out, hand it to me, and I'd wash the mouthpiece. That was particularly important if there was blood on it. A lot of fighters have their mouthpiece put back in without cleaning. And then if they get hit, they swallow their own blood. So I would always take the mouthpiece and wash it in good cold water, ice water. I'd leave a little water on it so it would be moist, and then I'd give it back to Angelo. Against Norton, each round I was taking out the mouthpiece, and there was more and more blood on it. I could see it was a lot of blood after each round, because my bucket with the water and ice in it became red. In every other fight, between rounds I'd take the mouthpiece out and put it in the bucket and there was just slobber on it. But here, after each round, I had to shake the mouthpiece to get all the blood out of it into the water."

FERDIE PACHECO: "The jaw was broken in the second round. Ali was missing a tooth at the point of fracture, and that plus the pressure from Norton's punch broke his jaw. He could move the bone with his tongue and I felt the separation with my fingertips at the end of the second round. That's when winning took priority over proper medical care. It's sick. All of us—and I have to include myself in this—were consumed by the idea of winning that fight. When the bell rang, I was no longer a doctor; I was a second. My whole thing was to keep Ali fighting. As a doctor, I should have said, 'Stop the fight.' There's no disgrace in having a broken jaw. It goes down as a TKO; in six months you have a rematch, and life goes on. But Norton was a guy Ali was supposed to beat hands down, and at that point in Ali's career he couldn't afford a loss. Also, with Ali there was always politics involved. We didn't fight in a sterile atmosphere. We didn't fight in a room closed off from the rest of the world. Everything had to do with Muslims and Vietnam and civil rights, and if Ali lost, it was more than a fight. So you didn't just have a white guy say, 'Stop the fight'; especially if Ali didn't want it stopped. And when we told Ali his jaw was probably broken, he said, 'I don't want it stopped.' He's an incredibly gritty son-of-a-bitch. The pain must have been awful. He couldn't fight his fight because he had to protect his jaw. And still, he fought the whole twelve rounds. God Almighty, was that guy tough. Sometimes people didn't realize it because of his soft, generous ways; but underneath all that beauty, there was an ugly Teamsters Union trucker at work."

Going into the twelfth and final round, one judge had Ali ahead by two points, one had Norton ahead by a point, and the third judge had the fight scored even. Norton dominated the final round to win an upset of enormous proportions. Afterward, Ali underwent ninety minutes of surgery at Claremont General Hospital. Dr. William Lundeen, who performed the operation, called the injury "a clean break, all the way through." "I can't fathom how he could go on the whole fight like that," Lundeen added.[10]

Meanwhile, Ali's detractors gloated, salivating at the prospect of an over-the-hill Ali being beaten up by young up-and-coming fighters. "It isn't a big achievement," wrote Jimmy Cannon, "but a kid coming up can be made by knocking out Ali. Promoters deal in names. He has a big name and not much to defend it with. He is the guy the hungry kids want to get their hands on. No one appreciated being a winner more than Muhammad Ali. He is a loser now, and they match old losers with young winners."[11]

HOWARD COSELL: "Losing to Norton was the end of the road, at least as far as I could see. Certainly, it was the worst moment I shared with Ali until those awful beatings at the end of his career. So many of Ali's fights had incredible symbolism, and here it was again. Ken Norton, a former Marine, in the ring against the draft-dodger in San Diego, a conservative naval town. Richard Nixon had just been reelected with a huge mandate. Construction workers were marching through the streets supporting the war in Vietnam, which showed no sign of winding down. After that loss, it seemed as though Ali would never get his title back again. And then, to come back the way he did; to beat Norton, to beat Frazier, to beat Foreman. And then as champion, to beat Frazier and Norton again! The man was awesome."

The comeback began with a rematch against Norton.

"I took a nobody and created a monster," Ali said of the man who'd defeated him and broken his jaw. "I put him on *The Dating Game*. I gave him glory. Now I have to punish him bad."[12] But as the rematch approached, Ali's aura of invincibility was gone. Before the exile, he had seemed unbeatable. Now, after two brutal losses, those around him held their breath when they watched him step into the ring.

WALI MUHAMMAD: "It took six months before the jaw healed and Ali was able to fight Norton again. This time, we knew Norton would be tough. Ali took it more serious; he trained harder; he wasn't underestimating Norton anymore. But still, the fight was very hard. Every man who fought Ali got himself in the best condition of his life. If he wasn't a great fighter, he'd become great for that night. And if he couldn't be great, at least he'd be as good as he could be, because it was a once in a lifetime chance to fight Muhammad Ali. Also, Norton had a style that was troublesome for us. He was kind of awkward, which made him hard to hit. And after his first fight with Ali, he got brave. Norton was afraid of guys with a big punch. Against Earnie Shavers, George Foreman, Gerry Cooney, he was nothing. If you made Norton step back, he couldn't fight. But Ali always let him come forward. He made Norton look like a better fighter than he was."

In the rematch, as with their first fight, Ali and Norton were even entering the twelfth and final round. This time, though, Ali captured the last three minutes on the judges' scorecards and won a close but unanimous decision. Six weeks later, on October 20, 1973, he fought again, decisioning Rudi Lubbers in Jakarta, Indonesia. Then came his second bout against Joe Frazier.

Ali-Frazier II, like Ali-Frazier I, was fought in Madison Square Garden. Each fighter was guaranteed $850,000 against 32.5 percent of the net income from the fight. Given those percentages, they were paid roughly the same amount as for their first encounter. But more important, there was the matter of pride. Ali wanted desperately to average his earlier loss, and Frazier flat-out didn't like Ali.

DAVE WOLF: "In the ring they were equal, but out of the ring, Joe couldn't match Ali. In their first fight, Joe had done what he had to do. He'd won fairly, and had every right to expect acceptance as heavyweight champion. But Ali managed to taint the victory and tarnish Joe with his harangues. I guess Joe had an unrealistic expectation of what would happen after he beat Ali. He thought all of the Ali-related problems that existed in his mind, particularly in terms of acceptance by the black community, would go away. And they didn't. Joe still wasn't perceived as the total champion, and he blamed that entirely on Ali."

In the weeks leading up to their second fight, Ali and Frazier traded insults repeatedly. "Clay and I; we want each other bad," said Frazier. "I still call him Clay; his mother named him Clay. If you've been around this guy long enough, you can have a lot of hate in your heart when the bell rings, but otherwise you kind of look at him and you laugh. There's something wrong with the guy. I'm aware now that the guy's got a couple of loose screws someplace."[13]

Ali, in turn, took pleasure in branding Frazier "ignorant," a label Frazier hated more than any other. "Joe Frazier says he's gonna train his son to be a fighter," Ali proclaimed, drawing the contrast between himself and his adversary. "Me, I'm gonna make my son a lawyer or a doctor. I'm gonna brainwash him, educate him. A good tutor is gonna teach him to read and write and learn foreign languages. I'm not educated so good, but I have enough money and enough sense to know how important education is. My daughter is now brainwashed enough to become a doctor. She's four. She says, 'I want to be a doctor.' You gotta keep drilling it in them from when they're young."[14]

On Wednesday, January 23, 1974, five days before their fight, the bitterness between the two men came to a boil.

HOWARD COSELL: "That Saturday, ABC Sports was going to broadcast a tape of Ali-Frazier I. It was the first time the fight had been shown on home television, and we arranged for Ali and Joe to be in the studio to comment round by round. Joe almost didn't come. He and Eddie Futch, who had become Joe's manager after the untimely death of Yank Durham, felt Ali would use the opportunity to make personally abusive comments before a national audience, and I gave my word that I would not allow that to happen. I told Joe that I would insist upon both men limiting their remarks to the fight, and that I would cut Ali off at the first sign of a personal diatribe. And of course, my word was good enough for Joe. When they arrived at the studio, the producer set us on the stage, with Joe in the middle flanked by Ali and myself on either side. And everything went smoothly until Joe—not Ali, Joe—made a remark about Ali having to go to the hospital after the fight. Up until that time, Ali had been relatively controlled. Occasionally, he'd gone off on a tangent, but whenever he did, I brought him back to the business at hand. It was after Joe's comment about the hospital that the situation exploded."

As soon as the hospital comment left Frazier's lips, Ali responded: "Why'd you say that about the hospital, Joe? Why'd you bring up the hospital? I wasn't gonna talk about the hospital. Everybody knows I went to the hospital for ten minutes. You were in the hospital for three weeks. You're ignorant, Joe."[15]

"Ignorant" was the catalyst. Frazier stood up, leaned over Ali, and demanded, "Why'd you call me ignorant?" At that point, Ali's brother Rahaman, who was in the studio, jumped onto the stage and moved toward Frazier, who snapped, "You want to get in this, too?" Then Ali rose from his chair and grabbed Frazier in the manner of a wrestler applying a bear hug.

Ali was playing. Frazier wasn't.

DAVE WOLF: "The fight was real. Joe was angry. Ali had called him ignorant once too often, but there was more to it than that. Rahaman had been heckling Joe from the first round of the tape on. He was only about ten feet from the stage. And every time the tape showed Ali landing a punch, Rahaman would shout, 'Amen! Praise Allah! There it is again!' And Joe started burning. It wasn't just what Ali was saying; it was what Joe was hearing in the other ear as well. If we'd known how loose the security was going to be and that Rahaman would be allowed to act the way he did, there's no question that Joe wouldn't have gone. Rahaman was more of an instigator than Ali that afternoon. He got Joe mad enough to get into that thing about the hospital, and then Ali came back with his 'ignorant' comment. I wonder if Ali didn't know that ignorant was the trigger word. I think he did. I don't think he meant to trigger that much, but certainly he meant to unsettle Joe. And Joe obviously made a mistake by opening the Pandora's box about the hospital, because he was in no position to explain why he'd been in the hospital for so long after the fight.

"The truth is, Joe's medical problems began before he fought Ali. He was suffering from hypertension, high blood pressure. In fact, in the month preceding their first fight, the situation was serious enough that there was talk of postponing the fight and getting Joe treated immediately, but Joe wouldn't consider it. Then, when the fight was over, it was obviously time to deal with the hypertension. That's why Joe checked into the hospital. It was not primarily for fight-related reasons.

"So you had all that history leading up to the studio fight. And I remember, when Ali grabbed Joe, Joe just threw him to the floor. Then Rahaman tried to pile on, and a couple of Joe's people went after him. Cosell seemed terrified by it all, and Ali looked scared too. At that point, he realized Joe wasn't playing. And I'll tell you, if nobody in the studio had intervened, if everyone had ducked out of the room, I don't know what Joe would have done to Ali. One thing I do know is, Joe is not the type of guy you'd want to fight in the street, and Ali was a guy who wouldn't scare you in the street. If they'd been left alone, I think Joe would have taken Ali's head off, and that was certainly what he intended to do.

"After they were separated, Eddie Futch said, 'Let's get out of here.' My recollection is, Eddie was cursing at Cosell. Maybe he wasn't cursing, but he was livid, because there'd never been any hint beforehand that Joe and Ali would be sitting next to each other without someone in between or that Ali's entourage would be a problem. But our feeling in the limo going back to camp was that the whole thing had been a plus. Remember, Joe had won the only fight he and Ali had fought in the ring, and now he kept talking about the studio brawl, saying, 'Did you see how wide that nigger's eyes opened up? Now I really got him scared.' "

Two days after their studio brawl, Ali and Frazier were fined $5,000 each by the New York State Athletic Commission for "deplorable conduct demeaning to boxing." The penalties were announced by Chairman Edwin Dooley, who admitted that neither he nor the other commission members had seen tapes of the incident or interviewed either fighter. Hoowever, Dooley defended the heaviest fines in commission history on grounds that he and his brethren had read about the incident in the newspapers.

Meanwhile, public interest in the fight was building. Despite having lost in their first encounter when he'd been a seven-to-five underdog, Ali was now a six-to-five betting favorite. Once again, Madison Square Garden was sold out. But Ali-Frazier II was very different from Ali-Frazier I. The fighters inflicted relatively little damage on one another. Ali avoided the ropes, tied Frazier up when they got in close, and flurried at just the right times. There were two points of controversy during the bout. The first came late in the second round, when Ali staggered Frazier with a straight right. At that moment, thinking the round was over, referee Tony Perez stepped between the fighters, giving Frazier precious seconds to recover. But on the other side of the coin, Frazier's camp complained bitterly that Perez allowed Ali to grab Joe behind the neck and pull his head down throughout the fight. Regardless, the outcome was clear—a unanimous decision for Ali.

TONY PEREZ: "Both of those controversies had to do with me, so let me answer both of them. First, Ali grabbing Frazier behind the head. Frazier's people complained that it kept Joe from working on the inside. And it's true; Ali was very strong. He'd pull guys down by the back of the neck and no one was strong enough to pull back. If you let a guy do that all night, it wears you down. But I couldn't do anything because it was like Joe was happy laying on Ali's chest, waiting for me to break them apart. That's the way it was the whole fight. Joe would come in, punching, bobbing, weaving. He'd score one or two shots, and then just lay there in a clinch like he was resting. All he had to do was bend at the knees. Get down low so Ali can't hold anymore. He's shorter than Ali, so Ali can't hold him below a certain point. And once Joe's free, he'd be in position to come up punching. His own corner kept telling him to do that, but it seemed like he was content to be in a clinch.

"The other problem came in the second round. Ali connected with a good punch, and I thought I heard the bell. Then the time-keeper yelled at me, 'Tony, the round isn't over,' so I put them back to fight. It was only a thing of about five seconds. Later, Ali claimed that Joe was hurt, but he wasn't that hurt. Frazier wasn't going to get knocked out. They fought three times, more than forty rounds, and Ali was never able to knock Frazier down. So what makes him think he would have knocked Frazier down that night?"

After the fight, Frazier was quick to demand a rematch. Glossing over the fact that he'd forced Ali to wait thirty-five months for a return bout, he told reporters, "I want him again; one more time."

Ali, for his part, responded in kind. "I'm not gonna duck Joe. I'm gonna give Joe all the chances he wants."[16]

But first there was the matter of Ali versus George Foreman in the heart of Africa in a bid to recapture the heavyweight championship of the world.

10

Zaire

JACK NEWFIELD: "Muhammad Ali has gone through more periods and assumed more identities in his life than any person I've known. Manchild, con man, entertainer, poet, draft-dodger, rebel, evangelist, champion. You name it; he's done it. But if I had to put one label on him, it would be as a symbol of the 1960s. Those were rebellious conflict-ridden times, but they were also a period of great hope. And Ali, along with Robert Kennedy and the Beatles in the persona of John Lennon, captured the sixties to perfection. Ali, like Robert Kennedy and the Beatles, was full of passion and willing to challenge authority. In a rapidly changing world, he underwent profound personal change and influenced rather than simply reflected his times. And he survived. John Kennedy, Robert Kennedy, John Lennon, Martin Luther King, Malcom X; all the other great heroes of the sixties are dead. So are the icons like Elvis Presley and Marilyn Monroe. But Ali is alive, and not just in the flesh. He's in the hearts of everyone who experienced those times."

In 1974, the spirit of the sixties was very much alive. Indeed, within the span of twelve weeks, two events seemed to vindicate the decade. First Richard Nixon resigned his presidency. And then Muhammad Ali regained his crown.

There have been other sporting events that captured the imagination of the world. But no athletic contest in history inspired as much global joy as the battle between Ali and George Foreman, which took place in the predawn hours of October 30, 1974, in Kinshasa, Zaire. Like Sonny Liston, Foreman was considered unbeatable. His professional record was forty wins and no losses with thirty-seven knockouts. His eight most recent bouts had ended in the first or second round, and among his victims in those fights were Joe Frazier and Ken Norton—the two men who had beaten Ali. "My opponents don't worry about losing," Foreman bragged. "They worry about getting hurt." That view was seconded by Dave Anderson of *The New York Times*, who wrote, "George Foreman might be the heaviest puncher in the history of the heavyweight division. For a few rounds, Ali might be able to escape Foreman's sledgehammer strength, but not for fifteen rounds. Sooner or later, the champion will land one of his sledgehammer punches, and for the first time in his career, Muhammad Ali will be counted out. That could happen in the first round."[1]

JEREMIAH SHABAZZ: "That night in Zaire will stay with me for as long as I live. It was more than a fight. It was a vindication of everything that we in the Nation had struggled for over the years. Everything about it was right. Ali, the underdog; an awesome foe. I even thought we had a promoter we could be proud of, because Zaire was where Don King made his mark. Later, I learned that black doesn't matter to Don, except when he's using it to rob some fighter. The only color Don cares about is green. But in Zaire and for a short time afterward, I thought Don King was all right. And even today, I'll give Don credit for one thing. Other promoters could have made that fight, but Don was the one who brought it to Africa."

Don King and Ali met for the first time in the mid-1960s. King was a numbers czar in Cleveland, who later spent four years in prison for manslaughter. Ali was heavyweight champion of the world, and had not yet been stripped of his title. The man who introduced them was Lloyd Price, who wrote and recorded such rock hits as "Personality" and "Stagger Lee."

LLOYD PRICE: "Ali was a kid when I first met him. Sixteen years old, sitting outside the Top Hat Lounge in Louisville, Kentucky, because he was underage and they wouldn't let him in. That was in 1958. 'Stagger Lee' had just reached number one on the charts. I was on tour, and when I got to the lounge, this crazy kid rushed over, saying, 'Mr. Price, I'm Cassius Marcellus Clay; I'm the Golden Gloves Champion of Louisville, Kentucky; someday I'm gonna be heavyweight champion of the world; I love your music; and I'm gonna be famous like you.' I just looked at him, and said, 'Kid, you're dreaming.' But what happened was, we got along. You couldn't help but like him. The Top Hat Lounge was a popular place, and each time I played there, I saw Ali. After a while, I started looking for him and bringing him in with me. And he had all sorts of questions—about music and traveling, but mostly he wanted to know about girls. There were a lot of things he didn't know, and he asked me how to make out with girls. He was very sincere about it. I told him, 'Just be yourself, and the girls will like you.' Although as part of the lesson, I gave him a couple of dollars and said, 'Always have some money. That's the beginning of hanging out with the foxes.'

"Anyway, that's how our friendship started. Then, after he turned pro, he came to New York and stayed with me at my apartment several times. Right before he fought Doug Jones, I drove him around town to publicize the fight. That was my red Cadillac he was in. And around the same time, I met Don King. I used to go to Cleveland because my song-writing partner, Harold Logan, lived there. I knew all the people Harold knew, and through him, I got friendly with Don. One day, I was over at Don's place, in the kitchen talking about Muhammad. Don's daughter Debbie said, 'I want to meet him.' It was her birthday; she was about five. So I telephoned Muhammad, and he sang 'Happy Birthday' to her over the phone. Then Don got on and started talking. He was strictly a Cleveland man at the time. He didn't know anything about New York or Chicago or Los Angeles; and he was into numbers, not boxing. But that was the introduction. He and Ali got together—once I think it was—and then Don went to prison. But when he got out, you could see the wheels turning in his mind."

The events that followed Don King's release from prison read like the script of a television miniseries. On March 8, 1971, he had listened to reports of the first Ali-Frazier fight from his prison cell in Marion, Ohio. Three years later, he was a key player in putting together Ali-Foreman. And one year after that, he promoted the historic third Ali-Frazier confrontation in Manila. In a little more than four years, he'd become one of the most successful black businessmen in America, and the cornerstone of his power was Muhammad Ali.

DON ELBAUM: "It began with a boxing exhibition. Don went to Lloyd Price, and asked Lloyd to call Ali to box a charity exhibition for the Forest City Hospital in Cleveland. Ali agreed to it for free, but Don needed someone to orchestrate the show. That's where I came in. I was doing some fights in Cleveland, and had gone to Buffalo for a fight card at the Buffalo Auditorium. Around five in the evening, I got a phone call from a fellow named Clarence Rogers, an assistant district attorney in Cleveland. Clarence told me, 'Don, there's someone in my office that I'd like you to meet. His name is Don King, and he wants to do something with boxing.' I'd never heard of King before. But all of a sudden, there's this voice on the phone—and it still hasn't changed—shouting, 'Don Elbaum! Don Elbaum!' I'm all the way in Buffalo, and I can hear him without the telephone. And King says, 'There's a black hospital here in Cleveland that's going under, and we've got to save it. I want to do a boxing show for that black hospital and bring in Muhammad Ali. But there's no boxing in Cleveland without Don Elbaum because Don Elbaum is boxing, and you're the only guy who can save this hospital. And Don, I'm at Clarence's office, and we're staying here until you get here.' I said, 'Don, I'll be glad to work with you, but I'm in Buffalo, and I'm staying overnight.' And King said, 'No, no, no! We're not moving till you come back to Cleveland. I don't care if it's two, three, four o'clock in the morning.' I said, 'Don, I can't come. I'll get there tomorrow.' And in the course of the conversation, he asked, 'What do you charge for things like this?' I said, 'Five thousand dollars. I'm the matchmaker. I have to cover my phone calls, pay expenses, and have a little left over for myself.' And of course, before the conversation was done, he had me down to a thousand, and I hadn't even met the guy yet. And sure enough, I wound up leaving Buffalo that night, going to Cleveland, and meeting a little after midnight in Clarence's office.

"That was how I met Don King. And we decided to arrange the show by matching three or four guys who meant something in the Cleveland area, and then having Ali's exhibition as the main event. I set up the whole card, made all the matches, and Don King fell in love with boxing. At the fight, he said, 'Boy, this is fantastic.' And I gotta tell you, I flipped over Don King. I thought he was the real thing. I said to him, 'You've got to get out of the numbers business. You've got to get out of Cleveland. You've got to come to New York.

Boxing needs a black promoter. It's about time, and you're the one.'
I would sit with Don and his wife, Henrietta, and tell her, 'Let me
get him into boxing. I promise you, he'll make it big.' I was mesmerized by the man, and that was the beginning. We were partners
for eight months, and after that, I walked. I brought him to New
York, gave him half of my end of Earnie Shavers, and before long
he had the whole fighter. He just took what he wanted and ran over
everybody. Like the Forest City Hospital exhibit. The show grossed
eighty-six thousand dollars; I remember that figure. And when
everything was done, when Don finished with it, the hospital got I
think it was five thousand. That's one figure; that's the generous
figure. Later on, someone told me the hospital only got fifteen
hundred. I remind myself of that from time to time, because whenever I see Don now, he tells me, 'Elbaum, if you'd stuck with me,
you'd have been a millionaire. And my answer is always, 'Don, if
I'd stuck with you, I'd have wound up in jail!' "

After parting ways with Elbaum, King promoted several small
fight cards on his own in Ohio. Then, in early 1974, he was brought
into the Foreman-Norton championship bout as a consultant to Video
Techniques, the closed-circuit firm that promoted the match. "I was
their token nigger," King said later. "A black face to deal with the
blacks."[2] But all the while, King had his eye on Ali. Periodically, he
asked for the right to promote Ali's fights, and each time he was
rebuffed by Herbert Muhammad. However, in mid-1974, the situation changed. Foreman was now ready to fight Ali, but Ali's camp
wanted five million dollars. The amount was unheard of. "People
thought I was crazy," Herbert Muhammad would say later. But Don
King took him at his word. The only problem, King warned, was
that for that kind of money, Ali would have to fight in a foreign
country. "No problem," Herbert Muhammad assured him. "For five
million dollars, Ali will fight anywhere on the planet Earth."

TEDDY BRENNER: "Actually, King didn't promote the fight, although he did his best to make it seem that way. Video Techniques
put it together, with front money from a British corporation and the
rest from the government of Zaire. King was helpful in lining up
the fighters, but the deal could have been made without him. For
ten million dollars, which is what Ali and Foreman split, anybody
could have done the job. My only regret, and it has nothing to do
with personalities, is that the fight killed our own promotion. Madison Square Garden had negotiated a deal for Ali to fight Jerry

Quarry. He'd beaten him twice, but then Quarry knocked out Earnie Shavers, and Ali agreed to fight him again in New York for a million dollars. Herbert had an apartment in Manhattan. I went over there with a contract ready for signature, and Bundini met me at the door. He said, 'Teddy, Don King is hiding in the bedroom. He's making a match for Ali to fight Foreman. He's giving Ali five million dollars.' Well, that seemed like nonsense. It was twice what any fighter had gotten before. Then I saw Herbert, and he told me the same thing. So all I did was shake hands, give Herbert the contract, and say, 'If you can get five million dollars, take it. If not, I want this contract signed.' And before I left, I shouted out, 'King, wherever you're hiding, you're full of shit. But if you can really pay him five million dollars, he'd be a fool not to take it.' "

Ultimately, Ali received $5,450,000 for fighting George Foreman. That was more than Joe Louis ($4,600,000), Jack Dempsey ($3,500,000), or Rocky Marciano ($3,000,000) grossed in an entire career. The money was available primarily because Zaire's President Mobutu Sese Seko wanted to spread his name and that of his country across the globe, and was willing to part with ten million dollars to do it. Several public relations problems followed. A fight poster trumpeting, "From the slave ship to the championship," offended Zairians and had to be replaced. When tickets for the bout arrived in the African nation, they were returned to Philadelphia for reprinting because Mobutu's name had been misspelled. And Ali himself caused something of a stir before leaving the United States, when he told reporters, "All you boys who don't take me seriously, who think George Foreman is gonna whup me; when you get to Africa, Mobutu's people are gonna put you in a pot, cook you, and eat you." "Two days later," Gene Kilroy recalls, "we got a call from Zaire's foreign minister. I answered the phone call, and the minister asked, 'Where's Ali?' I said he was sleeping, and the minister told me, 'Well, please tell Mr. Ali that we are not cannibals; we don't eat people. We're doing the fight to create trade and help our country, and Mr. Ali's remarks are damaging our image.' "

The fight itself was scheduled for September 25 at 3:00 A.M. to accommodate closed-circuit audiences in the United States. Ali flew to Zaire several weeks in advance, accompanied by a thirty-five-person entourage that included family members, friends, sparring partners, training assistants, and various other personnel. Zairians had never seen anything like the Ali roadshow, and a number of reporters took to playing a game called "What Do He Do?" designed to determine the function of each member of the entourage. "It was hard coming up with jobs for some of them," Ed Schuyler of the Associated Press recalls. "Blood took care of the gym equipment and tasted Ali's sweat after each workout to determine if it had the proper salt content. Kilroy answered the telephone and got people to where they were supposed to be. Someone asked Muhammad what his brother Rahaman did, and Muhammad answered, 'I give him fifty thousand dollars a year for jiving and driving, and that's not bad.' And that was true of most of the entourage. They didn't do much. A few pulled their own weight. Angelo certainly had a job. Lana Shabazz did her share of cooking. Luis Sarria worked hard. And Howard Bingham wasn't a leech. Howard was a friend who enjoyed being around Ali, but made a living as a photographer on his own. As for the others, my guess is they loved Ali and some of them probably had work to do, but I sure don't know what it was."

Once Ali arrived in Zaire, he settled into the presidential compound in N'Sele. forty miles from Kinshasa. On occasion, there were complaints from the press. "They're holding the world heavyweight championship fight in the Congo," groused Jim Murray of the *Los Angeles Times*. "I guess the top of Mount Everest was busy. I don't know why they can't hold it in Yankee Stadium like everybody else."[3] But Ali understood the stakes involved, and publicly, he had nothing but praise for his hosts.

"It's a great feeling being in a country operated by black people," he told reporters. "I wish all black people in America could see this. In America, we've been led to believe that we can't do without the white man, and all we know about Africa is jungles. All we see of Africa is a bunch of natives leading white men on a safari, and maybe one of the white men is trapped by a gorilla and the natives save him. We never get shown African cars and African boats and African jet planes. They never tell us about the African TV stations. And everything here is black. The soldiers, the president, the faces on the money. It don't seem possible, but twenty-eight million people run this country, and not one white man is involved. I used to think Africans were savages. But now that I'm here, I've learned that many Africans are wiser than we are. They speak English and two or three more languages. Ain't that something? We in America are the savages."[4]

"Watching Ali in Zaire was wonderful," recalls Ferdie Pacheco. "He'd go on walks into areas where I don't think they had electricity, let alone television sets, and everyone knew him. To see the looks on people's faces when they saw him, the love, the power he had over them; it was spine-tingling. And Ali was having a ball, talking about black doctors, black lawyers, black heads of state, black airline pilots; I'm not sure I ever saw him that excited."

"The black pilots were what did it," adds Ed Schuyler. "Ali kept talking about black pilots and black flight crews and black jet-airplane mechanics. And then one day he told me, 'Of course, once they get the plane up in the air, they bring a white man out of the closet to fly it.' "

Meanwhile, there was a fight to be fought, and the prefight buildup was vintage Ali, reminiscent of his first bout against Sonny Liston. All a reporter had to do was open his notebook, and the quotes tumbled forth:

• George Foreman is nothing but a big mummy. I've officially named him "The Mummy." He moves like a slow mummy, and there ain't no mummy gonna whup the great Muhammad Ali. See, you all believe that stuff you see in the movies. Here's a guy running through the jungle, doing the hundred yard dash, and the mummy is chasing him. Thomp, thomp, thomp. "Ooh, help! I can't get away from the mummy! Help, help! The mummy's catching me. Help! Here comes the mummy!" And the mummy always catches him. Well, don't you all believe that stuff. There ain't no mummy gonna catch me.

• George hits hard; I know that. But hitting power don't mean nothing if you can't find nothing to hit. When Dick Sadler [Foreman's trainer] holds the heavy bag, George can punch a hole through it. But when we get in the ring, ain't nobody gonna be holding me. No one hits me with seven or eight punches in a row like George hit Joe Frazier. And George telegraphs his punches. Look out; here comes the left. Whomp! Here comes the right. Whomp! Get ready; here comes another left. Whomp! I'm not scared of George. George ain't all that tough. What you white reporters got to remember is, black folks ain't afraid of black folks that way white folks are afraid of black folks.

• George Foreman ain't nothing. He's a big old bully from Texas who used to beat up people in the streets. He's a gang boy, who went into the Job Corps and got lucky. He hasn't been through no test. I got a punch for George. It's called the ghetto-whopper, and the reason it's called the ghetto-whopper is because it's thrown in the ghetto at three o'clock in the morning, which is when me and George are gonna fight.

• George Foreman don't stand a chance. When I finish going upside that sucker's head, he'll have so many nicks and cuts, it'll look like he had a bad morning shave. Except for Joe Frazier and one or two others, he ain't even fought nobody. Listen to the people George has fought. [Reading from a list] Don Waldheim. He was a nobody. Fred Askew. He was a nobody. Sylvester Dulliare. I can't even pronounce his name. Chuck Wepner. He was a nobody. John Carroll. He was a nobody. Cookie Wallace. He was a nobody. Vernon Clay. [Pause] Clay? He might be good.[5]

Foreman, by contrast, appeared surly and mean in the mold of Sonny Liston. Later in life, he would evolve into a genuinely likeable man, but in Zaire he was a hostile ominous presence.

"Are you concerned that Ali might be faster than you?" he was asked.

"It's all a matter of what you call fast," Foreman answered. "I can hit a man on the jaw fast enough."

"How do you feel about fighting at three o'clock in the morning?"

"When I was growing up in Houston, I had a lot of fights at three and four in the morning."

"What do you think of Ali's promise that he's going to tell you something just before the fight that will affect your mind?"

"I guess he'll have to say it."

"Do you like to talk during a fight?"

"I never get a chance to talk much in the ring. By the time I begin to know a fellow, it's over."[6]

GEORGE FOREMAN: "There was a time in my life when I was sort of unfriendly, and Zaire was part of that period. I was going to knock Ali's block off, and the thought of doing it didn't bother me at all. But to be honest with you, Ali had been important to me for a long time. I remember being in junior high school, and walking home with a friend who had a record of Cassius Clay reading poetry. I went over to this friend's house; we listened to the record; and I just about fell in love with Ali. Then, when I was sixteen, working in the Job Corps, people would say to me, 'George, you're always picking on someone. Why don't you become a boxer?' And I said okay; I'd become a boxer, because I wanted to be like Muhammad Ali. He talked; he was handsome; he did wonderful things. If you were sixteen years old and wanted to copy somebody, it had to be Ali. So I started boxing and won an Olympic gold medal. But all through the amateurs, I was a puncher. Then I turned professional and told Dick Sadler, my trainer, that I wanted to fight like Ali. I could dance, jab, box, move. Sadler said, 'Okay, I'll make a finesse fighter out of you.' And he let me train that way, moving around the ring in the gym. But right before my first professional fight, in the dressing room, he told me, 'Go out and knock this guy out. That's the strategy. Push him off, hit him hard, and knock him out.' I said, 'Wait a minute. I'm a boxer; I fight like Ali.' But I followed Dick's instructions and knocked the guy out. After that, I went back to the gym, and again, sparring, Dick let me bounce around. He always let me dance in the gym. But every fight, right before we went to the ring, he'd say, 'Forget about being like Ali tonight. Punch!'

"Finally, I actually met Ali. It was around the time of my fourth professional fight. I was working in a gym in Florida. Ali came in, walked over to me with a briefcase in his hand, and said, 'George Foreman, I'm Muhammad Ali.' My knees were shaking; that's how proud I was to meet him. Then he said, 'I'm gonna show you something that will blow your mind. Don't tell nobody, but when you get to be champ, you'll have something like this.' And he sort of motioned me to the side, to a place where no one else in the gym could see us. He was pointing to his briefcase, and I said to myself, 'He's gonna open it up, and there's gonna be thousands of dollars inside.' And sure enough, he opened the briefcase. And inside, there was a telephone. He said, 'Man, what do you think of that?' And what I thought was, I love him, but this guy is crazy."

In Zaire, Foreman stayed in seclusion. Ali, by contrast, was often visible, attending press conferences, mingling with his fans, promoting both the fight and himself. Leon Gast, who was in Kinshasa as director of a hundred-man film crew, recalls some of the events surrounding the scene.

LEON GAST: "Ali was supremely confident. At least, that's how it seemed. It was as though the championship belonged to him, and getting it back in the ring was a formality to be dealt with at the appropriate time. Bundini was running around, shouting, 'The King has come home to reclaim his crown.' The other crazies in the entourage were doing their thing. And nothing seemed to bother Ali, except maybe Don King. Once or twice, you could see King was getting on Ali's nerves; and that was hard to do, because nothing seemed to bother Ali. One incident in particular that sticks in my mind happened at a press conference. Ali and King were seated on the dais, with Angelo in between. Bundini had a funny line he wanted to pass to Ali, so he whispered it to King. Then King leaned over Dundee to tell Ali whatever it was Bundini said, and Angelo asked, 'What did you say?' King told him, 'I ain't talking to you.' And Ali got furious. He leaned forward, put his finger in King's face and said, 'Don't you talk to Angelo like that. Don't you ever talk to him like that again.' Dundee made light of it. He put his hands up in the air, and said, 'Come on, fellows,' and they went on with the press conference. But I thought it was admirable the way Ali stuck up for Dundee. As soon as he saw King was trying to belittle Angelo, he got right on King. And then, later on, he socked it to King again. One of the women Don brought to Zaire was a friend who he was passing off as a translator. And Ali was having all sorts of problems with translations over there. None of the Zairians understood American idioms. Ali was constantly telling them, 'You don't talk American nigger; you don't understand our slang.' Finally—and it might have been at the same press conference—when the local translator couldn't understand something, Ali turned to King's woman, who'd been standing around doing nothing for days, and told her, 'You translate.' And she didn't know a word of anything except English. So Ali looked right at King and said, 'You mean, you brought that girl all the way over here just to let me down?' "

As September 25 approached, tensions mounted but Ali remained confident. On several occasions, he read a lengthy poem entitled "A Bad Morning Shave" to reporters, "because the fight's at three o'clock in the morning, and after the fight, George will look like he had a bad shave."[7] On other occasions, shorter poetry sufficed:

> You think the world was shocked when Nixon resigned?
> Wait till I whup George Foreman's behind.

> Float like a butterfly, sting like a bee
> His hands can't hit what his eyes can't see
> Now you see me, now you don't
> George thinks he will, but I know he won't.

I done wrassled with an alligator
I done tussled with a whale
Only last week I murdered a rock
Injured a stone, hospitalized a brick
I'm so mean I make medicine sick.[8]

Then came a hitch—a big one.

Eight days before the fight was scheduled to take place, Foreman was sparring with Bill McMurray, a thirty-three-year-old journeyman fighter. Raising his arms to defend against a barrage of blows, McMurray accidentally jammed an elbow into the champion's face, slicing open the skin above Foreman's right eye. Now, suddenly, the fight was in limbo and rumors were flying. Foreman was going back to the United States and might never fight Ali. The government of Zaire was planning to put both fighters under house arrest to ensure that they stayed in the country. Foreman's cut wasn't that bad. Foreman's cut was so bad that it might be six months before he could fight again.

HOWARD BINGHAM: "I was with Ali when they told him the fight was off because of the cut for at least a month and maybe longer. He wasn't happy about it. He'd worked harder to get himself in shape for that fight than anytime before in his life. And to be truthful, he'd had his fill of Zaire. Publicly, he was telling everybody how much he loved the country, how wonderful it was, and how beautiful the women were. But when we were alone, he was saying things like, 'I'd give anything to be training in the United States. They got ice cream there, and pretty girls and miniskirts.'

"Angelo, Bundini, Ali, and me were in the room when we heard about the cut. And Ali just about went crazy. First, he wanted to go ahead with the fight, and let George wear a headguard to protect his eye. Then he realized that wouldn't work, and he started saying they should bring in Joe Frazier. Give Frazier a million dollars; Ali would take three million instead of five. And when Angelo said that wouldn't work, Ali wanted to move the whole show back to the United States, to the Los Angeles Coliseum or the Astrodome in Houston. He was saying, 'They've seen us over here in Africa. It would be easier to fight in the United States, especially for George.' I mean, he was upset. He was tired of worrying about the food and drinking only bottled water. There was no telling when George would be able to fight or whether the cut might open up again in training. Ali had a couple of bad hours, but then pretty soon he was back to his old self again. By the end of the day, he was in much better spirits, saying everything happens for a reason and God plans everything, so probably something bad would have happened if the fight had gone on when it was supposed to happen."

The bout was rescheduled for 4:00 A.M. on October 30. Probably, Ali suffered less from the layoff than Foreman, because he was able to continue training without interruption. Both fighters were warned by the government of Zaire that it would be unwise to try to leave the country. And while the champion brooded about his cut, the challenger busied himself with predictions:

- It's befitting that I should go out of boxing just like I came in, beating a big bad monster who knocks everybody out and nobody can whup him. This man is supposed to annihilate me, but ten years ago they said the same thing about Sonny Liston. George Foreman don't stand a chance. He's in trouble. The whole world is gonna bow down to me, because the stage is set. Everybody's talking about how great George Foreman is, how hard he hits; but I'll be king again. I'm fighting another Sonny Liston.

- George Foreman is relying on one thing. He's relying on his power, but I'm relying on lots of things. I've got speed of hand, I'm fast on my feet, I can take a punch, and I've got experience. I've gone fifteen rounds a number of times, and he's only been ten rounds twice. I can go the route. If someone knocks me down, I get up again. My jaw gets broke, and I keep on fighting. We don't know how George will be after five rounds with a man who's sticking and moving. We don't know what happens to George when he finds hisself taking a whuppin'. I never seen George tired yet, huffing and puffing, get winded and have to take a few punches. And when George gets tired, I'll still be dancing. I'll be picking my shots, beating him at will. If George Foreman don't get me in seven, I'm telling you now, his parachute won't open.

- Tell everybody to get to their theaters and don't be late, because I might end this in one round. I never wanted to whup a man so bad in my life. I'm getting angry just thinking about it. How much longer do we have to wait? I'm ready to whup George Foreman right now.

October 29, 1974, the day before the fight, was hot and muggy in Kinshasa. Ali slept sporadically. He had been in Zaire for fifty-five days. Meanwhile, at the stadium where the fight would be fought, a scene that would lead to controversy was unfolding. Many of the pivotal fights in Ali's career were steeped in rumor and innuendo. Against Henry Cooper, the issue was whether Angelo Dundee deliberately slashed his fighter's glove to give him time to recover from a fourth-round knockdown. Later, when Ali fought Sonny Liston, there were allegations that Liston quit. In Zaire, after the fact and in light of how the fight evolved, debate centered on whether Dundee deliberately loosened the ring ropes before the bout. Dundee emphatically denies the charge. Bobby Goodman, who was with him in the ring the afternoon before the fight, discusses those crucial hours.

BOBBY GOODMAN: "Before any fight, Angelo would go down to check the ring and make sure it was all right. In Zaire, the fight was at four in the morning, so we went at noon the day before. And the ring was awful. It was brand new, but it hadn't been set up right. One corner was sinking into the mud, so we had to put concrete slabs under the cornerpost. The padding was Ensaflor, which is the universally approved safety flooring. It's a foam rubber that provides maximum safety for the boxer if he hits his head, but it has to be kept in a cool environment. Once you put Ensaflor in heat and humidity, like any foam rubber, it gets soft and mushy. We'd asked the ring crew not to put it down until the evening of the fight, but they'd put it down early. That meant the ring would be slow, which was definitely to Ali's disadvantage. The canvas was new and much too slippery, so we put some resin on it. Then some guy came along with a bucket and sponge, trying to wipe the ring clean. Angelo asked, 'What are you doing?' And the guy answered, 'The television people told us the ring was dirty.' Angelo said, 'That's not dirt, that's resin. You gotta put resin in the ring.'

"So all those things were going on, but the worst problem was the ropes. New ropes stretch after one night's use. They have to be readjusted because they become loose. And because these ropes were new and had been left out in heat and humidity, they'd already started to stretch. Plus, to make matters worse, you can tighten ropes by turning the turnbuckles in each corner, but here the workmen had already tightened the turnbuckles as far as they'd go. So we had to readjust the ropes. We didn't loosen them; we made them tighter. If we hadn't, with the heat and humidity and preliminary

With Howard Cosell and Wilt Chamberlain, 1971. *(Howard Bingham)*

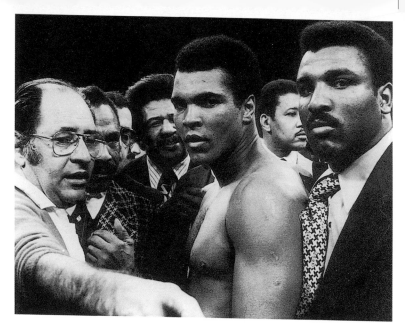

Flanked by Ferdie Pacheco,
Cassius Clay, Sr. (plaid
coat), and brother Rahaman
before the Ernie Terrell
fight, 1966.
(*Howard Bingham*)

Trainer Angelo Dundee.
(*Howard Bingham*)

With Bundini Brown in Zaire, 1974. *(Howard Bingham)*

Fighting on the ropes with George Foreman in Zaire, 1974. *(Howard Bingham)*

ABOVE LEFT–Pat Patterson.
(*Howard Bingham*)

ABOVE RIGHT–James Anderson.
(*Howard Bingham*)

MIDDLE LEFT–Wali Muhammad.
(*Howard Bingham*)

MIDDLE RIGHT–Lloyd Wells.
(*Howard Bingham*)

ABOVE LEFT–Bobby Goodman.
(*Howard Bingham*)

RIGHT–Gene Kilroy.
(*Howard Bingham*)

Jeremiah Shabazz and Abdul
Rahaman (Captain Sam), 1980.
(Howard Bingham)

With Lana Shabazz at Deer
Lake, 1978. *(Howard Bingham)*

During the filming of *The Greatest*, 1976; Bundini is on Ali's right, Wali Muhammad to his left. *(Howard Bingham)*

With President Gerald Ford at the White House, 1974. *(Howard Bingham)*

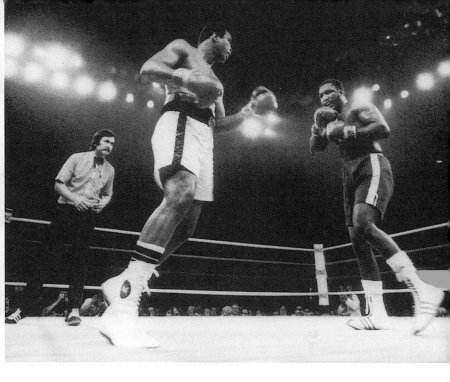

Fighting Joe Frazier in Manila, 1975. *(Howard Bingham)*

Don King and Bob Arum. *(Howard Bingham)*

A wedding portrait: Cassius Clay, Sr., third wife Veronica, Ali, and Odessa Clay.
(Howard Bingham)

bouts, by fight time they would have been draped on the floor. The way we did it was, we took off the clamps, pulled the ropes through the turnbuckles, lined everything up, and cut off the slack. We took about a foot out of each rope, and retightened the turnbuckles by hand so they could be tightened more just before the fight. Angelo even told the ring chief that, right before the first bout, he should tighten the ropes by turning the turnbuckle. And then, before the main event, they were supposed to tighten them again. That never happened. They just didn't do it, so by the time Ali got in the ring, the ropes were slack; but there was nothing underhanded in what Angelo did. In fact, Dick Sadler and Archie Moore, who were Foreman's cornermen, saw us that afternoon in the ring. Angelo and I were sweating our butts off, cutting the ropes with a double-edged razor blade because nobody could find a knife. We were pulling them through, taping up the ends. And we said, 'Come on! You know, you guys can help.' But it was hot, and they wouldn't give us a hand."

The night of the fight, Ali watched a horror film called *Baron of Blood* on television. Then he went to sleep, woke up at 2:00 A.M., and dressed in a black shirt and black trousers. Foreman was a three-to-one betting favorite. The challenger's own camp doubted his ability to win. "Before Ali fought Joe Frazier," Wali Muhammad would say later, "we thought he just couldn't lose. But we were wrong, and against Foreman we were worried. George had been built up to be such a great fighter. People thought he'd kill Ali. And then, right before the fight, Ali told me he had a plan. He was gonna go out and hit Foreman with a straight right hand as soon as the bell rang. I said, 'No, champ; no! You're gonna dance.' And he told me, 'No, I'm going out and hit Foreman upside his head, so he'll know he's in a fight.' And that's just what Ali did, but that wasn't the only surprise he had for George that night."

Ali and his entourage were driven by bus from N'Sele to the Stade du 20 Mai, where sixty thousand fans were waiting. "In the dressing room," recalls Bernie Yuman, a longtime Ali friend, "everyone's teeth were chattering. We were shaking like leaves on a tree. Ali looked at us and demanded, 'What is it? What's the matter?' "

No one answered. Then Ali grinned. "This ain't nothing but another day in the dramatic life of Muhammad Ali," he told them. "Do I look scared? I fear Allah and thunderstorms and bad plane rides, but this is like another day in the gym."[10] Minutes later, Herbert Muhammad entered the dressing room with a message for

Ali from his father, Elijah Muhammad. "He told me I was fighting for our people," Ali remembers. "He said I should do my best, and that if I did, Allah would be with me."

Then Ali left for the ring. And over the course of the next hour, he performed one of the "miracles" that went into the making of the Ali legend. Years later, suffering from terminal cancer, Lana Shabazz would reminisce, "I wasn't worried during that fight. I just died three or four times. Oh, my goodness; I flat out died. I couldn't look. I just covered my face with my hands, and every now and then I'd ask, 'Is he still alive?' Never mind winning or losing; I feared for his life. I don't know what was wrong with that boy; standing by the ropes, taking all those punches. But Ali won; he found a way. Lord Almighty, he found a way."

FERDIE PACHECO: "What Ali did in the ring that night was truly inspired. The layoff had taken away his first set of gifts, so in Zaire he developed another. The man had the greatest chin in the history of the heavyweight division. He had as much courage as anyone who ever fought. He could think creatively and clearly with bombs flying around him. And he showed it all when it mattered most that night with the most amazing performance I've ever seen. Somehow, early in the fight, Ali figured out that the way to beat George Foreman was to let Foreman hit him. Now that's some game plan. Watching that fight, seeing Ali take punch after punch, and knowing that with his strength and courage he wouldn't go down, a person could have been forgiven for thinking that sooner or later the referee would be forced to step in to save his life. But Ali took everything Foreman could offer. And at that most crucial moment in his career, instead of losing, which was what most people thought would happen, he knocked George out and embarked on another long wondrous championship ride."

During round one, Ali tested Foreman at long range. Then, thirty seconds into the second round, he retreated to the ropes—the last place an opponent wanted to be against the most feared puncher in boxing. The move so violated conventional wisdom that George Plimpton, who was at ringside, turned to Norman Mailer and shouted, "It's a fix." Ali's corner was screaming at him to dance. But the challenger remained in place, determined to fight out of a defensive posture, blocking some punches, leaning back against the ropes to avoid others, and absorbing the sledgehammer blows that landed. For the next six rounds, that was how he fought. But Ali didn't just take punches, he threw them as well. Fighting off the ropes, he won three of the first four rounds. Then, in round five, Foreman began landing thunderous right hands to the challenger's body. Ali looked tired; the end seemed near. But he rallied at the end of the round, survived rounds six and seven, and at the start of round eight, told Foreman, "Now it's my turn."

Five men who were in Zaire tell the story of the bout, starting with Foreman's most experienced cornerman, who was also Ali's first professional trainer—Archie Moore.

ARCHIE MOORE: "George was the most dangerous puncher of his time. And what I remember most about that fight was, Ali rushed out at the opening bell, showing no fear, and struck George on top of the head. Plans upset; do you know what I mean? Right at the start, George knew he had something different to contend with. But George only knew one way to fight, so he swung and he swung, and he pinned Ali up against the ropes, determined to wear him down. At first, that seemed like a fine strategy. Everything we'd planned was designed to get Ali on the ropes, where George could hit him. But once George got him there, and when Ali stayed there, George didn't know what to do.

"I was not the instruction-giver in Zaire. That was Dick Sadler's job. I was yelling from the corner, 'Go underneath; go between the arms.' But George had other ideas. He wanted to beat on Ali's arms, because fighting like that he'd actually broken one of Gregorio Peralta's arms. He was going to beat Ali's arms down so he could get to the rib cage. And as I recall, George also threw some rather lethal punches in the direction of Ali's cranium. And everything George did would have been well and good, except for several small details. Ali protected his body with his forearms and elbows. He was able to avoid the devastating experience of George hitting him in the head by leaning way back against the ropes. And when George's blows did land, Ali took them with a marvelous show of disdain and managed to convince George that George couldn't punch. Then George got tired. Ali had him thinking, and worrying, and he'd wasted too much ammunition on Ali's arms. And when George got tired against a skilled warrior like Ali, that was the beginning of the end. In fact, that was the end."

WALI MUHAMMAD: "In the first round, Ali danced like we knew he would. Then, I guess it was near the end of the round, he got caught on the ropes and leaned away from a big left hook. It was one of those punches—I don't want to think about what would have happened if it landed, but Ali leaned way back and it missed by six inches. Then Foreman threw another punch, and the same thing happened. Between rounds, me and Angelo were working the corner. I was cleaning Ali's mouthpiece, and Angelo was giving him instructions. We had seen the ropes were loose, so Bundini got on the ring apron to tighten them. And Ali shouted, 'No, don't! Leave 'em alone.' Then he went out for round two, and I thought he was crazy. He went to the ropes. We were hollering, 'Get off the ropes! Dance, champ; dance!' But Ali stayed where he was almost the whole round. Afterward, in the corner, Angelo told him, 'Get back on your toes. Move! Don't let Foreman tee off on you like that.' But the next round, it was the same thing. I thought George would break him in two. The plan was to dance for six or seven rounds, tire Foreman out, and when he got tired, move in on him. And instead, Ali was standing in one place, taking punches. A couple of times, I asked Angelo, 'What's happening?' Angelo said, 'I don't know.' Then, in the sixth round, I think it was, Foreman started slowing down. Between rounds, I said, 'Champ; he's getting tired.' Ali told me, 'I know; I'll get him in a couple of rounds.' And that's what he did. He knocked him out in the eighth round. Fighting off the ropes was the wrong thing to do, but it was the right thing to do. Ali just had that ability to see things nobody else saw."

ANGELO DUNDEE: "I won't kid you. When he went to the ropes, I felt sick. Going into the fight, I thought Muhammad would win but not that way. The way I saw things happening was Ali dancing for five or six rounds. Foreman was a stand-up fighter who didn't move his head much, so I figured Muhammad could do a number with his jab. Then I imagined him picking up the pace when George got tired, and knocking him out in the late rounds. Styles make fights, and George had the perfect style for Ali. But everything we planned was built around not getting hit. Muhammad was going to move, stay on his toes, show George all kinds of angles. What can I say? That shows what I know. It was a great fight, and I had a hell of a seat to watch it."

MUHAMMAD ALI: "I didn't really plan what happened that night. But when a fighter gets in the ring, he has to adjust according to the conditions he faces. Against George, the ring was slow. Dancing all night, my legs would have got tired. And George was following me too close, cutting off the ring. In the first round, I used more energy staying away from him than he used chasing me. I was tireder than I should have been with fourteen rounds to go. I knew I couldn't keep dancing, because by the middle of the fight I'd be really tired and George would get me. So between rounds, I decided to do what I did in training when I got tired. It was something Archie Moore used to do. Archie was a smart fighter. He fought till he was as old as I am now, and he did it by conserving energy. He let younger men take their shots and blocked everything in scientific fashion. And then, when they got tired, Archie would attack. Not everyone can do that; it takes a lot of skill. But I figured I'd be able to handle George off the ropes early in the fight when I was fresh, and if he hit too hard, I'd just start dancing again. So starting in the second round, I gave George what he thought he wanted. And he hit hard. A couple of times, he shook me bad, especially with the right hand. But I blocked and dodged most of what he threw, and each round his punches got slower and hurt less when they landed. Then I started talking to him. 'Hit harder! Show me something, George. That don't hurt. I thought you were supposed to be bad.' And George was trapped. I was on the ropes, but he was trapped, because attacking was all he knew how to do. By round six, I knew he was tired. His punches weren't as hard as before. And because of the way George fought, one punch at a time with his head not moving, it was getting easy to hit him with counterpunches. The punch I knocked him out with, if I'd knocked him down in the first round, he would have gotten up. But by the time I got him, he was so exhausted that to pull himself up was just too much."

GEORGE FOREMAN: "Muhammad amazed me; I'll admit it. He outthought me; he outfought me. That night, he was just the better man in the ring. Before the fight, I thought I'd knock him out easy. One round, two rounds. I was very confident. And what I remember most about the fight was, I went out and hit Muhammad with the hardest shot to the body I ever delivered to any opponent. Anybody else in the world would have crumbled. Muhammad cringed; I could see it hurt. And then he looked at me; he had that look in his eyes, like he was saying I'm not gonna let you hurt me. And to be honest, that's the main thing I remember about the fight. Everything else happened too quick. I got burned out. Muhammad started talking to me. I remember Angelo shouting from the corner, 'Muhammad, don't play with that sucker,' but Muhammad just kept playing. The 'rope-a-dope' was what he called it later, and it worked. You see, Muhammad's antennas were built to look out for big punches. And with the style I had, my height, and my tendency to throw big punches—no matter how hard I hit, Muhammad had the instinct to get ready for each punch, ride it through, and be waiting for the next one. I was the aggressor; there was no doubt about that. I was throwing the most punches, but I knew that in some way I was losing. In fact, I remember thinking during the fight, hey, this guy wasn't champion before because someone bought the title for him. He's good.

"I remember the punch that knocked me down, too. I was going after him. I was tired, but I still didn't respect his punching power, so I was chasing with my hands down. Muhammad was near the ropes. I missed with a right hand, turned around with my hands down, and he moved with speed that he wasn't supposed to have at that point in the fight after taking all those blows. He moved, threw a right hand. And boom! Right on the button. It caught me off balance, and I went down. I could have gotten up, but I'd been taught, when a man gets knocked down, he looks to his corner. So I looked to my corner, and they were signaling for me to wait. Then they signaled for me to get up, but it was too late. If I'd gotten up—you know, I've been hurt and knocked down in other fights, and gotten up off the floor to win. Anyone who saw me against Ron Lyle knows that. But to be honest, against Muhammad, he was such an intelligent boxer, even if I'd gotten up, that night I think he would have won. He was just a little too sharp for me then.

"After the fight, for a while I was bitter. I had all sorts of excuses. The ring ropes were loose. The referee counted too fast. The cut hurt my training. I was drugged. I should have just said the best man won, but I'd never lost before so I didn't know how to lose. I fought that fight over in my head a thousand times. And then, finally, I realized I'd lost to a great champion; probably the greatest of all time. I was drugged all right. Muhammad gave me a dose of that big right hand. He won fair and square, and now I'm just proud to be part of the Ali legend. If people mention my name with his from time to time, that's enough for me. That, and I hope Muhammad likes me, because I like him. I like him a lot."

Shortly after the fight ended, a torrential thunderstorm began, flooding the stadium and knocking out satellite communication between Kinshasa and the rest of the world. Hundreds of fans remained in the stands, chanting, "Ali, bomaye" (Ali, kill him)—the battle cry they'd chanted during the night. Meanwhile, Ali returned to the compound in N'Sele, which for eight weeks had been his home. He and his wife were in the back seat of a Citroen, with a police car in the lead. The bus carrying his entourage followed behind. "It was like the return of a victorious army," Ferdie Pacheco recalls. "All through the jungle, people were lined up along the road with children in their arms, waiting for Ali in the pouring rain."

An hour later, with the rain still falling, *Newsweek*'s Pete Bonventre followed Ali's route as the African darkness turned to dawn.

PETE BONVENTRE: "The fight was over. Ali was the champ. Everyone had rushed to the locker room for interviews, and then the guys working for the daily papers sat down to write their stories. I was on a weekly deadline, so I had some time before I filed. It was five in the morning, and Ken Regan [a photographer on assignment in Zaire] said, 'Let's drive out to N'Sele.' So we got a driver and were en route when the thunderstorm really hit. We couldn't see five feet in front of the car. Once or twice, we had to pull off the road. Finally, two hours after we started, we got to N'Sele. There was no press. The entourage was gone. We went over to Ali's cottage. And three hours after the greatest victory of his life, Muhammad Ali was sitting on the stoop, showing a magic trick to a group of black children. It was a rope trick, where the rope is cut in half and then it's suddenly back together again. And it was hard to tell who was having a better time, Ali or the children. All I could think was, I don't care what anyone says, there'll never be anyone like him again."

Ten years after he'd beaten Sonny Liston, seven years after he'd been stripped of his title, Muhammad Ali had at long last reclaimed the heavyweight championship of the world.

11

The King

Ali's triumph over George Foreman lifted spirits throughout the world. It was the classic tale of a handsome prince, unfairly stripped of his crown, who battles back against adversity to recapture what rightfully belongs to him. Past emnities were all but forgotten. Long-time detractors became friends. Eight years earlier, *Ring* magazine had declined to designate a "fighter of the year"; acknowledging that Ali deserved the award on the basis of his ring performance, the publication nonetheless declared, "Cassius Clay most emphatically is not to be held up as an example to the youngsters of the United States."[1] Now, in the aftermath of his victory in Zaire, Ali was named *Ring*'s "Fighter of the Year," "Sportsman of the Year" by *Sports Illustrated*, and awarded the Hickock Belt, given annually to the nation's outstanding professional athlete. Maury Allen put the out-pouring of good will in perspective:

> There are certain heroes of sports who transcend the games and contests they participate in. They become folk heroes, figures of such enormity they cross the standard barriers. In the last four decades, maybe half a dozen athletes have become historical figures, preserved landmarks of American life. Joe Louis was such a figure, a man of quiet dignity and pride, an American dream fulfilled. Joe Di-

Maggio came from the windswept fishing docks of San Francisco's Italian back streets to typify style and elegance in his sport. Jackie Robinson crossed those lines from the field of play to the fields of life. And Ted Williams in his way did it, and Vince Lombardi in his, and Bill Russell in his.

Muhammad Ali does it best of all. It is time to recognize Ali for what he is; the greatest athlete of his time and maybe all time and one of the most important and brave men of all American time. The time has come to end the bitterness and forget the past. It seems time to appreciate and enjoy this incredible athlete, this wondrous man.[2]

Then came an occasion that would have been unthinkable several years earlier. On December 10, 1974, at the invitation of Gerald Ford, Ali visited the White House.

GERALD FORD: "I recall it quite well. I've always been interested in boxing. I guess it goes back to my youth, when I can recall very vaguely Jack Dempsey and Gene Tunney, and then later, Joe Louis. And I've always been a sports enthusiast. I read the sports pages first every morning, because I have a fifty-fifty chance of being right there. With the editorials and front page, the odds aren't as good. As president, I felt it was appropriate to recognize those who had achieved excellence in sports. I always liked to meet the best in any part of the sporting world, and certainly Muhammad Ali was representative of that group. But beyond that, when I took office, we as a nation were pretty much torn apart. There were conflicts between families, in colleges, and on the streets. We'd gone through some serious race problems; the Vietnam War had heightened differences; and of course there was the heritage of Watergate. And one of the major challenges my administration faced was how we could heal the country. Not that everybody had to agree, but at least we should lower our voices and listen to one another. I think that, during the two-and-a-half years I was president, we did that, and having Muhammad Ali come to the Oval Office was part of our overall effort. I felt it was important to reach out and indicate individually as well as collectively that we could have honest differences without bitterness. So I wanted to meet Muhammad, not only because of my interest in sports, but because it was part of my overall effort to heal the wounds of racial division, Vietnam, and Watergate.

"His visit was an enjoyable time for me. You know, Muhammad

never lacked for words, and it was a real pleasure to chat with him. He was a magnificent-looking man; big, handsome, fit. We talked about some of his successes and my interest in sports. I've always respected what he accomplished in boxing. He represented what a young man can do in developing his talent and reaching the pinnacle of his chosen profession. And he was a man of principle. I know there were some who thought he evaded his military responsibility, but I've never questioned anybody's dedication to whatever religion they believe in. I give people the maximum benefit of the doubt when they take a stand predicated on conscience. That's always been my philosophy, so I never joined the critics who complained about what he did and didn't do during the Vietnam War. I accepted his decision. And because of his principles, I firmly believe that as time goes on, Muhammad Ali will be remembered for more than just excellence in athletics. I suppose it's premature to say how history will be written, but I'm quite sure that his page will talk about him as more than just a superb athlete."

"The heavyweight champion," it has been written, "is a King without a country. And on the rare occasions when he chooses to fight, his sport lives again like a fairy-tale kingdom."[3] But Ali, who broke the mold so many times, broke it again in that, when he was champion, his kingdom flourished all the time. "He served the world a banquet of dreams and opportunities," says Bob Dylan, "a mixed bag of attitudes and desires culminating in the fulfillment of hopes and aspirations of the young and old alike."

"There was so much intuitive grace in what Ali did," recalls David Halberstam. "He had that touch. He knew how to play the role of champ, inside and outside the ring. God, he knew how to play that role."

GEORGE PLIMPTON: "Ali was by far the most interesting athlete of my generation. Some came close: Bill Russell, Joe Namath, Willie Mays. But Ali was electrifying when he was at his best and champion. He towered above everyone else. I remember the discouragement I felt, and others felt, that we hadn't done enough for this extraordinary man when his title was taken away from him. Of course, he won vindication in the courts, but that wasn't enough. He had to get his title back, and that had to be done in the ring.

"There are so many memories I have of Ali. He took me around Chicago once, chauffeuring me in this big car. I sat in back, because he said you can't have a chauffeur without someone sitting in back.

We drove by Elijah Muhammad's house at seventy miles an hour. I doubt he wanted to be seen with a white man in back. I remember sitting on the grass with him at night, looking up at the stars, and his telling me about Wallace Fard's spaceship in the sky. And I was with him when he visited the prison on Riker's Island. He'd just come back from Africa. All the prisoners were gathered together in a big assembly hall, and when Ali was introduced, there was a roar of acclaim. He walked on stage, did the Ali Shuffle, and the cheering got even louder. But then he lost them. He began talking about how he'd been in jail in Florida for a traffic violation, how much he'd hated jail, and what were they doing in jail? And it was the wrong approach. The prisoners started hooting. So he looked out at them and said, 'All right! You think you're bad? Anybody who thinks they're badder than I'm bad, come up here and I'll show you who's bad.' That won them all back again. They cheered and carried on and loved him. Even today, when I think about Ali, I smile, and there aren't many people who have that effect. There was an aura about him. He glowed, sort of a strange golden color; like a statue bronzed gold. He shone as though he was possessed of some wonderful power that his skin just couldn't contain."

Ali's looks were part of his appeal. That was obvious. The same person in another man's body would have constituted a totally different phenomenon. "He was a beautiful man," recalls Julian Bond. "Not just his face, but his whole physique. I remember a picture of him on the cover of a book; one where he was sweaty and staring right into the camera. I looked at that photo and said to myself, 'There must be women, white and black, all over America, who wouldn't be caught dead at a boxing match, who are contemptuous of boxers, who are buying this book because of the photos." "He was the best-looking man in the world; that's all," says Lana Shabazz. "And don't think that didn't make us proud."

Four men and a woman who've spent a good part of their adult lives painting, photographing, and otherwise analyzing looks comment on Ali's appeal.

LEROY NEIMAN: "I saw him in person for the first time in 1962 when he fought Billy Daniels at St. Nick's Arena. I'd just moved to New York, and before the fight Jack Drees, who did some announcing, came over to me and said, 'You've got to see this kid.' I knew what Ali looked like, because like everyone else, I'd seen photographs of him at the Olympics. But Jack told me, 'You have to see him; it's different in person.' So we went back to this dingy dressing room, opened the door, and there was Ali—he was Cassius Clay then—sitting by himself on a table. Very friendly, very cool and relaxed; in a good mood, happy to meet anyone. I asked if I could draw him and he seemed to think that was a good idea, so I sat down and started to sketch. And he was golden, no hair on his body, just beautiful. He looked like a piece of sculpture, with no flaw or imperfection. His features and limbs were perfectly proportioned; and over the years, the way he looked that night never really changed. He was an extraordinarily handsome, charismatic man."

HOWARD BINGHAM: "He had that face; he was born for the camera. There's lots of people with kind faces and lots of people with happy faces, but no one ever photographed like Ali. It's like there was magic between him and the camera. He always knew what to do to make a picture come out right. I've probably taken more photographs of Ali than any person took of another person ever. I don't like doing it as much now as before because, with that look he has on his face sometimes, it's not as good as it used to be. But when he's happy, when he's up, it's still good. No one in the world has a face like Ali. You know, I can take a hundred pictures of most people, and maybe one will turn out real good. But with Ali, when he was in his prime, forty or fifty would turn out right."

NEIL LEIFER: "Ali was a photographer's dream. He was so good-looking. He was what you wanted a fighter, or anybody else, to look like. And in person, his size always surprised me because he was built so perfectly to scale. People who never met Ali might have thought he was too delicate for boxing, but in the flesh he was huge. And there are some subjects who are comfortable posing and some who aren't. Ali knew how to pose. I think it was vanity that made him concentrate on the camera. But beyond that, he was spectacularly cooperative. A photographer couldn't miss with Ali. He made your job a success just by showing up."

RAY CAVE: "I spent close to thirty years at Time Inc., starting as a writer for *Sports Illustrated* and ending up as editorial director for all of Time Inc.'s publications. During that period, I must have looked at close to a million photos. And there's a handful of people who, when the camera clicks, something wonderful happens. They're just different from you and me. John Kennedy was one; Arnold Palmer was another. There's Cheryl Tiegs, and Ali. When the camera was on Ali, it always seemed to catch something. And

I'll tell you a story that's central to what we're talking about. When I was managing editor of *Time*, *Newsweek* was about to excerpt a major book. It was one of the Watergate memoirs. They had a two-part cover story coming up, and had done marvelously with similar book excerpts in the past. And our publisher asked if I could think of something to keep our newsstand sales up for those two weeks, because we figured to take a beating. At the very least, he wanted better-than-average covers, and I said okay. This was near the end of Ali's career. And keep in mind, we're talking about *Time*, not *Sports Illustrated*. But in all my years at *SI*, the people who had always sold best on the cover were Ali and Cheryl Tiegs. So I put Ali on the cover the first week and Tiegs the next, and both covers sold 70 percent more than *Time*'s normal newsstand sales. They far outsold *Newsweek*. And I think Ali would sell well on the cover of most magazines even today, which is extraordinary when you realize how long he's been out of the limelight. But his personality has gotten into the American psyche, and he has that look."

CHERYL TIEGS: "He's an extraordinarily handsome man because of his charm, his charisma, his whole being. In many ways, he exudes confidence. But I've met him several times, and each time, even though he recognized me and said hello, he never looked me in the eye. It was always down or to the side, and I wondered if he's not very shy. In a way, it confuses me, because like everyone else, I've seen him shouting, 'I'm the greatest.' I've listened to him recite poetry and all the rest. And I'd like to know what he's really like. Does he hide behind his image? Is he proud of it? I don't know. But if the answer is that he's shy and finds it hard to deal with people one-on-one, then I think what he's done is brilliant; to be noticed and to overcome his shyness. And the way he looks, the way he photographs, is extraordinary.

"I feel totally comfortable in front of the camera. All it takes is a little concentration to look at that black hole in the circle and forget everything else. But I've been trained, so every second I'm being photographed I'm aware of every part of my body as well as what's going on inside. After years of training, it comes naturally to me, and I'd think that Ali, as a trained athlete, has that same awareness of his face and body. Look at these pictures of Ali. This one [Ali in boxing trunks, smiling, posed against the ring ropes] radiates total confidence in his being. He's looking straight at the camera, not hiding anything at all. He obviously cares about his appearance, and looks perfect without even trying, but that's not what makes him so good with the camera. It's the confidence that puts him so at ease. Now this picture [Ali squared off in mock battle with a well-muscled adversary on an inner-city street] is different from the last one. In the first picture, Ali was performing for the camera. Here he's doing it for the people around him. The people on the street are his audience. He might not be aware of how he looks to the camera, but he's aware of how he looks to them. He's having a great time, and obviously he knows he's turning them on. This one [Ali in a tuxedo] is the sweet side of the man. Handsome, charming; he looks so gentle. And this [Ali standing over Sonny Liston with his fist cocked, screaming at Liston to get off the canvas]; Ali's not doing this for anybody but himself. And I don't blame Liston for not getting up."

But Ali's appeal went far beyond his looks. At its core was the fact that he loved people. "He draws strength from the people," wrote Richard Durham, one of Ali's biographers. "They nourish him and he keeps what they give him. Some men cannot take from the people. If the people give to them, it doesn't get through or it just seeps away. He has the power to keep it. It strengthens him the way a parent's love strengthens a child. And when he has enough of that strength, he can do anything the people want of him."[4]

Ali received more people on a daily basis than any pope or president ever. More than any other public figure of his time, he belonged to the masses. Most celebrities live life removed from their idolators. Ali chose to walk among them, never looking down at those who looked up to him. He loved to be recognized, and virtually never declined when asked for an autograph, handshake, or kiss. As far as he was concerned, people were people, and all people were meant to be loved. "I think it's his secret wish to be seen by every man, woman, and child on the planet earth," wrote Wilfred Sheed.[5] And those who met Ali were rarely disappointed. He wasn't special only to black Americans, Muslims, or any other group. Muhammad Ali belonged to the world.

HOWARD BINGHAM: "Ali loves people; he always has. He believes God put him on Earth to be good to people, and that's the way he is. A lot of celebrities are only interested in hanging out with other celebrities, but with Ali, the celebrities were the ones who pursued him. He wasn't any more interested in being with someone famous than being with anyone else. Except for old rock stars. Ali loved Fats Domino, Little Richard, Jackie Wilson, Sam Cooke, Lloyd

Price, Chubby Checker, all those guys. He still does. Even today, he'll run across a room, all excited, if Chubby Checker comes in. And he doesn't realize how excited those guys are to meet him. It's like he's still a kid, looking up, and they're the ones on the pedestal."

RALPH THORNTON: "Ali loved just about everyone. It wasn't something he did for show. No reporter had to be around for him to spend time with a hotel maid or the maid's children. He'd do his magic tricks for a truckdriver the same way he'd do them for a president or king. And people couldn't help but like him. Even the bigots, people who thought they hated him; there was something about Ali that, once they were in his presence, it didn't matter what they'd thought before, they'd hold up their babies for him to kiss and line up to shake his hand. And don't think it was just in the United States. It was like that all over the world. In Africa, in Asia, Ali could be doing roadwork, and little kids would come running out of huts. These kids had never seen a television. Probably, they didn't even have a radio. But their faces would light up. They'd point and say, 'Muhammad Ali!' They all knew him; he was the most recognizable person in the world. And no one ever got shut out. Ali was accessible to everyone."

One of the remarkable aspects of Ali's life is that, despite being a lightning rod for all sorts of emotions, he scorned most security precautions. The 1960s were a time of violence and assassination in the United States. Ali, in some quarters, was the most hated man in America. Yet he never stopped moving freely in public. In the 1970s, that violence extended throughout the world. Terrorism became the weapon of choice for the disaffected and disenchanted. Yet Ali continued to mingle at will. "I don't need no bodyguard or guns," he said often. "God is my bodyguard; Allah watches over me. If I walk into a stadium with a hundred thousand people, no human can keep somebody from putting a bullet in me. But I can't be worrying about things like that. A man filled with fear don't live and enjoy life. So I trust in God to look after me. Allah fixes the time when all of us will be taken."

Thus, handling "security" for Ali often meant little more than directing traffic and hoping for the best. Pat Patterson, who had the job for the better part of a decade, recalls what it was like.

PAT PATTERSON: "My meeting Ali goes back to when I was a policeman in Chicago and had the assignment of escorting Elijah

Muhammad home after a Savior's Day convention. This was after Malcolm X had been assassinated, and there were rumors Elijah would be killed in retaliation. Three other policemen and me were taking Elijah up the back stairs to his house when two guys came out of the shadows. I pulled my pistol; I was ready to shoot. But they threw their hands in the air, and it turned out that one of them was Elijah's son, Herbert Muhammad. They'd been out patrolling the grounds. Then, some months later, Herbert sent for me and asked if I'd take care of his fighter. Ali was going to Canada to fight George Chuvalo. So on my own time, vacation days and days off, I went to Toronto. And from that point on, I was the man in charge of security, although for quite a while it wasn't my regular job. I stayed with the police until 1974. That's when Ali moved to Chicago, and beat George Foreman. And after that happened, when we came back from Africa, Ali went to Mayor Daley and asked if I could be assigned to guard him full-time.

"Over the years, there were all sorts of bomb threats and rumors of people coming to hurt Ali, but none of that ever materialized. At Deer Lake, I'd walk around the camp at night to make sure everything was all right. And on the road, wherever we went, Muslims from the different mosques would volunteer to help, so I'd have ten or fifteen people working with me. I always got along with the brothers. When we got to wherever it was we were going, I'd take the head man of the local mosque aside and tell him what I wanted done. And after that, I'd step back out of the way to let them do the job. I didn't have to be the main guy. I didn't have to stand next to Muhammad. Do you follow me? I could have blocked these brothers and not had them around. But most of them were very competent at security. They'd stand in the hallway by your door all night if that was what you wanted, and having them present made for good relationships. It's easy to get along with people if you don't have a big head. Even when we were in countries with military police, I was able to work well and get along with everyone.

"And I'll tell you something else about Ali. Being with him affected the kind of policeman I turned out to be. I was a relatively young man when I met him. I was about twenty-nine, but I hadn't been on the force that long. And young police, they're always interested in locking people up. But with Ali, I realized it was more important to be a peace officer, that people needed help. He taught me to take time and listen to people. Watching him, I learned that power shouldn't be used in a bullying way. The man was so caring; he cared so much about people. And after a while, you had to know that the way he felt about people was right."

Patterson's view of Ali is shared by James Anderson, who assisted the Chicago policeman from 1974 until the end of Ali's ring career.

JAMES ANDERSON: "It was a unique experience, every day was different. Pat was very authoritative when the situation called for it, but the biggest problem we had was Ali going off into crowds. Sometimes he'd get out of his car, like on Forty-second Street and Eighth Avenue in New York, and stand there just to see how large a crowd he could draw. And let me tell you, Ali had a knack for drawing crowds. There were quite a few times when I was worried. The crowd would grow and it would be hard to move in any direction. People would be pressing and pushing and closing in because they wanted to touch him, and we'd have trouble getting back to the car. Pat Patterson and I would try to stay close and watch people's faces to see if there was signs of trouble. But the way Ali let people around him, there was just so much we could do. I mean, if you want to know the truth, he almost never listened when it came to security. If we wanted him to go out the back door, he'd want to go out the front. If we wanted him to go out the front, he'd start looking for a door on the side. Since then, I've worked as a bodyguard for Richard Pryor, Donna Summer, Sugar Ray Leonard, and a bunch of other celebrities. And I'll tell it to you straight: After you've been security for Muhammad Ali, everybody else is easy."

But even as Ali was surrounded in public, the media's access to him remained. Over the years, a new generation of sportswriters and broadcasters had come into being, and he welcomed them as he had their predecessors. Three members of that new generation—Mike Katz, Vic Ziegel, and Ed Schuyler—are joined by Wilfred Sheed in recalling Ali after he regained his crown.

MIKE KATZ: "I guess it's common for sportswriters—and I put myself in the group—to lull ourselves into thinking we're smarter than the athletes we cover. And Ali was one of those wonderful people who, every now and then, remind us that, hey, this guy is sharper than we are.

"The first fight of his that I covered was in 1971 against Jurgen Blin. This was nine months after Ali had lost to Frazier. There were only three American writers there. Angelo arranged for an interview a day or two before the fight, and as soon as we started, Muhammad took out some religious writings and began to read Muslim theory to us. You know, the sun is good and it is warm, and this went on for about an hour. The man was very into his religion, and God bless him for that, but it wasn't what I wanted to hear. If you interview the pope, you don't want to talk about boxing. But I listened, and eventually we got to what I'd come for, and I had a good time. That was the biggest difference between covering Ali and covering other fighters. It was fun, and I don't think there's been an athlete in history who gave as much of himself to the media as Ali. He liked attention; he thrived on it. If there were no people around, he'd probably recruit the attention of a cat. But he also worked cooperatively with the media and understood it as well as anyone I've ever known. It wasn't thought out; it came naturally. He liked attention, he knew how to get it, and he accepted writers as part of his world. And not just reporters from the major newspapers and television stations. Ali would spend as much time talking to a tenth-grader from the local high school newspaper as he would to the boxing writer for *The New York Times*. Unlike some athletes, he never regarded the press as his enemy. And now that it's over, I feel the way most sportswriters feel. It was a privilege to cover Ali."

VIC ZIEGEL: "I don't think anybody who covered Ali ever stops thinking about him. I know one of the things that impressed me most and I remember most fondly is that he had that rare ability to be at his best when the spotlight was most intense. Most people are intimidated by the spotlight, but Ali welcomed it. Part of his magic was that it pushed him to his greatest performances in and out of the ring. It seemed to make him a better person. And I always marveled at how he could be so true to himself and shine so brightly in that light. You know, it's funny. I'm not sure he even knows my name. He used to call me 'my press man' whenever he saw me, but that was all right. Like most press men, I thought Ali was a writer's dream."

ED SCHUYLER: "There's never been a heavyweight champion, and maybe not any superstar athlete, who was more accessible to the media than Ali. His training camp was always open. You could cover him twenty-four hours a day. We never worried about whether he'd meet with the press after a fight. Hell, he'd meet with you the morning and afternoon before. And you could ask him anything without his getting angry. I never felt more comfortable with an athlete in my life than with Ali.

"The best time to talk with him if you wanted to do it alone was at Deer Lake. He was a different person when he was alone. He'd talk very quietly and somberly, but you rarely had him alone for long, because the phone would ring or someone from the entourage or another writer would come in, and pretty soon it was showtime. And it was really more fun to interview him in a group. Once he saw a microphone or if two or three of us were taking notes, it was like someone threw a switch and a light went on. You know the routine. I'm the greatest. So and so—whoever he was fighting next—doesn't stand a chance. And when Muhammad was on, he could make you believe almost anything he wanted as long as you wanted to believe it too. Like those hokey magic tricks. I remember one press conference before a fight. Muhammad stood up and announced he was going to levitate. He stood on a chair so we could all see him. And then he went up in the air. I looked at it, and I said to myself, 'My God! The man is levitating.' And you know he can't, but there it is. He's in front of you, and he's doing it anyway. I'm telling you; there's never been a fighter like Ali. If you couldn't write about Ali, you couldn't write. He made us all look good."

WILFRED SHEED: "I met Ali after he beat George Foreman, when I contracted to write a book about him. I'd always been a boxing fan, but that's not why I undertook the project. I wanted to write about Ali. He's one of those madonnas you want to paint at least once in your life. The book was planned to go on sale before Ali's autobiography, which was being published by Random House. Naturally, Random House tried to make it difficult for me to gain access. Howard Bingham was put in charge of keeping me away, but he was too nice a person for the job. It pained him; he just couldn't do it. And Ali was never able to resist anyone with a pad and pen, although I'd expected him to be more spontaneous than he was. I'd hoped he made up his funny lines as he went along, when in fact I discovered he had a formidable memory bank of them. And while he was always friendly and polite, after I got to know him a bit I realized there was no point in asking a lot of questions. The closest we came to a personal rapport was one night when he was pulling me onto his bus. I suffered from polio when I was younger. Ali offered me his hand, and I told him the handrail was better than the strongest human being; that I could pull myself up by the handrail, but his pulling wouldn't help because at that point I'd become dead weight. He seemed interested in that. He said, 'I didn't know that.'

"I differ from some people in that I never saw Ali as a major social or political figure. I think he was basically an entertainer. Without him, I don't think society would be significantly different today. He was more a symbol than a doer, but I suppose importance is what you make of it. And I do believe that any interesting black person makes white people realize the possibilities and potential of blacks, so Ali was useful in that respect. You know, we're still only getting to know each other, and Ali was a step forward. Also, I'd have to say that if Muhammad Ali never existed, life certainly would have been duller. Whatever you think of the man and his meaning, the world would have been far less interesting without him."

In the months that followed his victory over George Foreman, Ali reveled in having regained his crown. "Now that I got my championship back," he told a reporter, "every day is something special. I wake up in the morning, and no matter what the weather is like, every day is a sunny day."[6]

There were boasts as to Ali's next fight:

I want to fight two people now. Joe Frazier and George Foreman in the same night; ten rounds apiece, not fifteen. Frazier first. After I beat him, knockout or by decision, right away let George Foreman jump in the ring and start round eleven for me which will be round one for him. They won't take this fight in America because it's against the law, but we'll take it to Russia. Russia will accept it and China will too, but I'd like to have it in Russia. George Foreman and Joe Frazier in the same night with no rest. And then if Howard Cosell is there, I'm gonna jump over the ropes and slap him and pull his toupee off his head.[7]

There were epic poems:

This is the legend of Muhammad Ali,
The greatest fighter that ever will be.
He talks a great deal and brags, indeed,
Of a powerful punch and blinding speed.
Ali fights great, he's got speed and endurance;
If you sign to fight him, increase your insurance.

Ali's got a left, Ali's got a right;
If he hits you once, you're asleep for the night.
[Etcetera, etcetera, and so forth][8]

And through it all, there was one thing more that didn't change: Ali steadfastly maintained his allegiance to Elijah Muhammad and continued to speak his mind,

On brotherhood: "We're not all brothers. You can say we're brothers, but we're not. White and black are not brothers. Brothers would help brothers. Brothers wouldn't let us be in the shape we're in. Brothers would cry when they see us. White people don't cry over our condition. Maybe one or two of them do, but it's so few it don't count. No, they ain't our brothers. A brother don't lynch a brother, cut his privates off and put it in his mouth; tie him to horses to pull him apart, and burn him up and kill pregnant women before their babies are born, enslave him for four hundred years. And they're still doing it. White people just don't want their slaves to be free. That's the whole thing. Why not let me go? I don't pick cotton no more. You don't need me no more. We're on welfare; we're robbing in the streets; we're fighting and killing, having babies every day. Why not let us go and build ourselves a nation?"[9]

On Christianity: "Christianity might be a good philosophy if the white man lived up to it, but he don't. All he does is use it to control black people, and the way the white man teaches Christianity is full of lies. I'll show you an example. Jesus lived around Egypt; he went to school in Egypt. The Bible said he had hair like lamb's wool and skin like burnt brass. That's something black. Don't that shake you up? Jesus was a black man, but the Christians don't tell you that."[10]

And on the need for a separate black homeland: "America is pregnant with the truth. In 1930, the seed of truth was planted. Allah came to America, taught Elijah Muhammad, told him to unite black people, bring them back to Islam, back to their right names, culture, and religion. It's time for us to separate. Now this truth has been planted and it's growing. The baby, the black man, is kicking; he wants to be

free. It's like a woman nine months pregnant. The baby
wants to get out. And if they don't get that baby out, the
woman and the baby will both die."[11]

And then, suddenly, there was a change. On February 25, 1975,
Elijah Muhammad died.

MUHAMMAD ALI: "I was at Deer Lake, training, when I heard
the news, and it made me sad. Elijah Muhammad dedicated his life
to helping black people. Not everything he said was right, but everyone in the Nation of Islam loved him because he carried what was
best for us in his heart. His life was dedicated to lifting people up,
and it was his teaching that started me thinking.

"After Elijah died, his son Wallace took over as leader. That didn't
surprise us, because we'd been told Wallace would come after his
father. But what surprised some people was, Wallace changed the
direction of the Nation. He'd learned from his studies that his father
wasn't teaching true Islam, and Wallace taught us the true meaning
of the Qur'an. He showed that color don't matter. He taught that
we're responsible for our own lives and it's no good to blame our
problems on other people. And that sounded right to me so I followed Wallace, but not everyone in the Nation felt that way. Some
of the ministers didn't like what he was teaching. Jeremiah Shabazz
didn't like it. Louis Farrakhan didn't like it either. They believed
Elijah was a prophet, and they've kept the exact ways Elijah taught
them. But I've changed what I believe, and what I believe in now
is true Islam."

HERBERT MUHAMMAD: "When my father passed, I expected
Wallace to take the Nation of Islam in a new direction. I knew it
was the correct direction, and I believe my father knew the direction
Wallace would take. You see, my father had a message to black
people. Black people knew their life was bad. They wanted something to make it better. And my father's message was to gain dignity
and self-respect and make black people the master of their own
needs. As long as other people controlled what we needed, then
those people would be able to control us. So my father sought to
make black people self-reliant, and take them away from gambling,
alcohol, prostitution, and drugs. He taught that the answer to what
black people need is in God and in ourselves. And you have to ask
what it was that enabled my father to get a man or woman off drugs,

when right now the whole government can't do it. You have to ask what it was that could bring a man out of prison, and the next month have that man be clean-shaven, wearing clean clothes, completely clean. My father helped people to do that, and one of the things that troubles me today is when people take my father's words and teachings out of their proper context. You see, my father saw that black people had a deep inferiority complex. He saw that white people had a great superiority complex. And by the whites being in an upper-hand position, blacks would never come up unless someone gave them a philosophy that they were better than whites. Black people had to shoot higher to get up near. If people feel they're nothing compared to what they're looking up to, they'll always stay down. But if you can give them aspirations and have them shoot higher than those other people, when they get up to a certain level they'll find they're no better than those other people but no less either. That was my father's philosophy, and that was what he tried to accomplish with his life."

Elijah Muhammad's death marked a turning point for the Nation of Islam, and foreshadowed a significant change in Ali's public pronouncements on race. In the past, the public and private Ali had seemed almost at war with each other over whether white people were truly evil. Now Ali was able to say openly, "I don't hate whites. That was history, but it's coming to an end. We're in a new phase, a resurrection. Elijah taught us to be independent, to clean ourselves up, to be proud and healthy. He stressed the bad things the white man did to us so we could get free and strong. Now, his son Wallace is showing us there are good and bad regardless of color, that the devil is in the mind and heart, not the skin. We Muslims hate injustice and evil, but we don't have time to hate people. White people wouldn't be here if God didn't mean them to be."[12]

JEREMIAH SHABAZZ: "Ali changed all right, and so did the Nation. There's been a metamorphosis, and I don't like it. After the Messenger died, his son Wallace led everyone to believe that he would carry on his father's work and perpetuate his father's teachings, but he didn't. His thing was to turn the Nation of Islam around and make it follow the teachings of orthodox Islam. And what I truly regret is, because of our discipline at the time and because of our respect for Elijah Muhammad, we didn't oppose Wallace. We accepted him; and another reason for that actually was our fear and dislike of the white man. We didn't want to show the white man that we were divided. We wanted to appear united as far as the enemy was concerned. And what happened was, Wallace turned everything around until now there's no more Nation of Islam. That's the worst thing that happened. If we'd continued on the path we were traveling, we'd be a powerful religious force to be reckoned with today. The Messenger had the best program for black people, and if we'd continued his programs and everything else the Messenger taught us, we'd be the envy of the Third World today. We'd have something all black people could be proud of."

BOBBY GOODMAN: "I remember going back to training camp not long after Elijah Muhammad died. Now keep in mind, color and religion had never been an issue between me and Muhammad. I'm white, I'm half-Jewish, and it hadn't bothered him a bit. In fact, if you look at the tape of Muhammad in the locker room after the Foreman fight, I'm the first guy he hugs. But regardless, I walked into the kitchen at Deer Lake. Muhammad came over, grabbed me; he was all excited. And he said, 'Bobby, did you hear? The religion is changing. Now you can become a Muslim.' And I said, 'Muhammad, we've had a good relationship for a long time, right?' He said, 'Yeah, real good.' And then I asked, 'Would my converting to Islam change anything?' Well, he thought about it, and finally he answered, 'I guess not.' But he was all excited at the prospect of my being able to become a Muslim."

Four weeks after Elijah Muhammad's death, Ali resumed his ring career against a journeyman fighter named Chuck Wepner. From the start, the bout shaped up as "no contest"; an easy payday for the champion before his next major title defense. The thirty-five-year-old Wepner was a liquor salesman from Bayonne, New Jersey, with a professional record of thirty wins, nine losses, and two draws against mostly mediocre opponents. Because of his tendency to cut when hit, he'd accumulated more than three hundred stitches in his face and earned the nickname "the Bayonne Bleeder." Up until his fight with Ali, Wepner's greatest claim to fame had been a loss on cuts to Sonny Liston in the last bout of Liston's career. Asked if Wepner, who needed 120 stitches after the bout, was the bravest man he'd ever seen, Liston replied, "No, his manager is."[13]

In the past, for fighting opponents of Wepner's caliber, Ali had received in the neighborhood of $250,000. The fact that he was coming off a victory over George Foreman and had regained his championship was expected to double or triple that amount. Still, when contracts were signed, the numbers were staggering: Wepner was such a pronounced underdog that there wasn't even a formal betting line on the fight, yet Ali was to be paid $1,500,000.

BOB ARUM: "The payday was largely Don King's doing. King wanted to stay in the heavyweight picture. If possible, he wanted to control Ali. So he went to some mob guys in Cleveland, and got financing from the mob. That enabled him to offer more for the fight than anybody else could afford. And financially, it bombed. Ali-Wepner lost a bundle, which wasn't surprising, because Don King doesn't know how to promote anything but himself. He's good at getting his name in the papers. He's good at extracting large sums of money from other people. He's good at stealing fighters that someone else has developed. But he can't promote well now, and he certainly couldn't do it then. So the Wepner fight became a real monkey on King's back. I know that for a fact, because some FBI people told me that the interest he owed on the loan from the mob kept building and building, and King wasn't able to pay it off until after Holmes-Cooney in 1982. That's how long it took him to get clear again."

DON ELBAUM: "King financed the Wepner fight with mob money. I've heard that since he put the fight together, and while I can't prove it, I believe it to be true. I heard he borrowed a million and a half from the mob in Cleveland, and then had trouble paying it back. In fact, I heard that part of how he paid it off was by giving them his numbers business. And by 'them' I mean the people he borrowed the money from. He had the numbers business going after he got out of prison. There's no question about that; I know that. Like I told you before, Don King is quite a guy."

The fight against Wepner was dull and one-sided, with Ali in complete command. The only moment of drama came in round nine, when the champion tumbled to the canvas after taking a punch to the chest. Referee Tony Perez ruled the incident a knockdown. However, after the bout, photographs bolstered Ali's claim that he'd fallen because, at the moment of impact, Wepner was stepping on his foot. The end came with nineteen seconds left in the final round. For the first time in his career, Wepner was knocked down. He staggered to his feet, his nose broken, bleeding over both eyes. Perez then stopped the fight, and Wepner sagged into his cornermen's arms.

CHUCK WEPNER: "Fighting Muhammad Ali was the greatest time of my life. Of all the fights I had, of everything I did, that was the best. It's the only time I got to train full-time for a fight. Every other time, I had to work during the day and train at night. For Ali, I had seven weeks in the mountains, and everybody did everything for me. All I had to do was snap my fingers and someone would be there. I got myself into the best shape of my life. And I figured, probably he'd take me lightly, not train as hard as he should, and maybe I'd have a shot at winning. You know, I was never a great fighter. I was a brawler. I never had a lot of ability, but I could take a punch. With my style, I'd come in and take two shots to land one and wear guys down. So against Ali, I thought maybe I could wear him down and catch up to him in the late rounds. I was pumped up, really looking forward to the fight.

"I'm an ex-Marine, so they played the Marine Hymn as I walked down the aisle to the ring. I was wearing a red, white, and blue robe. It was great. The referee gave us our instructions, and I said to myself, 'Wow! I've made it. I'm face to face with Muhammad Ali.' I wanted to do well; I gave it my best shot, but Ali was just too good for me. When the fight started, I tried cutting off the ring, but he was too fast and elusive. Every time I thought I had him in a corner, somehow he managed to slip away. His punches were hard. Not as hard as some guys I fought, but he was a strong puncher, and it was the number of punches he hit me with. He wouldn't hit you with just one punch; it was two and three in combination. In the ninth round, I knocked him down. That was the high point for me. I threw a jab, he pulled away—you know how he used to lean back—and I hit him with a right hand under the heart. It was a good punch. He was off-balance, and it dropped him. Afterward, they said my foot was on top of his, but the referee declared it a knockdown. After that round, I felt great. I went back to my corner and said, 'Look at that; I knocked him down.' And my manager told me, 'Yeah, but he looks pissed.' And Ali wasn't really hurt. He came back from the knockdown with four- and five-punch combinations. Then he started sticking and moving again, and I had trouble keeping up with him. The last five rounds, I was totally exhausted. I'd never gone fifteen before, and I just couldn't put it together. I might have been the best heavyweight in New Jersey, but he was the greatest heavyweight of all time. Finally, Tony Perez stopped it in the last round. I was disappointed; I wanted to go the full fifteen. I argued, but it wasn't any use. And I suppose it doesn't make that big a difference. The record book shows that Chuck Wepner fought Muhammad Ali and took him into the fifteenth round."

The fight itself might have been ordinary, but the aftermath of Ali-Wepner was anything but. Shortly after the bout, Ali appeared on ABC's *Wide World of Sports* with Howard Cosell and vehemently attacked referee Tony Perez. Angered by the fact that Perez had allowed Wepner to pursue roughhouse tactics, and perhaps more upset by the referee's ruling that the ninth-round slip was an official knockdown, the champion launched into an uncharacteristically vicious and unfounded tirade. Perez, he said, was "a dirty dog; he's not black and he's not white; he's Puerto Rican. He's more black than white, but he's trying to be white." Then, referring to the second Ali-Frazier fight when Perez prematurely halted action in the second round, Ali declared, "He was paid probably by some gangsters or somebody, or he had some money bet on Frazier."[14]

Perez's response was a $20 million lawsuit, filed against Ali in the United States District Court for the Southern District of New York.

TONY PEREZ: "I was mad. Ali had no business saying what he said about me. If you look at the fights I refereed with Ali, in the Quarry fight he had nothing to complain about; I stopped the fight. Against Frazier, he complained about my hearing the bell, but Frazier's people complained I let Ali hold Frazier. Then, with Wepner, Ali cried about two things. Number one, he complained about the rabbit punches—punches to the back of the head. But Wepner was a brawler; he always punched that way, roundhouse rights. Did you ever see a referee take a point away from Wepner because of that? Never. And my style is to let the fighters fight. I'm consistent; I treat all fighters the same. Everybody knows what to expect when I referee a fight. And the other thing Ali complained about with Wepner was the knockdown. All I saw was the right hand to the chest. Later, Ali said Wepner stepped on his foot, but a referee can't watch everything at once. If I'm watching a fighter's feet I can't see his hands and head.

"Then, after the fight, Ali went on television and said those things about me. And eight lawyers called me that night. We went to court, and the judge was very harsh to me. In the middle of the trial, he brought me into his chambers and said, 'Mr. Perez, I'm going to talk to you like a father. I don't see no damage here. Why don't you shake hands with Ali and forget the whole thing?' I looked at him and I asked, 'Your Honor, do you mean to say to me that if someone goes on television and says you're with the Mafia, there's no damage to you?' So he went on with the trial, but you could see the judge was very affected by having Muhammad Ali in his court. Ali's lawyer would ask me a question, and I'd try to explain because maybe the jury wouldn't know much about boxing, and the judge would say, 'Just answer the question.' Then Ali would get on the stand and talk for half an hour, and the judge wouldn't stop him. And it was the same thing, when I finished talking, the judge would say, 'Okay, step down.' But when Ali finished, he would say, 'All right, Mr. Ali; you may step down, please.' And the charge the judge gave the jury; oh my God, what a charge. He almost told the jurors there's no case here. And what the jury decided was, Ali believed what he said was true when he said it, so even if it was false, I couldn't win the case. After that, for a while, I was angry. What happened didn't seem fair. But then, not many years ago, Ali and I ran into each other. He put his arms around me and kissed me. You know, he was a little slow talking, but he said to me, 'Tony, we're friends. We don't fight no more; I love you.' And I told him, 'Thank you, Ali. I love you too.'"

But the ramifications of Ali-Wepner weren't limited to boxing. One of the fans who watched the bout was an unemployed actor named Sylvester Stallone, who paid twenty dollars to see the contest on closed-circuit television. Stallone was so inspired by Wepner's courage that he sat down and wrote a screenplay entitled *Rocky*.

SYLVESTER STALLONE: "I had perfected the art of failing in my chosen profession as an actor. And since I was going nowhere and had so much time on my hands, I thought why not do a story about people who can't fulfill their desires? I was looking around for a suitable vehicle, one that would be appropriate for me. Someone had shown me a tape of Rocky Marciano fighting Ali; it was a computer analysis of what would happen. I saw the juxtaposition of styles and contrast, and I was interested. I thought, 'Not bad.' Then, as fate would have it, I saw the fight between Ali and Chuck Wepner. And the fight was really undistinguished until the man who was considered an absolute pushover knocked the unbeatable champion down. I saw how the crowd reacted, and I said to myself, 'This is what it's all about.' Everybody wants a slice of immortality, whether it's for fifteen rounds in a fight or two minutes in their own life.

They want that sensation that they have a shot at the impossible dream, and that solidified the whole thing for me.

"*Rocky* came out of that fight between Wepner and Ali. I was a fan of Ali's. Rambo and some of the other characters I've played are essentially right-wing, but those aren't my beliefs. A lot of people think I'm inseparable from my characters, but that's not true at all. For example, when Ali refused induction, I wasn't as opposed to him as some people assume. I thought Vietnam was an exercise in futility, as most wars are. There were a couple of times I took exception to what Ali said and did. He could be infuriating, but I realized that was part of his psyching. A lot of the time, he was just transferring his own fears onto his opponent. And his fights were a celebration of life. The fight game is dangerous, but the way he presented it, it was simply a contest, a challenge that you might see on a TV game show. He made light of it. He added fun. He made people smile. Being around him was like, let's go to another adventure. And of course, Apollo Creed was a thinly disguised impersonation of Ali. If Ali didn't exist, I don't think people would have bought the premise of *Rocky*. But the fact that Ali did exist gave the film validity and pushed it into a believable vehicle for what I wanted to say. And part of what I wanted to say was what Ali represents. I think of him as a manchild, and I mean that in a positive sense. He had a vitality and vigor and drive to topple giants, and that basically is what youth is all about—taking on the icons that have been set before us, toppling old values and trying to replace them with new ones."

CHUCK WEPNER: "The best time for me was after the fight. I'd done a lot better than people thought I would. I put up a good fight, and that gave me prestige. Everywhere I went, people congratulated me. I was getting calls for personal appearances. I'd go to clubs down on the Jersey shore, and they'd bring me on stage to take a bow. I even did a short film on dental hygiene with Ali. It was for grammar school kids, and he knocked out Mr. Tooth Decay, who was me. We spent some time filming together in Washington, D.C., and he was great. What a guy. I'm still grateful for the opportunity he gave me.

"Then, a few years ago, I got myself in trouble. When you become famous, when you become a celebrity, everywhere you go someone is offering you something, and I got addicted to cocaine. It was the first time in my life anything like that happened to me. I pled guilty to possession and conspiracy to distribute. I could have gone to trial, but I didn't. It would have hurt too many people I care about, so I admitted my mistake and took my punishment. Unfortunately, it was one of those times when celebrity status worked against me. The prosecutor said, 'We can't give you a break, because if we do, everyone else will say how come Chuck Wepner got a break when we didn't?' So where somebody else might have gotten less time, they gave me the maximum on the plea bargain, ten years. Right now, I'm in Northern State Prison in New Jersey. I've put in for a couple of work release programs, so maybe by the time this is printed I'll be out. Not much good happens here; except not long ago, Sylvester Stallone came to see me. He was at the prison to do a movie. They called me down, and he gave me a big hug. Then we chatted for a while, and he told everybody I was the real Rocky.

"I like Stallone. After the first movie, he called me up and told me who he was. He said they were doing *Rocky II* and that he'd like me to be in it. My part was going to be a guy named Ching Weber, one of Rocky's sparring partners. I had thirty-two lines, but nine days before filming began, the film company cut me out. I should have taken acting lessons, that's what I should have done. But whatever else happens in my life, I proved to people that I was a fighter. I showed them I belonged in the same ring as Muhammad Ali.

"And you know something? It's funny. More than anything else except for the knockdown, there's one thing I remember about the night we fought. I'd told everybody that, if I won, I was going to rent a bus, put all my friends in it, drive from here to California, pick up every female hitchhiker, and party for days and weeks and months. I would have gone completely into orbit; it would have been great. I mean, nobody partied more than me. I loved to party, I had two ex-wives and a hundred girlfriends, and I was always known as a big party guy; a womanizer, my wives used to call me. If I'd been heavyweight champion of the world, I would have tried to take on the whole female population of the United States. But instead, what happened was, the day of the fight, I gave my wife a very sexy blue negligee. And I told her, 'I want you to wear this tonight, because after the fight you'll be sleeping with the heavy-weight champion of the world.' And when the fight was over, after I'd gotten stitched up, twenty-three stitches, I went back to the hotel. I was pretty much exhausted. And my wife was in the room, waiting for me, wearing the negligee. And she said to me, 'Okay, bigshot. Do I go to the champ's room, or does he come to see me.' "

On May 16, 1975, eight weeks after defeating Wepner, Ali fought
Ron Lyle in Las Vegas. The bout was broadcast in prime time by
ABC, only the second time in nine years that an Ali fight had been
shown live on home television in the United States. For ten rounds,
the champion looked mediocre. Two of the judges had him trailing
on their scorecards, and the third saw the bout as even. Then, in
the eleventh round, Ali set Lyle up with a jab and followed with a
straight right that landed flush on the jaw. Dazed, the challenger
staggered back, and Ali pursued, raining punches on his opponent's
head. Then he stopped, and gestured for referee Ferd Hernandez
to halt the fight. But Hernandez refused and Ali resumed, battering
Lyle until the bout was halted.

For defeating Lyle, Ali received a gross purse of one million
dollars. Seven weeks later, he was in the ring again, this time against
Joe Bugner in Kuala Lumpur, Malaysia. Foreign money was the
primary lure—two million dollars for the champion. But there was
added incentive for Ali in that, for only the second time in his career
(his bout against Rudi Lubbers in Indonesia was the first), he would
be fighting in a Muslim country.

VIC ZIEGEL: "Ali was in splendid form in Malaysia. He and Bugner had already fought each other once, and at first it seemed there
wouldn't be much to write about the second time around. But then,
a few days before the fight, there was a rules committee meeting.
And you've been to those meetings; you know how boring they are.
The three-knockdown rule will or won't be waived; the ring doctor
can or can't stop the fight. Ali and Bugner picked out their gloves,
and gave them to someone from the local boxing commission for
safekeeping. And then the commissioner explained that the gloves
would be kept in a local prison until the fight. I thought that was
odd, but I kept taking notes. And all of a sudden, Ali, who was just
trying to stay awake, perked up, raised his hand like a kid in school,
and said, 'Wait a minute! You're putting my gloves in jail?' Well,
from that point on, he was unstoppable. And what we heard with
perfect comedic timing for the next ten minutes was, 'This is awful!
How can you do that? How can you put my gloves in jail. They ain't
done nothing—yet.' "

BOBBY GOODMAN: "Ali-Bugner II was another closed-circuit
fight, and it was a hard sell because no one thought Bugner had a
chance. We were racking our brains to come up with a new publicity
angle, and then John Condon asked, 'How would it play if Muham-

mad announces that this is his last fight?' And I said to him, 'John, that's not totally beyond the realm of possibility. When Muhammad gets tired, sometimes he says casually in passing maybe he should pack it in.' So I went to Muhammad and told him, 'This is the idea, but you have to sound serious. In fact, you have to be close to tears for this to be believable and help the fight.' And Muhammad agreed, like he always did. We rehearsed what he'd say, and then I called the press to his suite. And Muhammad was magnificent. He started out, 'The reason I called you guys together is to say that this is my last fight. All the years I've been on the road, all the training camps and time away from my wife and children; it's just too much. I miss my family. My life with them is more important than boxing. I want to retire while I'm still on top.' And you could see his eyes getting a little watery as he reminisced about when he'd started his career and how many years he'd been in boxing. And then one of the reporters asked, 'What about Joe Frazier? Aren't you going to fight Frazier again?' And I knew what was coming, but there was nothing I could do to stop it. Muhammad's eyes lit up, and he started in. 'Joe Frazier! I want him bad. How much money do you think I can get if I go and whup Joe Frazier?' "

The Bugner bout went as expected, with Ali dominating over fifteen rounds. "He should have quit after Bugner," says Ferdie Pacheco. "The time was right; he had his health. If Ali had retired after Malaysia, he'd be far ahead of the game today."

But Ali was like a child raised in a circus trunk. Boxing was the world he knew. It was where he'd been bred and born and raised. And like most performers, he was compelled to go where the lights shone brightest. "Ali does not necessarily sit around thinking of how he can become famous," wrote Wilfred Sheed. "It is a blind biologic groping for the limelight, awesome in its accuracy."[15] And so Ali journeyed next to Manila to meet Joe Frazier and pursue his destiny.

12

Manila

MIKE KATZ: "Looking back, people say that Ali-Frazier III was a great fight. And it was; one of the greatest of all time. But going in, a lot of people didn't even think it would be a good fight. Frazier had been turned into a yo-yo by George Foreman. Ali hadn't looked good after Zaire, although he figured to have more left than Joe. There just wasn't that much anticipation, but these are two guys who would probably do it to each other if they fought in their eighties. That's just the way they are. Frazier was a warrior, and he brought out the warrior in Ali. And don't kid yourself; there's something inside Ali; even in his current condition, if they fought, Ali would find a way to make it hard on Joe."

The spectacle of Ali versus Frazier in Manila was vintage Ali from beginning to end. In keeping with his status as the greatest drawing card in sports, the champion was guaranteed $4 million against 43 percent of all fight-generated income. "I remember signing the contract," says Frazier's trainer and manager, Eddie Futch. "Ali wound up getting six million dollars, and Joe received half that amount. But one thing about the contract that sticks in my mind is, Joe required accommodations for seventeen people, and Ali needed rooms for fifty. That's how big his entourage had grown. And later, the president of the Hilton Hotel in Manila told me that, even though Ali had fifty rooms, when he got there he needed two more."

By the time Ali reached Manila, his entourage was in full bloom. Not even Sugar Ray Robinson in his prime supported as many workers, hangers-on, and friends. The entourage basked in Ali's glow, like the moon in the light of the sun. Because of him, they had the world on a string, but not everyone was enamored of their role.

ALEX WALLAU: "If you judge somebody by their friends, you'd have thought Ali was a lowlife, because he had an awful lot of scum around him. It was a horrendous collection of hypocrites and hustlers, people who had their hands in his pocket and were looking to make side deals whenever they could. Howard Bingham was the main exception. I'm a big Howard Bingham fan. Over the years—and he's proven it time and time again—he was a guy who sincerely loved Ali. I'm not saying he never made money around Ali as a photographer, but that's not why Howard was there. And I liked Angelo; he's special too. It wasn't just Angelo's ability as a cornerman, which is his greatest strength; or his ability as a trainer, which is considerable. I was fascinated by Angelo's ability to survive. He could be in the middle of that whole collection of crazies, from militant Muslims to the most corrupt con men on earth, and get along with everyone. Angelo was the greatest diplomat I've ever seen. He had his views but he kept them to himself, and you never saw him trying to make a fast buck off Ali. So to my way of thinking, Howard and Angelo were the most attractive people in the entourage. There were a lot of people tied for last.

Bundini, to me, was the most obvious exploiter. I'm not saying he didn't have genuine feeling for Ali, and he was an entertaining guy, but Bundini knew no limits when it came to exploitation. And there were more than a few more who fit that mold. That might be an unfair assessment of some of the others. There were a few I liked. Lana Shabazz, the cook, was a wonderful woman. And I liked Pat Patterson. But I always felt that most of the entourage was just along with Ali for the ride and would disappear when the ride was over."

FERDIE PACHECO: "Everyone in the entourage had one thing in common: They loved Ali. And very few of them were people to whom love came naturally. A lot of them were street people. And sure, when they had the chance to make a buck, they took advantage of it. But most of them served a need, even if they didn't understand what that need was. Otherwise, Ali wouldn't have put up with them.

Luis Sarria was the greatest exercise man in the world. Lloyd Wells—I'll let someone else tell you about Lloyd. But if you saw Lloyd Wells with four great-looking chicks, what else should you expect? That was his job, and that's what he was. If a guy knew how to hustle and get things done like Gene Kilroy, fine. Some people would rather go to the dentist than spend time with Kilroy. But Gene was a facilitator, and on a few occasions he was actually a voice of sanity in camp. Everyone in the entourage served a purpose. They were there because Ali wanted them to be. Sometimes they fought like naughty children. There was a lot of jealousy and struggling for status on the totem pole. But in one way or another, they all helped restore what the world drained out of Ali every day. Most of them did what they were supposed to do, and Ali loved them like a man loves his children. If you have ten children and two of them are sons of bitches, you love those two just as much as the other eight."

Well and good.

But when Ali arrived in Manila, one member of his entourage played a special role. Her name was Veronica Porche. For almost a year, she'd been Ali's mistress. By September 1975, their relationship had reached a point where it was threatening Ali's marriage. And it was about to become public knowledge.

HOWARD BINGHAM: "Ali caused a lot of his own problems, and that was true of some of his problems with women. His habits were bad. When we met in 1962, he looked at girls a lot but didn't touch. Maybe he'd flirt a little, but even if someone was interested, which a lot of them were, it didn't go beyond talking. Then Sonji turned him on, and after they split up, there were a lot of women. You know, most men have to wine 'em and dine 'em, but all Ali had to do was look at a woman and she'd melt. He got an awful lot of encouragement. I don't think there was ever a white woman. Some people have written and some women have bragged that I'm wrong about that. But I know Ali as well as anyone, and I don't think there ever was a white woman."

BELINDA ALI: "When we got married, he was an innocent guy, but he changed during the course of our marriage. Some of it, I guess, wasn't his fault. So much was happening around Ali that he couldn't always see himself. The world was spinning by so fast; he didn't have time to stop and think. And he was influenced by certain people in the religion who he looked to for guidance, and they led him wrong. Some of them were married and fooling around themselves. And instead of trying to be like him, they tried to make him like they were, and they were successful. It could happen to anyone. I don't think he would have been the way he was with other women if he'd been surrounded by the right people. But in order for someone bad to influence you, you have to want it, or at least part of you has to want it. So maybe those other people just brought out that side of him.

"For a long time, his seeing other women confused me. I was young, just learning about life, and there were a lot of things I didn't know. I dressed modestly all the time, and was a loyal wife. I tried to be like Jackie Kennedy was for white people. And when Ali was with those other women—I guess Kennedy did it too—there wasn't cause for him to be that way. At first he did it behind my back. Then I found out, and he tried to use the religion as an excuse. The Qur'an allows a man to have more than one wife, but there are rules and regulations. You don't do it the way Ali did. You're allowed to have more than one wife if your first wife is barren, or if there's a shortage of men because of war. But the Qur'an also says that sex is supposed to be limited to marriage. And I'm a healthy woman; I wasn't barren. I had four children; I had twins. So Ali had no reason being with other women. And as much as he tried to stretch Islamic law, it didn't make what he was doing right. And for a long time, because I was being manipulated, I let it go. There was one time he did it right before a fight. And that really made me mad, because I looked at those fights as the most important thing as far as our security as a family was concerned. If he messed up a fight, he was taking from our children. I was hurt a lot by what was going on, but mostly I kept the hurt inside. That's how we lasted nine years together. But finally it got to be too much, and that's when we started to clash."

"We're talking about the most attractive man in the world in the most charismatic position in the world," acknowledges Ferdie Pacheco. "He'd have had to be a monk not to fool around with women."

"I guess, after a while, you get the picture," adds Howard Bingham. "Ali liked women; women liked him. And there were a couple of folks who helped arrange introductions. Lloyd Wells was the biggest help. Lloyd was a talented man in the area of women. He's older now, but he's still pretty good. And Lloyd always made sure that there were a lot of women around Ali whether it was good or bad for him."

LLOYD WELLS: "I met Ali in 1965. At the time, I was sports editor for the *Houston Informer* and a sportswriter for the *Pittsburgh Courier*. And I also was a photographer for various high school and college yearbooks in Texas. What happened was, a guy named Isaac Sutton, who's now the West Coast bureau chief for *Ebony* and *Jet*, came to Houston. He was there to photograph some centerfolds for *Jet*. And because of my yearbook work, I had quite a few contracts, so I got the girls for him. Then Isaac started talking about Muhammad Ali and asked, did I know him. Naturally, I knew of Muhammad, but I'd never met him. And Isaac was from Chicago; he was friendly with Ali, so he telephoned him. We talked on the phone for about an hour. The conversation was interesting; we hit it off. And Ali told me he'd come to visit if I picked him up at the airport in Houston.

"Then in 1966, I became a full-time scout for the Kansas City Chiefs football team. They moved me to Atlanta, and had me scouting East Coast colleges. I was a single man in my early forties, considered handsome, with a beautiful new Eldorado car every year. I had status, prestige, an expense account, and the ability to travel. And of course, because of my job, I was always on college campuses, meeting football players, cheerleaders, majorettes, and the sophisticated seniors. I had a lovely highrise apartment in downtown Atlanta. The Delta Airlines stewardess school was in Atlanta, and I used to give a graduation party every year. I had some pretty wild parties. So I knew a lot of football players, and after a while I met a lot of other athletes. I got friendly with some beautiful girls. And I got to be known for having good parties, good connections, and a good address book.

"Then in 1975, the Chiefs fired Hank Stram. He was their coach, and my best friend. They gave him the shaft, so I quit. And the next day, Gene Kilroy called me. I'd stayed friendly with Ali over the years. He used to visit me in Atlanta, and I'd visit him in Chicago. Gene told me that Ali wanted me to come work for him, so that's what I did, and I stayed full-time with Ali until he retired. I guess you could say my job in camp was as an advisor, close confident, and friend. I did some work as a video photographer, but mostly Ali liked just having me around. We'd look at wild-West movies together. John Wayne; shoot 'em up at the OK Corral. He loved that stuff; he watched it like a kid. We'd eat together—gobble gobble, we called it—and had other good times.

"I was a great admirer of Belinda. She was a great mother, a great cook, a great organizer, a great hostess. In a lot of ways, she was perfect for Ali. Belinda was the first woman I'd ever seen who could do all the cleaning herself in a house as large as the one they lived in. She steam-pressed the clothes, and took care of the children. Ali had all kinds of company coming and going. Celebrities like Bill Cosby and Nancy Wilson, and lots of folks you never heard of. Belinda fed 'em all, welcomed them to spend the night. She did whatever Ali wanted her to do. She was a great matriarch; everybody liked her. But you know, great men are men of great passion. In other words, they like women. Kennedy, Martin Luther King; they were passionate men, and Ali was the same. But I'll tell you one thing, and I'm being honest. Ali was never involved with a white woman. Never, never, never! Now, I'm a guy that tells it like it is, and I don't think Ali ever had sex with a white woman. He had all sorts of opportunities. They'd throw themselves at him; some big names too. I saw them, but I never saw Ali date a white woman, and I'm sure he never had sex with a white woman. That's just not the way it was. And I'd know if he had, because on that score, when it came to women, I was closer to him than anyone. I was the one he talked with. I was the one he came to before and after."

MUHAMMAD ALI: "I used to chase women all the time. And I won't say it was right, but look at all the temptations I had. I was young, handsome, heavyweight champion of the world. Women were always offering themselves to me. I had two children by women I wasn't married to. I love them; they're my children. I feel just as good and proud about them as my other children, but that wasn't a right thing to do. And running around, living that kind of life, wasn't good for me. It hurt my wife; it offended God. It never really made me happy. But ask any man who's forty years old—if he knew at twenty what he knows now, would he do things different? Most people would. Things you do early in life, sometimes you're embarrassed about later on. So I did wrong; I'm sorry. And all I'll say as far as running around chasing women is concerned is, that's all past. I've got a good wife now, and I'm lucky I have her."

The primary hurt to Belinda came in the person of Veronica Porche. Veronica was tall with light mocha-colored skin, shapely, and breathtakingly beautiful. Her mother was a nurse, her father a Los Angeles construction worker. "Creole," was how Veronica described herself. "In our family, it's black, French, Spanish, Indian, and my mother's grandfather was Jewish," she told one reporter.[1]

In 1974, Veronica entered a beauty contest to choose poster girls for the upcoming Ali-Foreman fight. Out of seventy entrants, four were chosen to travel around the United States promoting the bout and ultimately to go to Zaire. Veronica was one of them.

LLOYD WELLS: "Ali met Veronica in Salt Lake City, Utah. There was some kind of press conference to promote the fight. We were at the airport, and Gene Kilroy came over and said, 'Ali, I just saw the prettiest colored girl I've ever seen.' Ali asked, 'Where, where?' And Kilroy told him, 'Over there with the girls Don King is bringing to Africa.' So we went over to take a look, and Ali was smitten on sight. Veronica is one of the most beautiful women in the world. Not one of the most beautiful black women; one of the most beautiful women, period. Ali didn't talk to her that day. In fact, he told Kilroy and me to act like we weren't interested so she wouldn't get cocky. But you better believe he noticed, and Veronica was beautiful. Tall, intelligent, well-educated for her age. I think her mother quarterbacked her to the point of being ambitious enough that before long she had her sights set on marrying Ali. But it wasn't anything like Robin Givens and her mother. No way! You'd never mention Veronica and Robin Givens in the same breath as far as personality or looks is concerned. Hell, compared to Veronica, Robin Givens must look like Buckwheat when she wakes up in the morning."

BELINDA ALI: "I knew something was going on in Zaire. I just didn't know Veronica was the one. One night at the Intercontinental Hotel, I caught him coming in late with Veronica. They came in around one o'clock. And I smacked him good; scratched him a bit. I would have whupped Veronica worse, but she ran and I didn't know who she was. He kept Veronica a pretty good secret. For a while, I thought she was just one of the bunch."

LANA SHABAZZ: "I knew what was going on with Veronica. How could I not know? The closest thing to a person is when you feed them. And I was heartbroken for Belinda. The first time I laid eyes on Veronica, I knew she was trouble. I used to go to the hotel in Kinshasa and pick up pastries to bring back to N'Sele. One day, C. B. Atkins, who was driving for Ali, was putting Veronica in a car. I said, 'Come here, C. B. Where do you think you're taking that woman?' Because I knew the moment I saw her that, if I could go and pick somebody Ali wanted, she'd be the one. C.B. said, 'Ali told me to bring her to camp.' And I started using bad language, saying don't take her. C.B. looked at me like I was crazy, and hollered back, 'Okay, Lana; I won't take her. I'll just call the champ and tell him you told me not to do it, and you're giving all the orders from now on.' He took her, of course. Here we are, training for a championship-of-the-world fight so Ali can get his title back, and Ali is messing around with this girl. It made me mad. And I was sad for Belinda, because I knew this girl was gonna turn everything around."

In the months following his victory over George Foreman, Ali and Veronica were frequent companions. At first, their liaisons were held in private. But as time passed, they grew more bold.

LLOYD WELLS: "Once Belinda learned about Veronica, she tried to fight it. And then, when she realized Ali wasn't gonna stop seeing this woman, she sort of acquiesced. They explained Veronica's presence on trips by saying she was a babysitter or cousin and things like that. That's what they did in Las Vegas, when we were there for the Ron Lyle fight. Veronica was very prominent at that point. She and Ali used to go shopping together, arm-in-arm. And I felt real bad for Belinda. She's such a good person, and she was such a good mother with those four kids. She struggled to try to keep her husband; but it was a no-win situation because Veronica was so beautiful, Veronica was new, and Ali was in love."

LANA SHABAZZ: "If I'd been Belinda, the first time Veronica showed up I'd have whupped her to within an inch of her life. There wouldn't have been anything like, we're gonna have a happy medium and share this man. I wouldn't have put up with that. That's not my style. A man has to make me think it's just me, and I'll make him think it's just him. That's the way I believe, because my mother and father taught me that. I knew what was going on was wrong, and I knew in the end it was gonna hurt Ali. But there wasn't nothing you could tell that boy. One time, he came to me and said, 'Lana, you're a wise woman. You can solve my problem.' And I told him, 'Ali, I can solve your problem, but you're not gonna listen to me. All you're gonna do is go right back to Veronica and tell her what I said.'"

LLOYD WELLS: "We were coming back from Malaysia after the Bugner fight, up on a 747. Ali called me over and said, 'I want to talk with you. I respect you for knowing more about women than any man I ever met. When it comes to women, you know more about them than anyone because of your experience and expertise, so I want to ask you something. What do you think I should do about this situation with Belinda and Veronica?' And I told him, 'What I think and what anybody else thinks isn't gonna have any bearing on it. You're gonna do what your heart wants to do, wrong or right. You love your family; you don't want to hurt Belinda; you respect your religion and all that; but you're in love. I don't have to tell you what to do or not, and my knowledge isn't gonna help because you're caught. You're hooked, you're in love, and you want that woman more than anything in the world.' "

So, when Ali journeyed to Manila, Veronica Porche went with him. Belinda knew she was there, and chose to stay in the United States. Meanwhile, tensions between Ali and Frazier, which had always been high, were turning ugly. In Malaysia, the day after the Bugner fight, the fighters had attended a joint press conference to announce their upcoming confrontation.

"I'm gonna—" Frazier began.

"I'm going to," Ali interrupted. "Not 'I'm gonna.' Talk intelligent."

Frazier went on, trying to ignore him. "I'm gonna go inta training—"

"Not inta," Ali corrected. "Into. How far did you go in school?"

"As far as you went."

"You don't talk that way. Why do you say 'dat-uh'?"

Several onlookers began to laugh.

"Dat-uh," Ali repeated. "What's that?"[2]

Then, in Manila, Ali went further, labeling Frazier "the gorilla":

> It will be a killer
> And a chiller
> And a thrilla
> When I get the gorilla
> In Manila

That hurt Frazier badly enough, but the champion went further. Reaching into his pocket, Ali pulled out a black rubber gorilla, and announced, "This here is Joe Frazier's conscience. I keep it everywhere I go. This is the way he looks when you hit him." At that point, Ali began pummeling the gorilla. "All night long, this is what you'll see. Come on, gorilla; we're in Manila. Come on, gorilla; this is a thrilla."[3]

Most of the reporters in attendance laughed. Frazier didn't think it was funny. "Look at my beautiful kids," he said afterward. "How can I be a gorilla? Well, I guess he's gonna talk. Ain't no way to stop him, but there'll come that moment when he's gonna hear that knock on the door, gonna hear it's time to go to the ring, and then he's gonna remember what it's like to be in with me, how hard and long that night's gonna be."[4]

REGGIE JACKSON: "I loved Ali; I still do. As a young black, at times I was ashamed of my color; I was ashamed of my hair. And Ali made me proud. I'm just as happy being black now as you are being white, and Ali was part of that growing process for me. But in the days before their fight in Manila, I felt for Joe. That was one time I wasn't charmed by Ali.

"You have to remember what Joe Frazier is. Not who he is; what he is. He's a hard-working honest decent man, with small-town roots and very little formal education. He's a proud man. And there's a great honor about Joe. That was evident in the way he fought. And Muhammad ridiculed Joe; he humiliated him in front of the world. And outside the ring, Joe had nothing to fight back with. You know, Ali almost never attacked anyone's character. He never called anyone a liar or said someone was a bad family man or anything like that. He'd say this guy is a bum and that guy can't fight, and this one is ugly and that one is a mummy. But he never attacked people's morals, and he usually knew when to stop. The one time he stepped over the line—and he did it several times with him—was with Joe Frazier. Ali had fun with Joe; calling him a gorilla, calling him ignorant. He took the English language and ripped Joe to death with it. And Joe couldn't match wits with Ali; he didn't have the verbal skills. So his response was to get more angry and bitter. It hurt Joe that black people loved Ali more than they loved him; that Ali had made him the bad guy to black America. Joe would say, 'Hey, I'm blacker than he is. Look at me; I got black features. Look at him, talking about his pretty face.' And I don't think we can be angry at Joe for the negative feelings he has toward Ali. Muhammad was pretty hard on Joe, and it was as bad as ever in Manila."

In the days leading up to their fight, Frazier's rage clearly showed. "It's real hatred," he told reporters. "I want to hurt him. I don't want to knock him out. I want to take his heart out. If I knock him down, I'll stand back; give him a chance to breathe, to get up."[5]

Ali, for his part, was introspective at times. "I'm gonna have another test soon," he told Mark Kram. "Things have been going too good lately. Allah must make me pay for my fame and power. I feel something out there."[6] But for the public at large, he remained supremely confident. "This fight won't even be close," he predicted. "Not one round will the judges say Frazier won. By round three, the fight will have to be stopped. Joe Frazier is completely washed up; nothing but a punching bag. People will be yelling, 'Stop it; don't kill him; stop it!' "[7]

Ali was an all-encompassing force. He had a remarkably active mind, and at times seemed to be orchestrating everything that went on around him. It was as though he had his own movie, and he was the director, the producer, the cameraman, and main actor. He almost always controlled the show, but every now and then the production didn't go as planned. That was true of the fight in Manila, and there was a foreboding of the unexpected when the situation between Belinda and Veronica got out of hand.

The event that served as the catalyst for bringing Ali's relationship with Veronica into the spotlight occurred at Manila's presidential palace. Ten days before the fight, Ali and Frazier were invited to meet with Ferdinand Marcos and his wife. Patti Dreifuss, who was in the Philippines as a publicist for Frazier, recalls what happened next.

PATTI DREIFUSS: "Each fighter was told he could bring four people, including himself. I went as part of Joe's group, with Eddie Futch, Joe, and Joe's son Marvis. Ali actually had five; himself, his parents, Angelo, and Veronica. The room was set up with a desk in the middle, and we were lined up on either side, with photographers and reporters looking on. Marcos came out. Veronica was standing next to Ali. And in his remarks, Marcos nodded toward Veronica and said something to Muhammad like, 'You have a beautiful wife.' It was very embarrassing, but nobody corrected him. It would have been difficult to do that under the circumstances, with the media snapping photographs and writing down everything that was said. But in the long run, it was too much to let pass. You couldn't dismiss it with, 'Oh, well; that's Ali.' And at that point, it became just a matter of time until the story broke."

The man who broke it was Pete Bonventre, in a high-profile feature for *Newsweek*.

PETE BONVENTRE: "About three weeks before the fight, my editor called me in and said, 'Listen, I want to do the ultimate story on Ali. Who is this guy; what's he all about? Go to Manila ahead of the rest of the press, and give me everything you get.' So I went over with Ali. I even sat next to him for a while on the flight, and found out lots of interesting little things. I interviewed as many people as I could, and spent time with the entourage. I watched what was going on, and I was struggling with myself—do I write about Veronica? Because at the time, fifteen years ago, you didn't write about that stuff. Nobody wrote about it, whether you were covering politics in Washington or baseball in New York. And I had pretty much made up my mind not to do it, even though with Ali's Muslim faith it was a legitimate part of the story. But then we went to the presidential palace. And I'll never forget; Marcos looked at Ali and said, 'Your wife is quite beautiful,' meaning Veronica. Ali answered, 'Your wife is beautiful, too.' And I said to myself, 'Oh, shit.' Now, Ali didn't introduce Veronica to Marcos as his wife. It was a presumption on Marcos's part, but as the day went on, with various members of the Filipino press, he began to introduce Veronica as his wife. And I said to myself, 'Okay, *Newsweek* is spending thousands of dollars to send me here. Ali is pretending this woman is his wife. If this gets into the newspapers with her picture and I don't write about it, *Newsweek* is going to wonder what the hell I'm doing over here.' So I was stuck, and finally I wrote about it. I told it like it was; that here was this complex man with so many contradictions fused into one cosmic personality, and one of the contradictions was his devotion to the Islamic faith at the same time he had a mistress. *Newsweek* had a system back then where, on Sunday night before the magazine hit the stands, they'd issue press releases to radio and television, describing some of that week's stories. They featured this thing about Ali, and after that it was out of my hands."

Bonventre's story, entitled "The Ali Mystique," covered four pages in the magazine. Among other things, it noted the change in Ali's entourage over the years and declared:

Solemn Muslim guards have given way to streetwise hustlers. Liberals who cherished him as a symbol of pro-black antiwar attitudes have been replaced by wry connoisseurs of his pure showmanship. Even Ali's women, invariably beautiful and black, have now been brought out of the back rooms of his life and openly flaunted. As of last week, Belinda was still at home in Chicago, and the stunning Veronica Porche, sometimes known as "Ali's other wife," was touring Manila with the champ.[8]

The article went on to describe Ali's meeting with Ferdinand Marcos, and made it clear to readers that Belinda had apparently been relegated to second-class status. Yet even then, the storm might have passed had Ali not made a rare media miscalculation.

JERRY IZENBERG: "Taking Veronica to the presidential palace was a tacky, stupid thing to do. Ali should never have done it, and Veronica shouldn't have allowed it to happen. It was one of those times when Ali needed a friend to step in and say, 'Don't; it's the wrong thing to do.' But even after the story broke, it didn't have to spread. Everybody had known about Veronica before. One article didn't mean we were going to write about her. And that's when Ali made a colossal mistake. Every day in Manila, he held a press conference. It wasn't formal. Usually what happened was, he'd get up and say whatever was on his mind, and then the rest of us would ask questions. But the day after the *Newsweek* story, he began the press conference by talking about Veronica. No one even asked the question, and quite possibly, no one would have. But Ali started off by telling us about the needs of a man and how we all had girlfriends, trying to justify the whole thing. To my knowledge, it was the first time in history that a major celebrity, or anyone else for that matter, called a press conference to announce his marital infidelity. And of course, at that point, we had no choice. It forced everybody to write about it."

What they wrote was what Ali had said. "I know celebrities don't have privacy," he'd told the press in Manila. "But at least they should be able to sleep with who they want. Anybody who worries about who's my wife, tell them, you don't worry who I sleep with and I won't worry about who you sleep with. This is going too far. They got on me for the draft. They got on me for my religion. They got on me for all sorts of things. But they shouldn't be able to get on me for having a girlfriend. I could see some controversy if she was white, but she's not. The only person I answer to is Belinda Ali, and I don't worry about her."[9]

Twenty-four hours later, Belinda was on a plane to Manila. Five observers recount her journey and what happened afterward.

DAVE WOLF: "I was on the same plane. Belinda got on in San Francisco with a phalanx of guys who looked like they had come from the Chicago Bears training camp. And this was not a happy camper. She looked like she was going to war. I sat across the aisle, and I don't remember her saying much of anything on the flight other than snapping an order when she wanted something to eat or something like that. I had read the newspapers and been on the phone with people in Joe's camp, so I knew what was going on. And from the vibrations I got, I had the feeling that Belinda was going to fly into Manila and there might be physical violence. This woman was mad. She was a big strong woman. At that point, she had almost a Sonny Liston–type glare, and I didn't envy Ali when she caught up with him. I had visions of Belinda tossing Veronica out a window and maybe Ali after her. That was a long flight. She didn't sleep; she didn't read; she didn't talk. She just sat there and stared ahead. Her demeanor was something I'll never forget."

HAROLD CONRAD: "We got word that Belinda was flying to Manila. Ali told me, 'She's coming in; you'd better go to the airport and meet her.' So I went to the airport. Belinda got off the plane, took one look at me, and said, 'You're with him. I'm not going with you.' And she didn't. She walked by me, got another car, and took that to the hotel. And she was pissed."

PETE BONVENTRE: "I'll never forget the scene in the hotel lobby. All the press was there. We knew Belinda had flown in from Chicago and was about to arrive at any minute. The limousine pulled up; Belinda got out. She's a tall woman; about six feet, very regal. She was wearing a flowing white dress and, I think, a white turban. She didn't look left; she didn't look right. We all stared, but she didn't deign to look at us. She just walked through the lobby into the elevator. And I remember, one of the Brits shook his head and said, 'The queen herself couldn't have done it better.' "

DICK SCHAAP: "I was with Ali in his suite when Belinda came in. I was doing a story on the fight for *The Today Show*, so I had a camera crew with me. Angelo was there too. We were in a sitting room off the main entrance, when there was a very loud knock on the door. Ali got up, opened the door. It was Belinda. And we turned the cameras and microphone off, damn it. There was a bedroom further down the corridor, and the two of them went past the room we were in. Ali didn't ask to be excused, which under the circumstances was understandable. He just disappeared into the bedroom with Belinda, and loud shouting began to emanate from the room. I could hear both voices, and there's no doubt that Belinda's was the louder. Having gone through two divorces myself, I know it was fairly standard dialogue. Then Angelo looked at me and said, 'I think we should go downstairs for a cup of coffee.' "

LLOYD WELLS: "I was in the bedroom. Belinda cussed Ali out, threw furniture around, and raised hell for about an hour. She looked at me and said, 'You're part of it too.' I said, 'Nah, it ain't me,' and she threw her championship ring at me. And you better believe, when she started throwing things, Ali got out of the way. The last thing she said was, 'You tell that bitch, if I see her I'm gonna break her back. If I see her anywhere, I'm gonna break her back.' And then she went downstairs, back out to her limousine, rode to the airport, and went home on the same plane that brought her."

LEON GAST: "At that point, people were talking about Belinda-Veronica as much as they were talking about Ali-Frazier. And you could see, even Muhammad began to feel it was getting out of hand. The day before the fight, they had the weigh-in. Howard Cosell was getting ready to interview Ali by satellite from New York. And before they went on the air, Ali said, 'I don't want you to mention anything about Veronica.' Well, you know Cosell. He went into his schtick about how, 'There are sixty million people who watch me on ABC, and all of them know I tell it like it is, and this is news, and I stood up for you when you refused induction into the Army, and I'm a journalist and I have integrity, and this is the story and we have to talk about it.' And Ali said, 'If you say one word about Veronica, I'm going to tell your sixty million viewers about that woman you had in the hotel room in London before I fought Henry Cooper.'

"Now, I don't know if Howard Cosell had a woman in his hotel room before Ali fought Henry Cooper or not. Everything I've read leads me to believe that he had a wonderful wife and a wonderful marriage. It may very well have been that Cosell simply wanted to avoid being the butt of one of Ali's jokes with sixty million people watching on television. But I do know that Cosell didn't say one word about Veronica that morning when he was interviewing Ali."

Dave WOLF: "It's funny how times change. I have a piece of paper that Ali signed just before the first Liston fight. It's a piece of lined paper taken from somebody's notebook, and Ali's signature—he was Cassius Clay then—is witnessed by Howard Bingham and Jack McDermott of *Life* magazine. In that paper, Ali swore he was a Muslim. *Life* was about to run the story, but it seemed so incomprehensible that they weren't prepared to do it unless Ali acknowledged in writing that it was true. Otherwise, *Life* was afraid he'd sue for libel. And now, in Manila, instead of the Nation of Islam or the war in Vietnam, the prefight story was Ali's women.

"As far as the fight itself was concerned, the feeling in Joe's camp was that Ali's problems would work to our advantage. We were sitting back, waiting for intramural war to break out in the Hilton. Ali's personal life was so tumultuous, it seemed he'd almost have to suffer. But in retrospect, I think Ali thrived on this stuff. I doubt that he enjoyed the embarrassment of the situation, but he liked being the center of attention and being in the limelight. Back in the sixties, none of the turmoil around him had impacted adversely on his performance as a fighter. He'd kept on fighting and winning then, even though he was facing jail. So I think, instead of being a distraction, this type of thing actually helped Ali get ready. It allowed him not to get tied up in knots worrying about the fight itself."

Ali-Frazier III took place on October 1, 1975, in Quezon City, six miles outside Manila. Ali entered the ring a two-to-one favorite. Although the fight was held at 10:45 A.M. to accommodate closed-circuit television in the United States, the twenty-five-thousand-seat Philippines Coliseum was jammed. Shortly before the bout began, Herbert Muhammad visited Ali's dressing room and spoke privately with the champion. "He told me success comes from believing in yourself," Ali remembers. "We prayed to God to give me strength, not for myself, but because there were millions of Muslims all over the world who were praying for me; and if I lost, they'd lose too."

"That was the key," Gary Smith of *Sports Illustrated* would say later. "Ali, more than any other fighter, or any person I ever wrote about, understood that in order to be great you need something outside of yourself to flow into. Most fighters aren't fortunate enough to have something like that in their life. And when you fight for yourself, maybe it's you against the world and that gives you some fuel, but it will never give you the strength Ali had. Muhammad was fighting for more than himself. He fought for God; his mission was huge. And that's why, in places like Manila, he was able to prevail when other men would have lost."

Then came the fight.

ED SCHUYLER: "The Thriller in Manila was the best fight I've ever seen. As it unfolded, everybody at ringside understood they were watching greatness. From the third round on, it just kept building. The ebb and flow was incredible. In the sixth round, Frazier hit Ali with a left hook that's the hardest punch I've ever seen. It had to be harder than the punch he knocked Ali down with in their first fight. Ali's head turned like it was on a swivel, and his response was to look at Frazier and say, 'They told me Joe Frazier was washed up.' And Frazier answered, 'They lied.' The pace never eased; it was hell the whole way. I've never seen two people give more, ever. And I've never seen the film of that fight. I don't have to. I remember it like it was yesterday."

ALEX WALLAU: "The most obvious thing that impressed me about Ali was his speed, but the thing that impressed me most was his heart-slash-chin. He had the most amazing chin I've ever seen, and that includes all the fighters I've watched on old fight films. He had a remarkable capacity for recovery, and also remarkable ability to fight through pain. And he had guts. That's one of the things that surprised people, especially the hard-bitten old-line fight crowd. They dismissed Ali as a creation of the media, a loudmouthed pretty-boy who would fold when the going got tough. But whatever was left of that criticism came to an end in Manila. What Ali did there was take his courage and show it to the world on terms any redneck could understand. Here it is; I'm giving it to you on a silver platter. I'm as tough and brave as any of those tough guys you admire."

JERRY IZENBERG: "What it came down to in Manila wasn't the heavyweight campionship of the world. Ali and Frazier were fighting for something more important than that. They were fighting for the championship of each other, and it was an epic battle. I think about Manila, and really, I don't even think about who won. Usually that's paramount, but what matters most about that fight is how great it was. Both men gave it everything they had. They both knew that probably it was the last time they'd face each other. And if you do what we do for a living, you wanted to be at ringside for that fight."

In a way, Ali-Frazier III was three fights. The early rounds belonged to Ali. He outboxed Frazier, landing sharp clean blows, and staggered the challenger several times. Still, Frazier kept coming forward, and in the middle rounds the tide turned. Now Ali was tiring, and Frazier rocked him with thunderous blows. Slowly, Ali's arms came down as the challenger trod inexorably in, bludgeoning the champion against the ropes, pounding away to bring him down.

DAVE WOLF: "As the fight went on, I began to think that the judges' scoring was irrelevant, because there was no way it was going fifteen rounds. By the seventh round, neither man had any mobility left at all. They were just standing there, pounding on each other. And there was frustration in watching it, because part of the strategy Eddie Futch had worked on with Joe was to batter Ali's arms. We knew Ali would do the rope-a-dope, and it would be hard to come up the middle against him at first. But if you beat the crap out of his arms, a space would open up; and Joe didn't do that enough. He threw fewer body punches than he normally did. I think it came down to this emotional thing, where he was fighting with so much hatred that it was almost as though he couldn't be bothered to go after the arms. He wanted Ali's head. I really believe that if Joe had fought the way Eddie wanted him to, he would have won, because he came close to winning anyway. There were times when I thought Joe had the fight won. On a number of occasions, he hurt Ali more than it would have appeared to somebody who was watching on television or even as far back as the third row. But he didn't go to the body enough, because he wanted to hit Ali in the head. And then Ali reached into that incredible reservoir of strength, physical and emotional, just when it looked like he was gone."

ANGELO DUNDEE: "You know, Muhammad was a much better puncher than people gave him credit for. Even though other guys had bigger reputations as bangers, when he got off his toes, there weren't a lot of heavyweights around at the time who could bang with him. And Muhammad was always at his best as a fighter when he felt he had something to prove. So was I worried in Manila? You bet I was; it was a brutal fight. But like I told the press when it was over; both guys ran out of gas, only my guy had an extra tank."

In round twelve, Ali regained the initiative, staggered Frazier, and began measuring him for blows. One round later, a jolting left hook knocked the challenger's mouthpiece into the crowd. Frazier was shaken, but finished the round. Then, in round fourteen, Ali resumed his assault. Frazier's left eye was completely closed, and vision in his right eye was limited. He was spitting blood. Ali's punches were landing cleanly, and Frazier couldn't see them coming. Finally, Frazier's chief cornerman, Eddie Futch, had seen enough.

EDDIE FUTCH: "Joe had a tendency to swell and puff up. He didn't cut, but he'd swell; and after the eleventh round in Manila, it started to impair his vision. At that point, instead of being low and close, he had to stand up and back off in order to see with just one eye. And Ali was a great opportunist, so he took advantage of the situation by stepping up the attack and landing those big right hands. The thirteenth round was very bad, but I thought maybe Ali had punched himself out and would be arm-weary after landing so many good blows. That's the reason I let Joe go out for the four-teenth, and it was worse than the round before. Joe kept getting hit with the right hand. His left eye was completely closed; his right eye was closing. It had been a grueling fight, and that's when fighters get hurt; when they get hit with good clean punches they don't see and still don't go down. I didn't want Joe's brains scrambled. He had a nice life and a wonderful family to live for. So I decided at the end of the fourteenth round to stop it. I just didn't think Joe should go on anymore.

"Joe came back to the corner after the round. He sat down, and I said, 'Joe, it's over. I don't want you to go out for the next round.' He started to protest. He was getting up off the stool, so I put my hands on his shoulders and he stayed down. Then I told him again, 'Joe, the fight's over. I'm stopping it. You're taking too much pun-ishment, and I don't want to see you take any more.'"

DAVE WOLF: "Joe wasn't happy with Eddie's decision, but in my mind it was the right thing to do. If one tries to be objective about it, we were behind on points; Joe had shown no indication that he'd be able to score a knockout in the final round because he couldn't even see Ali. There really wasn't anything to be gained by sending him out, because either he'd be knocked out, or if he lasted the final three minutes he'd lose anyway. The fight was lost. At least, that's how it seemed.

"And then, after it was stopped, I distinctly remember Ali col-lapsing in his corner. He stood up, his legs were like jelly, and he sort of oozed to the floor. Now there are all sorts of possible expla-nations for that. Relief, joy, happiness, whatever. But I had a pretty clear view of it; and I remember thinking that, if Joe had actually come out of his corner, Ali might not have been there for the final round. So I think the decision to stop the fight was a good one, but I'm not sure what would have happened if Eddie had let it go on."

What might have happened is subject to speculation. Inside the arena, it was sweltering and the air-conditioning didn't work. Both fighters were exhausted, and the humidity was reminiscent of a night in 1952 when Sugar Ray Robinson fought Joey Maxim. That night, Robinson was well ahead on points at the end of thirteen rounds, but then he hit the wall. Suffering from heat prostration, weaving around the ring like a drunk, he was led to his corner by his handlers and failed to come out for the fourteenth round.

In Manila, as Sugar Ray Robinson had, Ali hit the wall. Whether he would have come out for the final round is open to question, but Ali himself acknowledges, "Frazier quit just before I did. I didn't think I could fight anymore."

WALI MUHAMMAD: "After the fourteenth round, Ali came back to the corner and told us, 'Cut 'em off.' That's how tired he was. He wanted us to cut his gloves off. And Angelo ignored him. He started wiping Ali's face, getting him ready for the fifteenth round. We sponged him down, and I gave him a drink of sweetened water, honey and water, from a bottle I'd made up. I don't know if he'd have gone out for the last round or not. Ali's not a quitter; he'd never quit. But I'd never seen him exhausted like that before.

"Then somebody—I think it was Kilroy—looked across the ring, and saw Eddie Futch call the ref over. Kilroy started shouting, 'It's over! It's over!' And the feeling I had then; I can't express it. In the dressing room afterward, Bundini and me, we just broke down and cried."

DAVE WOLF: "In the dressing room after the fight, Joe was hurt, depressed, dehydrated, exhausted. He had the kind of face that swelled up in lumps, so even when he won he looked like he'd lost, and after Manila he looked like a wreck. He was lucid and angry at Eddie for stopping the fight, but he didn't have a lot of strength left to move around. And there was no immediate sense of glory in defeat. Later, it sank in that this had been a great fight, but at the time all that mattered was we'd lost. There was a feeling that Joe could and should have won the fight. The heroic aspects didn't sink in until later."

FERDIE PACHECO: "Ali was badly beaten up. There were welts and bruises all over his body, and huge hematomas over both hips—collections of blood where Frazier had hit the hip sockets. His face was puffy. He wasn't disoriented, but he was as exhausted as a man can be to the point where he could barely talk. Later, he said that fight was the closest thing to death he knew of. And he was right. It took about twenty-four hours for his brain to recuperate, for his thought processes to become complete. And the effects on the rest of his body lasted for weeks. It was the toughest fight I've seen in my life."

That night, Ali attended a reception given by Ferdinand Marcos at the Manila Antique House. "The champion's face resembled a mask that had been stretched to fit," Dave Anderson wrote. "His narrowed eyes appeared to be underlined in purple crayon. His forehead had small lumps on it. The bridge of his nose was scraped pink. When he walked, he moved stiffly, almost in a limp."[10] "Ali was hurting," remembers Ed Schuyler. "He sat like a man who was afraid that if he let his breath out, his stomach would fall out with it."

Frazier's wife came over to congratulate Ali, and the champion extended his fingers and smiled. Frazier himself wasn't there. "His eyes are just about completely shut," said Eddie Futch, explaining his fighter's absence.

Several miles away, Frazier lay on a bed in semidarkness. Later, Mark Kram described the scene:

Only his heavy breathing disturbed the quiet as an old friend walked to within two feet. "Who is it?" asked Joe Frazier, lifting himself to look around. "Who is it? I can't see! Turn the lights on!" Another light was turned on, but Frazier still could not see. The scene cannot be forgotten; this good and gallant man lying there, embodying the remains of a will that had carried him so far—and now surely too far. His eyes were only slits, his face looked as if it had been painted by Goya. "Man, I hit him with punches that'd bring down the walls of a city," said Frazier. "Lawdy, Lawdy, he's a great champion."[11]

Then Joe Frazier roused himself to attend the "victory party" given by his supporters. "Joe's eyes were closed up so bad he couldn't recognize Red Smith," says Ed Schuyler. "But he still got up and sang with the band."

JOE FRAZIER: "I hated Ali. God might not like me talking that way, but it's in my heart. I hated that man. First two fights, he tried to make me a white man. Then he tried to make me a nigger. How would you like it if your kids came home from school crying, because everyone was calling their daddy a gorilla? God made us all the way we are. He made us the way we talk and look. And the way I feel,

I'd like to fight Ali-Clay-whatever-his-name-is again tomorrow. Twenty years, I've been fighting Ali, and I still want to take him apart piece by piece and send him back to Jesus.

"I'm a hard man. I can look at you hard enough to make tears come out of your eyes. And I'm a proud man. I do what I got to do, whatever it is that's got to be done. That's the kind of man I am. And I know things would of been different for me if Clay hadn't of been around. I'd of gotten a lot more respect. I'd of had more appreciation from my own kind. But the Good Man planned it for us to come at the same time, and I'm sure he had a plan.

"We were gladiators. I didn't ask no favors of him, and he didn't ask none of me. I don't like him but I got to say, in the ring he was a man. In Manila, I hit him punches, those punches, they'd of knocked a building down. And he took 'em. He took 'em and he came back, and I got to respect that part of the man. He was a fighter. He shook me in Manila; he won. But I sent him home worse than he came. Look at him now; he's damaged goods. I know it; you know it. Everyone knows it; they just don't want to say. He was always making fun of me. I'm the dummy; I'm the one getting hit in the head. Tell me now; him or me; which one talks worse now? He can't talk no more, and he still tries to make noise. He still wants you to think he's the greatest, and he ain't. I don't care how the world looks at him; I see him different, and I know him better than anyone. Manila really don't matter no more. He's finished, and I'm still here."

MUHAMMAD ALI: "I don't think two big men ever fought fights like me and Joe Frazier. One fight, maybe. But three times; we were the only ones. Of all the men I fought in boxing, Sonny Liston was the scariest; George Foreman was the most powerful; Floyd Patterson was the most skilled as a boxer. But the roughest and toughest was Joe Frazier. He brought out the best in me, and the best fight we fought was in Manila. That fight, I could feel something happening to me. Something different from what I'd felt in fights before. And God blessed me that day. He's blessed me many times, and that fight in Manila was one of them. It was like I took myself as far as I could go, and then God took me the rest of the way.

"So I'm sorry Joe Frazier is mad at me. I'm sorry I hurt him. Joe Frazier is a good man. I couldn't have done what I did without him, and he couldn't have done what he did without me. And if God ever calls me to a holy war, I want Joe Frazier fighting beside me."

13

The Lion Grows Older

ROBERT LIPSYTE: "Back in 1960, a fan jumped out of the stands at Yankee Stadium and hit Mickey Mantle. This was before recreational violence, and in any event, it was rather extreme. The *Times* wanted to cover it, but on stories like that, they didn't send their ambassador to the sport, the real baseball writer. They'd send a kid from the rewrite desk, like me. I went to the stadium before the next game. Mantle and Yogi Berra were tossing a ball back and forth in front of the dugout. I introduced myself very politely, explained who I was—I remember, I called him 'Mr. Mantle'—and asked for some comment on what had happened. And Mantle said, 'Why don't you go fuck yourself.' I thought I'd heard wrong or done something wrong. There was no reason to suspect that a great athletic hero would treat anyone, let alone a young obsequious member of the press, like that. So I rephrased the question, at which point Mantle signaled Berra and they began throwing the ball through my hair, and I realized the interview was over. That was a consciousness-raiser for me. It taught me what kind of people certain heroes really are. And then I compare that with Ali—always accessible, always friendly, always basically decent and helpful. And finally, after many years, the world at large saw him that way. Even people who had once thought he was awful let go of their emotional baggage and accepted him for what he was."

In the aftermath of his victory over Joe Frazier in Manila, Ali's popularity and his greatness as a fighter were confirmed. Once, his every move in and out of the ring had been criticized by the media. Now it seemed, he could do no wrong. "People loved him," says Ed Schuyler. "It was that simple. If Ali had stood up at a press conference, as Larry Holmes later did, and said, 'Rocky Marciano couldn't carry my jockstrap,' we'd have fallen down laughing. Holmes was crucified for saying that. And Ali said things a lot worse, but he got away with it because he was Muhammad Ali."

"I've been in this business for forty years," says Jerry Izenberg. "And there are lots of people who can stop a room if they're in the right town. Joe Namath in his prime could stop a room in New York, but not in Boston. Michael Jordan can stop a room in Chicago, but they won't even recognize him in a lot of places. The only two people I've known in sports who could walk into a room anywhere at any time and stop it cold were Joe DiMaggio and Muhammad Ali. And Ali still does it everywhere he goes. That's something to marvel at; it's a special gift. But fame and notoriety don't necessarily mean you're a good person. And what's nice about Ali's fame is, people like him; it's well-deserved; and ironically, after all he went through, the affection for him is largely colorblind. Late in his career, Ali developed a quality that only a few people have—except maybe he didn't change; maybe it was the rest of the world changing. Ali reached a point where, when people looked at him, they didn't see black or white. They saw Ali. And for a long time, that mystified him. He expected black people to love him and crowd around him, but then he realized white people loved him too, and that made him very happy."

HOWARD BINGHAM: "Ali is aware of what color people are; sometimes he knows their religion. But it doesn't affect how he feels about them. A couple of weeks after he beat Joe Frazier in Manila, we were in New York for a reception at the United Nations. Ali was watching the news on television, and a story came on about a Jewish community center that was closing because it didn't have enough money. It was a place for old people. They were handicapped, and a lot of them had been persecuted by the Nazis in Germany. The next morning [December 2, 1975], we went up to the building where the center was. Ali looked around, talked to some of the people, and gave them a check for a hundred thousand dollars. That's just the way he is. And when someone asked why he did it, all he said was he had a soft spot in his heart for old people."

Ali, after Manila, was the best-known and possibly the most popular person in the world. When he did battle in the ring, people held their breath. More than a boxing match was at stake; more than a world title was involved. Ali's fights were about ideology at one extreme, and watching a loved one risk danger at the other. Indeed, in some ways, his fans preferred mismatches to competitive fights. With a mismatch, they could sit back and enjoy Ali the entertainer. An Ali mismatch was a performance to be savored without fear of injury or loss. In a mismatch, the ring was Ali's stage and he was a performing artist. And never was that more clear than on the night of February 20, 1976, when Ali fought "The Lion of Flanders"— Jean-Pierre Coopman.

Coopman was a twenty-nine-year-old sculptor of religious statues, who happened to be the heavyweight champion of Belgium. By all accounts, he was a very nice man; he just couldn't fight. Ali himself defended the choice of Coopman as an opponent by pointing to his brutal bout in Manila and projected rematches against Ken Norton and George Foreman. "Let me have a little rest in between," he pleaded at a New York press conference.[1] It was hardly the way to build drama for a fight; but certainly, Ali was being honest. "The Lion of Flanders," as Coopman was known, might not have beaten Bert Lahr.

George Kanter, who served as Coopman's business representative in the United States, recalls the events leading up to the bout.

GEORGE KANTER: "I didn't know much about Coopman, but I was in Belgium when he beat a fighter named Charlie Green. Green is in jail now; he killed some people in Harlem. But he became rather famous anecdotally after an incident at Madison Square Garden. Jose Torres was scheduled to fight, and at the last moment, his opponent pulled out. Gil Clancy was Green's manager. He looked around the arena, found Green eating a hot dog, and told him, 'Put down that hot dog; you're fighting tonight.' They negotiated Green's purse rather quickly. But then in the dressing room when Clancy was taping his hands, Green told him, 'Don't put the bandages on till you give me eight dollars.' Clancy asked, 'What do you want eight dollars for? You're getting paid for the fight.' And Green said, 'I paid eight dollars for my ticket, and I'll be damned if I'll pay to see myself in the ring.'

"Anyway, Green lost to Coopman in Belgium. I was at the fight, and afterward Coopman's manager asked if I would help him in America. I wasn't sure what I could do. European heavyweights weren't much at the time, and the heavyweights in Belgium were even less. But then Ali said he was tired of fighting tough opponents, and that after Manila he was entitled to an easy bout. And Coopman was perfect, so I went back to Belgium to see Coopman's manager. He owned a barber shop in the small country town where Jean-Pierre lived. And he was so excited he could hardly talk, because his fighter was going to fight the great Muhammad Ali. Finally I told him, 'Look, calm down; let's talk money.' And the guy said to me, 'It's such an honor to fight Muhammad Ali, we would fight him for nothing.' I said, 'Well, don't tell the promoter that, because if you do, that's exactly what you'll be fighting for.' So we agreed on a purse, and there was a press conference to announce the fight at one of the New York hotels. Coopman arrived; I went to the airport to get him. I figured, this is going to be a tough sell; I have to do something to build the fighter. And it occurred to me, Belgium is cut up into three parts. There's Flanders, there's Brussels, and there's the Walloon country. Coopman was from Flanders, and on their flag—it's a yellow flag with a lion on it—I said to myself, 'Well, this is the obvious thing; we'll call him the Lion of Flanders.'

"So we had the press conference, and one of the main problems was, Coopman was so in awe of Ali and so pleased to meet him that he wanted to kiss him all the time. And Ali was saying, 'Get away from me. How am I ever gonna get mad at this guy?' I kept close to Coopman, because I saw he wasn't, as they say, too hep. But at one point, I was taken aside by a reporter and Coopman was left to the other newspapermen. And the next thing I heard was someone asking him, 'Why are you called the Lion of Flanders?' And Coopman answered, 'I don't know. Mr. Kanter just told me that was my name.'

"Now, generally speaking, if you're trying to sell a mediocre fighter in the United States, you're at an advantage if he's European. That's because nobody knows him. As the French say, it's easy to lie when you come from far. But Coopman strained that bit of logic. He trained a little in New York, and it was obvious, to put it politely, that he was not world-class. Then we went to Puerto Rico, which was where the fight was held, and I had to find a sparring partner who would make him look good. I scouted around, and someone suggested, 'Why don't you try Galvan?' I've forgotten his first name. He was a fighter I'd used years before as a middleweight in Paris. He was Puerto Rican, and they told me, 'Galvan is broke, he needs the money.' So I went looking for Galvan, and finally found him. He was really a middleweight, but at this point his stomach got him to being a heavyweight. I said to him, 'Galvan, would you like to make some money?' and he told me, 'Sure, I'll be at the gym tomorrow. What time do you want me?' And he was there on time. The sparring started, and Galvan, who had not fought in seven or eight years, who was in no shape at all, grossly overweight, was kicking the hell out of Coopman. So I stopped it and announced, 'Coopman is still suffering from jet lag, there will be no more sparring today.' Then I talked to Galvan, and said, 'You know, you can't do this.' And he told me, 'I haven't fought for seven years; I'm not even trying hard.'

"Anyway, we had a tough time getting through the training. We decided to have secret workouts, as we called them, to shield Coopman from the press. It was announced that this was being done because Coopman had devised a master plan for beating Ali, and we didn't want anyone to know what it was. Periodically, the two fighters would run into each other, and whenever they did, Coopman would want to kiss Ali. I'd beg him, 'Please don't ask for his autograph.' And Ali kept saying, 'How am I gonna get mad at this guy? How am I gonna get mad at him?' Finally, I had lunch with Bobby Goodman, who was doing publicity for the fight, and I said, 'Bobby, we've got to somehow build Coopman up. Bobby told me that was impossible, but then something wonderful happened. There was a very famous witch in Puerto Rico who wanted to work with Ali, and of course, Ali wanted nothing to do with her. So I called the witch and told her we wanted her to work for Coopman. Now, the strange part was, on top of everything else, Jean-Pierre Coopman believed in witches, and he really felt this was going to bring him the heavyweight championship of the world. We went to the witch's studio, or whatever she called it, and she told us, 'We're going into another room to chase all the evil spirits away, but everybody must first take off their watches.' Now, seeing the kind of place it was and her son, who didn't look particularly honest, I didn't go inside. I stayed with the watches, because otherwise I felt we might not have them when we were through. But she took Jean-Pierre in, put him in a big hole, poured some witch water on him, and so forth. And then she explained that some invisible general whose name I've forgotten—a Puerto Rican general, who was dead of course—and his entire army would be in trenches behind Coopman so there was no way that Ali could beat him. I wasn't sure how effective this general would be when the bell rang, but Coopman seemed to believe it was true. And more important, it was a good story. It got us into the papers to build the fight."

In the end, the bout was a tribute to Ali's magic as a drawing card. No one thought it would be competitve. Yet CBS broadcast it in prime time; the Coliseum in San Juan was sold out, and an overflow crowd of 11,500 paid to watch it on closed-circuit television at an arena adjacent to the live action. As for the fight itself, Bert Sugar recalls, "After the first round, Ali leaned over the ropes and shouted down to one of the TV network people, 'You guys are in trouble; ain't no way you're gonna get all your commercials in.' "

GEORGE KANTER: "On the night of the fight, I was in Ali's dressing room watching his hands being taped. Then I went back to Coopman's dressing room. Jean-Pierre had his wife in his arms, and they were drinking champagne. This was before the fight. I asked, 'What's going on here? Am I in a house of ill repute, or is this a boxer's dressing room?' But that's how it was. Coopman had quite a bit of champagne before the fight, and then they gave him champagne between rounds. He was the happiest loser I ever saw. The more champagne he drank, the more he smiled, and he had the stupidest smile on his face the whole night. Anyway, they played the national anthems before the fight. Then round one began. And Ali at that time, when he fought anybody, right at the beginning of the fight he'd go inside and feel his opponent's strength. And any doubts I might have had about the outcome of the fight evaporated in the opening seconds when the fighters clinched. Ali tested Coopman's strength, and when he came out of the clinch, he was laughing. The rest is history. He knocked Jean-Pierre out when he wanted to, which I think was the fifth round. But that fight was the beginning, not the end, for Coopman. Afterward, he went back to Belgium and got five hundred dollars a speech to lecture in virtually every town in Belgium about his fight with Ali. I said to myself, 'This will be the shortest lecture of all time.' But it made him a local hero; he wasn't at all discouraged. And the heavyweights in Belgium were quite poor, so he remained the dominant Belgian heavyweight for a long time. And of course, from that point on, every time Coopman went into the ring, he was introduced as 'The Lion of Flanders.' "

Two months after the Coopman bout, Ali fought what was expected to be another "breather" in Landover, Maryland, against Jimmy Young. Young was a journeyman heavyweight, who'd lost to opponents like Clay Hodges, Roy Williams, and Randy Neumann. He had relatively little personality so to speak, so again the burden of promoting the fight was on Ali. Three days before the bout, the champion met with President Ford's daughter, Susan, put his arm around her for photographers, and started singing, "If you knew Susie like I knew Susie . . ." Then he entertained a group of college students from the University of Maryland, and promised a thousand dollars to anyone who brought him Howard Cosell's toupee.

As always, the prefight rituals made for good copy; but the fight itself was awful. Ali came into the ring at 230 pounds, the heaviest of his career. He was slow, overweight, and clearly out of shape. Young, who might have won with a more aggressive battle plan, was a largely passive figure. On six occasions when Ali had him cornered, the challenger literally stuck his head outside the ropes, forcing a halt in the action. The result, wrote Mark Kram, was "some of the worst and most numbing rounds in heavyweight history."[2] Ali won a unanimous decision, but as a showman he'd failed. Even Angelo Dundee, who was legendary for looking at the bright side of things, acknowledged that Ali's performance had been "the worst of his career."[3] Yet Ali's appeal was such that twenty-four days later, on May 24, 1976, he was on prime-time television again—this time, against England's Richard Dunn.

The Dunn bout was held in Munich and promoted by Bob Arum in conjunction with a West German promotional firm. Ali was aware that his previous fight had gone badly. Indeed, before facing Dunn, he told the press, "I don't want to look bad again. I let the public down last time."[4] Still, tickets for Ali-Dunn sold poorly. Dunn was perceived as a retread of Jean-Pierre Coopman, and the spectre of empty seats in Munich's Olympiahalle haunted the West German promoters, who were having trouble paying their bills. Finally, on the eve of the fight, Ali agreed to cut his purse by one hundred thousand dollars in exchange for two thousand tickets, which he distributed to United States military personnel stationed in Germany. "I can see myself sitting in the barracks," he told Mike Katz. "Let's say I got no money, I'm an American, and here's Muhammad Ali, the heavyweight champion of the world. If I was a soldier, I'd want to see me; and I got nothing against them for going in the Army. I didn't go because of my religion, but them soldiers are just doing their job."

Meanwhile, as the public readied for Ali's performance in the ring, a battle behind the scenes was brewing. Don King had promoted or been part of the promotion in six of Ali's seven previous fights, starting with "The Rumble in the Jungle" in Zaire. But now King had tasted big money and wanted more. He wanted to control Ali.

BOB ARUM: "I know for a fact that King made a move on Ali. King was innovative. At the time, his press wasn't bad. And there were a lot of people in Ali's camp who were on King's payroll, getting money to report what was happening and to say good things about him to Ali. I wouldn't pay those bastards, but anybody that looked like they were close to Ali, King tried to put them on his payroll. And it wasn't just handing out hundred-dollar bills when he went into camp. It was much more organized than that; it was real payments in return for services. Herbert's reaction at first was to deal with it by compromising; Herbert tends to go with the flow. But then it got worse, and for a short time, he might have felt his position was threatened. In the end, of course, Herbert won. His bonds with Ali were tremendously strong. But in 1976, when he realized how bad it was, Herbert made an affirmative move away from King. If you look at the fights Ali had after that—Dunn, Norton, Evangelista, Shavers, Spinks twice—Evangelista was the only one King promoted. And I'm not sure Herbert even felt comfortable about that deal."

BUTCH LEWIS: "Definitely, Herbert made a move away from King. And Don didn't like it; he fought it hard. After Joe lost to Ali in Manila, I wanted to try my hand at promoting, but I wasn't experienced enough to do the nuts and bolts work myself. So what I did was make a deal with Arum, where if I brought in Ali, he'd promote it through Top Rank. Then Ali gave me the Dunn fight. I was the one who brought it to Arum. And King was pissed about losing Ali. He kept using all that black shit against me, saying, 'Butch Lewis is just an Uncle Tom; he's just a front man for Arum. You don't want to go with that nigger over there. Let me do the fight.' "

HERBERT MUHAMMAD: "I was never able to travel all the time with Ali, because my religious obligations came first. And in 1975 when my father passed, I felt an obligation to keep the community strong and help my brother, Wallace D. Muhammad, so then especially I wasn't in camp every day. And what happened was, certain people took that as a sign that maybe they could seize the opportunity to get to Ali. Now Don King, it seems he tries to destroy the image of managers. Don wants to make any fighter feel he doesn't need a manager. I don't care who it is, it behooves Don to get a relationship with the fighter where he can tell him, 'Why pay a manager one-third of your purse? I'll get you the fights; just sign with me. Forget the manager; what do you need him for? Make me the promoter, and you'll keep 100 percent of everything for yourself.' And some fighters believe that. What they don't understand is, Don doesn't care about them the way a good manager does. He won't get them top dollar; he won't necessarily choose the right opponents. If they lose, he don't necessarily care, because if two fighters get in the ring, he's got both of them. So Don King might say, 'I'll put you on my farm; I'll get a trainer for you; just sign with me, and I'll take care of you.' But in the end, he'll pay his fighters as little as he can. Believe me; if you're a fighter, you don't want to deal with Don without a manager.

"Now I have positive things to say about Don, too. Don has been a great motivator for black people, because he's shown that you can come up and meet the challenge of society. He made a lot of black people feel like they can make it if they try. He's a heck of a promoter; I gotta say that. He knows how to make money for himself out of boxing, which is his job, but sometimes he goes too far. A lot of fighters, the black ones, feel they're not doing what's right if they don't go with a black promoter, and Don takes advantage of that. I know from my own experience, if Bob Arum offered me more money for Ali's services than Don did, I'd go with Arum. Then Don would come to me and say, 'Because you're black, you should help a black brother.' And I'd tell him, 'Don, I did help you. You'd just come out of prison, and I didn't even know you other than you were a black man like myself trying to make it, and I let Ali go over and do an exhibition for you in Cleveland.' And sometimes Don goes further than he should in other ways, too. I know he paid people in the camp. I know he tried to talk to Ali behind my back. Ali was hearing from certain people, 'Herbert's taking one-third and he's not even here. Maybe we should get rid of Herbert.' But I never confronted Don about it, because I had confidence in my closeness with Ali. I knew Don would never be able to come between us. And Don resented that. To this day, he doesn't like me. He hates my guts, really. He might have some respect for me because of my father, but nothing else. And he really hasn't done what he should for Ali. None of them have. If it wasn't for Ali, Bob Arum wouldn't be where he is today; Don King wouldn't be where he is today. What's the other cat's name, Butch Lewis, he'd never be where he is today. Without Ali, they'd never have been known; yet none of them wants to turn around now and make Ali a partner. Like Don King right now could say to Ali, 'Okay, I got a promotion and I want you to come in,' and give him some real money. Not just five or ten thousand dollars; I'm talking about really helping. But I haven't seen it in Don's nature to help anyone like that."

With the struggle for control hidden from view, Ali knocked Rich-ard Dunn down five times before stopping the Englishman in the fifth round. There was no way of knowing it at the time, but those were the last knockdowns Ali would register in his career. Although he was to fight ninety-six rounds in seven championship bouts over the next five-and-a-half years, he never put an opponent on the canvas again. His skills were eroding, and in his next major public appearance, the Ali luster noticeably dimmed.

The opponent was Antonio Inoki. And he wasn't a fighter; he was a professional wrestler. Ali and Inoki met in Tokyo to do battle for what was called "the martial arts championship of the world." Their encounter occurred on June 25, 1976, and the motivating force behind it was money. Ali was guaranteed six million dollars, although financial irregularities and broken contracts would cut that amount to $2,200,000. Inoki was "guaranteed" two million dollars, but wound up with only a token amount.

In the days leading up to the contest, Ali did his best to generate public interest. He dubbed his opponent "the Pelican" because of Inoki's prominent jaw, and promised to knock him out with a newly developed "acupunch." "I'm ready," the champion told the world. "I can't let boxing down. I can't let the American fans down. I can't lose to an old fat-bellied wrestler. I'll destroy Inoki. This will be the biggest one-sport event in the history of the world."[5]

Not everyone was convinced. Many suggested that Ali-Inoki was degrading for boxing and also for the heavyweight champion. But as always, Ali was quick to respond. "People expect these things of me," he told a national audience on CBS's *Face the Nation*. "I have a great imagination; I'm always doing something. And it's in-teresting. People want to know what would a boxer do with a wres-tler. What's going to happen if Ali gets his arm twisted? What will happen if he throws Ali on his back? What will happen if he kicks Ali? I'm betting I can hit him before he can grab me. With my dancing and moving, I can't see him getting close enough to hit me without me hitting him. This man is a wrestler. He's not used to taking hard shots to the head. The minute I go upside his head, it's over."[6]

BOB ARUM: "Ali-Inoki was embarrassing. What happened was, some Japanese guys came to Herbert with the deal. Herbert asked me to do the closed-circuit, and the whole thing was supposed to be fixed. The scenario was set. I met with Ali and Herbert at Her-bert's office in Chicago, and at that meeting we went over the script for the fight. Ali would pound on Inoki for six or seven rounds. Inoki would be pouring blood. Apparently, he was crazy enough that he was actually going to cut himself with a razor blade. Ali would appeal to the referee to stop the fight. And right when he was in middle of this humanitarian gesture, Inoki would jump him from behind and pin him. Pearl Harbor all over again.

"Except when Ali got to Japan, his conscience started bothering him. He decided it was wrong to trick the public, and he refused to go to any of the rehearsals. So all of a sudden, we had a real fight; and from that point on, the whole thing was bizarre. No one had any control; no one knew what was happening. Someone put together a set of nonsense rules, with fifteen three-minute rounds. Essentially, Ali was supposed to box; Inoki was supposed to wrestle. Inoki would get knocked out, or Ali would be pinned. And it was awful, because the Japanese guy was terrified of Ali, so he came out and lay on his ass the whole fight, kicking to keep Ali away from him. At that point, any moron knew it wasn't fixed, because a fixed fight wouldn't have been that awful. It was the nightmare to end all nightmares, and the best thing would have been not to do it at all."

Ali-Inoki was insufferably boring. For fifteen rounds, Inoki crab-walked around the ring, horizontal to the canvas, kicking at Ali's legs. That was the fight. Ali threw six punches. Two of them, both jabs, landed. At the end, the contest was declared a draw, and Ali was suitably embarrassed. "I wouldn't have done this if I'd known he was gonna fight like that," the champion told reporters. "Nobody knew this was gonna happen, so we had a dead show."[7] But the repercussions went beyond boredom. During the course of fifteen rounds, Inoki had kicked Ali in the legs dozens of times. After the bout, the left leg in particular was badly bruised and swelling. Yet proper medical care was not forthcoming.

FERDIE PACHECO: "Fighting Inoki was an incredibly stupid act. To subject a great legendary fighter to a carnival atmosphere like that was wrong. Ali was a showman, but this wasn't much of a show, and it put his entire career in jeopardy for some dollars that he could have made just as easily without risking his reputation and his health. So it was bad, but what happened afterward was worse.

"Because of the kicks, Ali suffered ruptured blood vessels and his left leg filled up with about a quart of blood. The proper treatment for that is to pack the leg in ice and elevate it. I was going home to

Florida from Tokyo, and I told him, 'Either stay here and elevate the leg or go home and elevate the leg. But whatever you do, don't, repeat don't, go to Korea.' That's because Ali was supposed to go from Japan to Korea to box an exhibition; and from there, he was scheduled to go to Manila to dedicate a shopping mall. And I told him, 'For God's sake, cancel the thing. You could get blood clots. They could go to your lungs or heart or brain.' And of course, he went to Korea and Manila anyway, because half the entourage had home remedies to get him in shape. Bundini told him to put heat on his legs. Someone else brought in a Turkish masseuse to massage the leg, like you need to massage a broken blood vessel that's pumping. And the upshot of it was that, by the time Ali got back to the United States, he had to be hospitalized for blood clots and muscle damage."

Three months after his exhibition against Inoki, Ali returned to legitimate boxing. However, this time, after bouts against Jean-Pierre Coopman, Jimmy Young, and Richard Dunn, he was facing a tougher foe. The opponent was Ken Norton, who had broken Ali's jaw in their first confrontation and barely lost in their twelve-round rematch. Ali was installed as an eight-to-five favorite, and guaranteed six million dollars by the bout's copromoters, Top Rank and Madison Square Garden.

Ali got in shape for Norton. He had no illusions about the nature of the fight. Physically and mentally, he was as ready as he could be. Initially, he trained in Arizona. Then, at the request of the promoters, he moved to the Concord Hotel in upstate New York to be more accessible to the media. Finally, several days before the bout, which was to be held at Yankee Stadium, he moved into Harold Conrad's New York City apartment.

"The night before the fight," Conrad remembers, "I woke up and heard Ali's voice coming from his bedroom. This was maybe four o'clock in the morning, so I went to the door and looked in. Ali was sitting on the edge of the bed. I had a VCR hooked up to the television, which was a relatively new thing then, and he was watching a tape of his second fight against Norton. And the whole time he's watching, he's pumping his arm up and down in the air, chanting, 'Norton's gotta go! Norton's gotta go!' "

The bout took place on September 28, 1976; and from beginning to end, it was a mob scene, literally. The New York City Police Department was experiencing a "job action" over work schedules and deferred raises, and a thousand off-duty cops were demonstrating outside the stadium. They blew whistles, stopped traffic, and were joined by their on-duty brethren. That led to a general breakdown of order, as pickpockets and purse-snatchers ran amuck.

Inside the stadium, the scene was no better. "A lot of undesirables crashed the gate," James Anderson remembers. "There was no police and no crowd control; it was total chaos. Going from the dressing room to the ring that night was the longest walk I've ever taken. Everyone wanted to touch Ali and grab him. We tried to find a secure route, but there wasn't none. A couple of times, I was afraid we'd be crushed just by the pressure of the crowd. And you know, with a fighter, all you gotta do is step on his foot too hard, and all of a sudden the fight is off."

As for the bout, the early rounds belonged to Norton. He was doing what he wanted to do, and Ali was a shadow of his former self. After eight rounds, referee Arthur Mercante and the two judges had the challenger well ahead. Then, slowly, the tide turned. Drawing on every resource at his command, Ali won rounds nine through eleven, lost the twelfth, and won the next two. Going into the final round, both judges had the fight scored even, and Mercante favored Ali by a single point. As in the first two Ali-Norton bouts, the last round would decide the victor.

ARTHUR MERCANTE: "I'd refereed two previous Ali fights, including his first bout against Frazier at Madison Square Garden. And by the time he fought Norton at Yankee Stadium, he wasn't the same fighter anymore. His timing was off; he tired more easily. But he was still the best boxer I've ever seen at coming up instinctively with what was necessary to win. Sometimes, the things he did were annoying. Those ring gyrations, taunting opponents, playing to the crowd, always bothered me. And of course, he was a master at clinching. Technically, clinching is illegal; and as the referee, it was my job to stop it. But for a fighter who's tired or hurt and needs a rest, clinching makes sense; and Ali was the best fighter I ever saw in terms of clinching. Not only did he use it to rest, but he was big and strong and knew how to lean on opponents and push and shove and pull to tire them out. He knew all the tricks, and he used every one of them against Norton that night. He was so smart; you could see his mind working. Most guys are just in there fighting, but Ali had a sense of everything that was happening, almost as though he was sitting at ringside analyzing the fight while he fought it.

"Against Norton, it came down to the last round. And before the round, I went to both corners like I always do. Angelo Dundee was telling Ali, 'You've got three more minutes. Fight like hell; we need this round.' And then, in Norton's corner, I heard his manager, Bob Biron, tell him, 'Be careful; stay away from him. Don't take chances, because you have the fight won.' And I said to myself, 'Gee, that's not such good advice, to tell Norton to coast. This fight is close.' But Norton did coast. He gave away the first two-and-a-half minutes of the last round to Ali. And even though he came on strong in the last thirty seconds, it wasn't enough. Ali won the round."

KEN NORTON: "As far as my third fight with Ali is concerned, I look back and wish I could fight that last round over again. I wasn't tired; I was in good shape. I could have fought the whole three minutes all-out and won it easily, but my corner said I had the fight won and don't take any chances. That's why I was so cautious. And if you saw the look on Ali's face at the end, he knew I beat him. He didn't hit me hard the whole fight. People said he had trouble with me because I was awkward, but what they're really saying is, I was a good defensive fighter. I hate that word 'awkward.' Awkward, to me, means someone is clumsy and can't do things right. I was the one who made Ali look awkward because of my defensive skills, and I won that fight. Then they announced the judges' decision; and I was bitter, very bitter. Not toward Ali; I can't say I was bitter toward him, because he wasn't a judge. He'd done his job; he was just there to fight. But I was hurt; I was mad; I was angry; I was upset. And it still upsets me. I've never watched a tape of that fight. I've never scored it for myself. I already judged it when I was in the ring, so why bother to judge it again? There's nothing I can do to make it better for me now, except live with it and try to put things in perspective.

"You know, the first time I fought Ali, I felt it was an honor just to be in the same ring with him. That was when I broke his jaw. The second fight was closer than the first, and I thought I won but the judges gave it to him. And the third fight; well, I'm getting mad again, talking about it. But Muhammad brought out the best in me. He was the best fighter I ever fought, and I respect him. Very few men would give up the things he gave up for their beliefs, and I admire that. Hell, I even liked Ali. I liked him before we fought; I liked him after we fought; just not during.

"And I'll tell you something. When it counted most, Ali was there for me. In 1986, I was in a bad car accident; real bad. I was unconscious for I don't know how long. My right side was paralyzed; my skull was fractured; I had a broken leg, a broken jaw. The doctors said I might never walk again. For a while, they thought I might not ever even be able to talk. I don't remember much about my first few months in the hospital, but one thing I do remember is, after I was hurt, Ali was one of the first people to visit me. At that point, I wasn't sure whether I wanted to live or die; that's how bad I was hurt. And like I said, there's a lot I don't remember. But I remember looking up and there was this crazy man standing by my bed. It was Ali, and he was doing magic tricks for me. He made a handkerchief disappear; he levitated. And I said to myself, if he does one more awful trick, I'm gonna get well just so I can kill him. But Ali was there, and his being there helped me. So I don't want to be remembered as the man who broke Muhammad Ali's jaw. I just want to be remembered as a man who fought three close competitive fights with Ali, and became his friend when the fighting was over."

After his third bout against Norton, even the most ardent of Ali's fans had to acknowledge that his skills were in decline. "There is no question now," wrote Mark Kram, "that Ali is through as a fighter. The hard work, the life and death of Manila, the endless parade of women provided by the fools close to him, have cut him down. Unlike the Jimmy Young defense when he obviously was out of shape, there is no excuse for Ali's showing against Norton. He threw only one good combination all night. His jab, which once drained and depressed aggression, was only a flick. Only a sure hand on his craft saved him."[8]

Seven-and-a-half months would pass before Ali stepped into the ring again. And when he did, it was against another nonentity—Alfredo Evangelista of Spain. Evangelista had been fighting professionally for only nineteen months. He'd never fought beyond eight rounds in his life. "It was one of the worst fights ever fought," Howard Cosell, who broadcast the bout for ABC television, would say later. "The only interesting thing about it was how the WBC phonied its ratings to get Evangelista in the top ten in order to receive a sanctioning fee for the fight. Evangelista couldn't fight a lick, and by then Ali wasn't fighting much either. The fact that the bout went fifteen rounds told you that Ali was shot."

Ali-Evangelista was deadly boring. The crowd put up with it because they weren't necessarily boxing fans. They were Ali fans, and as long as Ali won, they were happy. But as was happening with increasing frequency, Ali's attention wasn't on boxing. His marriage to Belinda was about to end. He and Veronica had a nine-month-old child and were planning to get married. An Ali "autobiography" was on sale at bookstores, and a movie version of his life was about to be released.

It was the marital problems that weighed most heavily on Ali's mind. Although it wasn't publicly known, Cassius Marcellus Clay, Sr., and Odessa Clay had separated years earlier. "Mr. Clay fooled around sometimes," Howard Bingham recalls. "The marriage to Mrs. Clay was kind of stormy. They stopped living together in the early seventies. Partly, that's because Cash was drinking, but mostly it was because of the women. Mrs. Clay got tired of it, and the kids were grown. So Ali bought his mom a house, and she moved out; although afterward, for the public, she and Cash sometimes acted like they were still living together."

Now Ali was following in his father's footsteps. On September 2, 1976—four weeks before Ali fought Ken Norton—Belinda Ali had filed for divorce, charging desertion, adultery, and mental cruelty. Seventeen weeks later, after a negotiated property settlement, a judgment of divorce was granted. Belinda received $670,000 payable over five years, a home in suburban Chicago, and miscellaneous personal property. In addition, Ali placed one million dollars in a trust fund to benefit their four children.

BELINDA ALI: "I tried; God knows, I tried. I loved Ali. When he was in the ring, I felt the blows with him. When something happened to him, I felt it too. The whole time we were married, I tried to accept what he was about and what he liked. He'd buy these big mansions, and I'd fix them up as best I could. Visitors would come in all the time, and I entertained every one of them because that was what he wanted me to do. And I'm not talking about company just on weekends. I'm talking about people in the morning, people in the afternoon, people in the evening, meals, staying overnight, seven days a week. I was the hostess; I was the mother. I cooked, I cleaned, I did all those things; and I was happy doing it because it made him happy.

"And then everything got destroyed. For a while after we broke up, I was angry. But that's all past now. Anybody can look back and say things should have been done different; but once they're done, you can't change them. It hurts me to see Ali the way he is today. I knew him when he talked so fast and clear, and I miss that part of him. It scares me; I hate it, the way he is now. I don't see him often, but he calls me from time to time, and I think he's a better person now than he once was. I believe that souls can be mended. I believe that people can change if they want to. And I think probably Ali is more at peace with himself now than before."

On June 19, 1977, Ali and Veronica Porche were married in a civil ceremony in Los Angeles. Two hundred fifty guests were present. Howard Bingham was the best man. After the wedding, Ali and Veronica honeymooned in Hawaii. "It wasn't your average honeymoon," Lana Shabazz remembers. "A couple of days before they left, Veronica came to me and said, 'You know, Ali and I are getting married, and he gets bored quickly. I want to take someone on our honeymoon with us, and I'm not sure who that should be.' So I told her to bring Howard Bingham. Howard was Ali's best friend, and wouldn't bother either of them. And that's what they did. They took Howard on their honeymoon, and it probably worked out better that way."

"The honeymoon didn't last long," Bingham adds in passing. "It was just a formality; no big thing. Ali and Veronica were already living together, and Hana was ten months old, so the thrill was gone. We got to Hawaii on a Monday evening, and they were back home Wednesday afternoon. Ali was bored most of the time. He was never one for hanging out on the beach; not with Veronica or anyone else. All he did in Hawaii was sign autographs, which was the same thing he did all the time."

Meanwhile, as Ali's marital status was changing, a variety of commercial ventures were underway. In 1976, Random House had published the Ali "autobiography," written by Richard Durham. Given Ali's popularity, the book had enormous potential but it was plagued by problems from the start. Ali was uninterested in the project, and spent relatively little time with Durham. Indeed, he never read his "autobiography" until after it was published. Moreover, even though Durham was an editor for *Muhammad Speaks*, before any material was submitted to Random House, each page had to be approved and initialed by Herbert Muhammad. "I'm not sure the book is the true story of Ali's life," former Random House editor-in-chief James Silberman, who helped edit the book, later acknowledged. "Where corroborative sources were available for events such as fights, it was accurate; but there were stretches where there was no source other than Herbert or Ali himself. I imagine, though, if you check Winston Churchill's version of history, you'd find it somewhat at odds with other versions by historians. And certainly, that would be true of books by many other public figures."

The Ali autobiography was followed by a movie distributed by Columbia Pictures in May 1977. Entitled *The Greatest*, it starred Ali, with cameo appearances by Robert Duvall, James Earl Jones, Paul Winfield, and various members of the Ali entourage. Like the book, the film—which purported to be accurate—was fictionalized. Its saving grace, apart from Ali's performance, was the song "The Greatest Love of All." Written for the soundtrack, recorded by George Benson (and later by Whitney Houston), it enchanted with the words:

> If I fail, if I succeed
> At least I live as I believe
> No matter what they take from me
> They can't take away my dignity.

But beyond that, *The Greatest* was mediocre. "Of all our sports heroes," Frank Deford wrote, "Ali needs least to be sanitized. But *The Greatest* is just a big vapid valentine; it took a dive. A genuine film about this unique man and his times must wait until Ali can no longer indulge himself as star and censor alike."[9]

As 1977 progressed, Ali-related commercial ventures continued to proliferate. His name and image were licensed by DC Comics for a special edition entitled "Superman vs. Muhammad Ali: The Fight to Save Earth from Star-Warriors." A pesticide manufacturer enlisted Ali's aid as national spokesman for a household roach-killer. For the first time, there was serious speculation in the press regarding whether Ali should, and would, retire, from boxing. But on September 29 he was in the ring again, at Madison Square Garden against Earnie Shavers.

Shavers was a particularly dangerous foe. Not that he was invincible; he wasn't. In sixty fights, he'd lost five times with one draw. But with George Foreman's retirement earlier in the year, Shavers was regarded as the hardest puncher in boxing. Fifty-two of his fifty-four wins had come by knockout, twenty in the first round. "Earnie Shavers takes no prisoners" was the tag-line attached to his career. And because Ali was at a point in his own career where he was getting hit, the bout was viewed with mixed emotions by the Ali entourage and by Ali himself.

JERRY IZENBERG: "I remember sitting with Ali in the old Hotel Statler across the street from Madison Square Garden. It was a day or two before he fought Shavers. We were alone, and Ali said to me, 'Do you know how many years I've been fighting? Do you know how tired I am? Do you have any idea how hard that man is going to beat on my head tomorrow night?' And I asked him, 'Why do you do it?' He didn't really give me an answer, although it was clear that money and glory and other people's expectations were all part of it. And then I said, 'Let me tell you something. Do yourself a favor. Sit down and play back that roach-spray commercial you just made, because I listened to it ten times before I was able to make out the word "fog." I couldn't understand what you were saying. And then take any of the tapes you made over the years, and listen to your voice the way it used to be.' And I told him, 'You know, there was once in this world a pathologist named Martland. And Martland might not have had all the answers, but it was his theory that, if you stop fighting tomorrow and never get in the ring again, it will still take two more years for the disintegration of your brain to stop. That's something you should think about after you fight Earnie Shavers tomorrow night. Because it would be a horrible tragedy if you were to wind up punch-drunk, which is what Martland's Syndrome is all about.' "

Like Ali's previous fights, Ali-Shavers was a testament to the champion's drawing power. Although the bout was broadcast live on home television, Madison Square Garden was sold out. NBC attracted 70 million viewers, and while the bout was in progress, enjoyed a 54.4 rating and 77.0 share. That meant more than half of all the television sets owned in the United States and more than three-quarters of those actually in use were tuned to the fight.

HARRY MARKSON: "An hour or two before the fight, Ali showed up at the employees entrance with fifty or sixty hangers-on he'd collected on his way to the Garden. One of the guards stationed at the door sent word to me that I'd better come down because there was a problem. So I ran down, and there was Ali, insisting that all these people be allowed in for free. He said, 'Harry, these are my friends, and they can't buy tickets. There are no tickets, so you gotta let them in.' I said, 'There's no place for them. The Fire Department won't allow it. There's nothing left; we're even sold out of standing room.' Then Ali told me, 'If they can't come in, I ain't fighting.' And he turned around and started to walk away. Angelo went running after him and brought him back, and finally we compromised. I figured with twenty thousand people in the building, twenty more walking around wouldn't make much difference, so we let twenty in, and after that, we said no more. Probably, Ali wouldn't have walked if I'd refused altogether, but with Ali, who knows?"

It was an exciting fight. Not "good" in the traditional sense, because for much of it Ali was as much a performer as a fighter—posturing, mugging for the crowd. But there were moments of high drama. In round two, Shavers landed a devastating overhand right. Ali was hurt. "Next to Joe Frazier," he said later, "that was the hardest I ever got hit." But Shavers had a history of tiring late in his bouts, and was pacing himself to go fifteen rounds. So instead of firing a barrage of punches, he continued to move methodically forward, and Ali was able to survive the round.

Still, the champion wasn't out of the woods yet. For the entire night, he fought on the edge, getting by on guile and courage to complement his fading skills. Due to an NBC promotional twist, Angelo Dundee was able to follow the judges' scoring, which was announced on television after each round. While the Shavers camp failed to take advantage of the situation, Dundee arranged for a Baltimore matchmaker named Eddie Hrica to watch the broadcast on a portable television in the arena and relay the scoring via hand signals as it was announced. After twelve rounds, Ali was leading eight to four on the cards of two judges and eight-three-one on the third. But three rounds remained, and Shavers was coming on strong.

"The thirteenth round was Shavers's best round to that point," Pat Putnam wrote later. "The fourteenth was even better. Rocked by hard right hands, Ali survived, but the legs that had carried him through fifty-six professional fights were beginning to fail. At the end of the fourteenth round, the champion had to dip into his reserve of strength just to get back to his corner. Wearily he slumped on his stool, he eyes glazed by fatigue. When the bell for the fifteenth round rang, Ali could barely stand."[10]

PAT PUTNAM: "That fight with Shavers, and particularly the last round, sums up for me what Ali was about, even though he was long past his prime. Shavers could have taken him out. He had him hurt early. Ali was ready to be taken, because if Shavers hit you, you were gone. But he suckered Earnie. He faked being more hurt than he was, and conned him out of going for the kill. He fought through that; he fought through fourteen rounds. And people talk about Manila; they talk about Foreman; they talk about Liston. But to me, the fifteenth round against Shavers was as magnificent as any round Ali ever fought. He was exhausted. I don't know where he found the strength and stamina to go on, because when he went back to his corner after fourteen, there was nothing left in his body. But he came out for the last round and fought three minutes as good as any three minutes I've ever seen. Not many people remember it now, but late in the round, he even had Shavers in trouble. Only the ropes kept Shavers from going down."

EARNIE SHAVERS: "Fighting Ali was hard for me to do because he was such a good man. He was my idol. Before we fought, he'd helped me out several times: letting me use his training camp for free, giving me advice on what to do against other fighters. I loved him personally, and you hate to see a legend defeated. But at the same time, I was fighting for my family and myself.

"It was a good fight. In the second round, I hit him with a right hand that hurt him. He wobbled, and then he wobbled some more. But Ali was so good at conning, I thought he was playing possum with me. I didn't realize how bad off he was. Later, when I watched the tape, I saw it, but at the time I was fooled. He could do that; that's why he was Ali. And he beat me. When the fight was over, I thought I'd won. But looking at the tape over and over, it was close but I can see how the judges voted for him.

"That fight had a big impact on my life. After I lost, I was down on myself for letting the title get away. I wanted to be champion of the world, and I came close twice—against Ali and later against Larry Holmes. Winning those fights would have meant financial security for me, and beating Ali would have been extra special, because when you fought Ali the whole world was watching. But God had different plans for me, and everything worked out just fine.

"Six years ago, I met a lady from Warren, Ohio, named Miss Paula Johnson. By that time, I owned a meat company, and she was one of my customers. I'd always see her with a beautiful smile on her face; she was cheerful all the time. Finally, I asked her what made her so happy, and she told me she had Jesus in her heart. It took a while for me to understand. She didn't push it on me, but finally I learned. That's when I opened my heart to Jesus, and that changed my life around. If I'd beaten Ali, I probably never would have known the Lord. All that money and glory would have led me down a different path, but now I'm in good hands. In a way, I guess it's like when Ali turned to religion. He got to the pinnacle of his profession, saw all that glory and material things, and still he didn't have peace of mind. He and I are of different religions. I'm a born-again Christian. But both of us believe in God, and we both have peace in our hearts. I preach all over the world these days. People know me on every continent because I fought Muhammad Ali. They open their hearts to me because of him. And that's why I say, most of what I am today I owe to God, but I also owe a lot to Ali. I'll never forget his kindness to me. The man has such a big heart. He just wants to help everybody. And seeing how he is today, his health, it kind of hurts me. But wherever I go, wherever I speak, I ask people to pray for Ali."

The Shavers fight reaffirmed Ali's heart and courage, but also his advancing age. He was in a sport where men grow old before their time, and at thirty-five, he could only impersonate the fighter he used to be. It was an odd transition that Ali had made. Once, he'd gloried in the fact that opponents couldn't lay a glove on him. Now he was taking pride in the fact that they could hit him again and again and not visibly hurt him. He'd gone from a proponent of the proposition that the hand can't hit what the eye can't see, to a fighter who lay on the ropes taking punches, refusing to go down. He seemed capable of absorbing unlimited punishment and after each bout being reborn. But the gift was a mirage, as those in the know could see.

The day after Ali defended his title against Earnie Shavers, he attended a press conference at Madison Square Garden. "Before Ali entered the room," Teddy Brenner remembers, "I took him aside and said, 'Champ, why don't you announce your retirement?' He asked, 'What for?' And I told him, 'Because sooner or later, some kid that couldn't carry your bucket is going to beat you. You're going to be beaten by guys that have no business being in the ring with you. It's just a matter of time. If you take a big piece of iron and put it down on the center of the floor and let a drop of water hit it every ten seconds, eventually you'll get a hole in the center of that piece of iron, and that's what's happening to you. You're getting hit; you're gonna get hurt. You've proven everything that a great champion can possibly prove. You don't need this. Get out!' "

And then Brenner did something that doesn't happen often in professional boxing: He put his money where his principles were. He went out and told the assembled media, "As long as I'm here, Madison Square Garden will never make Ali an offer to fight again. This is a young man's game. Ali is thirty-five; he has half his life ahead of him. Why take chances? There's nothing more for him to prove. I don't want him to come over to me some day and say,

'What's your name?' The trick in boxing is to get out at the right time, and the fifteenth round last night was the right time for Ali."[11]

Brenner's declaration was a clear-sounding alarm, and a week later that warning was bolstered by another event—the departure of Ali's longtime physician, Ferdie Pacheco. In part, Pacheco's leaving may have been occasioned by public comments he'd made regarding Ali's penchant for women, comments that had angered various members of the champion's entourage. But Pacheco's concern over Ali's deteriorating physical condition was also a factor.

FERDIE PACHECO: "Athletes get old early. John McEnroe today is like an over-the-hill fighter. Once, he was the greatest tennis player in the world. Now he loses in the second round at Wimbledon. But there's a major difference between boxing and tennis, because when McEnroe takes a beating, it's not in the form of concussive blows to the brain.

"It all progresses in a fighter's life. The legs go; his reflexes aren't what they used to be; he cuts more easily; the injuries accelerate. And the older you get, the less your recuperative powers are. Ali at age twenty-three could have absorbed Frazier in Manila and shaken it off, but age thirty-three was another story. If I had to pick a spot to tell him, 'You've got all your marbles, but don't go on anymore,' no question, it would have been after Frazier. That's when it really started to fall apart. He began to take beatings, not just in fights but in the gym. Even sparring, he'd do the rope-a-dope because he couldn't avoid punches the way he did when he was young. And I don't care how good you are at rope-a-doping. If you block ninety-five punches out of a hundred, the other five are getting in.

"The Shavers fight was the final straw for me. After that fight, Dr. Nardiello, who was with the New York State Athletic Commission, gave me a laboratory report that showed Ali's kidneys were falling apart. Instead of filtering out blood and turning it to urine, pure blood was going through. That was bad news for the kidneys; and since everything in the body is interconnected, we were talking about the disintegration of Ali's health. So I went back to my office in Miami, sat down, and wrote Ali a letter saying his kidneys were falling apart. I attached a copy of Nardiello's report, and mailed three extra copies, return receipt requested: one to Herbert, one to Angelo, and one to Veronica, who at the time was Ali's wife. And I didn't get an answer from any of them; not one response. That's when I decided, enough was enough. Whether or not they wanted me, I didn't want to be part of what was going on anymore. By then, they were talking about 'only easy fights,' but there was no such thing as an easy fight anymore."

Then an "easy" fight surfaced—Ali against Leon Spinks. The self-proclaimed "greatest fighter of all time" against a novice with seven professional bouts to his credit.

BUTCH LEWIS: "After Ali fought Earnie Shavers, he started talking like maybe he'd retire. My job at the time was, Bob Arum had made me executive vice-president of Top Rank, and Leon Spinks was one of my fighters. Technically, Leon was signed to Top Rank, but in reality he was my man. He did all of his business through me. So I went to Ali and told him, 'If you retire, fine; but if you fight again, I'd like you to give Leon a shot.' Ali thought I was nuts. Leon had fought only five professional fights, and Ali told me, 'I can't fight this kid; it would make me the laughingstock of the world.' He wouldn't even consider the idea, so Leon fought Scott LeDoux instead. LeDoux was a middle-of-the-road heavyweight. The bout was on TV, because Leon was an Olympic gold-medal winner, and the two of them fought a draw. Then, as soon as the fight was over, I got a call from Ali, and he's saying, 'Butch, I want him. I want your boy bad.' What happened was, Ali had figured out an angle. He was shouting, 'I beat Floyd Patterson, who won a gold medal. I beat Joe Frazier, who won a gold medal. I beat George Foreman, who won a gold medal. I'm gonna beat 'em all before I retire, to prove I'm the greatest of all time.' And it wasn't hard to figure out what had happened. Ali and Herbert were looking for a soft touch. They'd just seen Leon fight life-and-death with Scott LeDoux, and you can't get much softer than that.

"Anyway, I brought the fight to Arum. We didn't think Leon would win, but it was worth doing because he was the only fighter we controlled that Herbert and Ali would accept. First, we had to go through some politics, because Leon wasn't ranked in the top ten, which you have to be to fight for the title. But we worked it out with Jose Sulaiman [president of the World Boxing Council] that we'd fight an Italian named Alfio Righetti, and the winner of that fight would be the next opponent for Ali. Righetti was a typical European heavyweight, which meant he wasn't very good. Leon beat him; they both looked awful. But I figured Leon, if he trained right, would be respectable against Ali, because Ali was slipping; he was slipping a lot."

Ali-Spinks was a hard sell. Virtually no one took the fight seriously. CBS finally bought television rights, but only after ABC and NBC declined to bid. Then, to compound Top Rank's problems, Ali decided to stop talking to the press. "The gold-medal hype didn't catch on," Lewis remembers. "That hurt Ali's feelings, and the way he dealt with it was by keeping quiet. Arum sent me to see if I could juice him up. But when I got there, Ali told me, 'Spinks only has seven fights. What am I gonna tell people; that I'm gonna destroy him? Talking that way makes me look stupid, so I just ain't gonna talk.' "

But if Ali wasn't talking, he wasn't training much either. He was eating more, working less, and sloughing off in the gym. Reporters who went to watch him train saw him threaten to run, threaten to work out, and threaten to hit a sparring partner. All totaled, he sparred less than two dozen rounds in preparation for Spinks, after starting to train at 242 pounds.

BUTCH LEWIS: "One of Ali's problems was, there were too many ass-kissers in his camp. I remember, after he fought Jimmy Young, we were back at the hotel. Ali was sitting on the sofa in his suite. All these guys were stepping over each other trying to get close to him. Ali asked, 'How did I look?' And they're saying, 'Oh, champ, you were wonderful, you were great.' I didn't say nothing until he looked at me, and then I told him, 'You looked like shit.' And that wasn't anything he didn't know already. The ass-kissers in the room started to get on me, and Ali said, 'All you people in here are lying. I know I looked bad. Why are you telling me I looked good?'

"Well, it was the same thing when Ali was training for Leon. Nobody could tell him what to do, and nobody had the guts to say he looked like shit. He just didn't take Leon seriously. And the one thing I promised myself was, whatever else happened, Leon was going into the ring against Ali in shape. I had him all set up in the Catskills, the first time he'd been in a training camp in his life. My own mother was there to cook. I slept on a cot outside the door to Leon's room, so he couldn't sneak off to a bar or disco. I mean, I covered all the bases. Leon was gonna be in shape if it killed me. So what happened was, one morning, Sam Solomon, Leon's trainer, woke me up and asked, 'Where's Leon?' I said, 'He's in his room,' and Sam said, 'No, he ain't.' And the motherfucker—I mean, I thought I was gonna kill Leon—he'd gone out the window. You know how some houses have a roof that goes over the porch? Well,

Leon went out the window, walked across the roof, jumped down, and ran off. Finally, we found him in a poolroom in Monticello, and he told me, 'Butch, I was all cooped up. I just had to have some freedom.'

"But we were making progress. Leon was in shape, looking good, and I was starting to think maybe he could beat Ali. Then, with about ten days left, he was sparring with Roy Williams. We wanted Roy to hold Leon and wrestle with him the way Ali would. So Roy pulled Leon behind the head with his right hand, hit him with a left hook to the ribs, and boom, Leon went down. We stopped the sparring, put some ice on Leon's ribs. The next day against Roy, he threw a right hand and collapsed in pain. We take him to a doctor; the doctor looks at Leon, and says there's nothing wrong with him. But back in the gym, he throws the right hand—same thing. 'Ow! Ow! It hurts; I can't stand it!' And I'm saying to myself, 'Wait a minute. Maybe Leon is starting to have second thoughts about this fight.' So that night, I sat him down and asked, 'Listen, do you want to fight, or are you trying to find a way out?' And Leon said, 'Man, I've never been in this kind of shape. I want this fight; I can win it.' So I took him to another doctor, a specialist. This doctor asked, 'When does it bother you?' Leon told him, and the doctor said, 'I want you to throw your right hand and hold it the way it is when it hurts.' Then he took X-rays and saw there was a muscle tear around the rib cage, and when Leon raised his hand a certain way, it opened up.

"So now the fight was really gonna look like a farce. Leon couldn't even throw his right hand, but nobody was gonna believe he was injured after Ali knocked him out. They were just gonna say that Leon was a bum. And if we postponed the fight, probably it wouldn't ever come off. The public wasn't exactly begging for Ali-Spinks, and ticket sales were taking a beating. And then we came up with a solution to the problem. At that time, there was no urine test in Nevada, which was where the fight was gonna be. So what we did was get a painkiller, shoot it into Leon's ribs, go to the gym, and have him work out. 'Leon, throw the right hand. Come on; throw the right.' And he didn't feel pain. So in the hotel, right before the fight, we had a doctor shoot Leon up. And after that, we just had to hope that Leon made it through the night."

Other than the fact that Ali was a participant, it wasn't a particularly interesting fight. But the stakes and personalities involved invested the bout with an aura of high drama. Ali gave away the

In the ring with the Lion of Flanders, Jean-Pierre Coopman, 1976.
(*Howard Bingham*)

With Cassius Clay, Sr. and President Jimmy Carter in the White House, 1980.
(*Howard Bingham*)

ABOVE–The third fight against Ken Norton, at Yankee Stadium, 1976.
(*Howard Bingham*)

BELOW–Herbert Muhammad and Ferdie Pacheco before the Norton fight, 1976.
(*Howard Bingham*)

ABOVE–Playing around at a school assembly, 1974. *(Howard Bingham)*

BELOW–Harold Smith with Larry Holmes, 1990. *(Howard Bingham)*

On these two pages, Ali poses with his children: here, from left, Maryum, Rasheeda, Jamillah, and Muhammad Junior, 1980. *(Howard Bingham)*

With Veronica, Hana, and
Laila, 1983. *(Howard Bingham)*

With Khaliah, 1989.
(Howard Bingham)

With Miya, 1989.
(Howard Bingham)

Clowning with Maryum, 1990.
(*Howard Bingham*)

Howard Bingham, 1990. *(Denise Turner)*

With Joe Frazier and George Foreman, 1990. *(Howard Bingham)*

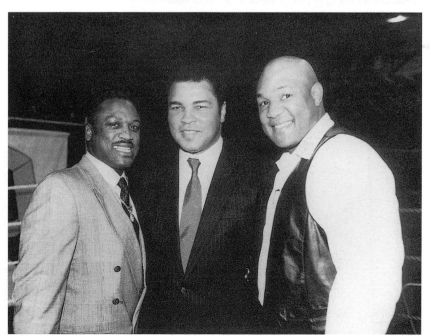

With Lonnie, 1989. *(Both photos Howard Bingham)*

early rounds, laying on the ropes, waiting for Spinks to punch himself out. But it never happened. Instead, the challenger punched nonstop the entire night, battering the champion's arms and body. He was crude and unpolished but also young and strong, facing a once-great warrior who simply didn't have it anymore.

As the fight wore on, Ali's corner told him he was losing. "I'll get him; I'll get him," the champion promised. But the late-rounds rally never came. Instead, it was Spinks who continued to score. In round eleven, the painkiller began to wear off, but Leon was psyched and fought through the pain. In the last round, Ali make one final charge, gathering his resources and backing Spinks up against the ropes. But it was too little too late. The fight was over. Judge Art Lurie scored the bout for Ali by a point. The other judges—Lou Tabat and Harold Buck—properly gave the decision to Spinks. For the first and only time in his life, Ali had lost his title in the ring. He'd been dethroned and beaten up.

MUHAMMAD ALI: "Of all the fights I lost in boxing, losing to Spinks hurt the most. That's because it was my own fault. Leon fought clean; he did the best he could. But it was embarrassing that someone with so little fighting skills could beat me. I didn't train right. I gave away the first six rounds figuring he'd tire out, and then it turned out it was me that got tired. The last three rounds, I knew I was losing, or if I was lucky, the fight was even. But when I tried to come on, I wasn't in shape. Everything I did before the fight was wrong, and my plan for fighting him didn't work. So after that, I had to fight him again. I wanted to get my title back. What they paid me didn't matter. I just couldn't leave boxing that way, losing an embarrassing fight like that."

After the bout, Ali's entourage was disconsolate. Some claimed he had been "robbed"; others said he'd simply been out of shape. But it was Ali who hurt the most. At the postfight press conference, he was gracious in defeat. "I messed up; I was lousy," the now-former champion said. "But I don't want to take anything away from Spinks. He fought a good fight and never quit. He made fools of everybody, even me. We all lose in life," Ali continued. "You lose your wife; you lose your mother. We all have losses, and what you have to do is keep living, overcome those losses, and come back. You can't just go and die because you lose. I did my best."[12]

But out of sight, a more tormented scene was unfolding. Harold

Smith—a California promoter who later used Ali's name to build an empire that collapsed in scandal—was with the former champion after he lost to Spinks.

HAROLD SMITH: "The day after the fight, we flew back to Chicago. Ali went to bed early. I was staying over as a guest; and sometime around two in the morning, I heard him downstairs. I got up to see what was happening. And you know, no fighter runs right after a fight, and no one runs at two in the morning. But there was Ali, getting ready to go out the door, talking to himself. 'Gotta get my title back. Gotta get my title back.' So I put on some clothes and went with him. He was running; I was driving his car behind him. I saw it; I heard it. He was in pain. Two o'clock in the morning, running down the damn freeway; punching, shouting, 'Gotta get my title back. Gotta get my title back.' Then he pulled off the main road, stopped under a streetlight, and started shadow-boxing. 'Gotta get my title back! Gotta get my title back!' I was scared; I thought he was going off the deep end. I kept saying, 'Don't worry, champ. You'll get it back. Come on, champ. You'll get it back.' His hands were blazing, real fast. It was February, but sweat was streaming down his face. And he kept at it for almost an hour. He kept going until he was exhausted."

Given Ali's popularity, a rematch with Spinks was all but inevitable. The World Boxing Council threatened to strip Spinks of his title if he defended it against anyone except Ken Norton. But Ali-Spinks was what the public wanted, and that's where the big money was.

BUTCH LEWIS: "The first thing out of Arum's mouth in Vegas; the moment we knew Leon won, Arum turned to me with a big shit-eating grin on his face and said, 'I finally got Herbert Muhammad where I want him.' It was payback time. Because anytime before, if you did business with Ali, Herbert had you by the balls. And now Arum was in a position where he could make Herbert squirm. But we owed Ali a chance to win back the title. And let's be honest; Ali was the only big-money fight out there for Leon. So we had a meeting in New York—Ali, Bingham, myself, a couple of other people. I was feeling sort of important, because even though Leon was under contract to Top Rank, I was the one who really had him. And at that meeting, Ali said to me, 'I know you guys got the title. You can make me wait a year, two years, to get a chance to win it back. I never asked you for a favor before, but I'm asking for one now. Give me a shot before I'm too old to win.'

"Now you have to understand, at this time Don King was working hard against Ali. He had Norton, Larry Holmes, and a bunch of other heavyweights wrapped up, but he was shut out as far as Ali and Leon were concerned. So King went to Jose Sulaiman, and the WBC threatened to strip Leon of his title if there was a rematch. But we figured, fuck the WBC. Even if we lost the WBC sanction, the WBA was still with us. And as long as we had Ali and Leon, we had what the public would pay to see."

On March 29, 1978, the World Boxing Council stripped Leon Spinks of his title and proclaimed Ken Norton "heavyweight champion of the world." Norton was awarded the title retroactively on the basis of a fifteen-round decision over Jimmy Young the previous November in a bout promoted by Don King. Also, more than coincidentally, Norton's first title defense was to be against Larry Holmes in a bout promoted by Don King in June. Meanwhile, Ali and Spinks agreed to a September rematch. Then in June, after contracts were signed, the former champion embarked on a twelve-day goodwill tour of Moscow and Soviet Central Asia.

Ali was well-known in the Soviet Union. Years earlier, *Pravda* had reported at length on what it termed "the campaign of persecution against Muhammad Ali by racists who wanted to curtail forever the career of The Black Hope."[13] Thereafter, the world's most recognizable face had been a familiar presence on Soviet television, and his arrival was eagerly awaited in Moscow.

"It feels just like landing in America or any other country," Ali announced as he stepped off the plane at Sheremetyevo Airport. "Oxygen is oxygen; trees are trees; grass is grass; and humans are humans."[14] Forty-eight hours later, it seemed as though Ali was as popular in Moscow as he was in New York. "In slightly less than two days," *The Washington Post* reported, "he has captured the state-run media and captivated Muscovites in random man-in-the-street encounters. He took his quest for meeting the people to Red Square at six A.M. today, jogging up in workout togs to a line of people queuing for Lenin's Tomb, shook some hands and gave some autographs. Soon, an eager throng gathered and he clowned and chatted, then jogged off. Last night, he was mobbed at the circus, a crush so heavy the performance was delayed as hundreds tried for his signature."[15]

From Moscow, Ali flew to Samarkand and Tashkent. Then he

returned to the Soviet capital for a meeting with Communist party leader Leonid Brezhnev and a night of exhibitions against Soviet amateur boxers. The thirty-five-minute meeting with Brezhnev went well. The three two-round exhibitions didn't. Ali was overweight, out of shape, his reflexes were poor, and he tired quickly. Although there was no formal scoring, he was clearly outclassed in the first contest and fought only on even terms in the third. "I wasn't at my best," he acknowledged afterward. "I wish I was twenty-eight. Let me come back here, and let each guy be thirty-six."[16] But the danger signs were clear. In three months, Ali would be in the ring again with Leon Spinks. And there was no reason to believe he would be any more successful in their second encounter than he had been in their first.

Still, as always, Ali's confidence was there. "Leon Spinks borrowed my title; that's all," the former champion told reporters. "This is perfect for me. I've learned you got to lose to be great. Think of what it will mean to be the first man in history to win the heavyweight championship three times. That's something I'll have for the rest of my life. Every morning when I wake up as long as I live, whether the sun is shining or it's raining or snowing, I'll be three-time heavyweight champion of the world. That's worth taking some pain and hurt."[17]

And hurt is what Ali did. Preparing for his rematch with Spinks, he pushed himself harder in training than ever before in his life. Every morning before breakfast, he ran three to five miles. Then Luis Sarria would lead him through a series of tortuous ring exercises. He sparred more than he had in years, a total in excess of two hundred rounds. "All my life, I knew the day would come when I'd have to kill myself," Ali confided in Pat Putnam before the fight. "I always dreaded it, and now it's here. I've never suffered like I'm forcing myself to suffer now. I've worked this hard for fights before, but never for this long. All the time, I'm in pain; I hurt all over. I hate it, but I know this is my last fight, and it's the last time I'll ever have to do it. I don't want to lose and spend the rest of my life looking back and saying, 'Damn, I should have trained harder.' "[18]

Meanwhile, Spinks was living in the spotlight as heavyweight champion, on the verge of being overwhelmed by it all. "Sometimes I gotta swoop," he told one reporter. "Everybody's making plans for me all the time, but what they don't understand is I ain't gonna let nobody plan my life for me. So I just swoop; I say, gotta go. I want everybody to love me, but I gotta be me. I'm a ghetto nigger; people shouldn't forget that about me. People may be disappointed because I'm not Ali. People want the heavyweight champion to fit a certain image, and they're afraid I'm nothing but a dumb nigger. But I'm just Leon."[19]

BUTCH LEWIS: "Leon is a very sweet guy. People might make fun of Leon, but it's hard to dislike him, because the only person Leon hurts is himself. I mean, before the first fight, the biggest problem we had was psyching him up to be aggressive. Ali was his hero. And all the time I had to remind him, 'You know, Leon, it's not personal. You can love Ali, but you gotta hit him to win the fight.' And after Leon won, it wasn't like he went around bragging, 'Yeah, man; I kicked his ass.' What he said was, 'I still love Ali; he's my hero. Ali's the greatest; I'm just the latest.' So what happened was, people liked Leon. He was a regular sort of guy.

"After he won, we came back from Vegas, and my secretary had a stack of messages six inches high waiting for me. These were people interested in endorsements. The U.S. Dairy Association, Coca-Cola, 7-Up, Prudential Life Insurance. And I was rolling in it; it's making my day. I'm the new kid on the block, and I've taken a kid with seven professional fights to the heavyweight championship of the world. I'm setting up interviews with advertising agencies. We're ready to make a fortune in endorsements. But Leon had gone through eight weeks of serious training, and he hadn't had a chance to bust loose. I had him staying in my apartment in Manhattan. I didn't put him in a hotel because I didn't trust him. And Leon told me, 'Butch, you gotta let me go. I need free time. You gotta let me swoop.' Because in his mind, nothing had changed from being Leon Spinks to being Leon Spinks, heavyweight champion of the world. So finally I said, 'Okay, I can't keep you in a cage. I'm gonna be working, setting up endorsements; I'll give you a few days.'

"Two nights later, I'm lying in bed; four o'clock in the morning, and the telephone rings. It's Ed Schuyler, Associated Press, asking, 'Butch, do you have a statement for this story about Leon?' Obviously, Ed knew something I didn't know, because otherwise four o'clock in the morning was a bad time to be calling. So I asked, 'What story?' and he told me, 'Leon just got busted for cocaine.' The motherfucker. Here we are, about to make millions of dollars, and he's got five dollars worth of cocaine in his hatband. So they put a picture of Leon in handcuffs on the front page of every newspaper in the country. The endorsements are gone. And because Leon's got money from the last fight, leeches like you wouldn't believe are coming out of the woodwork. And he's not training; he's

everywhere except the gym. Leon is partying his life away, and all
the leeches are telling him, 'Right on, Leon; do it your way,' because
they want the money that they can suck out of him.

"Then Leon disappeared completely. It was time to start serious
training, and nobody knew where he was. Finally I tracked him
down in North Carolina, in a little shack drinking moonshine whiskey. He's smoking dope, groggier than hell, like this is a dream and
he's gonna enjoy it because any day he might wake up. And that's
how it was the whole time he was champ. Leon was supposed to
be here; he'd be there. He's supposed to be there; he'd be here.
Take him in the front door of a hotel, and he'd keep on walking
right out the back. At most, he trained ten days for the rematch.
He even disappeared in New Orleans. The fight was in the Superdome in Louisiana. There was a big motorcade from the airport to
the hotel. We got to the hotel; we're all getting out of our limousines,
not paying much attention. Leon got out of his limo, got into another
limo that was left with the motor running, and drove off by himself—
not even with a driver. Now we're in the lobby of the hotel, and I
ask, 'Wait a minute; where's Leon?' No one knows. We've got Mr.
T before he became famous. He's supposed to be Leon's bodyguard.
I mean, how hard is it to watch a guy walking from his limo to the
hotel? But I ask Mr. T, 'Where's Leon?' And Mr. T says, 'I don't
know.' Then, finally, Leon telephones. He's having a good time.
He tells me, 'I'm okay, but I ain't gonna say where I am.' And I
blew my stack. I said, 'What the fuck is the matter with you, Leon?
Are you fucking crazy?' And then I said to myself, 'Fuck Leon. The
fight is sold, and if he don't care enough to do things right, then it's
gonna be his ass and his problem. I mean, enough is enough. As
long as Leon shows up for the fight, I just ain't gonna worry about
him no more.'

"And I'll tell you something. Ali didn't win that second fight.
Leon lost it. Forget all that stuff about Ali going back and working
hard and being better the second time around. Ali wasn't better the
second time against Leon. Ali was worse. Ali had slipped even more
than before, but Leon went against him with nothing at all."

On the eve of the fight, New Orleans was flooded with fight fans.
Despite the fact that ABC was broadcasting the bout, 63,532 people
would pack the Superdome—the largest indoor fight attendance in
history. More important from the promoters' point of view, those
fans would pay $4,806,675 in live gate receipts, shattering the fifty-
one-year-old mark established by Gene Tunney and Jack Dempsey

by more than two million dollars. ABC, in turn, would enjoy the second-largest audience in television history, surpassed only by the final episode of *Roots*.

Predictions as to the outcome of the fight varied. Even the Ali entourage was cautious. "Spinks is a natural fighting animal who just keeps coming with punches," Harold Conrad told a reporter. "Some are good and some are nothing, but there are so many of them that he'll lay plenty of hurt on Muhammad. People say Muhammad threw away the first fight with bad tactics, by playing in the early rounds. But with the condition Ali had then, if he'd warred with Spinks early, he'd have been knocked on his ass. As it was, Spinks kicked the shit out of him. This time, Ali is in shape; but that old bum with the white beard will be on the stool along with him."[20]

Still, Ali remained optimistic. "You can't write a movie no better than this," he announced at a press conference just before the fight. "When I beat Sonny Liston, I shocked the world. When I joined the Muslims, I shocked the world. When I beat George Foreman, I shocked the world. I am from the House of Shock."[21]

MUHAMMAD ALI: "Against Spinks the second time, my plan was simple. Jab, jab, and throw the right hand. If he got in close, tie him up. No rope-a-dope; fight the whole time in the center of the ring. And throw lots of punches at the end of each round. Closing a round right impresses the judges, and I wanted to give Spinks something to remember between rounds."

In truth, it was a slow sluggish fight, but that was what Ali wanted. It was the most likely way for him to win. In round five, he was penalized for holding. Still, his fight plan remained unchanged. Meanwhile, Spinks kept plodding forward, but without the intensity of their first encounter. The rounds passed; the drama grew. Muhammad Ali, fighting from memory, on the verge of regaining the heavyweight championship of the world. "Objectively speaking, it was a terrible fight," Howard Cosell later recalled. "Ali won a unanimous decision, and neither man fought at all." But given the drama of Ali's presence, it was a memorable night for everyone involved.

The late rounds passed with Ali in control and sixty thousand fans urging him on. Around the world, millions watched as the final minutes and seconds ticked down. Flush with emotion, Cosell sought to convey to his audience what was at hand. America's child of the 1960s, desperately clinging to his youth. And if somehow Ali were able to prevail, perhaps every man might stay young. Thus, at the end of what he later called "the greatest broadcast of my life," Cosell quoted another icon of the sixties, Bob Dylan:

> May your hands always be busy,
> May your feet always be swift,
> May you have a strong foundation
> When the winds of changes shift.
> May your heart always be joyful,
> May your song always be sung,
> May you stay forever young.

LEON SPINKS: "Ali was my idol; I looked up to him. Going in the first fight, I just fought to win. Throw punches. Don't worry about what he's doing. I knew I had it won in the ring, but you know how judges are. When the fight was close, they always gave it to Ali, so it surprised me that I won. The second time we fought, he wasn't better. He just held a lot, and I had a lot of things on my mind. I don't think about that second fight no more. Don't matter now. It's done; it's over. But sometimes what I think about is how my life changed, being champion. It wasn't right, the way people treated me. I was fighting to get ahead. All I wanted was to make a living, and the world wanted me to be like Ali. I couldn't do what I used to do, because everything I did got blown out of proportion. I couldn't be like I wanted to be. Not getting respect didn't matter to me. I don't mind people making fun of me. People always make fun of me, and if they don't do it to my face, they're gonna do it behind me. But when I was champion, no one would leave me alone. That's what really bothered me. Everyone wanted me to give them something or do something or act a certain way. And I couldn't do it. I'm Leon Spinks; I'm not Ali. And then, when I lost, people still didn't leave me alone. Even now, they don't let me be."

[Then Spinks is asked about Ali's physical condition today and whether he feels sorry for Ali.] "What for should I feel sorry for Ali? Don't you hear what I been saying? The man's still living; the man's still eating; he's making money; there's a roof over his head. And best of all, whatever happens, he'll always be Muhammad Ali."

14

The Money

After his victory over Leon Spinks, it seemed unlikely that Ali would fight again. Ali himself said as much when he told a reporter, "I'd be the biggest fool in the world to go out a loser after being the first three-time champ. None of the black athletes before me ever got out when they were on top. My people need one black man to come out on top. I've got to be the first."[1]

As expected, there were offers to continue fighting. Some were for bouts against credible opponents. Others were less so, and one, by any standard, was absurd. Twenty-one years earlier, sixteen-year-old Cassius Clay had been stopped in the second round of an amateur bout in Chicago by an older, more experienced opponent named Kent Green. Clay wasn't actually knocked down, but he was "getting shellacked pretty good," his coach Joe Martin later remembered. "I tend to stop fights a little earlier than most guys. I hate to see my boys hurt. He wasn't hurt, but he was gonna get hurt, so I threw in the towel."[2]

Now, in early 1979, even Kent Green was mentioned as a possible opponent. He hadn't been in the ring for years. He'd never been a world-class amateur or professional fighter. But he was the only man to have knocked out Ali, and that was enough in the minds of some to warrant a return bout for revenge.

On June 26, 1979, nine months after defeating Spinks, Ali put an end to the nonsense by announcing his retirement from boxing. The timing of his declaration was widely reported to have been occasioned by a three-hundred-thousand-dollar payment from Bob Arum. Under World Boxing Association regulations, Ali could have waited until September to defend or relinquish his crown. But Arum was anxious to stage a WBA title bout between John Tate and Gerrie Coetzee in South Africa, and reportedly paid the champion to step aside. As for Ali's motivation, "Everybody gets old," he told reporters. "This time, I'm thinking about my family, my children, the record books. I'd be a fool to fight again."[*3]

Meanwhile, a four-hour television miniseries entitled *Freedom Road*, starring Ali and Kris Kristofferson, was completed and aired. Ali played the fictionalized role of Gideon Jackson, an ex-slave who fought in the Civil War and eventually became a United States senator. Kristofferson remembers his costar well.

KRIS KRISTOFFERSON: "The first thing that struck me about Muhammad was his genuine love for everybody he met. People were always asking him to pose for pictures or sign autographs, and he gave everyone what they wanted. You know, a lot of celebrities make a show of concern for the public, but in reality they hold their public in contempt and feel people are infringing on their life, which sometimes is true. But Muhammad never begrudged the intrusions. There were times he'd be so weary from the demands people made on him that he'd nod out and fall asleep in the middle of an interview. But he never let a person go by without an autograph if that was what the person wanted. He told me once, 'You don't realize how much it means to these people. A lot of them have never met anybody famous.' And he told me how, when he was a little boy, his father took him to a tree that Joe Louis had leaned against in Louisville, and he realized how much that could mean to someone.

"There was a scene in the film that Muhammad asked me to rehearse all the time with him. I don't know how many times we did it. I played a Georgia cracker, and it was where I called him a nigger. Something about that tickled him to death; maybe because

---

*Ali vigorously denies receiving the three-hundred-thousand-dollar payment, and says that he wouldn't have timed an announcement of that nature for monetary gain. Arum says that the payment was made, and that it was his practice during that period to pay all money due Ali to Herbert Muhammad. However Mr. Muhammad denies any recollection of receiving the money. Stories about the payment were reported by United Press International and carried in newspapers across the country.

I was a skinny little white guy, and he could have torn me apart if he'd wanted. And I thought he was an honest performer. In my view, he could have had a career as an actor, but nobody took the time to train him properly. Once, some of the people around him asked me, 'Which actor makes the most money?' At the time, it was Brando, who made maybe two million dollars a picture. And I could see the wheels turning. They were thinking, Muhammad gets more than that for a fight, and as an actor he'll never make as much as Brando. And of course, if he'd pursued a career in acting—or any endeavor except boxing—a lot of the people who hung around him wouldn't have been along for the ride."

After *Freedom Road* was completed, Ali and Veronica moved to a mansion in the Hancock Park section of Los Angeles. By any measure, it was the most luxurious residence that any heavyweight champion had ever owned. There were seven bedrooms, a living room, dining room, reception hall, library, billiard parlor, conservatory, breakfast room, kitchen, and sleeping alcoves for household domestics. A Tiffany stained-glass window oversaw the second-floor landing. Earth-tone tilework by Ernest Batchelder covered much of the ground floor. In keeping with Veronica's taste, the mansion was furnished like a museum, with gilded furniture, Renaissance paintings, Oriental rugs, and huge standing urns. Antique chairs were protected by ropes strung between the armrests to prevent guests from sitting where they didn't belong.

In addition to Hana, now age three, Ali and Veronica had a second daughter, Laila, who was one year old. Ali's four children by his marriage to Belinda stayed in Chicago, where they were raised by Belinda's parents. Maryum, the oldest, was eleven. The twins, Rasheeda and Jamillah, were nine. Muhammad Junior was seven. Throughout their lives, they had lived with a father who was the most famous man in the world. Now that relationship was further complicated by the geographical distance between Ali and his children.

MARYUM ALI: "I was in third grade when my parents split up. I was young, but I could see what was going on. And even in third grade, I got disgusted. Veronica was around a lot. My mom was bitter. There was a lot of tension. The divorce was written up in the papers, and it was hard for me in school. The other kids never teased me about it, but I'd overhear people talking. I guess what made it easier for me was my grandparents explaining things as I went along. They were really the ones who raised us from the time I was in second grade on. We lived in Chicago. I had an Islamic upbringing, and there was no hypocrisy. My grandparents set a good example for us, because they led good clean lives. At night, we talked about whatever was on our minds. And I think that's one of the reasons my sisters and brother and I are so loving toward one another now. We get into arguments but we're very close, and none of us have ever been in trouble. We were brought up to believe that God sees everything, and we're just more comfortable when we're doing right.

"The best memories I have of my father when I was young were the everyday things we did together. I was Daddy's girl. I loved my mom, but I always wanted to be with him. He'd come home from training camp after a fight, and I'd have grown during that period. He'd stare and say, 'Man, you've gotten big. You know how to dress yourself, and you can comb your own hair.' And I remember a trip we took to Florida. We stayed at a hotel, and each morning we ate cornflakes by the pool. But there weren't enough of those times when we were a family unit alone. I loved the feeling of being a family; even when it got complicated, like when we found out my father had two more children at the same time he was married to my mother. I didn't know about them when they were born [in 1972 and 1974], but I learned about them when I was young. At first I was mad. I asked myself, why does it have to be this way? But my father said, 'These are my children, these are your sisters,' and he taught us to accept them completely. Then Hana was born, and after that, Laila. And my grandparents did a real good job of keeping everything in perspective for us all.

"Another thing I remember from when I was little was my father teaching me how fortunate I was; that we were a wealthy family, and it was our obligation to share our wealth with those in need. Sometimes we'd be driving through a poor neighborhood. There'd be homeless people on the streets, and he'd get out of the car and buy them dinner. This was before most people thought about the homeless, but he thought about them a lot. And he always wanted me to know that material things come and go, so I shouldn't get too hyper over a new car or money. You can like them, they're nice to have, but they don't matter a whole lot compared to the importance of loving God.

"So all that was good. But what I didn't like was, when we were growing up, too much of his life revolved around the public. My father likes lots of people around him. He never says no to anyone, and there was a constant stream of people in our home. When he wasn't entertaining, he was traveling. Things never revolved around the family; the family revolved around other things. I mean, there are people in this world who, no matter how wealthy and busy they are, at certain times they say, 'It's my daughter's birthday,' or 'It's this holiday, and I don't care what else is happening, I'm going to spend it alone with my family.' But my father wasn't like that. I used to wish he was, but he wasn't. He'd never say, 'I can't go to Saudi Arabia this month because I have to spend time with my children.' And that upset me a lot. But then I'd tell myself, 'I just have to put up with these things.' As I got older, I understood it better; although sometimes I still got jealous, particularly with women. We'd be at an airport or a restaurant or someplace else, and all these women would want to get next to him. I'd check them out, and I'd want to say, 'Get away from him; that's my daddy.' But after a while, I got used to that too, as long as there wasn't anything messy involved. I guess what happened was, I got used to how famous he was. I remember, in school one time, we had our books open and there were three people mentioned in the lesson we were doing—Count Dracula, Ronald Reagan, and Muhammad Ali. I looked, and it hit me. And I guess, even now, sometimes it hits me. Like not long ago, we went to a basketball game at the Los Angeles Forum. And when we left, the whole crowd stood up and gave him an ovation. Or one time, we met Prince. I was excited; I was dying to meet Prince. We got there. Prince was looking at my dad, saying, 'Muhammad Ali, I love you so much!' And I said to myself, 'God, this is incredible.'

"So I guess what I'm saying is, things have worked out well for me. I could have gone in a lot of different directions. I could have said, 'I'm Muhammad Ali's daughter,' and had a chip on my shoulder all the time. Or I could have been irresponsible, and used his name to get by if I did things wrong. But I've looked at what my father and mother taught me. I learned from what they did right and from their mistakes. My grandparents helped interpret the world for me, and I was guided by my religious beliefs. So I'm happy; I'm at peace with myself. I know my dad feels bad about not having watched us grow up. He's always asking questions now about what my life is like and what I believe. And one thing I believe is that I'm truly blessed to have him as my father. I love being Maryum Ali."

On the surface, Ali's retirement to Los Angeles seemed like the idyllic close to an illustrious ring career. He was handsome, a man of extraordinary achievement, revered around the globe, married to one of the most beautiful women in the world, rich. The list went on ad infinitum, but much of it was illusory. For twenty years, the ring had been Ali's pulpit, and it was a different world without it. His marriage was only two years old, but already under serious strain. And he wasn't rich enough to sustain the lifestyle that Veronica had chosen.

During his career, Ali had made tens of millions of dollars. His three fights with Joe Frazier had brought him gross purses of $11,000,000. His third fight against Ken Norton carried a $6,000,000 price tag. He'd been paid $5,450,000 to fight George Foreman, and $6,750,000 for two bouts against Leon Spinks. Seven-figure purses had accompanied his championship defenses against Earnie Shavers ($3,000,000), Alfredo Evangelista ($2,750,000), Joe Bugner ($2,000,000), Jimmy Young ($1,600,000), Chuck Wepner ($1,500,000), Richard Dunn ($1,500,000), Ron Lyle ($1,000,000), and Jean-Pierre Coopman ($1,000,000). All totaled, Ali's ring earnings surpassed the *combined* earnings of every heavyweight champion who had come before him. Moreover, he'd been well-situated to take advantage of numerous business ventures and endorsement opportunities. But by 1979 when Ali retired, most of the money he'd earned was gone. Much of it had been generously spent and used to pay his taxes, but a lot had been lost to bad deals, exploitation, and outright theft by people he'd trusted.

LLOYD WELLS: "I've been around athletes all my life; and some of them are generous, but a lot of them are stingy shits. And Ali was such a giving person. He made sure everybody got paid for their services. If someone took a suitcase out of his car, Ali always tipped him right. He never left a restaurant without making sure the waitress got a good tip. He understood that those people had bills to pay for clothes and food and a place to live. He just never felt he was using his money right if he spent it on himself instead of helping other people out.

"I'll never forget, one time we were in Haiti. We were driving to the airport, and all of a sudden, Ali said, 'Stop the car; stop!' There was an old Haitian lady sitting by the road; just sitting, not doing nothing else. And Ali got out of the car, walked over to her, reached into his pocket, and gave her a handful of bills. The woman looked at it, and started to cry. She couldn't believe it. And Ali did things like that all the time. Money and possessions never mattered to Ali. He'd spend on everybody but himself. I can't tell you how many times he'd get a check for five or ten thousand dollars, and say, 'Send this to my mother,' or, 'Send this to my father.' And not only did he give away the money; he'd pay the taxes on it. I'm telling you, if someone cut Ali open, they'd find his heart was made of pure gold."

MICKEY DUFF: "Ali was incredibly generous; not just with his money, but with his time. Shortly after the second Spinks fight, I set up some exhibitions in Europe. And right in middle of it, Ali came to me and said he was flying to the United States for a charity dinner he'd promised to attend. The only way he could do it was to go back and forth within twenty-four hours, and I was worried about his coming back on time. We went to the airport in London; he caught his plane. And I asked Herbert, 'Do you think he'll really be back tomorrow?' Herbert told me, 'Not if he's dead. If he's dead, his wife will want his body. But if he's not dead, he'll be here.' And he was. He flew all the way to the United States, went to the dinner, got right back on a plane, and was in London the following morning. And that was typical of Ali. He hated to say 'no' to anybody.

"I remember when he fought Richard Dunn; it was the same time I was planning a benefit dinner for a British fighter named Chris Finnegan, who had lost an eye. So I went to Ali, and asked if we could have his gloves to auction off after the Dunn fight. He agreed. Now, it's a week later, the fight is over. Ali has just knocked Dunn out in five rounds. I jumped into the ring to get the gloves, because I was afraid Ali might have forgotten his promise. Angelo took the gloves off and handed them to me. And as I was walking away, I felt a tap on my shoulder. I turned around, and I swear this is a true story. It was Ali, and he said to me, 'Look inside the gloves.' So I looked inside, and there in Ali's handwriting, in one glove it said, 'Ali wins,' and in the other glove it said, 'KO, round 5.' Isn't that remarkable? He'd stopped predicting publicly by then, but he'd wanted to do a little something extra for Chris Finnegan."

Wherever he went, whoever he was with, Ali's generosity was evident:

Howard Bingham: "We were in Los Angeles one time, and this Vietnam veteran was on the ninth floor of a building. He was having flashbacks, threatening to jump, and the police couldn't get to him. People on the street were yelling, 'Jump, jump!' The guy was crying; he was on a balcony. Ali just walked out to him, put his arms around him, and brought him back. And then he spent eighteen hundred dollars on him for clothes and an apartment so the guy could have a place to live."

Chuck Bodak: "I remember a dinner at the Aladdin Hotel in Vegas. They were honoring all the living heavyweight champs, and each one was presented with a diamond ring. These were beautiful rings, full of stones; the kind you get if you win the Super Bowl or World Series. Ali got his. He was walking off the stage, and he passed a little girl who was sitting in a wheelchair. The girl's mother asked if Ali would pose for a picture. And without batting an eyelash, Ali hugged the girl, kissed her like he always does with children, and put the ring in her hand. That ring was worth thousands of dollars, but it didn't mean a thing to him compared to the pleasure he got from giving it to that child."

Ralph Thornton: "We were in New York, going to Madison Square Garden; I think it was for the Shavers fight. And there was this bum; he was filthy. I mean dirty, dirty, dirty. Ali saw him, and said, 'You look like you don't got no money; you ain't taking care of yourself.' Then he gave him a hundred-dollar bill. The man just stared; held it and stared was all he did. And he asked, 'Is this real? Is this a real hundred-dollar bill?' Ali said, 'Yeah'. And then he realized he'd made a mistake, that the guy would have trouble cashing something that big. So he told him, 'Here, let me give you five twenties instead.' And the man didn't want to give back the hundred; he'd never seen one before. So Ali let him keep the hundred, and gave him the five twenties too."

Lloyd Wells: "Ali had all these plans. We'd sit and talk, and he'd want to solve the problems of everybody in the world. In the locker room before his fights, we'd be waiting, wondering like you do sometimes. And out of nowhere, Ali would ask some question about what he could do to help the poor. And believe me, you can walk into any locker room in professional sports—baseball, football, basketball; I don't care what sport we're talking—and those guys aren't thinking about helping poor people. But that's the way Ali was. He wanted to buy clothes for every person he saw in rags, pay the rent for every homeless person on the street; feed every man, woman, and child who was hungry. And one man can't do it all. Governments can't do it; one man sure can't. But God knows, Ali tried."

Meanwhile, Ali's resources were being depleted on many fronts, starting with his own entourage. Some of the people in Ali's camp were scrupulously honest. They never took a dollar that wasn't theirs, and worked for everything they got. But others followed a different set of rules, and were always hustling to make money on the side.

Sometimes the hustle was aggravating but not serious. "I'd show up for a photo session," Neil Leifer remembers. "There'd be a dozen guys waiting with their hands out, and I'd have two choices. I could pay them, in which case they'd say, 'Wow, these pictures are great; you look incredible, champ.' Or I could refuse to pay, in which case there'd be a campaign to end the session. 'Come on, champ; it's getting late. He shot that picture four times already. How much time you gonna take? Hurry up; we don't got all day.' It was that sort of thing; psychological warfare, really. And it was easier to take care of the hustlers than fight them."

"Life around Ali was a constant hustle," John Condon recalls. "A lot of people in the entourage were only there to serve their own needs, and too often Ali's interests took a back seat. I don't want to think about how many times these guys picked up money on the side by bringing someone into camp or up to Ali's hotel room to meet the champ. And anyone who paid, if they'd known the score, could have come in just as easily for free. And these guys, the way they spent Ali's money. For years, they billed everything to him. Travel, phone bills, meals, you name it. It must have been like having a dozen kids in college and paying for all of them at the same time."

BOBBY GOODMAN: "Ali was good to so many people, and a lot of those people took advantage of him. When he went to Germany to fight Richard Dunn, the entourage stayed at the Bayerischer Hof. It's a landmark hotel; one of the best in Germany. And these guys ran up charges like you wouldn't believe. Phone bills, restaurant bills, bar charges, gift shop purchases; all of it charged to Ali. And for the first time—at least, it was the first time I saw—Muhammad got mad over the way people were spending his money. He called everybody to his hotel suite, and started off very firm. 'How can you guys treat me like this? I pay you; I feed you; I take you all over the world; and all you do is take advantage of me.' He grabbed

Bundini, shook him, and said, 'Bundini, I heard you ordered two steaks in the restaurant last night and left one on your plate.' And Bundini looked at him and sort of whined with puppy eyes. Then Ali turned on someone else who'd run up a phone bill of a couple of hundred dollars. And you could hear his voice start to soften. He was trying to stay mad but it just wasn't in him, so what came out was, 'Listen, I know it's tough to be away from home, so just make one call home a day.' Now if you're talking about a whole group of people, and each one makes one call a day from Germany to the United States, do you know what that costs? And with these guys, it was going to be more than one call no matter what he said. But before I knew it, Ali was back to Bundini, saying, 'Don't order two steaks at the same time and leave one. But if you're hungry after you eat the first steak, you can order a second.' And it was frustrating for me to see the way people took advantage of him. It frustrated Angelo; it drove Howard Bingham crazy. But there was nothing any of us could do to change him."

But some in the entourage did more than spend Ali's money. They stole from him. "Ali finds it very hard to say no," says Belinda Ali. "In some ways, he's much more insecure than people realize. He wants everybody to like him, and he'll look away rather than confront someone who takes advantage of him. And what happened was, certain people understood that about Ali and took advantage of the situation."

Gene Dibble was an investment advisor to Ali in the 1970s. Born in Alabama, he moved to Chicago upon his discharge from the United States Air Force in 1954. Dibble recalls the frustrations inherent in his financial dealings with the Ali entourage.

GENE DIBBLE: "There's very few of them that didn't steal from Ali in one way or another. Most of them didn't start out wanting to hurt Ali, but the opportunities came along and, well, you know human nature.

"You should have seen the training camp expenses. Say someone was buying groceries. They'd go to town, bring a receipt to Ali; he'd give them the money, and then they'd send the receipt to Chicago to be paid a second time. Sometimes they'd inflate the receipt, too. They'd come back to camp with a receipt for a hundred dollars, bringing fifty dollars worth of groceries. Same thing with gas. If the bus took sixty dollars worth of diesel fuel, they'd show up with a bill for eighty dollars. Ali just wouldn't deal with it. I'd bring it all to his attention, but he refused to confront anybody on unpleasant matters, so they stole from him like crazy. All the trophies, plaques, and rings he got are gone. They disappeared; people took them. And in camp, you had guys walking out with sheets and towels, like it was a hotel or something. Anything that wasn't nailed down got taken.

"And don't think it was just petty theft. When Ali was interested in the farm in Berrien Springs where he lives now, he and I and a couple of friends went to check the place out. We took a look around the farm. Then Ali pulled me off to the side and asked, 'What do you think it's worth?' I didn't know, but I figured I could find out quick, because I had two friends who lived in Benton Harbor, fifteen miles away, and one of them was a large real estate investor. So I called my friend—his name was Hackley Woodford—and said, 'Hack, we're looking at this farm. The man wants $450,000. What do you think it's worth?' Hack told me, 'If you pay more than $300,000, you're crazy.' So I went back and offered the seller $250,000. Ali came over and asked what we were talking about, and I told him, 'Ali, just be quiet for a few minutes; maybe we can work this out.' Anyway, I got the seller down to $325,000, and then I told Ali, 'Let's take a walk. Tell the guy it's still too much, and maybe we'll come back next Saturday to make a deal.' Meanwhile, while I'm with Ali, some of his good friends are with the seller. Then I went to make a telephone call, and they started telling Ali, 'Don't listen to Gene Dibble. This is a great deal, pay the man what he wants.' Well, to make a long story short, by the time I got back, the seller was back up to $400,000, and Ali paid it. I told him, 'You're making a big mistake.' And Ali told me, 'I don't care; I want it.' Later I found out that Ali's friends cut a deal with the seller while Ali and I were talking, and Ali overpaid by $100,000.

"And that was common; things like that went on all the time. It drove me crazy, and I used to get on Howard Bingham. I'd say, 'We've got to lead Ali in the right direction, because no one is looking out for him financially.' Howard was Ali's greatest friend. Outside of Lonnie, who he's married to now, Howard is the best thing that ever happened to Ali. But Howard didn't have the wherewithal— the business background or the strength—to fight all these people and guide Ali. So it ended with Ali getting cheated and taken advantage of most of the time."

HOWARD BINGHAM: "I used to go to bed at night crying because of the way people were ripping off Ali. In the early days, it was rough because I wasn't a Muslim, so he didn't believe much of anything I said. All someone had to do was walk in the door and say, 'As-salaam-alaikum.' That was the easiest way to plug him. Then it got so anyone could rip him off as long as they made friends with the right people on the inside. And even today, I see people ripping off Ali. I'll say something, but he doesn't always want to listen. And if I warn him too much about too many people, it starts to aggravate him. So the way we leave it is, if he asks for my opinion about someone, I give it. And if I see something real bad, I'll warn him. But otherwise, I let things be."

But theft from within was only part of the problem. Ali was a target for a wide range of con men. "My father is incredibly trusting," says Maryum Ali. "He's always had a blind belief in people, and he lets people get close to him who shouldn't be allowed in. I grew up with it. I saw it all the time, and it just about drove me crazy. People would come to our house, crying, drenched in tears. 'Muhammad, I have eight kids; my wife's in the hospital, and I can't pay the doctors' bills.' He'd give them money, and a week later, the same guy would be back again. 'Oh, Muhammad, woe is me. Now my children are sick; please give me more money.' So he'd give the same guy money again. And just looking at that guy, I might have only been eight years old, and I'd know it was someone he shouldn't trust. But my father is stubborn. You can argue with him. You can say, 'I don't trust this person for these reasons.' But in the end, he's going to trust who he wants to trust, and who he trusts is most of the world."

GENE DIBBLE: "It didn't take a genius to hustle Ali. In the ring, he might have been the smartest man ever. But when it came to money and knowing who to trust, his decisions weren't very smart. I've never seen a man who made so much money, tried to make so much money, and at the same time had such tremendous disregard for money. I've just never met anyone like that. I hated the way people stole from him. I'd say, 'Ali, if you don't care about yourself, think about your children. These people are stealing from your kids.' But it went on and on and on forever.

"Even when Ali tried to do right, he got taken. After a fight, he always put aside money for taxes. He knew how Joe Louis wound up, broke and a million dollars in debt to the IRS. And he swore that would never happen to him. So what happened? Jeremiah Shabazz introduced him to a lawyer named Spiros Anthony. Anthony took $2,400,000 of Ali's money to hold in escrow for taxes. Then, in addition, he got Ali involved in some program in Washington, D.C., where they were supposed to start a global organization to fight world poverty. That was another million dollars. And the next thing you knew, Spiros Anthony had run off with Ali's money.

"There was an accountant in Philadelphia who put Ali into a couple of movie deals that cost him about a million. There's another fellow, a man named Arthur Morrison, who's been exploiting Ali for years, bouncing checks, forging Ali's signature, and costing him thousands of dollars. And I guess what aggravates me the most is, after these people betray his trust, Ali always forgives them. And no matter what any of them do, he never says a word against them."

Ali's relationships with Spiros Anthony and Arthur Morrison are instructive because they fit so clearly into a pattern. Anthony claimed that the money Ali gave him was properly invested in ventures that unexpectedly failed, or in some cases, was spent pursuant to Ali's direct orders. However, James Bierbower, who was Ali's attorney in the litigation that followed, has a distinctly different view.

JAMES BIERBOWER: "Anthony was a lawyer who wormed his way into Ali's affections and became part of the hangers-on in Ali's camp. Finally, he got to the point where he was holding the tax money; and when tax time came, the money wasn't there. It was the tax money and something more that was missing. I filed a civil lawsuit against Anthony, who testified that every time he wrote a check on Ali's account, the money had been spent on behalf of Ali. Then I took some depositions in Las Vegas. And it turned out that, every time Anthony was substantially behind and in debt to a casino, he'd go to the cashier and write a check on Ali's account. It was obvious, really. The proof was there. We got a judgment expeditiously. After that, Anthony was disbarred, and we started searching for his assets. There were a few antiques and a little real estate, but not nearly what Ali was entitled to. I was in favor of filing criminal charges. I didn't believe Anthony when he came up empty. I thought he had rat-holes full of money stashed away, and I wanted him in jail unless he started talking. But Ali refused to file charges. I wanted to keep after Anthony for the rest of his life, but the champ had a belief that people make mistakes and the Lord requires forgiveness."

Like Spiros Anthony, Arthur Morrison has been a thorn in Ali's side. Morrison says the two men met in jail in 1968, when Ali was serving time for a traffic violation. Ali doesn't recall their meeting, but at one point he signed a contract giving Morrison the right to manufacture and market certain products bearing Ali's name. Morrison has continued to use Ali's name, and over the years has engaged in a long trail of abuses. On at least two occasions, he was reportedly on the verge of being arrested for fraud, but charges were dropped because Ali made good for him on his obligations. On another occasion, he allegedly forged Ali's signature and that of a notary public in an effort to get $250,000 from a California marketing company. "Arthur Morrison is one of the dirtiest nothings I've ever seen," says Jeremiah Shabazz. "He keeps coming back with one bad deal after another, using Ali, disgracing his name. If Ali would just press charges against him, it would end and the other exploiters would get the message. But Morrison knows he can use Ali again and again. Because sooner or later, whatever else happens, Ali lets his guard down and Arthur Morrison waltzes back again."

GENE DIBBLE: "Arthur Morrison has used Ali's name all over the country and never put anything worthwhile together. Ali always lets it go. He just shrugs and says that, if someone only uses his name, it doesn't cost him any money. But he's wrong. Ali's name is the best earning asset he has. Right now, it's the only earning asset he has. So when someone misuses his name and exploits his image, it costs him a lot.

"But it's not just Arthur Morrison. I can't tell you how many times people—some of them well-intentioned—have come to Ali over the years with poorly-thought-out fly-by-night proposals. There was something called 'Champburgers', a fast-food hamburger chain that was undercapitalized and folded. There was an Ali candy bar; Mr. Champs Soda; African Feeling sheets. And even when the proposals were solid, Ali would wind up with the short end of the stick or with no deal at all.

"Ali had a piece of property in Chicago that he bought on my advice for three hundred thousand dollars. It's worth ten times that now, but Spiros Anthony talked him into selling it at cost so he could invest in property in Washington, D.C., that eventually went into foreclosure. I had Ali investing in bonds. Some of his people nearly crucified me for that, because it meant his money wasn't available for their purposes. Ali today should be richer than Bill Cosby. But he let anybody and everybody into his business, and signed his future away in the dark."

Muhammad Ali Sportswear Ltd. was a typical Ali venture. Harold Schulman (who had previously founded and served as chief executive

officer of Nik-Nik) was president of the Ali sportswear corporation.
He explains what went wrong.

HAROLD SCHULMAN: "I was approached by three men, one of
whom was Larry Ashinoff, who I'd grown up with in the Bronx.
They had a license to manufacture Muhammad Ali sportswear, and
I didn't want to get involved. I'd done my time in the men's apparel
business, and was happy with the consulting career I'd adopted.
Larry kept putting more and more money in front of me, and I kept
saying, 'No.' But all of us have a catchword that turns us on, and
finally Larry hit mine. He said, 'Harold, I've known you for thirty-
five years; and I promise, working with Muhammad Ali will be fun.'

" 'Fun' was the word that suckered me in. So I took the job, and
it was a poor strategic venture from the start. First, we were undercapitalized. Ali got sixty-five thousand up front, and I think one
more payment of fifteen thousand. That was his minimum guarantee
against royalties. But of course that meant he was locked into an
exclusive arrangement with us, so he couldn't accept something
more profitable to him that might come along. Sixty-five thousand
was cheap for somebody like Ali; it was nothing. But after we paid
it, there wasn't much left for product development and cuttings.
And we had all sorts of problems. Ali was at Deer Lake, training.
I'd go out there, usually every other Thursday, to get measurements
from him and the like. And it was always hurry up and wait. I'd
wait while he sparred, and I'd wait while he took a nap, and I'd wait
while he entertained visitors with magic tricks and gave interviews
to every high school newspaper reporter in the state. Finally, I'd
get him to stand still for some measurements, and right in the middle
of what we were doing, some lady from Watkinsville, Iowa, would
knock on the door and want his autograph, and everything would
stop dead. Or worse, we'd be there with a photographer to take
color shots of a catalogue or some other publication. Now you're
talking about heavy money, and in the middle of the shooting, Ali
would walk away and talk to tourists for half an hour. And of course,
while we were waiting, the light would change, and the jacket he
was wearing wouldn't be appropriate anymore.

"At one point, Bundini threatened to sue us. It had been decided
to use a logo of a butterfly and a bee, based on the slogan, 'Float
like a butterfly, sting like a bee.' It was a great logo, very attractive.
But Bundini's lawyer sent us a letter saying he'd coined the phrase
and copyrighted it for commercial purposes. That struck me as nonsense; I thought it was in the public domain. But the last thing we

needed was a lawsuit, so we paid Bundini five thousand dollars. And to be honest, another problem we had was, a lot of our clothing was schlock. I was trying to create a line of quality merchandise—jogging suits, shorts, sweatshirts, knit tops; 'active sportswear' was the terminology within the industry. But what happened was, the items we created for Ali were commingled with lesser goods that Larry was stuck with from other ventures, so we weren't selling an across-the-board quality product.

"Then it was time to go public. First, we had a press conference at the New York Athletic Club. And the NYAC was rather exclusionary in its membership practices. What I remember most about the press conference is, before the press got there, we were testing the microphone. Ali picked the microphone up and said, 'Ladies and gentlemen, the Jews and niggers and all the other members of the NAACP welcome you to the NYAC.' Later that day, we introduced the sportswear at Madison Square Garden, in the Felt Forum. We'd counted on filling the place up. It seated forty-five hundred people; and instead, we had eight or nine hundred. The buyers didn't show; the public didn't show. And with all the other headaches we had, there was one more problem.

"I went to a lot of people at major department stores trying to sell Muhammad Ali sportswear. These were buyers, store presidents, CEOs. And invariably, the response I got was, 'Harold, you're crazy! For years, we've been trying to keep blacks out of our store. They shoplift; they turn off other customers. Why should we carry as product line that invites them in?' We offered Ali for personal appearances, and only one big retailer—a store in Washington, D.C., called Cavalier—wanted him. Nobody in New York wanted him; nobody in Chicago wanted him; nobody in Los Angeles wanted him. And below the Mason-Dixon Line, forget it. And at that time, which was 1980, let's face it, no black athlete had been successful in selling his name. Michael Jordan does it now, Magic Johnson does it now, but it wasn't really happening then."

The man most responsible for Ali's financial affairs over the past quarter-century has been Herbert Muhammad. As Ali's manager, advisor, and friend, he negotiated fight contracts, business ventures, and commercial endorsements. Very little went on without Herbert's knowledge, and people are divided as to how well he did his job.

Ali clearly reveres his mentor. To this day, he says, "I know there are people who don't like Herbert, but I love and respect him. Make sure the world knows, I love and respect Herbert Muhammad." But the relationship is more complicated than that. "Ali," Wilfred Sheed observed, "has always been managed by someone else, and perhaps he always will be. There is a dependent strain beneath the self-assertion, an insatiable need for daddies."[4]

Herbert Muhammad plugged into that need. And over the years, his influence over Ali has been enormous, as he himself acknowledges.

HERBERT MUHAMMAD: "When I started to manage Ali, my father told me, 'Make sure Ali gets his just dues. Make sure nobody robs him or takes advantage of him. Get the most money you can for his services. Don't let anybody buy him cheap, where he goes in the ring and risks his life for nothing.' So those were my guiding principles. I don't care about glorification for myself. All I was interested in was the best deal for Ali. I always tried to stay out of the spotlight. One person in the spotlight was enough, and that was Ali. You never saw pictures of me in the ring after a fight holding up Ali's hand, or pictures of me signing contracts or standing behind Ali when he signed to fight. To this day, I'm happy in the background.

"But to understand my relationship with Ali, you got to understand, the strongest motivation in Ali's life is his love for my father. The spiritual strength Ali gets from me comes from his love and respect for my father, and from the fact that I have great knowledge of our religion. When we first met, and we were much younger then, I told Ali, 'I don't think we were put together just because you're a fighter. I think we have a much bigger mission together.' And that's been proven to be right. In our religion, once Allah puts two people together, no one but Allah can take them apart. I believe Allah put Ali and me together. My father might have been the inspiration for the relationship, but Allah is the force that keeps Ali and me together. For twenty-six years, I've been teaching Ali about the religion. His father didn't teach him; his mother didn't teach him. He wasn't trained by the Fruit of Islam. My father put that job on me, and asked me to show him the way. And then my father told Ali, 'When I'm not here, ask Herbert what you'd ask me, and Herbert will say to you what I would say.' "

Still, Herbert Muhammad has his detractors. "Did you ever see that movie, *Return of the Jedi?*" asks Belinda Ali. "You know that character, Jabba the Hut? That's what I think of Herbert. He was a great manipulator. Sometimes he'd tell Ali good things and do things that on the surface seemed right, but then he'd mix it with something devious. That's what I have to say. I won't bite my tongue; I'll say it."

"It makes me angry, the way people exploited Ali," adds Howard Bingham. "But who let it happen? Herbert Muhammad. Now a lot of it was Ali's fault, not Herbert's. But if Herbert had told Ali to stop what was going on, I think it would have stopped; at least some of it would. But Herbert had his own things going, and I don't know how much he really cared about Ali."

JEREMIAH SHABAZZ: "Herbert is smart when it comes to the religion. We don't always see eye-to-eye about it, but with the religion he's very smart. But business is another matter. That's one place where Herbert leaves a lot to be desired. I don't think it was maliciousness on Herbert's part. I think it was ignorance, but Ali still suffered.

"You know, there's something about people like Herbert who didn't have a chance to complete their schooling. Sometimes they have an inferiority complex, and they try to hide it by appearing superior and refusing to admit what they don't know. Ali had the opportunity to be the richest black man in America, but Herbert didn't steer him right, and he wouldn't let anybody else steer him either. He completely messed up Ali's potential. Someone convinced him that rather than put Ali in the hands of experts who could really make money, they should sell him piecemeal. So they sold his ties to one man, his shirts to another, his shoes to a third; and pretty soon there were deals in so many places that no one could keep up with them. Herbert allowed a deal with some people in England for exercise equipment with Ali's name on it. They sold it around the world for ten or fifteen years, and did millions of dollars worth of business. Do you know what they paid Ali? Fifteen hundred dollars. And then some people in Canada I knew wanted to do an exercise-equipment deal with Ali and give him a hundred thousand dollars. But the people from England came in and said, 'You can't do that. We have rights to him for fifteen hundred.' That was the sort of thing that messed Ali up. He could have had big soda commercials, but some brother in Detroit claimed he was going to get a brewery to convert from making beer to soda pop. He got hold of Ali's name for a couple of thousand dollars and tied him up to the point where, for a long time, Ali couldn't endorse Pepsi or Coke. It went on and on and on and on. And to this day, it hasn't stopped."

HAROLD CONRAD: "It's a myth that Herbert got Ali top dollar from the promoters. Sure, he could barter a little like anyone else. If you offered Herbert fifty, he'd say, 'I want seventy-five,' but that's about all. I first met him when he showed up in Maine for the second Ali-Liston fight. After the fight, we came back to New York for a black tie dinner. Ali didn't own a tuxedo, so I took them to a clothing place called After Six. I knew some people there. And Muhammad Ali, heavyweight champion of the world; they were happy to give him a tuxedo. They gave Herbert one too, for free. And that was when Herbert found out he could get something for free with Ali. It started him off and he never stopped. Before you knew it, he was a silent partner in Ali's promotions. I think he made more money out of some of those fights than Ali. Arum and King both cut him into the promotions, and I doubt he shared that money with Ali.

"That was one way Herbert made an extra buck. Another was, for a promoter to make a fight with Ali, before money for the letter of credit was raised, the promoter had to put up a hundred thousand dollars, or whatever it was, with the promise that the rest would be delivered by a certain date. The promoters always figured, if they had Ali, getting the rest of the money wouldn't be a problem, but that wasn't necessarily the case. I don't know how much of that front money Ali ever saw, but it was paid to Herbert. And with the big fights like the first one with Frazier, Herbert didn't realize what they were worth. When Jerry Perenchio offered $2,500,000 for each fighter, all Herbert had to do was hold out for $2,500,000 against 35 percent. Just add those three words—'against 35 percent'—and Ali would have been seven million dollars richer."

GENE DIBBLE: "I think Herbert was interested first and foremost in Herbert. And I also think Herbert just didn't know much about business. He thought he was a good negotiator, and he wasn't. Instead of getting first-rate lawyers, he listened to a lot of bad advice. And when you put everything he did together, really, you had a terrible mess. Herbert just didn't prepare Ali financially for this time in his life. I used to tell Ali, 'Listen, you have to plan for what comes after boxing. Boxing won't last forever.' Ali would say, 'Yeah, I understand,' but he never planned properly. And there was really nothing I could do because of Herbert's influence and control over Ali."

But Herbert Muhammad also has supporters and admirers. "I think basically Herbert cared about Ali," says Howard Cosell, who dealt with him often. "From what I saw, he relied on people he thought were qualified, and studied to learn what he could about investments." "Another thing about Herbert," adds Mickey Duff, "is every deal I ever made with him, he kept his word. That was true when I promoted Ali's fights, and it was true when someone else promoted. Several times when Ali fought for Don King, King played games with the closed-circuit. Each time, I called Herbert and he did right as far as I was concerned."

As for the allegation that Herbert was a silent partner in Ali's promotions in addition to being Ali's manager, Bob Arum acknowledges, "During the period between the first two Frazier fights, Herbert had a piece of the action. Whatever small amount we made on those fights, yeah, it was understood Herbert was a silent partner. That was also true of the Thriller in Manila [where Arum handled closed-circuit bookings]. I know that for a fact, because King wanted me to sign some papers and I refused. And on the second Ali-Frazier fight, certain payments were made; I paid part of the profits to Herbert. My way of justifying it was, I assumed Herbert told Ali about the arrangement. I don't know that for sure, but the bond between them was so strong and Ali followed Herbert so blindly, that Herbert could have told him, 'This is what you're getting and this is what I'm getting as a silent partner in the promotion,' and Ali would have said, 'Fine.' Also, I'd have to say that, given Ali's susceptibility to every con man in the world, on balance Herbert was very good for him. And don't forget, Ali would never have gotten all the money and recognition he got from boxing if he hadn't internationalized the sport. Part of that was due to circumstances and his being there at the right time in terms of the electronic revolution, but part of it came about as a consequence of Herbert and the Muslim influence."

Teddy Brenner: "The last ten years of Ali's career, he was so much in demand that it was hard to make a bad deal for him. Anybody who was representing him could have known that whatever a fight was projected to gross, Ali was worth at least half. The other fighter was worth what you had to pay him, and the rest of the money would go to staging the fight, distributors, and the promoter's profit. Herbert didn't always follow that formula, but he was a good businessman. He let the promoters make money, so they were always fighting over Ali. And he didn't have just one promoter. He let everyone bid for Ali's services, and then he'd go to the highest bidder.

"One thing Herbert did very well was the way he played Don King. He read King right. He brought the dollars out of King and got bigger paydays from King than anybody else, because he made King prove again and again that he was the best promoter, and the only way King could prove that was by coming up with big dollars. It was hard for King to work the black-white line on Ali when Herbert was there. And of course, there were boundaries King might have been afraid to cross with Ali for fear that someone like Jeremiah Shabazz might have been behind Herbert as an enforcer. So I think Herbert did a pretty good job of bringing in top dollar for Ali's services; at least, as far as the fights were concerned. What happened to the money afterward, I don't know."

FERDIE PACHECO: "I respected Herbert. I think he had Ali's best interests at heart, and I have a certain grudging admiration for him. Some people complained that he didn't earn his job, that he fell into it. What was he, a photographer before he was Ali's manager? But given Herbert's educational background, where he came from, and what he was; to be thrown into that high-speed Ali circus, I think he handled it very well. There were so many deals being offered, mountains of con men, half the world trying to steal. And to sort out the real from the unreal, check everything that was happening on the side, judge who was being adequately taken care of; it would have taken a combination of Solomon and Macchiavelli to handle everything to perfection at the same time. There must have been days when Herbert felt like a one-armed paper-hanger, running all over the place, trying to patch up feuds and close deals. And one of the things that made Herbert's job so difficult was, Ali was such a forgiving guy. It's not like Herbert could fire someone for stealing or poor performance. All the guy had to do was run to Ali, and Ali would take him back again.

"People say, and it's true, that Herbert made a fortune off Ali. And it's also true that Ali might not be as well off financially as he could be today. But the bottom line there is, if Herbert had never taken a penny, if he'd worked for twenty years for free and brought in every dollar possible for Ali, Ali would have given it all away. Now, I hear, things are different. Ali has a wife—a very smart good woman—who helps keep an eye on the money. But when Ali was fighting, Herbert didn't want the entourage; Ali wanted it. Bundini and all the rest of those guys weren't Herbert's men; they belonged to Ali. The people Ali traveled with, the way he lived; that wasn't Herbert's idea, that was Ali's. Ali gave his money away, and he was smart enough to know what he was doing. Money just wasn't Ali's main concern. Otherwise he wouldn't have supported an entourage of half a million people.

"And along with everything else, there were times when Herbert was a very sick man. He had high blood pressure, completely out of control; diabetes; he was badly overweight. So he was fighting on all those fronts too, any one of which could have killed him. I thought he might drop dead at any moment. So whatever Herbert got from Ali in terms of money, glory, anything else—believe me, he earned it. That was a mind-boggling twenty-four-hour-a-day job."

LONNIE ALI: "I can't comment on Herbert's relationship with Muhammad before I met Herbert, but there's something you have to understand about them. Some people see Herbert as a shadowy figure. They're aware of his role as Muhammad's manager, but they're totally unaware of the personal relationship between them. And to judge Herbert's service only in monetary terms is wrong, because money means relatively little to Muhammad. Muhammad's spiritual condition has always been more important to him than his financial condition. And the things Herbert has given Muhammad are more important than dollars. Herbert has been Muhammad's confidant, teacher, and friend. He's given him inspiration, guidance, and religious instruction. Now, what all that has been worth to Muhammad, only Muhammad can tell you. But Muhammad loves Herbert like an older brother. Herbert has contributed enormously to Muhammad's belief in himself. And those are things you and I can't judge, and no one can put a price tag on."

Still, despite all the chaos surrounding Ali's finances, there was one period of hope and promise. In 1978, a man named Robert Abboud had read an article in *The New York Times* detailing Ali's precarious financial condition. Abboud was no ordinary citizen. He was chief executive officer of the First National Bank of Chicago. Ali's plight bothered him enormously, and he was determined to do something about it.

ROBERT ABBOUD: "It started with an article in *The New York Times* [after the first Leon Spinks fight]. Muhammad was living in Chicago. He was such a great citizen, such an asset to the country, and I was afraid he'd have no money left. I'd seen it so many times with athletes, and we at the bank had started to serve some of them. They'd be brought into our trust department by Phil Wrigley of the

Cubs or George Halas of the Bears, and we'd arrange for financial counseling to protect them. So I telephoned Muhammad, explained who I was, and said, 'Champ, I think we should get together and talk. You might find it useful, you might not; but in any event, why don't you come in for lunch?' I think he was curious as to why the chairman of the First National Bank of Chicago would take the time to call, so he said, 'Fine,' and we set a date.

"He came into my office with Howard Bingham, and we had a very frank talk. I thought, in terms of native intelligence, he was one of the smartest people I've ever met. He was very quick, with an agile mind and eyes that seemed to drink in information. But his financial condition was bad; that's no secret. He was way overextended, with commitments to participate in projects which in some instances can only be described as bizarre. There were any number of transactions where he'd ostensibly loaned money to people, but those people didn't seem to have any intention of paying it back. And I told him, I said, 'Champ, let us help you. We don't want anything for ourselves. We just want to preserve your financial assets for you and your family.' He acknowledged that there was a problem, both with the advice he'd been receiving and his inability to say no to people. And he told me, 'I want to do this. This is the first time I've talked to someone who hasn't wanted something from me, and I trust you.'

"So that's how it started. There was a young officer at the bank named Bob Richley. Bob was assigned to work with Muhammad, take inventory of his assets and obligations. Then we arranged for Michael Phenner, who was a partner at Hopkins & Sutter, to do some legal counseling. And we sought out Barry Frank, who worked with Mark McCormack at IMG [International Management Group] to line up commercial endorsements. It was a good group of people, and I was optimistic about the way things were going to work out."

ROBERT RICHLEY: "I met Muhammad the day he came in to see Robert Abboud, and I went to work almost immediately. At first, the biggest problems we had were figuring out what had happened before we got involved and getting control over Muhammad's future business dealings. One of the fundamental agreements we reached with him in the beginning was that he wouldn't sign contracts without running them through Mike Phenner. But it wasn't long before we got word that things weren't being handled that way at all. Muhammad was training for the second Spinks fight at Deer Lake, and people were coming out of the bushes, trying to get him to endorse this and sign that. And the people around him were putting pressure on him, promoting their own deals and pushing their own interests. It seemed like we were losing control of the situation, so I was sent to Deer Lake to tell Muhammad that we weren't going to be involved if he didn't stick to the agreement.

"At Deer Lake, I watched Muhammad work out and had dinner with him at the training table. Then we went back to his cabin, and there must have been thirty people there. He was lying down on this huge sort of chaise longue, and I said, 'I need to talk with you in private.' He told the others, 'Okay, this is a private conversation; everybody leave.' And about half of them left, the rest stayed. So I told him again, and he told them again. And finally we got it down to where there were only two unnecessary people left, and I said, 'Look, this is private; you have to leave too.' They weren't happy with that, but they did leave. Then I pulled a chair over to Ali and said, 'We're telling people they have to go through Mike Phenner, and you're undercutting us by making deals on the side. Our arrangement won't work if you undermine our credibility. If that happens, we won't handle your business anymore.' And I'll never forget, Ali reached up, grabbed me, made that mocking fist he does sometimes, and said, 'Do you know who you're talking to?' I answered, 'Yeah, to the greatest.' Then he laughed, and said, 'You guys don't make a dime off me, do you? All right; you got my word. I won't do it anymore.' "

MICHAEL PHENNER: "Robert Abboud brought Hopkins & Sutter into the picture when he realized that Muhammad wasn't independently represented by counsel. Ali's lawyer was Charles Lomax, who was also Herbert's lawyer, and that was a dangerous potential conflict of interest.

"The first few meetings we had together, Muhammad struck me as larger than life. He had a personality you couldn't dislike. If you had every bias known to mankind and were sitting with Ali, you'd have to like him. But nothing in my legal training prepared me for the years I spent with Muhammad. His legal situation was in total disarray. There were no comprehensive records to indicate what contracts he'd signed or what he'd endorsed. There just wasn't any order to his legal life, and his financial condition was pretty much the same. Obviously, he'd gone through a lot of money, but very little of it had been spent on himself. Mostly, he'd just given it away, or invested it poorly because he couldn't say no.

"The first thing we did was negotiate a revision of the managerial contract between Ali and Herbert. We represented Ali in the negotiations, and Herbert was represented by Charles Lomax. It wasn't so much a question of cutting down the percentage Herbert took, which we did, but rather a matter of who decided which deals Muhammad should be involved with. Then we reviewed every contract we could find, made sure payments were made when they were supposed to be made, and saw to it that the money was invested wisely. In the past, Ali had survived financially because he'd had huge chunks of money coming in from his fights. But we knew that was about to end, and it was important to find alternate sources of income. So the next thing Robert Abboud did was contact Barry Frank."

BARRY FRANK: "Just before the second Spinks fight, I got a call from Robert Abboud. He was upset that Ali was in financial difficulty, and wanted to put together a group of legitimate business people to correct the situation. Mike Phenner would handle Ali's legal affairs, the bank would handle his finances, and IMG would handle his income-producing activity. I had some misgivings about getting involved, because I'd heard about Ali's penchant for saying one thing and doing another when it came to monitoring his business conduct. But I flew out to Chicago; Ali agreed to this triumvirate we were setting up. And one of the very important things we agreed to— maybe the most important as far as I was concerned—was that I'd deal directly with Ali, not with Herbert. To this day, I've never met Herbert Muhammad, although that relationship ran very deep, as all of us later found out.

"In the beginning, when IMG tried to do things for Ali, we were hamstrung by deals he'd previously made. For years, he'd signed everything his people put in front of him. Sometimes they'd had no idea what the contracts they told him to sign meant. And other times, they'd obviously been pursuing their own interests instead of his. So our first problem was, Ali didn't control his own name; he'd sold it eighteen ways to Sunday. Ninety percent of the time when we tried to put something together with a legitimate company, Ali would say, 'There's no problem.' Then we'd start to get the deal done, and some guy would pop out of the woodwork and tell us, 'You can't do that; I have Ali signed for life.' We were very close to a deal with Converse for a Muhammad Ali line of footwear, but it fell apart because he already had a shoe commitment, which to my knowledge never paid him a dollar. We couldn't do what we wanted to with Chrysler, because of some half-baked contract Ali had signed to manufacture a Muhammad Ali automobile. Now, I know a little about the automobile business, because I worked on the Ford account for J. Walter Thompson for six years. It takes hundreds of millions of dollars to launch an automobile, and these people had no idea what they were doing. But even with all the obstacles we faced, we managed to get things going. Mike Phenner did a wonderful job making sense of the contracts Ali had signed and bailing him out of trouble, left, right, and in-between. The people at the bank were terrific. And of course, we had Ali. After he won his title back from Leon Spinks, his popularity was at its peak, and we were ready to go ahead.

"We put together a deal on *Freedom Road* that brought him seven or eight hundred thousand dollars. Robert Walker [president of the American Program Bureau] set up a lecture tour; that was maybe another half-million. We got $250,000 from Idaho potatoes, and $800,000 from a televised 'Farewell to Muhammad Ali' in 1979 after he formally retired. Then we came up with the concept of a ten-city farewell tour of Europe that generated a million dollars for Ali.

"When we were in Denmark on that tour, I went to see the castle at Elsinore because *Hamlet* is my favorite Shakespearean play. When I came back, Ali asked where I'd been. I told him, and he wanted to know what the play was about, so I sat down and told him the story of Hamlet. He was fascinated, like a little kid listening to a fairy tale. When I finished, he asked, 'Man, did Shakespeare make all that up?' I told him, 'Well, there's a little truth to it, but basically he made it up.' And Ali said, 'That's great. Was the ghost real, or did Shakespeare make up that part?' We also went to Europe for a *This Is Your Life* telecast in England that paid him something like $350,000. And all of this happened in less than two years. We built up a trust fund of $2,500,000. Everybody was happy. I remember, Ali had a favorite line he'd use when I called. I'd ask, 'How are you doing, Ali?' And he'd say, 'Aw, just another nigger trying to get bigger.' So one day he asked how I was, and I told him, 'Aw, just another Jew trying to get through.' He loved it; he just about fell on the floor laughing. He acted like it was the funniest thing he'd ever heard."

ROBERT WALKER: "I was happy as hell when I got the call from Barry Frank to represent Ali. Over the years, I've booked some of the biggest speakers in the country: Martin Luther King, Jane Fonda, Ralph Nader, Ronald Reagan. But Ali was as much in demand as any of them.

"We did one major tour; several dozen college campuses. Ali was wonderful. He didn't necessarily tell his audiences what they wanted to hear; he told them what he believed. But in the end, he gave them what they wanted; he gave them the real Muhammad Ali. The only problem we had was, Ali didn't like to fly; he wanted to go by bus. And when you charge fifteen thousand dollars a speech, which is what we were charging, you have to be flexible regarding dates and distance. In other words, you have to fly. So we had this predicament, and finally I convinced Ali that, if we had a jet at our disposal, we could fly when we wanted to and maybe even do two speeches a day. Then I called another one of my clients. At the time, I was representing Ben Abruzzo, Larry Newman, and Maxie Anderson—the three balloonists who'd crossed the Atlantic Ocean in Double Eagle II. Ben and Larry owned a Lear jet. So I called Larry to ask if I could rent the jet. And when Larry heard it was Muhammad Ali going on tour, he said, 'I'll go you one better; I'll fly the thing for you.' So there I was with Muhammad Ali, the greatest name in sports, and Larry Newman, who was a hero in his own right, in the air together. The first time they went up in the plane, Larry figured he'd make Muhammad less frightened and more at ease by bringing him into the cockpit and putting him where the copilot normally sat. Larry said, 'I'll show you how to fly.' He put some headphones on Muhammad. The plane was on automatic pilot, and he showed Muhammad what to do, which is really quite simple. Ali was ecstatic. Now he's reciting poetry while he's flying the plane. 'I sting like a bee / It's really me / Muhammad Ali!' And as Larry tells it, the pilot on a nearby commercial airliner heard him and said, 'Oh, my God. I'm afraid it's really him.' Ali asked, 'What did he say?' And Larry told him, 'Don't worry; he said you're flying beautifully.' "

Meanwhile, as the "triumvirate" did its job, an administrator named Marge Thomas was brought in to handle bookkeeping and other day-to-day financial activity.

MARGE THOMAS: "I had a friend who was working for an employment agency in Chicago. The First National Bank had brought him a list of qualifications they were looking for in an employee, and he told me I was the only person he knew who fit the job. I'd previously been the manager of a nursing home and an administrative supervisor at a Chicago hospital. I'm not an accountant but I know accounting, and can do just about everything necessary for day-to-day administrative work.

"My friend wouldn't tell me what the position was, but he asked if I'd go to First National for an interview. I spent three-and-a-half hours with a bank official named John Clark. After that, they checked up on me pretty thoroughly. I was put through a police check to see if I had a criminal record, which I don't. My past employers were contacted. Then Mr. Clark called back and said his principal would like to meet me. And all this time, they hadn't told me who I'd be working for or what I'd be doing. It was quite mysterious. I asked, 'How do you know I'll even want to work for this person?' And Mr. Clark told me, 'I'm sure you will.'

"By now it was December [1978], close to Christmas, and the only time we could set the appointment for was a Sunday morning. First Mr. Clark said they'd send a car for me, and I told him, 'No, I prefer driving myself. Just tell me where I'm supposed to be, and I'll take myself there.' I mean, this thing had gotten to a point where it was just too much cloak and dagger. I was even thinking about the Mafia; I'd started thinking a whole lot of things. And at any rate, I was going to have my own transportation so I could leave when I wanted. Then he told me the location and I immediately put it together, because anybody who lived in Chicago knew that Muhammad Ali owned this big house on Woodlawn Avenue. I went to the house, but he wasn't there, so I talked with Veronica. We spent a couple of hours together, and she said as far as she was concerned I was hired, but that she wanted to let Muhammad make it official. I said, 'Fine,' and the next morning I got a call to come back again. When I got there, Muhammad had a whole bunch of people around him. He looked up and said, 'Oh, yeah, you're Miss Thomas.' We went upstairs and talked, sitting at the top of the stairs with all these people down in the living room. He said, 'Well, if my wife likes you, you're hired. Make sure you see my wife before you leave.' So I went to see Veronica, and she put two weeks pay in cash in my hand. I asked what it was for, and she told me, 'It's not your fault that we were out of the country and you haven't been able to work these past two weeks. Muhammad wants to pay you for it.'

That's how we met. There's no description for what I was hired to do other than to say, whatever had to be done, I did it. I suppose you could say I was a day-to-day administrative aide and financial manager. I maintained the bank accounts, monitored expenses, wrote and signed checks. The checks led to problems, because people would come to me for checks and get upset when I refused to write them without a direct authorization from Muhammad or Veronica. Another part of my job was to cut down on the expenses I was monitoring, but that was difficult because Muhammad does not like people telling him what to do with his money. I can't tell you how many times he instructed me to give money to someone he'd never seen before in his life. One person was a derelict he picked up off the street, drunk, and brought into the house. That day, when I came to work, he told me, 'Give this man five thousand dollars.' I said, 'What are you talking about, Muhammad?' And he said, 'Well, this man hasn't had a bath, he needs clothes, he needs someplace to stay.' I said, 'Muhammad, don't you know that if you give this man five thousand dollars, he'll get rolled for it or drink it away? The money will just go down the drain.' And then he gave me the business, 'Well, who's the boss, me or you? Whose money is it?' I said, 'Muhammad, this makes no sense. If you want to take him out and buy him some clothes, get him a hotel room so he can take a bath and has a place to stay, and give him a few dollars for a decent meal, that's fine. But to hand somebody like this five thousand dollars, it's just ridiculous.' With that particular man, I had about five hundred dollars in my purse. Muhammad took the money, bought him some clothes, got him a hotel room, and gave him whatever amount was left.

"Our first big fight came about because I wouldn't reconcile my own bank accounts. I wanted a tax accountant, and Muhammad said he didn't see the need for one. He told me, 'You write the checks; you know what's in the bank.' And I said, 'That's neither here nor there. One person shouldn't write checks, sign them, and reconcile the accounts. You're setting yourself up so I could take anything I wanted and cover it any way I want.' He told me he knew I wouldn't steal from him, and I said, 'That's been the problem your entire life. You're right; I won't steal from you, but other people have. You need someone besides me to reconcile the accounts. You've got to learn to do things right.' So finally he gave in and let Michael Phenner hire a tax accountant, but he was mad. He told me—and I guess it was in jest—he told me I was lucky he liked me, because otherwise he'd fire me.

"And there were other things I tried to do for Muhammad. I brought health insurance, which he'd never had before, into his organization. Before that, if someone working for him got sick, Muhammad would pay the medical bills out of his own pocket. I tried to cut down on the exploitation around him, because what I saw was sickening to me. And there were some people around Muhammad who I just refused to deal with. In fact, some of his friends tried to have me fired, but Muhammad never had any problem with my work or me. He told me once, he said, 'You know, Marge, I should have had you around twenty years ago.' And I said, 'No you shouldn't, Muhammad. Because if you had, by now we'd probably both be dead.' "

Ali and Veronica moved to Los Angeles in early 1979, but the triumvirate continued to function. Marge Thomas moved to California and got a home nearby. IMG kept putting together deals that maximized Ali's income. Hopkins & Sutter tied up loose legal ends, and the First National Bank of Chicago maintained Ali's investment portfolio. "I really thought we were on our way," Robert Abboud remembers. "Everything was in place, and I said to myself, 'My God, this is going to be one of those stories with a happy ending. Muhammad and his family will be financially secure for life.' But then, for whatever reason, Ali reversed course, and everything started to fall apart."

BARRY FRANK: "Even when things were going well, there'd been a lot of headaches and hassles. I remember, on the farewell tour of Europe, we'd had something like eight seats on the Concorde. And that was a pretty expensive ticket, maybe fifteen hundred dollars each way. We were at the counter checking in, and here comes Bundini, who wasn't on the list. He's got two huge steamer trunks with him. And he's literally crying, tears streaming down his face, begging Ali to take him along. So Ali tells me to get him a ticket. I said, 'Ali, he isn't on the tour and we're not paying for it.' And Ali said, 'It's okay; I'll pay for it.' The trunks were like five hundred dollars extra weight. I wondered what was in them, and it turned out that Bundini had a whole supply of Ali T-shirts, caps, and all that crap. Every place we went, he'd set up shop and sell mementos. And of course, he was going into competition with the same people who'd bought the tour and were paying Ali a million dollars. We'd go into a city like Copenhagen. The promoter would have the rights to sell this stuff, and there's Bundini competing with the promoter. I told Ali, 'You can't do this, we've got contracts.' Ali would say, 'Oh, he don't hurt nobody.' And of course Bundini was a pain in the ass. Everywhere we went, he was always late. We had a private jet, and he'd always hold up the jet. He had these huge trunks that we had to get people to schlepp. It drove me crazy, because we had the whole tour mapped out. We had hotel rooms booked. We had a private plane with the right number of seats on it. And here's Bundini, who served no useful purpose, who was along only to rip off some money, screwing everything up. It didn't bother Ali at all, but it bothered the hell out of me.

"Then, I guess it was about a year after we started, I began to get bad vibrations. There was a guy from Wisconsin, I can't remember his name, who came up with a deal where Ali would supposedly make a lot of money. But there was no money up front, no guarantees, and no controls. I flew out to Los Angeles and went through the usual drill with Ali, which was sitting at his house waiting for him to get done with twenty other people who were sitting there waiting to talk with him, and then trying to have a business discussion while eight other people were sitting around listening. And my saying, 'Ali, I don't want to discuss this in front of anybody else,' and his saying, 'These are my friends, you can talk.' And my saying, 'Ali, this is nobody's business but yours and mine.' And Ali just not being prepared to do it that way.

"Anyway, I told him not to do this deal, and he went ahead and did it anyway. And I could sense that what was happening was, with the exception of Howard Bingham, the many hangers-on had become very jealous and upset with our role. They were upset because they were no longer getting a cut of the action from all the fly-by-night deals they'd brought around before. For the first time, Ali was starting to make real money outside the ring, and that was threatening, because if he really never fought again, what would they do for jobs? Most of them were just out for themselves, and the situation deteriorated from that point on.

"I'd bring Ali a deal, and he'd say, 'That's no good.' I'd tell him, 'Ali, I think it's pretty good. You're leaving two hundred thousand dollars on the table.' And he'd say, 'Well, that's nothing. I don't want to do it.' Then he moved toward a relationship with Qaddafi. Some of the people around him put it in his head that he was Muslim and Qaddafi was Muslim, and he could get rich by tapping into Libyan oil money the way Jimmy Carter's brother tried to do. And the Qaddafi relationship was a terrible negative; a lot of people were turned off by that. Ali insisted on dealing with Qaddafi, and I told him, 'Look, who you want to be friends with is your business, but a lot of people think this isn't such a hot dude.'

"But the final straw was when he fought Larry Holmes. When he announced he was making a comeback to fight Holmes, I said, 'Ali, you've done two things here. First, you've made liars out of all of us, because we had a farewell tour. You swore it was your farewell tour, and you ain't farewell at all. And second, I don't want to be at your funeral, because you're going to get the shit kicked out of you. It's a huge mistake; it will be bad for your image; and you're going to get hurt.' Then he told me Herbert Muhammad had brought him the fight and he was going to do it. And I said, 'Well, if you're back with Herbert, that's fine. You certainly have that right, but IMG is going to take a walk.'

"So that in a nutshell is what happened. I loved Ali and still do. I think he's a wonderful guy. On those occasions when I got him alone, he was terrific; very bright, rational, much wiser than one might think. But obviously he was torn between doing what was right for his family and himself and doing what the hangers-on wanted for their own selfish interests. Sitting here, thinking about it now, makes me mad and sad. Ali was such a wonderful guy. In some respects, he was very sophisticated; but in others, he was so foolish and childlike and easily led. Even with all his previous mismanagement, if he'd stayed with us and hadn't fought Holmes or Trevor Berbick, he'd easily be making two million dollars a year, probably more, every year for the rest of his life. There'd be long-term relationships with solid companies in place. He wouldn't even have to work for the money, other than occasional goodwill appearances. And maybe the saddest thing of all now is, Ali has been hustled and misused and exploited by so many people that his endorsement doesn't mean much anymore. He's given away the credibility that attached to his name. It's ironic, really. Muhammad Ali, who stood for principle throughout his life, and I would think continues to do so, has lost his credibility because he didn't realize the value of his name."

IMG was the first component of Ali's financial triumvirate to leave the fold. The First National Bank of Chicago followed. "Things started to come unglued when he fought Holmes," Robert Abboud recalls. "After that, Muhammad began making unwise financial decisions against our advice, and there was no way we could keep the situation under control. I guess the whole system broke down."

"It was frustrating," Robert Richley remembers, "because we wanted to do nothing but good and add nothing but value. And Muhammad kept going off, making these horrendous deals on the side, forcing us to spend time untangling rather than building."

Finally, Hopkins & Sutter withdrew as well.

MICHAEL PHENNER: "When Ali moved from Chicago to Los Angeles, it became harder and harder for us to know what was going on and maintain any semblance of control. I was increasingly worried about whether the situation was being managed correctly, and two things, I guess, led to our withdrawal. The first was, we could advise Ali, but we couldn't tell him what to do. You can give people advice till it's coming out of their ears, but legally, unless you have a custodian appointed, you can't stop someone from signing a contract. And that was a continuous problem for us. Sometimes Ali would follow our advice, and other times he'd sign horrendous contracts because he didn't know better or was trying to help someone else out. Also, I was troubled by Ali's association with a lawyer from Virginia named Richard Hirschfeld. At one point, Hirschfeld tried to borrow money on behalf of Ali against the trust fund, which he couldn't do, and he also involved Ali in several other things I didn't approve of. So finally, I called Muhammad and said, 'That's it. We can't represent you while someone else represents you and you continue to ignore our best advice. I'm sorry, but we have to resign.'

"I hated to say that. I felt badly about it, and worse about the fact that we hadn't done as much good for him as I would have liked. Our goal was to get something in place that would leave Muhammad financially secure for life, and we weren't able to achieve that. And I told Muhammad at the time we resigned, I said, 'I have wonderful love and admiration for you. I think you're fantastic, but you don't seem to want us to help. You act like you want to prove that you have a constitutional right to go broke.' "

The leaders of the triumvirate have gone on with their lives and continue to excel in business. Robert Abboud is chairman of the board of the First City Bancorporation of Texas. Robert Richley is president of the same bank, and works with Aboud on a daily basis. Barry Frank is senior group vice-president at IMG, which currently manages twelve of the top twenty-five commercial-earning athletes in the world. Michael Phenner is the managing partner at Hopkins & Sutter in Chicago.

As for Ali, he's comfortable financially but not as well-off as he might be. His wife, Lonnie, has an MBA from UCLA and manages their finances as well as possible. But Ali on occasion is still exploited and mixes bad deals with the good.

"I worry about the exploitation," says Ramsey Clark, who befriended Ali and has maintained contact with him over the years. "I've worried about his relationship with Herbert, and many of the financial decisions Muhammad has made. But it's extremely difficult to be as rich and famous and powerful as Muhammad Ali, and come from his background, and manage money efficiently and effectively for the good deeds he sought to achieve. The risk of exploitation is very high. It's like colonialism in a way, with this very rich human resource, like uranium or gold; and the colonialists were out to get as much of him as they possibly could for themselves. So the money was dissipated, but I can't criticize Ali for that. We are who we are; he wasn't a financial analyst. And in terms of the goals he sought to achieve, his desire to use his money for good; what's fifty million dollars? What's a hundred million dollars? That's an insignificant fraction of one minor weapons system. So suppose Ali had gotten his money all together, organized it, spent only 17 percent on administrative costs, and used the rest to provide the best nutrition you could find for people in need. Sure, that would have been important, but it wouldn't have changed the world."

15

The Beating

As Ali's retirement extended into a second year, he was less fit than ever to return to boxing. His weight ballooned to 255 pounds, and his reflexes continued to deteriorate. He was out of shape and thirty-eight years old. But too many people had a vested interest in his fighting again for him to remain out of boxing.

The sequence of events that culminated in Ali's return to the ring began in early 1980. For years, he'd traveled around the world, being honored by diplomats and heads of state. In Moscow in 1978, he'd met with Soviet leader Leonid Brezhnev, and afterward told reporters, "Brezhnev didn't talk about small things such as fights. He talked about peace and love for humanity. He told me he'd like me to do all I can to better relations between our countries, and he made me an unofficial ambassador for peace to the United States, so don't be surprised if you see me in the White House soon. It felt good to be a little black boy from Louisville, Kentucky, who couldn't hardly meet the Mayor of that place a few years ago. Now I'm sitting in Russia, talking to the most powerful man in the world."[1]

Ali took his diplomatic skills seriously, on occasion referring to himself as "the black Henry Kissinger." And he wasn't alone in that regard. Jimmy Carter acknowledges that, soon after the Iranian takeover of the United States embassy in Tehran, "We very seriously contemplated having Ali serve as an intermediary, perhaps in conjunction with Andy Young [United States ambassador to the United Nations] to find an avenue of communication to release the hostages. But the Ayatollah was so totally against contact with any American that we decided it wasn't feasible."

But then another diplomatic opportunity arose. The Soviet Union invaded Afghanistan, and the Carter administration sought to orchestrate a boycott of the 1980 Moscow Olympics.

JIMMY CARTER: "When the Soviets invaded Afghanistan in December of 1979, there was aroused throughout the world a tremendous abhorrence of that act. The Congress voted almost unanimously not to send an Olympic team to Moscow. And the United States Olympic Committee, which is independent of any influence by the president, voted two to one not to send a team. I was also against sending a team to Moscow while they were invading Afghanistan, but many of the Third World countries didn't understand the significance of rewarding Moscow, in effect, while they were an aggressor nation. I was always interested in having the African nations know that our country is comprised of people who have a deep interest in them. I appointed Andy Young to be my representative to the United Nations. And another of the things I did in that regard was ask the most famous person in our country to represent me and the government of the United States in Africa. There was a specific interest on my part in having Muhammad Ali explain our country's position on the Olympic boycott, and also in his pointing out what our nation is, what its basic policies are, our commitment to freedom and human rights, and the fact that we have black Americans who have been successful with a diversity of religious commitments."

Ali was in India on a twelve-day tour to raise money for various Indian charities when he received President Carter's request to go to Africa. Howard Bingham picks up the story.

HOWARD BINGHAM: "Ali was in New Delhi when the State Department called and explained what it wanted, and he agreed to fly right to Africa. But then the Russians found out what was happening, and around midnight the Russian ambassador came to our hotel. We were scheduled to leave the next morning. And the ambassador spent a lot of time, more than an hour, telling Ali why he shouldn't go. He looked Ali right in the eye, and said the only reason the Russians were in Afghanistan was because the people of Afghanistan had asked them to come in. Ali believed him; he almost didn't go.

But finally, he decided in favor of going, and we left on a State Department plane in the morning. There was him and me and some State Department people on the plane. We had a compartment all to ourselves and could call home and eat anything we wanted. At first, Ali was worried because he thought the Russians might shoot us down, but one of the State Department guys said, 'Don't worry; this plane is being watched.' Then we landed in Tanzania, and there was a problem because, you see, Ali wasn't really involved in politics. He didn't know what was what and who was who in Africa, and when we got there, he caught hell."

Ali's trip was later described by *Time* magazine as "the most bizarre diplomatic mission in recent U.S. history."[2] At best, it was ill-conceived; at worst, a diplomatic disaster. The Islamic world might have been receptive to a Muhammad Ali presidential mission, but black Africa clearly wasn't.

Upon his arrival on Tanzania on February 2, 1980, Ali was granted an audience, not with President Julius Nyerere, but with the country's minister for youth and culture, thereby denominating his visit as a sports event. Other Tanzanian officials expressed anger at what they considered a racial insult, asking, "Would the United States send Chris Evert to negotiate with London?"[3] Moreover, Ali was unable to explain to his hosts why African nations should boycott the Moscow Olympics when, four years earlier, the United States had refused to join twenty-nine African countries in boycotting the Montreal Olympics over South Africa's place in the sporting world. Nor was he aware that the Soviet Union was backing popular revolutionary movements on the continent. "They didn't tell me about that in America," Ali acknowledged at an impromptu press conference. "Maybe I'm being used to do something that ain't right. You're making me look at things different. If I find out I'm wrong, I'm going back to America and cancel the whole trip." At that point, a State Department official tried to cut short the questioning, but Ali continued. "I'm not a traitor to black people. If you can show me something I don't know, I want to be helped. You all have given me some questions which are good and are making me look at this thing different."[4]

Despite his doubts, Ali journeyed next to Kenya—a country that had already voiced support for the Olympic boycott. There, he complained that Carter had put him "on the spot" and sent him "around the world to take the whupping over American policies," and announced that if he'd known "the whole history of America and South

Africa," he probably would have declined to tour Africa at the president's request. However, he reaffirmed his belief that "It's wrong for anybody to go to Moscow for the Olympics, knowing what the Russians are doing in Afghanistan." In Nairobi, Ali also found a new rationale for his trip, saying his real aim was to avert nuclear war between the United States and the Soviet Union. "If these two white men start fighting," he declared, "all us little black folks are going to be caught in the middle."[5] Then it was on to Nigeria, where the minister of youth and sports reaffirmed his country's commitment to participate in Moscow. Stopovers in Liberia and Senegal concluded the tour.

HOWARD BINGHAM: "When the trip was over, we went to the White House. Ali told the president about what had happened, which I guess Carter knew already, and we were there for about half an hour. The most interesting part was, toward the end, they started talking about what was happening in Iran. Ali asked what we'd do if the Iranians harmed any of the hostages. And all Carter said was, 'If they do that, we'll pop 'em.' He didn't say what he meant by 'pop 'em,' but he looked serious when he said it. And you could tell, Ali was disappointed at how the African trip worked out. I don't think he felt misused by Carter, but he was down at the way the Africans received him. I guess he thought he was a diplomat, and it kind of hurt when he found out he wasn't."

Talk of an Ali comeback began as soon as he returned from Africa. The motivations were many. Money was a factor, since a comeback bout could be expected to pay between five and ten million dollars. Also, the embarrassment of Ali's mission had made it clear that he was a less effective diplomat than performer. "Ali needed a platform to do his thing," Jim Brown explains. "He was a spirit who had an impact on people all over the world. But he wasn't a nuts-and-bolts person, a pragmatist who could leave boxing and run an organization that would impact upon society. I got out of football in my prime, and formed an organization [the Black Economic Union] with eight offices across the country. I had Harvard MBAs working for me, and was interfacing with people like Tom Bradley and the NAACP. But Ali didn't have the background and intellectual understanding to do what I did. He had all these dreams for helping people, but to be effective, he had to be in the spotlight."

The spotlight as an end in itself was also a consideration. "Ali was a junkie," says Drew Brown, Jr. "He needed to see his name in lights; he had to hear the crowd. There's only one sport in the world where they say, 'And in this corner, the undisputed heavyweight champion of the world, Muhammad Ali.' That's addictive; everything always revolving around you, everyone telling you you're the greatest. Ali never messed with drugs, but he was a junkie for fame."

"I don't know if he came back because he was pushed into it or because so many people told him not to," says Marge Thomas. "You know, Muhammad is a funny person. You can use reverse psychology on him quite well. If you don't want him to do something, just say he has to do it and he'll back up like a mule. But I asked him once why he fought Larry Holmes, and he told me, 'Marge, I don't care how much money you have; I don't care who your friends are. There's nothing like the sound of the crowd when you come down that aisle and they're yelling, "Ali, Ali!" You'd give your life to hear it.' I said, 'Not me, Muhammad. I wouldn't let anybody hit me for nothing.' But you have to understand what he was saying. Think about a man who's had that kind of adulation from the time he was twelve years old; the world at his feet, little old ladies walking up to him at airports, pleading, 'Can I touch you, Mr. Ali? Please, let me touch you.' "

But the simplest explanation might be the most honest. "Muhammad fought again because he wanted to," says Angelo Dundee. "I've heard all sorts of reasons. He wanted the money; there was this and that. Some people say he fought as long as he did because he felt cheated by the years he wasn't allowed to fight. But I'll tell you something. Muhammad was never happy outside the ring. He loved boxing. The gym, the competition. It was in his blood, and win or lose, he loved it to the end."

On March 5, 1980, Bob Arum announced that Ali had agreed to fight World Boxing Association heavyweight champion John Tate in a bout scheduled for late June. That afternoon, Ali returned to the gym, but three days later his plans were put on hold. Sparring with Jeff Sims, Ali spat out his mouthpiece to taunt his foe and got punched in the mouth. The blow caused an inch-long gash that extended through the muscle tissue in his upper lip. Ten stitches, including four internally, were needed to close the wound.

The cut was another warning that Ali didn't belong in the ring. Then, on March 31, Tate was knocked out by Mike Weaver, and the search for an opponent began anew. Weaver, Scott LeDoux, Duane Bobick, and Bernardo Mercado were considered but found wanting. Meanwhile, for the first time, Ali's mother publicly voiced the view that her son shouldn't return to boxing. "I don't want to see him fighting anymore," Odessa Clay told a reporter. "I talk to him on the phone two or three times a week, and I've told him every time. He says he knows what he's doing. He looks fine to me. I just don't want him to fight anymore."[6]

But retirement was no longer an option, and inevitably, attention centered on Larry Holmes. Holmes was no stranger to Ali. He'd been at Deer Lake as a sparring partner from 1973 to 1975, and going back further, had trained with Joe Frazier before Ali-Frazier I. "Joe took his anger at Ali out on me," Holmes recalls. "He broke one of my ribs, and hurt me in places I didn't know I had." But more important, despite the proliferation of sanctioning bodies and world titles, Holmes was considered the true heavyweight champion. After decisioning Ken Norton in June 1978, he'd knocked out seven consecutive opponents, including WBA champ Mike Weaver in twelve rounds.

GENE KILROY: "Larry and Ali went back a long way. Larry was a nice kid. I'd seen him fight a couple of times in the amateurs and always liked him. Then he lost to Duane Bobick in the [1972] Olympic trials. And after that, he came to Deer Lake to ask if he could meet Ali. I introduced them. Ali said, 'Let me see your jab.' Larry put it out. And we weren't doing anything that day; the gym at Deer Lake wasn't ready yet. So I drove them down to the Police Athletic League in Reading, and they sparred together. Afterward, Ali said, 'You're good, kid.' He always praised everybody he boxed with. And Holmes told him he wanted to be his sparring partner. I think he was working in a car-wash or something. Ali said, 'Nah, it's not the style I like to spar with.' But I said, 'Come on, he's a nice kid.' So Ali hired him and bought him some decent boxing equipment, because all Larry had was junk that was falling apart. And the other thing I remember about that day was, Ali closed Larry's eye. I said, 'Come here, kid; I'll put some ice on it.' And Larry told me, 'No way. I want to go back to Easton and show everybody the black eye I got from Muhammad Ali.'

"Larry was with us for a couple of years after that. We took him to Zaire, and at the airport going over, we had three sparring partners—Larry, Roy Williams, and Boss Man Jones. Don King called Larry over and told him to carry his bags. Larry started to pick them up, and I said, 'Wait a minute! You're not a porter. Let him carry his own bags.' Then in Zaire, he got homesick and came back to the States, so we only had two sparring partners.

"Also, I remember one time when Larry was still Ali's sparring partner, he gave somebody an interview and said, 'Ali's the champ, but I'm the better fighter.' Well, Ali was always easy on his sparring partners, but Bundini told him about that in the dressing room, and I put my two cents in too. So that day, when Ali went out to spar with Holmes, first round, he moved on him. Pop-pop-pop-pop, backed Holmes into a corner and told him, 'Larry, my legs are gone.' And Holmes said, 'No, they're not, champ.' Second round, Ali beat on him again, and at the end, shouted across the ring, 'I'm old!' And Holmes said, 'No, champ; no, you're not.' Third round, he beat the shit out of Larry, went back to his corner, and yelled, 'Larry, you're the better fighter. I just got the title.' Holmes was crying, 'No, champ; that's a lie.' Bundini and I laughed our heads off, although I don't think Larry thought it was funny."

Richie Giachetti, who managed and trained Holmes through most of his career, recalls his tenure with Ali.

RICHIE GIACHETTI: "They started sparring together in 1973. I was there to coach Larry. His job was to get Ali in shape, but I made sure that Larry got better too. As time went by, he went from being outclassed to holding his own to finally fighting even with Ali. His best sessions were when only the camp was there. When there was a crowd, Larry backed off. He had a job to do, and part of that job was to not outshine Ali. Then, after the Wepner fight, I figured it was time to quit. Larry wasn't learning anything anymore, and I didn't want him to fall into the syndrome of being just a sparring partner. Larry wanted to stay. He liked Ali. At the time, Ali was paying tremendous money and Ali fought all the time, so Larry was working a full year. Plus when Ali fought, Larry was on the under-card, so he got purses from that too. It was a good living; but I figured, if Larry kept getting better, Ali would let him go anyway, and if they saw how good he was there was no way they'd give him a title shot. Also, I wanted Larry to get hungry again, because I thought he was becoming complacent as a fighter. So we left, but we left on good terms. I told Ali, 'There's nothing more Larry can learn here. It's time he went out on his own.' And I'll tell you the truth; when the time came, Larry didn't want to fight Ali. He knew Ali had nothing left; he knew it would be a horror. But once the offer was on the table, there was no way to turn it down. If Larry had refused to fight Ali, the public would never have respected him as champion."

MICHAEL PHENNER: "We were still representing Ali when he told us he was going to fight Holmes. I didn't like it; I thought it was a mistake. But he said, 'Mike, one more fight and I can be set for life. Where else can I make that kind of money in an hour?' That was part of it; Ali wanted the money. And I also think he wanted to shake up the world. Everyone was saying he couldn't do it. And you know Ali. He was a sort of contrary spirit. I think he wanted to show people he could win, that he could beat Larry Holmes.

"The key contract negotiations took place at Don King's home—over Mother's Day weekend, as I recall. Ali, Herbert, and King were there. So were Holmes, Richie Giachetti, and King's lawyer. We spent most of the weekend putting the contract together on a rinky-dink typewriter. Ali was to get $8 million, Holmes something like $2.3 million. And it was clear to me that Holmes revered Ali. He kept telling everyone who was there that Ali shouldn't fight again. He just didn't want to fight Ali, but there was no way he could turn the fight down."

After contracts for the bout were signed, there was the usual early prefight hoopla. Ali named Holmes "the Peanut" ("because his head is shaped like a peanut, and I'm going to shell him and send him to Plains, Georgia"). At the Felt Forum in New York, he sparred with one hand behind his back ("because I'm so great, I haven't decided yet if I'm gonna fight Holmes with one hand or two"). And he grew a mustache ("because I'm the new Dark Gable"), although he soon shaved it off.

Meanwhile, training in earnest began at Deer Lake with a new set of sparring partners. One of them—Tim Witherspoon, who later reigned briefly as heavyweight champion—recalls his days with Ali.

TIM WITHERSPOON: "I was just starting out; twenty-two years old. And I was happy to be there. I mean, this was Muhammad Ali, and it was an experience to be around. People were always bugging him about different things. It seemed like everybody always wanted something. I used to hang low, out of the way. All I wanted was to give him good work, and he always treated me right.

"It was a happy camp. Later on, I trained at Don King's camp in Ohio, and that was horrible. Everybody who was in Ali's camp loved him. Just about everybody who was in Don King's camp hated Don's guts. Hell, at Don's camp, lots of times there wasn't even enough to eat. We had to buy our own food. And I remember, one time at Don's, I asked for beef bacon because I didn't eat pork, and Don made a big laugh out of it. He said, 'I know where you learned that; from Ali. Well, Ali's gonna be eating pork bacon before he's done.'

"Ali was chubby when he started training, maybe 250 pounds; but outside of that, he was in pretty good shape. He did a lot of work on the up-and-down bag; you know, the bag that goes from the ceiling to the floor with elastic at both ends. He worked on that and the speed-bag for timing. He shadow-boxed and hit the heavy-bag. He had a style of hitting the heavy-bag where, instead of asking someone to hold it, he'd let it swing and move around. Sparring, the first few days he told me to work the body, so that's what I did. Then he got kind of sore and asked me to stay off the body for a day or two, and I concentrated on the head. But we had regular sparring sessions. He hit me, and I hit him back. I got in my share of shots to the head, but not too many. They never told me to stay off the head."

Still, regardless of whether the people in Ali's camp were concerned about his health, a growing number of others were worried. "Ali should not try to come back," Ferdie Pacheco said publicly. "At his age, with the wear and tear he's had as a fighter, there's no way for him to escape the attrition his body has undergone. All the organs that have been abused will have to work harder. His heart, lungs, kidneys, liver. Even Muhammad Ali is human and subject to the laws of nature."[7]

As summer began, the controversy over Ali's health escalated. Various news organizations began to question the propriety of the Nevada State Athletic Commission licensing an Ali-Holmes bout. Ali was speaking more softly and slowly than in the past, and his reflexes were continuing to deteriorate. Thus, on July 23, 1980, as a precondition to the commission's granting a license, Ali checked into the Mayo Clinic in Rochester, Minnesota, for a two-day renal and neurological examination. Ken Johannsen, a spokesman for the clinic, recalls Ali's visit.*

KEN JOHANNSEN: "He was a boxer; there was a certain amount of controversy over his medical condition; and he had to resolve some of those issues before he could fight again. That's why he came

---

*In 1989, Muhammad Ali sent letters to all medical personnel interviewed for this book, asking that they release his medical records and speak freely to Thomas Hauser. There has been no breach of medical confidence in this or the following chapters.

to the Mayo Clinic. He needed the examination in order to get a license for a fight.

"The doctors who examined him didn't have any specific experience with professional fighters as such. They examined Mr. Ali as they would any other patient, and provided him with a report of their findings. I don't think we sent anything specifically to the Nevada commission, because we deal with all of our patients as private individuals. And it goes without saying that, if Mr. Ali had come to the clinic and told us the specific findings he wanted in the report, we wouldn't have complied without a scientific basis for it. That's just not the way we operate."

The Mayo Clinic's evaluation of Ali was forwarded to the Nevada State Athletic Commission, and on the basis of it, Ali was granted a license to fight. That fact alone is scandalous. First, as noted by Ferdie Pacheco, "Just because a man can pass a physical examination doesn't mean he should be fighting in a prize ring. That shouldn't be a hard concept to grasp. In fact, most trainers can tell you better than any neurologist in the world when a fighter is shot. You watch your fighter's career from the time he's a young man; you watch him develop into a champion; you watch him get great; then all of a sudden he doesn't have it anymore. Give him a neurological examination at that point and you'll find nothing wrong. Sugar Ray Robinson could pass every exam in the world at age forty-four, but he wasn't Sugar Ray Robinson anymore. It doesn't change, whether it's Wilfred Benitez and Edwin Rosario, who were shot by the time they reached their mid-twenties; Thomas Hearns, who's shot at thirty; Ali, Joe Louis. Anybody in the gym can see it before the doctors can, because the doctors, good doctors, are judging these fighters by the standards of ordinary people and the demands of ordinary jobs, and you can't do that because these are professional fighters."

But far more telling than Ferdie Pacheco's observation is the content of the Mayo Clinic evaluation that was forwarded to the Nevada State Athletic Commission. There were two reports: one by Dr. John Mitchell of the Department of Nephrology and Internal Medicine, the other by Dr. Frank Howard of the Department of Neurology. Dr. Mitchell was charged primarily with evaluating Ali's kidneys, and his report declared, "Preliminary examinations would indicate that the patient is in excellent general medical health with no evidence of renal impairment or chronic or acute medical illness."

Well and good. But Dr. Howard's report was another matter. In whole, it read:

I saw Muhammad Ali for a neurological evaluation on 7-23-80. He was concerned about some comments that he might have brain damage, because following a filmed TV interview in London, it was commented that he staggered and that his speech was slurred. The patient attributes this to excessive fatigue from an all-night flight to London, and claims that he has always had some mild slurring of his speech for the past ten to twelve years. He stated that he was tired on the day of the examination here and that he had gotten little sleep. He denied any problems in coordination as far as jogging, sparring, or skipping rope. He also says that his memory is excellent and that he can deliver five forty-five-minute lectures without notes.

He has never been knocked out, even though he had his jaw broken in a fight. He has been dazed on two occasions—once in a 1964 fight with Sonny Liston where his mentation was fuzzy for a considerable length of time, and in 1972 in another fight he was briefly dazed. He has never been in any car accidents where he sustained an injury, he has not had any infections with any high fever, and he takes no medication. Other than occasional tingling of the hands in the morning when he awakens which clears promptly with movement of the hands, he denied any other neurologic symptoms. On neurologic examination, he seems to have a mild ataxic dysarthria. The remainder of his examination is normal except that he does not quite hop with the agility that one might anticipate and on finger to nose testing there is a slight degree of missing the target. Both of these tests could be significantly influenced by fatigue.

A CT scan of the head was performed and showed only a congenital variation in the form of a small cavum septum pellucidum. The remainder of the examination was normal, and the above mentioned structure is a congenital abnormality and not related in any way to any head trauma. On extensive psychometric testing, he showed a minimal decrease in memory that was more pronounced when he was fatigued, but all other intellectual functions appeared to be intact.

In summary, there is no specific finding that would prohibit him from engaging in further prize fights. There is minimal evidence of some difficulty with his speech and memory and perhaps to a very slight degree with his coordination. All of these are more noticeable when he is fatigued.

It's hard to understand why the Nevada State Athletic Commission allowed Ali to fight without following up on this report. The commission's members had to be aware that Ali was dazed on more than the two occasions cited (his bouts against Sonny Liston in 1964 and Bob Foster in 1972). What about the blows he took from Joe Frazier, Earnie Shavers, and George Foreman? Did Nevada authorities really believe it was proper for Ali to fight when "he does not quite hop with the agility that one might anticipate, and on finger to nose testing there is a slight degree of missing the target"? Weren't they bothered by "the occasional tingling" of his hands in the morning or the "small cavum septum pellucidum" in Ali's brain (a hole in the membrane separating the ventricles that can be enlarged by concussive blows to the head). And what about Ali's claim that he'd "always had some mild slurring of his speech for the past ten to twelve years"? All the commission had to do was requisition tapes of Ali from 1968 to 1970 to hear how his voice had changed. Perhaps then it would have been more concerned about his "mild ataxic dysarthria"—difficulty in coordinating the muscles used in speaking. The Mayo Clinic report was billed as clearing Ali to fight, when in fact it raised far more questions than it answered.

ALEX WALLAU: "Going into the Holmes fight, it was obvious to me that this wasn't the same Ali. And had it just been the Nevada commission doctors who okayed the fight, there would have been a much bigger outcry against it. But I was swayed, and I assume others were swayed, by the fact that Ali had been examined at the premier medical institution in the United States and, we'd been told, given a clean bill of health. I still didn't think he should fight Larry Holmes, but who was I to say he shouldn't? The best medical minds in the country had examined him and supposedly taken a contrary position. Still, I remember trying very hard to get the commission to release the Mayo Clinic's report. Ali initially agreed to release it to me. But then, I'm told, Duke Durden, who was with the commission and soon after became a member of Don King's staff, talked him out of it. All I know for sure is, I went to the commission office for a copy of the report and they wouldn't show it to me."

Thus, Ali-Homes was allowed to proceed, with the fighters exchanging barbs and matching wits in the familiar Aliesque mode:

Muhammad Ali: "He's no Liston. He's no Foreman. He's no Frazier. He's only Larry Holmes, and he's nothin'. He's just the man between me and my fourth title, and I'm going to beat him so bad it's going to be a total mismatch. You think I'd come back now and go out a loser? You think I'd be that stupid? Everybody else goes out loser, but not this one. Four-time champion, how does that sound?"[8]

Larry Holmes: "That's the same old broken record I've been hearing as long as I can remember. That kind of talk don't win no fights. It might convince Ali and it might convince some people, but the guy he's got to convince is Larry Holmes. If Ali stays in front of me, he's gonna get knocked out early. If he's still there after eight rounds, he's lucky. I feel better than I ever felt. I've had four fights in the last year, and what was he doing? Blowing up past 250 pounds."[9]

Muhammad Ali: "I'm the underdog. Great! I love that. I need a fight like this to motivate me. I've been off two years, no activity, thirty-eight years old, and I promise you, this will be no contest. I'll be supremely superior. I'm serious. I was 252 pounds when I started training. Now I'm 227, and I hope to fight around 222. I predict a miracle."[10]

Larry Holmes: "I don't believe in miracles, and I'm sure none is gonna happen that night. To me, Ali isn't a God. He's a human being, just like you and me. He got his weight down, and he thinks that will make him young again, but it won't. Ali can't turn back the clock; no one can. Just about everybody he fought was old. Now he's going to find out how it feels to be an old man fighting a good fast young man. I really believe I'll knock him out."[11]

Muhammad Ali: "Holmes must go. I'll eat him up. I'll hit him with jabs and right crosses. He can't dance; I'm gonna dance fifteen rounds. This old man will whup his butt. Pow! Pow! Pow! I see it all now. He's exhausted. Bam! The right hand over the tired jab. And Holmes is down! Ali goes to a neutral corner. Seven, eight, nine, ten! And for the world-record-setting never-to-be-broken fourth time, Muhammad Ali is the heavyweight champion of the world."[12]

Larry Holmes: "Ali was a great fighter, but he stepped out of his time into my time. I know all there is to know about how he fights. Whatever he tries, I'll beat him. At a distance, I'll out-jab him. If he covers up, I'll break his ribs or murder his kidneys. If he wants to rassle, I'll show him a few holds. I'll beat him to death. He's in trouble. You know it; everybody knows it. They just feel sorry for the old man. He thinks he can pull a rabbit out of a hat, but there's no more rabbits. His ass is grass, and I'm the lawnmower."[13]

MIKE KATZ: "Before Ali-Holmes, the biggest prefight story was, how would Larry Holmes handle the pressure, which was enormous on anyone who fought Ali. But Ali couldn't get under Larry's skin. In fact, he complained to me one day; he said, 'I can't do anything with Larry, because he's been around me too much. He knows my lines before I finish them.' And it was true. Ali would start a line, and Larry could finish it. Larry kept his cool. He was very calm, very professional. In fact, I remember a week or so before the fight, some nut was going to jump a motorcycle over the fountain at Caesar's Palace. It wasn't Evel Knievel; it was some other lunatic. Ali was talking about it, saying how this was another example of someone doing the impossible. He'd done the impossible against Sonny Liston; people were going to the moon, which was impossible; and he was was going to beat Holmes, which was impossible. Anyway, I asked Larry if he was going to watch the jump. And Larry told me, 'No way; I measured it. I know motorcycles, and the guy can't make it.' And of course, the guy didn't make it. He wound up breaking a bunch of bones. But that was Larry Holmes; he was into realism. He knew what was possible and what wasn't."

As the fight approached, public interest grew, with an ever-increasing number of people giving Ali a legitimate chance to win. The odds, which had once been three-to-one, dropped to thirteen-to-ten in Holmes's favor. Pat Putnam of *Sports Illustrated* wrote, "Whatever happens when Ali meets Larry Holmes, one irrefutable fact will stand out. Ali will be in better physical and mental condition than at any time since he battled George Foreman. His face is slim and firm. So is his body. It's as if he has turned the clock back to 1971, when he was twenty-nine."[14]

But Ali's appearance was a mirage. His hair was black only because dye covered the gray. His reflexes were slower than they'd ever been. His followers thought that beating Larry Holmes wouldn't be any more extraordinary than beating Sonny Liston. But in reality, Ali had no chance at all. He was an aging fighter about to face a very good champion. And along with everything else, Ali's physical condition was worsening. Not only wasn't he ready to fight, he wasn't in condition to shadow-box for fifteen rounds.

The true nature of Ali's health wasn't known to the public, nor was the most immediate cause—medication that had been improperly prescribed and abused. In mid-September, several weeks before the fight, Ali had been visited by Herbert Muhammad's personal physician, Dr. Charles Williams. Williams advised Ali that he was suffering from a hypothyroid condition, and gave him one hundred tablets of a drug called Thyrolar. Among its many side effects, Thyrolar speeds up the body's metabolism and interferes with its self-cooling mechanisms. Thus, Ali continued to lose weight, and began to feel fatigued and sluggish. But internally, even more dangerous changes were occurring.

"When Ali left Deer Lake after training," Gene Kilroy recalls, "he was in great shape. His spirits were good; he was ready. Then in Vegas, he started taking those drugs. I was in the room with him at Caesar's Palace when Dr. Williams came in and said, 'Ali, I have something for you that will make you strong.' I told Ali, 'This is crazy. It's the worst thing in the world; don't fool with it.' But Ali took it, and afterward he was dehydrated and urinating all the time. He couldn't run; he was losing weight like mad. And the closer the fight came, the worse it got. I was worried but I wanted to build him up, so I told him, 'You're gonna win. I'm betting everything on you.' And Ali told me, 'No, don't do it. Something is wrong.'"

MIKE KATZ: "I remember watching Ali spar right before he fought Larry Holmes. And outside the ring, maybe he looked magnificent. But in it, he had nothing at all. I mean nothing; he was an empty shell. I told Angelo he looked awful, and Angelo said, 'I know, I know; but he always looks awful in the gym.' Which was true. Ali's idea of training, especially late in his career, was to let sparring partners hit him. There were a couple of times when he hit back for real, but mostly, even if there was an obvious opening, he wouldn't do anything more than tap whoever he was in with. He didn't believe in beating on his sparring partners. The heavy-bag was where he sharpened his combinations. But even knowing how Ali trained, what I saw in the gym before Holmes was awful.

"Ali was sparring with a heavyweight named Marty Monroe, who was a decent fighter. He would be a cruiserweight today. And Monroe was beating the shit out of him. Ali was trying as hard as he could, and not only couldn't he keep Monroe off, he couldn't get out of the way of his punches. Monroe was landing everything he threw. And you know, Angelo thinks every one of his fighters is going to win before a fight. So he was telling me, 'Yeah, Ali looks bad now, but his most important piece of equipment is the mirror. Every morning, he stands in front of the mirror and admires how good he looks. It gives him confidence, and that's what he needs to pull something out of the bag to beat Holmes.'

"And that's what a lot of people thought. There were people, some of them far more knowledgeable than I am, who actually gave Ali a chance because they had this incredible faith in the man and were sure he'd find a way to win. Even Angelo was hoping against hope; but I told him, and I think he knew, 'Angelo, you don't beat Larry Holmes with mirrors.' "

Gene Dibble: "I've known Ali a long time, since before he fought Sonny Liston. I know when he's happy; I know when something is bothering him. And before Holmes, things just weren't right. He was slow and debilitated physically. He couldn't run. Hell, he could hardly stay awake. My brother and I saw him the day before the fight. And my brother, who's a physician, took one look at Ali and said there was no way he should fight. That was enough for me. I said, 'Ali, why don't you postpone this thing?' But he shrugged it off, and said there were people coming from all over the world to watch him. Then he stood up and threw a few jabs, shadow-boxing like he usually does, but he wasn't his regular self. After that, I talked to Bingham; I talked to Kilroy. I talked to everyone I could, trying to stop the fight. But what it came down to was, there was only one person who could tell Ali not to fight, and that was Herbert Muhammad. So I went to Herbert. I saw him in the lobby of the hotel, and I told him I didn't think Ali should fight. And Herbert told me I didn't know what I was talking about."

Jerry Izenberg: "A day or two before the fight, I had a talk with Larry Holmes. Larry was saying, 'This is going to be terrible. Ali has nothing left.' And then he asked me, 'What would you think if I came out hard, just to establish something, and then eased off? Would that be wrong?' And he wasn't asking in terms of what he should or shouldn't do to win the fight. He was worried about hurting Ali. And it was eerie, because I had a feeling of déjà vu with Ali and Cleveland Williams, except this time Ali was the fighter who was shot. I kept thinking about Manila, and how Eddie Futch had stepped in to keep Joe Frazier from taking more punishment. And I wondered, if it came down to that, who would come out of Ali's corner? That's what worried me most about that night. And when fight night finally arrived; well, I tried to be professional. But then, that round when Holmes unloaded and landed that awful hook to the kidneys, when Ali stood there covering his face with his hands; I died, I felt horrible. I said to myself, 'Please, don't let him get hurt.' And I started shouting, 'Stop it! Stop the fight!' I was very sad that night; and, I guess, relieved when it was over, because Ali got out alive. And you know, I've seen that happen too in boxing."

On October 2, 1980, Muhammad Ali and Larry Holmes entered a temporary arena constructed in the parking lot at Caesar's Palace in Las Vegas. The 24,740 fans in attendance paid $5,766,125, breaking the previous record for a live gate set in Ali's most recent bout against Leon Spinks. Ali weighed 217 pounds, the lightest he'd been since facing George Foreman. Holmes weighed in at 211.

It wasn't a fight; it was an execution. Most of the world might have been rooting for Ali, but in the ring, like every other fighter, he was alone. "Every fighter has the same nightmare," Ali had said years before. "You dream you've boxed six or seven fast rounds, and then you get tired, exhausted. You have nothing left. It's all gone. You have to quit."[15]

Against Holmes, that nightmare became a reality, except Ali had nothing from the opening bell on. Each judge awarded Holmes every round, until the slaughter was stopped at the end of ten rounds.

RICHIE GIACHETTI: "Larry and I were confident going in. We'd seen Ali both times against Spinks, and knew there was nothing left. The only problem I saw was, mentally it would be a hard fight for Larry because of how he felt about Ali. When Larry was a kid, he'd idolized Ali, and when he got to know him, he loved him.

"I thought they should have stopped it in the sixth round. After that, there was no point in going on, and that's when the mental thing started to get to Larry. He didn't want to hurt Ali, and began backing off because Ali wouldn't go down. After that, he'd come back to the corner and say, 'What am I supposed to do with this guy?' And I told him, 'Larry, this guy is trying to take away everything you have. The best thing you can do is knock him out, for him and for yourself.'"

"I sat next to Herbert Muhammad during the fight," Dave Kindred, then with The Washington Post, remembers. "Herbert never said a word. Mostly, he just hung his head and looked like he was in pain. Right before the fight ended, he signaled to someone.

I don't know who it was, but Herbert shook his head and Angelo stopped it. Herbert must have missed half the fight, the way he was looking down. And it was awful; the worst sports event I ever had to cover. Ali had that great fighter's heart, boundless courage, all that pride. And he got his brains beat out by Holmes. It was like watching an automobile accident that kills someone you love. Round after round, he kept going out. And if they'd let him, he would have gone out for more."

In the ninth round, Holmes stunned Ali with an uppercut that draped the challenger against the ropes. Turning away involuntarily, Ali covered his face with his gloves, and the champion followed with a right hand to the kidney that caused Ali to cringe and double over in pain. Round ten was more of the same—"Like watching an autopsy on a man who's still alive," Sylvester Stallone said later.

And then at last it was over. Herbert Muhammad gave his signal, and Angelo Dundee told referee Richard Greene, "That's all."

"One more round," Bundini pleaded, grabbing onto Dundee's sweater.

"Fuck you! No!" Dundee shouted. "I'm the chief second. The ballgame's over."

MUHAMMAD ALI: "Before the fight started, I thought I could win. I wouldn't have fought if I didn't think I'd beat him. But after the first round, I knew I was in trouble. I was tired, nothing left at all. A couple of times before, when I had hard fights, in the middle of the fight I'd ask myself, 'What am I doing here?' With George Foreman in Zaire, against Joe Frazier in Manila, I told myself I had to be crazy. But when the fights were over, it always seemed worth it, except when I fought Holmes. I didn't want Angelo to stop it. I wanted to go the fifteen rounds. But I guess what he did was right, because if it had gone on, maybe I would have gotten hurt more."

LARRY HOLMES: "After the fight, I went to Ali's room in the hotel and told him, 'You're still the greatest; I love you.' I meant it; and I felt awful. I felt terrible before I went to his room, and when I got there I felt worse. Even though I won, I was down. And Muhammad saw it, so he said to me, 'Man, now you got me mad. I took care of you; I fed you; I taught you how to fight. And look what you did to me. I'm coming back again to whup your ass.' And that made me feel better, listening to him say, 'I want Holmes; gimme Holmes.' And the only other thing I want to say is, I want people to know I'm proud I learned my craft from Ali. I'm prouder of sparring with him when he was young than I am of beating him when he was old."

Four days after he fought Larry Holmes, Ali checked into the UCLA Medical Center. "His condition was bad," Howard Bingham remembers. "He was sitting around at home, real tired, worse than I'd seen him ever. And he didn't want to go. He didn't want people reading in the newspaper that Larry Holmes put him in the hospital. But we told him it was better reading that Holmes put him in the hospital than it would be reading that Holmes killed him."

Ali underwent two days of tests at UCLA, after which the outline of what had occurred emerged. Several weeks before the fight, he'd been visited by Dr. Charles Williams, who was Herbert Muhammad's personal physician. Dr. Williams advised Ali that he was suffering from a hypothyroid condition, and prescribed one tablet of Thyrolar (three grains) per day. The doctor's diagnosis was speculative and apparently incorrect. Moreover, Thyrolar is a potentially lethal drug, and no one on Thyrolar should engage in a professional fight. Also, Ali was not advised of the drug's side effects, and there was no subsequent verification whether he was taking the proper dosage. Ali then compounded the problem by taking three tablets a day, because in his words, he "thought the pills would be like vitamins." Tests administered at UCLA also revealed the presence of Benzedrine in Ali's system. Benzedrine is a stimulant, and when it wears off, the user is more fatigued than he otherwise would have been. The use of these drugs over a period of several weeks was consistent with Ali's condition immediately before, during, and after the fight. In the fight itself, according to the medical history taken from Ali at UCLA, he felt weak, fatigued, and short of breath from round one on. His body wasn't able to cool itself properly, and his temperature rose. That, Dr. Williams later acknowledged, "led to heat exhaustion that went into heat stroke with an intermediate period of slight stupor and maybe delirium. I may have placed him in jeopardy inadvertently."[16]

Or, phrased differently, the medication given to Ali before the fight, in conjunction with the fight itself, had the potential to kill him. Dr. Williams explains his actions.

DR. CHARLES WILLIAMS: "I was Elijah Muhammad's doctor. He had confidence in me, and then Herbert got confidence in me and asked if I'd like to go to Japan with Ali as a guest for the Mac Foster fight. After that, they invited me to be one of the doctors in the group on most of the trips, although Pacheco was the main doctor. Each time, it was a fantastic journey. I'd never been treated like anything other than a nigger in my life, and now we're on this big plane up in the sky, and we'd have the front of it, the whole first-class section, and in back was where all the white people sat. It thrilled me that black people could reach up that high. And I did whatever Herbert and Ali wanted me to do. I wanted to be the best servant of all.

"It was right before the second Spinks fight that I learned Ali's thyroid wasn't working properly. This is the first time I've told anybody about that. Ali told me things weren't quite right. I noticed a little slowing down, and Herbert was worried. So I took some samples of Ali's blood and urine over to the Oschner Clinic. That's a famous clinic in New Orleans. Ali never went there himself, but the pathologist at the clinic knew it was Ali's specimen. They did a battery of tests to check his thyroid function. And the pathologist told me his thyroid function was far below normal, so I corrected it. I won't say how. I only had a day or two to correct it. Let's just say I corrected it, and Ali whupped Leon Spinks. But based on that, I knew his internal environment wasn't being regulated like it should by the body. The equilibrium in the body wasn't being maintained.

"Then after that, we had the Holmes fight, and I knew Ali had something wrong with his thyroid. He gained a huge amount of weight. He went up to about 260 pounds. I saw him on TV and said, 'Jesus Christ, his thyroid is way out of line.' And it was made worse by all the stress he was under. The effect of stress on the human body is poorly known by most doctors. I probably know more about stress than any doctor in America. But Herbert didn't call me until two weeks before the fight, so it forced me to correct things in too short a period of time. It was just too much. Ali's metabolism had to be increased to normal, plus he was getting older; too old, really. My job, as I interpreted it, was to do the best I could. The contracts were signed, Ali fights the fight; he conforms to the stipulations of the contract; and he gets paid. I didn't worry about whether he was going to win. It was stupid to think he was going to win. I just wanted to get him in good enough shape, and sure enough, he looked good. What the hell; he was almost thirty-nine. He'd fought a million fights. He'd already proved himself three times world champion, and I knew it had to end sometime. Don King showed me something that said, 'See the great man fight; his last tango.' I said to myself, 'Well, people aren't expecting him to win.

People are just coming to see the great Ali fight.' He was always interesting whether he won or lost.

"Anyway, I only had a few weeks to get Ali ready, and I was in a dilemma. So I told him, 'Well, try this.' And as soon as I gave him just a little bit of Thyrolar, whoom, he shot back up. He felt like he could whip a gorilla. He responded well; he was looking good. People were saying I really knew what I was doing, and as soon as he lost, they started blaming it on me. At UCLA, when they checked Ali, they didn't find any evidence of a thyroid problem but that's because I'd corrected it. I'm positive I was correct. I don't take a back seat to any doctor. When I told Ali something, I'd put my life on it. And if I had it to do over again, I'd do exactly the same thing. I know I've been criticized for the way I treated him, but when you know you're right you just accept that."

Dr. Williams's statement raises numerous questions. Several days before the Spinks fight in New Orleans, Ali had in fact complained of weariness. However, tests showed that his blood was low in salt, iron, and potassium. There was no mention of a thyroid deficiency. Dennis Cope, who supervised Ali's stay at the UCLA Medical Center and continues to monitor Ali's health, casts further doubt on Williams's evaluation. "The thyroid extract was given to Muhammad because, in the opinion of Dr. Williams, he looked hypothyroid," Dr. Cope states. "Unfortunately, there wasn't any testing done to verify that this was actually the case. I don't know for sure, but I can infer that prior to medical intervention, Muhammad's thyroid gland was functioning properly, because since then without medication it has functioned properly. And when a person's thyroid gland malfunctions, it's usually a long-term problem."

FERDIE PACHECO: "Ali is lucky he lived through the Holmes fight. And as far as Charles Williams is concerned, I don't like to talk badly about another doctor, but I think the facts speak for themselves.

"I first became aware of Charles Williams in Zaire, when he announced that Ali was tired because he had hypoglycemia. That means low blood sugar. Now for starters, you can't diagnose hypoglycemia without a battery of tests—glucose tolerance and things like that—none of which were performed in Africa. But worse than Dr. Williams's diagnosis was his proposed cure. There's a delicate needle in the pancreas that determines how much insulin is released into the blood to burn how much sugar. And what happens with hypoglycemia is, the needle goes crazy and releases too much insulin when you take in sugar. Now what does the body do with that excess insulin? It goes to the brain and makes you groggy. That's hypoglycemia, pure and simple. It's not a killer; it's something you can adjust. The endocrine system is an interlinking of several glands, and everything can be balanced out so the insulin is kept within a certain limit. It's not a big thing. It's just something that requires a little attention on the part of an internist or endocrinologist. But the one thing in red letters that you cannot in any way, shape, or form do is give someone with hypoglycemia more sugar. That's the last thing you do unless you're trying to kill them, because whatever additional amount of sugar you put in, you'll get that much more insulin proportionally. And if you put enough sugar in, the patient will go into an insulin coma. You'd get thrown out of medical school if you reached third year and didn't know that.

"So there we were in the heart of Africa, and here's Charles Williams telling Ali he has hypoglycemia. And his cure was for Ali to eat a peach cobbler with ice cream right before the fight. In other words, his blood sugar was supposedly low, so we'll put some more sugar in. Let's fill his tank up with gas. And it was a problem. I wasn't sure what to do. I knew what I couldn't do, which was give Ali more sugar. But here's a doctor; he treats Herbert. I can't tell him he's an ignoramus. So what I said was, 'Look, this is a boxer; he's not a regular patient. He can't eat a peach cobbler right before the fight, because the possibility exists that George Foreman will punch him in the stomach. So what we'll do is, fill a bottle with orange juice and sugar; make sort of an orange syrup, and give that to Ali between rounds.' Williams said, 'Great!' We mixed the bottle. And that bottle is still out in the jungle somewhere between N'Sele and Kinshasa.

"Then came the Holmes fight. And as you know, I wasn't with Ali by then. But one thing I can tell you with great certainty is, in the absence of appropriate laboratory tests, you can't diagnose a hypothyroid condition. Ali had just been to the Mayo Clinic, with no evidence at all of a thyroid problem. To my knowledge, the condition never surfaced in any physician's evaluation of Ali other than Charles Williams's before or after Larry Holmes. And beyond that, if a fighter needs Thyrolar, it's like Russian roulette for him to be in the ring. His heart rate accelerates; his basic metabolism changes; his muscles are affected, because muscle tissue as well as fat is burning off. He can't sweat; he's debilitated by loss of water.

Thyrolar has never been given to another fighter in the history of boxing that I know of. And I don't know of anybody who ever had a thyroid condition who fought.

"Ali was a walking time bomb in the ring that night. He could have had anything from a heart attack to a stroke to all kinds of bleeding in the head. It's not up to me to make a judgment as to whether Charles Williams is competent to practice medicine. That's up to a medical board in the state of Illinois, where he practices. He's got his credentials, and that's that. But Ali-Holmes was a horrible end for a great champion, and years later, I'm still pissed off about it."

But the questions about Ali-Holmes go beyond Charles Williams. And foremost among them is why the fight ever happened. Why were contracts signed to begin with? And why was the bout allowed to proceed given the sudden marked deterioration of Ali's physical condition?

Ali himself is partly to blame for a fight that should never have taken place. He wanted the glory, he wanted a platform for his views, and he wanted the money. And in pursuit of those ends, he deceived himself, massively. "Getting ready for Holmes," says Ferdie Pacheco, "Ali was like a vain actress who's forty and wants to look twenty again. Maybe he looked young, but he was past his age in terms of his physical condition."

In the end, none of Ali's prefight objectives were realized. Once the bout began, glory was replaced by pain and humiliation. "I embarrassed myself," Ali acknowledged afterward. "I felt embarrassed for all my fans. I fought like an old man who was washed up."[17] Rather than give Ali a platform for future crusades, the fight diminished his credibility. And as in the past, the money he earned was siphoned into many hands. Herbert Muhammad took his one-third share. Taxes, training expenses, and the entourage ate up a significant amount. There were gifts, more bad business ventures, and ultimately a short paycheck from Don King.

MICHAEL PHENNER: "The contract for the fight called for Ali to receive eight million dollars. It had a clause saying there could be no amendment except in writing, and that was that. Ali was entitled to eight million dollars. Then, maybe a week before the fight, King started complaining about financial problems, and claimed Ali had agreed orally to fight for seven million. He had a lawyer chasing me all over Caesar's Palace trying to get me to amend the contract, and

I refused. I was Ali's lawyer. My job was to protect Ali, not bail Don King out of financial trouble. Then, after the fight, when it was clear King had done quite well, I talked with Ali and we agreed the contract should be enforced the way it was written—that we'd go after Don for the million dollars, which he was refusing to pay. It was an open-and-shut lawsuit; summary judgment. But about a month later, I saw Ali. He was very chagrined. He told me he'd met with Don King; that King had put fifty thousand dollars in cash on the table in front of him. And fifty thousand dollars in cash looks like a lot of money, so Ali had taken it and signed a release. When I heard that, a tear rolled down my cheek. Here we were, trying to get Ali set financially. He'd just taken a horrible beating, in large part for the money. And then he'd gone and signed a piece of paper that cost him $950,000."

But Ali isn't the only person who should shoulder responsibility for the fight. The Nevada State Athletic Commission had a copy of the Mayo Clinic report. It also supposedly gave Ali its own physical examination just before the bout. By then, Ali was showing the effects of Thyrolar. Indeed, two days before the fight, he'd tried to do his usual roadwork, but been so fatigued after a half-mile that he'd had to stop. Yet the Nevada commission, whose first mission is to protect fighters within its jurisdiction, let the fight go on.

Herbert Muhammad also bears responsibility for Ali-Holmes. He's the manager who made the fight. "On things like that," says Howard Bingham, "Ali might not have listened to other people, but he always listened to Herbert. If Herbert had told him not to fight, that fight wouldn't have happened."

Moreover, it's hard to understand why Herbert wasn't aware of his fighter's deteriorating physical condition after Ali began taking Thyrolar. "I watched Ali the day of the fight," Bernie Yuman remembers. "And he was debilitated, terribly slow. You've got to understand, there was a difference between Ali being slow and Ali being serene. Ali had a serenity about him right before his fights; it was a mind-over-matter sort of thing. Everybody else could be freaking out in the heat of the moment, and he'd be incredibly peaceful and serene. But this was different. He wasn't peaceful; he was slow. He wasn't serene; he was drugged out. He was a sick man."

The charge most often made against Herbert Muhammad with regard to Ali-Holmes is that he sold Ali out for the money—one-third of Ali's purse, plus the possibility of more. Herbert Muhammad responds.

HERBERT MUHAMMAD: "I wasn't in boxing for the money. I was in boxing because my father put the obligation on me to look after Ali, and that's what I did. Other fighters constantly contacted me to manage them. Even now, I'm contacted by fighters who are having problems with managers or promoters, and I turn them all down. I once even had paper in Larry Holmes. When he was sparring with Ali, I had him on paper as manager, but I never did pursue it. I never managed but one fighter, and that's the only one I wanted.

"As far as Ali fighting Holmes, I believed he could beat Larry. That's not the fight I was worried about. The fight where I was worried was against George Foreman in Zaire. Before that fight— and I shouldn't tell you this, because people will take it and twist it around—but before that fight, one of our people went to Zack Clayton, the referee, with my knowledge. He offered him five thousand dollars cash, and told him, 'This is for one thing, and one thing only. If Ali gets in trouble, stop the fight. Don't let Foreman keep beating on him if he's hurt.'*

"And against Holmes, I was the one who stopped the fight. Most of the time at Ali's fights, I sat in the front row, right by Ali's corner. Usually I didn't look at the fight, unless it was clear there was no danger. I didn't like seeing Ali get hit. Usually I'd be praying with my head down. When he fought Frazier, the time he lost, I almost fainted. And against Holmes; well, I was watching, and I wondered what was wrong with Ali. He was getting hit and not hitting back. I started talking with Lloyd Wells, and Lloyd thought it should be stopped. So I didn't leave my seat, but I sent word to Angelo. I sent Lloyd and Pat Patterson to say, 'If there's one more round like this, stop it. If it looks like this at the end of the next round, throw the towel in.' And that's what happened. The next round, Ali was still getting beat, so I made the sign for them to stop the fight."

The decision to approve Ali-Holmes will be debated well into the next century, but one thing is clear. The fight was significant for a lot of people and affected many careers. For most of the past hundred years, whoever controlled the heavyweight champion controlled the lion's share of professional boxing. When Tex Rickard controlled Jack Dempsey, when Mike Jacobs controlled Joe Louis, when James Norris controlled Rocky Marciano, they turned that position into an

---

*Herbert Muhammad maintains that he doesn't know if Clayton accepted the money or for that matter if it was ever actually offered to him. The $5,000 was never returned by the member of Ali's entourage who was authorized to make the offer.

empire. Herbert Muhammad never did that with Ali; he didn't want to control boxing. But the man who promoted Ali-Holmes did. Don King was Larry Holmes's exclusive promoter. It was very much in his interest for Holmes to fight and beat Ali. Once that occurred, King was well on his way to achieving a stranglehold on the heavyweight division, and that translated into a massive amount of money for anyone who had a share.

MIKE KATZ: "I don't know what happened behind the scenes in Vegas. I just know that it was essential to Don King for Ali to go ahead with the fight. This was one of the few times King had his own money on the line, as opposed to someone else's. If Ali-Holmes had fallen through or failed at the gate, King would have been in trouble. And of course, it was clearly in Don's interest to have Holmes win. He was Larry's exclusive promoter. And from beginning to end, Don was able to play Larry like a violin. He reeled him in with his black-brother line, jerked him around, and paid him millions of dollars less than Larry could have gotten from another promoter. When Ali and Frazier fought the first time, Frazier was champ, Ali was the draw, and Frazier got parity. When Ali fought Foreman, Foreman was champ, again Ali was the draw, and Foreman got parity. But when Holmes fought Ali, even though Larry was champ, he got five million dollars less than Ali. Who do you think got the five million? And it happened again when Larry fought Gerry Cooney. Larry was champ; he was at the peak of his career. But Cooney got nine million dollars, and Larry, if he was lucky, got half as much. And I felt for Larry, because I thought he was basically an okay guy and a great fighter. But I felt more for Ali. I was crying, literally crying, when the two of them fought. Tears were rolling down my cheeks. There was a total emptiness inside me. All I could see was Ali slumped on his stool, and I was like listening to echoes. 'Ali! Ali!' "

Ali is reluctant to criticize Don King for promoting Ali-Holmes or any other deed. "Other promoters acted the same as Don for years," he says, "and no one complained about them. Some of what Don does is good; maybe some is bad. But I don't want to judge Don King, because that's God's position to judge."

However, others are less reluctant to judge, particularly where Ali-Holmes is concerned. King has many critics, and John Schulian, formerly of the *Chicago Daily News* and *Chicago Sun-Times*, is one of them.

JOHN SCHULIAN: "I hated Don King for promoting that fight, and I hated Herbert Muhammad for letting it happen. You didn't have to be a rocket scientist to know at that point that Ali was facing brain damage. He wasn't talking the way he used to. He wasn't moving the way he used to. If Herbert cared about Ali, he would have taken care of him. He would have talked to him, counseled him, done everything in his power to keep him out of the ring that night. But instead, all Herbert did was send him out to get some more of his brain cells scrambled. And Don King; that lying thieving motherfucker. That he could stand there and say, 'Oh, Muhammad; I love you, Muhammad. I'm with you, Muhammad; you're the greatest!' And then make a fortune off Ali getting brutalized that way. Well, fuck you, Don King. The man is a total scumbag; he really is. He always has been and always will be. I have so little regard for Don King. It's hard to imagine how hard his heart must be. I'll bet King has a lump of coal in his chest. I hate to think that's what life is about or that's what boxing is about, but that's certainly what it was about that night. They sacrificed Ali. That's all it was; a human sacrifice for money and power. And it was more than a matter of Ali getting beaten up. That night went far beyond Ali. One of the great symbols of our time was tarnished. So many people—blacks, whites, Muslims, Americans, Africans, Asians, people all over the world—believed in Ali. And he was destroyed because of people who didn't care one bit about the things he'd stood for his entire life."

HOWARD BINGHAM: "Ali should never have signed for that fight, and they should never have let him fight after he started feeling sick. I don't know that there was a deal on the side, but people talk. You hear rumors about who got what, how much the promoters made, stuff like that. And then you wonder how a doctor can let a situation like that develop by accident. Even when Ali weighed 250 pounds and was out of shape, he could throw punches. And against Holmes, all he could do was put his arms up. By the time he got in the ring, he was gone. I've heard people say there was a big bet. Other people say that Larry Holmes made a lot of money for people who used to do business with Ali. I'm not accusing; there's nothing I can prove. But there's lots of questions people should ask, and maybe someday we'll get some answers."

16

Burial

After his loss to Larry Holmes, Ali returned to Los Angeles where his image suffered another blow. For years, the sporting press had been aware of the hustling and exploitation around him. But since Ali seemed to tolerate it and was the primary victim, it had passed with little public comment. However, in early 1981, a new scandal broke. Once again, Ali had been misused. This time, though, it was to defraud others, and the amount in question was too large to ignore—$21,305,000.

The key figure in the new Ali scandal was a man named Ross Fields, who had adopted the alias "Harold Smith." Over the previous four years, Smith had formed two organizations—Muhammad Ali Amateur Sports (MAAS) and Muhammad Ali Professional Sports (MAPS)—designed to promote amateur and professional boxing. For the use of his name, Ali was to receive 25 percent of the net profits from all MAPS-sponsored events, plus personal appearance fees for various promotions. Meanwhile, Smith began promoting fights, paying huge purses to fighters, and apparently losing money. But he kept spending until it was learned that $21,305,000 was missing from the Wells Fargo Bank of California as a consequence of his manipulation of funds in tandem with a bank employee named Ben Lewis.

HAROLD SMITH: "I met Ali in the early 1960s, when I was a student at Tennessee State University. He visited the campus. I went over and shook his hand, but at that point I was no different from a hundred other students he said hello to that day. Then, years later, I got involved with a sprinter named Houston McTear. It looked like he was going to the [1976] Olympics, and there'd been stories in the newspapers about how this young black man was going to represent the United States and his family was living dirt poor in a shack in Florida. I knew Ali by then because I'd sort of hung out with the group before his fights. I told Ali about Houston, and it struck him as wrong for these people to be living in such poverty. So Ali instructed one of his attorneys to buy the family a home. We found one for about seventy thousand; four bedrooms, red brick. And after that, Ali sort of became Houston's sponsor. One day they were talking. Ali was kidding around, saying, 'You're pretty fast, aren't you?' Houston said, 'Yes.' And Ali started asking about different sprinters, like, 'I hear Harvey Glance is fast. Did you ever beat Harvey Glance?' Houston said, 'I beat him twice.' And Ali asked about some other sprinters. He kept naming people. And if I remember right, Lloyd Wells was there. He named a few sprinters too. And then Ali said something that started the whole thing rolling. He looked at me, and these were his exact words; he said, 'Harold, wouldn't it be something if we could get all these niggers together and find out which one is really fastest?'

"Well, I took that idea; I worked on it. And out of that came the Muhammad Ali Invitational Track Meet [at Cerritos College on Memorial Day 1977]. CBS televised it. We even had a celebrity race with Ali running against Marvin Gaye, Tony Orlando, Angel Cordero, and some others. Marvin Gaye won. Ali finished next to last; I think he beat Tony Orlando. And the centerpiece was the hundred-yard dash, which went just like we'd planned. The greatest sprinters in the world were there: Houston McTear, Harvey Glance, Johnny Lam Jones, Hasely Crawford. Ali was the starter, and Houston won. It was a big success, and it started me thinking. Ali was a fighter; why don't we do some amateur boxing? That's how the Muhammad Ali Amateur Boxing Team came about. I went around the country, spent a lot of time on the road at local tournaments, and selected twelve fighters. Of those twelve, seven eventually fought for world titles, and five became world champions. The five who made it were Tony Tubbs, Tony Tucker, Bernard Benton, Lindell Holmes, and J. B. Williamson. We had a hell of a team, and it only seemed right to form some sort of organization that would protect them when they turned professional, and that's how Muhammad Ali Professional Sports began. Then other fighters started coming our way, and I guess you know the rest.

"Ali wasn't involved in the business end of things. If one of our guys was fighting, he was usually there, but that's about it. I don't like to talk about the business end, because that's been talked about so much. You know, the banking situation. But my problem as I see it was a banking problem, not a boxing problem. Certain people in the bank looked at me and said, 'Here's a guy who's got a lot going for him. He's got all these amateur fighters; he's got some good professional fighters; he's a friend of Ali.' And Ali was a big part of it; no doubt about it. The people in the bank felt that by getting involved with Ali through me that Ali could do something for them later. I could never have gotten that money from the bank without Muhammad Ali's name. And if you think what I did was wrong; well, I'm not going to tell you that I wasn't guilty of something, but look at all the savings and loan institutions. They've been ripped off for billions of dollars—not millions, billions—and none of them white guys is gonna do one day in jail. My situation was the same sort of thing, but I'm a nigger and I got caught being involved with the wrong people."

When the MAPS scandal broke, Ali held a press conference at his Los Angeles home to deny knowledge of any wrongdoing. "A guy used my name to embezzle $21,000,000," he told reporters. "Ain't many names that can steal that much."[1] But no amount of humor could obscure the fact that once again Ali's name had been tarnished. And the fact that Harold Smith would ultimately spend more than five years in federal prison served simply to underscore the problem.

Dean Allison, who was chief of the United States Attorney's Special Prosecutions Unit in Los Angeles and lead prosecutor in the MAPS case, recalls the matter from his perspective.

DEAN ALLISON: "The case involved what was then the biggest bank embezzlement in American history, which was accomplished by an ingenious computer manipulation scheme. Harold's only defense at trial was that he lacked criminal intent; that he was running a boxing program out of purely altruistic motives for the black youth of the community and for the betterment of amateur boxing, and that he had no idea this money was stolen, because he thought the bank, based on some alleged loose remarks by bank personnel, had given him an unlimited line of credit. That claim was proven ludicrous and had no factual basis. In fact, the jury convicted him on thirty-one of thirty-two counts in the indictment. And the only reason it wasn't all thirty-two was, they couldn't find one of the checks we'd introduced as an exhibit at trial.

"As far as Ali was concerned, the only time I met him in connection with the case was in the courthouse. Harold talked him into coming down and sitting in the gallery during his lawyer's closing argument, presumably as a way of lending credence to Harold's claims and showing moral support. But as a tactical maneuver, it was a terrible blunder. Ali's attention span was limited. Anybody's attention span would have been limited given the length of Harold's attorney's closing argument. And in addition, Ali had no grasp of the details of the case, so he wasn't in a position to follow a coherent summation, much less the one that was given. There was a little girl sitting near him, so he spent most of the time playing with her and fidgeting. And apart from that, his mere presence distracted the jurors, who were more interested in watching the celebrity than listening to what Harold's lawyer was saying.

"I came to the conclusion that Ali had no knowledge of the wrongdoing that was going on at MAPS and certainly no knowledge of their finances. From a mechanical standpoint, he had nothing to do with accomplishing the embezzlement, concealing the embezzlement, or any of the criminal activity whatsoever. Whether the crime would have actually happened without Ali being used by Harold Smith as bait to get Ben Lewis involved, I don't know. It's very speculative as to whether Smith would have gotten a hold on Ben Lewis had he not had Ali to wave around. But there was never any prospect or thought other than uninformed speculation in the newspapers that Ali would be involved in the case in the sense of being a target, a defendant, an unindicted coconspirator, or accused of wrongdoing in any other way, directly or by implication. Harold Smith used him; that's all."

Meanwhile, as the MAPS scandal unfolded, Ali, incredibly, was planning to fight again. Some of his advisors were telling him that Thyrolar, not age, was to blame for the Holmes debacle, and that he could still win in the ring. Also, Ali wanted to finish his career on his feet, not slumped on a stool in his corner. "I thought I should go out of boxing with a win," he said later. "And if I couldn't go out with a win, at least I wanted to be throwing punches at the end."

Finding a site for yet another comeback bout was a problem. After Ali's poor performance against Holmes, the Nevada State Athletic Commission had begun hearings to determine whether he should be precluded from fighting again. To forestall that ruling, on December 29, 1980, Ali voluntarily relinquished his license to box in Nevada, and pledged not to seek a new one. But that left the rest of the world to fight in. Then, in autumn 1981, a bout between Ali and Trevor Berbick was announced by a company called Sports International Ltd.

The main force behind the promotion was James Cornelius, who had been arrested nine times, convicted of theft in connection with a used-car dealership, and was the target of a continuing FBI bank-fraud investigation. After trying unsuccessfully to stage Ali-Berbick in the United States, Cornelius found a home for it in the Bahamas. But when Ali tried to hype the fight, his words had a melancholy ring. "They say I'm washed up," he told reporters. "They say I'm too old. That I'm finished. That I can't talk no more. That I've got brain damage. That I have bad kidneys. That I'm broke. That I'm sad. Ooooooh, man, I've got so many critics to whup. So many newspaper people who think I'm dead. So many boxing commissions. So many doctors. I'm gonna mess 'em all up by whupping Berbick and then becoming the first forty-year-old man to ever win the heavyweight title. Get ready for the shocker. I'm gonna mess up the world."[2]

In truth, it was a fight virtually no one wanted. Ali's mother told the press, "I worry about my son getting seriously hurt. His whole family worries about him. He's almost forty years old; too old to be fighting."[3] There was no closed-circuit interest in the bout. The three major television networks declined to bid. And a number of writers who had covered Ali throughout his career refused to attend.

Meanwhile, as the fight approached, an ugly behind-the-scenes battle was raging. In April 1981, Berbick had challenged Larry Holmes for the title and lost a unanimous fifteen-round decision. But in order to get a championship bout, he'd been forced to give Don King options on his next three fights. Thus, when Ali-Berbick was announced, King demanded a piece of the promotion. James Cornelius refused; King threatened to sue to block the fight. And that's how things stood until Saturday, December 5, six days before the bout, when King flew to the Bahamas to press his claim for "perhaps as much as $200,000."[4]

Ali and his entourage were staying in Nassau, where the fight was scheduled to be held. But rather than approach Ali or Herbert

Muhammad, King went to Freeport, where Berbick was training. That night, he met with the fighter and demanded satisfaction. Then, the following morning, there was a knock on King's hotel-room door. Eight hours later, he was in a Florida hospital, the victim of a savage beating.

Jeremiah Shabazz: "Not many people stand up to Don King, but Don doesn't have the heart for real confrontations. If you stand up to him, he'll back off, and that's what happened in the Bahamas. Ali's career was pretty much over. It was just a matter of one last payday, and I felt Don should have stepped aside. Ali was in his twilight years; Don had made millions off him. But there was Don, hanging on for the last dollar, and interfering with Muslim business. [James Cornelius was a member of the Nation of Islam.] He was doing everything he could to stop the fight or get money he wasn't entitled to; so some of the brothers took offense.

"What happened as I understand it was, Cornelius went over to Freeport to confront Don and tell him to stop interfering with the promotion. They had some words, and Don made the serious mistake of shoving one of brothers who was with Cornelius. I heard it said later that there were four or five brothers present, but I think that's an exaggeration. To my knowledge, Cornelius only had two body guards with him that day, but they were top karate-trained professionals. In the past, they'd been unhappy because they'd never had a chance to practice their skills on a real live opponent. It was always bricks and boards and things of that sort. But then Don gave them the chance to break a real live head, and they went to work on him pretty good.

"Charles Lomax was there with Don, but he begged off on account of a bad heart, so he was excused. Don wasn't that lucky. I hear he was begging and pleading, but the brothers gave him a sound thrashing, with broken teeth and blood all over. Later, Don blamed me for what happened, but nothing could be further from the truth. I didn't even know about it until afterward when the brothers came to my room and told me. I was pleased; I won't deny that. I can't think of a more deserving fellow than Don King for that kind of treatment. Because if you want my view, Don is one of the dirtiest rottenest pieces of scum that ever lived. On a couple of occasions, he gave me some bucks to bring Ali to him, and I'm ashamed to say, that's what I did. But Don King is an evil megalomaniac. He's a closet Hitler, a tyrant in the police-state mold. Sometimes he'll make alliances the way dictators work with the armed forces in their country, but in the end he wants everything for himself. He came to prominence because of our Muslim brother, Ali. But he's never had a Muslim working for him in any position of importance; only as a chauffeur, gofer, or cook. As far as Don is concerned, the only thing Muslims are good for is to bring him drinks and shine his shoes. He once told me he'd give me a job if I'd show the same respect and loyalty to him that I gave to Elijah Muhammad, to which I told Don I'd never give him that kind of loyalty and respect.

"The way Don King views it, he's bigger than any boxer who ever lived. He used Ali; he used Larry Holmes. Don views fighters like a snake views frogs. They're only good as something to eat. He charms them, and then he swallows them. And after they're used up, all you see is their bones. He spouts a mixture of Americanism and black nationalism, and says whatever he has to say to win fighters over. But after they're used up, they mean nothing to him and he discards them like they were firewood.

"I'll give you an example of what I mean. A couple of years ago, Leon Spinks was at Don's office in New York, using Don's telephone. Don was upstairs; Leon was downstairs. And Don sent word that Leon should stop using his phone. Then Leon had to catch a train from Penn Station to Philadelphia. Don's big white limousine was standing right outside. Don wasn't going anyplace, but he wouldn't ask his chauffeur to give Leon a ride to the train station. Instead, he put Leon out on the street and left him there at rush hour, standing on the corner waving his arms trying to catch a taxi, and he couldn't get one. And I thought about how, when Leon was champion, Don couldn't get enough of him. Don figured Leon might reign for a while, and he did everything he could to get control of Leon. He played up to him; he flattered him, just like he treats Mike Tyson now. And I feel sorry for Tyson when I see him being played for a fool by Don King. So in my view, the beating Don got in the Bahamas was justified."

As fight night approached, Ali's followers gathered for one last farewell. His weight was back at 236 pounds, nineteen pounds heavier than when he'd fought Larry Holmes. But he looked worse than ever in the gym, and often walked on his morning run. The end was near and everyone knew it, including Ali's twelve-year-old daughter, Maryum.

MARYUM ALI: "When you're born and have a dad who fights, it seems normal because it's the only thing you know. Most of his

fights I don't remember because I was too young. And I didn't go
to many of them, because when I was little, I was usually in school.
I was supposed to go to Zaire for the Foreman fight. Before that
one, I remember my dad was really psyched at home. I was six; I
didn't understand what was going on, but I knew something special
was involved and that it was very important for him to win. I got
my shots and everything for the trip, and then my parents changed
their mind and said I had to stay in school. I was mad; I'd gotten
those shots for nothing. I yelled and cried and screamed, but it
didn't do any good. When they went, they still left me home.

"I saw my dad fight a couple of times, and it always scared me.
Even when he won, I'd cry because he was getting hit, and it wasn't
just the physical danger. I sensed what was involved for him emotionally, and felt the intensity of it all. But he was good in the ring,
and that helped. He won most of the time, and that made it easier.
But after a while—how can I explain this—you know how, when
you're a kid and you go to the doctor and smell alcohol, you know
you're going to get a shot? Well, after a while when I was a kid,
every time I heard Howard Cosell's voice on television, I'd start to
shake because I knew, 'Oh, boy; here it comes again.'

"Still, I pretty much accepted my father fighting up until he fought
Trevor Berbick. That was the only fight I wanted him to lose. I
wanted him to win but I didn't, because if he won he'd keep fighting,
and I didn't want him to fight anymore. I was in the last row of the
first level of the stadium that night. And I remember saying to
myself, 'If he loses, he won't fight again and I'll be happy. But if he
wins, he'll go on and on.' "

On December 11, 1981, Muhammad Ali entered the ring for the
last time. "The show started two hours late," Ed Schuyler remembers. "That's because the promoters couldn't find the key to the
front gate of the baseball field where the fight was held. Then someone realized there were only two pairs of gloves for the entire un-
dercard, and after each fight the cornermen had to unlace the gloves.
They couldn't cut them off, because the next fighter needed them.
There was no bell. Finally, someone found a cowbell in a truck. I
don't think they had regular corner stools either. And it was heart-
breaking, because Ali had so much class, and this was how his career
came to an end."

The fight was suited to its surroundings. Ali had nothing left, and
Berbick showed little skill. Berbick was the aggressor throughout,
landing to the body almost at will. "I'd see Ali get hit," Wali Mu-

hammad recalls, "and the expression on his face showed me he was in pain. One of the writers who was sitting nearby said, 'He's getting hurt, Blood.' And I told him, 'That's right; he is.' "

All three judges scored the bout for Berbick. The following morning, there was a press conference at which the victor arrived first but refused to answer questions until Ali was there. "I don't know if he was being gracious or what," Ed Schuyler remembers. "But of course, once Ali arrived, none of us could have cared less about Trevor."

Speaking to the press, Ali at last accepted the inevitable. "Father Time caught up with me," he said. "I'm finished. I've got to face the facts. For the first time, I feel that I'm forty years old. I know it's the end; I'm not crazy. After Holmes, I had excuses. I was too light, didn't breathe right. No excuses this time, but at least I didn't go down. No pictures of me on the floor, no pictures of me falling through the ropes, no broken teeth, no blood. I'm happy I'm still pretty. I came out all right for an old man. We all lose sometimes. We all grow old."[5]

At the end of the press conference, Schuyler spoke for his brethren: "Muhammad, thank you. You gave us a hell of a ride." And then it was over. The most exciting and one of the greatest careers in ring history at long last had come to an end.

The ensuing years were difficult for Ali. The profession by which he'd defined himself was gone. His health continued to deteriorate, and his marriage was about to fail. Visitors to his Los Angeles mansion came away with a feeling of sadness.

"I remember going to his home," Alex Wallau recalls. "It was beautiful, with Persian rugs and wonderful art. If you gave it to the ambassador to the Court of St. James's as his official residence, he'd have been thrilled. But that home, with all its beauty, wasn't part of Ali. Mentally, he was someplace else. People told me he wasn't well; that they'd be on the telephone with him, and in the middle of the conversation he'd forget who he was talking with. So I expected someone who wasn't there mentally, but that wasn't what I found. What I saw was a man who was fully aware of his surroundings, but somehow detached from life in a very strange way. I thought it was as much an ailment of the heart as of the head, but clearly, something was wrong. And it was very sad; I felt for him."

ALEX HALEY: "You could tell it was a difficult time for Ali. I saw him at a fund-raiser in his home. Some organization had gotten him to make the house available; and I don't usually go to those things, but I went to this one. Twenty years had passed since I'd interviewed him at the Hotel Theresa. Since then, Malcolm's autobiography had been published; *Roots* had happened. Ali told me how happy he was for my success, and introduced me to his wife, who was a beautiful woman. But even though he had the big mansion and the gorgeous wife, he seemed very much alone. He was kind of just floating around. The entourage wasn't there anymore; he knew he'd never fight again. He looked lonely, and I felt sorry for him."

GEORGE PLIMPTON: "I was in Los Angeles [in 1984] and went to Ali's house to see him. He showed me some magic tricks. And one thing about Ali as a magician is, his religion says you can't deceive anyone. So after he performs a trick, he shows you how it's done, which has probably made him the bane of all magicians. That afternoon, I learned how to make a handkerchief disappear and how one gives the appearance of levitating. But then Ali started looking for his championship belt. He wanted to show it to me, and he couldn't find it. I saw him sitting at his desk, working laboriously to sign his name. He wasn't even a shadow of what I'd seen before. And despite being filled with beautiful things, the house seemed so empty and bare."

Meanwhile, concern over Ali's health was mounting, and in September 1984 he checked into the Columbia-Presbyterian Medical Center in New York for a series of diagnostic tests. "I'm not suffering," he told reporters. "I'm in no pain. It's really nothing I can't live with. But I go to bed and sleep eight, ten hours; and two hours after I get up, I'm tired and drowsy again. Sometimes I have trembling in my hands. My speech is slurred. People say to me, 'What did you say; I can't understand you.' I'm not scared, but my family and friends are scared to death."[6]

After eight days of tests, Ali was released, and a brief public statement was issued by his supervising physician, Stanley Fahn:

To Whom It May Concern:
    With regard to my patient, Muhammad Ali, no definitive diagnosis can be given at this time. However, the following has been determined:
    1. Muhammad Ali does not have Parkinson's disease.
    2. Ali exhibits some mild symptoms of Parkinson's syndrome.

3. Ali is responding well to medication. It is anticipated that his symptoms can be reversed with medication, and that he can lead a normal life.

4. There is strong reason to believe that Ali does not have a progressive degenerative condition. It is anticipated that with medication his condition will stabilize with Ali doing very well.

5. Ali does not suffer from dementia pugilistica, commonly referred to as "punch-drunkenness." Ali's mind is impressively alert and well-oriented.

6. Ali's life is not threatened by his condition. His life expectancy is in no way diminshed by his condition.

7. Ali's condition is not contagious.

8. Ali should be fully able to effectively carry out personal appearances and other business activities indefinitely.

However, Fahn's statement raised as many questions as it answered; foremost among them being, "What was wrong with Ali?" Clearly, he was ailing. Just as clearly, he needed someone to care for him. But the nature of his infirmity was still undefined, and there was doubt as to how long Veronica would be there for him.

MARYUM ALI: "I never liked Veronica. I can sense people; I have that gift. And the first time I met her, I saw the future. My parents weren't even divorced yet, but I could see them splitting up. And I knew that when my father stopped fighting and the bright lights and money disappeared, Veronica would be gone. I'm not saying everything was her fault. When I got older, I confronted my father about what happened, and he admitted to me that he did wrong. But Veronica was a cold person inside. I was always worried about my father with Veronica. She was like a stage wife. She didn't cook. They had somebody else take care of the kids, while she was off being a star. I didn't trust her. Veronica was a beautiful woman, but there's a difference between being a beautiful woman and being a beautiful person inside."

LLOYD WELLS: "At the start, Ali was smitten with Veronica. I remember once, on a television show, he said that she was the best thing that ever happened to him. And me and Gene Kilroy jumped all over him. I said, 'You're crazy; what about your momma? You got one momma, and at the rate you're going, you're gonna have a hundred wives. This wife will be gone, but your momma will still be your momma.' We gave him hell, me and Kilroy. We jumped down his throat on that one. And later we asked him, 'If your momma and your wife was drowning, who would you save?' He wouldn't say; he didn't want to think like that. And we told him, 'Fool, you can always get another wife, but your momma, she's always your momma. Ain't but one of those; ain't nothing like a mother's love.'

"But then things soured between Ali and Veronica. He got sick, and some people say she treated him bad. But I don't fault Veronica as much as others do. Ali was pretty hard to live with at that point in his life. He's different now, but back then, he wanted to have his cake and eat it too. Things fell apart, but don't blame it all on her. In my view, if Ali had treated Veronica right, she'd probably still be his wife today."

LONNIE ALI: "After a while, from what I understand, the marriage became difficult for both Muhammad and Veronica. I don't know everything that happened. To this day, I don't really know Veronica well. But I know Muhammad; he has insecurities like the rest of us, and I think he was captivated by Veronica's beauty. Now you and I know it takes more than that for a marriage to work. And Muhammad knows it now, too. But when they met, all he could see was Veronica's face. She might have had other qualities that attracted him as well, but certainly her looks were the most obvious. She was, and still is, a very beautiful woman, and Muhammad was totally enamored of her looks.

"As for assigning blame, I don't believe that's my function, but clearly, it wasn't all one person's fault. In starting a relationship with a married man, I'm sure Veronica felt she was only doing what Muhammad wanted. But let's face it. There are lots of things that Muhammad might want that Muhammad doesn't get because Muhammad shouldn't have them. And even when I was Veronica's age I knew that. Plus, Muhammad might take what you give—and certainly, a lot was offered to him during that period—but if you put your foot down and say no, he's always accepted that. Muhammad was never one to pursue and chase and cajole women into giving more than they were comfortable with. And thankfully, over the last five or six years, he's grown more respectful of marriage in general.

"As for the divorce, it wasn't a question of Veronica leaving Muhammad or Muhammad leaving Veronica. Rather, they came to the mutual understanding that their lives were going in different directions and they weren't suited for each other anymore. And that was a sad time for Muhammad. I've known him since I was six years old; I grew up with him before we were married. And the first time I saw Muhammad cry was when he and Veronica decided to split up, and he realized he wouldn't be living with Hana and Laila anymore; that that type of life, his family life, was about to come to an end."

Once it was clear that Ali and Veronica were getting a divorce, the focus shifted, as it often does, to money. For a while, it looked as though Ali would be protected. His primary assets were four pieces of real estate and a municipal bond trust fund. The property included his Los Angeles mansion, an apartment complex in Virginia, the training camp at Deer Lake, and the Berrien Springs farm. All totaled, Ali had a net worth in the millions. But equally important, before he and Veronica were married, a prenuptial contract protecting his interests had been signed.

MICHAEL PHENNER: "Hopkins & Sutter didn't draft the prenuptial agreement. It was in place before we became involved, but it was an excellent agreement and an excellent idea. Then, after we started representing Ali, he and Veronica moved to California, which is a community property state. And around that time, Ali started asking me to void the agreement. At least once a month, he'd say, 'Mike, let's get rid of it; tear it up.' And I'd tell him, 'Ali, why do you care? It's only there to protect you.' That always satisfied him, but then Veronica started calling. Whenever she called, I'd say it wasn't appropriate for me to discuss it with her. But clearly, voiding the agreement was an item on her agenda, and she also seemed very aware of the status of Ali's money. Around the time of the Holmes fight, we'd created an irrevocable trust with something like two million dollars in it. My recollection is that it paid him close to fifteen thousand a month after taxes. Unfortunately, when we put the trust in place, the longest period Ali would agree to was five years. And Veronica knew it was a five-year trust. We weren't representing Ali by the time of the divorce, but I understand it was timed pretty carefully to coincide with the dissoluton of the trust."

GENE DIBBLE: "If Ali had chosen to enforce that prenuptial agreement, he'd have come out of the divorce in good shape financially. But you know Ali. Veronica convinced him that, even though she'd signed the agreement, she'd given up her career for him. Then she said she needed lots of money for Hana and Laila, and that was all Ali needed to hear. The result was, Ali ordered his attorneys to disregard the agreement, and Veronica got an extraordinarily generous settlement. She got the house and everything in it, which included a half-million dollars worth of rugs, paintings, and things like that. The trust fund was divided fifty-fifty, although the money she got wasn't tied specifically to Hana and Laila, so you can make your own guess as to what happened to it. And there were other twists, like Ali paying certain taxes, so by the time they were done, despite the prenuptial agreement, Veronica walked away with more money than Ali."

Ali's divorce became final in the summer of 1986, leaving him temporarily alone and in failing health. Meanwhile, the endless stream of questionable business ventures continued. One typical deal involved the sale of a powdered milk called "Primo" to Third World countries, but the company was undercapitalized and failed. Other plans were more grandiose, to the point of being farcical. Perhaps the most unrealistic was formation of a Muhammad Ali Financial Corporation, whose officers were authorized "to apply for and negotiate a loan in the amount of One Hundred Billion Dollars ($100,000,000,000.00) for the corporation."[7] The money, it was explained, would be used to build three hundred mosques and one hundred thousand low-income apartment buildings in the three hundred largest cities in the United States.

Then another problem arose. Over the course of several years, Ali had endorsed a number of Republican candidates for office. In 1984, he'd nominally supported Ronald Reagan's reelection bid. In 1988, he'd lent his name to George Bush and Utah Senator Orrin Hatch. Reaction to his political activity was mixed; Edwin Meese, who served as counselor to the president and later as attorney general during the Reagan administration, called Ali "a great patriot." But others were saddened by what they saw. Andrew Young bemoaned Ali's support for "candidates whose policies are harmful to the great majority of Americans, black and white." "I don't know why he's doing it," Julian Bond observed, "but it makes me feel bad. Ronald Reagan and George Bush have been tragedies for black Americans, and Orrin Hatch in my opinion is an awful person politically. I'd love to sit down with Ali and discuss it. I wish I could say to him, 'Listen, don't do that.'"

Then, in December 1988, the *Atlanta Journal-Constitution* published a three-part investigative report by Dave Kindred. "In an act of political deception aimed at the U.S. Senate," the first article began, "an imposter using Muhammad Ali's name and voice has made hundreds of telephone calls to dozens of politicans, journalists, and Capitol Hill staffers."[8] Among those receiving the calls, Kindred reported, were six United States senators, a former governor, and the attorney general of the United States. The caller spoke articulatley, seemed conversant with politics, and sought to advance three goals:

(1) The appointment of a University of Virginia law professor to a job in the Justice Department.
(2) The investigation of a federal prosecutor, who had pursued a case against a Virginia businessman; and
(3) Enactment of special legislation which would enable Ali to sue the United States government for damages suffered as a result of being prosecuted for refusing induction into the armed forces two decades earlier.

The calls struck Kindred as odd. In twenty-two years of dealing with Ali, he'd never known him to be interested in political minutiae. Moreover, the caller's verbal skills were in marked contrast to what was known about Ali's health. Kindred decided to investigate, and found a common denominator in the person of a Virginia attorney named Richard Hirschfeld. Hirschfeld was friends with the law professor in question. He was a former business associate of the man who had been investigated by the federal prosecutor in question. He himself was under investigation by the same prosecutor. And he was one of Ali's attorneys, with a presumed interest in Ali's litigation against the government. Growing more curious, Kindred investigated further and was deeply disturbed by what he found.

DAVE KINDRED: "I read in *The Washington Post* about Ali's political involvement and the telephone calls he was supposed to be making on behalf of various political projects. And it rang completely false to me. I'd known him for over twenty years, and to my knowledge, he'd never had a long political conversation with anyone. Then I remembered something that an aide to Herbert Muhammad had told me: that there were a dozen people around the country who imitated Ali's voice on the phone. And at that point, an alarm went off in my head.

"A few years earlier, Ali had been on *The David Letterman Show*, and Letterman asked him something about a business venture in Virginia Beach. Ali couldn't answer the question, so he told Let-

terman to call his lawyer, Richard Hirschfeld, out of the audience
to give him a response. Anyway, on a hunch, I called one of the
people Ali had become political buddies with, Orrin Hatch, and said
I needed to talk to Hirschfeld. Then when I got hold of Hirschfeld,
I told him that since the Democratic convention was going to be in
Atlanta, I wanted to talk to Ali about politics. Two weeks later, I
was at home one night and the telephone rang. A voice said, 'David,
it's Ali. I hear you want to talk about politics.' Whoever it was, we
talked about politics for forty-five minutes. And when we finished,
I didn't know who I'd been on the phone with, but I knew it wasn't
Ali. That voice was good. It was a practiced impression, with Ali's
rhythm, Ali's language, Ali's breathing, all by someone who knew
Ali very well. But what it was, really, was someone doing Ali's voice
as that person wished Ali were today; admitting the brain damage,
admitting the voice problems, yet retaining the wit, charm, and
quickness of the young Ali. And you can't have all those things
together, so the next questions were: who and why? I pursued the
story, and after a while, I became convinced it was Hirschfeld. I
think he did it for two reasons—to get himself out of a couple of
jams he was in with the federal government, and to push several
projects and appointments he was interested in.

"If you look at the record, on three occasions Hirschfeld was
involved in the violation of federal securities laws. [In 1974] he tried
to start a Hirschfeld Bank of Commerce in Virginia and was charged
by the Securities and Exchange Commission with fraud. [In 1984]
he sold stock in an Ali boxing camp, and the SEC charged him with
hiding the fact that a six-hundred-thousand-dollar note which was
the company's principal asset was worthless. [In 1986] he pled guilty
to criminal contempt in connection with another of his companies,
Hirsch-Chemie Limited. He's been barred for life from practicing
as a lawyer before the SEC, and has had other problems as well.

"I don't know why Ali is with Hirschfeld. My guess is, early on,
he produced some money for Ali, and Ali responded to that. And
I'm sure Hirschfeld treats Ali well on a superficial level. I would
too if he was my ticket to every shady business deal I could dream
up, and Hirschfeld is a very imaginative guy."

RICHARD HIRSCHFELD: "First of all, I never called anyone on
the telephone and pretended to be Ali. You might not believe me,
but that's the truth. Do I coach Ali as to what I think he should do
and say politically? Yes, I do. But I don't think that's out of line or
unusual.

"As for my business dealings with Muhammad, there's a difference between making money around Ali and making money off Ali. I won't tell you I never made money around Ali. But I can say in all honesty that I've never taken a penny from Muhammad, and he's never lost money in any deal I put him into. That's the beauty of the things I got him into. He didn't have to do anything to be paid, except on occasion be there. I negotiated a deal with a gentleman from Switzerland [Wilhelm Wolfinger] that paid Ali twenty thousand dollars a month for a year. He got a salary of seventy-six thousand dollars from a company called Champion Sports that I founded. I put together a deal in connection with a refinery in the Sudan which paid a million dollars split three ways between Ali, Herbert, and myself. We left that money in the refinery. Since then, they've devalued the Sudanese pound and had some economic problems over there, so our stake is worth considerably less than a million dollars. But none of those projects required Ali to put up any money or endorse any obligations. He couldn't lose; there was no personal exposure. All we did was benefit jointly from his name.

"So that's what I have to say about my business dealings with Ali. And let me say one more thing for the record. No matter what you or anybody else writes, it won't be as bad as some other things which are true that you could write about me. No matter what you say, you'll only hit scar tissue. I know that sounds like a very self-deprecating remark, but it happens to be accurate. Some people trust me; some people don't. Some people love me; a lot more have me on their hate list. And you know something? I don't care. I'd rather have one or two close friends than be one of those guys who says, 'I love all mankind; I love everybody, and everybody loves me.' Because the guy who thinks he has a hundred friends really doesn't have any. You only need six people to carry your coffin."*

Richard Hirschfeld has supporters and critics. Ali remains fond of him to this day. But others question Hirschfeld's motives and judgment. Kindred speaks for them when he says, "Nobody steps up and says, 'Yeah, I hustled Ali.' Nobody admits they exploited him and screwed him over. But that's what happens. They act like Ali has an infinite number of lives and skins, and anyone can take

---

*On November 28, 1990, Hirschfeld was indicted by a federal grand jury in Virginia on four counts of conspiracy and tax fraud. On March 5, 1991, as this book went to press, he was convicted on three of them, with the jury deadlocked on the fourth count. An appeal is expected.

what they want and it won't matter. But it does matter. It takes a toll, and it's a tragedy. Ali could have been anything, and he winds up being so much less than he might have been because of the way the exploiters took advantage of him. He could still be such a force for good. And to see him in the shadows, still being taken advantage of by people who too often abuse his kindness; to see all that when he should be standing in sunlight, that's very sad to me."

Meanwhile, as Ali's finances continued to be the subject of rumors and speculation, so was his physical condition. "For many years, I refused to accept the fact that he was sick," Patti Dreifuss remembers. "Even when he was young and healthy, there had been times when it was hard to hear him. He might yell and shout in public, but then we'd be alone and he'd be so quiet I'd have to bend over to understand what he was saying. So for a long time, I told myself, 'He's stopped performing; that's all. It's just a question of his being the same person in public now as he was behind the scenes before.' But after a while, as his voice kept getting worse, you got the feeling, you knew."

GARY SMITH: "After Ali retired, I ran into him a half-dozen times in connection with stories I was writing for *Sports Illustrated*. And each time, there was never any connection with the previous encounter. It wasn't like, 'Oh, I remember you.' I never heard, 'You were here last month,' or, 'I saw you a couple of weeks ago.' It was always like we were starting fresh. And I didn't know if that was the physical impairment, or because he dealt with so many thousands of people that he couldn't possibly remember each one. All his life he'd seen so many people that, even in his good days, it must have been hard to see the world in any way other than a colossal blur. Most of the time we spent together, he was fully aware of what was going on. Everything seemed clear in his head. But then he'd kind of fade away. His thought processes seemed to come and go, kind of like a radio, and I'd wonder if it was voluntary or not.

"I spent a day with him for a story I wrote about the entourage in the winter of '87–'88. Ali asked if I wanted to watch him work out. I did, and he took me to a little gym to show me he could still shadow-box and hit the heavy-bag. What I remember most about that experience was the difficulty he had getting in and out of the gym. It was locked, and it took him several minutes to get the key in the lock and open it. But instead of acting sheepish or making excuses, he kept plugging away. There was something honorable in

how he went about it. There was great dignity in the way he dealt
with his condition. He wasn't going to stop until he got the lock
open and accomplished what he was there for. So when people ask
me, do I feel sorry for Muhammad Ali, the answer is no. And this
might sound strange, but I think in some ways he almost welcomes
his condition as a buffer. I'm sure at times it's frustrating for him
not to be able to talk and do things the way he did before. But I
also think that part of him, the more spiritual side, doesn't want it
to be the way it used to be. After running like crazy for twenty-five
years, I think he's happy for an excuse to slow down."

JOHN SCHULIAN: "I got a look at what life was like for Ali a few
years ago when the Boxing Writers Association of America gave me
an award for writing about boxing. There was a dinner at the United
Nations. I was sitting on the dais next to Ali, who was getting a
lifetime achievement award, and it was a madhouse. He came in,
sat down, and immediately was besieged by fans, everybody just
swarming around him. 'Muhammad, sign this! Muhammad, sign
that!' There was an unemployed actor who was saying, 'Muhammad,
I've been following you since I was a kid in Nebraska; I cried the
night Ken Norton broke your jaw.' A waitress was saying, 'Muhammad, I named my son after you.' There were Wall Street brokerage
house and lawyer types asking, 'Would you sign this for my daughter;
her name is Muffy.' They'd spell out the name, and he'd very slowly
write it on the program or whatever it was he was signing. Then
somebody shoved a boxing magazine from 1965 in front of him. The
cover story was, 'Can Cassius Clay Beat Sonny Liston a Second
Time?' He opened the magazine and stared at the pictures, absolutely transfixed. Meanwhile, all these people were still clamoring
around. Ushers and security people were saying, 'Come on, give
the champ some room, let him breathe.' And more and more people
were coming over, asking for autographs on anything they had in
their hands. Then a woman came up behind us. A very attractive
woman; I'd say she was in her early forties. She tapped him on the
shoulder. Ali looked up. She smiled at him and asked, 'Do you
remember me?' He didn't have the slightest idea who she was. And
you sensed that somewhere along the line, this had been a one-time
meeting that had probably been the crowning achievement of this
woman's history, but for Ali it had just been one more pretty girl
in a long long line. Then she went off. He signed more autographs.
Finally they started serving dinner. The people drifted away, and
all of us at the dais were chatting to the person sitting next to us,

who in my case was Ali. He had a water glass which was empty, and turned it upside down on his napkin. Then he took a pen, traced around the edge so there was a circle on the napkin, and did some more drawing. Then he nudged me, and said, 'See that?' I looked, and he'd drawn a globe. He'd drawn some continents inside the circle, and created his own little globe. And he said to me in a hoarse whisper, 'See that? I used to be champion of all that. I was the heavyweight champion of the world.' And then during the speeches, before it was time for him to get up and accept his award, he fell asleep."

In July 1987, there was another flurry of medical activity around Ali. Appearing at a World Boxing Council symposium in Mexico City, Ali was introduced to a Mexican surgeon who offered his services for an operation to transplant tissue from Ali's adrenal gland to his brain. Ali's family and Dennis Cope, his supervising physician from the UCLA Medical Center, strongly opposed the procedure, which was experimental and had a 10 percent mortality rate. It was never performed, but a year later, another healer was on the scene.

Dr. Rajko Medenica was born in Yugoslavia and moved to Switzerland in 1968. Thereafter, he was convicted of fraud in absentia in Yugoslavia, and served sixteen months in a Swiss prison in connection with various medical-related charges. The primary allegations against him, which Medenica says were politically motivated, involved bills for seven hundred Yugoslavian patients who Medenica claimed to have treated in Geneva. The Yugoslavian government alleged that more than two million dollars in fees relating to 180 of those patients was fraudulent.

Medenica moved to the United States in 1981 and became a U.S. citizen in 1986. He has authored more than three hundred articles in the fields of immunology, oncology, and blood disorders, and held a series of impressive teaching and clinical positions around the world—all of which has won him the trust and admiration of a number of prominent patrons, including South Carolina Governor John West and Senator Strom Thurmond. Recently, the Yugoslavian government sought his extradition in connection with additional criminal charges, but Thurmond interceded with State Department officials and extradition was blocked. A similar Swiss attempt was stymied when a federal judge in South Carolina ruled that Medenica's absence from the state would imperil the lives of his patients.

Ali and Medenica met in June 1988. Thereafter, Medenica told Ali that the cause of his slurred speech and slowed movement wasn't

brain damage. Rather, according to Medenica, Ali's symptoms were
the result of an extraordinarily high level of pesticides in his blood.

On July 5, 1988, Ali began undergoing treatment with Medenica
at Hilton Head Hospital in South Carolina. Since then, despite some
skepticism in the medical community, he has returned to the hospital
roughly at three-month intervals for "plasmapheresis"—a procedure
by which his blood is removed, filtered through a machine to elim-
inate toxins, and returned to his body in a purified state.

DR. RAJKO MEDENICA: "Ali suffers from an immunological and
metabolic neurological disorder. When I examined him, there was
a domestic pesticide, I won't say which one, that was in his blood
seven hundred times what was normal. Why it was in his blood, I
don't know. It could have been breathed in or come through the
food he ate or the water he drank. Probably, it was introduced over
a period of time, maybe as long as five or six years. He started to
show symptoms in 1980, and I think the pesticides were introduced
at least one year before that. Then his body began producing antibodies to fight the pesticides. The antibodies caught the hapten
[small molecules] of pesticides, joined with them, and created an
immune complex. This immune complex is what causes his problems. It circulates in Muhammad's blood, and has sedimentated in
the small blood vessels of his nerves and brain. His condition does
not appear anywhere in classical medical literature. I have discovered it, and I called it 'The Muhammad Ali Syndrome.'

"By cleaning Muhammad's blood, I remove the immune complex
that is in his plasma. At the same time, I replace the plasma with
a combination of albumin, gammaglobulin, minerals, and vitamins
in the same percentage as you find in his blood. What happens next
is, there is movement of cellular fluid from his nerve and brain
tissues to his blood. When that occurs, the immune complexes that
have sedimentated travel into the blood, where they can be removed
the next time I take out plasma. In other words, each time I take
out plasma, I remove more immune complex.

"The healing process will involve many cleanings and take several
years to complete. It will take as long for him to recover as it took
for the condition to be caused. His voice will take even longer to
make right, because his vocal cords haven't been used properly for
a long time. If somebody has been in bed for months, their legs
become soft; they have trouble walking. It is like that now with
Muhammad's vocal cords. They have lost their elasticity.

"Each plasmapheresis treatment that I give him lasts for five to six hours. During that time, I filtrate fifteen to twenty liters of blood. That's two to three times Muhammad's volume of blood, so I'm recirculating his blood between two and three times. During the procedure, he lies down and watches television. There's no anesthesia. He wears a normal hospital gown. As soon as the procedure is finished, he gets up and walks out of the room. There are still pesticides in Muhammad's blood, but not as many as before. And the pesticides in his blood aren't the true marker of his condition. The true marker is the pesticides that have sedimentated—the ones that remain in his nerves and brain. Eventually, those pesticides will be gone, and Muhammad will be very good. His speech will improve; his movement will be better. I think he will be recovering completely."

Medenica acknowledges that he never discussed his findings or treatment with Stanley Fahn or Dennis Cope. "They are in different medical institutions," he says. "I have their reports and the information from their examinations. If they want to talk with me, I would be happy to talk with them, but I don't see that they can give me more information than I have already read from their reports. I have everything I need for the complete picture."

Still, Dennis Cope, who monitors Ali's health at UCLA, voices doubt. "I don't want to attack another physician," says Cope, "but I've found no evidence that would support Dr. Medenica's findings. After his report, we ran tests to determine the presence of chlorinated pesticides in Muhammad's blood. The tests were run on September 14, 1988, and sent to the Smith-Klein Bioscience Laboratory, which can detect one part per million. No chlorinated pesticides were detected. There was no evidence of them whatsoever."*

FERDIE PACHECO: "Forget about what Medenica says. Ali is injured, he's hurt. That's all there is to it. People come to him all the time with this or that cure, and none of them work. And then you have the people who claim he's in marvelous health with nothing wrong. They're the ones who you hear say, 'I talked to Ali this morning, and he sounded great.' Really? I talked to him last month, and I couldn't understand what he said. We were on the phone. He

---

*Lonnie Ali voices support for Medenica's findings and treatment, a view encouraged by recent studies suggesting a link between Parkinsonism and agricultural chemicals. "I believe Dr. Medenica is helping Muhammad," she says. "I know many people don't feel that way, but they don't live with Muhammad and I do."

called me, and I asked him for his number because he changes it more often than the CIA. He gave it to me, and I had no idea what he was saying. I told him, 'Thanks, now let me speak to Bingham.' And I got the telephone number from Howard.

"Ali was, and still is, a very special person. His face had all the emotion in the world. If he was joyful, every muscle showed it. Now, most of the time, he's got that dull flat look. And I hate it. If this is what boxing does, then it shouldn't be a sport. But this is not what boxing does. This is what boxing does if you stay on too long. Age thirty is the cusp. Thirty-five is over the line. I don't care how good you are, after age thirty-five you're getting brain damage. If Ali had quit when he should have quit, he wouldn't be having these problems today. But he didn't, and now you see what happened.

"I don't know what it was that made him fight those last few fights. I don't know why he wasn't satisfied in terms of his desire for public recognition and achievement. I don't know why, but I guess I do. It's said about all great fighters who can't give it up. It's what they do; they're fighters. If you're a fighter, you fight, and it's very difficult to walk away from what makes you great. The three greatest fighters of all time—Joe Louis, Sugar Ray Robinson, and Muhammad Ali—each fought past the age when they should have stopped, and they all wound up physically impaired. There's a message in that for anyone who's paying attention."

As the 1980s ran their course, Ali's glory seemed more and more distant. In 1988, Bundini became the first member of the entourage to die, when he suffered a stroke and was found by a maid in a motel room.

"Muhammad didn't say much about it when Bundini died," Lonnie Ali recalls. "But I knew he was upset, because for a month or two afterward, I'd catch him looking out into space. He and Bundini spent a lot of time together, and Muhammad had never had anybody that close to him die. It cast a shadow over his life, knowing there was someplace else and not knowing where that place was for Bundini."

RALPH THORNTON: "Bundini; oh my God, what a man. God rest his soul. He was a magnificent uncontrollable force that might do or say anything at any moment. I don't know what it was that tore at his soul, but I know it was bad. He'd go on binges, drink for two or three days without stopping. Once, I remember, we were up at camp and he was drunk, shooting into the air at three o'clock in the morning. Pow! Pow! The neighbors' lights were going on. Bundini was screaming, 'Me and Shorty are gonna straighten this out.' But Bundini was one of the main forces behind Ali. He knew how to motivate him, make him mad, make him work. A lot of times, Ali made Bundini his whipping boy; and I guess there were times he deserved it. But there was a spiritual bond between them, and it's a sorrow that Bundini isn't here anymore."

Two years after Bundini's death, Lana Shabazz died from cancer. "She was a wonderful woman," Gary Smith remembers. "Very big-hearted; part Harlem, part Alabama. She'd been like the mother of the camp, and she'd looked after Muhammad like her own child. She worried about everything he ate, whether his room was too cold with the air conditioner on, if he was sleeping right, every little thing like that. When Ali left boxing, it was as though Lana had lost her little boy. You could tell something was missing from her life. She'd joke about it and say she was getting along, but it was obvious that someone very important to her was gone."

LANA SHABAZZ: "What was Ali like? In my feelings, the way I saw him, there's never been anyone like him in the world, and I don't think there will be again. What made him special was the way he gave to people, and the joy he brought to everyone. I gave myself to him because I thought he deserved it, and I'm loving him up until the end.

"Sometimes now I get mad at Ali. Me and Blood and some of the others are getting on in years, and we always thought that when he retired, he'd provide for us. You know, everybody works to retire some day. We're too old to start a new life now, and we worked hard for Ali. I was never a hanger-on. When Ali met me, I was working in the Muslim restaurant. I had a job; I was doing just fine. I was making as much money as I made later on with Ali. And the people who love Ali, the ones who were the most loyal—we thought Ali would take care of us later, and it didn't work out that way.

"I know if I'd asked Ali for money, he'd have given it to me. Everybody used to ask him for money, and he always gave it. But my momma always taught me, if you give everything you have to someone the way I gave to Ali, you aren't supposed to ask for nothing back. They're supposed to give it to you without the asking. So like I said, sometimes I get mad at Ali. I'm still working; eight, nine hours a day. I just got out of the hospital. You know I haven't been feeling good lately. I live in an apartment where there are all those stairs to climb. But then I'll see Ali, like the last time he was in New York, and I love him to pieces all over again.

"There'll never be anyone like Ali. A while ago, some people asked if I wanted to work for Mike Tyson. I'd never met Tyson before, and the money they were offering was good, so I figured I should take a look. He was fighting at Madison Square Garden. They gave me a ticket, and I went to the fight. But then Tyson came into the ring and started after the other guy, and I said to myself, 'Lana, you don't want to work for that boy. He's gonna kill somebody; he's crazy.' You see, I needed the money, but I want to work for someone I can get close to and love. I'm not just a cook; I want to be with family. That's the way it always was between me and Ali.

"And I had a dream about Ali, real recent like. In the dream, there were two Alis. One was like he is now with the sickness; and he treated me bad, like he didn't want to have anything to do with me. But then I went further in the dream, and I came to Ali the way he used to be. He was healthy and happy and he treated me right. That's when I woke up, and it was like—how can I say this— being with Ali, every day was a sunshine day; and being without him, there's no sunshine. But I realize that God brought him special into the world to do what he did and be who he was, and Ali is what he's supposed to be."

As the years pass, more members of the Ali entourage will pass away. Several are currently in poor health; others are getting on in years. But whatever happens, for all those who were part of the Ali entourage, the world has irrevocably changed.

"A lot of the people who attached themselves to Ali never had any other family," observes Gary Smith. "Muhammad brought something special into their lives. They lived it; they enjoyed it. They weren't people who planned ahead and asked themselves what they'd be doing when they were sixty years old. They were on the same train and they stayed on it with Ali up until it came to the end of the line. A few of them got off all right. Ferdie Pacheco is doing well professionally. Howard Bingham has his own career as a photographer, and one or two of the others are doing okay. But for all of them, life will never be the same. And it won't ever be as good as it was when they were with Ali."

PAT PATTERSON: "I had so many great moments with Ali. A lot of them might not have mattered to the rest of the world, but they were very special to me. The best times I had were up at Deer

Lake. It was like we had our own little village. Everybody got to be themselves; the family really came together. We'd sit there, talking about whatever crossed our mind. And believe me, it was very special to have those moments with Ali. The rest of the world saw the fights and the glory. But we were there at six o'clock in the morning, when he came back from running with ice under his nose. We laughed with him at night, shared good times and bad.

"I remember once at camp, Ali had finished working out. He was getting a rubdown; he was dead tired. There were twenty or thirty people waiting outside, which is like it always was. And Ali said, 'Tell them I'm not coming out. I'm not signing autographs or taking pictures today. I'm too tired; I want to rest.' But then he looked at me kind of funny; you know that look. And he said, 'Those people came from all over the world to see me. It's wrong if I make them go away disappointed.' So he went out and gave them what they wanted. And that's the way it always was with Ali."

LLOYD WELLS: "When I see Ali today, I still get a rush, a feeling in my heart. The man is such a beautiful person. Sure, he made his share of mistakes. But when Ali thought something was right, he'd do everything he could to defend it. He never turned his back on his beliefs. And in the end, the whole world loved him. At the end, hardly anybody wanted to see him get beat. I had an old man tell me something once. And I'll never forget it, because it describes Ali best to me. The man said, 'Hell, even the people who don't like Ali like Ali.'"

One arena where Ali is very much loved is in the world of sports. "Ali is the King of Athletes," says Reggie Jackson, "and everyone joyously gives him that. You could sit Ali down with Jim Brown, Bill Russell, Wayne Gretzky, Jack Nicklaus, Kareem Abdul-Jabbar, Michael Jordan, Willie Mays, all the greats. These are guys who were, and in some cases still are, as great in their field of endeavor as Ali was in his. But for all of them, Ali would be King. He was bigger than boxing; he was bigger than sports. When people call Muhammad Ali 'the greatest,' they know what they're talking about."

Jackson's thoughts are echoed by another great athlete—Henry Aaron—who in 1974, the year Ali dethroned George Foreman, hit his 715th career home run to eclipse Babe Ruth's hallowed mark.

HENRY AARON: "I was born in Mobile, Alabama, in 1934. I came up with the Braves when I was twenty, and coming from Mobile,

I was very shy. I wasn't satisfied with the way things were, but I felt like I had to do something special in baseball in order to get people to listen to me. By the time Ali came along, things were a little different but not that much. My first awareness of him was when he won the gold medal, and I saw greatness stamped all over him. How great, I didn't know, but I was impressed by his ability and his confidence.

"Being a gifted athlete, being one of the best in the world at what you do, is a great feeling. But sometimes it's kind of eerie, because you wonder why you're blessed with so much ability. I'd go up to the plate to face a pitcher, and I'd know that before the night was over I was going to hit one out of the ballpark. I felt that, and I'm sure Ali felt the same way. That no matter who he got in the ring with, he was better and he'd figure them out. He had all kinds of confidence, and I was the same way. The only thing that scared me was, when I was approaching Babe Ruth's record, I got a lot of threatening letters. I'm sure Ali went through the same thing, with letters from people who didn't want him to be heavyweight champion. Most of that stuff is nothing but cranks, but one of them might be for real, and you never know which one.

"I don't think there'll ever be another fighter like Muhammad Ali. I'm not putting anybody else down. Maybe someone could have beaten Ali in his prime, but I'm not concerned about that. There's just no one who could possibly be as beautiful in the ring as he was. For a guy to be that big and move the way he did; it was like music, poetry, no question about it. And for what he did outside the ring, Ali will always be remembered. When you start talking about sports, when you start talking about history; you can't do it unless you mention Ali. Children in this country should be taught forever how he stood by his convictions and lived his life. He's someone that black people, white people, people all across the country whatever their color, can be proud of. I know, I'm glad I had the opportunity to live in his time and bear witness to what he accomplished. God gave Ali the gift, and Ali used it right."

Ali's hold over athletes exists to this day, but he's also an inspiration to those who teach. "From a coach's viewpoint," says Red Auerbach, "he's the kind of guy you want, because first, he's super-competitive, and second, he's got balls. Ali was a winner. Whatever it took, he'd rise to the occasion and do the job in the clutch. Without a doubt, if he's on your team, he's the guy you want taking the last shot."

"Ali would be easy to coach," adds Auerbach's protégé, Bill Russell. "Because he's great, and you don't coach greatness. All you do is counsel."

But for those who view themselves as teachers and "molders of young minds," Ali's greatest appeal lies in what he accomplished outside the ring. John Thompson is a nationally renowned college coach. Harry Edwards is a professor of sociology who sprang to prominence in 1968 when he organized a boycott by black American athletes of the Mexico City Olympics. Both of them reflect on Ali.

JOHN THOMPSON: "For me, it started with curiosity; I found Ali to be entertaining. Then I realized that, in addition to being loud and outspoken, he was a fine athlete. And if he'd never done anything more with his life, that alone would have been an enormous contribution, because he pulled us away from that docility, where black people who were successful sat around acting humble. Ali gave us a role model we could look to, someone who was talented, confident, cocky, and a whole lot more that black people weren't supposed to be. But more important, when the time came, he stood up for what he believed.

"You know, most people, when they reach the plateau Ali was at as heavyweight champion, tend to conceal their true feelings. There's so much to lose; there are risks they won't take. But society needs people who are visible to stand on principle. We need encouragement; we need to see examples. Even as adults, we need role models who will say this is wrong and that's right. And I'm not talking now just about black and white. I'm talking about integrity and dignity and courage for all people. Those qualities are important to me. I can't measure exactly where I learned them, because I've benefited from many people in my life. But certainly Ali was an inspiration to me. Very definitely, he contributed to the man I am today."

HARRY EDWARDS: "Ali is probably the single greatest athletic figure of this century in terms of the black community, largely because he turned around the image of the black athlete. If you look at the sojourn of the black athlete, from 1900 to the 1930s we were struggling for the acceptance of black athletic legitimacy. By the time you get to Jesse Owens and Joe Louis, our legitimacy had been established and we began to struggle for access. That was epitomized by Jackie Robinson in the 1940s, but there were others who carried the struggle past that point. Althea Gibson oftentimes wasn't allowed to live in hotels and practice at the country clubs where the tennis tournaments she participated in were held. Draft rights to Bill Russell were traded by St. Louis to the Boston Celtics, largely because it was felt that St. Louis wasn't ready for a black basketball player. Then you come to the 1960s, when our legitimacy and access were pretty much on track, but we were still struggling for dignity and respect from the sports mainstream and American society. The principals in that struggle were people like Tommie Smith, John Carlos, and Arthur Ashe. But the greatest figure in that regard was Muhammad Ali. And because of the impact of sports on American society, there was a carryover of dignity and pride from Ali's efforts that accrued to all black Americans.

"Later in his life, as Ali's star began to fade, black people in particular and sports in general began to look for another Ali. But there won't ever be another Ali, because the age was different, the time was different, and the individual was unique. I've been around great athletes all my life, and I've long since gotten over being awed by them. These are men and women who happen to do one thing better than anyone else in the world. Box, run, play basketball, hit a baseball. But in my line of work as a sports sociologist, I wind up dealing with their problems. I see their human side, and it was from that perspective that I really came to appreciate Ali.

"I don't know of anyone who doesn't like Ali as a person. Even when he did things that rankled, he carried himself in such a way that forgiveness was easy because there wasn't a malevolent bone in his body. He always seemed fresh and exuberant. He was a wonderful guy to be around. Obviously, there are aspects of his life we could talk about that are less positive. Ali's relationships with women were a downside to his life. He made a lot of money, and there are questions as to whether that money was wisely used or squandered. But all that says is, Ali was a total human being with assets and liabilities and victories and defeats. He was a good man, which I guess is about the greatest thing you can say about any man. I think we're all better off because Muhammad Ali passed this way."

Ali is revered throughout the world of sports, but nowhere is he as beloved as in boxing. Officially, his three reigns as champion totaled less than seven years. But his persona dominated the sport for the better part of two decades.

Ali made boxing a glamour industry. He took it out of smoke-filled rooms, and turned it into a socially acceptable business. Anyone in boxing who makes big money today owes part of it to Ali. In his presence, "mere mortals" (like Sonny Liston), institutions (such as the press), and even countries (the Philippines and Zaire) were reduced to props. "Nobody heard of Vietnam until there was a war," Ali once proclaimed. "Nobody heard of Korea until there was a war. Nobody heard of Zaire until I fought there, and paying me is a whole lot cheaper than fighting a war."[9]

The esteem that Ali enjoys today wasn't always there. Twenty-five years ago, with Vietnam swirling around him, he was the most vilified athlete in America. "Cassius Clay has been the world's heavyweight champion for two years," wrote Milton Gross. "Nobody has ever done less with time and the title, and destroyed his image more."[10] Five days after Ali annihilated Cleveland Williams, Jim Murray of the *Los Angeles Times* wrote a column in which he labeled Ali "the white man's burden."[11]

But times change, people change, and so has the public perception of Ali. Certainly, he still has critics. But even his critics now temper their remarks with fondness toward Ali.

MARK KRAM: "Muhammad is an extraordinarily decent person, and always has been, innately so. There's nothing fake about him; maybe a little street hustle here and there, but he's a good human being. Still, I don't know how to say this except to say it—I don't think Muhammad is very bright, and over the years, I found him somewhat boring. Thrilling as a fighter, but tedious as a person. And if you look back, Ali never said much of worth other than, 'I ain't got no quarrel with them Vietcong.' Other than that, it was a lot of redundant material that kept getting recycled like those wrestlers you see ranting and raving on television.

"The least attractive thing to me about him has always been his Muslim affiliation. I'm not questioning his or anyone else's right to choose their religion. But Muslim doctrine as taught by Elijah Muhammad in the 1960s was like Louis Farrakhan today. If Ali wanted to fight racial injustice, he could have followed Martin Luther King. And if he'd wanted to be a Muslim, there were more peaceful factions he could have chosen. So I think Ali was misguided about his religion then. And even though the more radical elements of Islam in the United States have moderated over the years, I think he's too fanatical about it now. Islam is all he talks about these days. It's a crutch. And I guess he finds that a secure way to go through life, but to me that's a negative in his makeup.

"Now, please, don't misunderstand what I'm saying. I have no ax to grind with Ali. I go back with him to the first Liston fight in

Miami, and I like the man immensely. I just never shared that great fascination the American people have for Ali. I could never understand the mythologizing. Maybe it would be easier to explain if I put what I'm saying in terms of Ronald Reagan. I look at Reagan, and when people talk about him as a great this and a great that, I see him as an amiable man but someone with a clearly limited intellect. And I have similar reservations about Ali. I know a lot of people feel differently about him, but that's how I feel. And even now I'll ask myself, am I the only one who sees this?"

Three writers who covered Ali respond.

BERT SUGAR: "I don't think Ali was boring. Sportswriters become deadly dull when they describe what happens technically in the ring, on the football field, at the track, wherever. And one of the things that was marvelous about Ali was, there was always so much else going on around him. Imagine traveling to the heart of Africa to watch a fight for the heavyweight championship of the world. Or listening to the greatest athlete on earth spout poetry like a precocious child. But all those things are very small compared to the true meaning of Ali.

"Muhammad is one of the few Americans, and certainly the first American athlete ever, to transcend the borders of this country and become an international hero. He was the greatest sports hero of all time. He contributed a man's share times ten to this world, and he's still giving.

"I have a problem in that as a writer I'm supposed to be totally objective, and I am about boxers. But Ali was more than a boxer, and I can't really be objective about him. He stood for an entire era and always said what was on his mind. Everything about him bespoke of individual rights. If he wanted to change his name for religious reasons instead of changing it the way Joe Louis or Ray Robinson did it, that was his right. The pope changes his name for religious reasons when he's elected, and no one complains about that.

"We had a government in the 1960s that gave us Vietnam, and Ali was the wonderful person who gave them back no Vietnam. It didn't take long for the morons and bigots who controlled boxing to steal his title away. When he refused to step forward in Houston, within hours he was defrocked. And you know, all kinds of people can lose their jobs, but with athletes it's different. Their professional lives are very short. They can never recover those golden years. But Ali stood up for what he believed was right. He believed he had a debt to God and society, and that it was incumbent upon him to use his talent for more than knocking people out. And if there's a future for this country, it will be as a result of people like Ali. Outside of Don Quixote, no one ever tilted at windmills more often. And when Ali tilted at windmills, thank God, he usually won."

PAT PUTNAM: "I tend to look at Muhammad in personal terms, rather than in a political way. And as a person, I don't think he's changed much from the young man I knew in Miami in 1960. We all learn about life as we grow older, but his core is still the same. And it's like he's always been family to everyone. When you see him coming, you feel good all over.

"I'll tell you a story about what I mean. Late in Muhammad's career, I went to Deer Lake for *Sports Illustrated,* and I took my son Sean along. Sean was maybe fourteen years old. We stopped for the night at a small motel near Deer Lake. We were planning to go to camp the next morning. Sean and I were in the dining room. He was facing the door; my back was to the door. And all of a sudden this look came over his face. I'd never seen it before; I've never seen it since. It was a look of total awe and reverence. And I knew immediately what had happened; that Muhammad Ali had walked into the room. He'd snuck out of training camp for some ice cream, and was like a little kid, saying, 'Don't tell anybody about this. I shouldn't be here.' But I'll never forget the look that came over my son's face. I even got a little jealous that someone else could have that effect on him, although I enjoyed it at the same time."

JOHN SCHULIAN: "I think Ali is the most interesting and one of the most important people of my lifetime. That might sound like an exaggeration, but the more I've thought about it, the more I think it's true. He touched so many more people than anyone else was capable of touching. There are people in the middle of Africa and Asia who haven't the slightest idea who the president of the United States is, but they know Muhammad Ali. He was more important than any athlete has a right to be or could expect to be. He was important in the antiwar movement; he was important in matters of racial pride; he was important in teaching people how to love. He was such an extraordinary person that, when I think of him, I have to remember almost as an afterthought, 'Oh, yeah; besides everything else, he was a great fighter!' "

But Ali was a great fighter, and thus the question becomes, "How great?" In that regard, the first thing to realize is that Ali before his exile from boxing and Ali afterward had very different abilities and relied on markedly different skills.

"There were two Alis," Cus D'Amato once said. "Before the layoff, the only time anyone could touch him was at the start of a fight when the referee instructed both men to touch gloves. I don't care how many fights he won after the layoff. The young Ali was the real Ali."

When Ali returned to boxing in 1970, his speed was diminished and his legs weren't the same. In their stead, he was more experienced and stronger, with added determination and will. But what the world saw then was an old man's greatness, and most geniuses are at their best when they're young.

Two men—Floyd Patterson and George Chuvalo—fought Ali before and after his exile from boxing. Both think he was better before. "After the layoff," says Chuvalo, "he never regained the efficiency and skill he'd had. He wasn't able to fight at a fast pace for more than a few rounds, whereas he kept it up for fifteen when he was young. For a while, after he came back, you could see him improving. But after Foreman, he started on the way down again. He just couldn't move the way he wanted to anymore."

"Ali was better before," concurs Patterson. "That's when he was in the prime of his life, when he had his speed and all his skills. When he came back, there was still a lot of movement, but not as much as he had before."

MUHAMMAD ALI: "If you put the Muhammad Ali who fought Cleveland Williams and Zora Folley against the Muhammad Ali who fought Joe Frazier and George Foreman, the young Ali would win. I was more experienced when I was older. I was stronger. I had more belief in myself. Except for Sonny Liston, the men I fought when I was young weren't near the fighters that Joe Frazier and George Foreman were. Williams and Folley were light work. But I had my speed when I was young. I was faster on my legs, and my hands were faster. The young Ali would dance, move, get in and out. He'd beat the older Ali all around the ring. The older Ali wouldn't quit. When I was old, against a young version of me, I'd use the rope-a-dope, make charges, and try to knock him out. But I was better when I was young."

ANGELO DUNDEE: "Ali before the layoff was a better fighter than Ali after. But what a lot of people don't realize, and it's very sad, is we never saw him at his peak. The Ali who fought Cleveland Williams and Zora Folley was the best he could be at that time; but he was still improving. He hadn't lost any of his speed, but he was getting bigger and stronger and more experienced in the ring. What was he, twenty-five years old when they made him stop? Those next three years would have been his peak. And if he'd continued getting better at the rate he was going, God only knows how great he would have been."

Greatness in fighters is hard to measure. Comparative statistics like how many seconds it takes to run a mile or how many home runs a man hits don't exist in boxing. But it is possible to compare fighters by watching them on film. And while careers in the ring are relatively short, the memories last forever.

Four respected voices of boxing—Jim Jacobs, Eddie Futch, Al Bernstein, and Mike Katz—comment upon Ali's greatness as a fighter.

JIM JACOBS: "You have to be smart to be a great fighter. And here, let me say, there are many different kinds of intelligence. Mozart was a musical genius, but he probably would have made a very poor rocket scientist; and your average rocket scientist probably isn't a very good financial analyst or banker. But Ali was an absolute genius in the ring—as smart as any fighter who ever lived. And he had one other advantage that no one could match. He was the fastest fighter who ever lived. Not the fastest heavyweight; the fastest fighter I've ever seen, live or on film. No matter what his opponents heard about him, they didn't realize how fast he was until they got in the ring with him.

"People say that, pound for pound, Sugar Ray Robinson was the greatest fighter who ever lived. And I've said that several times myself. But Ali was Sugar Ray Robinson squared. I took some fight films and measured Ray's punches through a synchronizer. Sugar Ray Robinson threw his jab in eight-and-a-half frames. Ali threw his jab in six-and-a-half. Robinson as a welterweight was close to perfection, but when he moved up in weight to 160 pounds, he was beatable. If you made Sugar Ray Robinson a two-hundred-pound fighter with no loss of speed and coordination, I still think Ali in his prime would have beaten him."

EDDIE FUTCH: "I first saw Ali in 1962 when he was in Los Angeles to fight Alejandro Lavorante. He'd caused so much comment by virtue of the fact that he talked so much that before the fight I went to the gym to watch him train. He was working with a pretty good heavyweight, playing with him, doing whatever he wanted. Angelo told me he was going to be champion of the world someday. And of course, you take that sort of thing with a grain of salt, because whenever a trainer gets a fighter, the minute he starts to shadow-box, there's talk about a future champion. But I was impressed by what I saw, and after that I spent a lot of time watching Ali. He continued to improve, and I was amazed at the way he did it. He did things other fighters couldn't get away with, like pulling away from punches with that great sense of speed, balance, and timing. His jab was incredibly fast and accurate, and he had a classic right. His left hook wasn't the best in the world, but it was serviceable. He almost never punched to the body, which I considered a fault; and except for the tactic of pulling his opponent's head down, which is against the rules, he wasn't much of an inside fighter. But he got the most out of what he had. What he could do, he did so well that he became a truly great fighter.

"I'd rank Ali with Joe Louis and Jack Johnson as the three greatest heavyweights of all time. Maybe I'm prejudiced because I came along with Louis, but I think he would have beaten Ali. People remember how hard Louis punched; what they don't remember is what a good boxer he was. I always thought Joe would have seen the flaws in Ali's style and been able to take advantage of them. And being such a great defensive fighter, Jack Johnson might have beaten Ali, too. But Ali was great; no doubt about it. It was a privilege to be in boxing during his time."

AL BERNSTEIN: "I have a theory that there are certain athletes and certain teams for whom good things are going to happen. The New York Yankees of the 1950s, the Green Bay Packers under Vince Lombardi, the Boston Celtics with Bill Russell, the UCLA basketball teams coached by John Wooden. It's not just that they had the ability; it's not just that they were well-coached. I don't believe in destiny and fate, but something always happened for those teams. Were the Dallas Cowboys better than the Green Bay Packers? Absolutely. More talented, a better game plan. But twice in a row, the Packers found a way at the end to win. That game in the freezing cold in Green Bay; everybody's slipping on the ice, and Donny Anderson, who's slow as molasses, is the only one who can keep his footing. I don't know what it is, but those teams had it. And Ali had it. It wasn't that he had the most talent, although obviously he had an awful lot. It's that, more than any athlete ever, he always found a way to win.

"It's hard to compare fighters across generations, but I think Ali was the greatest heavyweight ever. Joe Louis was a better puncher, but so were a lot of the guys Ali beat. Ali wasn't a great finisher like Louis, but he beat three pretty good ones in Sonny Liston, Joe Frazier, and George Foreman. He was a champion's champion."

MIKE KATZ: "Ali was the embodiment of the human spirit; you just couldn't keep him down. A lot of fighters are broken by defeat. They fly so high that when they're shot down it destroys them, but losing never destroyed Ali. If you look at his career, not counting Holmes and Berbick at the end, there were three fighters who beat Ali. Frazier beat him, and he came back to beat Frazier twice. Norton beat him, and he beat Norton twice. Leon Spinks beat him, and at age thirty-six, he came back and beat Leon. Each time he lost, he learned from defeat and came back stronger to win. Ali coming back to beat George Foreman is the ultimate sports fantasy of all time.

"And God, could he fight. I remember against Jurgen Blin, he landed a triple hook. I said to myself, 'You don't see triple hooks.' You don't even see double hooks often now, but nobody throws triple hooks, and Ali wasn't even known as a hooker. He had moves to get away in any direction. Most guys, if they're in trouble and want to escape, they'll go either to their left or their right. Ali could go either way. I think, if he'd wanted, he could have gone up the middle. There are very few guys who could move like Ali. And he always seemed to be in control of exactly where he was and what angle he was presenting. It was as though, if you freeze-framed any particular moment, he was there for a reason. I'm sure he didn't think those things out. Some of them, maybe; but a lot of it was, he was just a great instinctive fighter. And he was able to prove himself against the best opponents of any heavyweight in history. Joe Louis might have been champion longer, but he never had the inquisitors that Ali had. Look at what Ali did. He started out by demystifying Sonny Liston, and went through a pretty good crop of heavyweights: George Chuvalo, Cleveland Williams, Ernie Terrell, Zora Folley. Then he went through another generation headed by Joe Frazier and George Foreman. And there were the other guys like Jerry Quarry, Oscar Bonavena, Ken Norton, and Earnie Shavers, each of whom would be ranked in the top five in the world today. That's an amazing group of opponents. And I'll tell you something. If fighters could fight like baseball teams and play a 162-game schedule; and if you could match the greatest heavyweights of all time at their peak, so Ali was in a league with Jack Johnson, Joe Louis, Jack Dempsey, Rocky Marciano, Gene Tunney, Larry Holmes, Sonny Liston. You know who the best heavyweights are; you can put them all on the list. Ali wouldn't be undefeated; there are guys who would give him trouble on a given night. But I think, when the season was over, Ali would be in first place."

Ali's own heavyweight rankings place himself first, Jack Johnson second, and Joe Louis in third place. Even before Mike Tyson's loss to James "Buster" Douglas, Ali said in private about Tyson, "He's predictable, the way he moves his head. He has fast hands, but he's slow on his feet and my hands were faster than his. The way to beat Tyson is with a fast jab, a hard right hand, and if he hits you, you have to be able to take a punch."

Larry Holmes, who fought Tyson when "Iron Mike" was at his peak, says, "Ali would have slapped Tyson all over the ring. Tyson hits hard but he's a bully, and Ali had a way of dealing with them. Can you imagine the things Ali would have said about Tyson before that fight? He'd have made Tyson so mad, Tyson would have been running into the ropes when they started the fight."

Holmes's view of Ali's ring supremacy is shared by Tyson's early boxing family. Jose Torres and Floyd Patterson were guided to world titles by Tyson's mentor, Cus D'Amato. Bill Cayton served with Jim Jacobs as Tyson's first comanagers. Kevin Rooney and Teddy Atlas worked with D'Amato as Tyson's trainers. When asked to match Ali in his prime against the best Tyson has been to date, all five said Ali would prevail.

JOSE TORRES: "You can't explain Ali in a conventional way because he consistently did the wrong thing in the ring. He didn't bend down. He didn't go to the body. He punched going backwards. He held his hands too low. He pulled straight back from punches. He didn't even throw combinations; he threw punches in flurries. And then he would win for two reasons—speed and magic.

"Against Liston, Ali wanted to quit because of his eyes, but he got pushed out by Angelo Dundee and he wins. It's magic. Against Foreman, he had no business to win, but he destroyed Foreman's mind like a wizard. It's magic. If Ali at his best fought the best Mike Tyson, Mike would have more power, but there would be too much magic. Because of Cus, my heart would be with Tyson. But Ali would box Mike for twelve rounds, fifteen rounds, as many rounds as you want easily."

FLOYD PATTERSON: "I don't want to say anything derogatory about anybody. All I know is, anybody who moves like Clay moved is going to give his opponent a lot of problems. I've seen Tyson with guys who moved a bit, and he had difficulty, so imagine putting him in with Clay. Mike can be hit with the left jab if you time it properly. I don't think he would have gotten by Clay's left. And he wouldn't have knocked Clay out, because Clay took a very good punch and almost never got hit. Clay beats Tyson."

BILL CAYTON: "I honestly believe that Mike Tyson at his best was the second-greatest heavyweight of all time, but he wasn't Muhammad Ali. Mike is quick, but Ali was quicker. Mike has power, but Ali had the greatest chin ever. And Mike, unfortunately, is prone to frustration, which would be his Achilles heel against Ali, because Ali was the best fighter in history at playing mind-games with his opponent. If Ali in his prime fought Mike at his best, I see Ali winning a decision; say, eight rounds to four, or nine rounds to three."

KEVIN ROONEY: "Ali had that special belief in himself that allowed him to impose his will on other fighters. This is a guy who took on three of the toughest heavyweights in history—Sonny Liston, Joe Frazier, and George Foreman—and beat them five out of six. And when he fought Frazier and Foreman, he wasn't even in his prime.

"The young Ali would have frustrated Mike. I see Ali coming out, jabbing, moving, talking a lot. If Mike had me in his corner and his head was screwed on right, it would be close. I'd advise Mike to keep his hands high, be elusive, slip, move in; whenever possible, work the body. Lots of feints, because Ali was a terrific counter-puncher. Believe it or not, I'd work the jab, even if it was only to Ali's chest. It would have been an interesting fight, with both guys missing a lot. But even with Mike at his best, I'd give the edge to Ali."

TEDDY ATLAS: "Ali at his best beats Tyson at his best. At his core, Ali is a much stronger, more stable person. Probably, the way he'd have fought Mike was to rely on what he did best: jab, score from the outside, stay off the ropes, show a lot of side-to-side movement, neutralize the pressure, make Mike pay when he missed, tie him up when he got inside. After a while, Mike would get anxious and be throwing one punch at a time. Then I think he'd break down mentally, which is the area where Ali was strongest. And when that happened, Ali would start putting punches together to punch Mike downhill even more. Finally, when the time was right, without it being too dangerous, Ali would give Mike a reason to fall. I think Ali would knock him out around the ninth or tenth round. But before that, Mike might get so discouraged and beaten mentally that he'd quit the way Liston quit."

One of the few remaining questions about Ali in the ring is the extent to which Angelo Dundee contributed to his success. The belief often exists that a fighter makes the trainer rather than the other way around. "I'm the greatest trainer who ever lived," George Gainsford once boasted. "I trained Sugar Ray Robinson." And the response was, "George, you've had hundreds of fighters. Why weren't they all as good as Sugar Ray?"[12]

Still, most observers believe that Dundee was important to Ali. "Muhammad would have evolved roughly the same no matter who was training him," says Ray Arcel, one of boxing's most venerated trainers. "A lot of what he did in the ring was unorthodox, and no one could teach him to fight like that. In fact, no trainer in his right mind would dare. But Angelo took Ali's God-given talent, improved it where possible, and guided him properly. He was an excellent tactician in the corner. To my mind, he was a tremendous asset to Ali."

"Angelo was a great psychologist," adds Gil Clancy. "Ali at times could be difficult to handle, but Angelo was always able to keep him happy. I don't know if I could have done it Angelo's way. To me, the trainer is supposed to be the boss. He's the guy who tells the fighter, 'Today you're gonna hit the heavy-bag. Today you're gonna box four rounds.' Ali would come into the gym, and Angelo would ask, 'What do you want to do today?' Ali would say he wanted to box ten rounds or whatever, and Angelo would go along with it. I guess he was right to do it that way. Ali was a free spirit, and the results speak for themselves. But if I'd been Ali's trainer, I don't know how long I would have lasted."

ANGELO DUNDEE: "Muhammad was a great natural talent, and he would have been a great champion without me. I'll be the first one to say it wasn't me; he was the guy. And outside the ring, it was him who taught me. He taught me patience; he taught me decency. I watched how he reacted to everything. I saw things done to him that made me sick to my stomach. And all he'd say was, 'You have to forgive people.'

"Muhammad came along at a time when he was needed. He changed a lot of things in and out of boxing. There's so much I remember about being with him. Before the first fight with Sonny Liston, he just about drove Liston crazy. One time, Liston shouted at him, 'You can't punch hard enough to break an egg.' And Muhammad shouted back, 'Oh boy! You stand there, and pretend you're an egg.' He loved being a practical joker. I was afraid of snakes, so he'd go out to do roadwork and come back with a piece of rubber or a stick that looked like a snake and come after me with it, and I'd play along like I was scared. One time, at a hotel in Los Angeles, he lit a towel outside my room, blew smoke under my door, and had me thinking there was a fire. Another time, in Puerto Rico, I was asleep in my room and the curtains were rattling. This was like on the tenth floor with no balcony. So I got out of bed, opened the curtains, looked out. Nothing. I went back to bed; five minutes later, more rattling. Again, nothing. And it went on like that for an hour until I realized it was Muhammad. He'd tied a string to my curtains, run it out the window to his room, and was having a wonderful time driving me crazy.

"The saddest time in his career for me was when they forced him out of boxing in the 1960s. Muhammad suffered when he wasn't allowed to fight, and I don't mean financially. Money was the least of it. He suffered because he loved boxing. Sometimes he'd call me up and say, 'Hey, Ange; how about letting me come down to the gym and work out?' I'd tell him, 'Stop that. It's your gym; you can work out any time you want.' Harold Conrad and the rest of the guys tried everything they could to get him a fight, but nothing worked. I remember once we thought we had it, but the governor of the state where the fight was supposed to be got cold feet, and it was canceled. I went up to Muhammad's room and told him, 'It don't look like it's gonna be.' All Muhammad said was, 'It don't make no difference; life goes on.' I said, 'Man, what are you talking about? I just dug a hole in my backyard. I was gonna build a swimming pool, and now I got to shovel the dirt back because I can't afford it.' And I could see, Muhammad didn't feel bad for himself. The person he felt sorry for was me. God, he was special. You know, the whole time he wasn't allowed to fight, I never heard him complain or show animosity toward anybody. He's not bitter about the years he lost, and that amazes me.

"I used to tell people—and it's true—I wish I was as good a Catholic as he is a Muslim. There's so much more to him than meets the eye; so many things that people don't see. Even now, I'll be sitting around or at a fight, and I'll think of some crazy thing we did together or something that happened to him and me. And with everything he's done, he belongs to boxing. Boxing should be proud of its association with Muhammad. I know I'm proud to have been associated with him. It would be nice if people remember me as Muhammad Ali's trainer, but it's more important to me to be Muhammad's friend."

MUHAMMAD ALI: "When will they ever have another fighter who writes poems, predicts rounds, beats everybody, makes people laugh, makes people cry, and is as tall and extra-pretty as me? In the history of the world from the beginning of time, there's never been another fighter like me."

In the history of the world from the beginning of time, there's never been another anything like Ali.

17

Rebirth

Outside, the air is chill. Autumn leaves have begun to turn. No one else in the house is awake. The most famous man in the world is alone, praying in the minutes just after dawn. "Most people don't pray until they're in trouble," he will say later. "When people need help, they pray a lot. But after they get what they want, they slow down. If a man takes five showers a day, his body will be clean. Praying five times a day helps me clean my mind."

Muhammad Ali spends much of his time on a farm in the southwest corner of Michigan. After he bought it, the rumor spread that Al Capone had been a previous owner. That spurred Bundini Brown to spend countless hours digging for buried treasure, but none was ever found. The house Ali lives in was built in the 1920s. It's spacious and comfortable, with a den, kitchen, and storage room on the ground floor. The den is the most often used room on the farm, with a large sectional sofa, worktable, and forty-six-inch-screen television. The living room and dining room are on the second floor, adjacent to an enclosed porch and two small bedrooms. There are four bedrooms on the third floor. Except on rare formal occasions, the Alis eat in the kitchen and entertain in the den.

Each day, after his morning prayer, Ali goes downstairs to the den. He gives out two thousand autographs a week. Rather than simply sign his name, he sees each request as an opportunity to propagate Islam. In recent years, he has spent two hundred thousand dollars on books and pamphlets, which he carries in a large briefcase wherever he goes. "If I just hand out pamphlets," he explains, "most people would throw them away. But if I sign each one and put on the person's name, people will keep them and read what the pamphlets say."

For two hours, Ali autographs religious tracts. On each one, he writes the word "to" followed by a space and the legend "from Muhammad Ali." The pamphlets will go in his briefcase. Then, whoever he meets, if they want his autograph he'll ask their name, insert it in the space, and date the pamphlet beneath his signature. "I'm not trying to convert anybody," he says. "Only God can do that. I just want to open people's minds, so they'll think about God and Islam."

After signing three hundred pamphlets, Ali eats breakfast—cereal and toast. Then he goes outside for a walk. Recently, Dennis Cope of the UCLA Medical Center told him he needed to exercise. His weight had ballooned to 255 pounds. The once-beautiful sculpted body was gone. A friend jibed, "Man, you weigh more than George Foreman." In response, Ali began walking two hours a day and lost thirty pounds.

Around eleven, Ali returns home and shifts his attention to the daily mail. He gets more than a hundred letters a week, and personally answers every one. After an hour of tending to that chore, he puts aside the mail and reaches for the Qur'an. Years ago, Ali admitted, "I haven't read ten pages in all the books written about me. I can't read too good; I'm a bad speller too. Oh, I wish I could read better."[1] But since then, spurred by a desire to study Islam, he has improved his reading skills. Now, reading the Islamic holy book, he stops periodically to copy passages he likes longhand on lined paper.

He eats lunch with Lonnie, and says his second daily prayer. Then he drives to Andrews University, a Seventh-Day Adventist school nearby. Ali enjoys visiting with students, and they enjoy him. Soon after he gets out of his car, he's surrounded. Undergraduates, faculty members, maintenance workers, black, white, old, young. The men want handshakes; the women, hugs. Everyone wants an autograph and Ali obliges, distributing the pamphlets he signed that morning. Someone thrusts a fifteen-year-old copy of *Sports Illustrated* in front of him. Ali is on the cover, dressed in a tuxedo with a red carnation pinned to his lapel. He asks the person's name, and signs, "To Robert—The heart is a net where love is caught like fish. Love, Muhammad Ali."

An hour later, the pamphlets are gone. Ali keeps signing; notebook pages, scraps of paper. Finally he leaves, and in the car going home he confides, "Sometimes I wish I'd gone to college. Those students don't know how lucky they are. I could have done more if I'd gotten a better education and gone to college."

At the farm, Ali says his afternoon prayer; then goes to the den and turns on the television. Several mothers whose children joined cult groups are on a syndicated talk show, and he hangs on every word. Lonnie comes in, points to a wad of chewing gum stuck on the end table by the sofa, and asks, "Muhammad, did you put that gum there?"

"Yes."

"Haven't we talked about that before?"

"Well, I'm supposed to throw my gum in the garbage, but I wasn't finished. I think I might chew it some more."

For the rest of the afternoon, visitors filter through the home. Neighbors, strangers, tourists, friends. Late in the day, a guidance counselor from the local junior high school comes by with a thirteen-year-old boy. Ali has been told that the student has a drug problem. He offers him a seat, and puts a tape in the VCR. An Ali documentary appears on the screen. The boy watches in total awe. Ali watches too, and is entertained. "Man, I can't believe I said those things to Sonny Liston," he admits as the tape goes on. "I was something. I shook up the world."

The boy asks if Ali hated Liston.

"I never hated anyone I fought. And some of the guys—Jimmy Ellis, Buster Mathis, Zora Folley—I liked a lot. It's wrong to hate. Sonny Liston, Joe Frazier, George Foreman; we were all in it together. It was good; we had our day."

Then Ali turns the television off and speaks to the boy about drugs. It's the standard speech—pride in one's self; respect for the law; achievement and good health; there are people who care about you. But at the end, Ali does something remarkable. He tells the boy, "You know where I live. Anytime you get down, if you need a lift, get on your bike and come over here. Bring a friend if you want. When I'm home, the door is open. But I don't want you taking drugs. Remember, I'm here when you need me."

After the boy leaves, Ali goes upstairs to pray as the sun falls beneath the horizon. Then he answers mail until dinner is ready.

Lonnie cooks because "Muhammad burns water." Afterward, for effect, she asks him to help wash the dishes.

"I ain't washing no dishes, and I don't have to. I already ate."

"Maybe so, but you'll be hungry again tomorrow."

"It still don't matter. I can make my own breakfast, and by lunch, you'll forgive me."

Ali washes a few dishes, then watches television for the rest of the night. "I like the farm," he says at one point. "When I was young, the bright lights attracted me. I used to see old men sitting on the porch, rocking back and forth in their chairs, and I wondered how they could just sit. Now I know. I like hearing the birds in the morning, and looking out at the grass and the trees. Boxing was good to me while it lasted, but it was only a start to what I want to accomplish in life. Here on the farm, I can rest up for my true mission—loving people and spreading the word of God."

At eleven o'clock, Ali says his night prayer, the fifth obligatory prayer of the day. Soon after, he goes to sleep. The following day will be much the same, and central to it all is his wife, Lonnie.

Muhammad and Lonnie have been married since 1986, but their relationship dates back to 1962, when Lonnie's family moved into a house across the street from Mr. and Mrs. Clay. "Lonnie was in awe of Muhammad," her mother, Marguerite Williams, recalls. "She was five, and he was twenty. He'd take her to the playground, recite poetry, tell her what he intended to do to whoever he was fighting next. Then he'd get on one of the children's tricycles, and race the kids around the block." And while Ali's life is often tangled today, there's unanimity about the importance of Lonnie:

Maryum Ali: "I feel real good about Lonnie. She looks after my father in terms of meals, doctors, going places, and stuff like that. But the most important thing is, she really loves him. And he needs that; he needs to be loved. Lonnie makes me feel very secure about my father."

Jeremiah Shabazz: "Lonnie is the best thing that ever happened to Ali; the absolute best. I don't care what color you are or what you believe. Anyone who cares about Muhammad has to be grateful for Lonnie."

Howard Bingham: "Everybody who meets Lonnie likes her, because she's nice, she's smart, and she loves Ali. He's pretty happy and content these days, and it wouldn't be that way without Lonnie. That's not taking anything away from anyone else, but Ali is very fortunate that Lonnie's his wife."

Lana Shabazz: "When Lonnie married Ali, he wasn't King of the Mountain anymore. But she loves him, she stands by him, and she cares about the person inside. I think Allah sent Lonnie to give Muhammad comfort in his later years and strengthen him to fulfill his mission in life."

LONNIE ALI: "I met Muhammad when I was five-and-a-half. I was in first grade, and had come home from school one day. My mother was standing in the doorway of our house, and Muhammad was sitting on his mother's front porch, directly across the street from ours. He was wearing a white short-sleeved shirt, black pants, and a black bow tie. He was twenty, which looked very grown-up to me. And his parents' driveway was overrun with bicycles. All the kids in the neighborhood were there. Muhammad was surrounded by children, and my mother said, 'Look, Lonnie—there's Cassius Clay.' I didn't know Cassius Clay from Joe Smith. But Muhammad saw me standing in the doorway, and asked the children, 'Do you know who that little girl is?' My brother Albert was there at the time. He's a year older than me, so he was six-and-a-half. He said, 'Yeah, that's my sister,' and Muhammad told him to go get me. I resisted; I was very shy. I didn't want to go over, and I started crying, but finally I went. Muhammad picked me up; put me on his lap. And I don't remember what happened after that. I blanked. But from then on, whenever Muhammad came to Louisville, he'd get together with me. I was like his little sister. Once, I was playing in a treehouse and he sent one of the neighbors to find me. Other times, he'd take me out in his car, buy me ice cream or whatever. I remember, right before he fought Sonny Liston, which would have been when I was seven, he came to town with a big bus. It had a loudspeaker system and it was painted different colors with the name 'Cassius Clay' on the side. He put as many kids as he could on the bus, and we drove all over town. He'd shout out, 'Who's the greatest?' And we'd shout back, 'You are.'

"I was still seven when Muhammad married Sonji, and I thought she was the nicest person in the world. I only met her one time. I was in front of my house playing jump rope, and she came by to say hello. She didn't know us kids from Adam, but she jumped with us and taught us how to double dutch. Then, maybe a year later, I saw Muhammad with another lady who was tall and wearing what looked to me like foreign clothes; someone from another world. I kept wanting to ask, 'Who's that lady?' but I didn't want to be rude.

Finally I asked, and Muhammad told me her name was Belinda and she was his new wife. That seemed weird to me, because as far as I was concerned, Sonji had been a perfectly good wife, and I didn't understand why he needed a new one.

"I saw Muhammad a lot after that; whenever he came to town. Sometimes he'd just sit around our house, talking with my parents or playing with me. As I got to know him, it felt a lot like he was my brother, because he always looked after me. He was kind, gentle, handsome, terribly sure of himself. I thought he was the most magnificent person in the world. Around the time I was seventeen, I developed an enormous crush. And this might sound strange, but I knew at seventeen that someday I'd marry Muhammad. Even though he was fourteen years older than I was, which at that age is a lot; even though he was married to someone else; I knew that someday I'd be his wife. I can't really explain what it was, except to say I guess I always felt inside that I could never be happy with anyone else. There always seemed to be that bond between us, as though it were divine will.

"Then I went off to college, and Muhammad had a lot to do with where I went. I was planning to go to Fisk, which is an all-black college in Nashville. My brother-in-law taught there; my best friend was going there. But Muhammad told me to check it out first. He said I should seek out the best school possible, one with a big library and good laboratories, regardless of whether it was black or white. So at Muhammad's suggestion, I got on a bus and visited Fisk. And sure enough, there was no way I could have gone to that school at that point in my life. There's no way I could have lived in that environment. It would have consumed me, because I wasn't raised in an all-black anything. I lived in a black neighborhood; I knew I wasn't white. But I'd never gone to an all-black school before, and my parents never talked like that. By coincidence, around that time, my brother-in-law left Fisk for a position at Vanderbilt, and I went to Vanderbilt instead.

"After college, I was accepted into the clinical psychology program at the University of Illinois. And at the same time, I was offered a job at Kraft Foods. There'd always been a lot that I disliked about business. It was too cutthroat, and I was a big humanitarian. At college, I wouldn't even take a business course. But after college I had to choose—go on with school or go to work. I knew it would take five years more years to get a Ph.D. in clinical psychology, and I started to think about what it would cost as well as how much money in earnings I'd lose in the process. And then I focused on my emotional makeup. How attached I am to children; whether I could deal with a career where I saw battered children during the day and still be able to sleep at night. Knowing myself, I realized I'd take each child home with me emotionally, so I decided to work for Kraft. I started as a sales representative, became an account representative, and it was a good first job. I also began work toward an MBA degree at the University of Louisville. Then, in 1982, Muhammad made one of his visits to Louisville and asked if I'd meet him for lunch.

"He was staying at the Hyatt-Regency Hotel, and came down to meet me in the lobby. He got off the elevator, and he was stumbling. He stumbled across the carpet; he wasn't speaking clearly. We went out to eat, and he stumbled on the street. He was despondent. It wasn't the Muhammad I knew. He'd always been in control of his life and sure of himself, and I didn't know what to do. Gene Dibble was in Louisville at the time, and he told me, 'Lonnie, Muhammad isn't well. And if somebody doesn't do something to help him, I think he's going to die.'

"That scared me. I knew there were problems at home with Veronica, but this was obviously something more. I thought a lot about what Gene said, and decided to move out to Los Angeles to look after Muhammad. I was aware that I would be taking a risk—giving up a good job, not to mention what people might say about my being in Los Angeles because of Muhammad. But I didn't feel I could place a lot of emphasis on that. I felt, wisely or unwisely, that Muhammad's well-being was more important than the sum total of anything negative in my going. So I moved to Los Angeles to look after him and go to business school at UCLA at the same time. I was twenty-five. In some ways, I was very naive and green, and Muhammad still thought of me as a child. But I got a condominium nearby. Muhammad took care of all my expenses, with Veronica's knowledge and consent. And I did everything I could for him.

"It was in Los Angeles that I started to study Islam. I was raised a Catholic, and was a very devout Catholic until my freshman year of college. But then I began to question my religion. I went to visit a black Baptist church in Nashville, and the place was packed. There were chairs in the aisles; people were standing. There was gospel singing. The minister gave a powerful sermon. It moved me. I'd never witnessed anything like it before. I knew I'd never become a Baptist, but it made me ask, 'Why do I feel so good here, and I don't feel like this when I go to a Catholic church?' So I kept going to Catholic church, but began to look at other religions to find something I felt more compatible with. Muhammad had loads of books and pamphlets about Islam. He gave some to me, and explained some of Islam's basic tenets. There was a mosque in Los Angeles that I went to several times. In many respects, Islam was similar to what I'd learned in Catholicism. The discipline was the same. I'd stopped eating pork when I was seventeen. I never drank in my life, so that wasn't a problem. The main thing I had to consider was the fact that in Islam there is only one God and there are no other gods. And the way it was put to me—I'd never really thought about it before—was that Catholics say Jesus is God, too. Catholics tell us that God is three people—the Father, the Son, and the Holy Ghost. And once I started thinking about it, I realized that God is too powerful to have had a human son and been here in human form. Jesus was a great prophet, but there's only one God. He is worthy of our worship, and no other god is worthy of that.

"Finally, in July of 1986, Muhammad and Veronica got divorced, and Muhammad asked me to marry him; although he didn't put it quite that way. It would have been nice if he'd gotten down on one knee and proposed marriage, but that's not Muhammad's style. He's not romantic in that sense. What happened was, our friendship had become very strong, which is the way I think all marriages should start; because if two people aren't friends, I don't see how they can be in love. We knew we wanted to be together, but that would have been totally against the tenets of Islam without our being married. I was going home to visit my parents. And Muhammad's way of proposing was to say, 'Why don't you see if you can get a marriage license, and we'll get married in Louisville.'

"We were married on November 19, 1986. Harvey Sloane, who was a former mayor of Louisville, performed the ceremony at his home. It was a quiet wedding, maybe twenty people. Just family and a few friends. I don't think I could have walked down an aisle with everybody gawking at me, but fortunately I didn't have to do that. And there's something I have in my relationship with Muhammad that his other wives didn't have: I've known him for so long that I have a little better sense of who he is and where he comes from. I've been able to watch him grow over the years."

Ali's fourth marriage formalized the union of two families that had been close for decades. Over the years, Marguerite Williams and Odessa Clay had become best friends—"like sisters," both of them say. Indeed, in 1975, Ali had "retired" Mrs. Williams from her job so she could be his mother's traveling companion. "We were together every day, not just when we traveled," Mrs. Clay recalls. "We stayed together; we made our own fun. We're very close. There's nothing I wouldn't do for Marguerite, and nothing she wouldn't do for me."

MARGUERITE WILLIAMS: "I've known Muhammad for almost thirty years. I've watched him grow to be a fine person. He lives an exemplary life today, and seeing him with Lonnie makes me feel good. It pleased me when they got married, because I knew they'd be happy together.

"Muhammad understands that famous people are regular people; no better, no worse than anyone else. And that's how he wants to be treated. I don't care how powerful or poor a person is; Muhammad will treat him like an equal. He's down to earth. And, of course, he says and does and gets away with things like nobody else because he's Muhammad Ali. People feel good because it's Muhammad who's doing it.

"But I guess what I like most about Muhammad is the way he gives of himself to people. And I'm not just talking about money. In every way, he's the most giving person I know. He'll talk with anybody who comes over to say hello; no matter who it is, no matter what he's doing. He'll put his fork down in the middle of a meal and let his food get cold to sign autographs and give someone a hug. I don't know how he does it. I'd go crazy or wind up exhausted in bed, but Muhammad is accessible to everyone. There are no barriers. If someone doesn't come over to say hello, it's their reservation, not his. And he's the same to everybody, big and small. If you think about the range of people on this planet—Wall Street lawyers, tribesmen in Africa, factory workers in Asia, farmers in South America—Muhammad loves them all. And on those few occasions when he's tired and doesn't want to be bothered by people, even then he doesn't have the heart to say no. He feels an obligation to respond to anyone who intrudes. He knows how important meeting him is to people, and making people happy is the theme of his whole life.

"Also, another thing I like about Muhammad is, he's never forgotten where he came from. A lot of people, when they get famous, they forget old friends, or at least they expect you to come to them. But not Muhammad. Whenever he comes back to Louisville, he goes to the neighborhood he grew up in. He visits all the people he knew. He's just wonderful, and like I said before, I'm happy Lonnie is married to him. She's part wife, part mother, part friend, part everything. She truly loves him, and he's a good husband for her."

LONNIE ALI: "Muhammad is a paradox. As soon as I start to explain Muhammad, he'll do something to contradict what I think I know about him. So I can't explain Muhammad; I can only experience him. We've known each other for twenty-eight years, and every day he does something that surprises me.

"One of the things that amazes me about Muhammad is how much he knows even though his education never went beyond high school. There are things he's not aware of because he hasn't taken a certain course or been part of a particular college program. But sometimes he'll come out and say something that leaves me asking, 'How in the world does he know that?' Sometimes he'll act like he's ignoring a conversation, when in reality he's paying very close attention. Other times, he won't let on that he understands what's happening, but then he'll ask a question or make a comment that cuts right to the heart of the matter. I don't know why he didn't do better in school, but I have several theories. In my family, education was all my father talked about for his children. He made great sacrifices to send us to private school. He always told us, 'Get as much education as you can, because it's important.' I don't think Muhammad had that type of motivation from his parents. The push just wasn't there. And on top of that, two of Muhammad's children have been diagnosed as dyslexic, and I think Muhammad might be dyslexic too. He hasn't been clinically examined. But certainly, if he had that type of problem, it might have caused him to shy away from his studies.

"Where our daily life is concerned, Muhammad is remarkably easy to get along with. He's not a macho individual. He makes compromises, and cares about how I feel. If I want to go to Louisville to visit my family, or anyplace else for that matter, he'll say, 'Okay, let's go.' When it comes to the house, he lets me make most of the decisions. And if he disagrees with what I want to do, he's always willing to sit down and discuss it.

"One of the compromises I've made in our marriage is, I don't have a career of my own. When I was in Los Angeles, I got an MBA degree from UCLA. If Muhammad was a different type of person, I'd probably have my own business now. Certainly, I'd have a job. But Muhammad doesn't want me to work. It's not that he doesn't want me to grow. It's that I'm his wife, and he wants me with him all the time. Before we got married, I had to decide; was I going to pursue my career, or be the wife Muhammad wants and needs? I've also compromised, or at least changed my style, with regard to how I deal with other men. I was brought up to be friendly to everyone, and I'm a seeker of information, which leads me into conversations with any number of people. But Muhammad can't stand my talking to most men. He thinks I'm too casual, too approachable, too nice. And I have to admit, by Islamic standards, he's right. Sometimes he contrasts me with Veronica, who nobody came up to and started talking with because of the way she held herself aloof. And even though I know there's an element of jealousy on Muhammad's part, I also know that he's older and wiser than I am and sometimes sees things that I don't see. So I do what I can to maintain an appropriate distance between myself and most men. I try to be friendly, but I think it's clear that I belong 100 percent to Muhammad. And I can say—knock on wood, because no woman can ever say this with complete certainty—I believe Muhammad is completely faithful to me. He'd never do anything to deliberately hurt me. And at this point in his spiritual growth, he wouldn't do anything that would be an affront to God. He knows he has a life after this life, and he takes that very seriously.

"The most difficult thing for me to deal with as Muhammad's wife is the stream of strangers in our house. Muhammad, apart from everybody else, is easy to live with. He makes no demands. He never complains. His tastes are simple. He avoids confrontations. Sometimes he'll get moody about something, and it's hard to predict what that might be. The same thing that bothers him today might not matter at all tomorrow. But usually I can cheer him up and get him in a better mood. Aside from that, he's very quiet. Sometimes I don't even know he's home. He reads the Qur'an or answers mail for hours almost every day. As I said, the one negative, at least it's a negative for me, is the number of strangers in our home, our hotel room, wherever we are.

"Muhammad loves people and loves having people around him. I respect the fact that people want to see him, and I also know I can't shut him up in the house alone for twenty-four hours a day. Muhammad isn't my property. Muhammad belongs to the world. That's why, when we're out in public, even in the middle of a meal, I don't try to keep people away. I just sit back and say, 'Here he is. This is your time with Muhammad Ali.' But I'd like it to stop at our door, and it doesn't. Too many people think they should have access to Muhammad whenever they feel like it, and they intrude on our privacy in ways that offend me. When we're traveling, they're always up in our hotel room. Of course, Muhammad lets them in. And I don't care if it's a suite or a single room, either I have to stay in the bedroom with the door closed or be in the same room, and I lose all my privacy and freedom. That's not fair to me, and a lot of these people are freeloaders. They make long-distance telephone calls; they call room service for lunch. I'd never impose on someone else like that.

"And at home, it's the same thing. Muhammad has an open-door policy. Whoever comes to the door, no matter what time it is, whether we're eating or in a meeting or entertaining guests, he invites them in. Now this isn't anything new. I understand that when Muhammad lived in Chicago and Los Angeles there were lines of people outside his home. I don't know how Belinda and Veronica lived through it, because there are times it drives me up the wall. I don't mind it when students from Andrews or Notre Dame come by, because they keep Muhammad fresh and in tune with a new generation. They exchange ideas, and that's good. And the people we know, friends and neighbors, that's obviously all right too. But then there are the tourists. People learn that Muhammad lives here, and this is the highlight of their summer vacation. They come from all over the world, not to mention every corner of the United States. I don't know what they're doing here, but they wind up at our front door and Muhammad invites them in. And to be honest, there are times I resent it. I know it's the chance of a lifetime for these people, but I'd like to draw the line at our property and keep the uninvited away.

"Aside from that, I love being married to Muhammad. We're compatible. We have the same ideals and share the same values on things that are important like family and religion. Some people treat me differently because I'm Muhammad's wife, but I try not to let that happen. I've always wanted to be myself, and I certainly don't want to be thought of as an appendage to another person. Now that we're married, I don't go around saying to myself, 'Oh my God, I'm married to Muhammad Ali.' I know he's special; I know people love him. But he's just Muhammad to me. I couldn't be married to someone I put on a pedestal. That's no way to live."

The affection between Muhammad and Lonnie is mirrored in Ali's love for his children. "I didn't have as much time as I wanted to teach them," he says today. "Because of the divorces and the way I lived, I wasn't really around to raise them. But they turned out good, all eight of them. None of them are into drugs; they live right. And whatever they need, I try to give it to them."

"Ali is one proud poppa," adds Howard Bingham. "And he listens to the kids; he doesn't just lecture them. Like with Maryum. When she was in college, she started a rap group and comedy act. At first, Ali wasn't happy about it. But they talked. Maryum is very intelligent and mature. Her head is screwed on right. And after a while, Ali came to the view that the singing and comedy were all right. Then, one night when I was at the farm, we turned on the television, and there was Maryum. Ali sat there with this big smile on his face. He kept saying, 'Look at that; she's all grown now.' As soon as the show was over, he was on the phone calling just about everyone he knew, saying, 'Did you see her? Wasn't she good?' And what made him proudest was, Maryum had gone out and done it on her own. She hadn't used his connections for help."

MARYUM ALI: "I've gotten close to my father in the past few years, and it's a nice feeling; real nice. I guess it started in 1985, when I moved to Los Angeles for my senior year of high school. I hadn't lived with him since second grade, and I wanted us to have at least one good year together before college. He and Veronica were getting ready to split up, but I lived with them and Hana and Laila. And in terms of quality time with my father, it was good. We did all the things together that he'd never had time for before. Little average ordinary stuff, like he wanted to take me to school every day.

"Right now, as a family, we're kind of spread out. The twins, Rasheeda and Jamillah, are at the University of Illinois in Champaign. They're very beautiful; they look like models. When I was young, I was a tomboy type, but they're much more quiet and shy. My father is more protective of them than he is of me; probably because they're so good-looking. I remember once when they were sixteen, they told him they were going out with some friends. He assumed it was girlfriends they were seeing, and then they came home with two real handsome boys. The guys were nice; they were the right age and everything. But my dad was shocked. I don't think he even spoke to them. It's not that he wanted to be rude, but he couldn't believe that the twins were old enough to be going out with boys. And he led such a wild life when he was young, I don't think he understands how calm it is for them and me. When he was my age, he was heavyweight champion of the world. Beautiful women were throwing themselves at his feet. And he was gorgeous. I mean, one time we were looking at pictures of him when he was young. I said, 'Ooh, Daddy. Ooh, ooh! If you were my age now, I'd go for you.' He looked at me; then he looked at the pictures; and all he said was, 'Yeah, I was pretty.'

"Muhammad Junior is finishing high school. He's getting real tall and skinny, the way my dad used to be. He's a lot like the twins, very quiet and shy. Growing up, I think it bothered him more than the rest of us that my father wasn't around. Also, being the only son, there's more pressure on him from people who think he has to be a great athlete, and he's not much into sports. He lives with my grandparents in Chicago, and we see each other whenever we can. My dad visits with him pretty often, and there's a lot of love there.

"Hana and Laila are LA kids. They're much more aware that their father is Muhammad Ali than I was at their age and more aware of what that involves. Hana looks just like my dad. Laila looks like Veronica. And both of them are good kids. I see Miya maybe twice a year. She lives in New Jersey with her mom. I don't see my other half-sister, Khaliah, much at all. That's not her fault. It's because her mom keeps her distant from the rest of the family. Miya and Khaliah have it difficult sometimes, because my dad was never married to their mothers and sometimes their names aren't mentioned in stories about Muhammad Ali's children. But I know he loves both of them a lot, and there's nothing he wouldn't do for any of us kids."

In addition to his children, there are several other people who are central to Ali's life today. Herbert Muhammad is still his spiritual mentor, business advisor, and friend. Ali's father died in February 1990, but Ali and his mother are close, as they have been over the years. But with the exception of Lonnie, no one is more important to Ali's day-to-day existence than Howard Bingham.

"I love Howard," says Maryum Ali. "I've been seeing his face since I was born. He's part of the family, and I trust him completely. A lot of people have come and gone, but Howard has always been there; for my father, for me, for anyone who needs him. I adore him. And what people should understand is, Howard Bingham is the best person ever to be around Muhammad Ali."

HOWARD BINGHAM: "I guess I see Ali a hundred days a year. It would be more, but he lives in Michigan and I live in LA. So we travel together, visit each other's homes, and talk on the phone every day. And what can I say? I love Ali. He's family to me. He's not perfect but he's the best person I know, and my bottom line is always Ali. It always has been and always will be, and everybody who knows me knows that.

"One of the things that amazes me about Ali is, despite all the attention he gets, he really doesn't understand why people love him. He knows they want kisses and autographs. When they crowd around, it makes him feel good, but he doesn't see the whole picture of his life. One time, I was on the farm, and we were watching a TV documentary, *Eyes on the Prize*. You know, that series about the civil rights movement. The producers were planning some new shows and wanted to interview Ali, so we were watching the original ones. There was James Meredith at the University of Mississippi, Ernie Green at Central High School in Little Rock, Rosa Parks, Martin Luther King, all those people. Ali was watching, and when one of the shows was over, he asked Lonnie and me, 'Why do they want me to be in this film? What did I do to be with all these great people?' Because, you see, he really doesn't understand how important he is and what he gave to this country. He doesn't think of himself as great or important or better than anyone else. And the God's honest truth is, we relate to each other as equals. But every now and then I'll still say to myself, 'I'm a very lucky guy.' And that's not because I'm friends with a famous celebrity. It's because of the kind of person Ali is. I couldn't wish for a better friend than Ali."

BELINDA ALI: "I'll tell you straight out: With everything I went through with Ali, the one person I always could count on was Howard Bingham. He's such a nice man, so sweet. Since before Ali and I knew each other, he's been Ali's truest friend. But there's one story I have to tell you. Howard and I were driving in California. I was driving, actually. He was giving me directions. And Howard stutters; sometimes he stutters bad. Well, we were on this road, and he'd say, 'T-t-t-turn right; t-t-t-turn left.' And I drive kind of fast, so one time, by the time he got the words out of his mouth, I missed the turn. But I got him. There was a truck coming toward us, and I pulled out to pass a car, pretending like I didn't see. And Bingham thought he was gonna die. He screamed, 'Look out for the truck!' I mean, he was scared. Anyway, I maneuvered back into the lane where I was supposed to be. And then I said, 'Bingham, you didn't stutter.' And do you know what he told me? He said, 'I couldn't. I didn't have t-t-t-time.'"

LONNIE ALI: "There are times I'm not sure I'd survive without Howard, particularly when Muhammad is traveling. Last year

[1989], Muhammad went to Senegal, Yugoslavia, Saudi Arabia twice, Geneva, Pakistan, London, and India. Muhammad took sixty-seven trips inside the United States, and was on the road for 236 days. That's exhausting for anybody under any circumstances, and the way Muhammad travels, forget it. I think it was Bundini who used to say, Muhammad would wind up killing everybody off and he'd probably live forever. I don't know about Muhammad living forever, but as far as killing the rest of us, Bundini might have been right.

"Moving Muhammad from place to place is an almost impossible job. For starters, we can never get anywhere on time, because people are always pulling on him. We'll be getting into a cab. Someone will spot Muhammad, as they always do. They'll beg and plead for his autograph. Muhammad will sign. And of course, once you stop for one, you stop for a hundred.

"Then we get to wherever we're going. And in most public situations, the security breaks down, because Muhammad makes it impossible for the security people to do their job. If someone cuts through a barricade or gets into a restricted area, he insists on talking with them and giving them his autograph instead of letting security take that person away. Obviously, what happens after that is, everyone else sees what's going on and breaks through and there's a mob scene. Sometimes, if we're staying in a hotel, Muhammad goes downstairs and takes over the lobby for hours. He'll walk through any area of any city in the world at any hour. And when he does things like that, fifteen or sixteen hours a day, I just can't keep up with him. No one person can. So thank God for Howard Bingham. Muhammad listens to him at least some of the time. And when Howard travels with us, I can relax knowing that, as long as Muhammad and Howard are together, Muhammad is in good hands."

Ali on the road is a sight to behold. Imagine what it's like to walk the streets of any city in the world and have hundreds, sometimes thousands, of people following you. That's what Ali experiences every day he's away from home. Oddly, he's afraid of flying. "The only time I've seen my father scared," says Maryum Ali, "is when we're in the air and the plane starts shaking. That's when his eyes get real big and he definitely wants to be on the ground. Other than that, he's okay on planes, except sometimes he'll fool around. Once, I remember, he found the intercom the stewardess uses, turned on the loudspeaker, and announced, 'Ladies and gentleman, this is the captain speaking. We're having problems with the engine, and we're gonna crash.'"

Ali's most memorable airplane ride occurred on a shuttle flight from Washington, D.C. to New York, when a stewardess asked him to buckle his seatbelt before takeoff. "Superman don't need no seatbelt," Ali advised the stewardess. "Mr. Ali," the stewardess responded sweetly, "Superman don't need no plane." But once the plane lands, wherever he is, Ali is a show-stopping scene.

BERNIE YUMAN: "There are places where people have never heard of the Super Bowl. They've never heard of the World Series or the NBA playoffs. But they know Ali, and they love him. Take Mike Tyson to Japan, and people there can't stand him. Bring Evander Holyfield to Korea, and no one will know who the hell he is. But wherever Ali goes, he draws crowds. It boggles the mind to see five thousand, ten thousand, fifteen thousand people struggling to catch a glimpse of the man. When he arrived at the airport in Kuala Lumpur [in 1975], twenty-five thousand people were waiting. He was mobbed at the airport; he was mobbed at the mosque. He went to visit a refugee camp in Hong Kong. There were stacks of beds up to the ceiling along the walls. The kids loved him. They touched his face; they climbed over his body. The outpouring of love was incredible, and it's still that way all over the world. To this day, there's no one who works a crowd better than Ali; no one who's more loved."

JOSE SULAIMAN: "The best moment I ever spent with Ali was when he came to my home town in the mountains of Mexico. There was an aura about him, and the Indians all knew him. They came to him as if he was a god. But Ali didn't act like a god. He made himself one of the people. He played with the children; he spoke softly with the old men and women. To this day, I remember the sweetness in his eyes."

JOSE TORRES: "Ali's hold on the public is incredible. No one in the world is more loved. I was in Atlantic City the morning after one of Mike Tyson's fights. I was in the hotel restaurant, when all of a sudden I heard someone applaud. Then more people applauded, and began to stand up. It was Muhammad Ali coming into the room, and I got goosebumps from what I saw. Mike Tyson was heavyweight champion of the world, and if he'd walked in, people would have looked. One or two would have gone over and asked for an autograph. But with Ali, everybody stood up and applauded, like a president or king was entering the room."

HAROLD CONRAD: "Five years ago, on one of those trips we took together, Ali visited a women's prison in California. All the women were lined up to shake his hand. Ali walked down the line signing autographs, and every now and then he stopped and kissed one of them. And every one he kissed was ugly. The first one he kissed, if they'd had an ugly-woman contest, she would have won. He leaned over, hugged her and kissed her, and she just about fainted. She was crying, 'Oh, my God! He kissed me! He kissed me!' Then the next one he kissed, she would have done pretty well in that contest too. And all the way down the line, he kept kissing the ugly ones. Afterward, I asked why, and he told me, 'The good-looking ones ain't got no problem. But them ugly ones, who's gonna kiss them? If I kiss them, they got something to talk about for the rest of their lives.' And the other thing I remember about that day is, there was a woman standing in line who was crying her eyes out, sobbing and sobbing. I asked what the matter was, and she said to me, 'All my life, I've been in love with Ali. Ever since I was a little girl, I've dreamed about him. And now, finally I get to meet him, except the dream is a nightmare because I'm meeting him in prison.' She'd killed a guy. She was in for manslaughter. Some guy she was living with started beating up on her, so she'd shot him."

LONNIE ALI: "I've never seen Muhammad unhappy in a crowd. When there are people around, he's alive; he feeds on it. Muhammad can be getting off an airplane with that bedraggled weary-traveler look on his face. He'll be exhausted and uninterested in everything that's going on. But all it takes is a couple of people, particularly children, to come over and ask for an autograph, and his face starts to change. With children, his eyes light up completely. That's the best part of traveling for Muhammad—all the people he gets to meet."

HERBERT MUHAMMAD: "I worry about all the people Ali hugs and kisses because of the diseases he might get. He'll go to Africa or Asia, any country in the world, really. And any baby that's there, he'll kiss it. That baby can have bumps and sores all over, but Ali is so soft and affectionate, all he sees is a child to love. And all the other people he embraces. They might be sick with contagious diseases; he don't know what germs they're carrying. He says that Allah will protect him, and if not, then he's not supposed to be protected. But if I was Lonnie, I wouldn't just make him take a shower when he comes back to the room. I'd spray him down with something every time he comes back from seeing all those people."

HOWARD BINGHAM: "Traveling with Ali is something else, and don't think it's just when we're overseas. Last year, we visited the New York Stock Exchange. There was Ali, Joe Frazier, Larry Holmes, and Ken Norton. It had to do with a video they were promoting. First, the other three guys walked onto a balcony looking over the stock exchange floor. There was applause and a little cheering. Then Ali walked out, and the place went wild. They were shouting, 'Ali! Ali!' like the other guys weren't there. And Ali likes the attention he gets. That same trip, we were in the car talking, and he asked, 'If I walked down one side of the street, and Larry Holmes, Joe Frazier, George Foreman, and Mike Tyson walked down the other, which side would get more attention?' I told him his would. Then he asked, 'If I walked down one side of the street and Jesse Jackson walked down the other, who'd get more attention?' And I told him the same thing. So finally he asked, 'If I walked down one side of the street and Elvis Presley walked down the other, who'd get more attention?' That one was harder, and I told him, 'Overseas, you'd have more people, but in the United States it would be pretty close; maybe even a little for Elvis.' That didn't bother him. All he said was, 'I guess that's right. Elvis has been dead for a lot of years, so people would want to see if it was really him.' "

MUHAMMAD ALI: "I like traveling because it gives me a chance to meet people and see different things. There are billions of people in the world, and every one of them is special. No one else in the world is like you. No one else looks the same. Everyone has two eyes and a nose and mouth and ears, but the way they're arranged makes their faces different. No two people are the same. Ain't that amazing? Billions of people, and every one of them is special.

"Howard was just talking about Elvis. All my life, I admired Elvis Presley. When I was in Las Vegas, I heard him sing, and it was a thrill to meet him. Later, I saw him again in private. He said he was a fan of mine, and had me measured for a robe that said 'People's Champion' on the back. I wore it for two fights. Then I got my jaw broke, and stopped wearing it. But I felt sorry for Elvis, because he didn't enjoy life the way he should. He stayed indoors all the time. I told him he should go out and see people. He said he couldn't, because everywhere he went, they mobbed him. He didn't understand. No one wanted to hurt him. All they wanted was to be friendly and tell him how much they loved him.

"Sometimes I get tired and don't want to be bothered. But most of the time, I like it when people come up to me. I remember how excited I was when I was a kid and met Lloyd Price and Willie Pastrano. Willie Pastrano gave me his autograph, and I took it home, kept it in my room, showed it to everybody. And I remember how bad I felt one time when I met Sugar Ray Robinson and asked for his autograph, and he told me, 'I'm busy, kid.' The only thing that bothers me about giving autographs is I can't give them to everyone. I'll sign for an hour. Then maybe I'll have to catch a plane or something, but there'll be a lady crying, 'Muhammad, all my life I've wanted to meet you. I'll die if I don't get your autograph.' So I sign for her, and then there's another person, saying, 'Muhammad, I drove a thousand miles, you're the greatest,' and I got to sign for her too. Then I'll really have to go, and people start jumping on the car or trying to put their hand through the window, and I'm afraid someone will get hurt. That always worries me, having an injury because of me. Like there'll be five hundred people running toward me, and some old lady is getting squeezed. I try to help her, but the people think I'm coming to shake hands with them, and the old lady gets pushed more. And the other thing I should worry about is, Herbert tells me it's wrong under the teachings of the Qur'an for me to be kissing women, even on the cheek, or even shaking hands with them. I'm so pretty, they all want to kiss me, but it's not proper. Probably, I should be polite and tell them I can't because of my religion."

Ali is welcome anywhere in the world, and no journey is too distant if he considers the cause just. In November 1990, against the advice of some of his closest friends, he travelled to Iraq and met with Saddam Hussein in the hope that his presence would promote dialogue and forestall war. There was danger in the possibility that a visit from history's best-known gladiator would feed Hussein's ego and stiffen his resolve. Yet for Ali, the trip was the logical extension of what he has believed for decades—that all life is precious and war is wrong.

After ten days in Iraq, Ali returned to the United States with fifteen of the estimated three hundred American hostages then being held. One of them, Harry Brill-Edwards, was bleeding heavily internally as a consequence of having been struck in the kidney with a rifle butt when he was taken hostage. For seventeen weeks, he'd been used as a "human shield." Brill-Edwards recalls the end of his ordeal.

HARRY BRILL-EDWARDS: "I was told by my captors that I was going to be released. I didn't believe them. I'd been lied to in that fashion so many times, and each time all that happened was I'd been taken to another detention site. I'd been held at a plant where crude uranium was processed, a power station, an oil field. And of course, none of us had any way of knowing that all the hostages would be released before the end of the year, or for that matter that we'd be released at all.

"I suppose what impressed me most about Ali was the way he cared for everyone. He had a kind word or gesture for absolutely every person he saw. When we landed in Amman, I had the opportunity to fly back to the United States on a State Department charter flight. It would have been much quicker than the flight we were on, and I was anxious to get home. I was ready to leave. But Ali hadn't been invited on the State Department charter, and I wanted to thank him and say goodbye. So I went to him; I looked in his face. And how can I say this? He'd made such a torturous trip; he'd secured our release. And I said to myself, I can't do this. We should be in Muhammad Ali's presence when we go home.

"In the end, six of us stayed on the flight with Ali. We did it out of sheer gratitude and respect for the man, and it's the best decision I've made in a long time. I told my family when I got home, 'I've always known that Muhammad Ali was a super sportsman; but during those hours that we were together, inside that enormous body, I saw an angel.' "

Ali's good deeds are universally acknowledged today. Yet in considering his life, people often express concern about two areas—his financial condition and his health.

Ali's financial condition is reasonably good. Most of his holdings are in real estate—the farm where he lives, some property in Virginia, and the training camp at Deer Lake. The training camp is currently leased for a dollar a year to a home for unwed pregnant teenagers. Ali and Lonnie have a mutual fund, and trusts are in place for his eight children. Ali dresses nicely, travels as he chooses, and has all the material comforts he wants.

"Ali's tastes are simple," Howard Bingham elaborates. "Like, when he's in Las Vegas, where just about everything for him is free, if he has a choice between the best restaurant in the hotel or the $4.99 buffet, he'll take the buffet. In the expensive restaurant, he can't see what he's getting until after he orders, but a buffet means he can walk into the room, see what he wants, take as much as he wants, and if he's hungry when he's finished, he can go back for more. The only luxury Ali has is, in addition to his Chevy Blazer and Cadillac, he owns a Rolls Royce. And he wouldn't miss the Rolls if it was gone."

Ali's income derives from various sources. There are some endorsements and business ventures, but personal appearances are the mainstay of his earning power. He has also found a niche in the burgeoning sports collectibles market. The fact that he gives away a hundred thousand autographs a year undercuts their value, but the going rate for his signature is still twenty-five dollars. Only Joe DiMaggio, $40, and Ted Williams, $30, are higher. Each year, Ali signs an estimated fifteen thousand signatures for profit. Most of those are marketed through a company called Sports Placement Services, which also represents Mickey Mantle, Sandy Koufax, Kareem Abdul-Jabbar, Jim Brown, and Joe Namath on a nonexclusive basis. SPS President Harlan Werner comments on Ali's marketability.

HARLAN WERNER: "Muhammad could do a show in a different city every week and sell as many autographs as he's physically capable of signing, but we've limited the number to three or four annually. The way it works is, he agrees to sign a certain number of autographs. For example, there's a show coming up in New York, where he'll sign fifteen hundred autographs over the course of two three-hour sessions. The organizers will pay him a lump sum and charge above that for the autographs, which is how they'll make their profit. Also, there's a big business in Ali memorabilia. Posters, lithographs, statues, everything. If Muhammad signs a pair of boxing gloves, they're worth close to two hundred dollars. Gloves he actually wore in a fight are worth ten to fifteen thousand. The same is true of Ali's robes, but the problem is, the market has been saturated with phony merchandise. Some of the people associated with Muhammad bought new gloves and robes, soiled them, and sold the stuff for major dollars. There's a radio deejay in Los Angeles who has a pair of gloves in his office that he thinks are from the Thriller in Manila. They're his pride and joy, but I know who he got them from and they're not real. Old *Life* magazines with Ali on the cover have value. So do tickets from Muhammad's fights; not stubs, but the whole ticket. The same is true for original fight posters, Ali rings, and any one-of-a-kind memorabilia.

"At the sports collectible shows, Ali is the greatest guest you could ask for. Most celebrities sign their name as quickly as possible, like it's an assembly-line job. But Muhammad takes pictures, kisses babies, and does whatever anyone wants. Wherever he is, the whole place goes crazy. In fact, Muhammad and Joe DiMaggio made a joint appearance for me a few years ago in Los Angeles. People had bought tickets for autographs and were standing in line for Joe. Meanwhile, Muhammad finished his own signing, went over to say good-bye to Joe, and left. And when Muhammad left, it was like everyone who'd been on line forgot who Joe DiMaggio was. They swarmed all over Muhammad, begging for hugs, pictures, kisses, you name it. Joe got more and more agitated, until finally he said, 'I'm not going to take this,' and he left. I don't think Joe DiMaggio had ever been upstaged like that in his life. Maybe Marilyn Monroe did it; I don't know. But he stormed out; he simply walked out on the show, and I had to refund eight thousand dollars worth of signature tickets."

Herbert Muhammad still puts together deals for Ali. Ali has also been instrumental in raising money for a foundation controlled by Herbert, which is soliciting funds to build a mosque in Chicago. Other ventures come and go, some of them profitable, some not. At present, Ali spends a considerable amount of time traveling to promote a Muhammad Ali Cologne, marketed by Crystal Fragrances, Inc. So far, profits have been minimal, but he remains optimistic.

HOWARD BINGHAM: "One of the problems, as you know, is Ali still lets people take advantage of him and doesn't always listen to the right people. Deals that should go for a hundred thousand dollars wind up selling for ten or twenty or maybe less. Guys come in and embezzle money, and Ali lets them get away with it. We had a situation this year; someone Ali knew took a couple of thousand dollars to deliver him to a Police Athletic League banquet in Oregon. The money was supposed to go to Ali, but he didn't know anything about it. In fact, he didn't know about the dinner until the organizers called and asked what time he was coming. Now, what Ali should have done was refused to go and got the guy arrested. But instead, he worried about the charity and people saying Muhammad Ali was a no-show. So he went to Oregon; the guy kept the money. And he'd already done the same thing once before with a sports collectibles show in West Virginia.

"Now, Lonnie knows what's going on. She's a smart woman. More and more, she's getting involved in Ali's business decisions. He

respects her and understands it when she says that he should get
what he's entitled to. But you can't tell Ali what to do. He does
what he wants, and there are things that are more important to him
than being rich."

LONNIE ALI: "I was raised in the South, and the people I grew
up with were basically good. My parents taught me to always be
nice, and I trusted everybody I met until they gave me a reason
not to. But I'd never met schemers like some of the people who
latch on to Muhammad. I'd never seen that level of exploitation. I'd
never dreamed people could be like that. It's as though Muhammad
is a golden egg. These people come by and say, 'I want a chip.' And
then they take another and another.

"Muhammad puts up with it. God blessed him not to hold malice
in his heart, so he forgives whatever people do to him. There are
people who've misrepresented him, forged his signature on checks,
misused his name, stolen literally millions of dollars. Muhammad
knows who they are, but he always forgives them. The same person
can come back six months later, and Muhammad will treat him like
nothing wrong happened. I'll say, 'Muhammad, don't you see? Look,
he's doing it again.' But Muhammad believes in the essential good
of people. He has a soft heart, and he'll tell me, 'Lonnie, God is
merciful, and when He judges us, He'll judge us in part on our
compassion for others.' That's Muhammad. He's so conscious about
not hurting anyone else that sometimes I think he carries it to a
fault. But that's also one of the things I love and admire about him.

"Lately, I've gotten more involved in Muhammad's business dealings. He'd rather be reading the Qur'an, and I have the educational
background to be of service. At first, he got a lot of flack because
Muslim women aren't generally involved in business; although that
seems to me to be more cultural than religious, because under the
Qur'an, one of a wife's duties is helping to protect her husband's
possessions. Now we're at a point where Herbert also consults with
me, which I appreciate. That represents a big compromise for both
of them, but I care. Muhammad and I are a unit. We're not one
person, but what happens to him happens to me. What affects him
affects me. What's good for him is good for me. And if I can help
protect Muhammad, you know I'm going to do it. If anyone out
there hurts Muhammad, I don't care who it is, there's no hole deep
enough for them to hide in that I won't find them. Maybe that's too
vindictive; maybe that's something I should pray about, but that's
the way I feel. A lot of the exploiters are gone now, but some of

them are still around. I try not to blow up in front of them, because it upsets Muhammad. But by the same token, I make Muhammad aware of what's happening, and I let them know that I understand what's going on. I think it would be a sin for me to do less, because after God, my loyalty and allegiance are to Muhammad."

Thus, Ali's finances today are on a relatively even keel, and what concerns people more is his physical condition. His voice is weak; he moves slowly. When he's tired, his hands tremble. "I look at tapes of Ali when he was young," says John Schulian. "Not in the ring but when he was talking, and it breaks my heart. He spoke so clearly and had so much to say. There was so much joy and life about him."

"What's happened to Ali saddens me," concurs Bert Sugar. "It betrays my youth and makes me feel that I'm mortal and growing old. Seeing him the way he is is like watching someone I love in a wheelchair—or maybe myself."

Still, the most important aspect of Ali's health is that it's not as bad as many people believe. Dr. Dennis Cope of the UCLA Medical Center examines Ali four times a year. Cope attributes Ali's physical symptoms to boxing, and acknowledges, "So far as I know, if Muhammad hadn't been a professional fighter, none of these problems would have occurred." That view is shared by Dr. Stanley Fahn of the Columbia-Presbyterian Medical Center, where Ali underwent extensive testing in 1984. But Cope and Fahn agree that, generally, Ali's health is good. According to Cope, "Muhammad's kidney, liver, lungs, and heart are in excellent shape. The thyroid medication he took before the Holmes fight has had no long-term effect. And while it's unlikely that there will be any dramatic future improvement in Muhammad's physical condition, I don't expect any progressive deterioration either. Also," Cope adds, "it's enormously important for people to realize that Muhammad is not incapacitated. He travels all over the world. He performs magic tricks. He can still do the Ali Shuffle, although more slowly than before. He speaks to large audiences when he wants to. And his thought processes are clear; his reasoning ability is good. He thinks perceptively and makes appropriate decisions. Muhammad's problem is one of expression. He is not what is commonly known as 'punch-drunk.' "

Cope and Fahn are nationally respected physicians with impressive credentials. Cope is a professor of medical medicine at UCLA, director of the UCLA General Internal Medicine Residency Program, and chairman of its Educational Policy and Curriculum Committee. Fahn is director of Columbia-Presbyterian's Parkinsonism and Movement Disorders Clinic, a professor of neurology at Columbia University, and scientific director of the Parkinson's Disease Foundation, which is an independent foundation.

Dr. Fahn elaborates on Ali's physical condition, and discusses his evaluation and treatment of Ali at the Columbia-Presbyterian Medical Center.

DR. STANLEY FAHN: "Muhammad Ali doesn't have Parkinson's disease, as has sometimes been reported. He has Parkinsonism. Parkinsonism, or Parkinson's Syndrome, is a neurological problem with several key features. One is a tremor. Another is slowness of movement. A third is rigidity of muscles, including those muscles used in speech. There can also be difficulty maintaining balance. The most common cause of Parkinsonism is a progressive neurological disorder known as Parkinson's disease. However, there are many other causes. You can get Parkinsonism from encephalitis or little strokes in the brain. It can be caused by Wilson's disease, which is a treatable disease that results from excessive copper accumulation in the body. Chemicals and certain kinds of drugs can cause Parkinsonism. In fact, some of the major tranquilizers prescribed for schizophrenic patients today can cause drug-induced Parkinsonism. Most of these causes decrease the dopamine function in the brain. With Parkinson's disease, the cells in the brain stem that produce dopamine progressively degenerate and die and produce less dopamine. In Muhammad's case, there's damage to these cells from physical trauma.

"I was Muhammad's primary physician during his two stays at the Columbia-Presbyterian Medical Center. He was referred to me by another physician, since I specialize in the field of neurology known as movement disorders, including Parkinsonism. He came to us because his condition had begun to worsen and was something he could no longer ignore. This was in September of 1984. I haven't seen Muhammad since then, but I have no reason to believe that our diagnosis at that time was wrong or that his condition has changed significantly since then. To the contrary, based on what Dr. Cope has said, I'd say that our findings were accurate and his condition is substantially the same.

"When I examined Muhammad, I had all his records from the UCLA Medical Center and Mayo Clinic, so that's a good place to start. Some slurring of his speech was noted as early as 1978. He was evaluated at the Mayo Clinic in July 1980, but no signs of organic brain disease were discovered. In preparation for his October 1980 fight against Larry Holmes, he modified his dietary intake, increased exercise, and lost thirty-eight pounds. Approximately three weeks before the fight, his personal physician from Chicago made the judgment that Muhammad appeared myxedematous [hypothyroid characterized by dry skin and loss of mental and physical vigor], and thyroid replacement was initiated. Didrex [benzamphetamine hydrochloride] was also administered. Two days prior to the fight, Muhammad became severely fatigued while jogging. Within one round of the fight itself, he felt weak, fatigued, short of breath, and his sweating was minimal despite the fact that the temperature at ringside was 105 to 110 degrees. After the fight, he was hospitalized at the UCLA Medical Center under the care of Dr. Cope, and the thyroid medication was discontinued.

"In June 1981, Muhammad was diagnosed as having pneumococcal pneumonia, and was treated with antibiotics. Subsequently, he was notified that his sputum was growing two colonies of mycobacterium tuberculosis—that is, the sputum was positive for tuberculosis—and in August 1981 he was hospitalized again at UCLA. They did a tuberculin skin test; they did a chest X-ray and another sputum analysis; and it all came back negative, so they couldn't confirm the finding of tuberculosis. But it was on that admission that the people at UCLA began to notice slurred speech. He was examined by a neurologist, who found mild imbalance on walking quickly, but the rest of his examination was normal. It wasn't clear what he had, and no firm diagnosis was made. Then, a year later, Muhammad was hospitalized again, in July 1982, because he continued to feel fatigued and have slurring of speech. He complained, in his words, that he was walking like an old man. His right leg felt sluggish, his handwriting was deteriorating, and friends said that he was drooling saliva from time to time. At that time, the hospital staff observed that his responses were slowing, and that he had slurring of speech with low volume. But his walking and balance were said to be normal. The sensory examination was also normal. They did an EEG; that was normal. They also performed what we call visual-evoked-responses and brain-stem-auditory tests. Those are physiological tests designed to examine the visual pathways from the eye to the cortex and the hearing pathways from the ear to the cortex. And although the waves were not delayed in any way, the people at UCLA thought that the amplitude, the wave forms, were less than they should be. They also did what we call a somatosensory test—evoked responses from the leg—and thought that was abnormal. Again, a CT scan was done of the brain; that was normal. And the conclusion reached was that the patient's fatigue was most likely due to a lack of relaxation and his lifestyle, along with some degree of underlying central nervous system dysfunction from prior head trauma.

"In October of 1983, Muhammad was admitted again to UCLA. His speech and walking had continued to worsen, and he'd developed a tremor in his hand as well. He also reported, in his words, that he was moving about as if he was a mummy. This time, a repeat CT scan showed a prominently enlarged third ventricle with an abnormality known as a cavum septum pellucidum. There was also some enlargement of the space around the brain stem reflecting atrophy of the stem. He had an EEG, which showed some disorganization of rhythm but was still not highly abnormal. And he underwent comprehensive neuropsychological testing, which revealed deficits in the tracking trains of learning anything but the simplest new material, thereby suggesting early organicity. Organicity means due to brain damage, rather than psychological causes. At that time, he was put on Sinemet, which is the most potent drug used for treating Parkinsonism, and there was immediate improvement. But the overall problems remained, which was why he came to us at the Columbia-Presbyterian Medical Center.

"Muhammad's first stay began on the evening of September 6, 1984. I examined him the following morning, and he told me that he was constantly fatigued; that he thought his thinking had slowed; that his facial expression wasn't as animated as it used to be; that he was having trouble with coordination; that there was an intermittent tremor of his hands, mainly on the left; and that people had trouble understanding him when he spoke. His voice was a major problem. He also acknowledged that he wasn't taking the Sinemet as often as prescribed by Dr. Cope.

"Our examination revealed that there was decreased facial expression—what we call in neurology a 'masked face.' His tests for rapid-succession movements were slow; his left side was clearly worse than his right. There was some stiffness of his neck muscles and limbs. He got out of a deep chair easily. For short distances his gait was brisk, but there was a slight decrease in arm swing. There was some reflex blepharospasm; that is, his eyelids tended to close as we tried to examine his eyes. And we found upgoing toes, which is a neurological sign of abnormalities in the nervous system. In other words, when you stroke the sole of a person's foot, the toes normally go down. If they go up, it's a sign of damage, either in the brain or spinal cord. He had great difficulty in the articulation of gutturals, linguals, and labials, and was slow in most of the movements around his face. Even his tongue movements were slightly slow. All of the signs I'm talking about now are signs we see in Parkinsonism.

"We did a high-resolution CT scan which confirmed that Muhammad had a dilated third ventricle and a cavum septum pellucidum. It also suggested some atrophy around the ventricular structures, particularly around the third ventricle. We did an MRI scan, which was a fairly new test, and that showed evidence of changes in his brain stem. He was still very strong, and scored very high on the strength tests. There was no evidence of memory loss. He was a little slow in his response to questions, but there was no hard data to suggest that he was declining in intelligence.

"We also did a sleep study, because Muhammad had complained of drowsing during the day and waking up frequently during the night. We performed two all-night studies and one daytime study, and found that his sleep was highly disrupted with frequent punctuations of awakening from sleep. I don't know if you know the words REM sleep and non-REM sleep. REM stands for rapid eye movement. It's a very characteristic part of sleep, and everybody should have some elements of REM sleep during the night. That's the part of your sleep when dreams occur, and if you don't get some REM sleep, you could become psychotic. But the awakenings were happening even with REM sleep, and those awakenings definitely were not normal. Also, his naps during the day were fragmented. They were brief naps, and he'd enter REM quickly, suggesting he wasn't getting enough REM at night. The fragmented sleep and lack of REM sleep were another indication of damage to the brain stem, which is where the sleep centers are located.

"We didn't have time for a thorough evaluation during Muhammad's first visit. He had several public appearances scheduled in Europe, so we discharged him after five days. But we booked him to return on September 18, so we could work with his medicines and find the best dosage.

"Muhammad's readmission was marked by a great deal of publicity. When he was in the hospital the first time, it was a well-kept secret. He'd been admitted under the alias of 'Paul Jefferson,' and nobody knew he was there. But during a news conference in Europe, he mentioned the hospital and said he was coming back, and that brought a media onslaught. The press was everywhere, and this was during the 1984 presidential campaign. Jesse Jackson was campaigning for Walter Mondale in New York, and wanted to make an appearance with Muhammad. I'd taken Muhammad off his Sinemet, because I wanted to run a test without any drugs in his system. And of course, at that point, he became much more Parkinsonian. I was making the rounds one evening, and went in to see him while he was eating dinner. He told me that Jesse Jackson was coming and asked if he could take his Sinemet. I said I'd rather he not. And that was when Muhammad showed his street smarts. He said, 'Look, I'll be leaving the hospital soon. I'd like you to write out exactly the dosage of medicine I should take, so there won't be any mistakes in the future.' And I did that. I wrote it out for him, left the hospital and went home, and turned on the TV news. And there was Muhammad meeting with Jesse Jackson just outside the hospital. He looked wonderful. And what he'd done of course was taken his medicine in the dosage I'd written out, and then gone outside to show the world he wasn't as sick as people thought. I thought that was pretty clever of him, although it didn't do much for the tests I was conducting.

"We ended up adjusting Muhammad's medication, giving him a combination of Sinemet and Symmetrel, and discharging him on September 21. At that time, he requested that I not state publicly what in my view was the cause of his Parkinsonism. But he's asked that I speak freely and completely [for this book], so I'll tell you my diagnosis that it was a post-traumatic Parkinsonism due to injuries from fighting. Muhammad himself told me he thinks that most of the damage came from the third Frazier fight, the one in Manila. That may be where he started to get his damage, but it's highly unlikely that it all came from one fight. My assumption is that his physical condition resulted from repeated blows to the head over time. One might argue that his Parkinsonism could and should have been recognized earlier from the changes in his speech. That's speculative. But had that been the case, it would have kept him out of his last few fights and saved him from later damage. It was bad enough to have some damage, but getting hit in the head those last few years might have made his injuries worse. Also, since Parkinsonism causes, among other things, slowness of movement, one can question whether the beating Muhammad took in his last few fights was because he was suffering from Parkinsonism and couldn't move as quickly as before in the ring, and thus was more susceptible to being hit.

"As for the type of life Muhammad can expect to lead in the future, we rated him as being able to perform all the activities of daily living at 90 percent of what would be normal for him without his physical problem. What I'm talking about here is, how long does it take to shave, make breakfast, get dressed? He's slightly slow, but certainly functioning. His condition is not in any way life-threatening. And I saw no indication that he was suffering from 'puglistica dementia.' In other words, the symptoms were in his motor skills: movement, speech, and facial expression. His condition did not affect his level of intelligence or the quickness of his mind. In fact, I was very much impressed by his street smarts and his ability to handle people, particularly the press.

"To the extent that people see Muhammad today and he's moving unusually slowly or speaking particularly poorly, that simply suggests to me that he's not taking his medicine at that time. Nothing will make him 100 percent again. But with proper medication, exercise, and diet, the quality of his life should be good. Also, it's been a while since I've seen him. There are new drugs available today that might be better for him than Sinemet, or perhaps his dosage should be adjusted.

"Outside of that, the only other thing I can tell you is, Muhammad was one of the easiest patients to deal with that I ever had. He never complained. He was very cooperative. Except for the one incident with Jesse Jackson, he did every test just as we wanted. He went out of his way to be nice to everyone. Doctors, nurses, other patients, everybody, absolutely fell in love with him."

Dennis Cope is in accord with Fahn's evaluation, and has continued Ali's prescription for Sinemet. "Of course, getting Muhammad to take his medicine is a problem," Lonnie Ali acknowledges. "Muhammad doesn't like putting foreign substances in his body. He doesn't like pills; he has trouble swallowing them. And he looks on the need for medication as a weakness, a reminder that something is wrong with his health. When I'm around, he's pretty good, because I give him the pills with meals and he's used to taking them with me. But when I'm not there, if he's traveling with Howard or someone else, he tends to forget or act stubborn."

Lonnie's point is born out by a recent exchange between Ali and Howard Bingham:

Bingham: Ali, take your medicine.
Ali: I just took it.
Bingham: No, you didn't. I was watching. You put the glass to your lips, but your Adam's apple didn't move.

Ali: That's because the pills work better if you take them without water.

Bingham: But they don't work better if you keep them in your hand. Open your hand, Ali.

Still, despite his aversion to medication, Ali remains active. "One of the extraordinary things about him," says Dennis Cope, "is that he doesn't allow himself to be handicapped. He has a bit of denial in him, which is one of the things that made him great. I mean, here's someone who could jump into the ring with Sonny Liston and say, 'There's no way this guy can hurt me.' To do that, you have to have some denial, and part of that denial is a belief in his ability to do the impossible. I see it with his current condition. He feels he can accomplish whatever he wants, and that's a very important part of Muhammad's strength."

GEORGE FOREMAN: "Even though Muhammad is six years older than me, I look on him like a little brother. I see him now, and it preys on my mind that I might have contributed to his physical condition. But the man still amazes me. Ninety percent of the people who get sick go off and hide in a corner, but not Muhammad. Maybe his words don't come out the same. He has days now where he might not feel as good as he used to, but he does the best he can each day. I admire that. I really do. I'm proud of Muhammad. I'd rate him deep down inside as the strongest individual of my lifetime. People talk to me about Muhammad now, and they say, 'Man, he's sick. He has trouble talking; he has trouble moving. Don't you feel sorry for him?' And I say to those people, 'Hey, Muhammad Ali is still the greatest show on earth.' "

LONNIE ALI: "When Muhammad started having trouble physically, when his speech began to change, I don't think he was aware at first that there was anything wrong with him. Then he realized something was happening, but didn't want to admit it. He was reading all those stories in the newspapers about how he was dying and only a shadow of the man he used to be. And let's face it, it's scary for anybody to experience a physical decline. But when the whole world is watching and so much of your life has been defined by your physical skills, to lose that is very difficult. And what happened was, for the first time in Muhammad's life that I know of, he became intimidated. He stopped speaking as freely as before because he was afraid that, as soon as he opened his mouth, people would say, 'Listen to Muhammad; he can't even talk.' Then other people tried in good faith to explain away the situation by saying, 'Muhammad is bored; Muhammad is tired. Muhammad is fine; he's just a little depressed.' And those people might have been trying to help, but the truth is, Muhammad does have a physical problem. And that problem shouldn't be treated in hushed tones as an embarrassment any more than cancer or a stroke. Muhammad faces up to his condition, and so should everybody else.

"You know, part of the problem is, Muhammad was what people wanted him to be for so many years that it's hard for them to accept the fact that he isn't that way anymore. People want Muhammad to be healthy. He was part of their youth, and they love him. When they look at old films of Muhammad, it's like watching an old family movie. And for many people, Muhammad represents the best time of their lives. So the world wants the Muhammad Ali of fifteen or twenty years ago. People don't want Muhammad to age. They want him to always be bold and sassy. They want that brash young man with the loud voice, boasting about what he could do. But even apart from his illness, Muhammad has matured and mellowed. Even if he was completely healthy, he wouldn't be shouting, 'I'm the greatest,' because that's not what he's about anymore. He's become more spiritual and introspective. He's a much more developed person than before; far more in tune with his religion and himself. Other famous people grow old and change. John Lennon married Yoko Ono. Paul McCartney became a homebody. Look at Jimmy Carter. We got a letter from him the other day. Do you know what Jimmy Carter is doing now? Physically building homes for the homeless. If John Kennedy were still alive, he'd be different from the person he used to be. So would Elvis Presley. People like to remember their heroes in a particular way, but Muhammad has left his old ways behind. In fact, if he were the same person now that he was when he was thirty, it would mean he'd wasted the past twenty years by not growing at all.

"The tendency people have now is to feel protective of Muhammad and treat him as though he were fragile. But there's no need to do that. Muhammad travels more than anyone else I know on this earth. I'm a healthy woman. I don't have any physical frailties, and I can't keep up with his traveling schedule. I've begged off of trips that Muhammad went on because I just couldn't do it, and I'm fourteen years younger than he is. People don't understand when they see Muhammad what his previous days might have been. People say, 'Muhammad come here; Muhammad go there.' And he'll get on a plane and do it without any concern for his health or how tired he might be. And then someone will interview him after he's been in Pakistan and flown back for twenty-seven hours, and they expect him to pop off the plane and be fresh as a daisy. Well, you can't do that after twenty-seven hours of flying. I guarantee you, if any reporter in the world followed Muhammad around and did what Muhammad does for fifteen or twenty days in a row, he'd come back looking worse than Muhammad.

"So don't worry about Muhammad. To relate to Muhammad, you shouldn't worry about his speech. You can't be intimidated by his health or celebrity status. Just talk with him like you'd talk to any other person. Ask him anything, and he'll give you an answer."

HOWARD BINGHAM: "I'm like everybody else. I want Ali's health to be the way it used to be, but deep down I know it's not going to happen. Some of it is laziness, and he gets tired from not resting right. If he took care of himself, he'd do better than he does. His mind is like it used to be. You have to remember, his thinking was always different. Twenty years ago, Ali might have asked what month it was and everybody would have laughed. Because the truth is, he never paid attention to stuff like that. Now if he asks the same question, people turn their eyes away because they think it's a sign of the illness, but it's not.

"I'm not saying there's nothing wrong. But when I look at him, it's not like, 'Poor Ali.' Physical disabilities can happen to anyone. It could happen to you or me, and you have to live with it. There's no other way. Also, I have to say, there's a lot of good deeds left in Ali. For the first time in a long time, he's exercising right. His weight is down. Lonnie's got him taking his medicine. And the most important thing is, he's started speech therapy. I don't know if he'll keep it up. But if he does, he'll be talking a lot louder and more clearly. So don't write Ali off. He might raise a ruckus in the next few years, and some people will love it but others might not like what he says. In fact, I wouldn't be surprised if some people decide they liked him better when his voice was bad and he wasn't talking so much."

Ali's decision to undertake speech therapy was made in July 1990. Subsequently, he has met with Tom Bishop, who is director of the Mercy Memorial Medical Center Speech and Hearing Clinic in

Berrien Springs and also a faculty member at Andrews University.
Bishop comments on his patient's prognosis.

TOM BISHOP: "Muhammad does not have intellectual deficits.
There's an underlying motor problem; and if you look at people
suffering from stroke phenomena, Parkinsonism, head injuries, and
the like, his difficulties are common. At this point, we're still in the
assessment stage. But my goal is to educate Muhammad as to what
his skills are and how to improve them, and give Muhammad exercises he can work on. Then I'll be able to bow out and see him
every six or eight weeks just to make sure he's following the program.
Our objectives are geared toward compensatory strategies. That is,
to compensate for his underlying condition by exaggerating or
overdoing movements. That's a developed skill. It takes conscious
purposeful awareness to talk that way; none of us do it naturally.
But even if Muhammad's underlying condition were to deteriorate,
which isn't anticipated, through the use of the compensatory strategies he could exploit the skills he has to perform within normal
limits. His prognosis for increased speech intelligibility and improved verbal communication is good to excellent. The prognosis
for increased spontaneous performance—that is, improved performance when he's not really thinking about it—is fair to good.

"One of the first things I told Muhammad—and it's true for all
my patients—was, 'I'm not going to bathe you in skills. In fact, I'm
not going to do anything for you. You're the one who has to do this.
All I can do is teach you what I know.' And I refrained from telling
him that I knew how he felt, because I don't. But I did say that I've
worked with many people who've had difficulties similar to his own,
and I can use my skills to help and guide him. Success will depend
on how badly he wants to succeed and how hard he's willing to work.
Certainly, in the past, Muhammad has shown the ability to work
hard and discipline himself to be great at what he chose to do. In
fact, one way I explained the process to him was to say, 'I can take
a young man and show him a few boxing basics, but that won't make
him a champion. And for you to be really good at this will take more
than a quick look.'

"It's easy to fantasize about therapy, and that's particularly true
for someone like Muhammad, who has a storybook personality and
has led a storybook life. So I've also emphasized that he needs to
be very honest and realistic about what we're doing. He can't fantasize about therapy and, without more, expect his fantasies to come
true. But within the framework we've laid out, I believe he has an

excellent chance to present himself successfully and communicate more clearly, both publicly and in private, in the future."

Given Ali's physical condition, some people feel sorry for him, and others wonder, 'If he had his life to relive, would he do the same things over again?'

Certainly, Ali was aware of the risks inherent in boxing. Five years before the end of his career, he appeared on CBS's *Face the Nation* and acknowledged, "I think boxing is dangerous. The brain's a delicate thing. If a fellow is not qualified, he shouldn't be allowed to fight. My jaw's been broken, and one nerve is just coming back from where I couldn't feel for a year or two. I got my eardrum busted in Manila training for Joe Frazier, and I just had it rebusted; the same one. I would advise nobody to box if they get hit too much and it's too dangerous."[2]

But Ali did box; he continued to box; and several people who knew him well from different perspectives offer their view.

RAHAMAN ALI: "My brother's health? What can I say. He became the most famous man in the world, and there's a price he had to pay. Ten years ago, he didn't know where he'd be today. He didn't care. And I don't think he has any regrets about what he did with his life. He didn't mean for some of these things to happen to him, but none of us can know the future. You make mistakes, but what are you gonna do? Life's that way."

ALEX WALLAU: "When I see Ali today, I feel sad, but I don't feel as badly as some people do because I know Ali doesn't feel sorry for himself. He's had a great life. He's done more in his first forty-nine years than most people could do in forty-nine lifetimes. He's reached heights that almost anyone would envy. He's not bitter. He understands what boxing did for him, and nobody had a better ride than Ali.

"When Ali was growing up—and I guess, unfortunately, it's still true—there weren't many avenues to excel available to a black kid from Louisville. So when people say, 'Boxing is horrible; look what it did to Ali,' I have to ask, 'What kind of a life would he have had without boxing?' Probably, it wouldn't have been much. Certainly, it wouldn't have compared favorably to the life he's led. So even with foreknowledge of how things would turn out, I think if he had it to do all over, he'd live his life the same way. He'd still choose to be a fighter."

LARRY MERCHANT: "I guess what saddens me is to see how Ali today is a prisoner of his past. All most people want to talk to him about is the good old days, which is the definition of being old. And of course, as an athlete, he is old. Athletes have short intense lives. As an athlete, Ali is dead. But as a person, he's not dead. As a person, he's not even old.

"I think, even when Ali had his health, he was beginning to grow tired of being captive to his image. When the act was young, he loved every minute of it. But it was a time-consuming, energy-consuming, all-consuming job, and such a hard act to follow. Maybe, in a way, his illness, this slowness or whatever you want to call it, has freed him from that responsibility. He no longer has to be what everyone else wants him to be. He can live out his days the way he wants to. And he's entitled to that, because he carried a heavy burden for so many people for so long. I don't know. What do you do after you do what Ali has done? This is a man who by age thirty-three had done everything there was to do. He'd climbed every mountain possible in terms of fame and hero status. What do you do for an encore? I think if Ali was the same fast-talking gyrating guy now that he was then, life might be even more difficult for him. He might even find himself a little out of step with the times. Some of the people who worshiped him before might look at him differently now. But he still has that seminal spark of life, that desire to poke around corners and see what's coming next. He's smart enough to do new things and get into a new life."

JULIAN BOND: "I have the feeling that, despite his physical difficulties, Ali today is at peace with himself; that he's happy being Muhammad Ali, and that he's satisfied with the impact he's had on the world. I ran into him at O'Hare Airport in Chicago a few years ago. We embraced. And he had that voice. He was slow in articulating, but I had the feeling things were fine with him. He was able to walk and talk and get about. And he still has the prettiest smile in the business."

KAREEM ABDUL-JABBAR: "When I see Ali today, part of me feels sad, but I know what it's all about. It's the result of his having had every bit of fun that he wanted to have. Unfortunately, some of the lessons we learned from him were negative—what not to do. But that will never stop people from loving him, and that's Ali's ultimate triumph—that he won our hearts and still has them. It's not how loud he speaks but what he says that matters."

MUHAMMAD ALI: "I don't want anyone to feel sorry for me, because I had a good life before and I'm having a good life now. It would be bad if I had a disease that was contagious. Then I couldn't play with children and hug people all over the world. But my problem with speaking bothers other people more than it bothers me. It doesn't stop me from doing what I want to do and being what I want to be. Sometimes I think that too many people put me on a pedestal before and made me into an idol. And that's against Islam; there are no idols in Islam. So maybe this problem I have is God's way of reminding me and everyone else about what's important. I accept it as God's will. And I know that God never gives anyone a burden that's too heavy for them to carry."

Ali's faith runs deep.

"I have heard from many sources," says Jimmy Carter, "that Muhammad's religious faith is one of deep commitment, not a superficial belief designed to attract publicity or gain favor with the public. I've known others who share his faith—most notably, Anwar Sadat—who have also indicated to me the depth of their sincerity, and this is very impressive to me."

"God is the main force in Muhammad's life," adds Lonnie Ali. "I don't think I've met anybody ever who's more sincere about their religious principles than Muhammad."

MUHAMMAD ALI: "I became a true believer, I'd say, around 1983. Before that, I thought I was a true believer, but I wasn't. I fit my religion to do what I wanted. I did things that were wrong, and chased women all the time. Then, one day, someone I respect asked me, 'Would you go to bed with a woman where your mother could see you? No. Would you go to bed with a woman where your children could see you? No. So why go to bed with a woman where God sees you, because God sees everything all the time.'

"The first pilgrimage I made to Makkah [in January 1972] wasn't like a pilgrimage at all. People recognized me and I wished I could have met all of them, but I didn't appreciate where I was. Things weren't Westernized. There was no ice cream, no girls in short dresses, no one listening to Chubby Checker. Now I'm wiser. I've studied more, and each time I make a pilgrimage, it thrills me and makes me humble to be standing where the prophet Muhammad was when he received revelations from God.

"Everything I do now, I do to please Allah. I conquered the world, and it didn't bring me true happiness. The only true satisfaction comes from honoring and worshiping God. Time passes quick; this life is short. I see my daughter Maryum. Yesterday she was a baby. Now she's grown and ready to get married. My hair is gray underneath the dye. God doesn't allow you to go back and live your life over again. But the older you get, the wiser you get; and in the time I got left, I'm living right. Every day is a judgment for me. Every night when I go to bed, I ask myself, 'If God were to judge me just on what I did today, would I go to heaven or hell?' Being a true Muslim is the most important thing in the world to me. It means more to me than being black or being American. I can't save other people's souls; only God can do that. But I can try to save mine."

Islam is the youngest of the world's universal religions, with an estimated one billion adherents today. Its founder, Muhammad, is revered as the last prophet, chosen by God to deliver His final message to all mankind.

Muhammad was born in Makkah in the year 570. Critical of the idolatry practiced around him, he led a comtemplative life as he grew older. One night, at age forty, he was visited by the archangel Gabriel, who came to him in a vision and ordered him to "recite." Thereafter, Muhammad received a series of revelations, which continued until his death, and he became convinced that he was God's vessel for social and religious reform. In 622, threatened by the entrenched powers of Makkah who were outraged at his teachings, he fled to the city of Yathrib. That journey of 220 miles is known as the Hegira, and marks year one of the Muslim calendar. Eight years later, he returned to Makkah in conquest, and by his death in 632 was recognized both as a prophet and a secular ruler in the Arab world.

The words of God as given to Muhammad have been preserved in the Qur'an, which contains 114 chapters (suras). Much of the Qur'an parallels the Bible, and all of its words are held holy by Muslims. Its most important doctrines are pure monotheism and the concept of the Last Judgment. God is the creator of everything, the Qur'an tells us. He is the guardian over everything. Unto Him belong the keys of the heavens and the earth. He is One and the only One, who is similar to nothing, and nothing is comparable to Him. He is the First and the Last. He knows what is in land and sea; not a leaf falls, but He knows it. Not a grain in the earth's shadow, not a thing fresh or withered, but it is in a Book Manifest. It is He who recalls you by night, and He knows what you work by day.

As revealed in the Qur'an, God is also just. Evil must be punished and the virtuous rewarded. Thus, it is prophesied that a day will come when the world is destroyed and the dead will be resurrected to stand before God. That day will be the beginning of the life that will never end. The Day of Judgment must come, and God will decide the fate of each soul according to his or her record of deeds. But because God is also merciful, the door to forgiveness through true repentance is open to all until death.

Muslims believe the Qur'an to be the summation and culmination of all God's teachings. Muhammad is considered the final Messenger, but he is not God's only prophet. Adam, Noah, Enoch, Abraham, Ishmael, Isaac, Jacob, David, Solomon, Job, Joseph, Moses, Aaron, Elijah, Elisha, Jonah, Lot, Ezekiel, Zechariah, John, and Jesus are all honored as prophets. Indeed, some Muslim scholars suggest a total of 240,000 prophets, chosen by God from every region of the world to convey His message to mankind. Belief in the message of Moses and Jesus is an essential requirement of the Islamic faith. But Muslims are not to worship prophets; they are to worship God alone. And while the Qur'an acknowledges that Jesus had no human father, it rejects the concept of Jesus as the Son of God. "He was created in the same manner as Adam was created. He is the son of Mary, not of God. He is indeed the word of God, but since he is a human being in the full sense of the word, this should not be interpreted to mean that there is a Divine element in him. He is the word of God only in the sense that God said 'Be' and he was. Jesus was a loyal servant of God, who never claimed that he was in any way Divine."[3]

More than any of the other universal religions, Islam represents a total system of living, encompassing every aspect of life. Religion, politics, social structures, and economics are intertwined. God sees everyone at all times in all places, and his teachings must be obeyed. Every Muslim must practice what are known as the "Five Pillars of Islam":

(1) The Creed: Proclaiming the unity of God with the declaration, "There is no God but Allah; Muhammad is the Messenger of God."

(2) Prayer: Performed five times each day, facing Makkah.

(3) Fasting: Abstinence from food, liquid, and sexual intercourse from dawn to sunset during the month of Ramadan.

(4) Zakat: The payment of a certain percentage of one's wealth for distribution to the poor.

(5) Hajj: The performance of a pilgrimage to Mecca at least once in a person's life, provided means for the journey are available.

And finally, although people of all religions are invited to become Muslims, in no instance are they to be forced to convert or treated unjustly if they do not. For "God is the absolute and sole master of all men and the universe. He is the sovereign Lord, the Sustainer and Nourisher, the Merciful, whose mercy enshrines all beings. And since He has given each man human dignity and honor, and breathed into him of His own spirit, it follows that, united in Him and through Him, and apart from their other human attributes, men are substantially the same, and no tangible and actual distinction can be made among them on account of their accidental differences such as nationality, color or race. Every human being is thereby related to all others and all become one community of brotherhood in their honorable and pleasant servitude to the most compassionate Lord of the Universe."[4]

MUHAMMAD ALI: "I can talk all day about Islam, because more than anything in my life, I believe in God. There's one God, and He created everything in the universe. There's billions of stars and planets and moons and galaxies, and just thinking about how Allah created all that humbles me. Once upon a time, I didn't exist. Then I grew from a little cell and came into the world through my mother's tummy. Knowing God has power like that makes me humble too. If all the oceans on earth were ink and all the trees were pens, they couldn't write the knowledge that God has.

"This life on Earth is a test. Someday, God will judge every one of us according to what we've done. We're all gonna die. I don't care who you are, you're gonna die. But death on Earth isn't the end of life. It's the beginning of eternal life. Only God knows when Judgment Day will come, but it's coming for sure. It might be twenty thousand years from now, but when the dead are risen, all it will feel like was you slept for a night. And when Judgment Day comes, the good will be rewarded with eternal life in paradise, and the evil will be condemned to eternal life in hell. God will be the only judge. If you didn't know something, He won't be hard on you. But if you knew something was bad and did it anyway, then you're in trouble because God will have a perfect record of your life. He'll know what was in your heart and everything you did. Whatever you or me or anyone does, we'll be called to answer for it on Judgment Day.

"Nobody knows what heaven is like. The closest thing to say is, imagine all the gold and bank accounts and hotels and diamonds of this world. Add them up with all the fame and money and power of this world. And when you put it all together, it's nothing but a mosquito's wing compared to the joy of heaven and the eternal treasures of God. And hell isn't just fire. Hell can be so cold you burn yourself, or it can be hot. Your flesh burns and then you get new flesh and that burns too. You want to die but you can't, and hell is for eternity too. So it makes sense to live a good life. This life is nothing but a fraction of a second compared to eternity. You give God one good second, and God will give you heaven for eternity.

"People think you got to be an Arab to be a Muslim, but most of the Muslims in the world aren't Arab. I'm not an Arab; I can't be no Arab. And another thing; you don't have to be a Muslim to go to heaven. My mother is a Baptist. She believes Jesus was the son of God, and I don't believe that. I don't think God had sons. God don't beget; man begets. It sounds wrong—a woman saying, 'I got God's baby.' It don't make sense. God don't have babies. But what I was saying is, even though my mother believes different from me, when she dies, I believe she's going to heaven. There are Jewish people who lead good lives, and when they die, I believe they're going to heaven. If you're a good Muslim, if you're a good Christian, if you're a good Jew; it don't matter what religion you are, if you're a good person you'll receive God's blessing.

"Some people who call themselves Muslims do bad crazy things. But some people who call themselves Christian joined the Ku Klux Klan, lynched black people, and burned crosses on lawns. True Christianity teaches brotherhood and love, and true Islam teaches those things too. God created all people, no matter what their religion. We all have the same God; we just serve Him in different ways. Rivers, ponds, lakes, streams, oceans, all got different names, but they all are made of water. That's how it is with different religions. If you love God, you can't separate out and love only some of His children. If you believe in one God, you should believe in all people being part of one family. If you're against someone because he's a Muslim, that's wrong. If you're against someone because he's a Christian or a Jew, that's wrong. If you're against someone because he's black or white or yellow or brown, that's all wrong.

"The more I learn about God and Islam, the more I realize how little I know. So I'm still studying; I'm still learning. I'm not pure yet. I still do minor sins, but I'm working on that problem. Right now, it's two weeks since I swore at anyone. There's nothing as great as working for God, helping people lead better lives. The truly great men in history never wanted to be great. All they wanted was a chance to do things for other people and be close to God."

GEORGE FOREMAN: "I don't think Muhammad's conversion was a religious experience. I'll believe until the day I die that it was a social awakening that acquainted him with the Muslim religion. It was something that he needed at the time. The whole country needed it. Young people in particular were tired of walking around with a feeling of inferiority, and some of them were awakened socially by the call of the Muslims. Later on, what Muhammad believed began to turn more on religion. But at the start, I think it was something different.

"My own conversion was truly religious. A deep pull from God changed my life. I had an experience in Puerto Rico in 1977 where, for a split second in my dressing room after I fought Jimmy Young, I was out of this world. I was dead, and then I came back to life. Now you think about it. Everybody asks right before they die, if they could relive their life, how would they change it? And I had another chance. I was getting ready to die, and I said to myself, 'If I could relive my life, I'd be nicer to people; I'd believe in Jesus.' And that's what I did. I've given my life to Jesus. So the next time I go to meet God, I can tell him I've lived my life right.

"I've tried to convert Muhammad several times. I think he did the world a favor, and I think people are better off because he embraced something that made people take pride in themselves. But times have changed, and now it's time for Muhammad Ali and George Foreman to embrace something that will take us to the hereafter, and that is to get acquainted with the living God. I talked to Muhammad about it, more than once, until finally he told me, 'Hey, if God wants me to change, God will tell me. God will call me.' He didn't want me to push anymore, and that made me realize I should stop trying to put my beliefs on him. If Jesus wants to convert Muhammad Ali, Jesus will do it. And I don't know what it will be like in heaven for Muhammad, but I can tell you one thing for sure: Muhammad has had quite a life here on Earth."

LONNIE ALI: "Jimmy Swaggart wrote Muhammad a letter several years ago, and said in his letter how concerned he was for Muhammad's soul. He'd visited Muhammad in Los Angeles, and wanted him to accept the Lord Jesus Christ as his savior. He wanted Muhammad to be saved. Muhammad told me, 'Think about it, Lonnie. If Jimmy Swaggart can convert the best-known Muslim on Earth back to Christianity, what would that do for Jimmy Swaggart?' And then, of course, a month or two later, this big mess came out with Jim Bakker, and soon after, it came out with Jimmy Swaggart. I said to Muhammad, 'You know what you should do? You really ought to write Jimmy Swaggart a letter, saying that God still loves him and Jimmy Swaggart should accept Allah as his only Lord and savior.'

"Muhammad puts God ahead of everything today; before me, before his mother, before his children. He knows he's not a scholar himself, but he does what he can to learn and propagate Islam. Not everyone knows what Islam is. Here in the United States particularly, there's been a lot of negativity associated with the religion. Twenty-five years ago, we had the phrase 'Black Muslims,' which was associated with antiwhite feeling. Now many people in this country associate Islam with wars in the Middle East and terrorist groups. But true Islam doesn't promote terrorism. True Islam doesn't promote killing innocent men, women, and children. Muslims have been able to work and live peacefully with other people from the time of the Prophet. Islam addresses every problem we have in society. It teaches how to live, what kind of family life to lead. And I believe, if people would listen to Islamic philosophy, a lot of the problems society has today just would not be.

"Now Muhammad understands that not everyone has a philosophy of life that's the same as his, but he won't waver from his principles where his own conduct is concerned. He recently turned down a substantial amount of money from a casino in Las Vegas that wanted to use his name on a restaurant. There was a guarantee of six figures a year. But Las Vegas being what it is, there would have been alcohol; there would have been pork items on the menu; the restaurant would have promoted gambling. And Muhammad felt that, even though he personally wouldn't be doing anything against his religion, he couldn't in good conscience be part of something like that.

"Sometimes people ask me what it's like to live with a man who puts God ahead of everything, including his family. And the answer, which I've learned from Muhammad, is, I really wouldn't want to live with anybody who didn't feel that way. If Muhammad didn't put God first, there are lots of things he might be doing to hurt me. He might be going out with other women. He might be drinking; he might be gambling; he could be into drugs. There are things he doesn't do, not because I don't like them, but because Allah doesn't like them. I can't prevent Muhammad from doing things; only God and Muhammad can do that. He's not afraid of me, but he worships God and knows he has to answer to God in the end. And if he didn't have that type of mind-set, I don't think I could be with him. If Muhammad didn't have that attitude in his life, I don't think we'd make it, because Muhammad is a very powerful man. He's very strong-willed. I don't think there's anyone around strong enough to control his behavior when he decides to do something. It has to be someone or something greater than any person on Earth. So I'm glad he puts God first. I put God first too."

One of the saddest things about many people—and in particular, athletes—is that as they get older they lose whatever it was they defined themselves by earlier in life. But Ali has found a fulfilling replacement for what used to be. He can look at tapes of himself in the past, smile, and say, "Man, I was something." But he also genuinely believes that equally good times lie ahead.

As the years pass, there will be innumerable public offerings to Ali. There will be streets and parks named in his honor; trophies, plaques, awards, and the like. But no tangible offering can serve as an appropriate marker for Ali. His true legacy is that we're better people in a better world because he has been here. "He instilled courage and fear in the hearts of men, and remains a firelight of strength and independence," Bob Dylan has written. "He proved that you can stand up for your beliefs in the face of adversity and still remain standing."

Eight men and women from all walks of life put Ali in a final perspective.

BRYANT GUMBEL: "Obviously, we're not just talking about a fighter, and I guess it's very difficult to remove Ali from the context of his times. It's an interesting question: What would Muhammad Ali have been in the 1950s? What would he have been in the 1980s? God, I don't know. He was so much a product of his times and the times were so much created by him that it's hard for me to separate the two, but something about Ali lasts.

"He was a man of principle. Whether you agreed with his principles or not was almost irrelevant. It's very difficult for anybody, even his most ardent critics, to argue that he wasn't willing to accept the consequences of his beliefs. You could argue his beliefs till you were blue in the face, but by the time he was willing to go to jail

and be stripped of his title and lose the opportunity to make millions
of dollars, it was apparent that this wasn't a publicity gimmick. He
symbolized optimism and the hope that anything was possible, even
for the most downtrodden person. That a young black man with
limited education could rise to become the world's best-known
human being, the world's most loved figure; that's an extraordinary
accomplishment.

"And he was a hero. In my lifetime, there have been lots of martyrs
but very few heroes. And whenever we needed Ali, he was there.
He danced through our imagination as much as through real life,
and we loved him because he was our guy. When my generation
needed pride, he was it. When we needed victories, he supplied
them. He was bigger than life. I'll never say a bad word about him.
People like Muhammad Ali don't come along very often. They come
along, if you're lucky, once in a lifetime."

ALEX HALEY: "I worked closely with Malcolm X, and I also did
a *Playboy* interview with Martin Luther King during the same period, so I knew one very well and the other a little. And one of the
things I've reflected upon is that, as things went, they both died
tragically at about the right time in terms of posterity. Both men
were at a point in their careers where they were beginning to decline. They were under attack. People don't talk about it now and
many don't know it, but Dr. King had begun to be ridiculed, even
within his own immediate entourage. He was being called 'De
Lawd.' Terms like that, sort of poking fun in a way, which is a preface
to more. He was having problems keeping his thing together. Malcolm X, maybe even more graphically, had lost his power base,
which was the Nation of Islam. And Malcolm, I know, was having
a rough time trying to keep things going. Both of them were killed
just before it went really downhill for them, and as of their death,
they were practically sainted. Had the same thing happened to
Muhammad Ali at his peak, he too would have been sainted. However, since he's still with us, thankfully, people are inclined to take
a more rounded view of him.

"You know, there's a reality for anybody who studies history. And
that is that ninety-nine-point-nine-nine-nine percent of the people
who live will be totally forgotten a hundred years after they die.
And of those who are remembered, only a small proportion will have
made a significant and positive impact upon the world. But I think
Ali will be one of those people; and I think it's important for future
generations to know who Muhammad Ali was. So if I were to talk

to a young boy about Ali today—a young boy who wasn't alive in the 1960s, who didn't live through Vietnam, someone for whom Ali is history—I'd talk to that boy about principles and pride. I'd say, 'If you really want to know about people and history in the times before you were born, you owe it to yourself to go back, not read books so much, but to go to a library where you'll have access to daily papers and read about this man, every single day for years. That might give you some understanding of who Muhammad Ali was and what he meant to his people.' "

DICK GREGORY: "There are men who will let themselves down and play with their children in the privacy of their own living room. They become silly. They become children with their own children, but nobody else ever sees it. And Ali was like that with the whole world. He was what God meant people to be. Loving, kind, generous, good. His whole life was a prayer for peace, justice, and human dignity. He gave so much, and never asked for anything back. People didn't know where he came from; they didn't know where he was going; but they knew he was there. And when he entered people's lives, he made them feel good. Right then—not next week, not tomorrow. Right on the spot, you felt something. Being in his presence was like entering a warm room on a bitter-cold winter night.

"There were a lot of us against the war in our way, but nobody heard us, because we didn't command the worldwide attention that Ali enjoyed. Then he stood up and said, 'War is wrong; people get killed in wars.' And when he did that, he didn't embarrass the United States. He embarrassed armies all over the world. Had he used his energies differently, had he supported war, this planet would be an even more violent place than it is today. But instead, he taught love. He might be a prophet; a prophet of peace. Prophets come to change lives and bring the word of God into the world, and that's what Ali has done.

"I don't know of anyone who's had as great an impact on people as Ali. Not just black people; not just Muslims. This great monument of a human being is loved all over the world. There's no person on this planet who's had the same effect as Ali. He got our attention; he made us listen. And then he grew within people who weren't even aware that he was there. Whatever the universal God force meant for him to do, it's out of the bottle, and it isn't ever going back. Ali is inside all of us now, and because of him, no future generation will ever be the same."

LONNIE ALI: "Throughout Muhammad's entire career, there were people saying to him, 'Muhammad, just make this one compromise with principle. Muhammad, just make that one change in your beliefs.' And each one, if he'd made it, would have taken away from who he was. But he always held firm; he's a better person for it. And I think this country is a better country because of his struggle, particularly as it related to Vietnam.

"That war wasn't about serving the United States. It wasn't about national defense. This country wasn't under attack. It had to do with America prowling around in other people's affairs. And Muhammad was right. Back in the 1960s, black people didn't have justice in America. We didn't have a full place here. We were still slaves—mentally, if not legally—and even legally there were a lot of things we weren't allowed to do. There were places in this country where Muhammad couldn't even sit at a lunch counter, and yet he was expected to go over to Asia and annihilate people who'd never done anything wrong to him. The Vietcong had never done anything to Muhammad. There were white people here in America who did a lot to him every day and he wasn't at war with white people in America, so why should he go to war with people overseas? That was his frame of mind, and I think it was true of most other black Americans at that time, but Muhammad stood up for his beliefs. He didn't flee to Canada to escape what was put upon him. He didn't take any other circuitous route, honorable or dishonorable. He just said, 'I'm not going, and if you want to lock me up, go ahead and do it.' That took a lot of courage. He wasn't subjected to gunfire, but in his own way, it took as much courage as the people who went over there to fight. He was threatened with jail; his livelihood was taken away; people called him a traitor and worse. You have no way of knowing the ridicule Muhammad faced and how badly hurt he was by some of the things people said about him. But he never stopped believing in this country or the essential good of its people. And I'll tell you flat out; I think Muhammad would have been mentally destroyed if he'd gone to Vietnam. Given the type of person he is—his compassion, his decency—Muhammad wouldn't have come back from that experience whole. Muhammad could never pick up a rifle and kill someone. I don't care who it was; he just couldn't do it. He might have fought in the ring, but this man was never capable of shooting at another person. He won't even hunt. He absolutely refuses to do it. He can't kill an animal, so how could you expect him to kill another human being? All it would have taken was for Muhammad to see one person shot and killed, one child dead, I don't care what side they were on, and it would have destroyed him."

ANDREW YOUNG: "Martin Luther King made his most publicized speech against the war in Vietnam at Riverside Church on April 4, 1967—exactly one year to the day before he was assassinated. It was soon after that speech that Muhammad refused to take the step forward, and I know Martin was very proud of him.

"Muhammad was probably the first black man in America to successfully break with the white establishment and survive. He set his own course religiously, politically, and culturally. And in that sense, he was very important because he established a new concept of equality. I didn't necessarily think that his way was right. I believed in challenging the establishment from within. I was part of the Christian church. I was, and am, very much a part of the Judeo-Christian value tradition. But Muhammad gave young men who didn't feel a part of that tradition a way to respect themselves and express their rebellion constructively. A lot of criminal activity expresses rebellion, and a lot of violence and empty revolutionary rhetoric is an outgrowth of frustration against the establishment. But he gave people an alternative way to oppose what was essentially a white-Anglo-Saxon-Protestant-dominated culture, be religious, maintain self-pride, and at the same time, respect everyone's dignity. Certain things are right and wrong, and he never swayed from that. He was a very special gift for us all."

MARY TRAVERS: "War and racism are classic problems, which is also true of homelessness and hunger. If they were simple to resolve, they'd be gone by now. But they're still here; they're as old as man. As we speak, there are thirty-two wars going on, and twenty-eight of them are religious conflicts. Those of us who live in the West and read history books think of religious wars as something that belong in the Middle Ages, but they're still around. There's the bomb. We have holes in the ozone layer and all the other ecological problems on our incredible shrinking planet. And all any of us can do to help is the best we can, until someone else picks up the torch and carries it along.

"Muhammad Ali held the torch high, and given the structure of what surrounded him, his accomplishments were remarkable. If he'd never done anything else with his life, his refusal to go into the United States Army would still have been of monumental importance. He stood for dignity in a culture that afforded precious little dignity to black people. And he was a hero to people who'd never had a hero before. To be a hero, you don't have to be the brightest kid on the block. You don't have to be the strongest kid on the block. You don't have to be the most sophisticated kid on the block. What you do have to be is able to recognize the profound quality of right and wrong and want to be a constructive member of society, and Muhammad Ali was a hero. He rejected a value system that oppressed black people, not in the intellectual arena as someone like W. E. B. DuBois would have done, but by condemning it on moral grounds. He rejected the war, not with political sophistication, but for spiritual reasons that served him well. And the fact that he retained his principles and remained a Muslim is important.

"People have a tendency to be pessimistic today. The last decade had many moments of despair, and the issues of the nineties will be issues of survival; national survival, world survival. But human beings are the inventors of hope. It's a universal spirit that runs through the centuries, and hope is cyclical. I think of Pete Seeger's song from the Bible. To everything, there's a season. A time to hope; a time to mourn. You're born, and one door opens while another closes. You move from nothingness to being. Then you die, and you're wherever you are. I think we're at the beginning of another season of hope. I think the nineties will be very interesting. I can remember when I was fifteen years old, reading Jack London and Upton Sinclair, and saying to myself, 'I missed it. What an exciting time these people had, forming unions, crusading for important issues. And here I am. Eisenhower is President; Joe McCarthy is making people miserable. There'll never be times like the good old days again.' And then the 1960s came along.

"This country needed Muhammad Ali in the 1960s and I'm grateful for what he did, but the whole world needs people like him now. Being a hero isn't a permanent job. No one makes you sign up for life. But I understand that Muhammad wants to do more, and the opportunity for him is certainly here. He might not be able to articulate the way he used to. He's no longer heavyweight champion of the world. But with his spirit and what he represents, he can be a force for good for many years to come."

HOWARD BINGHAM: "When Ali was young, he was the greatest fighter in the world. He's not anymore, because like the rest of us, he got older. But right now, he's the most loved person in the world. And as far as I'm concerned, being the most loved person is better than being the greatest fighter. Love is what makes us different from other creatures; love and the ability to make a choice. Each of us can be an asshole or a nice guy, and Ali chose to be the nicest person in the world."

RAMSEY CLARK: "I don't like boxing. I oppose boxing, because I think it's violent and damaging to the young men who participate in it. It symbolizes our glorification of violence and the rule of violence over compassion and the rule of law. I also don't believe in fame. I think fame, like power, is a profound misunderstanding and distortion of what is good and desirable. One of the most damaging beliefs people have is that only those who are famous or hold power can change things or make a difference. True social change has to come from the people. Each of us has to want to be involved and has to believe that we as individuals can make a difference, and that our ability to make a difference doesn't depend upon our being elected to the House of Representatives or being the preacher of the biggest church in town or president of a corporation or heavyweight champion of the world. Those roles tend to be selfish and self-fulfilling and debilitating in terms of the pureness of one's commitment. You make so many compromises in pursuing those careers that it's an illusion to think that's how you make the changes you care about, if you care about justice and social change.

"But Muhammad Ali made an enormous difference. There was a quality of pure goodwill about him. There always has been, and I believe, always will be. Here was a young black man from American poverty. He could very easily have been embittered, hateful, racist. But through all his trials and tribulations, he never manifested any of those qualities, and when he spoke, he said loving things. In his mind, wishes came true, and that's the way a good portion of his life has been. He meant different things to different strata of American society. But to the poor, he meant you can do what you will; anything is possible.

"We wonder what people like Andrew Young and Martin Luther King have meant to black Americans. And if you talk to the black leadership, they might say of Andrew Young, 'He's not nearly aggressive enough.' Or they might have said something else about Dr. King. But if you go down to where the people are, they'll say, 'He gave us great hope for America.' I think Muhammad Ali gave people hope. He inspired and continues to inspire millions of people. And to everyone, he meant that you can be gentle and strong, that there's not a contradiction there; because for all his obvious physical strength, he always evoked gentleness and love. With Muhammad Ali, you saw grace; you saw joy; you saw wit. He meant charity in the truest sense of the word. He made people proud to be who they were. And I don't mean to put all this in the past tense, because I think all these things are still part of Ali.

"It's not an anomaly; it shows the way we are, really, that he came to the opportunity to do all that he did through fighting. But he's always had a vision that goes beyond the violence of boxing. His character causes him to want to help others. And character is destiny; that's the character we need. He hasn't been able to accomplish all that he wanted. Much of what he set out to do never materialized. But he's a person of unique good will and good works. He touched so many lives, and brought out the better angels in millions of people.

"You know, the joy of life is that you have to persevere and do what you can to make this a better world. We're going to have a billion more people on earth before the end of this century. The great majority of them will have dark skin and live in terrible poverty. Hundreds of millions of them will have shortened lives and suffer from hunger, malnutrition, ignorance, and disease. But if the rest of us can come through in the manner of Muhammad Ali, we can solve the problems that lie ahead. The most important thing he communicates is his love and desire to do good. That was what he taught us all. And if you can really communicate that, that there are people who love; well, then maybe you'll change the world.

"I see him from time to time. And the last time I saw him, I told him, and I meant it—I said to him, 'You'll always be my champion.' "

MUHAMMAD ALI: "People say I had a full life, but I ain't dead yet. I'm just getting started. All of my boxing, all of my running around, all of my publicity was just the start of my life. Now my life is really starting. Fighting injustice, fighting racism, fighting crime, fighting illiteracy, fighting poverty, using this face the world knows so well, and going out and fighting for truth and different causes.

"Talking about boxing bores me now. Boxing was just to introduce me to the world. People today, they want me to talk like I used to. 'I'm the greatest! I'm the prettiest! I'm this, and I'm that!' But I don't want to do that no more. There's bigger work I got to do. The whole world is in trouble. Crime is on the rise; the environment is deteriorating; you've got people fighting and the threat of nuclear war; no long-term friendships; corruption in government; evangelist preachers doing things they shouldn't do; no respect for elders; prejudice and injustice; people highjacking planes; Jews and Muslims in the Middle East and Protestants and Catholics in Northern

Ireland fighting each other. What's the reason? What's the cause? There's peace and tranquility among the animals. There's peace and tranquility among the birds. Everything in nature is in perfect order except man. Man is suffering because he has adopted a way of life that's against nature and the laws of God.

"All this hating in the world is wrong. Forget about nations. Forget about color. Forget about different religions. People are people; God created us all. The only thing that makes one man better than another is the goodness of his deeds in the eyes of God. And only God can judge good deeds. It's not for another man to judge. Here in this country, we've been making progress on how people get along. But there's still hatred, and hating someone because of his color is wrong. It's wrong both ways; it don't matter which color does the hating. All people, all colors, got to work to get along.

"There's hunger in the world, and that bothers me. Hunger isn't just being hungry. It means you feel sick. It means you can't work. It means you can't do well in school, because you're too weak to concentrate. And right in this country, there's millions of people homeless. People shouldn't sleep on the streets. They should have homes to go to. Struggling each day, not knowing where you're gonna sleep at night; this country is so rich, it's wrong we got people living that way. People talk about how I give my money away. But how can you be walking down the street and see an old lady so hungry and poor she's going through a garbage can for food; how can you see that old lady, and not give her some money from your pocket? I'll go someplace like Sudan, and when I come back, I get asked political questions about what I saw. I saw children starving to death. That's what I saw.

"So I'm sitting here with the most recognizable face in the history of the world. I'm the only man in history to become famous under two different names. And I feel like I should be doing more with what I've got to help people. My main goal now is helping people and preparing for the hereafter. I'm working harder now than I ever worked in boxing. When I was in boxing, I used to get up at six o'clock in the morning to run. Now I'm up at five o'clock, praying, signing pamphlets, and reading the Qur'an. I'm not looking to be idolized. Maybe I was great in the ring, but outside of boxing, I'm just a brother like other people. I want to live a good life, serve God, help everybody I can. And one more thing. I'm still gonna find out who stole my bike when I was twelve years old in Louisville, and I'm still gonna whup him. That was a good bike."

Author's Epilogue

To know anybody well is an opportunity. To know Muhammad Ali well is a special privilege. Over the course of two years, I've spent countless hours in his presence and traveled with him around the world. There have been many good times and none that were bad, but one moment stands out in my mind.

We were on a plane, returning to the United States from Indonesia, where Muhammad had been engulfed by admiring throngs. Thousands of people had come from distant villages to greet him at the airport when he arrived. Children who weren't alive when he fought stood in the rain, chanting his name. At the Grand Mosque in Jakarta, a crowd estimated by authorities at two hundred thousand converged when he appeared. They surrounded his car, pushing aside all pretense of security, shouting, "Ali! Ali!" The car moved forward, inches at a time, with Ali beseeching the driver, "Go slow; please, don't hurt anyone."

After ten days, we journeyed home on a seemingly endless flight through twelve time zones. Muhammad and Lonnie were seated next to each other. I was across the aisle, beside Howard Bingham. After a while, I drifted off to sleep, and awoke several hours later. Outside the plane, it was pitch black. The cabin was dark, and everyone else was asleep—except Muhammad. His overhead light was on, and he was wide awake, reading the Qur'an. And in that moment, bathed in light, he looked stronger and more at peace with himself than any person I've ever known.

Appendix

Muhammad Ali: His Life and Times couldn't have been written without the help of many people. I'm particularly indebted to the following individuals, listed alphabetically, who gave generously of their time and knowledge in the form of interviews for the project.

Henry Aaron

Kareem Abdul-Jabbar

Robert Abboud

Aminah Ali

Belinda Ali

Lonnie Ali

Maryum Ali

Muhammad Ali

Rahaman Ali

Dean Allison

James Anderson

Ray Arcel

Paul Ardaji

Bob Arum

Arthur Ashe

Teddy Atlas

Red Auerbach

Milt Bailey

Joe Louis Barrow, Jr.

Al Bernstein

James Bierbower

Howard Bingham

Tom Bishop

Chuck Bodak

Julian Bond

Pete Bonventre

Bill Bradley

Teddy Brenner

Harry Brill–Edwards

Drew Brown, Jr.

Jim Brown

Jimmy Carter

Ray Cave

Bill Cayton

Wilt Chamberlain

George Chuvalo

Gil Clancy

Ramsey Clark

Cassius Clay, Sr.

Odessa Clay

Sonji Clay

John Condon

Harold Conrad

Dennis Cope

Howard Cosell

Gene Dibble

Patti Dreifuss

Mickey Duff

Angelo Dundee

Bob Dylan

Harry Edwards

Don Elbaum

Jimmy Ellis

Stanley Fahn

David Falk

Gerald Ford

George Foreman

Bob Foster

Barry Frank

Joe Frazier

Eddie Futch

Leon Gast

Richie Giachetti

Bobby Goodman

Dick Gregory

Erwin Griswold

Bryant Gumbel

David Halberstam

Alex Haley

Richard Hirschfeld

Larry Holmes

Lou Holtz

Huston Horn

Tunney Hunsaker

Joe Ingraham

Jerry Izenberg

Reggie Jackson

Jim Jacobs

Ken Johannsen

Booker Johnson

James Earl Jones

George Kanter

Osman Karriem

Mike Katz

Evan Kemp

Ted Kennedy

Gene Kilroy

Dave Kindred

Marvin Kohn

Mark Kram

Kris Kristofferson

Neil Leifer

Butch Lewis

Robert Lipsyte

Mike Malitz

Mickey Mantle

Harry Markson

Michael Masser

Wilbert McClure

Chris Mead

Rajko Medenica

Edwin Meese

Arthur Mercante

Larry Merchant

James Michener

Archie Moore

Arthur Morrison

Herbert Muhammad

Wali Muhammad

Barney Nagler

Leroy Neiman

Randy Neumann

Jack Newfield

Ken Norton

Jack Olsen

Ferdie Pacheco

Joe Paterno

Floyd Patterson

Pat Patterson

Tony Perez

Mike Phenner

George Plimpton

Lloyd Price

Pat Putnam

Jerry Quarry

Abdul Rahaman

Rick Reilly

Robert Richley

Randy Roberts

Gil Rogin

Kevin Rooney

Irving Rudd

Bill Russell

Jeffrey Sammons

Dick Schaap

Budd Schulberg

John Schulian

Harold Schulman

Ed Schuyler

Attallah Shabazz

Dr. Betty Shabazz

Jeremiah Shabazz

Lana Shabazz	Ralph Thornton
Mort Sharnik	Cheryl Tiegs
Earnie Shavers	Jose Torres
Wilfred Sheed	Mary Travers
Jim Silberman	Carl Walker
Harvey Sloane	Robert Walker
Gary Smith	Alex Wallau
Harold Smith	Lloyd Wells
Leon Spinks	Chuck Wepner
Sylvester Stallone	Harlan Werner
Bert Sugar	Charles Williams
Jose Sulaiman	Marguerite Williams
Bob Surkein	Ted Williams
Mort Susman	Tim Witherspoon
Ernie Terrell	Dave Wolf
Marge Thomas	Andrew Young
Reggie Thomas	Bernie Yuman
John Thompson	Vic Ziegel

Not everyone listed above has been quoted in the book. But each person's contribution was valuable to me in understanding Ali, and I'm grateful to all of them. While I spoke at length with five of Muhammad's children, in deference to their age only Maryum Ali is quoted.

Ted Kennedy and Bob Dylan each submitted a written statement in response to questions. Larry Holmes and Joe Frazier were unwilling to grant me formal interviews, but I had numerous conversations with both men. Jim Jacobs died before I began work on the project, but I talked with him at length about Ali in connection with my earlier book, *The Black Lights*. Among the men and women I consider most important to Ali's personal and professional life, only Veronica Ali, John Ali, and Don King refused to speak with me in any fashion for this book. I mention this only to explain their absence from those quoted directly.

I'd also like to thank Dr. Ibrahim M. Oweiss, who has served as a founder of the Georgetown University Center for Contemporary Arab Studies and as a consultant to the Ministry of Education in Qatar, where his responsibilities involved reviewing the translation of the classical books of early Islamic philosophers to English. I've long been aware of the importance of religion in Muhammad Ali's life. And it was important both to Muhammad and myself, not only that this book reflect the depth of his religious commitment, but also that it be accurate with respect to all facets of Islam. Thus, when the manuscript was complete, at Muhammad's request, I asked that Simon & Schuster have it read by an Islamic scholar. Dr. Oweiss performed that task and noted two minor factual inaccuracies which were corrected. Dr. Oweiss also had this to say about Muhammad Ali: "Upon careful reading of the manuscript, I did not find anything that would be offensive in any shape or form to the principles of Islam which Muhammad Ali has finally been practicing. It was clearly documented that he repented and asked for God's forgiveness after having sometimes slipped on the road of human temptations. [He is] a religious man who adheres to the principles of Islam and who is devoted to the worship of God."

Notes

In reviewing the archival material on Ali's life, I often found the same quotation or different versions of the same quotation in a variety of newspapers, magazines, and books. However, for purposes of these chapter notes, I've omitted multiple listings and simply cited the source where I first saw the material quoted.

CHAPTER 1

1. The most comprehensive study to date of Ali's ancestry was prepared by Isabelle Warnas of the Family History Library in Salt Lake City, Utah, and presented to Muhammad and Lonnie Ali as a gift on January 25, 1989.
2. Jack Olsen, *Black Is Best*, Putnam, 1967, p. 74; Home Box Office Muhammad Ali special.
3. Wilfred Sheed, *Muhammad Ali*, Thomas Y. Crowell Company, 1975, p. 59.
4. September 25, 1961, *Sports Illustrated*; Robert Lipsyte, *Free to Be Muhammad Ali*, Harper & Row, 1977, p. 11 et seq.
5. Olsen, p. 74.
6. Home Box Office Muhammad Ali special.
7. August 29, 1960, *Sports Illustrated*.
8. September 25, 1961, *Sports Illustrated*.

9. September 25, 1961, *Sports Illustrated.*
10. John Cottrell, *Man of Destiny,* Muller Publishers, 1967, p. 29.

CHAPTER 2

1. Olsen, *Black Is Best,* p. 86.
2. Muhammad Ali with Richard Durham, *The Greatest,* Random House, 1976, p. 70
3. Don Atyeo and Felix Dennis, *Muhammad Ali: The Holy Warrior,* Fireside Books, 1975, p. 21.
4. September 25, 1961, *Sports Illustrated.*
5. October 16, 1961, *Sports Illustrated*
6. March 3, 1962, *The New Yorker.*
7. Atyeo and Dennis, *Muhammad Ali: The Holy Warrior,* p. 24.
8. *A/K/A Cassius Clay* film documentary.
9. George Plimpton, *Shadow Box,* Putnam, 1977, p. 82
10. *A/K/A Cassius Clay* film documentary.
11. November 26, 1962, *Sports Illustrated.*
12. Cottrell, *Man of Destiny,* p. 83.
13. November 13, 1962, *New York Times.*
14. February 24, 1964, *Sports Illustrated.*
15. February 15, 1963, *Life.*
16. *A/K/A Cassius Clay* film documentary
17. March 30, 1963, *The New Yorker.*
18. Cottrell, *Man of Destiny,* p. 101.
19. March 17, 1963, *New York Post.*
20. May 14, 1961, *New York Times.*
21. November 19, 1962, *New York Times.*
22. June 19, 1963, *New York Times.*
23. June 19, 1963, *New York Times.*
24. June 19, 1963, *New York Times.*
25. December 9, 1962, *New York Times Magazine.*

CHAPTER 3

1. October 1963, *Esquire.*
2. *The Greatest,* Columbia Records, 1963.
3. September 25, 1961, *Sports Illustrated.*
4. Lipsyte, *Free to Be Muhammad Ali,* p. 50.
5. September 25, 1961, *Sports Illustrated.*
6. March 25, 1961, *Saturday Evening Post.*
7. June 18, 1984, *Sports Illustrated.*
8. *The Greatest,* Columbia Records, 1963.
9. Cottrell, *Man of Destiny,* p. 116; July 23, 1963, *New York Times.*
10. November 18, 1963, *Sports Illustrated.*

11. February 15, 1963, *Life*.
12. Ali with Durham, *The Greatest*, p. 115.
13. Miscellaneous film footage, especially *A/K/A Cassius Clay*.
14. April 1964, *Ring* magazine.
15. Miscellaneous film footage, especially *A/K/A Cassius Clay*.
16. February 24, 1964, *Sports Illustrated*.
17. September 30, 1963, *Philadelphia Daily News*
18. January 23, 1964, *New York Herald Tribune*.
19. February 3, 1964, *Louisville Courier-Journal*.
20. February 24, 1964, *Sports Illustrated*.
21. August 5, 1963, *Sports Illustrated*.
22. November 18, 1962, *New York Journal American*.
23. February 23, 1964, *New York Times;* February 24, 1964, *New York Times*.
24. February 24, 1964, *Sports Illustrated*.
25. November 6, 1963, *New York Post*.
26. Jose Torres, *Sting Like a Bee*, Abelard-Schuman, 1971, p. 122.
27. Weigh-in quotations from many sources, inter alia, Cottrell, *Man of Destiny;* Olsen, *Black Is Best;* February 26, 1964, *New York Times*.
28. February 25, 1964, ABC Radio broadcast.
29. February 25, 1964, ABC Radio broadcast.
30. February 25, 1964, ABC Radio broadcast.
31. February 25, 1964, ABC Radio broadcast.

Chapter 4

1. March 1963, *Ebony*.
2. February 27, 1964, *New York Times*.
3. March 9, 1964, *Sports Illustrated;* February 27, 1964, *New York Times*.
4. February 27, 1964, *Washington Star;* February 28, 1964, *New York Times*.
5. Elijah Muhammad, *Message to the Blackman*, Muhammad's Temple Number 2 in Chicago, 1965, p. 304.
6. Muhammad, *Message to the Blackman*, pp. 32–33, 36, 51, 161, 221, 223; Malcolm X with Alex Haley, *The Autobiography of Malcolm X*, Ballantine Books, 1965, p. 253.
7. Malcolm X with Haley, *The Autobiography of Malcolm X*, pp. 212, 220, 251.
8. February 27, 1964, Associated Press report.
9. December 9, 1962, *New York Times Magazine*.
10. March 7, 1964, *New York Times*.
11. Cottrell, *Man of Destiny*, p. 178.
12. July 1964, *Boxing & Wrestling;* November 1984, *Playboy*.

13. March 24, 1964, *New York Journal American*.
14. March 24, 1964, *Washington Post*.
15. July 1964, *Boxing & Wrestling*.
16. Atyeo and Dennis, *Muhammad Ali: The Holy Warrior*, p. 52.
17. Atyeo and Dennis, *Muhammad Ali: The Holy Warrior*, p. 53.
18. Malcolm X with Haley, *The Autobiography of Malcolm X*, p. 168.
19. Malcolm X with Haley, *The Autobiography of Malcolm X*, p. 339.
20. Cottrell, *Man of Destiny*, p. 186.
21. Cottrell, *Man of Destiny*, p. 184.
22. May 18, 1964, *New York Times*.

CHAPTER 5

1. Olsen, *Black Is Best*, p. 184.
2. January 26, 1965, *New York Journal American*.
3. Robert Lipsyte, *Sportsworld*, Quadrangle, 1975, p. 118.
4. Cottrell, *Man of Destiny*, p. 195.
5. September 25, 1975, *Sports Illustrated*.
6. November 23, 1964, *Sports Illustrated*.
7. November 27, 1964, *Life*.
8. Ferdie Pacheco, *Fight Doctor*, Simon & Schuster, 1977, p. 76.
9. May 28, 1965, *New York Times*.
10. June 7, 1965, *Sports Illustrated*.
11. June 7, 1965, *Sports Illustrated*.
12. Chris Mead, *Champion: Joe Louis, Black Hero in White America*, Penguin, 1986, p. 292; Torres, *Sting Like a Bee*, p. 137.
13. February 5, 1967, *New York Times;* August 1966, *Esquire;* John D. McCallum, *The World Heavyweight Boxing Championship*, Chilton, 1974, p. 315; Cottrell, *Man of Destiny*, p. 343.
14. *A/K/A Cassius Clay* film documentary.
15. May 23, 1965, *New York Journal American;* Madison Square Garden press notes provided for Ali-Frazier I; Howard Bingham tape collection.
16. February 15, 1971, *Sports Illustrated*.
17. October 14, 1965, *Sports Illustrated*.
18. Torres, *Sting Like a Bee*, p. 143.
19. November 21, 1965, *New York Times;* Cottrell, *Man of Destiny*, p. 238; November 22, 1965, *Sports Illustrated*.
20. Cottrell, *Man of Destiny*, p. 238.
21. David King, *I Am King*, Penguin, 1975, unpaged.
22. December 3, 1965, *Life*.
23. November 23, 1965, *New York Times*.
24. November 24, 1965, *New York Times*.
25. November 20, 1965, *Sports Illustrated*.

CHAPTER 6

1. Sheed, *Muhammad Ali*, p. 13.
2. Atyeo and Dennis, *Muhammad Ali: The Holy Warrior*, p. 57.
3. Atyeo and Dennis, *Muhammad Ali: The Holy Warrior*, p. 57.
4. April 19, 1964, *Louisville Courier-Journal*.
5. Torres, *Sting Like a Bee*, p. 147.
6. February 23, 1966, *New York Herald Tribune*.
7. February 22, 1966, *New York Post*.
8. February 22, 1966, *New York Journal American*.
9. February 22, 1966, *New York Journal American*.
10. February 25, 1966, *Louisville Times*.
11. Cottrell, *Man of Destiny*, p. 252.
12. March 29, 1966, *New York Times*.
13. March 27, 1966, *New York Times*.
14. March 15, 1966, *Congressional Record*, p. 5580.
15. April 16, 1966, *Sports Illustrated*.
16. March 28, 1966, *Sports Illustrated*.
17. 397 Federal Reports 2d 901 (5th Circuit 1968).
18. 397 Federal Reports 2d 901 (5th Circuit 1968).
19. August 26, 1966, *New York Times*.
20. September 9, 1966, *Life* magazine.
21. Federal Bureau of Investigation files.
22. October 26, 1970, *Sports Illustrated*.
23. Cottrell, *Man of Destiny*, p. 302.
24. December 29, 1966, *New York Times*.
25. February 5, 1967, *New York Times;* February 13, 1967, *Sports Illustrated*.
26. February 13, 1967, *Sports Illustrated*.
27. February 8, 1967, *New York Daily News*.
28. February 8, 1967, *New York Times*.
29. February 7, 1967, *New York Post;* February 9, 1967, *New York Post*.
30. February 7, 1967, *New York World Journal & Telegram;* February 8, 1967, *New York World Journal & Telegram*.
31. February 21, 1967, *Congressional Record*, p. 4134.
32. WKCR-FM Radio broadcast, Thomas Hauser tape collection.
33. April 10, 1967, *Sports Illustrated*.
34. April 10, 1967, *Sports Illustrated;* April 23, 1967, *New York World Journal & Telegram*.
35. May 8, 1967, *Sports Illustrated*.
36. Federal Bureau of Investigation files.
37. Federal Bureau of Investigation files.
38. Federal Bureau of Investigation files.
39. Federal Bureau of Investigation files.
40. Federal Bureau of Investigation files.

CHAPTER 7

1. June 22, 1967, *New York Post.*
2. December 14, 1969, *New York Daily News.*
3. April 23, 1967, *New York World Journal & Telegram.*
4. June 19, 1967, *Sports Illustrated.*
5. June 21, 1967, *New York Times.*
6. June 21, 1967, *New York Times.*
7. Torres, *Sting Like a Bee*, p. 158; Lipsyte, *Free to Be Muhammad Ali*, p. 83; March 8, 1971, *Time.*
8. Home Box Office Muhammad Ali special.
9. Home Box Office Muhammad Ali special; *A/K/A Cassius Clay* film documentary.
10. August 1968, *Esquire.*
11. August 1968, *Esquire*; February 19, 1968, *Sports Illustrated.*
12. *A/K/A Cassius Clay* film documentary; WKCR-FM Radio broadcast, Thomas Hauser tape collection.
13. *A/K/A Cassius Clay* film documentary; WKCR-FM Radio broadcast, Thomas Hauser tape collection.
14. February 19, 1968, *Sports Illustrated*; April 1969, *Ebony.*
15. Howard Bingham tape collection.
16. April 1969, *Ebony*; *A/K/A Cassius Clay* film documentary.
17. August 1968, *Esquire*; *A/K/A Cassius Clay* film documentary.
18. Federal Bureau of Investigation files, July 25, 1967, memorandum.
19. Federal Bureau of Investigation files.
20. Federal Bureau of Investigation files.
21. Howard Bingham tape collection.
22. 397 Federal Reports 2d 901 (5th Circuit 1968).
23. 430 Federal Reports 2d 165 (5th Circuit 1970).
24. 430 Federal Reports 2d 165 (5th Circuit 1970).
25. October 12, 1987, *Sporting News.*
26. April 4, 1969, *Muhammad Speaks*; April 6, 1969, *New York Times*; Federal Bureau of Investigation files.
27. December 6, 1969, *New York Post.*
28. December 3, 1969, *New York Times.*
29. December 3, 1969, *New York Post.*
30. December 7, 1969, *New York Times.*
31. December 4, 1969, *Wall Street Journal.*

CHAPTER 8

1. Howard Bingham tape collection.
2. October 26, 1970, *Sports Illustrated.*
3. October 26, 1970, *Sports Illustrated.*
4. November 2, 1970, *Sports Illustrated.*

5. September 15, 1970, *New York Times.*
6. Thomas Hauser, *The Black Lights,* McGraw-Hill, 1986, p. 17.
7. Jimmy Cannon, *Nobody Asked Me But,* Penguin, 1983, p. 153.
8. March 8, 1971, *Sports Illustrated.*
9. Budd Schulberg, *Loser and Still Champion,* Doubleday, 1972, p. 162.
10. Howard Bingham tape collection.
11. March 8, 1971, *Sports Illustrated.*
12. Howard Bingham tape collection; *The Fighters* film documentary.
13. *The Fighters* film documentary.
14. Howard Bingham tape collection; February 1, 1971, *Sports Illustrated.*
15. February 22, 1971, *Sports Illustrated.*
16. Howard Bingham tape collection.
17. February 22, 1971, *Sports Illustrated.*
18. Howard Bingham tape collection; *The Fighters* film documentary.
19. Pacheco, *Fight Doctor,* p. 106.
20. Red Smith, *The Red Smith Reader,* Vintage Books, 1983, p. 271.
21. Lipsyte, *Free to Be Muhammad Ali,* p. 96.

CHAPTER 9

1. March 30, 1971, *Congressional Record,* p. 8630.
2. July 26, 1971, *Sports Illustrated.*
3. September 22, 1980, *Sports Illustrated.*
4. November 29, 1971, *Sports Illustrated.*
5. November 29, 1971, *Sports Illustrated.*
6. October 31, 1972, letter from Eric Weissman (vice president, Warner Brothers, Inc.) to Theodore Friedman.
7. January 2, 1973, memorandum from Bob Arum to Theodore Friedman.
8. Contract between Reliable N. E. Promotions, Top Rank, Inc., Muhammad Ali, and Al Jones.
9. April 23, 1973, *Sports Illustrated.*
10. April 1, 1973, *New York Times.*
11. April 7, 1973, *New York Post.*
12. Atyeo and Dennis, *Muhammad Ali: The Holy Warrior,* p. 93.
13. Howard Bingham tape collection.
14. Madison Square Garden press kit for Ali-Frazier II.
15. Howard Cosell, *Like It Is,* Playboy Press, 1974, p. 84.
16. January 29, 1974, *New York Times.*

CHAPTER 10

1. September 12, 1973, *New York Times;* October 27, 1974, *New York Times.*
2. Hauser, *The Black Lights,* p. 75.
3. September 15, 1974, *Los Angeles Times.*
4. Howard Bingham tape collection.
5. Howard Bingham tape collection.
6. Norman Mailer, *The Fight,* Bantam, 1975, p. 119.
7. Howard Bingham tape collection.
8. Howard Bingham tape collection.
9. Howard Bingham tape collection.
10. November 11, 1974, *Sports Illustrated.*

CHAPTER 11

1. March 1967, *Ring* magazine.
2. October 31, 1974, *New York Post.*
3. Wilfred Sheed, *Muhammad Ali,* p. 16.
4. Hugh McIlvanney, *McIlvanney on Boxing,* Beaufort Books, 1982, p. 41.
5. Sheed, *Muhammad Ali,* p. 89.
6. Howard Bingham tape collection.
7. Howard Bingham tape collection.
8. November 1975, *Playboy.*
9. Leon Gast tape collection.
10. Howard Bingham tape collection.
11. Bokris-Wylie, *Ali,* Freeway Press, 1974, p. 102.
12. David King, *I Am King,* unpaged; June 29, 1975, *New York Times Magazine.*
13. March 24, 1975, *Sports Illustrated.*
14. May 5, 1975, *People* magazine.
15. Sheed, *Muhammad Ali,* p. 16.

CHAPTER 12

1. May 2, 1980, *Los Angeles Times.*
2. July 8, 1975, *New York Post.*
3. Howard Bingham tape collection.
4. September 29, 1975, *Sports Illustrated.*
5. July 8, 1975, *New York Post;* September 29, 1975, *Sports Illustrated.*
6. September 29, 1975, *Sports Illustrated.*
7. September 30, 1975, *New York Times.*
8. September 29, 1975, *Newsweek.*
9. September 24, 1975, *New York Times.*

10. October 2, 1975, *New York Times*.
11. October 13, 1975, *Sports Illustrated*.

CHAPTER 13

1. January 8, 1976, *New York Times*.
2. May 10, 1976, *Sports Illustrated*.
3. May 10, 1976, *Sports Illustrated*.
4. May 23, 1976, *New York Times*.
5. June 23, 1976, *New York Times*.
6. May 2, 1976, *Face the Nation*, CBS Television; March 26, 1976, *New York Times*; March 23, 1976, *New York Times*.
7. June 27, 1976, *New York Times*.
8. October 11, 1976, *Sports Illustrated*.
9. May 30, 1977, *Sports Illustrated*.
10. October 10, 1977, *Sports Illustrated*.
11. October 1, 1977, *New York Times*.
12. John Schulian, *Writers' Fighters*, Andrews & McMeel, 1983, p. 14; February 27, 1978, *Sports Illustrated*; February 16, 1978, *New York Post*; Home Box Office Muhammad Ali special.
13. October 29, 1970, *New York Times*.
14. June 13, 1978, *New York Times*.
15. June 14, 1978, *Washington Post*.
16. June 25, 1978, *New Orleans Times-Picayune*.
17. Howard Bingham tape collection.
18. September 11, 1978, *Sports Illustrated*.
19. July 24, 1978, *Sports Illustrated*.
20. Hugh McIlvanney, *McIlvanney on Boxing*, p. 166.
21. Schulian, *Writers' Fighters*, p. 17.

CHAPTER 14

1. January 5, 1979, *Long Beach (California) Independent*.
2. Jack Olsen, *Black Is Best*, p. 74.
3. June 27, 1979, *St. Louis Globe Democrat*.
4. Wilfred Sheed, *Muhammad Ali*, p. 82.

CHAPTER 15

1. June 20, 1978, *New York Times*.
2. February 18, 1980, *Time*.
3. February 18, 1980, *Time*.
4. February 4, 1980, *New York Daily News*.
5. February 5, 1980, *New York Times*; February 6, 1980, *New York Times*.

6. April 26, 1980, *New York Times.*
7. March 2, 1980, *New York Times.*
8. September 29, 1980, *Sports Illustrated;* August 28, 1980, *New York Times.*
9. August 27, 1980, *New York Times.*
10. August 28, 1980, *New York Times;* Big Fights, Inc., film archives.
11. September 28, 1980, *New York Times;* September 29, 1980, *Sports Illustrated.*
12. Big Fights, Inc., film archives; September 29, 1980, *Sports Illustrated.*
13. Hugh McIlvanney, *McIlvanney on Boxing,* p. 176; Big Fights, Inc., film archives.
14. September 29, 1980, *Sports Illustrated.*
15. September 16, 1974, *New York Daily News.*
16. October 8, 1980, *New York Daily News;* October 8, 1980, *New York Times.*
17. October 8, 1980, *New York Post.*

CHAPTER 16

1. April 5, 1981, *Parade* magazine.
2. December 6, 1981, *New York Daily News;* December 10, 1981, *New York Post.*
3. December 6, 1981, *New York Daily News.*
4. December 11, 1981, *New York Times.*
5. December 13, 1981, *New York Times;* December 21, 1981, *Sports Illustrated.*
6. September 20, 1984, *New York Post;* September 20, 1984, *New York Daily News.*
7. Minutes of a special meeting of the board of directors of the Muhammad Ali Financial Corporation.
8. December 11, 1988, *Atlanta Journal-Constitution.*
9. Howard Bingham tape collection.
10. May 18, 1966, *New York Post.*
11. November 19, 1966, *Los Angeles Times.*
12. Thomas Hauser, *The Black Lights,* p. 42.

CHAPTER 17

1. September 25, 1975, *Sports Illustrated.*
2. May 2, 1976, *Face the Nation,* CBS Television.
3. Gaafar Sheikd Idris, *The Pillars Of Faith,* Islamic Teaching Center of Indianapolis, 1977.
4. *Human Rights in Islam,* The Institute of Islamic Information and Education of Chicago, undated.

Index

FOR MORE ON
ANNIE MURRAY

sign up to receive our

SAGA NEWSLETTER

Packed with features, competitions, authors' and readers' letters and news of exclusive events, it's a must-read for every Annie Murray fan!

Simply fill in your details below and tick to confirm that you would like to receive saga-related news and promotions and return to us at **Pan Macmillan, Saga Newsletter, 20 New Wharf Road, London, N1 9RR.**

NAME

ADDRESS

POSTCODE

EMAIL

[ ] *I would like to receive saga-related news and promotions (please tick)*

You can unsubscribe at any time in writing or through our website where you can also see our privacy policy which explains how we will store and use your data.